Chapter Title	Focus Company	Type of Organization	Company Website
7. Product Costs: Inventories and Cost of Goods Sold	The Goodyear Tire & Rubber Company	Manufactures tires, belts and hoses, and chemical and industrial products	www.goodyear.com
8. Allocating the Cost of Property and Equipment	AMR Corporation	Parent company to American Airlines, and includes passenger and cargo airlines, investment services and facilities	www.amrcorp.com
9. Accounting for Income Taxes	Campbell Soup Company	Manufactures and markets soup	www.campbellsoup.com
10. Investments in Intangible Assets	Amazon.com	Markets books and music on-line	www.amazon.com
11. Investments in Other Companies	The Coca-Cola Company	Manufactures, markets, and distributes nonalcoholic beverage concentrates and syrups	www.cocacola.com
12. Investments in Leased Assets	UAL Corporation	Cargo and passenger airline company that also provides airline support services	www.ual.com
13. Financial Instruments and Derivative Securities	The Procter & Gamble Company	Manufacturers of family, personal and household care products	www.pg.com
14. Pension and Other Postemployment Benefits	International Business Machines Corporation	Invents, develops and manufactures information technologies, including computer systems, software, storage systems and microelectronics	www.ibm.com
15. Shareholders' Equity	Intel Corporation	Designs, develops, manufactures and markets microcomputer components of desktop and server systems	www.intel.com
16. Earnings Management	General Electric Company	Technology and services company that creates products such as consumer appliances and lighting products	www.ge.com

Financial Reporting and Analysis

Financial Reporting and Analysis

David A. Guenther
University of Colorado at Boulder

McGraw-Hill
Irwin

Boston   Burr Ridge, IL   Dubuque, IA   Madison, WI   New York   San Francisco   St. Louis
Bangkok   Bogotá   Caracas   Kuala Lumpur   Lisbon   London   Madrid   Mexico City
Milan   Montreal   New Delhi   Santiago   Seoul   Singapore   Sydney   Taipei   Toronto

**McGraw-Hill
Irwin**

FINANCIAL REPORTING AND ANALYSIS

Published by McGraw-Hill/Irwin, a business unit of The McGraw-Hill Companies, Inc.,
1221 Avenue of the Americas, New York, NY, 10020. Copyright © 2005 by The McGraw-Hill
Companies, Inc. All rights reserved. No part of this publication may be reproduced or distributed
in any form or by any means, or stored in a database or retrieval system, without the prior
written consent of The McGraw-Hill Companies, Inc., including, but not limited to, in any
network or other electronic storage or transmission, or broadcast for distance learning.
Some ancillaries, including electronic and print components, may not be available to customers
outside the United States.

This book is printed on acid-free paper.

domestic   1 2 3 4 5 6 7 8 9 0 WCK/WCK 0 9 8 7 6 5 4 3
international 1 2 3 4 5 6 7 8 9 0 WCK/WCK 0 9 8 7 6 5 4 3

ISBN 0-07-250357-2

Vice president and editor-in-chief: *Robin J Zwettler*
Publisher: *Stewart Mattson*
Sponsoring editor: *Steve DeLancey*
Editorial assistant: *Emily Wong*
Marketing manager: *Richard Kolasa*
Media producer: *Elizabeth Mavetz*
Project manager: *Charlie Fisher*
Production supervisor: *Gina Hangos*
Coordinator freelance design: *Artemio Ortiz Jr.*
Photo research coordinator: *Kathy Shive*
Photo researcher: *Sabina Dowell*
Supplement producer: *Joyce J. Chappetto*
Senior digital content specialist: *Brian Nacik*
Cover design: *Artemio Ortiz Jr.*
Interior design: *Ryan Brown*
Typeface: *10/12 New Aster*
Compositor: *GAC Indianapolis*
Printer: *Quebecor World Versailles Inc.*

Library of Congress Cataloging-in-Publication Data
Guenther, David A.
   Financial reporting and analysis / David A. Guenther.
     p. cm.
   ISBN 0-07-250357-2 (alk. paper)
    1. Financial statements. 2. Corporations—Accounting. I. Title.
   HF5681.B2G842 2005
   657'.3—dc22

2003060757

INTERNATIONAL EDITION ISBN 0-07-111134-4
Copyright © 2005. Exclusive rights by The McGraw-Hill Companies, Inc. for manufacture and
export. This book cannot be re-exported from the country to which it is sold by McGraw-Hill. The
International Edition is not available in North America.

www.mhhe.com

This book is lovingly dedicated to my wife Dawn, whose constant support and encouragement made it possible.

About the Author

Dr. David A. Guenther is a Professor of Accounting and holds the Tisone Chair in Accounting at the Leeds School of Business at the University of Colorado at Boulder. He received his Ph.D. from the University of Washington in Seattle in 1990. Dr. Guenther's scholarly papers have been published in leading academic journals in accounting and finance, including the *Journal of Financial Economics,* the *Journal of Accounting and Economics,* the *Accounting Review, Contemporary Accounting Research,* and the *Journal of Accounting Research,* and his papers have been awarded the American Taxation Association's annual Tax Manuscript Award three times. Dr. Guenther has served on the faculty of the University of Connecticut, been a visiting professor at the Sloan School of Management at the Massachusetts Institute of Technology, and been an invited visiting scholar at Maastricht University in the Netherlands and the Chinese University of Hong Kong. Prior to his academic career he was a tax consultant and a certified public accountant for more than 10 years. He is married with three children and is a veteran of the United States Marine Corps.

Preface

The rigging of a sailing ship—the jumble of ropes, masts, and sails—seems confusing when you're unfamiliar with the mechanics of sailing. However, once you learn the purpose of each mast and rope, the whole structure makes sense. The same is true of accounting: Students need to understand how each piece of a financial statement relates to all of the other pieces and how each helps to accomplish the goals of the financial statement. This book is an attempt to give students that understanding.

WHY WAS THIS BOOK WRITTEN?

The book was written with three goals in mind, goals that I feel distinguish *Financial Reporting and Analysis* from any other book on the market.

First, the book is highly conceptual in nature, examining financial reporting practice through the lens of economics (specifically, information economics and contracting theory). Explaining financial accounting rules within the context of economic theory gives students a way of understanding how all of the rules relate to each other and to the overall goal of financial reporting. Rather than just presenting rules, this book explains the concepts behind the rules.

The second goal of the book is to give students a good sense of how financial accounting information is used. I have found in my own teaching that even the most complex rules are easier for students to learn if the students understand how the accounting information is used. Understanding how information is used also helps students to see how a particular rule relates to the whole structure of financial reporting.

The third goal is to be rigorous in terms of topical coverage, while at the same time avoiding much of the detail that seems to overwhelm students. My own experience is that students often lose sight of the big picture and miss important concepts because they focus too much on understanding small differences in accounting methods. On the other hand, sometimes subtle differences in accounting methods are extremely important and can be appreciated only after a detailed examination. My approach in this book has been to maintain a balance, avoiding complexity and detail where appropriate, while maintaining rigor where it is necessary for understanding. Thus, far from being a stripped-down or simplified version of a traditional intermediate text, this book is intended to challenge students with concepts and ideas rather than details and rules.

FLEXIBLE ENOUGH FOR ANY CLASSROOM ENVIRONMENT

This book is intended for three different audiences. First, the book is rigorous enough to serve as the text for a traditional two-semester sequence for accounting majors, for professors who want to emphasize a **conceptual understanding of financial reporting** rather than proficiency in completing CPA exam problems. That is how I use the book in my own teaching. Professors using the book for a two-semester sequence will likely supplement it with outside readings. Second, the book is intended to be concise enough to serve as a text for a **one-semester intermediate course** for nonaccounting majors. Finally, the book is ideally suited for an **MBA intermediate accounting course.**

AN INNOVATIVE APPROACH TO EACH CHAPTER

In addition to providing a rigorous explanation of financial accounting standards and placing an emphasis on fundamental concepts, three additional constructs are explored in each chapter:

- *Each chapter includes a discussion of how the financial accounting information discussed in the chapter is used to make decisions.* In my experience I have found that this puts the rules into a context and helps relate them to the whole structure of financial reporting, making it easier for students to understand and remember the details.
- *Each chapter explains the relationship between the accrual accounting concepts discussed in the chapter and cash flows.* By integrating the discussion of cash flows into each chapter, students are more likely to understand the cash flows statement and the link between net income and cash flows.
- *Each chapter notes the differences between U.S. GAAP rules and the financial reporting practices in other countries.* This explanation provides students with a better understanding of the similarities as well as the differences in financial reporting between countries and helps students take a global perspective with respect to U.S. financial reporting standards.

REAL-WORLD FINANCIAL STATEMENTS

Another unique feature of this book is the focus on real financial statements rather than simplified examples. One frustration that students face when reading actual financial statements is that the simple textbook examples don't correspond to what they find in real financial statements. The statement of cash flows is a good example: Traditional texts tell students that changes in current asset and liability accounts (such as accounts receivable, accounts payable, and inventories) should be reflected on the cash flows statement. However, in studying actual financial statements from public companies, students will find that changes in these balance sheet accounts are often quite different from the adjustments found on the cash flows statement. In this book students will come to understand why these differences occur and will have a better understanding of the complexity of real financial statements.

Unlike traditional intermediate texts, the topics in this book are not necessarily covered in balance sheet order. Rather, each topic is introduced at a particular time in the text for pedagogical reasons. Thus, bonds payable are covered before inventories, to allow an early introduction of time value of money concepts, and contingent liabilities are covered in the same chapter as asset impairments, since both topics involve the early recognition of expected future accounting losses.

HOW FINANCIAL REPORTING AND ANALYSIS IS ORGANIZED

Chapter 1 develops the conceptual foundation that will be followed throughout the text by introducing the two main uses of financial accounting: to convey managers' private information to users outside the company (the problem of information asymmetry) and to enable more efficient contracting. The key concept of the trade-off between relevant and reliable information is developed, as well as the trade-off of costs and benefits of accounting information. The idea that managers have incentives to influence accounting information is also developed, as well as different ways to think about the quality of financial accounting information.

Chapter 2 introduces the key concept of accounting accruals. Financial accounting uses accruals to modify cash flows to arrive at net income, and accruals are necessary because companies enter into transactions that affect more than one accounting period, and in many transactions the economic effect of the transaction takes place in a different accounting period from the cash flow effect. The concept of permanent and transitory income items and their effect on forecasting future earnings and cash flows is also addressed.

Chapter 3, dealing with the balance sheet, highlights the conflict between relevant and reliable accounting information. Fair values provide the most relevant information for decision making, but for many types of assets fair values are not reliable. Original cost provides reliable information but may not be relevant. The relationship between the balance sheet and the income statement is emphasized. Increases and decreases in the book values of assets and liabilities have corresponding effects on the income statement.

Chapter 4 introduces the statement of cash flows. While traditional intermediate texts defer this discussion until the end of the book, the approach I have taken is to present accrual-to-cash adjustments early, following Chapter 2's discussion of accruals and Chapter 3's discussion of the relationship between balance sheet book values and income statement effects. However, coverage of this chapter can easily be delayed for those who prefer to cover cash flows at the end of the course.

Chapter 5 introduces (or reviews) time value of money concepts. Unlike traditional texts, present value concepts are not introduced as an isolated topic but are developed in connection with accounting for notes receivable and notes payable, including bonds payable. Thus, an important conceptual topic (present values) is combined with a rigorous analysis of financial reporting rules for assets and liabilities.

Chapter 6 is perhaps the most unique feature of the book, covering the fundamental financial reporting concept of conservatism. This is a good example of how the economic theory underlying this book shapes the presentation of topical material. GAAP rules have the characteristic of recognizing expected future losses currently, while deferring the recognition of expected future gains until they are realized. This concept is illustrated in the chapter through a series of financial accounting rules that all have the feature of estimating and recognizing expected future losses. Thus, bad debts, lower of cost or market adjustments, asset impairments, restructuring charges, contingent liabilities, warranty expenses, and expected losses from discontinued operations are all presented as examples of the same underlying concept: accounting conservatism.

Chapters 7 and 8 complete the first half of the book, covering traditional topics usually found in the first semester of an intermediate accounting sequence: accounting for inventories, and accounting for property and equipment. Chapter 8's coverage of accounting for nonmonetary exchanges represents a good example of the trade-off that this book makes between presenting rigorous coverage of important conceptual topics, while at the same time limiting the amount of detail presented to students. Understanding accounting for nonmonetary exchanges is an important conceptual topic. For example, the restatement of Qwest's financial statements was largely due to Qwest's attempt to record gains from swaps of fiber-optic cable capacity. However, while the text covers the important conceptual rules relating to nonmonetary exchanges and presents basic journal entries to illustrate these concepts, details of the multiple ways that exchanges may be recorded (depending on whether cash is or is not received or paid with the exchange) are omitted.

Chapter 9 deals with accounting for income taxes. The topic is placed earlier in the book than most traditional intermediate texts. I wanted to cover accounting for income taxes as early in the book as was practicable, so that a discussion of the income tax effects of transactions could be incorporated throughout the remaining chapters of the book. For those professors who prefer to cover the topic later in the course, coverage of the chapter could easily be delayed.

Chapter 10 deals with the topic of intangible assets and incorporates the new FASB statement on purchased intangibles and goodwill impairment. Intangible assets are put into a framework that classifies all balance sheet assets and liabilities, and the unique characteristics of intangible assets are discussed.

Chapter 11 covers investments, including the fair value method, the equity method, and the consolidation method. The chapter provides an excellent opportunity to point out how U.S. GAAP rules can result in different accounting treatments for what is essentially the same asset, and how difference in balance sheet asset valuation methods affect the measurement of net income.

Chapter 12 covers lease accounting for both lessors and lessees. A fundamental discussion of the economics of leasing is presented, allowing students to understand the similarities between leasing and purchasing, which motivates the discussion of capital leases.

Chapter 13 deals with financial instruments and derivatives. As with leases, a fundamental discussion of the economics of hedging is used to motivate the accounting rules for derivatives. Students are shown how to understand both the need to record derivatives at fair value, as well as the offsetting of gains and losses that occurs with effective hedging.

Chapter 14 covers pension accounting. The chapter begins by discussing the underlying economics of pension liabilities and the role of pension trusts, putting the accounting rules into a context that makes them easier to learn. The chapter also points out that the purpose of many of the pension accounting rules is to smooth out the impact of pensions on reported earnings. Taking this perspective makes the rules for investment gains and losses and other deferrals much easier to understand.

Chapter 15 deals with several topics related to shareholders' equity, including accounting for employee stock options and earnings per share computations. The focus of the chapter is on understanding the fundamental concepts relating to the shareholders' equity section of the balance sheet. The chapter minimizes the amount of detail presented, while at the same time providing students with a good understanding of how the financial statements are affected by shareholders' equity transactions.

Chapter 16 provides a full chapter on earnings management, a vitally important issue for today's accountants, but a subject that is given scant coverage, if any, in other intermediate accounting textbooks. Reasons for earnings management are explained, incentives of managers are discussed, and arguments against earnings management are offered, together with arguments in favor of some degree of flexibility for managers to influence reported accounting numbers.

Two appendixes round out the text. Appendix A provides information about the standard-setting process in the United States, providing coverage of the SEC, the FASB, and the AICPA. A discussion of the role of accounting regulation and market failures is also included. Appendix B provides students with a review of recording accounting transactions, including a review of journal entries and debits and credits.

Finally, additional material related to topics that are not included in the text, but that are generally covered in a traditional intermediate book, are available on the textbook's supporting website (www.mhhe.com/guenther1e). These supplemental materials include coverage of accounting for long-term contracts; the retail inventory method; depletion; the effect of cash on nonmonetary exchanges; bonds issued between interest payment dates; troubled debt restructuring; leases with guaranteed residual values; and leases with bargain purchase options. With making this material available to both students and faculty on the website, those professors who want to include these topics as part of their course coverage may do so, using material that is presented in the same voice and format as in the text itself.

SUPPLEMENTS TO THE TEXTBOOK

Instructor Resource CD-ROM (ISBN 0072867345)

Provided solely for instructor use, this CD incorporates all of the teaching resources that support the textbook into an easy-to-use medium:

- *Solutions Manual:* Prepared by text author David Guenther, this provides solutions to all of the end-of-chapter questions and problems.
- *Instructor's Manual:* Also prepared by text author David Guenther, this provides suggestions on how to cover each chapter's topics, including key teach-

ing points and suggestions as to what supplemental materials might be used. Tips are provided regarding how to divide the chapters for use in different types of courses: one quarter, one semester, or two quarters or semesters. Guidance is also given in reordering the chapters for those professors who want to cover topics in a different sequence.

- *Test Bank:* Authored by Pamela Roush, University of Central Florida, this is a collection of test items tied closely to the format of the end-of-chapter materials found in the text. This test bank is also provided in a computerized format.

- *Microsoft PowerPoint Slides:* Prepared by text author David Guenther, these are designed to capture and display central points found in each chapter of the text.

Online Learning Center (URL: www.mhhe.com/guenther1e)

Instructor Edition:

- Password-protected, downloadable instructor resources include Microsoft PowerPoint Slides, Instructor's Manual, and Solutions Manual.

- Additional text material, written by author David Guenther, covers accounting for long-term contracts, the retail inventory method, depletion, the effect of cash on nonmonetary exchanges, bonds issued between interest payment dates, troubled debt restructuring, leases with guaranteed residual values, and leases with bargain purchase options. These additional sections are presented in a style consistent with the material in the text, allowing the instructor expanded coverage and maximum flexibility in the shaping of their course, while responding to the diverse needs of a wide range of students.

- PowerWeb delivers to instructors and students the latest news and developments pertinent to the course, including

  Access to current articles related to *Financial Reporting and Analysis.*
  Daily and weekly updates with assessment tools.
  Links to related sites.
  Web research guide.
  Access to Northern Light Search Engine, providing Internet access to additional articles.

Student Edition:

- Online Study Aid provides students with a variety of interactive online quizzing: multiple choice, true/false, and essay questions related to the text for student self-evaluation.

- Downloadable Microsoft PowerPoint Slides.

- PowerWeb is a unique website that extends the learning experience beyond the core textbook itself. It includes

  Current readings with assessments.
  Study tips and self-quizzes.
  Links to related sites.
  Web research guide.
  Access to Northern Light Search Engine, providing Internet Access to additional articles.

Online Course Support

- Course content cartridges are available for the course website and to support an online class delivery when using products such as WebCT or Blackboard.

PageOut

- McGraw-Hill's Course Management System.
- "Point and Click" Course Website Tool.

Additional Intermediate Accounting Products

Intermediate accounting products recommended as supplementary material include

- Abdolmohammadi/McQuade, *Applied Research in Financial Reporting: Text and Cases*, 1/e (ISBN 0070004803): This text uses real-world cases and issue-based research to help students develop critical-thinking and problem-solving skills for difficult accounting and reporting issues.
- Catanach/Croll/Grinaker, *Business Activity Model (BAM)* 2/e (ISBN 007282400X): BAM helps students gain technical competency, research and communication skills, as well as enhanced critical thinking as they replicate real-world accounting and financial processes. A website accompanies the Business Activity Model (ISBN 007282431X).

Acknowledgments

I would like to thank the following for their suggestions and recommendations that aided in the development of the text:

Noel Addy
Mississippi State University

Alex B. Ampadu
State University of New York at Buffalo

Matt Anderson
Michigan State University

Christine Botosan
University of Utah

Rodger Brannan
University of Minnesota–Duluth

Daniel E. Braswell
University of New Orleans

E. Lewis Bryan
Clemson University

Howard Bunsis
Eastern Michigan University

David Burgstahler
University of Washington

Otto Chang
California State University at San Bernadino

Marilynn Collins
John Carroll University

Catherine Craycraft
University of New Hampshire

Carol M. Fischer
Saint Bonaventure University

Dan Givoly
University of California at Irvine

Janet S. Greenlee
University of Dayton

Steven Grossman
Texas A&M University

Thomas J. Hogan
University of Massachusetts–Boston

Paula L. Irwin
Muhlenberg College

Scott I. Jerris
San Francisco State University

Florence Kirk
State University of New York at Oswego

Jerry G. Kreuze
Western Michigan University

David Law
Youngstown State University

Patsy L. Lee
University of Texas at Arlington

Kevin Leeds
St. Peter's College

Timothy M. Lindquist
University of Northern Iowa

Barbara Lougee
University of California

Susan Lynn
University of Baltimore

Gil Manzon
Boston College

Josephine M. Mathias
Mercer County Community College

Steve Moehrle
University of Missouri–St. Louis

Paula Heim Morris
Kennesaw State University

Paul Munter
University of Miami

Vaughan S. Radcliffe
Case Western Reserve University

Randall Rentfro
Florida Atlantic University

John Rigsby
Mississippi State University

Steve Rock
University of Colorado at Boulder

Pamela Barton Roush
University of Central Florida

William C. Schwartz, Jr.
University of Arizona

Margaret L. Shelton
University of Houston–Downtown

Thomas L. Stober
University of Notre Dame

Murat Neset Tanju
University of Alabama at Birmingham

Gary Taylor
University of Alabama

Peter M. Theuri
Northern Kentucky University

Mary Jeanne Welsh
LaSalle University

Stephen D. Willits
Bucknell University

Kathy Yeaton
University of Connecticut

I would also like to thank Marlene A. Plumlee from the University of Utah and Alice Sineath for their work in accuracy checking the text, as well as Pamela Roush, University of Central Florida, for the creation of the Test Bank. In addition, I am grateful for the creation of quizzes on the Online Learning Center.

I am also grateful to the editorial and production team at McGraw-Hill/Irwin for their help in the making of this textbook: Stewart Mattson, Steve DeLancey, Emily Wong, Rich Kolasa, Dan Wiencek, Charles Fisher, Gina Hangos, Elizabeth Mavetz, Joyce Chappetto, Kathy Shive, and Artemio Ortiz.

David A. Guenther

Brief Contents

Contents

Financial Reporting and Analysis

Chapter Learning Objectives

After reading this chapter you should understand

1. The two major uses of financial accounting information.
2. The trade-off between relevant information and reliable information.
3. How financial accounting quality can be evaluated.
4. The economics of accounting information.
5. The difficulties in comparing costs and benefits of financial accounting information.
6. How managers can influence financial accounting numbers.

Chapter 1

The Economics of Accounting Information

Focus Company: DaimlerChrysler

Introduction

This book is about information, why it is valuable, and how it is used. The specific type of information we focus on is financial accounting information—the information contained in the annual reports of publicly traded corporations. In this book we view accounting information as a product that is produced by corporations and consumed by many different types of users, such as security analysts, shareholders, creditors, potential investors (like yourself), employees, suppliers, customers, government regulators, and taxing authorities.

For example, DaimlerChrysler is a global company that produces automobiles, trucks, and other types of transportation equipment for a variety of different users, and these products are used in many different ways. Similarly, DaimlerChrysler also produces a variety of types of financial accounting information for many different users. Here are some examples of the financial accounting information produced by DaimlerChrysler in its 1999 annual report:

Revenues	$151.0 billion
Total assets	$175.9 billion
Research and development expense	$ 5.7 billion
Net income	$ 5.8 billion

Each of these items is a piece of accounting information, each is useful for making decisions about DaimlerChrysler, and each is produced in accordance with a set of financial accounting rules known as generally accepted accounting principles or GAAP.[1]

Although DaimlerChrysler has a great deal of discretion in deciding what types of cars to build and what features these cars will have, the company's cars must also meet government requirements relating to such things as safety, fuel efficiency, and emissions levels. Similarly, when DaimlerChrysler produces accounting information in the United States, it must also meet requirements imposed by both the government and the accounting profession. For example, the U.S. Securities and Exchange Commission (SEC) requires all publicly traded companies in the United States to file an annual report with the SEC, called Form 10-K for a U.S. corporation and Form 20-F for a foreign corporation, and the financial accounting information contained in these reports must conform to U.S. GAAP.

If you were asked the reason that DaimlerChrysler puts air bags in its cars, you could answer, "Because the government makes it do so," but that would not be a very useful answer. The real reason for the air bags is because they help prevent

---

[1] In general, each country has its own GAAP, and the GAAP presented in this book are those used in the United States, although throughout the following chapters we will also highlight important differences between U.S. GAAP and those used in other countries.

serious injury or death in an accident. In the same way, if you were asked why firms report certain accounting information, the answer "Because it is required under GAAP" is not very useful. In this book we want to go beyond that answer and look at the underlying reason for reporting the information in the first place. Just as some auto manufacturers included air bags in their cars before they were required to by government regulations, corporations also provided financial accounting information before they were required to by the SEC. In economic terms, firms are suppliers of accounting information, and they supply this information in response to a demand for information from users. Understanding why firms produce certain types of accounting information, and how that particular information is being used, is an important part of this book.

In this chapter we begin the study of financial accounting information by investigating accounting's underlying economics. We discuss how and why financial accounting information is used, what factors determine the quality of accounting information, what factors affect the costs and benefits of accounting information, and how and why managers influence firms' accounting numbers.

THE USES OF ACCOUNTING INFORMATION

In the United States there are two major uses of financial accounting information. First, financial accounting is a way to transfer information from managers to other users outside of the corporation, solving an important problem known as *information asymmetry*. Second, financial accounting information is often included in contracts between the corporation and other parties (such as managers, employees, and lenders), resulting in more efficient contracts. Each of these uses is discussed more fully below.

Information Asymmetry

Information asymmetry means that managers working inside a publicly traded corporation have access to information about the corporation's business and its future prospects that people outside the corporation don't have. Having access to this information could help people outside the corporation make more accurate assessments of the company's past performance, the company's expected future performance, the resources available to the company, and the riskiness of the company. Financial accounting provides the primary way for the company's managers to communicate some of this private information to other interested individuals who do not have access to it.[2]

Consider the hypothetical case of an investor deciding whether to buy shares of DaimlerChrysler. Her decision will be based on several factors, including forecasts she has made of DaimlerChrysler's expected future earnings and cash flows. These forecasts are based on DaimlerChrysler's financial statements, other news about DaimlerChrysler, and other information about the economy in general and the automobile industry in particular. However, she has financial statement information only from 1998 and would like to update her forecasts using more recent information about the company's 1999 performance.

The managers who run DaimlerChrysler have access to a great deal of information about the company's performance, and they have a better idea than outside investors about how the company performed during 1999. Assume that managers know the company's performance in 1999 was much better than in 1998. How can they convey that information to investors?

---

[2] *Transparency,* a term often used in the financial press, is related to the concept of information asymmetry. In a recent speech SEC commissioner Glassman defined *financial transparency* as "timely, meaningful, and reliable disclosures about a company's financial performance." The more transparent a firm's financial statements, the less information asymmetry there will be.

One way is for DaimlerChrysler's managers to report accounting net income of $5.8 billion for 1999. Reporting net income helps solve the information asymmetry problem by conveying some of the managers' private information about the company's performance to investors. Reporting a financial accounting number like net income has several other desirable features. First, the net income amount can be independently verified. An outside audit firm can be employed to audit DaimlerChrysler's financial records and provide a written opinion as to whether or not the $5.8 billion amount presents fairly the results of the company's operations for 1999. Second, the accounting net income has been computed in accordance with GAAP, so everyone who understands GAAP rules for measuring net income has a pretty good idea of how the $5.8 billion net income amount was computed. Third, since net income is reported as a specific dollar amount, it can be compared with the net income of Ford or Toyota for 1999, or with DaimlerChrysler's own net income for 1998.

Our hypothetical investor can use the financial accounting information provided by DaimlerChrysler—the reported net income of $5.8 billion—to update her forecasts and help her make her decision about buying shares. If the $5.8 billion amount is more than she was expecting, she could conclude that DaimlerChrysler is performing better than she thought and her forecast of future earnings and cash flows could be increased. On the other hand, if she was expecting net income to be more than $5.8 billion, she may decide that DaimlerChrysler is not performing as well as expected, and she should revise her forecasts downward.[3] The important thing to remember is that financial accounting information is useful to the extent it helps people make decisions. Through the process of financial reporting, managers are able to reveal some of their private information to people outside the company, and those people can use the information to make decisions.

Although solving the information asymmetry problem is only one use of financial accounting information, in the United States it is the most important use. Throughout the rest of this book whenever we talk about the usefulness of a particular type of accounting information, we will generally be referring to the information's usefulness in helping to reduce information asymmetry.

Accounting Information and Contracting

A second important use of financial accounting information is in contracting. Publicly traded corporations enter into many different types of contracts, and often the contracts refer to financial accounting numbers computed in accordance with GAAP. Basing contracts on information that is agreed upon by all parties, like GAAP-based financial accounting numbers, can reduce the costs of the contracts by reducing risk. Shown below are three examples of the use of financial accounting numbers in contracting: compensation plans, debt agreements, and implicit contracts with the government.

Compensation Plans

DaimlerChrysler has entered into employment contracts with its top managers, and these contracts specify, among other things, how much the managers are to be paid. In addition to a base salary, the DaimlerChrysler managers receive annual bonuses based on performance. DaimlerChrysler wants to reward managers for doing a good job, but it is not always easy to tell when they are doing a good job and when they aren't, especially when it comes to something as complex as running a large multinational corporation. A contract that simply said bonuses

---

[3] An actual investor would use more than just information about net income to update her forecasts. Information about sales, cost of goods sold, inventory turnover, cash flows, and income tax expense are just a few examples of other types of financial accounting information that investors would find useful.

would be based on whether or not managers did a good job would not be very useful.

Basing managers' compensation on financial accounting information helps solve this problem, since managers and the corporation's board of directors can agree on some accounting-based measures that will be used to indicate whether or not the managers are doing a good job.[4] Here is an excerpt from Daimler-Chrysler's employment agreement with its board of management explaining how the managers' bonuses are computed:

Annual Bonus

Annual bonuses are based on corporate performance, primarily in relation to profitability. Bonuses are expressed as a percentage of base salary and may be adjusted, upward or downward, based on other corporate objectives, such as shareholder return or revenue growth, and on individual performance.

Source: DaimlerChrysler Form 20-F.

Notice that the bonuses are based on "corporate performance, primarily in relation to profitability." Profitability is usually based on accounting net income, an objective measure computed under a set of GAAP that everyone understands and agrees to. In this way, both sides to the contract are able to easily determine whether or not the terms of the contract have been met. An additional accounting measure—"revenue growth"—is also referred to in this contract.

Use of accounting information in employment contracts makes the contracts more efficient, which is another way of saying the contracts are less costly to the corporation than other types of contracts that are not based on accounting information. For example, DaimlerChrysler could enter into a contract with managers that would pay a bonus based on a vote of its board of directors. This type of contract puts considerable risk on the managers. They may work hard and do an excellent job, and the board of directors may decide to vote a small bonus, or no bonus at all. Alternatively, managers may do a poor job, but the board of directors may decide to vote them a large bonus anyway. Adding this type of risk to the managers' compensation calculation may result in lower-quality managers taking jobs with DaimlerChrysler, or managers may require a higher salary or may work less to compensate them for the added risk. All of these results increase Daimler-Chrysler's costs. To the extent accounting-based contracts reduce or eliminate these costs, the employment contracts are more efficient.

One consequence of the use of accounting net income in managers' bonus contracts is that the managers of DaimlerChrysler may have a strong incentive to maximize reported net income to get the largest possible bonus. This means that managers may have a personal interest in the amount of net income the corporation reports, and to the extent they are able to choose accounting methods or estimates that affect net income, they make these accounting choices knowing that their own compensation is also affected. This idea is discussed more fully in a later section of this chapter.

Debt Agreements

Another typical use of financial accounting information is in contracting with lenders. When corporations borrow money, they enter into contracts with lenders (such as banks, insurance companies, pension funds, or individual bondholders), and these contracts—known as *debt covenants* or *debt agreements*—are often based on financial accounting information. The lenders are concerned that, after borrowing the money, the corporation may undertake risky activities that de-

---

[4] Basing managers' compensation on the company's performance helps align the incentives of managers with those of shareholders, reducing what are known as *agency costs.* Agency costs arise when shareholders delegate the management of a corporation to others.

crease the likelihood that the loan will be repaid. For example, DaimlerChrysler could borrow cash from a bank and pay all the cash out to its shareholders as a dividend. This would make the shareholders better off, but the lender worse off. To protect themselves from this type of risk, lenders would have to charge higher interest rates on loans, making the loans more costly to the borrower. To reduce these borrowing costs, the borrower can enter into a contract with the lender. Under this contract, the borrower agrees not to undertake a variety of activities that make the loan more risky. Usually, these activities are specified in terms of financial accounting information.

Here is an example from the loan contract entered into by Chrysler Corporation (a predecessor of DaimlerChrysler) in connection with a $2,550 million revolving credit agreement:

8.1 Indebtedness to Total Capitalization

Chrysler will not permit the ratio of Indebtedness to Total Capitalization as of the last day of any quarterly period of any fiscal year of Chrysler to be greater than 0.60 to 1.0.

"Indebtedness": . . . all liabilities secured by any Lien on any property owned by such Person or any of its Subsidiaries . . . in each case to be determined on a consolidated basis in accordance with GAAP.

"Total Capitalization": the sum of Indebtedness and Total Shareholders' Equity.

"Total Shareholders' Equity": the sum of (i) the par value (or stated value on the books of Chrysler) of the capital stock of Chrysler, (ii) the par value (or stated value on the books of Chrysler) of the preferred stock of Chrysler, (iii) the aggregate amount of additional paid-in capital of Chrysler and (iv) retained earnings (or minus accumulated deficit) of Chrysler less (v) treasury stock (at cost) of Chrysler, each of clauses (i) through (v) of this definition determined in accordance with GAAP.

Source: Chrysler Corporation Form 10-Q.

In this contract, the borrower is agreeing to limit the ratio of total indebtedness to total capitalization to 0.60 to 1.0. Notice that the definitions of "indebtedness" and "total shareholders' equity" are determined in accordance with GAAP. Both the lender and the borrower understand the complex set of rules that underlie GAAP, and so they are able to agree on a simple way to limit future debt levels to an amount that will not increase the risk to the lender. Entering into these types of debt contracts and basing the terms on financial accounting information reduces the risk to the lender and reduces the borrowing costs to DaimlerChrysler.

Implicit Contracts and Political Costs

In a democracy such as the United States, publicly traded corporations exist because most people believe they increase the overall welfare of society by making it possible for investors to more efficiently pool their capital in business activities. However, the government also has the power to impose costs, such as fines or penalties, on public corporations that are seen as acting against the public interest. A good example of companies acting against the public interest is when large corporations obtain monopoly power, or act to restrain trade, as happened recently in the case of Microsoft Corporation. In another example, the 1998 merger of Daimler Benz and Chrysler Corporation to form DaimlerChrysler required the approval of the U.S. government before it could be accomplished. The government had the power to impose costs on both corporations by refusing to allow the merger to proceed.

One way to view this system of government oversight is to imagine that an implicit contract exists between the public and every publicly traded corporation. The corporation contracts to act in a socially responsible manner in exchange for the legal rights granted by its corporate charter. If the corporation violates the terms of this implicit contract (for example, by acting as a monopolist), the government can act in the public's interest and intervene.

Often government regulators will look to financial accounting net income as a measure of corporate responsibility. Corporations that are earning what are considered to be excessive profits may be subject to government-imposed costs. These costs can take the form of additional regulatory restrictions, additional taxes, imposition of trade barriers, or even, in extreme cases, the breaking up of the corporation, as was done in the last century with the Standard Oil Company and AT&T Corporation, and as the government has recently proposed with Microsoft Corporation.

Any industry that appears to be unusually profitable may be subject to government intervention, particularly if the profits are seen as coming at the expense of the public. A recent example of this is the public scrutiny of profits of pharmaceutical companies, which some people argue are charging excessive prices for prescription drugs. Managers of large firms in politically sensitive industries are aware of the possibility of government intervention and may attempt to reduce the reported accounting net income of their corporations as a way to reduce this possibility.

THE QUALITY OF ACCOUNTING INFORMATION

Financial accounting information has value only if it helps people make good decisions. Information that would result in bad decisions is worthless and will simply be ignored. The more useful the information is in making decisions, the more valuable it will be to users. We can think of information that is very useful in making decisions as being of high quality. What are the characteristics of high-quality information?

The quality of financial accounting information can be assessed at two different levels—the country level, as reflected in the quality of a country's GAAP, and the firm level, as reflected in the quality of an individual firm's financial accounting information. Each of these ideas of quality is discussed more fully below.

The Quality of a Country's GAAP

Since information has value to the extent it helps people make decisions, the first question to ask when assessing information quality is: What is the decision being made? Different types of information may be more or less useful for making different types of decisions. For example, a security analyst trying to predict the future stock price of DaimlerChrysler may find information about research and development expense to be extremely useful, since the success of the company's future products will depend on current research and development activity. However, a banker making a decision to grant a short-term line of credit to Daimler-Chrysler may be more concerned with the marketable securities on the balance sheet and the operating cash flows generated in the past year.

In the United States the assumption is often made that financial accounting information should be useful for determining the price of a company's common stock. This means that accounting information should help investors, and potential investors, to forecast future earnings and cash flows. In academic accounting research, financial accounting information is considered to be useful to the extent it is found to be correlated with stock prices—or percentage changes in stock prices, called *returns*. For example, studies have found that stock prices and returns are correlated with net income. Therefore, accounting researchers believe that net income is a useful type of financial accounting information. The fact that net income has been found to be more highly correlated with stock prices and returns than are cash flows leads researchers to believe that net income is a more useful piece of information for determining stock prices.

In providing financial accounting information to the public, managers face a trade-off between providing relevant information and reliable information. Information is *relevant* to the extent that it would be useful in making a particular decision. For example, in determining a firm's stock price, knowing the market values[5] of all of the firm's assets and liabilities would be extremely useful, and hence this information would be relevant. The problem is that even the firm's managers do not know this information for many of the firm's assets and liabilities. Market value is often a subjective measure, and the best that managers could do would be an estimate of market value.

Suppose that the managers of DaimlerChrysler reported their estimate of the market values of all of the company's assets and liabilities. How useful would that be? Obviously, it would be useful to the extent it was an accurate estimate. But how accurate would it be? It is likely that any estimate of market value would differ from the "true" market value, so that even though this information might be relevant, it might not be reliable.

Reliable information is information that is accurate, precise, and not subject to error. For example, DaimlerChrysler reports that the acquisition cost of land and buildings owned by the company at December 31, 1999, was 20.2 billion euros.[6] Since the management of DaimlerChrysler knows the exact acquisition price of all the company's land and buildings, this information is extremely reliable. However, it is not clear that the acquisition price of land and buildings is very useful in any decisions that people will make about DaimlerChrysler. This information, although reliable, may not be very relevant.

From the above examples it is easy to see the trade-off that exists between relevant information and reliable information. High-quality information would be both relevant and reliable. In many cases it is not possible to achieve both relevance and reliability, and in these cases GAAP must choose one or the other. DaimlerChrysler reports its accounting information based on U.S. GAAP, despite being a Germany company; under U.S. GAAP, assets such as land and buildings are reported at their acquisition price. In the case of these types of assets, U.S. GAAP has chosen reliability over relevance.

Another feature that affects the quality of a country's GAAP is *timeliness*—in other words, how quickly do the GAAP financial accounting numbers reflect information about things that managers expect to happen in the future? For example, suppose that at the end of 1999 the managers of DaimlerChrysler knew that in the year 2000 the company would undergo a major restructuring that would cost the company $1 billion. Should that information be incorporated in the 1999 financial accounting numbers, or should managers wait and report this additional cost in the year 2000 annual report? Prior to 2003, the cost of this future restructuring would be reported in 1999, when management decided on the restructuring plan. Under a recent change in U.S. GAAP, these costs would not be reported until the year in which a liability is actually incurred. This change in accounting standards affects the timeliness of U.S. GAAP.

It is possible to compare the quality of U.S. GAAP with GAAP from other countries, and accounting researchers have attempted to do so in academic research. The results of this comparison will be discussed more fully later in the chapter when we focus on accounting information in a global environment.

The Quality of a Company's Financial Accounting Information

Even though all U.S. publicly traded corporations (and some non-U.S. corporations, such as DaimlerChrysler) report their financial accounting numbers under U.S. GAAP, the quality of the accounting information provided by companies can vary. Security analysts recognize this possibility, and they often consider earnings

---

[5] In the terminology of financial accounting, market values are known as *fair values*. The use of fair values is discussed in later chapters.

[6] Since DaimlerChrysler is a German company, most of the accounting information in their annual report is measured in euros, the currency unit of the European Union.

quality when evaluating the stock price of a particular company. Unfortunately, accounting academics are unable to agree on a definition of *earnings quality*.

For our purposes, earnings quality can be broadly thought of in terms of the following question: How likely is it that the net income reported for the current year will continue into the future? Another term that is often applied to this idea is *earnings persistence.* Here is an example. The reported net income for Daimler-Chrysler in 1999 was 5.7 billion euros, and that of 1998 was 4.8 billion euros. This represents an increase of 900 million euros, or 19 percent. The important question for investors is whether the additional 900 million euros in net income will also continue into the year 2000 and beyond, or was it just a one time increase that will not persist into the future? The more likely a company's net income is to persist into the future, the higher its earnings quality.[7]

Companies can get a reputation for reporting high-quality or low-quality earnings. A company that reports consistent earnings year after year will gain a reputation for high-quality earnings. Investors will feel confident that the net income that management reports will continue into the future. Similarly, a company that reports high earnings one year and low earnings the next may gain a reputation for low-quality earnings. Investors will never be confident that an increase in net income for one year will continue into the future.

Managers have some degree of control over the quality of a company's accounting numbers because of the choices they make in accounting methods. Some accounting methods under U.S. GAAP are more likely to result in consistent earnings over time. Managers who consistently choose these types of accounting methods for their companies will get a reputation for reporting high-quality net income. Managers who consistently choose accounting methods that result in the highest possible reported accounting net income in the current year will get a reputation for reporting low-quality net income. Investors using financial accounting information produced by different companies will take into account the quality of that information when using it to make decisions.

THE ECONOMICS OF ACCOUNTING INFORMATION

When the managers of DaimlerChrysler consider the production of cars, they apply basic economic theory that says the benefit the company receives from producing cars must be greater than the cost of producing the cars. In the case of cars, the benefit received by the company is the revenue from the sale of the cars.

This same basic rule of economics should also apply to the production of accounting information. DaimlerChrysler should only produce accounting information if the benefits received exceed the costs of producing the information. The problem is, unlike the production of cars, it is extremely difficult to measure the benefits and costs of accounting information. In this section we discuss some of these costs and benefits.

Costs of Accounting Information

The costs of accounting information might be thought of as the salaries of all the accountants that DaimlerChrysler has to hire to prepare its financial statements and the cost of computers necessary to keep track of all of its financial accounting information. Also included is the cost of the firm the company employs to audit its financial statements. In the case of DaimlerChrysler, this is the international auditing firm KPMG. For a company the size of DaimlerChrysler, the audit fee would be several millions of dollars. We can think of these types of costs as *direct costs* of financial reporting.

---

[7] Another term that is often associated with earnings quality is how *conservative* the reported earnings are. The notion of conservatism is an important one for financial accounting and is discussed more fully in Chapter 6.

There are other costs beyond the direct costs, and these may be thought of as *indirect costs* of financial reporting. One of the most important is the disclosure of confidential information to DaimlerChrysler's competitors. For example, DaimlerChrysler reported total research and development expenses for 1999 of $5.7 billion. By providing this information to the general public, DaimlerChrysler is also letting Ford, General Motors, and Toyota know the amount it spent on research and development. This may be giving away valuable competitive information to other companies that compete directly with DaimlerChrysler. Similarly, DaimlerChrysler reports accounting information for each of its major business segments—Mercedes-Benz Passenger Cars, Chrysler Group, Commercial Vehicles, Services, and Aerospace. This information also allows competitors to see the revenues and operating profit for the company's major products. Managers of publicly traded firms are aware that by providing financial accounting information to outside users they are also giving away valuable information to competitors.

A major problem with determining the costs of accounting information is this: The people who bear the costs of providing the information are not necessarily the same people who benefit from the information. For example, consider the costs of providing financial accounting information in the DaimlerChrysler financial statements. For simplicity, let's assume that these costs are borne by the shareholders of DaimlerChrysler. (In other words, assume these costs are not passed on in the form of a higher price to the people who buy Mercedes-Benz luxury cars or Chrysler minivans.) Although it seems clear that the DaimlerChrysler shareholders benefit from the financial accounting information the company provides, many other people also benefit from this information. For example, all of the people who are thinking about investing in DaimlerChrysler stock can obtain the annual report and use the accounting information to make their investment decision. Since these people are not actually shareholders of DaimlerChrysler, they are getting the benefit of the accounting information without bearing any of the cost.

This illustrates one of the basic problems with any type of information—the free-rider problem. In economics, a *free rider* is someone who receives the benefit of a good or service without having to pay for it. Since publicly traded corporations must make their financial statements available to the public, people who are not shareholders can have access to the information and use it without having to pay for it. If nonshareholders are asked to compare the costs and benefits of financial accounting information, they will always prefer more information, since the benefit of any information can never be less than the cost to them, which is zero.

Benefits of Accounting Information

The benefits of accounting information come from its usefulness in making decisions. This benefit is extremely hard to measure, and in some cases it is even hard to identify any benefit at all. For example, under U.S. GAAP DaimlerChrysler is required to report information relating to life and health insurance benefits that the company has agreed to pay to retired employees in the future—called *other postemployment benefits*.[8] This information is based on many complex actuarial assumptions about expected employee lives, retirement ages, and changes in health care costs many years in the future. It is costly for DaimlerChrysler to compile this information, which takes up an entire page of the notes to the 1999 annual report. While it may be possible to accurately compute the cost to DaimlerChrysler of providing this information, how can anyone determine the benefit?

---

[8] Accounting for other postemployment benefits is covered in Chapter 14.

To answer this question, we would have to know what decisions people make using this information and how those decisions would be different in its absence. Then we would have to somehow quantify the benefits of what are considered to be the "better" decisions that were made on the basis of the information about the company's other postemployment benefits. It is not clear that there is any way to do this. Comparing costs and benefits of particular items of financial accounting information may not be possible.

There is an additional concept of benefits that goes beyond the benefits to individual decision makers. This is the idea that society as a whole may benefit from corporate financial reporting. To illustrate this idea, consider that Daimler-Chrysler must install pollution control equipment on the cars it sells in the United States. The pollution equipment is costly and increases the price the customer must pay for the car. When an individual purchases a car from Daimler-Chrysler, the customer may not think that the personal benefits from the pollution equipment on the car exceed the additional price paid. However, the benefits of the pollution equipment are realized by society in the form of less air pollution for all of us. In other words, everyone in the country realizes a benefit from the fact that the new Chrysler you buy has pollution control equipment that you had to pay for. You incur the cost, but society gets the benefit.

Financial accounting information could be thought of in the same way. To the extent that financial accounting information helps investors make better investment decisions, this could in turn help to bring about a more efficient use of capital in the U.S. economy, which could benefit our whole society. Those companies most efficient at utilizing resources and producing goods and services that consumers demand will more likely be allocated capital in the form of more shareholders wanting to invest in those companies. If this is the case, then it may not be appropriate to measure only the benefits of accounting information to individual decision makers. A better measure may be to consider the benefits of accounting information to society as a whole, without regard to who actually bears the cost of providing the information.

MANAGERS' INFLUENCE ON ACCOUNTING INFORMATION

Almost all of the numbers reported on the financial statements of Daimler-Chrysler may be influenced to some degree by managers. Managers influence financial statement numbers in three ways—through their choice of accounting methods, through the use of estimates, and through the way they structure the company's transactions.[9]

Consider managers' choice of accounting methods. Even though Daimler-Chrysler's financial statements are prepared in accordance with GAAP, there are many cases in which GAAP allows a choice from among a set of different accounting methods, all of which are acceptable. For example, DaimlerChrysler computes its depreciation expense using both the declining balance method and the straight-line method. Both of these methods are allowed under GAAP, and the amount of depreciation expense the company reports will be different under the two methods. Through the choice of a method of depreciation, DaimlerChrysler's managers can affect reported net income and still be within the requirements of GAAP.

The main point to remember is that two different companies having identical assets and business activities may report different accounting numbers and still be within the rules of GAAP. The choice of accounting methods is one way that managers can affect the amount and timing of the company's reported earnings.

The second way managers influence reported accounting numbers is through the accounting estimates they make. Although the numbers reported in the

---

[9] The ideas briefly covered in this section are discussed in more detail in Chapter 16.

financial statements have the appearance of being exact, in reality many of them are the result of estimates made by managers. For example, in determining depreciation expense managers must estimate the useful life of the assets being depreciated. DaimlerChrysler's financial statements state that "The following useful lives are assumed: buildings—17 to 50 years; site improvements—8 to 20 years; technical equipment and machinery—3 to 30 years; and other equipment, factory and office equipment—2 to 15 years."

Notice that these lives are "assumed." There is no way to tell exactly how long any particular assets are going to be used by the company, and so the financial statements must base the depreciation calculations on managers' estimates of how long these lives should be. These estimates of useful lives become the assumptions used in the depreciation computations. If these assumptions are wrong, then the depreciation taken in any particular year will be overstated or understated.

The final way that managers can affect reported accounting numbers is through their structuring of the legal terms of particular transactions. In many cases, transactions that have similar economic consequences have very different financial accounting results, depending on the legal form of the transaction. One example is the decision to lease assets. Under GAAP, there are two different accounting treatments for leases, depending on the terms of the lease. Those considered to be capital leases under GAAP will be included as assets and liabilities, whereas those considered to be operating leases are not. The net income reported under these two types of leases will also be much different. From an economic perspective, capital and operating leases look quite similar, since the difference between the two relates to details of the lease terms.[10]

ACCOUNTING INFORMATION IN A GLOBAL ENVIRONMENT

As mentioned previously, DaimlerChrysler is a German corporation. You might wonder why its financial statements are prepared in accordance with U.S. GAAP. The reason is that DaimlerChrysler's common stock is traded on the New York Stock Exchange. Since the stock is traded in the United States, the corporation must follow U.S. financial reporting rules and is subject to regulation by the SEC. In addition to trading on the New York Stock Exchange, DaimlerChrysler's stock is also traded on the following exchanges: Frankfurt, Berlin, Bremen, Düsseldorf, Hamburg, Hanover, Stuttgart, Munich (Germany); Chicago, Pacific, Philadelphia (United States); Vienna (Austria); Montreal, Toronto (Canada); Paris (France); London (United Kingdom); Tokyo (Japan); and Basel, Geneva, and Zurich (Switzerland).

Rather than prepare many different sets of financial statements based on the GAAP of each of these countries, DaimlerChrysler has chosen to report its financial accounting information under U.S. GAAP. This avoids the problem that would arise if the company reported different amounts of net income in different countries. Investors would wonder which net income number was correct.

This raises an interesting question. If different countries have different GAAP, is one country's GAAP somehow better than another's? Results of academic research suggest that earnings measured under U.S. GAAP (and GAAP similar to those in the United States, such as in Canada, Australia, and the United Kingdom) are more closely associated with stock returns than are earnings measured under GAAP of other countries (such as Germany and France). This is particularly true with respect to bad economic news about a company, which is reflected quickly in accounting income under U.S. GAAP, making U.S. GAAP earnings timely.

This does not necessarily mean that GAAP from other countries is inferior to U.S. GAAP. Before you can judge the quality of a country's GAAP, you need to

---

[10] Accounting for leases is covered in more detail in Chapter 12.

understand how accounting information is used in that country. In the United States, the primary purpose of financial reporting is to help solve the information asymmetry problem for investors and potential investors. This may not be the most important role for financial reporting in other countries.

In addition to measurement differences between GAAP of different countries, there may be disclosure differences as well. In other words, even if net income is measured the same way under U.S. and Dutch GAAP, there may be requirements to disclose information in the financial statement notes that differ between the two countries. This may make it more difficult to make investment or other decisions about companies incorporated in particular countries. For example, assume that under Dutch GAAP all Dutch corporations must disclose the total amount spent on environmental cleanup and pollution control for the year. If investors think this information is important because they want to invest in environmentally responsible companies, and if this information is not required under U.S. GAAP, they may be more likely to invest in Dutch corporations than U.S. corporations.

There is an easy way for U.S. corporations to overcome the lack of environmental disclosures in the above example. Corporations are always free to voluntarily disclose any information they choose, even if it is not required under GAAP. Therefore, U.S. corporations could voluntarily disclose the amounts spent on environmental cleanup during the year, thus providing the information demanded by the hypothetical investors. Voluntary disclosure could also have an additional effect: If those U.S. corporations that were environmentally responsible voluntarily disclosed this fact, investors would automatically assume that any U.S. corporation that did not voluntarily disclose environmental information must have a bad environmental record. In this way, voluntary disclosure by some companies can lead to other companies being pressured to disclose the same information.

Another major difference in GAAP between different countries is the degree to which financial accounting rules must be the same as tax accounting rules. This concept is generally referred to as *conformity*. In the United States, there is very little conformity between financial and tax accounting rules. This means managers are free to report one net income number to shareholders while reporting a different taxable income number to the government. This is important because there are obvious incentives for managers to report the lowest possible taxable income to minimize the company's income tax payments. If financial accounting income had to match taxable income, this incentive to minimize taxable income may cause managers to report lower net income, thus reducing the ability of financial accounting to solve the information asymmetry problem.

You may wonder what causes different countries to arrive at different GAAP. One reason has already been mentioned: Financial accounting in other countries sometimes has a different objective than simply providing information to investors. A second reason has to do with who gets to set the financial reporting rules. In the United States, GAAP are primarily determined by an organization called the Financial Accounting Standards Board (FASB). The FASB is a private sector body, meaning it is not part of the government, nor is it controlled by the government. Therefore, we refer to accounting standards in the United States as being set by the private sector. Another country with private sector standard setting is the United Kingdom. In some countries, such as Germany, France, and Japan, financial accounting standards are set by the government. This is known as public sector standard setting. Since the goals, motivations, and incentives of individuals working in the private sector may differ from those of individuals in the public sector, particularly if they are elected politicians, it is not surprising that these two types of standard-setting systems result in differences in GAAP.[11]

---

[11] The way accounting standards are determined is discussed more fully in Appendix A.

Summary

This chapter discusses how financial accounting information can be thought of as a product that is produced by corporations and used by a variety of users outside of the company to make decisions. The two main uses of financial accounting information in the United States are (1) to reduce information asymmetry between managers and outside users and (2) to allow more efficient contracts, such as those for manager compensation.

The notion of the quality of financial accounting relates to how useful information is in making decisions, and this often results in a trade-off between relevant information that investors would like to have and reliable information that is accurate, precise, and verifiable. Companies can get a reputation for producing high-quality or low-quality earnings, and this issue of earnings quality is related to how likely it is that the reported earnings will persist into the future.

In providing accounting information, firms would ideally trade off the costs and benefits of the information they provide. There are additional costs to providing accounting information beyond just the direct costs, principally, costs associated with disclosing confidential information to competitors. It is difficult to measure the benefits of accounting information, and the measurement is made more difficult by the problem of free riders, who receive the benefits of information without incurring any cost. Financial accounting information may have social benefits beyond the benefits to individual investors.

Managers have the ability to influence accounting numbers through their choice of accounting methods, their use of estimates, and their ability to structure transactions.

There are international differences in financial reporting rules, how standards are set, and the uses of financial accounting numbers in different countries. These differences in GAAP can result in some countries' financial accounting numbers being more closely related to stock returns.

Discussion Questions

1. Discuss the two major uses of financial accounting information.
2. Explain what is meant by the term *information asymmetry*. How does this term relate to financial accounting?
3. Explain how financial accounting information can be used in contracting.
4. Discuss the trade-off between relevant information and reliable information. Which is more important? Why?
5. Give some criteria that might be applied to evaluate the quality of financial accounting standards.
6. In general, how are the economics of information different from the economics of physical commodities, such as coal or steel? Give some specific examples.
7. What are some costs of providing financial accounting information?
8. What are the benefits of financial accounting information? Who realizes these benefits?
9. Discuss some problems that arise when comparing the costs and benefits of financial accounting information.
10. Explain how managers can influence a company's financial accounting numbers.
11. Why don't multinational companies prepare financial statements using more than one set of generally accepted accounting principles?

Problems

1. Under GAAP, companies must report both net income and net cash flows from operating activities. Which is more relevant, net income or net cash flows? Why? Which is more reliable? Why?

2. Under GAAP, companies must report both the original cost and the current market value of some types of assets. Which is more relevant, original cost or current market value? Why? Which is more reliable? Why?

3. Under GAAP, companies must expense some types of software development costs but capitalize other types of software development costs. Which is more relevant, the cost expensed in the current year or the total of the costs that have been capitalized? Why? Which is more reliable? Why?

4. Under GAAP, the current value of employee stock options issued during the year may either be subtracted from net income on the income statement or disclosed in the notes to the financial statements. What are the costs and benefits associated with these two alternatives?

5. Under GAAP, some types of assets are reported at their current market value while other types of assets are reported at their original cost. What are the costs and benefits associated with these two alternatives?

6. Under GAAP, some types of gains and losses are reflected on the income statement as part of net income, while other types are reported only on the balance sheet as an increase or decrease to shareholders' equity. What are the costs and benefits associated with these two alternatives?

7. For the assets and liabilities listed below, indicate the degree to which managers' opinions and estimates might affect the reported financial statement amounts. (In answering this question, consider different ways that these items might be accounted for. You may ignore GAAP.)

   a. Cash.

   b. Accounts receivable, less an allowance for future uncollectible accounts.

   c. Equipment less accumulated depreciation.

   d. Cost of goods sold when raw materials prices have been changing during the year.

   e. Liability for future warranty expense claims.

   f. Income tax expense associated with foreign earnings.

   g. Possible future loss from a legal judgment not resolved at year-end.

   h. Marketable securities.

   i. Gains and losses from marketable securities.

   j. Rent expense.

Research Reports

1. Locate the most recent annual report of Philips Electronics (the large Dutch electronics company) on the company's website: **www.philips.com.** (You will find a downloadable annual report in the "Investor Information" section of the website. Make sure you download all of the parts of the annual report.)

   Answer the following questions about the Philips' annual report:

   a. Besides the financial statements, what other types of information are contained in the annual report?

   b. What types of financial statements are there in the annual report?

   c. What country's GAAP rules does Philips follow in preparing the financial statements contained in the annual report? (*Hint:* You should find this information at the beginning of the notes to the financial statements.)

   d. What are the differences between Philips' reported net income and the net income that would have been reported under U.S. GAAP? (*Hint:* At the end of the notes to the financial statements there should be a section that compares the company's net income with U.S. GAAP net income. In the

2001 annual report this is in a section called "Application of Generally Accepted Accounting Principles in the United States of America.")

2. Locate the most recent Form 20-F "Annual and Transition Report of Foreign Private Issuers" for Nokia Corporation (the large Finnish electronics company) on the SEC EDGAR database at **www.sec.gov/edgar/searchedgar/companysearch.html.** (Be sure to use the "[html]" version of the form.)

Answer the following questions about the Nokia Form 20-F:

a. Besides the financial statements, what other types of information are contained in the Form 20-F?

b. What types of financial statements are there in the Form 20-F?

c. What country's GAAP rules does Nokia follow in preparing the financial statements contained in the Form 20-F? (*Hint:* You should find this information at the beginning of the notes to the financial statements.)

d. What are the differences between Nokia's reported net income and the net income that would have been reported under U.S. GAAP? (*Hint:* At the end of the notes to the financial statements there should be a section that compares the company's net income with U.S. GAAP net income. In the 2001 Form 20-F this is in a section called "Differences between International Accounting Standards and U.S. Generally Accepted Accounting Principles.")

3. Shown below is part of the notes to the financial statements of ChevronTexaco Corporation for 2001. The note describes ChevronTexaco's method of accounting for costs associated with drilling oil and gas wells during the year.

The successful efforts method is used for oil and gas exploration and production activities. All costs for development wells, related plant and equipment, and proved mineral interests in oil and gas properties are capitalized. Costs of exploratory wells are capitalized pending determination of whether the wells found proved reserves. Costs of wells that are assigned proved reserves remain capitalized. Costs also are capitalized for wells that find commercially producible reserves that cannot be classified as proved, pending one or more of the following: (1) decisions on additional major capital expenditures, (2) the results of additional exploratory wells that are under way or firmly planned, and (3) securing final regulatory approvals for development. Otherwise, well costs are expensed if a determination as to whether proved reserves were found cannot be made within one year following completion of drilling. All other exploratory wells and costs are expensed.

Source: ChevronTexaco Form 10-K.

---

a. In your own words, briefly explain how ChevronTexaco accounts for costs of oil and gas wells.

b. Think of two other ways that these costs might be accounted for. These do not have to be actual accounting methods. You may feel free to use your imagination.

c. Contrast ChevronTexaco's actual accounting method with your two alternative methods on the bases of (i) relevance and (ii) reliability. In other words, which method is the most/least relevant and which is the most/least reliable?

d. Discuss the costs and benefits of ChevronTexaco's actual accounting method.

e. Discuss the costs and benefits of your two alternative methods.

4. The *New York Times* on December 14, 2002, reported the following in an article titled "Chief Quits at Bombardier; Railway Executive Gets Post." (Bombardier is a large Canadian corporation.)

Bombardier changed its chief executive today, citing its sagging share price and a need to improve its corporate governance practices as reasons.

The company, which makes commercial and corporate aircraft, motorboats and passenger trains, said that Robert E. Brown, its president and chief executive, had resigned, and that he would be succeeded by Paul M. Tellier, 63, chief executive of the Canadian National Railway. In his 10 years in that post, Mr. Tellier guided Canadian National through a transformation from a government-owned corporation into one of North America's most efficient and profitable railroads. Before that, he was the highest-ranking civil servant in the Canadian government.

Laurent Beaudoin, Bombardier's chairman and a member of the family that controls the company, said that Mr. Brown, a 15-year Bombardier veteran, had "asked to be relieved of his functions, and the board of directors accepted his resignation at the same meeting."

Cameron Doerksen, an analyst at the Dlouhy Merchant Group in Montreal, where Bombardier is based, said Mr. Brown had been "under a lot of pressure" because of the stock's weakness and an announcement in August that the company would miss its target of 10 percent growth in earnings this year. Analysts have also criticized changes in Bombardier's accounting methods that make comparing present and past performance difficult.

Note the last sentence: "Analysts have also criticized changes in Bombardier's accounting methods that make comparing present and past performance difficult." Answer the following questions with respect to this statement:

a. Why would analysts be critical of accounting changes that made comparing present and past performance difficult? In particular, what types of costs does this impose on the analysts?

b. Why would the management of Bombardier change their accounting methods? In particular, what benefits were they expecting? What costs did they incur?

c. Assume that Bombardier's new accounting methods are more relevant and reliable than the old methods. Would the analysts' criticism still be justified? Why or why not?

d. Suggest some approaches to accounting method changes that would allow companies to change to methods that are more relevant or reliable, or both, but would also allow investors to compare present and past performance. What are the costs of your approaches? Do the benefits outweigh the costs?

Chapter Learning Objectives

After reading this chapter you should understand

1. The nature of an accounting accrual.
2. The relationship between accounting periods and accruals.
3. The limitations of the cash receipts and disbursements method.
4. The revenue recognition criteria and what types of accruals affect revenue recognition.
5. The expense recognition criteria and what types of accruals affect expense recognition.
6. The matching principle.
7. The major categories of items reflected on the income statement.
8. The concept of materiality.
9. The treatment of transitory items on the income statement.

Chapter 2

Accrual Accounting and the Income Statement

Focus Company: Microsoft

Introduction

This chapter discusses the types of financial accounting information that are useful in answering questions about a company's economic performance, questions like, How profitable is the company? and How likely is it that the company's current level of profitability will continue into the future? To answer these questions, a person may use financial statements to find useful information about revenues, expenses, and gains and losses, as well as an overall performance measure called *net income,* or *earnings.* All of these items are presented in a company's income statement.

The chapter begins by introducing an important concept in financial reporting: the accounting period. Separating a company's entire economic life into short time periods results in a need for accounting accruals. Accruals are a fundamental concept in financial reporting, and understanding accruals is necessary for anyone using information found in an income statement. The chapter next discusses revenue and expense recognition criteria and explains how accruals are used to modify cash receipts and disbursements. The different components of an income statement are discussed next, followed by an explanation of income statements used in other countries and a brief discussion of how information in the income statement can be used to make decisions.

As an example to follow throughout this chapter, the income statements of Microsoft Corporation for the years ended June 30, 1998, 1999, and 2000 are presented on page 22. As additional examples, the income statements of The Boeing Company, IBM Corporation, Kmart Corporation, and Chrysler Corporation are presented at the end of this chapter.

ACCOUNTING PERIODS AND ACCRUALS

Microsoft's net income is computed separately each year because the income statement summarizes transactions that took place over some definite time period, referred to as an *accounting period.*[1] Annual accounting periods usually end on the last day of a calendar month, and often this month is December, although many companies in the United States use year-ends other than December. Microsoft has an annual accounting period ending on June 30. Kmart's year-end (known as a 52–53-week year) ends on a different calendar date each year (January 26, 2000; January 27, 1999; January 28, 1998) and is designed to end on the same day of the week each year (for example, the last Wednesday in January).

---

[1] The accounting period is usually a 12-month year (annual income statement) or a three-month quarter (quarterly income statement).

MICROSOFT CORPORATION Income Statements (in millions, except earnings per share)			
	Year Ended June 30		
	1998	**1999**	**2000**
Revenue	$15,262	$19,747	**$22,956**
Operating expenses:			
Cost of revenue	2,460	2,814	**3,002**
Research and development	2,601	2,970	**3,775**
Acquired in-process technology	296	—	**—**
Sales and marketing	2,828	3,231	**4,141**
General and administrative	433	689	**1,009**
Other expenses	230	115	**92**
Total operating expenses	8,848	9,819	**12,019**
Operating income	6,414	9,928	**10,937**
Investment income	703	1,803	**3,182**
Gain on sales	—	160	**156**
Income before income taxes	7,117	11,891	**14,275**
Provision for income taxes	2,627	4,106	**4,854**
Net income	$ 4,490	$ 7,785	**$ 9,421**
Earnings per share			
Basic	$ 0.92	$ 1.54	**$ 1.81**
Diluted	$ 0.84	$ 1.42	**$ 1.70**

Source: Microsoft Corporation annual report.

The separation of a company's economic life into small accounting periods, such as years and quarters, causes many of the measurement problems in financial accounting, and leads to the use of what are called *accruals* (discussed in more detail later in the chapter). Presented below is an example of why the use of accounting periods causes problems for financial reporting.

Assume you and two friends decide to start a software company. You each contribute $5,000 (a total of $15,000), buy some computer equipment, and develop an application that you sell by mail. You operate the business for three years, at which time you decide the market for the product has dried up, so you pay off all of the bills and liquidate the company. After scrapping the now-obsolete computer equipment and all the remaining supplies (shipping boxes, blank CDs, and so forth), the company ends up with a total of $37,500 cash in the bank, which is divided up among the three owners. Given these facts, computing the net income of the company over the three-year period is easy: $37,500 cash left for the owners, less $15,000 originally contributed, equals net income of $22,500.

But what if you couldn't wait three years to compute net income? Accounting information is not likely to be useful if profitability can only be measured when a business is terminated and liquidated. For example, the year 2000 was Microsoft's twenty-fifth anniversary, while other well-known U.S. corporations such as General Motors, Coca-Cola, and IBM are much older. For accounting information to be useful it must be timely, which means for U.S. public companies net income must be computed each quarter. This need for timely financial accounting information, produced for discrete accounting periods such as quarters or years, makes financial reporting much more complex than it would be if financial statements were prepared just once at the end of a firm's life.

Continuing with the example, suppose that after the software business had been in operation for one year the owners (that is, you and your two friends) needed to know how profitable the year had been. In other words, what was the net income for the first year of operation? One way to start is by looking at the bank balance at the end of the year, since that's how the net income over the three-year period was determined. Here's some information about cash receipts, cash disbursements, and bank balances for the first year of operation:[2]

	Increase/ (Decrease)	Bank Balance
Cash from owners	$15,000	$15,000
Buy computers	(9,000)	6,000
Pay rent (nine months)	(2,700)	3,300
Cash from customers (400 orders)	12,000	15,300
Buy blank CDs (1,000)	(500)	14,800
Buy shipping boxes (1,500)	(1,500)	13,300
Postage for shipping (300 orders)	(300)	13,000

Using the same procedure that was used in computing net income for the three-year life of the business, the $15,000 cash originally contributed would be subtracted from the $13,000 bank balance at the end of the year, resulting in a net loss of $2,000 for the year.

But how useful is the accounting information—a loss of $2,000—using this cash receipts and disbursements method? If the owners used this method of accounting, they might conclude that the business was losing money and abandon it, when in fact we saw that over the three-year period the business was profitable, earning net income of $22,500. Therefore, in this example relying on accounting information based on the cash receipts and disbursements method may result in poor decisions.

Contrast the above result with net income measured under the accrual method, as required under GAAP. Under the accrual method, net income is recognized in the accounting period in which it is earned rather than when it is received in cash. Let's go through each of the cash receipt and disbursement items and see how the accrual method might modify net income.

First, consider the purchase of the computers for $9,000. Under the cash receipts and disbursements method this is treated as a reduction in net income for the year. However, as we saw earlier, these computers were used for three years and scrapped at the end of the third year. Since the cost of the computers provides a benefit to the business for three years, under accrual accounting part of that cost is allocated to each of those years. For convenience we can allocate one-third of the cost to each year. Therefore, our expense[3] for computers for the first year is $3,000 rather than $9,000.

Now consider the $2,700 paid for nine months rent, or $300 per month. The owners of the business forgot to pay their rent for the last three months of the

---

[2] In presenting accounting numbers in financial statements, negative numbers or subtractions are shown in parentheses rather than with a minus sign.

[3] In accounting there is a subtle difference between the words *cost* and *expense.* The cost of something is how much we paid, or will pay, for it; an expense is the amount we record on the income statement as a reduction in net income. Therefore, the cost of the computer equipment is $9,000, but the expense for the first year is $3,000.

year. Their landlord sent them a past-due notice in January of the second year, and they promptly paid the back rent they owed. However, to properly measure net income for the first year under the accrual method the rent should be for twelve months, not nine, making the expense for rent $3,600 rather than $2,700.

During the year, orders for 400 copies of software were received, with each order containing a check or credit card payment of $30, for total cash receipts of $12,000. The software had to be tailored to each customer's specifications, and because of this only 300 units of software were actually mailed out by the end of the year. Early in the second year, the remaining 100 units were shipped to customers. Under the accrual method, only the revenue relating to the 300 units actually shipped by year-end is properly included in net income for the first year, a total of $9,000 (rather than $12,000).

The business purchased 1,000 blank CDs for $0.50 each (total $500) and 1,500 shipping boxes for $1.00 each (total $1,500). Since only 300 pieces of software were actually shipped to customers during the year, there were 700 blank CDs and 1,200 shipping boxes left at year-end. These leftover items were used in the second year, and under accrual accounting their cost does not reduce net income in the first year. Only the costs associated with the 300 units actually shipped are included in the first year, a total of $150 for CDs and $300 for shipping boxes. Finally, all of the postage of $300 related to the units shipped in the first year and is therefore properly used to reduce first-year net income.

Shown below is a comparison of the net income for the first year under the accrual method of accounting compared with the cash receipts and disbursements method:[4]

	Accrual Method	Cash Method
Sales revenue	$9,000	$12,000
Computer expense	(3,000)	(9,000)
Rent expense	(3,600)	(2,700)
Blank CD expense	(150)	(500)
Shipping boxes expense	(300)	(1,500)
Postage expense	(300)	(300)
Net income (Loss)	$1,650	$ (2,000)

Two things are apparent in this example. First, the problems that arose under the cash receipts and disbursements method came about only because of the necessity of ending the accounting period at the end of the first year (thus, dividing up the economic life of the business into discrete accounting periods) and measuring net income for the first year. If we could simply wait and compute one net income number when the business is wrapped up and liquidated, there would be no need for accrual accounting. Second, accrual accounting modifies cash receipts and disbursements to arrive at net income.[5]

An important point to note is that the use of the accrual method has no effect on the bank balance of the business. Under both the cash receipts and disbursements method and the accrual method, the bank balance at the end of the first year was $13,000, and the cash flow for the first year was negative $2,000. It is useful to complete this example by reconciling the negative $2,000 cash flow with the positive $1,650 accrual net income:

[4] The proper accounting terminology is to refer to the computer expense as *depreciation expense*. Depreciation is discussed more fully in Chapter 8.

[5] This will be covered in more detail later in the chapter.

Accrual net income	$ 1,650
Cash received for units not shipped	3,000
Additional rent expense owed at year end	900
Cost of computers relating to years 2 and 3	(6,000)
Cost of blank CDs used in year 2	(350)
Cost of shipping boxes used in year 2	(1,200)
Negative cash flow	$(2,000)

This relation between accrual net income and cash flows will be explored in more detail when the cash flows statement is covered in Chapter 4, but for now the most important points to remember are that accrual accounting uses accruals to modify cash flows to arrive at net income and that accruals are necessary because (1) companies enter into transactions that affect more than one accounting period, and (2) in many transactions the economic effect of the transaction takes place in a different accounting period from the cash flow effect. The sections below investigate in more detail the rules relating to accrual accounting and the income statement.

REVENUE RECOGNITION CRITERIA

Before discussing how accrual accounting affects revenues, it is important to understand the accounting rules governing revenue recognition. Revenue recognition refers to the GAAP rules that determine when revenue can be recorded on the income statement—that is, determining the proper accounting period in which the revenue belongs.

The term *revenue* means a net inflow of economic resources to the firm (usually represented by cash receipts or accounts receivable) arising from the ordinary business activities of the firm (usually selling a product or providing a service to customers). Borrowing money does not result in a net inflow of economic resources, because the cash received from the loan is offset by an obligation (a liability) to repay the loan in the future. Also, not all inflows of economic resources are considered revenue, only those that are related to the firm's ordinary business activities. For example, in the hypothetical software company, the cash you and your friends contributed to start up the business was not considered revenue.

For financial reporting purposes it is usually not difficult to determine whether a particular transaction represents revenue to the firm; the difficulty usually relates to determining in which accounting period the revenue properly belongs. This difficulty stems directly from the necessity of preparing income statements for discrete accounting periods. GAAP rules for revenue recognition deal with recording revenue in the correct accounting period.

The basic rule for revenue recognition is as follows: Revenue is recognized when (1) it is realized or realizable, and (2) it is earned. The requirement that revenue be realized or realizable is usually not a problem in most business settings. *Realized* means cash is received, or a promise to pay is received from the buyer—that is, an account receivable. *Realizable* means some other type of property is received that can be readily converted into cash, such as a piece of machinery with a known market value. Most of the complexity relating to revenue recognition stems from attempts to determine exactly when revenue is earned.

When Is Revenue Considered Earned?

Revenue is considered earned when the firm has done essentially everything it must do to be entitled to keep the revenue from the transaction. Here are some general rules that apply in most situations:

- Revenue from sales of products is considered earned when the product is shipped, or delivered, to the customer.
- Revenue from the performance of services is considered earned when the services have been performed.
- Revenue related to the use of property (for example, rental revenue or interest revenue) is considered earned with the passage of time as the property is used.

For the hypothetical software start-up company, orders for 400 copies of software were received during the first year, but only 300 units of software were actually mailed out by the end of the year. To be consistent with the revenue recognition criteria, only the revenue relating to the 300 units actually shipped by year-end is properly recorded for the first year, despite the fact that the company had actually collected the cash for the remaining 100 units. Revenue could not be recognized for those units in the first year because the revenue had not yet been earned. The revenue is considered earned when the software is shipped to customers in the second year.

To give you an example of how the revenue recognition criteria are applied to a real software company, here is a note from Microsoft's 2000 annual report discussing its accounting policies with respect to revenue recognition:

Revenue Recognition

Revenue is recognized when earned. The Company's revenue recognition policies are in compliance with all applicable accounting regulations, including American Institute of Certified Public Accountants (AICPA) Statement of Position (SOP) 97-2, *Software Revenue Recognition,* and SOP 98-9, *Modification of SOP 97-2, With Respect to Certain Transactions.* Revenue from products licensed to original equipment manufacturers is recorded when OEMs ship licensed products while revenue from certain license programs is recorded when the software has been delivered and the customer is invoiced. Revenue from packaged product sales to and through distributors and resellers is recorded when related products are shipped. Maintenance and subscription revenue is recognized ratably over the contract period. Revenue attributable to undelivered elements, including technical support and Internet browser technologies, is based on the average sales price of those elements and is recognized ratably on a straight-line basis over the product's life cycle. When the revenue recognition criteria required for distributor and reseller arrangements are not met, revenue is recognized as payments are received. Costs related to insignificant obligations, which include telephone support for certain products, are accrued. Provisions are recorded for returns, concessions and bad debts.

Source: Microsoft Corporation annual report.

As you can see from this note, applying the revenue recognition criteria to a company like Microsoft is an extremely complex undertaking. Microsoft recognizes revenues from different types of activities differently, such as revenue from products licensed to original equipment manufacturers and revenue from packaged product sales. Also, Microsoft follows certain technical accounting requirements for revenue recognition (for example, SOP 97-2, *Software Revenue Recognition*) set out by the American Institute of Certified Public Accountants. However, despite all of this complexity, the basic rule relating to revenue recognition is still fairly simple and is set out in the first sentence of Microsoft's note: "Revenue is recognized when earned."

The rules for revenue recognition are based on the notion that, given a choice, managers would be more likely to recognize revenue too early. Therefore, most exceptions to the general revenue recognition criteria are designed to delay the time at which firms can recognize revenue. For example, SOP 97-2 *Software Revenue Recognition* referred to above, contains the following general provision:[6]

---

[6] SOP 97-2 *Software Revenue Recognition* is an extremely complex regulation dealing with many subtle revenue recognition issues. The general rule discussed in the text has been highly simplified to make it easier for students to understand the major points of the regulation.

If an arrangement to deliver software does not require significant production, modification, or customization of software, revenue should be recognized when all of the following criteria are met: (1) evidence of an arrangement exists; (2) delivery has occurred; (3) the vendor's fee is fixed or determinable; and (4) collectibility is probable (Ernst & Young LLP explanation of SOP 97-2).

This looks quite similar to the general revenue recognition criteria of revenue being (1) received or receivable and (2) earned. However, SOP 97-2 goes on to state that, in those instances in which an arrangement to deliver software requires significant production, modification, or customization of software, the vendor must delay the recognition of revenue past the time of delivery and must recognize the revenue over the term of the arrangement as the production, modification, and customization operations are performed. This has the effect of delaying the recognition of revenue until it has been earned by the company, as evidenced by the completion of the production, modification, or customization requirements.

The U.S. Securities and Exchange Commission, which has the final authority over U.S. GAAP, has recently become so concerned that companies are recognizing revenue too early that it issued an official pronouncement, Staff Accounting Bulletin No. 101, in December 1999 to deal with the issue. According to the SEC, the results of a March 1999 study of accounting fraud found that more than half the cases of financial reporting fraud involved overstating revenue. The form of Staff Accounting Bulletin No. 101 is a series of examples, for which the staff of the SEC gives their interpretation of how the revenue recognition criteria should be applied. Consider the following example from Question 5 of Staff Accounting Bulletin No. 101:

> A company sells a lifetime membership in a health club. After paying a nonrefundable "initiation fee," the customer is permitted to use the health club indefinitely, so long as the customer also pays an additional usage fee each month. The monthly usage fees collected from all customers are adequate to cover the operating costs of the health club.

The question posed by the Staff Accounting Bulletin is as follows: When should the revenue relating to the nonrefundable up-front fee be recognized? Here is how the staff of the SEC answered that question:

> The staff believes that companies should consider the specific facts and circumstances to determine the appropriate accounting for nonrefundable, up-front fees. Unless the up-front fee is in exchange for products delivered or services performed that represent the culmination of a separate earnings process, the deferral of revenue is appropriate.
>
> In the situation described above, the staff does not view the activities completed by the company (i.e., selling the membership) as a discrete earnings event. The terms, conditions, and amounts of these fees typically are negotiated in conjunction with the pricing of all the elements of the arrangement, and the customer would ascribe a significantly lower, and perhaps no, value to elements ostensibly associated with the up-front fees in the absence of the registrant's performance of other contract elements. The fact that the company does not sell the initial rights, products, or services separately (i.e., without the company's continuing involvement) supports the staff's view. The staff believes that the customers are purchasing the on-going rights, products, or services being provided through the company's continuing involvement. Further, the staff believes that the earnings process is completed by performing under the terms of the arrangement, not simply by originating a revenue-generating arrangement.

In other words, a company cannot "earn" revenue simply by signing up customers and collecting a nonrefundable up-front fee. The revenue is considered earned as the company provides products or services to its customers.

Alternative Recognition Dates

Although the general rule for revenue recognition is to recognize revenue when products are delivered or services are performed, there are some important exceptions to this rule. In some cases, revenue is recognized prior to the delivery of a product or service; in other cases, revenue is not recognized until cash is collected from the customer. Both of these situations are discussed in this section.

Revenue Recognition Prior to Delivery

There are two cases in which revenue is recognized prior to the delivery of a product or service. The first case usually occurs only in mining or agricultural industries. When a firm produces a commodity (such as gold or wheat) for which there is a ready market for any quantity at a quoted price, revenue may be recognized at the time the commodity is produced (that is, the gold is mined or the wheat is harvested). The presence of a commodity market and a quoted market price means that the firm doesn't have to do anything else to convert the commodity into cash except agree to sell at the market price.

The second case in which revenue is recognized prior to the delivery of the product relates to what are called *long-term contracts*. These are contracts under which (1) a firm enters into an agreement that will take longer than a single accounting period to complete, and (2) the firm is allowed to periodically bill the customer as portions of the work are completed. Examples of these types of contracts are for completing a section of interstate highway, erecting a skyscraper, or building a nuclear submarine. Since the firm is actually earning revenue over several accounting periods, as work on the contract is carried out, it would not be very useful to report all of the revenue bunched up in the final year of the contract when the product is finally delivered to the customer. Therefore, in the case of long-term construction contracts, revenue is recognized throughout the contract period as work on the contract is completed.

Recognizing revenue as work on the contract is completed is known as the *percentage of completion method* of accounting. Under the percentage of completion method the amount of revenue recognized each period is based on the percentage of the total expected costs for the contract that have been incurred during the period. For example, if a company incurs $40 million in costs on a contract in the current year, and the total costs expected to be incurred on the contract are $100 million, the company would recognize 40 percent of the revenue from the contract in the current year.

Revenue Recognition as Cash Is Collected

In some unusual situations revenue has been earned and a product delivered, but there is some substantial doubt as to whether the sales price will ultimately be collected by the seller. In this case, the realized or realizable part of the revenue recognition criteria has not been satisfied, and revenue is not recognized until cash is collected in future accounting periods as payments are made from the buyer to the seller. For example, a company may sell an acre of land to a buyer, where the buyer agrees to pay the purchase price evenly over 10 years. If there is substantial doubt as to whether the full purchase price will ever be paid, revenue should not be recognized at the time of sale.

In these unusual situations two methods are used: the cost recovery method and the installment sales method. Both methods defer revenue recognition until cash is collected, but the cost recovery method delays recognizing any profit until after the full cost of the product sold has been received in cash, whereas the installment method recognizes some profit each time a cash payment is received. The installment method is sometimes used for income tax accounting purposes, but neither method is an acceptable accounting method under GAAP except in unusual circumstances. The methods are most often used in reporting sales of land and sales of new business franchises.

USING ACCRUALS TO MODIFY CASH RECEIPTS

Accruals are necessary to properly record revenue in two different situations. The first is the case in which cash is collected from the buyer in the accounting period after the revenue from the sale is recorded. The second is the case in which cash is collected from the buyer in the accounting period before the sale is recorded. If the sale is recorded in the same accounting period that cash is collected, no accrual is necessary.

Cash Collected after Year of Sale

To demonstrate the effect of accruals, consider a basic business transaction: the sale of a product to a customer on account, where *on account* means that the customer agrees to pay the purchase price in the future, creating an account receivable for the seller (and an account payable for the buyer). Assume that the terms of sale require payment within 60 days of shipment of the product, and the product is shipped on December 10, 2001. This transaction meets the criteria for revenue recognition under GAAP. If the seller uses the calendar year as an accounting period, the revenue from this sale should properly be recorded in the income statement for the year ended December 31, 2001, even though the cash from the sale will not be collected until the 2002 accounting period.

Accrual accounting allows the firm to record the sale in the year in which the economic inflow occurred (2001) rather than the year in which the cash was received (2002). Users of financial statements agree that, in most cases, accrual accounting net income is more useful than cash receipts and disbursements for (1) measuring the firm's past performance and (2) predicting the firm's future performance. This does not mean that accrual accounting information is more useful than cash flow information for all types of decisions made by users of financial statements. There are many types of decisions for which users will prefer cash flow information, which is why firms are required to provide cash flow information as part of their financial statements.[7] However, for measuring past profitability and predicting future profitability, accrual accounting measures are deemed superior to cash flow measures.

Microsoft reported accounts receivable of $3,250 million at the end of 2000, which were included in sales revenue in 2000 but not received as cash until the following year. Similarly, the accounts receivable of $2,245 million at the end of the previous year (1999) were included in sales revenue for 1999 but received as cash in 2000. Microsoft's sales revenue for 2000 was more than $1 billion greater than its cash receipts from selling products, as shown below:

Microsoft 2000 accrual basis sales revenue (in millions)	$22,956
Less: Accounts receivable at June 30, 2000	(3,250)
Plus: Accounts receivable at June 30, 1999	2,245
Estimated 2000 cash receipts	$21,951

If Microsoft reported cash receipts rather than accrual basis sales revenues, it would have ignored more than one billion dollars of economic inflows to the company (represented by the increase in accounts receivable) that occurred during the year.

Cash Collected before Year of Sale

The second way accruals are used to adjust cash receipts is when cash is collected from the buyer in the accounting period before the sale is recorded. In this

---

[7] The cash flows statement is covered in detail in Chapter 4.

situation, the firm has received cash but has not yet earned the revenue. An example of this occurred in the hypothetical software start-up company, where cash relating to 400 units was collected in the first year, but only 300 units were shipped by year-end. In that case, only the revenue related to the 300 units shipped was recorded under the accrual method. The company received $12,000 in cash, but it only recognized $9,000 of revenue. The journal entry to record this transaction would look like this:[8]

	Journal Entry to Record Cash Receipts for Software Orders		
+/−	Accounts [description of account]	Debit	Credit
+	Cash [balance sheet asset account]	12,000	
+	Sales Revenue [income statement revenue account]		9,000
+	Unearned Revenue [balance sheet liability account]		3,000

Cash is increased by the $12,000 received by the company. The Sales Revenue account is only increased by the $9,000 relating to the units shipped during the year. For the other $3,000 related to units not yet shipped, the entry is to increase an account called Unearned Revenue, a balance sheet liability account. The cash collected for units not yet shipped to customers is treated as a liability of the company, since the company is obligated to either ship the customers products in the future or refund the customers' payments. Revenue is not recognized for this $3,000 until the year the products are shipped. When the products are shipped in the second year, an entry is made to decrease the Unearned Revenue liability account and increase the Sales Revenue account, since the revenue has now been earned. Here is the entry to record revenue when the products are shipped in the second year:

	Journal Entry to Record Sales Revenue on Shipment		
+/−	Accounts [description of account]	Debit	Credit
−	Unearned Revenue [balance sheet liability account]	3,000	
+	Sales Revenue [income statement revenue account]		3,000

In this entry, the Unearned Revenue account that was originally increased at the time the cash was received for the unshipped units is now decreased, since the company has now earned the revenue and has no future liability to these customers. For the same reason, the Sales Revenue account is increased to reflect the fact that the $3,000 is now considered to be earned.

Unearned revenue can also arise with respect to future services that the company is obligated to perform for customers who paid an up-front fee for the service. An example of this is SEC Staff Accounting Bulletin No. 101 (discussed above), in which the SEC held that an up-front fee charged for a health club membership was actually earned over the period in which the customer used the health club services, not all at once when the membership fee was received.

This note from Microsoft's 2000 annual report demonstrates accounting for unearned revenue:

[8] In this journal entry and all subsequent journal entries in this textbook, the term *debit* refers to an increase in an asset or expense account, and a decrease in a liability, owners' equity, or revenue account. The term *credit* refers to an increase in a liability, owners' equity, or revenue account, and a decrease in an asset or expense account. The +/− indicates whether the particular account is being increased (+) or decreased (−). In actual practice the [description of account] and the +/− would not be included. For help with recording accounting transactions using journal entries, see Appendix B.

Unearned Revenue	

A portion of Microsoft's revenue is earned ratably over the product life cycle or, in the case of subscriptions, over the period of the license agreement.

End users receive certain elements of the Company's products over a period of time. These elements include items such as browser technologies and technical support. Consequently, Microsoft's earned revenue reflects the recognition of the fair value of these elements over the product's life cycle. Upon adoption of SOP 98-9 during the fourth quarter of fiscal 1999, the Company was required to change the methodology of attributing the fair value to undelivered elements. The percentages of undelivered elements in relation to the total arrangement decreased, reducing the amount of Windows and Office revenue treated as unearned, and increasing the amount of revenue recognized upon shipment. The percentage of revenue recognized ratably decreased from a range of 20% to 35% to a range of approximately 15% to 25% of Windows desktop operating systems. For desktop applications, the percentage decreased from approximately 20% to a range of approximately 10% to 20%. The ranges depend on the terms and conditions of the license and prices of the elements. In addition, in the fourth quarter of fiscal 1999, the Company extended the life cycle of Windows from two to three years based upon management's review of product shipment cycles. Product life cycles are currently estimated at 18 months for desktop applications. The Company also sells subscriptions to certain products via maintenance and certain organizational license agreements. At June 30, 1999 and 2000, Windows Platforms products unearned revenue was $2.17 billion and $2.61 billion and unearned revenue associated with Productivity Applications and Developer products totaled $1.96 billion and $1.99 billion. Unearned revenue for other miscellaneous programs totaled $116 million and $210 million at June 30, 1999 and 2000.

Source: Microsoft Corporation annual report.

Microsoft considers a portion of the cash it receives from software sales to be related to future services the company is obligated to provide to purchasers, such as browser technologies and technical support. In addition, Microsoft sells some products on a subscription basis. This is similar to a customer purchasing a three-year magazine subscription and paying the full three-year subscription price in advance. The recognition of the revenue is deferred and recognized as the company provides the product or service to the customer in future accounting periods.

Microsoft reported a liability for unearned revenue equal to $4,816 million at June 30, 2000, and $4,239 million at June 30, 1999. This means that as of June 30, 2000, Microsoft had received $4,816 million from customers relating to products or services that the company would provide in future accounting periods. Therefore, just like accounts receivable balances allowed us to reconcile revenues and cash receipts, unearned revenue balances also allow a reconciliation of Microsoft's 2000 accrual basis revenues with 2000 cash receipts. Assuming unearned revenue from 1999 was included in revenue (but not cash receipts) in 2000, and that unearned revenue from 2000 was included in cash receipts (but not revenue) in 2000, the reconciliation looks like this:

Microsoft 2000 accrual basis sales revenue (in millions)	$22,956
Less: Accounts receivable at June 30, 2000	(3,250)
Less: Unearned revenue at June 30, 1999	(4,239)
Plus: Accounts receivable at June 30, 1999	2,245
Plus: Unearned revenue at June 30, 2000	4,816
Estimated 2000 cash receipts	$22,528

Notice that this estimate of Microsoft's 2000 cash receipts is different from that computed earlier when we used only the accounts receivable balances. That's because all of the accruals relating to cash receipts must be used to arrive at an accurate reconciliation. The cash receipts estimated using only the accounts receivable balances left out an important accrual account: Unearned Revenue.

EXPENSE RECOGNITION CRITERIA

In the same way that there are GAAP rules for recording revenue using the accrual method, there are also rules for recording expenses. Expenses (along with revenues and gains and losses) are one of the three categories of transactions reported on the income statement. An expense is a net outflow of economic resources from the firm (usually represented by cash disbursements or accounts payable) arising from the ordinary business activities of the firm. In addition, an expense also arises when a firm's assets are used up or decrease in value. For example, in the hypothetical software company the using up of one-third of the economic life of the computer equipment was treated as an expense. Not all outflows of economic resources are considered expenses. The payment of a cash dividend to shareholders is not an expense. Also, the purchase of assets, such as computer equipment, does not result in an expense until the assets are used up by the company or are sold as inventory.

This section discusses two basic criteria for recording expenses: the concept of matching expenses with revenues, and the concept of matching expenses with accounting periods.

The Matching Principle

One of the fundamental principles underlying accrual accounting is that expenses should be matched with the revenue generated by those expenses. This is known as the *matching principle*. The term *matching* means recording an expense in the same accounting period as the revenue to which the expense relates. The reason the matching principle is necessary is to prevent revenues and expenses from being recorded in different accounting periods.

In determining the expense for blank CDs and shipping boxes for the hypothetical software company, only the costs of CDs and shipping boxes related to the 300 units shipped were charged to expenses in the first year, since only the revenue associated with those 300 units was recorded in the first year. Under the accrual method, the revenues and expenses associated with the 300 shipped units were matched, or recorded in the same accounting period. The costs of the additional CDs and shipping boxes were treated as an asset of the company; they will be treated as an expense in a future period when the CDs and shipping boxes are used to ship additional units of software.

Expenses that can be associated with a particular product or service in this way are referred to as *product costs*. Product costs often consist of wages paid to employees to manufacture products or perform services; raw materials costs, such as the blank CDs; supplies, such as the shipping boxes; and other types of manufacturing costs, such as a portion of the cost of a machine or a factory building.[9]

Matching Expenses with Accounting Periods

Not all types of expenses can be matched with a particular product or service. In the example of the hypothetical software company, rent expense was recorded on the basis of number of months that the company used the rented space rather than the number of units shipped during the period. That's because there was no direct relationship between the rent for the office space and the production of the software units.

Expenses that are not associated with a product or service are known as *period costs*. Other examples of period costs are salaries of corporate officers, legal and accounting fees, and advertising expenses. Since period costs are not associated with any particular products or services, they cannot be matched against

---

[9] Product costs will be discussed more fully in Chapter 7.

revenue. Instead, period costs are recorded as expenses in the accounting period to which the expense relates. That's why the rent expense for the hypothetical software company was recorded in the first year (the period during which the company rented the office space) rather than being matched with the shipment of products. Similarly, computer expense was recorded on the basis of the expected useful life of the computer equipment (three years) rather than being associated with the sale of products.

Presented below are examples of product costs and period costs from the notes to Microsoft's 2000 annual report. The items labeled cost of revenue on the income statement are product costs and are matched against revenue generated from the sale of products and services. In contrast, advertising costs are expensed as incurred, meaning they are treated as an expense in the same period that the advertising takes place.

Cost of Revenue

Cost of revenue includes direct costs to produce and distribute product and direct costs to provide online services, consulting, product support, and training and certification of system integrators.

Advertising Costs

Advertising costs are expensed as incurred. Advertising expense was $732 million in 1998, $804 million in 1999, and $1.1 billion in 2000.

Source: Microsoft Corporation annual report.

USING ACCRUALS TO MODIFY CASH DISBURSEMENTS

Just as accounting accruals like accounts receivable and unearned revenue were used to convert cash receipts into sales revenue, accruals also modify cash disbursements into accrual basis expenses. Two basic types of expense accruals are accrued expenses and prepaid expenses.

Accrued Expenses

Accrued expenses represent products or services that the company has acquired in the current accounting period but has not paid for by the end of the period. Common examples of accrued expenses are accounts payable for raw materials purchased, wages payable for wages earned by workers, and taxes payable for income taxes owed for the year. In the hypothetical software company example, the rent for the last three months of the year represented an accrued expense; the company had used the office space for those three months during the year but had not paid the rent by the end of the year. Here is how the journal entry would look to record accrued rent expense:

	Journal Entry to Record Rent Expense		
+/−	**Accounts [description of account]**	**Debit**	**Credit**
+	Rent Expense [income statement expense account]	3,600	
−	Cash [balance sheet asset account]		2,700
+	Rent Payable [balance sheet liability account		900

The Cash account is decreased by the $2,700 cash payments made for rent. The Rent Expense account is increased by the total amount of rent related to the year (12 × $300 = $3,600) rather than for the $2,700 rent paid. Finally, the Rent Payable account is increased to reflect the fact that the company has to pay an additional $900 of rent in the future.

Notice how the Rent Payable accrual reconciles the cash disbursement for rent actually paid ($2,700) with the accrual basis rent expense recorded on the income statement ($3,600). Microsoft reported the following accruals for 2000: Accounts Payable $1,083 million; Accrued Compensation $557 million; and Income Taxes $585 million.

Prepaid Expenses

Sometimes a company pays for products or services in an accounting period prior to the period in which the expense is properly recorded under the accrual method. Examples from the hypothetical software company are computer expense, CD expense, and shipping boxes expense. In all three cases, the company paid for something in the first year (a cash disbursement), but part of the payment was not treated as an expense until the following year under accrual accounting principles. This leads to a type of accrual known as a *prepaid expense.*

Prepaid expense is a generic term that can apply to all types of prepaid expenses. Typically, however, many types of prepaid expenses are given specific names. For example, the prepaid expense for computers in the hypothetical software company example would be called equipment rather than prepaid computer expense. The prepaid expense for blank CDs would be called raw materials inventory, and the prepaid expense for shipping boxes would be called supplies inventory. Typically, the term *prepaid expenses* on a company's balance sheet refers to such items as prepaid rent or prepaid insurance. Microsoft's 2000 balance sheet lumps these prepaid expenses together in a line labeled Other.

Here is how the journal entry would look to record an accrual for a prepaid expense (the Raw Materials Inventory for blank CDs) for the hypothetical software company example:

	Journal Entry to Record Blank CD Expense		
+/−	**Accounts [description of account]**	**Debit**	**Credit**
+	Blank CD Expense [income statement expense account]	150	
+	Raw Materials Inventory [balance sheet asset account]	350	
−	Cash [balance sheet asset account]		500

Cash is decreased for the $500 that the company paid for the blank CDs. Under accrual accounting, the cost of the CDs actually shipped to customers during the accounting period is treated as an expense of the first year, so the account Blank CD Expense is increased by $150. The balance of the CDs will be used in future accounting periods, and their cost is reflected in the increase in the Raw Materials Inventory account of $350.

COMPONENTS OF THE INCOME STATEMENT

This section focuses on presentation of the various types of revenues and expenses. In other words, it discusses where these items should actually appear on the income statement.

Sales Revenue and Gross Profit

Firms usually present some measure of total sales revenue earned from the normal operations of the business during the accounting period. For example, Microsoft's 2000 income statement reports revenue of $22,956 million for the year ended June 30, 2000. This amount may be called *revenue* or *sales,* and it often includes the term *net* (as in net revenue or net sales). Use of the term *net* reminds users that the reported sales amount has been reduced by (1) items returned (or expected to be returned) by customers, and (2) cash discounts or other sales allowances given to customers to increase sales or encourage faster payment.

Most companies also report an expense item called *cost of goods sold*, representing the costs of all items sold (or the cost of services performed) during the accounting period. The expenses under this category are all considered product costs, and they are being reported in the same accounting period as the revenue from sales of products or services in accordance with the matching principle. In Microsoft's income statement these costs are presented under the heading Cost of Revenue.

Firms sometimes present a subtotal on their income statement in which cost of goods sold is subtracted from sales revenue to arrive at a number known as *gross profit* (or gross margin). Gross profit is the net revenue generated from sales of goods and services during the year less the product costs associated with those same goods and services. Even for companies that don't compute gross profit on the income statement, such as Microsoft, users of the financial statements can compute the number by subtracting cost of goods sold from sales revenue. For Microsoft for the year ended June 30, 2000, gross profit is equal to $19,954 million ($22,956 million revenue minus $3,002 million cost of revenue).

The examples of other income statements at the end of the chapter show that presentations vary. The Boeing Company reported sales and other operating revenues as one item and subtracted an expense item for costs of products and services to arrive at a subtotal representing gross profit. IBM Corporation presented the separate components of both total revenues and total costs (for example, hardware, global services, and so forth) and then arrived at a total for gross profit. Kmart Corporation reported sales and cost of sales, buying, and occupancy and arrived at a total for gross margin. Chrysler Corporation did not report either a cost of goods sold or a gross profit number.

Users of a company's financial statements find it extremely useful to have information on both the cost of goods sold and sales revenue, since the ratio of gross profit to sales revenue shows how much gross profit, on average, the company is making for each dollar of sales. For example, using the numbers from Microsoft's 2000 income statement, we can see that the ratio of Microsoft's gross profit to total revenue is 0.87 (19,954/22,956). This means that, on average, every dollar of sales revenue Microsoft earns generates 87 cents of gross profit for the company. By comparing this gross profit percentage with those of other companies in Microsoft's industry, users of Microsoft's financial statements can tell how profitable Microsoft's products are compared with its competitors. For example, IBM's gross profit percentage for 1999 was 0.36, much smaller than Microsoft's.

Operating Income

Many companies report a subtotal called *operating income* on their income statements. Operating income represents sales revenue less all of the expenses associated with the operations of the company's normal business activities for the year. For example, on the statement shown on page 22 Microsoft reported the following types of expenses as operating expenses: cost of revenue; research and development; acquired in-process technology; sales and marketing; general and administrative; and other expenses. Microsoft reported a number for total operating expenses ($12,019 million for 2000), and subtracted this number from revenue to arrive at operating income ($10,937 million for 2000). The statements at the end of the chapter show that Boeing and IBM also reported a subtotal for operating income or earnings, whereas Kmart referred to this subtotal as continuing income.

Nonoperating revenues are usually investment revenue, such as interest or dividends. Interest expense is usually a non operating expense. Expenses or losses that are not expected to occur in the future are also shown as non operating expenses, although some companies refer to these as unusual or non recurring items. Gains and losses associated with sales of assets are often shown as non operating items. In Microsoft's income statements there are two non operating items: investment income and gain on sales. Boeing reported two non operating items on its income statement for 1999: other income, principally interest; and interest and debt expense; and IBM reported similar categories on its income statement.

Not all companies follow this format of presenting a separate subtotal for operating earnings. Some companies report a total revenue number and a total expense number, without regard for whether these revenues and expenses are considered to be operating or non operating. Chrysler Corporation did not separate revenues and expenses into operating and non operating categories on its income statement.

Taxes

Most companies report a subtotal for income before income tax expense. In the income statements of Microsoft and IBM, this is labeled *income before income taxes*, whereas the Boeing and Chrysler statements call this item *earnings before income taxes*. The Kmart statement does not present a separate line for income before income taxes.

All companies are required to report an item on their income statement for income tax expense. Many companies use the term *provision* rather than *tax expense*. For example, Microsoft, IBM, Kmart, and Chrysler used the term *provision* for income taxes on their respective statements.[10]

Transitory Income Statement Items

One important use of income statement information is to predict how profitable a company will be in the future. An investor would like to know what Microsoft's net income will be next year, the year after that, and over the next five years. With that information, an investor could estimate what she thinks the price of Microsoft's common stock should be relative to that of other public companies. The information from Microsoft's income statement that would be most useful in that regard concerns those revenues and expenses that are expected to continue into the future, and those that are expected to affect only the year ended June 30, 2000.

The concept that items affecting a company's net income in one year will continue to affect net income in future years is known as *earnings persistence*. Here is an example. Suppose that Microsoft introduces a new product in the year ended June 30, 2000, and that this new product causes net income to increase. We might expect that profits from this new product will also cause next year's net income to be higher. In the same way, if a company streamlines manufacturing processes to reduce costs, this may result in increased earnings for the current year, and these increased earnings would also be expected to continue in future years. Earnings that are expected to continue into the future are referred to as *permanent earnings*.

Not all types of earnings changes are expected to persist into the future. For example, on the 2000 income statement Microsoft reported an item called gain on sales of $156 million. Is it likely that this amount of income will continue into the future? Notice that Microsoft also reported a gain on sales in 1999, but none in 1998. Gains and losses from sales of assets are not usually the same each year, and thus they are unlikely to continue in the future. Earnings that are not expected to continue into the future are referred to as *transitory earnings*. Notice

---

[10] The computation of income tax expense is covered in Chapter 9.

that Boeing reported gain on disposition as part of operating earnings, even though this is usually a transitory item. For another example of a transitory earnings item, notice Kmart's expense for voluntary early retirement programs. This expense was $114 million in 1997, $19 million in 1998, and zero in 1999.

GAAP recognize that users of financial statement information are interested in firms' permanent earnings and do not want permanent earnings to be affected by one time or transitory earnings items. Therefore, GAAP require special income statement treatment for three major types of transitory earnings items: (1) income or loss from discontinued operations, (2) extraordinary items, and (3) the cumulative effect of a change in accounting principle.

All three of these items must be reported individually in a separate section at the bottom of the income statement following the company's income tax expense. Microsoft doesn't have any of these three items on its income statements. However, Kmart reported a loss from discontinued operations for 1999, and Chrysler reported an extraordinary item for 1996 and a cumulative effect of a change in accounting principle in 1995.

Usually a company that has one or more of these special items on its income statement reports a subtotal following income tax expense. The name used for this subtotal depends on which special item is being reported. For example, Kmart reported a loss from discontinued operations and used the subtotal title net income from continuing operations. Chrysler, reporting both an extraordinary item and a cumulative effect of a change in accounting principle, used the subtotal title earnings before extraordinary item and cumulative effect of a change in accounting principle.

All three of the special items have an unusual income statement treatment in common: they are all reported *net of taxes*. What this means is that the income taxes associated with the special items are not included in the firm's income tax expense. Rather, the income taxes associated with each special item are subtracted, or netted, from the before-tax income associated with the item. For example, in its 1999 income statement Kmart reported a loss from discontinued operations of $230 million. However, it also reported that this number is net of income taxes of $124 million. What this means is that the before-tax loss from discontinued operations was actually $354 million, but that the income tax savings associated with this $354 million loss (equal to a $124 million tax refund) was subtracted to arrive at the net-of-tax amount of $230 million reported on the Kmart income statement. Note that this $124 million of income tax savings did not reduce Kmart's other income tax provision of $337 million. The same income tax savings cannot be reported in two places on the income statement.

Materiality

Even though GAAP require special presentation on the income statement for discontinued operations, extraordinary items, and cumulative effect of a change in accounting principle, there is an important exception to this rule (and to all other GAAP rules as well). The exception deals with an accounting concept called *materiality*. The financial reporting rules contained in GAAP are only applicable to items that are material in amount. While there is no formal definition of what is meant by the term *material*, in general it can be thought of as follows: If a financial statement item would be large enough to make a difference in a decision that someone might make about the firm, then the item is material.

There are two features of any accounting item that should be considered in assessing whether the item is material. First, the size of the item, relative to other items on the firm's financial statements. For example, assume that Microsoft did in fact have an extraordinary item for the year ended June 30, 2000, in the amount of $1 million. Since Microsoft's net income for the year was $9,421 million, the hypothetical extraordinary item, if disclosed separately as required under GAAP, would be equal to 0.02 percent of Microsoft's net income. Since this amount is so small that it is unlikely to change any decisions anyone would make about Microsoft, it is not material and therefore would not require separate disclosure. A second consideration in assessing materiality is the nature of the item being considered. For example, if the item is small in amount but relates to a sensitive topic, such as illegal activities by employees, it may make a difference in users' decisions and therefore should be disclosed as material.

In the sections below, the GAAP rules for each of the three types of special income statement items are discussed in more detail. Under GAAP, the three special items are required to be reported in the order mentioned: discontinued operations first, followed by extraordinary items, with cumulative effect of change in accounting principle last.

Discontinued Operations

When a company completely disposes of a component of its business in a year, the gain or loss from the sale of the component is reported separately, net of tax. In addition, the results of operation of the component—that is, the revenues of the component less the expenses of the component—through the date of the disposition must also be reported separately, net of tax.

To illustrate this treatment, below is a portion of Kmart's income statements from 1994, 1995, and 1996. Notice that in all three years, Kmart reported two separate items related to discontinued operations. First, the line labeled discontinued operations reports the results of the operations of the components that were ultimately disposed of. These amounts represent the revenues less the expenses of the discontinued components. The reason for reporting these results of operations separately from continuing operations is to let users know that these revenues and expenses are not expected to continue. In other words, once the company decides to dispose of the component, these revenues and expenses cease to be permanent and become transitory.

Second, the line labeled gain (loss) on disposal of discontinued operations reports the gain or loss that Kmart realized on selling the assets of the components disposed of. All of the items relating to discontinued operations are reported net of tax. The discontinued operations are reported before the extraordinary item.

Years Ended January 29, 1997, January 31, 1996, And January 25, 1995 (dollars in millions, except per share data)			
	1996	**1995**	**1994**
Net income (loss) from continuing operations before extraordinary item	231	(230)	96
Discontinued operations, net of income taxes of $(3), $(139), and $64 . .	(5)	(260)	83
Gain (loss) on disposal of discontinued operations, net of income taxes of $(240), $88, and $282	(446)	(30)	117
Extraordinary item, net of income taxes of $(27)	—	(51)	—
Net income (loss)	$(220)	$(571)	$296

3. Discontinued operations and dispositions

Discontinued operations include Builders Square, Inc. ("Builders Square"), Borders Group, Inc. ("Borders Group"), OfficeMax, Inc. ("OfficeMax"), The Sports Authority, Inc. ("The Sports Authority"), Thrifty PayLess Holdings, Inc. ("TPH"), Coles Myer, Ltd. ("Coles Myer"), and Furr's/Bishop's, Inc. ("Furr's").

Source: Kmart Corporation Form 10-K.

Kmart also reported a loss from discontinued operations on its 1999 income statement. Here is how Kmart described this 1999 loss in the notes to it's financial statements:

On June 11, 1999, Hechinger Company ("Hechinger"), which had previously acquired substantially all of the operating assets of Builders Square, filed for Chapter 11 bankruptcy protection. In the second quarter of 1999, the Company recorded a non-cash charge of $354, $230 after tax, which reflected Kmart's best estimate of the impact of Hechinger's default on lease obligations for up to 117 former Builders Square locations which are guaranteed by Kmart. The foregoing non-cash charge does not reflect an amount, if any, which Kmart may ultimately recover on account of any claims previously filed by Kmart or an amount, if any, which may be sought by others against Kmart.

Source: Kmart Corporation Form 10-K.

In other words, in 1999 Kmart suffered an additional $354 million loss in connection with the previously reported disposition of the Builders Square business. Since this loss arose out of the sale of the Builders Square business, it is also reported as a loss from discontinued operations.

Extraordinary Items

Under GAAP, there is a strict definition that must be met for an item to be classified as *extraordinary*. The item must be both (1) unusual and (2) infrequent. If an item is unusual but not infrequent, or infrequent but not unusual, it may not be reported as an extraordinary item. Unusual means that this type of item would not normally be expected for the type of business that the firm is in. Infrequent means that this type of item is not expected to recur in the future, taking into account the location and business activities of the firm.

Prior to 2003, GAAP rules treated a gain or loss on the retirement of debt as an extraordinary item.[11] A company retiring its debt is a transaction that is neither unusual nor infrequent. However, including gains and losses from debt retirement in normal operating income could make it too easy for managers to manipulate operating income. By classifying these gains and losses as extraordinary, it is clear to users that they are not part of permanent earnings. Chrysler Corporation reported a loss from early extinguishment of debt in its 1996 income statement. Under current GAAP rules, gains and losses from debt retirement are only treated as extraordinary if they are both unusual and infrequent.

Change in Accounting Principle

The third type of special income statement item is the cumulative effect of a change in accounting principle, or method. Any time a firm changes from one accounting method to a different accounting method, it must calculate the difference between (1) the total net income actually reported for all prior years using the old method and (2) the total net income that would have been reported for all prior years if the new accounting method had been used. This difference is called the *cumulative effect of the change in accounting method.*

The cumulative effect represents the effect of the new accounting method on only prior years' net income. The effect of the new accounting method on the net income for the current accounting period is not shown as part of the cumulative effect. Instead, the firm simply computes net income for the current accounting period using the new accounting method, with no special adjustment necessary for the current year effect. However, the effect of the change on current year net income should be disclosed in a note to the financial statements.

The cumulative effect of a change in accounting principle is reported net of tax. This means that, when calculating the difference between the old and new methods for prior years, firms must also compute how the income tax expense would differ under the two methods.

Chrysler Corporation reported a cumulative effect of a change in accounting principle for the year 1995. Here is how Chrysler explained the change in accounting principle in a note to its 1995 financial statements:

---

[11] Retirement of debt will be covered in more detail in Chapter 5.

In 1995, the Emerging Issues Task Force ("EITF") of the Financial Accounting Standards Board ("FASB") reached a consensus on EITF Issue 95-1, "Revenue Recognition on Sales with a Guaranteed Minimum Resale Value." The consensus on EITF Issue 95-1 (the "consensus") affects Chrysler's accounting treatment for vehicle sales (principally to non-affiliated rental car companies) for which Chrysler conditionally guarantees the minimum resale value of the vehicles. In accordance with the consensus, these vehicle sales are accounted for as operating leases with the related revenues and costs deferred at the time of shipment. A portion of the deferred revenues and costs is recognized over the corresponding guarantee period, with the remainder recognized at the end of the guarantee period. The average guarantee period for these vehicles is approximately nine months. Chrysler changed its accounting treatment in accordance with the consensus effective January 1, 1995, which resulted in the recognition of an after-tax charge of $96 million (net of income tax benefit of $59 million).

Source: Chrysler Corporation Form 10-K.

Net Income

The final total of revenues and expenses on a company's income statement should be net income, or net earnings. Net income is a summary measure of the company's performance for the accounting period. For companies that have preferred shareholders[12] a final step is necessary. Dividends paid to preferred shareholders must be subtracted to arrive at net income available to common shareholders. IBM and Chrysler both made this adjustment on their income statements for preferred stock dividends, as shown at the end of the chapter.

Per Share Presentation

In addition to reporting net income, GAAP rules require firms to divide net income by the number of shares of stock the firm has outstanding to arrive at a measure called *earnings per share* (EPS). Two measures are given: basic and diluted.[13] Microsoft reported basic earnings per share of $1.81 and diluted earnings per share of $1.70 for the year ended June 30, 2000.

Earnings per share is the most widely quoted measure of a company's performance for an accounting period. When companies announce their quarterly earnings, they also announce earnings per share. When financial analysts give forecasts of what they think a firm's future earnings will be, they forecast earnings per share. However, you should note that earnings per share is simply a function of the number of shares of stock a company has issued in the past. Two companies could have identical net income, but if one company has more shares of stock outstanding (not necessarily more shareholders) it will have a lower earnings per share than the other company. Therefore, great care has to be taken when comparing earnings per share between companies.

INCOME MEASUREMENT IN OTHER COUNTRIES

Although every country has its own GAAP, there is a trend toward countries adopting similar accounting principles. This trend is primarily due to two factors. First, the International Accounting Standards Board (IASB), based in London, is working to establish a set of financial accounting standards that all countries could agree to. As these standards evolve over time, they appear to be moving in the direction of U.S. GAAP; thus, currently many academic accountants see little difference in quality between U.S. GAAP financial statements and IASB GAAP financial statements.

---

[12] Preferred stock is discussed in Chapter 15.

[13] The details of the earnings per share calculation are discussed in Chapter 15.

A second trend leading toward more universal accounting principles is the desire of companies in other countries to gain access to U.S. equity markets to obtain capital. One way to do this is to list the company's shares on a U.S. stock exchange. However, to do that means the foreign company has to follow the same financial reporting rules as U.S. companies. A second way to gain access to U.S. capital is for foreign stock exchanges to adopt U.S. (or IASB) GAAP as a requirement for companies to list their shares on the foreign exchange. For example, a new stock exchange recently started in Germany required all firms listed on the exchange to use either U.S. GAAP or IASB GAAP. In this way, these firms hope to attract capital from U.S. investors who are interested in investing in firms with high-quality financial statements.

At the end of this chapter is an example of an income statement prepared under foreign GAAP, the 1999 income statement of Reed Elsevier, a large international publishing company consisting of Reed International PLC (a corporation organized in the United Kingdom) and Elsevier NV (a corporation organized in the Netherlands). The income statement is prepared under U.K. GAAP, which is essentially the same as Dutch GAAP, and the numbers on the income statement are in millions of British pounds (£) rather than U.S. dollars. The number representing net income is called (loss)/profit attributable to parent companies' shareholders and is a loss of £63 million for 1999.

Notice how this income statement is different from those of the U.S. companies we have been studying. Many of the words used on the income statement are different from their U.S. counterparts, beginning with the title of the statement: profit and loss accounts rather than income statement, statement of earnings, or statement of operations as would be used by a U.S. company. The first line on the statement reports turnover, which is the U.K. term for sales revenue. There are also many similarities with U.S. income statements. The statement reports cost of sales and gross profit, and there are subtotals for operating profit and profit on ordinary activities. Notice that there are no per share numbers presented.

Another unusual feature of the Reed Elsevier income statement is the section at the bottom of the statement, titled adjusted figures. Even though the loss attributable to parent companies' shareholders on the income statement is £63 million, the adjusted profit attributable to parent companies' shareholders is a positive £527 million. Here is how the company explained the difference:

> U.K. and Dutch GAAP allow the presentation of alternative earnings measures. Adjusted operating profit is presented as an additional performance measure and is shown before amortisation of goodwill and intangible assets and exceptional items. U.S. GAAP does not permit the presentation of alternative earnings measures.

Source: Reed Elsevier Form 20-F.

Apparently, the management of Reed-Elsevier feels that their alternative earnings measure is more useful than the earnings computed under U.K./Dutch GAAP. Management has added back a very large expense—approximately £590 million of amortization of goodwill and intangible assets—to arrive at their alternative earnings measure.[14] As the explanation states, presenting an earnings measure other than net income would not be allowed under U.S. GAAP.

The notes to the financial statements of Reed Elsevier also discuss how the reported profit of the company differs from the amount that would have been reported under U.S. GAAP. Here are some of the differences pointed out in the notes:

---

[14] Amortization of goodwill and intangible assets will be discussed in Chapter 10.

29. Summary of Principal Differences between U.K. and Dutch GAAP and U.S. GAAP

The combined financial statements are prepared in accordance with U.K. and Dutch GAAP, which differ in certain significant respects from U.S. GAAP. These differences relate principally to the following items and the effect of material differences on profit and loss attributable and combined shareholders' funds is shown in the following tables.

Discontinued operations and sale of businesses

Goodwill and other intangible assets

Deferred taxation

Acquisition accounting

Pensions

Sale and lease back transactions of real estate

Exceptional items

Stock based compensation

Source: Reed Elsevier Form 20-F.

In the table below, Reed Elsevier's loss for 1999 under U.K./Dutch GAAP of £63 million is reconciled with the net loss of £73 million that would have been reported if U.S. GAAP had been used:

**Effects on Net Income of Material Differences between U.K. and Dutch GAAP and U.S. GAAP
(in pound millions)**

	Year Ended December 31		
	1997	1998	1999
(Loss)/profit attributable income under U.K. and Dutch GAAP	(14)	772	(63)
U.S. GAAP adjustments			
Amortisation of goodwill and other intangibles	1	(477)	(83)
Deferred taxation	32	77	67
Acquisition accounting	(1)	(10)	(1)
Sale and lease back	1	6	—
Pensions	23	30	6
Other items	1	—	1
Net income/(loss) under U.S. GAAP	43	398	(73)

Source: Reed Elsevier Form 20-F.

According to this reconciliation, differences in amortization of goodwill and other intangibles reduced earnings by £83 million, while differences in acquisition accounting reduced earnings by £1 million. Offsetting this were increases in earnings from deferred taxation differences of £67 million, pension accounting differences of £6 million, and other items of £1 million. The net effect of all these differences in accounting was to reduce Reed Elsevier's earnings by an additional £10 million. In other words, if Reed Elsevier was to prepare an income statement using U.S. GAAP, it would report a net loss of £73 million, not a very big difference. Notice, however, that for 1998 Reed Elsevier's profit under U.K./Dutch GAAP was £772 million, whereas under U.S. GAAP it would have only reported net income of £398 million, a much larger difference than that in 1999.

It is important to note that one set of GAAP is not necessarily better or worse than the other—they are just different. Both U.K. and Dutch GAAP are considered to be of high quality. Before making any decisions based on the financial statements of any company, a person must understand the GAAP rules being used to compute net income.

To give some comparison between U.K. GAAP and U.S. GAAP, below is Microsoft's income statement for the year ended June 30, 2000, prepared using U.K. GAAP. The reconciliation at the bottom of the income statement shows that Microsoft's net income is £7,048 million under U.K. GAAP compared with £5,922 million under U.S. GAAP. (Note that these statements are in British pounds rather than U.S. dollars, so the net income number won't agree with Microsoft's U.S. GAAP income statement.) The two differences between U.S. GAAP and U.K. GAAP for Microsoft are the visio pooling (a method of accounting for a business acquisition during the year) and the tax benefit of stock options (relating to a savings of U.S. corporate income tax when employees exercise employee stock options). Note that if you take Microsoft's net income from its U.S. GAAP U.S. dollar income statement ($9,421 million) and divide by the exchange rate of 1.5908, you get £5,922 million, the number computed below under U.S. GAAP.

MICROSOFT CORPORATION
Consolidated Profit and Loss Account (unaudited)
Year Ended June 30, 2000
(in millions £)

Turnover	14,430
Operating expenses	
Cost of sales	1,887
Research and development	2,385
Distribution costs	2,603
Administrative expenses	679
Other operating expenses	58
Total operating expenses	7,612
Operating profit	6,818
Interest receivable and similar income	2,000
Profit on sale of MSN Sidewalk	98
Profit before tax	8,916
Tax on profits	1,868
Profit on ordinary activities after taxation	7,048
Reconciliation to reported results presented in accompanying financial statements	
Profit for the financial year, as stated above (U.K. GAAP)	7,048
Visio pooling	38
Tax benefit of stock options	(1,164)
Net income per published U.S. financial statements	5,922

This unaudited consolidated profit and loss account has been converted from Microsoft's audited consolidated income statement into local currency and adjusted for accounting principles and format that are generally accepted in the United Kingdom. This presentation differs in certain respects from generally accepted accounting principles in the United States that are used in Microsoft's primary financial statements and its filings with the United States Securities and Exchange Commission. The Microsoft 2000 Annual Report to Shareholders and the Form 10-K are available on this website or copies may be obtained by writing to the Company.

All figures have been translated at the average exchange rate for the year (£1 = USD 1.5908).

Source: Microsoft Corporation website.

USING INCOME STATEMENT INFORMATION TO MAKE DECISIONS

There are two main ways in which income statement information is used to make decisions. First, net income is used as a measure of a firm's economic performance over the prior accounting period. Second, income statement information is used to forecast future earnings of the firm.

Net Income as a Measure of Economic Performance

Net income provides users with a consistent and reliable measure of economic performance over the accounting period. Although net income itself is used as a performance measure, it is often divided by a measure of the economic resources employed by the firm, such as total assets or total shareholders' equity, to arrive at a measure of return on investment, such as return on assets or return on equity.

Different components of the income statement are also used to evaluate the profitability of a firm. For example, sales divided by total assets, called *total asset turnover*, provides a measure of how efficiently a company is using its assets to generate revenue. Net income divided by sales, called the *profit margin ratio*, tells users how much profit the firm is earning on each dollar of sales.

Using these profitability measures, it is possible to compare different firms to determine which firm is being managed more profitability. When making these comparisons it is important to compare firms in similar industries, since these performance measures will differ by industry—grocery stores have high total asset turnover and low profit margin ratios, whereas designer clothing stores have just the opposite relationships.

Another use of profitability measures is to compare a firm's performance over time. For example, Microsoft's net income went from $4,490 million in 1998, to $7,785 million in 1999, to $9,421 million in 2000, while Kmart's net income went from $249 million in 1997 to $518 million in 1998, to $403 million in 1999. The patterns of net income for these two companies are quite different. The pattern of income statement items over time can provide useful information to users. Changes in such items as the gross profit percentage, return on assets, return on equity, asset turnover, and the profit margin ratio provide information about the trend in economic performance of a firm. Using this type of performance information over time is particularly useful when the information from one firm can be compared with the averages of these items for other firms in the same industry. For example, comparing the change in net income of Kmart over the three-year period 1997–99 with the patterns of net income of Sears, JCPenney, and Wal-Mart provides information about the relative economic performance of Kmart.

Firms are required to present net income on a per share basis on the income statement. One reason that earnings per share information may be useful to investors is that the price of a company's stock is quoted on a per share basis, so having a number for earnings per share allows users to easily compare the price of a share of a company's stock with the net earnings attributable to that same share. This comparison is usually made in the form of a price–earnings (PE) ratio, in which the price of a company's common stock is divided by the earnings per share. When used in this way, the stock price is thought of as a multiple of a firm's earnings. Using earnings multiples in this way is a method of estimating a firm's stock price for a given amount of earnings per share. The size of this multiple is thought to be related to (1) the expected future growth rate of the firm's earnings and (2) the riskiness of the firm's earnings, with higher expected growth resulting in a higher PE ratio, and higher expected risk resulting in a lower PE ratio.

Using Income Statement Information to Forecast Earnings and Cash Flows

The second major use of income statement information is to allow users to forecast the firm's future earnings and cash flows. By starting with current income statement items and projecting them into the future (based, for example, on historical trends, industry developments, or news about new products being introduced) it is possible to construct future income statements, called *pro forma income statements*. These pro forma income statements can reflect the relationships among revenues and costs, such as the firm's gross profit or profit margin ratios. New firm-specific information can be incorporated into these relationships, such as a cost-cutting program or the restructuring of a manufacturing division, so that the pro forma income statement reflects expected future performance. By understanding how accounting accruals modify cash flows to arrive at net income, users can use the pro forma income statements to also forecast a firm's future cash flows.[15]

Summary

This chapter discusses how accounting periods cause problems in measuring a company's economic performance over short time periods, and how accrual accounting can modify cash receipts and disbursements to arrive at a measure of economic performance—net income—that is useful both as a measure of past performance and as information for predicting future earnings and cash flows.

Revenue recognition criteria require that revenue must be both realized, or realizable, and earned before it can be recorded on the income statement. Accruals resulting from the application of the revenue recognition criteria are accounts receivable and unearned revenue. Expense recognition criteria and the concepts of product costs and period costs are introduced in the chapter. Under the matching principle, product costs are recorded in the same accounting period as their related revenue, whereas period costs are recorded in the period to which they relate. Accruals resulting from the application of the expense recognition criteria are accrued expenses and prepaid expenses.

Components of the income statement are cost of goods sold, gross profit, operating income, and tax expense. Three important transitory income statement items are discontinued operations, extraordinary items, and cumulative effect of a change in accounting principle. These three items must be reported separately at the bottom of the income statement.

---

[15] Forecasting future earnings and cash flows is covered in a course called "Financial Statement Analysis."

THE BOEING COMPANY AND SUBSIDIARIES
Consolidated Statements of Operations
(dollars in millions except per share data)

	Year Ended December 31		
	1999	**1998**	**1997**
Sales and other operating revenues	$57,993	$56,154	$45,800
Cost of products and services	51,320	50,492	42,001
	6,673	5,662	3,799
Equity in income (loss) from joint ventures	4	(67)	(43)
General and administrative expense	2,044	1,993	2,187
Research and development expense	1,341	1,895	1,924
Gain on dispositions, net	87	13	—
Share-based plans expense	209	153	(99)
Operating earnings (loss)	3,170	1,567	(256)
Other income, principally interest	585	283	428
Interest and debt expense	(431)	(453)	(513)
Earnings (loss) before income taxes	3,324	1,397	(341)
Income taxes (benefit)	1,015	277	(163)
Net earnings (loss)	$ 2,309	$ 1,120	$ (178)
Basic earnings (loss) per share	$2.52	$1.16	$ (.18)
Diluted earnings (loss) per share	$2.49	$1.15	$ (.18)

Source: The Boeing Company Form 10-K.

INTERNATIONAL BUSINESS MACHINES CORPORATION AND SUBSIDIARY COMPANIES
Consolidated Statement of Earnings
(dollars in millions except per share amounts)

	Notes	For the Year Ended December 31		
		1999	**1998**	**1997**
Revenue				
Hardware		$37,041	$35,419	$36,630
Global Services		32,172	28,916	25,166
Software		12,662	11,863	11,164
Global Financing		3,137	2,877	2,806
Enterprise Investments/Other		2,536	2,592	2,742
Total revenue		87,548	81,667	78,508
Cost				
Hardware		27,071	24,214	23,473
Global Services		23,304	21,125	18,464
Software		2,240	2,260	2,785
Global Financing		1,446	1,494	1,448
Enterprise Investments/Other		1,558	1,702	1,729
Total cost		55,619	50,795	47,899
Gross profit		31,929	30,872	30,609
Operating expenses				
Selling, general and administrative	Q	14,729	16,662	16,634
Research, development and engineering	S	5,273	5,046	4,877
Total operating expenses		20,002	21,708	21,511
Operating income		11,927	9,164	9,098
Other income, principally interest		557	589	657
Interest expense	K	727	713	728
Income before income taxes		11,757	9,040	9,027
Provision for income taxes	P	4,045	2,712	2,934
Net income		7,712	6,328	6,093
Preferred stock dividends		20	20	20
Net income applicable to common stockholders		$ 7,692	$ 6,308	$ 6,073
Earnings per share of common stock				
Assuming dilution	T	$ 4.12	$ 3.29	$ 3.00
Basic	T	$ 4.25	$ 3.38	$ 3.09

Source: IBM Corporation Form 10-K.

KMART CORPORATION
Consolidated Statements of Income
(dollars in millions, except per share data)

Years Ended January 26, 2000, January 27, 1999 and January 28, 1998

	1999	1998	1997
Sales	$35,925	$33,674	$32,183
Cost of sales, buying and occupancy	28,102	26,319	25,152
Gross margin	7,823	7,355	7,031
Selling, general and administrative expenses	6,523	6,245	6,136
Voluntary early retirement programs	—	19	114
Continuing income before interest, income taxes and dividends on convertible preferred securities of subsidiary trust	1,300	1,091	781
Interest expense, net	280	293	363
Income tax provision	337	230	120
Dividends on convertible preferred securities of subsidiary trust, net of income taxes of $27, $27 and $26	50	50	49
Net income from continuing operations	633	518	249
Discontinued operations, net of income taxes of $(124)	(230)	—	—
Net income	$ 403	$ 518	$249
Basic earnings per common share			
Net income from continuing operations	$ 1.29	$ 1.05	$.51
Discontinued operations	(.47)	—	—
Net income	$ .82	$ 1.05	$.51
Diluted earnings per common share			
Net income from continuing operations	$ 1.22	$ 1.01	$.51
Discontinued operations	(.41)	—	—
Net income	$ .81	$ 1.01	$.51

Source: Kmart Corporation Form 10-K.

CHRYSLER CORPORATION AND CONSOLIDATED SUBSIDIARIES
Consolidated Statement of Earnings

	Year Ended December 31		
	1997	**1996**	**1995**
	(in millions of dollars)		
Sales of manufactured products	$56,986	$57,587	$49,601
Finance and insurance revenues	1,636	1,746	1,589
Other revenues	2,525	2,064	2,005
Total revenues	61,147	61,397	53,195
Costs, other than items below (Notes 13 and 14)	46,743	45,842	41,304
Depreciation and special tools amortization (Notes 1 and 5)	2,696	2,312	2,220
Selling and administrative expenses	4,957	4,730	4,064
Employee retirement benefits (Note 12)	1,188	1,414	1,163
Interest expense	1,006	1,007	995
Total expenses	56,590	55,305	49,746
Earnings before income taxes, extraordinary item and cumulative effect of a change in accounting principle	4,557	6,092	3,449
Provision for income taxes (Note 8)	1,752	2,372	1,328
Earnings before extraordinary item and cumulative effect of a change in accounting principle	2,805	3,720	2,121
Extraordinary item - Loss on early extinguishment of debt, net of taxes (Note 7)	—	(191)	—
Cumulative effect of a change in accounting principle, net of taxes (Note 1)	—	—	(96)
Net earnings	$ 2,805	$ 3,529	$ 2,025
Preferred stock dividends (Note 11)	1	3	21
Net earnings on common stock	$ 2,804	$ 3,526	$ 2,004
	(in dollars)		
Basic earnings per common share (Notes 1, 7, 11, 17):			
Earnings before extraordinary item and cumulative effect of a change in accounting principle	$ 4.15	$ 5.09	$ 2.81
Extraordinary item	—	(0.26)	—
Cumulative effect of a change in accounting principle	—	—	(0.13)
Net earnings per common share	$ 4.15	$ 4.83	$ 2.68

Source: Chrysler Corporation Form 10-K.

REED ELSEVIER
Combined Profit and Loss Accounts
(in pound millions)

	Notes	Year Ended December 31		
		1997	**1998**	**1999**
Turnover				
Including share of turnover in joint ventures		3,519	3,271	3,464
Less: share of turnover in joint ventures		(102)	(80)	(74)
	3	3,417	3,191	3,390
Cost of sales		(1,282)	(1,092)	(1,185)
Gross profit		2,135	2,099	2,205
Operating expenses				
Before amortisation and exceptional items		(1,277)	(1,304)	(1,420)
Amortisation of goodwill and intangible assets		(278)	(323)	(369)
Exceptional items	6	(502)	(79)	(239)
Operating profit (before joint ventures)		78	393	177
Share of operating profit in joint ventures		16	9	3
Operating profit including joint ventures	3, 5	94	402	180
Non operating items	6	54	682	7
Profit on ordinary activities before interest		148	1,084	187
Net interest expense	7	(62)	(40)	(82)
Profit on ordinary activities before taxation		86	1,044	105
Tax on profit on ordinary activities	8	(99)	(271)	(167)
(Loss)/profit on ordinary activities after taxation		(13)	773	(62)
Minority interests and preference dividends		(1)	(1)	(1)
(Loss)/profit attributable to parent companies' shareholders . .		(14)	772	(63)
Adjusted figures				
Adjusted operating profit	3, 10	885	813	792
Adjusted profit before tax	10	823	773	710
Adjusted profit attributable to parent companies' shareholders . .	10	608	571	527

Source: Reed Elsevier Form 20-F.

Discussion Questions

1. What is meant by an accounting accrual?
2. How does the concept of an accounting period relate to accruals?
3. Why doesn't GAAP follow the cash receipts and disbursements method?
4. Explain the costs and benefits of the accrual method.
5. What are the revenue recognition criteria?
6. Explain what types of accruals affect revenue recognition.
7. When may revenue be recognized prior to delivery?
8. Explain the accounting treatment for cash collected prior to the year of sale.
9. What are the expense recognition criteria?
10. Explain what types of accruals affect expense recognition.
11. What is meant by the term *matching principle?*
12. What general categories do most income statements contain?
13. Explain what is meant by the term *materiality.*
14. What types of items are presented at the bottom of the income statement after income tax expense?
15. What is meant by the term *discontinued operations,* and how are discontinued operations treated on the income statement?
16. Explain the criteria for treatment as an extraordinary item.
17. How is a change in accounting principle treated under GAAP?

Problems

1. Below is some information about cash flows, sales, and costs for the year. Using this information, compute (a) accrual basis net income (ignore income taxes) for the year and (b) net cash flows for the year.

Cash collections related to prior-year sales	12,000
Cash collections related to current-year sales	85,000
Cash collections related to future-year sales	6,000
Value of products and services sold and delivered this year	100,000
Cash paid for expenses related to prior year	7,000
Cash paid for expenses related to current year	81,000
Cash paid for expenses related to future year	3,000
Cost of products and services sold and delivered this year	65,000
Other costs related to current year operations	20,000

2. Below is some information about cash flows, sales, and costs for the year. Using this information, compute (a) accrual basis net income (ignore income taxes) for the year and (b) net cash flows for the year.

Cash collections related to prior-year sales	15,000
Cash collections related to current-year sales	162,000
Cash collections related to future-year sales	9,000
Value of products and services sold and delivered this year	187,000
Cash paid for expenses related to prior year	3,000
Cash paid for expenses related to current year	176,000
Cash paid for expenses related to future year	2,000
Cost of products and services sold and delivered this year	163,000
Other costs related to current year operations	31,000

3. Below is some information about cash flows, sales, and costs for the year. Using this information, compute (a) accrual basis net income (ignore income taxes) for the year and (b) net cash flows for the year.

Cash collections related to prior-year sales	2,000
Cash collections related to current-year sales	205,000
Cash collections related to future-year sales	1,000
Value of products and services sold and delivered this year	233,000
Cash paid for expenses related to prior year	6,000
Cash paid for expenses related to current year	201,000
Cash paid for expenses related to future year	9,000
Cost of products and services sold and delivered this year	189,000
Other costs related to current year operations	27,000

4. Below is some partial income statement information. Using this information, construct the portion of the income statement beginning with income before income taxes and ending with net income.

Income before income taxes	180,000
Pretax income (loss) from discontinued operations	23,000
Pretax gain (loss) from sale of discontinued operations	(31,000)
Pretax extraordinary item	15,000
Pretax cumulative effect of change in accounting principle	5,000
Tax rate	35%

5. Below is some partial income statement information. Using this information, construct the portion of the income statement beginning with income before income taxes and ending with net income.

Income before income taxes	265,000
Pretax income (loss) from discontinued operations	(41,000)
Pretax gain (loss) from sale of discontinued operations	18,000
Pretax extraordinary item	(12,000)
Pretax cumulative effect of change in accounting principle	3,000
Tax rate	40%

6. Below is some partial income statement information. Using this information, construct the portion of the income statement beginning with income before income taxes and ending with net income.

Income before income taxes	492,000
Pretax income (loss) from discontinued operations	(16,000)
Pretax gain (loss) from sale of discontinued operations	31,000
Pretax extraordinary item	(10,000)
Pretax cumulative effect of change in accounting principle	(6,000)
Tax rate	42%

7. Here is a question from the SEC's Staff Accounting Bulletin No. 101. Give your own answer to the question, and provide the reasoning you used to arrive at your answer.

Facts: Company A receives purchase orders for products it manufactures. At the end of its fiscal quarters, customers may not yet be ready to take delivery of the products for various reasons. These reasons may include, but are not limited to, a lack of available space for inventory, having more than sufficient inventory in their distribution channel, or delays in customers' production schedules.

Question: May Company A recognize revenue for the sale of its products once it has completed manufacturing if it segregates the inventory of the products in its own warehouse from its own products?

---

8. Here is a question from the SEC's Staff Accounting Bulletin No. 101. Give your own answer to the question, and provide the reasoning you used to arrive at your answer.

Facts: Company R is a retailer that offers "layaway" sales to its customers. Company R retains the merchandise, sets it aside in its inventory, and collects a cash deposit from the customer. Although Company R may set a time period within which the customer must finalize the purchase, Company R does not require the customer to enter into an installment note or other fixed payment commitment or agreement when the initial deposit is received. The merchandise generally is not released to the customer until the customer pays the full purchase price. In the event that the customer fails to pay the remaining purchase price, the customer forfeits its cash deposit. In the event the merchandise is lost, damaged, or destroyed, Company R either must refund the cash deposit to the customer or provide replacement merchandise.

Question: When may Company R recognize revenue for merchandise sold under its layaway program?

---

9. Here is a question from the SEC's Staff Accounting Bulletin No. 101. Give your own answer to the question, and provide the reasoning you used to arrive at your answer.

Facts: Company A operates an Internet site from which it will sell Company T's products. Customers place their orders for the product by making a product selection directly from the Internet site and providing a credit card number for the payment. Company A receives the order and authorization from the credit card company, and passes the order on to Company T. Company T ships the product directly to the customer. Company A does not take title to the product and has no risk of loss or other responsibility for the product. Company T is responsible for all product returns, defects, and disputed credit card charges. The product is typically sold for $175 of which Company A receives $25. In the event a credit card transaction is rejected, Company A loses its margin on the sale (i.e., the $25).

Question: In the staff's view, should Company A report revenue on a gross basis as $175 along with costs of sales of $150 or on a net basis as $25, similar to a commission?

---

10. Below is the income statement from a U.S. corporation with the order of the lines scrambled. Rearrange the lines to show the income statement in its correct format under GAAP.

Consolidated Statement of Earnings (amounts in millions except per share amounts)			
	Years Ended June 30		
	2002	**2001**	**2000**
Interest expense	603	794	722
Income taxes	2,031	1,694	1,994
Marketing, research, administrative, and other expense	12,571	12,406	12,483
Cost of products sold	20,989	22,102	21,514
Net earnings	$ 4,352	$ 2,922	$ 3,542
Other non operating income, net	308	674	304
Operating income	6,678	4,736	5,954
Net sales	$40,238	$39,244	$39,951
Earnings before income taxes	6,383	4,616	5,536

11. Below is the income statement from a U.S. corporation with the order of the lines scrambled. Rearrange the lines to show the income statement in its correct format under GAAP.

Consolidated Statements of Income
(in millions except per share data)

	Years Ended June 31		
	2001	2000	1999
Interest income	325	345	260
Equity income (loss)	152	(289)	(184)
Net income	$ 3,969	$ 2,177	$ 2,431
Income before income taxes and cumulative effect of accounting change	5,670	3,399	3,819
Net operating revenues	$20,092	$19,889	$19,284
Other operating charges	—	1,443	813
Operating income	5,352	3,691	3,982
Interest expense	289	447	337
Cumulative effect of accounting change, net of income taxes	(10)	—	—
Other income, net	39	99	98
Gross profit	14,048	13,685	13,275
Gains on issuances of stock by equity investees	91	—	—
Income taxes	1,691	1,222	1,388
Cost of goods sold	6,044	6,204	6,009
Income before cumulative effect of accounting change	3,979	2,177	2,431
Selling, administrative, and general expenses	8,696	8,551	8,480

12. Below is the income statement from a U.S. corporation with the order of the lines scrambled. Rearrange the lines to show the income statement in its correct format under GAAP.

Consolidated Statement of Earnings
(millions, except per share data)

	Year ended December 31, 2001
Income taxes	322.1
Cumulative effect of accounting change (net of tax)	(1.0)
Selling, general, and administrative expense	3,523.6
Extraordinary loss (net of tax)	(7.4)
Interest expense	351.5
Net earnings	$ 473.6
Disposition-related charges	—
Cost of goods sold	4,128.5
Earnings before extraordinary loss and cumulative effect of accounting change	$ 482.0
Other income (expense), net	(12.3)
Earnings before income taxes, extraordinary loss, and cumulative effect of accounting change	$ 804.1
Restructuring charges	33.3
Operating profit	$1,167.9
Net sales	$8,853.3

Research Reports

1. When Intel sells products to distributors, the distributors are protected against price decreases and obsolescence by an agreement with Intel. Under this agreement, if Intel reduces prices, the distributors receive a refund for the price decrease for all Intel products still in stock. Also, the distributors have the right to return any obsolete products in stock. Because of this policy, Intel has a special accounting policy for recognizing revenue from sales to distributors. Shown below is the note explaining the revenue recognition policy from the 2001 annual report.

Revenue Recognition

The company recognizes net revenues when the earnings process is complete, as evidenced by an agreement with the customer, transfer of title and acceptance if applicable, fixed pricing and probable collectibility. Because of frequent sales price reductions and rapid technology obsolescence in the industry, sales made to distributors under agreements allowing price protection and/or right of return are deferred until the distributors sell the merchandise.

---

   a. In your own words, explain how Intel recognizes revenue from sales to distributors.
   b. Explain how revenue recognition is related to the cash flows from selling products. In other words, is the revenue recognized in the same period, a prior period, or a later period relative to the cash receipts?
   c. To properly match expenses with revenues, how should Intel report cost of goods sold related to the products sold to distributors?
   d. Locate the most recent annual report for Intel. Using the balance sheet information on "Deferred income on shipments to distributors," recompute Intel's net income for the most recent three years under the assumption that all income from sales to distributors was recognized in the year the products were shipped. (Don't forget to adjust income tax expense for the change in income.)

2. Here is the revenue recognition note from the 2001 annual report of the New York Times Company:

Revenue Recognition

Advertising revenue is recognized when advertisements are published, broadcast or when placed on the Company's websites, net of provisions for estimated rebates, credit and rate adjustments and discounts.

Circulation revenue includes single copy and home-delivery subscription revenue. Single copy revenue is recognized based on date of publication, net of provisions for related returns. Proceeds from home-delivery subscriptions and related costs, principally agency commissions, are deferred at the time of sale and are recognized in earnings on a pro rata basis over the terms of the subscriptions.

Other revenue is recognized when the related service or product has been delivered.

---

   a. In your own words, explain how the New York Times Company recognizes revenue from different sources.
   b. Explain how revenue recognition is related to the cash flows from the goods and services that are sold. In other words, is the revenue recognized in the same period, a prior period, or a later period relative to the cash receipts?
   c. Locate the most recent annual report for the New York Times Company. Using the balance sheet information on "Unexpired subscriptions," recompute the New York Times Company's net income for the most recent three years under the assumption that all income from subscriptions was recognized in the year the subscription was received. (Don't forget to adjust income tax expense for the change in income.)

3. Here is the revenue recognition note from the 2001 annual report of Halliburton (one of the world's largest providers of products and services to the oil and gas industries):

Revenues and Income Recognition

We recognize revenues as services are rendered or products are shipped. The distinction between services and product sales is based upon the overall activity of the particular business operation. Revenues from engineering and construction contracts are reported on the percentage of completion method of accounting using measurements of progress towards completion appropriate for the work performed. Progress is generally based upon physical progress, man-hours or costs incurred based upon the appropriate method for the type of job. All known or anticipated losses on contracts are provided for currently. Claims and change orders which are in the process of being negotiated with customers, for extra work or changes in the scope of work, are included in revenue when collection is deemed probable. Training and consulting service revenues are recognized as the services are performed. Sales of perpetual software licenses, net of deferred maintenance fees, are recorded as revenue upon shipment. Sales of use licenses are recognized as revenue over the license period. Post-contract customer support agreements are recorded as deferred revenues and recognized as revenue ratably over the contract period of generally one year's duration. With the exception of claims and change orders which are in the process of being negotiated with customers, unbilled work on uncompleted contracts generally represents work currently billable, and this work is usually billed during normal billing processes in the next several months.

---

a. For each type of revenue, explain the reasoning behind the accounting method used.

b. In general, do the accounting methods used accelerate or defer the recognition of revenue relative to the receipt of cash?

c. Locate the most recent annual report for Halliburton. Using the balance sheet information on "deferred revenues," recompute Halliburton's net income for the most recent three years under the assumption that all deferred revenue was recognized in the year the cash was received. (Don't forget to adjust income tax expense for the change in income.)

4. Here is some information about discontinued operations from the 2001 annual report of Halliburton:

Income (Loss) from Operations of Discontinued Businesses
(millions of dollars)

| | Years ended December 31 | | |
	2001	**2000**	**1999**
Revenues	$ 359	$1,400	$2,585
Operating income	$ 37	$ 158	$ 249
Other income and expense	—	—	(1)
Asbestos litigation claims, net of insurance recoveries	(99)	—	—
Tax benefit (expense)	20	(60)	(98)
Minority interest	—	—	(26)
Net income (loss)	$ (42)	$ 98	$ 124

Gain on Disposal of Discontinued Operations
(millions of dollars)

	2001	**2000**	**1999**
Proceeds from sale, less intercompany settlement	$1,267	$ 536	$ 377
Net assets disposed	(769)	(180)	(124)
Gain before taxes	498	356	253
Income taxes	(199)	(141)	(94)
Gain on disposal of discontinued operations	$ 299	$ 215	$ 159

a. Explain the difference between "income (loss) from operations of discontinued businesses" and "gain on disposal of discontinued operations."

b. Explain why GAAP requires companies to report these two types of information about discontinued operations separately.

c. Locate the income statement from Halliburton's 2001 annual report. Reconstruct Halliburton's income statement based on the assumption that the discontinued operations shown above did not qualify as discontinued operations under GAAP.

5. Information about the annual reports of Microsoft is available in the Investor Relations web page at: **www.microsoft.com/msft/ar.htm.**

a. Locate the annual report page and click on "2000 Annual Report." Find the pull-down menu that says "Financial Review." Select "Alternate Views" from pull-down menu. You should find yourself at a page with the following information:

Alternate Income Statements

In addition to standard U.S. accounting income statements, Microsoft income statements are presented using the local languages, local accounting conventions, and local currencies of the following countries:

Australian

Canadian

Deutsch

Français

Japanese

United Kingdom

---

b. From this web page, obtain separate income statements reflecting **GAAP** rules for three different countries. Select countries whose language you are familiar with. For example, if your only language is English, select Australian, Canadian, and United Kingdom.

c. For each of these three financial statements, summarize and explain the differences between Microsoft's net income under U.S. **GAAP** and the net income under the GAAP of the country selected.

d. Using the currency conversion rate shown on the bottom of the income statements, convert Microsoft's net income under the foreign country **GAAP** into U.S. dollars.

e. Comparing the U.S. dollar amounts of net income under different countries' GAAP, which country's accounting standards result in the lowest net income? Which country's result in the highest net income?

6. On its Investor Relations page, Microsoft provides an Excel spreadsheet as part of its "Stock Info and Analysis" tools. The spreadsheet, called "Microsoft Excel Financial Tools," is available at **www.microsoft.com/msft/tools.htm.**

Click on the location as shown below:

FY 2003 Microsoft "What-if?" (196 KB)

Do your own forecasting for Microsoft's FY 2003 income statements based on your assumptions with this Excel projection tool.

---

a. Using this spreadsheet, make your best estimate of Microsoft's 2003 net income.

b. Explain how information from Microsoft's prior year income statements was useful in deciding what numbers or percentages to input into the spreadsheet to forecast future net income.

c. Explain how the concept of earnings persistence relates to this assignment.

d. Obtain a forecast of Microsoft's 2003 net income (or, if available, Microsoft's actual net income for 2003). Forecasts of expected future net income are available from many different library or Internet sources (for example, Value Line, or Yahoo! Finance).

e. Compare your estimate with the forecast (or actual) net income. Explain whether your estimate was more or less than the forecast (or actual) net income and why.

Reuters NewMedia Inc./CORBIS

Chapter Learning Objectives

After reading this chapter you should understand

1. The major differences between the balance sheet and the income statement.
2. What assets and liabilities represent.
3. Why some expected future economic resources are *not* recorded as assets.
4. How the concepts of relevance and reliability apply to assets and liabilities.
5. The different methods for recording balance sheet book values for assets and liabilities.
6. What it means to capitalize an expense, and how this affects the income statement.
7. Why the use of original cost may provide useful information in some cases.
8. Why the use of market values may *not* provide useful information in some cases.
9. How the balance sheet and income statement are related.

Chapter 3

The Balance Sheet: Market Value versus Historical Cost

Focus Company: Microsoft

Introduction

The balance sheet of Microsoft Corporation at June 30, 2000, shown on page 62, reports total stockholders' equity of $41,368 million. What does this balance sheet value—known as the *book value* of Microsoft's equity—represent? On June 30, 2000, the common stock of Microsoft was selling for $80 per share, and the balance sheet indicates there were 5,283 million shares of common stock outstanding at that date. This means that the total market value of Microsoft's common stock was $422,640 million (that is, $80 × 5,283 million shares). Given this large discrepancy between the book value of Microsoft's equity ($41,368 million) and investors' valuation of the company's common stock ($422,640 million), how useful is the balance sheet information?

This chapter addresses that question and explains the financial accounting rules relating to balance sheets by focusing on three basic ideas: (1) the types of items that get recorded on the balance sheet; (2) the value at which these items are recorded; and (3) how investors and others use the information on the balance sheet to make decisions. For example, many valuable assets of Microsoft are not even listed on the balance sheet, and many of the assets that are listed are not recorded at their current market values. Yet despite these apparent limitations, in certain types of decisions balance sheet information can be extremely useful. In addition, there is a subtle but important link between the income statement—a measure of a firm's economic performance—and the balance sheet that adds to the usefulness of balance sheet information.

To give additional balance sheet examples, the balance sheets of The Boeing Company, IBM Corporation, Kmart Corporation, and Chrysler Corporation are included at the end of this chapter. Note that some of these companies use the term *statement of financial position* rather than *balance sheet*. The two terms mean exactly the same thing. The chapter begins by focusing on the idea that the balance sheet is a summary of economic resources of the firm and a list of the various claims against those resources.

THE BALANCE SHEET AS A SUMMARY OF RESOURCES AND CLAIMS

The income statement is related to a definite period of time, called an *accounting period*, and reflects the economic activity (revenues, expenses, and gains and losses) of the firm during that time period. In contrast, the balance sheet reports information as of a specific *moment* in time, called the *balance sheet date*.[1] For Microsoft, the balance sheet date is June 30 each year.

---

[1] In the terminology of economics, the balance sheet represents a stock of economic resources, while the income statement represents a flow of economic resources.

MICROSOFT CORPORATION
Balance Sheets
(in millions)

	June 30	
	1999	**2000**
Assets		
Current assets		
Cash and equivalents	$ 4,975	**$ 4,846**
Short-term investments	12,261	**18,952**
Total cash and short-term investments	17,236	**23,798**
Accounts receivable	2,245	**3,250**
Deferred income taxes	1,469	**1,708**
Other	752	**1,552**
Total current assets	21,702	**30,308**
Property and equipment, net	1,611	**1,903**
Equity and other investments	14,372	**17,726**
Other assets	940	**2,213**
Total assets	$38,625	**$52,150**
Liabilities and stockholders' equity		
Current liabilities		
Accounts payable	$ 874	**$ 1,083**
Accrued compensation	396	**557**
Income taxes	1,691	**585**
Unearned revenue	4,239	**4,816**
Other	1,602	**2,714**
Total current liabilities	8,802	**9,755**
Deferred income taxes	1,385	**1,027**
Commitments and contingencies		
Stockholders' equity		
Convertible preferred stock—shares authorized 100; shares issued and outstanding 13 and 0	980	**—**
Common stock and paid-in capital—shares authorized 12,000; shares issued and outstanding 5,109 and 5,283	13,844	**23,195**
Retained earnings, including other comprehensive income of $1,787 and $1,527	13,614	**18,173**
Total stockholders' equity	28,438	**41,368**
Total liabilities and stockholders' equity	$38,625	**$52,150**

Source: Microsoft Corporation annual report.

There are two major categories of items reported on the balance sheet. First, the balance sheet lists as assets many (but, and this is important, not all) of the economic resources owned or controlled by the firm. Second, the balance sheet lists the legal claims against those economic resources (both actual claims and probable future claims) in the form of liabilities and stockholders' equity. Liabilities represent claims for specific amounts of the firm's resources. For example, Microsoft reported accounts payable at June 30, 2000, of $1,083 million and income taxes payable of $585 million. These represent specific dollar claims of

Microsoft's creditors (in this case, its suppliers and the government) for a portion of Microsoft's assets.

Unlike the claims of Microsoft's creditors—represented by specific dollar amounts of liabilities—the stockholders[2] of Microsoft have the legal right to all of the assets of the company that remain after the creditors' claims are settled. For this reason, the shareholders are sometimes referred to as the *residual claimants* of a corporation. The shareholders are entitled to whatever is left over, that is, the residual, when the corporation's creditors are paid off.

In this sense, the total amount shown for shareholders' equity on a balance sheet is really a plug number that represents the difference between the total assets and the total liabilities of the company. Because of double-entry bookkeeping (where total debits must equal total credits) and the accounting balance sheet equation (assets = liabilities + owners' equity), anything that causes a change in the company's total assets without also causing a corresponding change in total liabilities *must* result in a change in shareholders' equity. Thus, from both a legal claims standpoint and a bookkeeping standpoint, shareholders' equity represents the residual difference between the firm's assets and liabilities.

This balance sheet focus on the shareholders as residual claimants has important consequences for the computation of net income on the income statement. Think of the operating profits of any firm as being divided up at the end of the year among three parties: (1) the creditors, in the form of interest; (2) the government, in the form of taxes; and (3) the residual claimants, that is, the shareholders, in the form of dividends and retained earnings. GAAP rules treat both interest and taxes as expenses on the income statement in arriving at net income. This means that net income represents the portion of the profits that belong to the shareholders. For example, all of Microsoft's net income for 2000 of $9,421 million belongs to the shareholders of Microsoft, since the interest payments to creditors and the tax payments to the government have already been subtracted. This net income results in an increase in Microsoft's stockholders' equity for the year.[3]

ASSETS: PROBABLE FUTURE BENEFITS

An asset represents a probable future economic benefit that is owned, or controlled, by a company. Thus, cash, accounts receivable, equipment, and land are all assets since they will all provide future economic benefits. In the hypothetical software company from Chapter 2, the unused blank CDs and shipping containers were also assets, since they would be used in the following year to ship new products to customers, thus providing a future economic benefit. For the same reason, paying in advance for future insurance coverage or rent also results in future economic benefits, and these assets are called *prepaid insurance* or *prepaid rent*. While this definition of an asset may at first seem simple and unambiguous, in practice determining what constitutes an asset can be extremely difficult, and much of the controversy surrounding current U.S. accounting practice deals with the issue of what is an asset. Here are two examples: intellectual property and human resources.

Firms such as Microsoft invest enormous amounts of money in developing new technologies and products, and this investment is usually called *research and*

---

[2] This book usually uses the term *shareholders* rather than *stockholders*. The two terms have the same meaning.

[3] There are also changes to Microsoft's stockholders' equity during the year other than the increase due to net income. For example, Microsoft had sales and repurchases of stock during the year, which also affect stockholders' equity. These other changes will be discussed in Chapter 15.

development, or *R&D.* If successful, the R&D activities result in the firm obtaining ownership of valuable rights such as patents, copyrights, secret processes, and similar property that is known collectively as *intellectual property.* For example, in the year ending June 30, 2000, Microsoft spent $3,775 million on R&D. Presumably, Microsoft would not spend this money unless management expected it to result in some future economic benefit to the company. However, under GAAP none of this R&D spending is treated as an asset on Microsoft's balance sheet. Instead, GAAP rules require all R&D to be expensed in the year incurred, essentially making R&D into a period cost.

The reason R&D is not treated as an asset is because there is too much uncertainty as to the amount, if any, of the probable future economic benefit. At the time the R&D expenditure[4] is made, management likely does not know exactly which R&D projects will end up resulting in the creation of valuable intellectual property and which will ultimately turn out to be worthless and a waste of money. It is only with hindsight that profitable outcomes from R&D activity can be determined.

Consider the example of a pharmaceutical company that invests in developing a new drug. It may be several years before the drug is finally proven successful and the company is able to begin selling the product. And there may be several wasted efforts for every profitable drug developed. Since users of the firm's financial statements want timely financial reporting, it is not possible to simply wait and see which R&D projects ultimately turn out to be profitable. Therefore, the R&D costs are all treated as an expense in the year incurred.

In the introduction to this chapter it was pointed out that the market value of Microsoft's common stock was far greater than the book value of Microsoft's equity. Now you can see one reason for this difference. Investors, when setting the price they are willing to pay for Microsoft's stock, know which R&D projects have proven to be successful for the company, and the value of the intellectual property that Microsoft has developed over the years (for example, the Windows operating system, or Office application software) is included in the market value of the company's stock. None of the costs of developing these products appear as assets on Microsoft's balance sheet, since these costs have all been expensed in prior years as R&D expense. One major difference between the book value of a company's equity and the market value of a company's stock is the absence of intellectual property assets on the balance sheet.[5]

A second example of an important asset that is not recorded on the balance sheet is *human resources*—the value of a highly trained, productive, and motivated workforce. Many companies spend a great deal on employee training, particularly companies in service industries such as accounting, law, consulting, and engineering. In addition, many employees develop valuable skills simply by working for a company. Just as with R&D expense, amounts spent on employee training and development are expensed as period costs each year. They are never recorded as an asset.

The reason for this is twofold. First, like R&D projects, it is difficult to tell in advance which employee training expenditures are going to result in a future economic benefit to the company and which are worthless. Second, unlike intellectual property, firms may not claim ownership of their employees; the employees are free to leave the company whenever they chose to do so. Even if the employee training is successful, and the employee becomes a valuable asset of the company, the individual may take his or her skills elsewhere and may even

---

[4] In this book the term *expenditure* is used any time a firm pays cash or incurs a liability (such as an account payable) to purchase a product or service. Used this way, the term is not intended to be synonymous with *expense,* which has a specific definition in Chapter 2.

[5] If Microsoft were to acquire title to intellectual property that is already developed, by purchasing it from a developer or inventor, that would result in an asset being recorded on Microsoft's balance sheet. Only internally developed intellectual property is subject to expensing as R&D.

start up a competing company. The probable economic benefits from employee training are too uncertain to result in an asset.

The balance sheets at the end of this chapter give examples of other types of assets that companies report. For example, Boeing reports short-term investments, deferred income taxes, customer and commercial financing, goodwill, and prepaid pension expense as assets. IBM reports sales-type leases receivable and software. Chrysler reports special tools and intangible assets. In all of these cases, managers are implicitly telling financial statement users that these items are expected to provide future economic benefits; therefore, these items are properly classified as assets on the companies' balance sheets.

Capitalization versus Current Expense

Any time a company spends money on something, or incurs a liability such as an account payable, there are only two places in the financial statements that the expenditure can show up: the income statement or the balance sheet. If the expenditure ends up on the income statement, it is treated as an expense for the accounting period. If the expenditure ends up on the balance sheet, it is treated as an asset and is considered to represent a probable future economic benefit.[6] Under no circumstances can the same expenditure end up in both the income statement and the balance sheet at the same time. The expenditure is either an expense in the current period or an asset, but not both.

One implication of this treatment is that managers, in making a decision to record an expenditure as an asset, are also implicitly making the determination that the expenditure is not an expense in the current period. Conversely, in making a decision to expense an item in the current period, managers are implicitly making a determination that the expenditure will not provide a probable future economic benefit. This way of thinking about the relationship between expenses and assets is also consistent with the definition of an expense given in Chapter 2: a net outflow of economic resources. Any time the firm spends cash to purchase an asset, such as a truck or factory building, there is no net outflow of economic resources. The firm has simply exchanged one type of economic resource (cash) for another type (a truck).

This distinction between a current expense and an asset is especially important when dealing with expenditures for repairs and maintenance of property. For example, if the firm replaces a leaky roof on an office building, is this a repair expense (a period cost) or a new asset (a roof)? If the new roof does not extend the useful life of the building, it is probably an expense. However, if the new roof will allow the firm to continue to use the building beyond its expected useful life, it should probably be considered an asset.[7] This is another example of the way managers' assumptions—in this case, about the effect of the roof on the building's life—can affect reported net income.

Mutually Unexecuted Contracts

Consider the news story below announcing that Eaton Corp. was awarded a $500 million multi year contract to supply General Motors with technology in the future. Clearly, this results in a probable future economic benefit to Eaton. Should Eaton record a $500 million asset on its balance sheet when the contract with GM was signed?

Eaton Wins $500 Million GM Contract

NEW YORK (Reuters)—Industrial manufacturer Eaton Corp. said on Monday General Motors Corp. awarded it a $500 million multi-year contract to supply the No. 1 U.S. auto maker with an advanced powertrain technology for an undisclosed future program.

---

[6] Recording an expenditure as an asset is referred to as *capitalizing* the expenditure.

[7] This issue will be discussed more fully in Chapter 8.

This contract does *not* result in an asset. The reason is that the contract represents what is known as a *mutually unexecuted contract*. A mutually unexecuted contract is one in which neither party has performed what is required of them under the contract. In this example, Eaton has agreed to provide future technology but has not yet done so. Likewise, General Motors has agreed to pay Eaton for the future technology but has no obligation to do so until the technology is provided. Therefore, at the time the contract is signed, both parties still have future obligations to perform. Under GAAP, mutually unexecuted contracts do not, in general, result in the recording of an asset.[8] However, note that investors will use their information about the existence of the contract in valuing the stock of Eaton Corp. This is another example of a difference between the market value of a company's stock and the book value of a company's equity.

LIABILITIES: PROBABLE FUTURE TRANSFERS

A *liability* represents a probable future transfer of economic benefits (either cash, services, or property) by the company to another entity (such as an individual, the government, or another company). Therefore, accounts payable, wages payable, and taxes payable are all liabilities, since the firm will have to pay cash in the future to satisfy the claims of suppliers, workers, and the government. When the firm borrows money from banks, insurance companies, or the general public, it issues notes or bonds payable, and these are also liabilities since they will have to be paid back in the future. Finally, when a firm receives revenue in advance from customers, this also represents a liability, since the firm has an obligation to either provide a future product or service or refund the customer's payment, either of which will result in a transfer of future economic benefits to the customer.

Recall that under GAAP some expected future economic benefits, such as intellectual property or human resources, are not recorded on the balance sheet as assets. When dealing with liabilities, just the opposite result can occur. Not only are all actual liabilities of the firm always recorded on the balance sheet, in some cases liabilities are recorded for items that may never have to be paid. For example, assume that a lawsuit has been filed against a company asking for $1,000,000 in damages. (For a real-world example, consider recent litigation against tobacco companies.) At the balance sheet date, the case may not even have gone to court yet. However, if it appears probable that the company will lose the case and will be required to pay the damages, a liability, called a *contingent liability*, must be recorded on the balance sheet at year-end.[9]

Presented below is a note from Microsoft's annual report discussing lawsuits against the company. In this case, Microsoft believes the claims are without merit. Therefore, under GAAP no liability is required to be recorded on Microsoft's balance sheet for these cases. If the managers of Microsoft thought it was probable that Microsoft would lose some of these cases, and if the amount were material, then a contingent liability would be recorded on Microsoft's balance sheet for the expected future payments.

A large number of antitrust class action lawsuits have been initiated against Microsoft. These cases allege that Microsoft has competed unfairly and unlawfully monopolized alleged markets for operating systems and certain software applications and seek to recover alleged overcharges that the complaints contend Microsoft charged for these products. Microsoft believes the claims are without merit and is vigorously defending the cases.

Source: Microsoft Corporation annual report.

---

[8] An example of a mutually unexecuted contract that *does* result in an asset under GAAP is a capital lease, discussed in Chapter 12.

[9] Contingent liabilities will be discussed more fully in Chapter 6.

BALANCE SHEET CLASSIFICATION

Under GAAP, firms usually classify assets and liabilities into *current* and *noncurrent* categories.[10] Current assets are those assets that are expected to be either converted by the firm into cash within one year or used up within one year. Current liabilities are those liabilities that are expected to be paid, or otherwise settled, by the firm within one year. To settle a current liability, the firm will either have to use up current assets or create another liability.

In some cases, a single asset can be partly current and partly noncurrent. In such an instance, the book value of the asset would be split, with the current portion reported as a current asset and the noncurrent portion reported as a noncurrent asset. For example, the Boeing statement at the end of the chapter reports current portion of customer and commercial financing as a current asset on its balance sheet, and the rest of customer and commercial financing as a noncurrent asset. A similar rule applies to liabilities, such as notes payable. For example, the Kmart statement reports long-term debt due within one year as a current liability, while the rest of long-term debt is reported as a noncurrent liability.

In those cases where the firm's operating cycle is longer than one year, the longer operating cycle period is substituted for the one-year period in the definition of current assets and current liabilities. The firm's operating cycle is the time it takes to convert cash into new inventory, sell the inventory, and collect the receivable from the sale.[11] For example, it takes years for whiskey distillers to convert cash into salable inventory, since the distillation and aging process is so long. Therefore, the operating cycle for the whiskey distiller industry is longer than one year.

Current assets are reported as the first assets in the asset section of the balance sheet, and current liabilities are reported as the first liabilities in the liabilities section of the balance sheet. In presenting current assets, those assets that are closest to being converted into cash are presented first. The usual order of presentation would be cash followed by marketable securities, sometimes called *short-term investments,* followed by accounts receivable, followed by inventory, followed by prepaid expenses. Chrysler Corporation is an example of a company that does not separate assets and liabilities into current and noncurrent classifications. Chrysler's current assets and liabilities, although not labeled as such, are still presented before noncurrent assets and liabilities. Chrysler's statement reports (1) payments due within one year on long-term debt, and (2) long-term debt as separate liabilities on the balance sheet.

BOOK VALUES VERSUS MARKET VALUES

The amount at which an asset or liability is recorded on a company's balance sheet is referred to as the *book value.* For example, at June 30, 2000, the book value of Microsoft's net property, plant, and equipment is $1,903 million and the book value of accounts payable is $1,083 million. But exactly what does book value represent?

This question is complicated because, although you might think accountants would have chosen one way to measure the values of all assets and liabilities, they haven't. Under GAAP, book value can represent one of several different values: original cost, net realizable value, net present value, current market value, or some value that accountants have made up that reflects none of these values at all. The value that is used depends on the type of asset or liability that is recorded. Throughout the rest of this book we will be learning the detailed rules that apply

---

[10] Sometimes the terms *short-term* and *long-term* are used instead of *current* and *noncurrent.*

[11] This is sometimes referred to as the *cash-to-cash cycle.*

to each type of asset and liability. For now, here is a brief summary of the valuation rules under GAAP for various types of assets and liabilities. Remember that the value of shareholders' equity is a residual number and thus depends on the book values of all the assets and liabilities.

Original (Historical) Cost as Book Value

If there can be considered a general rule for valuing assets and liabilities under GAAP it would be the use of *original cost,* also called *historical cost.* Original cost means the amount that the company originally paid for the asset, or the amount that the company originally received, or expects to pay, for the liability.

Land, buildings, and equipment—often referred to as *property, plant, and equipment*—inventory, and prepaid expenses, such as prepaid rent or prepaid insurance, are examples of assets recorded at original cost. Accounts payable, taxes payable, and bonds payable are examples of liabilities recorded at original cost.

Adjustments to Original Cost

In the case of depreciable assets such as buildings and equipment, the original cost is reduced each accounting period through the recording of depreciation expense. Depreciation is a method of allocating the cost of an asset to more than one accounting period. For example, if a building is expected to have an economic useful life of 40 years, the original cost of the building would be allocated over the entire 40-year period, with a portion of the original cost recorded as depreciation expense each year for 40 years. An asset's original cost reduced by the accumulated depreciation expense taken in prior years is called the *net book value* of the asset, where *net* refers to subtracting accumulated depreciation from prior years. The net book value of an asset will not necessarily be equal to the asset's current market value.[12]

Sometimes it becomes apparent that an asset's original cost is higher than the future cash flows the firm expects to receive from the asset. In this case, the original cost of the asset must be reduced to reflect the lower expected future cash flows. For example, in cases where the original cost of an item of inventory is more than the firm expects to sell the inventory for in the future, the inventory's original cost must be reduced—or *written down,* in accounting terminology—to reflect the net amount the firm expects to receive for the inventory in the future.

Net Realizable Value as Book Value

Under the accrual method of accounting, a firm records revenue when it is earned, even if the firm has not yet collected the cash from the sale. This means that the book value for accounts receivable reflects the sales price the firm charged the customer. However, in some cases customers will end up not paying for the products purchased. Accounts receivable that are never collected are referred to as *bad debts* or *uncollectible accounts.* Under GAAP, the book value of accounts receivable must be adjusted to reflect the net amount that management expects to receive from collection of the receivables. This is equal to the original selling price of the products sold on account, reduced by management's estimate of the amount of accounts that will never be collected.[13]

Net Present Value as Book Value

In the case of assets or liabilities for which the future cash flows are defined under a contract, it is possible to compute the net present value of those future cash

---

[12] Depreciation is discussed in more detail in Chapter 8.

[13] Accounting for uncollectible accounts is discussed in Chapter 6.

flows, which is then used as the book value. Two examples of this accounting treatment occur with leases and notes receivable.

When a company leases an asset, it agrees to use the asset for a certain period of time in exchange for a series of future lease payments defined in the lease agreement. For example, a company may lease an airplane for 10 years at a lease payment of $2,000,000 per year. In this case, since the cash flows associated with the airplane are reasonably certain, the present value of the future cash flows can be used to record the book value of both an asset (an airplane) and a liability (the future annual lease payments).[14]

Sometimes companies enter into transactions resulting in the receipt of a note: a written promise to pay certain amounts of cash at certain specified times in the future. Since the future cash flows are reasonably certain, the present value of the future cash flows can be used to record the book value of the note.[15]

One problem with applying the net present value approach to record assets and liabilities is the necessity of determining an interest rate to use in the present value computation. In some cases, the GAAP rules will specify an interest rate to use; at other times managers have to decide on an appropriate interest rate. This is another example of the influence managers may have on reported financial statement numbers.

Current Market Value as Book Value

Some assets and liabilities of a company may consist of publicly traded securities; therefore, these assets and liabilities have a readily determinable market value at any point in time. Simply by looking in the pages of *The Wall Street Journal* you can see the values of these securities on a daily basis. In this case, there seems little reason to not use the market value on the balance sheet date as the book value. Under GAAP, some types of marketable securities held by firms as investments (for example, common stock of other companies) have a book value equal to market value.

However, not all investments in marketable securities are accounted for in this way. For example, investments in debt instruments expected to be held to maturity and investments in more than 20 percent of the common stock of another company have different accounting treatments.[16]

For firms that issue publicly traded debt instruments, such as bonds or commercial paper, it is also possible to determine the market value of these liabilities on the balance sheet date. However, in most cases liabilities are recorded at their original issue amount, following the original cost rule, and are not adjusted to reflect their current market values.[17]

Other Values as Book Value

Finally, there are some methods of accounting for assets and liabilities that defy generalization. Three examples are accounting for pension assets and liabilities, accounting for deferred income taxes, and accounting for intercompany investments using the equity method. Although even a brief description of accounting for these items is beyond the scope of this chapter, keep in mind that the book values reported on the balance sheet for each of these items do not necessarily relate to original cost, realizable value, net present value, or current market value. The accounting rules for each of these items is discussed in more detail in later

---

[14] Leases are discussed in more detail in Chapter 12.

[15] Notes receivable are discussed in more detail in Chapter 5.

[16] Accounting for investments in other companies is discussed in more detail in Chapter 11.

[17] Accounting for financial instruments and derivative securities is discussed in more detail in Chapter 13.

chapters of this book: Chapter 14 for pensions, Chapter 9 for deferred income taxes, and Chapter 11 for the equity method.

The Trade-Off of Relevance and Reliability

In deciding how to value balance sheet items, accounting standard setters face the trade-off between relevant reporting and reliable reporting that was discussed in Chapter 1. Users of financial statements want information that is relevant to their decisions. In most cases, this means current market value information about assets and liabilities. Users also want reliable information, and current market values for most of a company's assets and liabilities are simply not available. To estimate a market value would require so many assumptions that the reliability of the information would be extremely doubtful.

The balance sheet accounting principles under GAAP are an attempt by standard setters to reach a compromise. For most cases in which market value information is reliably available—such as for marketable securities—GAAP rules require the use of market values on the balance sheet. When reliable market value information is not available, the more reliable original cost should be used as the balance sheet value.

Decision Usefulness of Original Cost

At first it may seem that recording assets and liabilities at original cost would not be very useful for investors' decision making, and in fact some people criticize GAAP as not being very useful, in part because of the focus on original cost rather than market values. However, some counter arguments suggest that original cost may do a reasonable job of providing useful information in many cases.

For current assets such as cash, accounts receivable, marketable securities, and prepaid expenses, book value is either equal to market value (cash and most marketable securities) or very close to market value (accounts receivable and prepaid expenses). The same can be said of current liabilities. Inventories are a current asset with a significant difference between original cost and market value, but recording inventories at market value would involve recognizing revenue at production rather than at the time of sale, which would likely lead to problems with overstating revenue, a worse problem than undervaluing inventory. Therefore, for current assets and liabilities, the GAAP rules seem to do a reasonable job of providing useful information. What about noncurrent assets and liabilities?

Market Value versus Original Cost: An Example from the Oil and Gas Industry

Consider as an example the case of financial reporting by oil and gas exploration companies. Under GAAP, these companies must provide supplemental financial statement information about the value of their oil and gas reserves still under the ground. This is an attempt to move from original cost toward a measure of market value, since the market prices of oil and gas can be easily observed on a daily basis. The supplemental market value information, called the *standardized measure*, is equal to the net present value of the after-tax cash flows associated with future sales of oil and gas. The standardized measure assumes that prices of oil and gas in the future will remain the same as the current prices, that future tax rates will remain the same as current tax rates, and that the appropriate interest rate for the present value computation is 10 percent.

Presented below is Mobil Corporation's computation of the standardized measure for 1997 and 1998. The measure of Mobil's oil and gas reserves under this standardized measure approach is $17,822 million at December 31, 1997, and $10,055 million at December 31, 1998. Does this mean that Mobil's oil and gas reserves decreased by more than 40 percent in 1998?

MOBIL CORPORATION
Standardized Measure

	At December 31	
	1997	**1998**
Future cash inflows	$74,065	$50,181
Future production costs	(21,730)	(19,868)
Future development costs	(6,151)	(5,904)
Future income tax expenses	(21,613)	(8,550)
Future net cash flows	24,571	15,859
10% annual discount for estimated timing of cash flows	(9,417)	(6,691)
Standardized measure of discounted future net cash flows	15,154	9,168
Standardized measure of discounted future net cash flows of equity companies	2,668	887
Total	$17,822	$10,055

Source: Mobil Corporation Form 10-K.

The answer is no. The following statement is a reconciliation showing what caused the change in Mobil's standardized measure from 1997 to 1998. As this reconciliation shows, the decrease in the standardized measure is due mainly to the decrease in the prices of oil and gas ($16,564 million) during the year. Since the standardized measure assumes future prices will be the same as current prices, the price decrease in 1998 has a dramatic effect on the standardized measure. However, since this oil and gas is still underground at the end of 1998, the current price may not have any relationship to the actual price at which Mobil can sell the oil and gas in the future when it is extracted and sold.

MOBIL CORPORATION
Change in Standardized Measure

	Year Ended December 31
	1998
Beginning of year	$17,822
Changes resulting from	
Sales and transfers of production, net of production costs	(3,783)
Net changes in prices and in development and production costs	(16,564)
Extensions, discoveries, additions and purchases, less related costs	457
Development costs incurred during the period	2,363
Revisions of previous quantity estimates	539
Accretion of discount	2,784
Net change in income taxes	8,218
Equity companies	(1,781)
End of year	$10,055

Source: Mobil Corporation Form 10-K.

How does this standardized measure of oil and gas values compare with the balance sheet book value based on original cost? Presented below is a reconciliation of the balances in the Properties, Plants and Equipment account from the notes to Mobil's financial statements. According to this reconciliation, the book value—that is, original cost less accumulated depreciation—of Mobil's oil and gas properties was $13,810 million at the end of 1997 and $14,307 million at the end of 1998. The depreciated original cost value on the balance sheet at the end of 1998 ($14,307 million) is substantially higher than the value based on the standardized measure ($10,055 million).

MOBIL CORPORATION		
Properties, plants and equipment are stated at cost, less accumulated depreciation, depletion and amortization of $25,074 million at December 31, 1997, and $23,954 million at December 31, 1998 (in millions).		
	At December 31	
	1997	**1998**
Petroleum operations		
Exploration & producing	$13,810	$14,307
Marketing	4,155	4,147
Refining	3,624	3,153
Other marketing and refining activities	899	793
Chemical	1,740	1,870
Corporate and other	328	457
Total	$24,556	$24,727

Source: Mobil Corporation Form 10-K.

If estimated market value information is more useful information than original cost, it would be reasonable to assume that the supplemental information about the standardized measure is more useful than the balance sheet book value. However, here is what the management of Mobil Corporation said about the usefulness of this supplemental standardized measure information:

> The standardized measure data are not intended to replace the historical cost-based financial data included in the audited financial statements. As such, many of the data disclosed in this section represent estimates, assumptions and computations that are subject to continual change as the future unfolds. For example, a significant decrease in year-end crude oil prices from 1997 to 1998 contributed to the lower discounted future net cash flow amount for 1998. Accordingly, *Mobil cautions investors and analysts that the data are of questionable utility for decision making.* (emphasis added)

Source: Mobil Corporation Form 10-K.

That last sentence—"Mobil cautions investors and analysts that the data are of questionable utility for decision making"—seems striking. If the purpose of financial reporting is to reduce information asymmetry, why do GAAP rules require the reporting of data that the company's management states are of questionable usefulness? This question clearly illustrates the trade-off that goes on between reliable and relevant financial accounting information. Accounting standard setters believe this supplemental information is relevant for investment decisions relating to oil and gas exploration companies, despite the data's lack of reliability. Management, however, believes that the data are so unreliable as to make them of questionable usefulness for decision making.

The conclusion from this example may be that unless reliable measures of market value are available, users may prefer to have reliable measures based on original cost rather than relevant but unreliable market value measures.

Contracting Usefulness of Original Cost

Recall that the second important use of financial accounting information, in addition to reducing information asymmetry, is in contracting. Basing management compensation plans on financial accounting earnings helps to align the incentives of managers with those of shareholders. Basing debt contracts on financial accounting numbers helps to align the incentives of shareholders with those of creditors. In both of these cases, the firm faces lower costs by reducing conflicts between managers and shareholders, and between shareholders and creditors.

When balance sheet book values are based on original cost rather than current market values, the usefulness of accounting for contracting may actually be enhanced. For those assets for which there are no publicly available market values, original cost numbers are more objective—that is, reliable—and are not subject to as much manager manipulation or estimation as are market value numbers. Contracting on a set of numbers that are in many cases simply estimates by managers would not make the contracts as useful to shareholders or creditors.

Another problem with using market values in contracting is they tend to fluctuate depending on macroeconomic factors that managers may have little control over. For example, if real estate prices are increasing throughout the country, using market values will increase the book value of land and buildings even though this increase may have little to do with how well managers are managing the business operations of the company.

The conclusion is that, although market values seem to be more relevant for solving the information asymmetry problem, it is not clear that market values are necessarily better than original cost for use in contracting.

Income Statement Consequences of Balance Sheet Valuation

Although the focus of this chapter has been on what items appear on the balance sheet and how those balance sheet items are valued, there is an important relationship between balance sheet valuation and the income statement. Consider the following example of what would happen if market value, rather than original cost, is used to value some securities that the company owns. Assume that the securities originally cost $1,000,000 when they were purchased last year, but that because of a rising stock market the securities have increased in value over the year and are now worth $1,200,000. What happens in the accounts when this increase in value is recorded? Here is a hypothetical journal entry to record the $200,000 increase:

	Journal Entry to Record Increase in Value of Securities		
+/−	Accounts [description of account]	Debit	Credit
+	Securities [balance sheet asset account]	200,000	
?	?		200,000

As you can see from the above incomplete entry, some other account needs to be credited for $200,000. Many accountants would argue that in this case the correct entry is to credit an income statement account for the increase in the value of the securities. This would have the effect of increasing net income.

Another example is the recording of depreciation. Consider the software start-up company from Chapter 2. At the end of the first year the company had an asset called equipment with a book value of $6,000. At the end of the company's second year of operations, another $3,000 of this asset's cost should be recorded as a period expense through depreciation. Here is how that journal entry would look:

	Journal Entry to Record Computer Depreciation for Year 2		
+/−	Accounts [description of account]	Debit	Credit
+	Depreciation Expense [income statement expense account]	3,000	
−	Equipment [balance sheet asset account]		3,000

The decrease in the balance sheet book value of the equipment is reflected in an additional expense on the income statement. Net income is decreased due to a change in a balance sheet book value.

These examples illustrate how increases and decreases in balance sheet book values are also reflected in income statement net income. When accountants debate how to record assets and liabilities, keep in mind that they are also trying to deal with how the increases and decreases in assets and liabilities will affect net income. There is a link between the balance sheet book values of assets and liabilities and the amount of net income reported on the income statement.

EVENTS SUBSEQUENT TO THE BALANCE SHEET DATE

The balance sheet reports a firm's economic resources and the claims on those economic resources at a particular time—the balance sheet date. However, firms are not able to issue complete financial statements on the balance sheet date. It often takes weeks or months between the end of an accounting period and the time the financial statements are finally sent to shareholders and the SEC. During this post balance sheet time period, things may happen about which users of financial statements would want to know. These are referred to as *subsequent events*. How should subsequent events be handled?

If the subsequent event provides additional information about prior events or account balances that *existed at the balance sheet date,* the balance sheet accounts should be adjusted to reflect this additional information. To ignore this information because it took place after the balance sheet date would be misleading to the users of the company's financial statements. For example, assume that a firm was valuing its inventory of computer disk drives at $50 per drive (its cost to manufacture the drives) on the balance sheet as of December 31. If early in January, before the financial statements have been issued, the firm discovered that the drives were in fact obsolete and it could sell them for only $20 per drive, it would have to reduce the balance sheet inventory amount reported at December 31 to report the expected net realizable value of $20 per drive.

If the subsequent event provides additional information about events or account balances that *did not exist at the balance sheet date,* no adjustment to the balance sheet accounts should be made. In many cases, these subsequent events should be disclosed in notes to the financial statements to alert the users that they have occurred.

Here is an example of a subsequent event from the notes to the financial statements of Boeing for 1999. Note that the balance sheet date was December 31, 1999, but the event being reported in the note took place on January 13, 2000.

Proposed Acquisition of Hughes Space and Communications Business

On January 13, 2000, the Company announced an agreement to acquire the Hughes space and communications business and related operations for $3.75 billion. The transaction is subject to regulatory and government reviews and is expected to be finalized by the end of the second quarter of 2000. Hughes is a technological leader in space-based communications, reconnaissance, surveillance and imaging systems. It is also a leading manufacturer of commercial satellites. Under the definitive agreement, Boeing also will acquire Hughes Electron Dynamics, a supplier of electronic components for satellites, and Spectrolab, a provider of solar cells and panels for satellites.

Source: The Boeing Company annual report.

Here is the same event described in the notes to the 1999 financial statements of General Motors Corporation, the parent of Hughes:

On January 13, 2000, Hughes announced that it had reached an agreement to sell its satellite systems manufacturing businesses to The Boeing Company (Boeing) for $3.8 billion in cash. The transaction, which is subject to regulatory approval, is expected to close in the second or third quarter of 2000. In addition, if Hughes were to enter into a settlement of the China investigation (see Note 16 to the GM consolidated financial statements) prior to the closing of the Boeing transaction that involves a debarment from sales to the U.S. government or a material suspension of Hughes' export licenses or other material limitation on projected business activities of the satellite systems manufacturing business, Boeing would not be obligated to complete the purchase of Hughes' satellite systems manufacturing businesses.

Source: General Motors Corporation annual report.

FINANCIAL LEVERAGE AND RISK

When firms finance their assets by borrowing, as opposed to obtaining cash from shareholders, it is referred to as *financial leverage*. The use of financial leverage is common in publicly traded corporations. Even Microsoft, a corporation without any direct borrowing, has some financial leverage in the form of accounts payable, accrued compensation, and income taxes.

Some companies utilize financial leverage more than others. For example, Boeing, IBM, Kmart, and Chrysler all reported long-term debt on their balance sheets shown at the end of this chapter. The use of financial leverage can provide benefits to a company in some situations. If the company can invest the borrowed money in productive assets, and if the earnings on these assets exceed the interest the company pays on the debt, the excess earnings represent residual income for the shareholders. The use of financial leverage is a way to increase earnings for the company's shareholders.

Using financial leverage also makes the company more risky, and this risk takes two forms. First, to the extent the company's productive assets generate earnings that are lower than the interest on the debt, the earnings of the shareholders are reduced. As residual claimants, shareholders may be charged with losses as well as residual income. Second, to the extent that the company is unable to make the required interest and principal payments on the debt, the creditors may force the company into bankruptcy and take over the company's assets, leaving the shareholders with nothing.

It is important to understand the benefits and risks of financial leverage to a firm, since one of the major uses of the balance sheet is to provide information about the company's leverage. The more liabilities a company reports, the more risk investors will likely perceive. One goal of managers is often to keep liabilities off the balance sheet to the extent possible under GAAP.

BALANCE SHEETS IN OTHER COUNTRIES

In Chapter 2 when we compared the income statement of Reed Elsevier, a U.K./Dutch company, with the income statements of U.S. companies, there were few apparent differences other than terminology. That is not the case with the balance sheet. If you look at the balance sheet of Reed Elsevier included at the end of this chapter you see that it looks nothing like the balance sheet of a U.S. corporation.

The first thing you notice is that, whereas a U.S. balance sheet would begin with current assets, Reed Elsevier reports fixed assets at the beginning of the balance sheet. (*Fixed assets* is another term for noncurrent assets.) The U.S. custom of reporting assets in order of liquidity is not part of European financial reporting.

Next, notice that current assets are reported together with the current liabilities, and the two amounts are combined to arrive at a figure for net current liabilities. Finally, the net current liabilities, as well as the remaining noncurrent liabilities, are subtracted from assets to arrive at a figure for net assets. The total assets of Reed Elsevier are never reported. The balance sheet concludes by reporting shareholders' equity (under the heading capital and reserves) and shows that the total combined shareholders' funds (that is, shareholders' equity) is equal to the total net assets.

In Chapter 2 we discussed the various differences between U.K./Dutch GAAP and U.S. GAAP and the effects those differences had on net income. These same GAAP differences also affect the balance of shareholders' equity. Shown below is a reconciliation of total combined shareholders' funds under U.K./Dutch GAAP with the balances that would result if U.S. GAAP were applied. Keep in mind that, while the differences in net income resulted only from GAAP differences in the current accounting period, differences in combined shareholders' funds reflect differences from all prior accounting periods. The net income of Reed Elsevier (see Chapter 2) was *lower* under U.S. GAAP, while the combined shareholders' funds is *higher* under U.S. GAAP.

Effects on combined shareholders' funds of material differences between U.K. and Dutch GAAP and U.S. GAAP (in pound millions):

	At December 31	
	1998	**1999**
Combined shareholders' funds under U.K and Dutch GAAP	2,130	1,855
U.S. GAAP adjustments		
Goodwill and other intangibles	637	553
Deferred taxation	(242)	(180)
Acquisition accounting	8	8
Pensions	57	63
Other items	(1)	(3)
Ordinary dividends not declared in the period	244	127
Combined shareholders' funds under U.S. GAAP	2,833	2,423

Source: Reed Elsevier Form 20-F.

In many countries it is possible to revalue assets periodically to reflect their current market value. However, Reed Elsevier stated in the notes to its financial statements that it reported tangible assets (that is, property, plant, and equipment) at cost rather than market value, consistent with U.S. GAAP.

USING BALANCE SHEET ITEMS TO MAKE DECISIONS

Balance sheet numbers are used to make decisions in two ways. First, balance sheet numbers are important when combined with income statement numbers in assessing the performance of a firm. Second, information about liabilities is useful in making decisions about the liquidity and riskiness of a firm.

In Chapter 2 it was noted that income statement numbers for sales or net income are often divided by some measure of the total amount invested in the company, such as total assets or total shareholders' equity, to arrive at a measure expressed as a rate of return on invested capital, such as return on total assets or return on equity. Often the denominator in these return measures is the average of the beginning and ending total assets, or shareholders' equity. This reflects the fact that the income statement number represents activity over the entire accounting period, whereas the balance sheet number only represents assets or equity as of the end of the accounting period. If a firm has been growing or shrinking, the average assets or equity for the year may differ from the year-end amounts.

Another useful measure based on balance sheet numbers is the inventory turnover ratio, equal to cost of goods sold divided by average inventory. This provides a measure of how much inventory a firm has on hand relative to the amount sold each year. Often this measure is expressed as an average number of days' inventory on hand. For example, a firm with an inventory turnover ratio of 12 has on average one month's inventory on hand at any one time.

A similar type of measure is the accounts receivable turnover ratio, equal to credit sales divided by average accounts receivable. This provides a measure of how long on average it takes a firm to collect its receivables. Like the inventory turnover measure, this is also often expressed as an average number of days' receivables on hand. In general, the faster a firm can collect its receivables the more profitable it will be.

The balance sheet also provides information about the liquidity of a firm, where liquidity is a measure of how likely it is that the firm will run out of cash. For this purpose, the classification into current assets and current liabilities is particularly helpful, as is the difference between these two measures, called *working capital*. The current ratio, equal to current assets divided by current liabilities, is another useful measure, with a high ratio indicating more liquidity and a smaller likelihood of running out of cash.

Finally, the balance sheet provides important information about a firm's use of leverage. Leverage ratios such as total liabilities divided by total assets, and long-term liabilities divided by total shareholders' equity, are measures of how much debt a firm has. Since the more debt a firm has, the greater the likelihood of not being able to make required interest or principal payments, leverage measures are a way of assessing the risk that the firm may end up in bankruptcy.

Summary

This chapter investigates the GAAP rules relating to firms' balance sheets by focusing on three basic ideas: (1) the types of items that are recorded on the balance sheet; (2) the value at which these items are recorded; and (3) how investors and others use the information on the balance sheet to make decisions. The balance sheet is a summary of a firm's economic resources at a particular point in time and the claims against those resources by creditors and shareholders, also called residual claimants.

Assets are defined as probable future economic benefits owned or controlled by a company. For some assets, such as intellectual property or human resources, the expected future benefits are too uncertain to result in an asset under GAAP. For any expenditure, managers must make a choice between expensing the item on the income statement or recording the item as an asset on the balance sheet. Liabilities are defined as probable future transfers of economic benefits by the company to another entity. Under GAAP, actual liabilities as well as probable contingent liabilities are recorded.

Assets and liabilities are classified as current or noncurrent. The rules for recording book values of assets and liabilities vary, with the following valuations used: original (historical) cost, original cost adjusted for depreciation, net realizable value, net present value, and current market value. In making the decision whether to use original cost or a measure of current market value, accounting standard setters have to trade off investors' need for relevant market value information with investors' preference for reliable information. Although market value information may be more relevant for some decisions, in most cases it is not as reliable as original cost. Also, for contracting purposes original cost measures may provide more useful information than market values. A decision to change the book value of an asset or a liability to reflect changes in market value means that net income, or shareholders' equity, must change as well.

Financial leverage results when firms borrow money to finance their investments in operating assets. Financial leverage has two consequences. First, it can increase the earnings to shareholders if the firm can invest the borrowed money in profitable projects. Second, financial leverage may make the firm more risky. The balance sheet provides information about the extent of a firms' use of financial leverage.

Balance sheet information is used primarily in two ways. First, information about liabilities is useful in determining the liquidity of the firm, as well as the risk of future bankruptcy. Second, information about assets can be combined with income statement information for the period to derive performance measures such as return on assets, return on equity, inventory turnover, and accounts receivable turnover.

THE BOEING COMPANY AND SUBSIDIARIES
Consolidated Statements of Financial Position
(dollars in millions except per share data)

	December 31	
	1999	1998
Assets		
Cash and cash equivalents	$ 3,354	$ 2,183
Short-term investments	100	279
Accounts receivable	3,453	3,288
Current portion of customer and commercial financing	799	781
Deferred income taxes	1,467	1,495
Inventories, net of advances and progress billings	6,539	8,584
Total current assets	15,712	16,610
Customer and commercial financing	5,205	4,930
Property, plant and equipment, net	8,245	8,589
Deferred income taxes	—	411
Goodwill	2,233	2,312
Prepaid pension expense	3,845	3,513
Other assets	907	659
	$36,147	$37,024
Liabilities and Shareholders' Equity		
Accounts payable and other liabilities	$11,269	$11,085
Advances in excess of related costs	1,215	1,251
Income taxes payable	420	569
Short-term debt and current portion of long-term debt	752	869
Total current liabilities	13,656	13,774
Deferred income taxes	172	
Accrued retiree health care	4,877	4,831
Long-term debt	5,980	6,103
Shareholders' equity:		
Common shares, par value $5.00—1,200,000,000 shares authorized; Shares issued—1,011,870,159 and 1,011,870,159	5,059	5,059
Additional paid-in capital	1,684	1,147
Treasury shares, at cost—102,356,897 and 35,845,731	(4,161)	(1,321)
Retained earnings	10,487	8,706
Accumulated other comprehensive income	6	(23)
Unearned compensation	(12)	(17)
ShareValue Trust shares—38,696,289 and 38,166,601	(1,601)	(1,235)
Total shareholders' equity	11,462	12,316
	$36,147	$37,024

Source: The Boeing Company Form 10-K

INTERNATIONAL BUSINESS MACHINES CORPORATION AND SUBSIDIARY COMPANIES
Consolidated Statement of Financial Position
(dollars in millions except per share amounts)

	Notes	At December 31 1999	At December 31 1998
Assets			
Current assets			
Cash and cash equivalents		$ 5,043	$ 5,375
Marketable securities	L	788	393
Notes and accounts receivable—trade, net of allowances		20,039	18,958
Sales-type leases receivable		6,220	6,510
Other accounts receivable		1,359	1,313
Inventories	E	4,868	5,200
Prepaid expenses and other current assets		4,838	4,611
Total current assets		43,155	42,360
Plant, rental machines and other property	F	39,616	44,870
Less: Accumulated depreciation		22,026	25,239
Plant, rental machines and other property—net		17,590	19,631
Software		663	599
Investments and sundry assets	G	26,087	23,510
Total assets		$87,495	$86,100
Liabilities and Stockholders' Equity			
Current liabilities			
Taxes	P	$ 4,792	$ 3,125
Short-term debt	J & L	14,230	13,905
Accounts payable		6,400	6,252
Compensation and benefits		3,840	3,530
Deferred income		4,529	4,115
Other accrued expenses and liabilities		5,787	5,900
Total current liabilities		39,578	36,827
Long-term debt	J & L	14,124	15,508
Other liabilities	M	11,928	12,818
Deferred income taxes	P	1,354	1,514
Total liabilities		66,984	66,667
Contingencies	O		
Stockholders' equity	N		
Preferred stock, par value $.01 per share		247	247
Shares authorized: 150,000,000			
Shares issued and outstanding (1999 and 1998-2,546,011)			
Common stock, par value $.20 per share	C	11,762	10,121
Shares authorized: 4,687,500,000			
Shares issued (1999-1,876,665,245; 1998-1,853,738,104)			
Retained earnings		16,878	10,141
Treasury stock, at cost (shares: 1999-72,449,015; 1998-1,924,293)		(7,375)	(133)
Employee benefits trust (shares: 1999-20,000,000; 1998-20,000,000)		(2,162)	(1,854)
Accumulated gains and losses not affecting retained earnings		1,161	911
Total stockholders' equity		20,511	19,433
Total liabilities and stockholders' equity		$87,495	$86,100

Source: IBM Corporation Form 10-K.

KMART CORPORATION
1999 Annual Report
Consolidated Balance Sheets
(dollars in millions)

	As of January 26, 2000, and January 27, 1999	
	1999	1998
Current assets		
Cash and cash equivalents	$ 344	$ 710
Merchandise inventories	7,101	6,536
Other current assets	715	584
Total current assets	8,160	7,830
Property and equipment, net	6,410	5,914
Other assets and deferred charges	534	422
Total assets	$15,104	$14,166
Current liabilities		
Long-term debt due within one year	$ 66	$ 77
Trade accounts payable	2,204	2,047
Accrued payroll and other liabilities	1,574	1,359
Taxes other than income taxes	232	208
Total current liabilities	4,076	3,691
Long-term debt and notes payable	1,759	1,538
Capital lease obligations	1,014	1,091
Other long-term liabilities	965	883
Company obligated mandatorily redeemable convertible preferred securities of a subsidiary trust holding solely 7¾% convertible junior subordinated debentures of Kmart (redemption value of $1,000)	986	984
Common stock, $1 par value, 1,500,000,000 shares authorized; 481,383,569 and 493,358,504 shares issued, respectively	481	493
Capital in excess of par value	1,555	1,667
Retained earnings	4,268	3,819
Total liabilities and shareholders' equity	$15,104	$14,166

Source: Kmart Corporation Form 10-K.

CHRYSLER CORPORATION
Consolidated Balance Sheet
(in millions of dollars)

	December 31	
	1997	**1996**
Assets		
Cash and cash equivalents (Note 1)	$ 4,898	$ 5,158
Marketable securities (Note 2)	2,950	2,594
Total cash, cash equivalents and marketable securities	7,848	7,752
Accounts receivable—trade and other (less allowance for doubtful accounts: 1997 and 1996—$52 million and $44 million, respectively)	1,646	2,126
Inventories (Notes 1 and 3)	4,738	5,195
Prepaid employee benefits, taxes and other expenses (Note 12)	2,193	1,929
Finance receivables and retained interests in sold receivables (Note 4)	13,518	12,339
Property and equipment (Note 5)	17,968	14,905
Special tools (Note 1)	4,572	3,924
Intangible assets (Note 1)	1,573	1,995
Other noncurrent assets (Note 12)	6,362	6,019
Total assets	$60,418	$56,184
Liabilities		
Accounts payable	$ 9,512	$ 8,981
Accrued liabilities and expenses (Note 6)	9,717	8,864
Short-term debt (Note 7)	3,841	3,214
Payments due within one year on long-term debt (Note 7)	2,638	2,998
Long-term debt (Note 7)	9,006	7,184
Accrued noncurrent employee benefits (Note 12)	9,841	9,431
Other noncurrent liabilities	4,501	3,941
Total liabilities	49,056	44,613
Shareholders' equity (Note 11) (shares in millions)		
Preferred stock—$1 per share par value; authorized 20.0 shares; Series A Convertible Preferred Stock; issued and outstanding: 1997 and 1996—0.02 and 0.04 shares, respectively (aggregate liquidation preference $8 million and $21 million, respectively)	*	*
Common stock—$1 per share par value; authorized 1,000.0 shares; issued: 1997 and 1996—823.1 and 821.6 shares, respectively	823	822
Additional paid-in capital	5,231	5,129
Retained earnings	10,605	8,829
Treasury stock—at cost: 1997 and 1996—174.7 and 119.1 shares, respectively	(5,297)	(3,209)
Total shareholders' equity	11,362	11,571
Total liabilities and shareholders' equity	$60,418	$56,184

Source: Chrysler Corporation Form 10-K.

REED ELSEVIER
Combined Balance Sheets
(in pound millions)

	Notes	At December 31 1998	1999
Fixed assets			
Goodwill and intangible assets	11	3,598	3,400
Tangible assets	12	399	386
Investments	13		
Investments in joint ventures:			
Share of gross assets		107	136
Share of gross liabilities		(32)	(47)
Share of net assets		75	89
Other investments		12	30
		87	119
		4,084	3,905
Current assets			
Stocks	14	101	113
Debtors: amounts falling due within one year	15	731	666
Debtors: amounts falling due after more than one year	16	136	148
Cash and short-term investments	17	708	440
		1,676	1,367
Creditors: amounts falling due within one year	18	(2,791)	(2,676)
Net current liabilities		(1,115)	(1,309)
Total assets less current liabilities		2,969	2,596
Creditors: amounts falling due after more than one year	19	(797)	(620)
Provisions for liabilities and charges	23	(36)	(113)
Minority interests		(6)	(8)
Net assets		2,130	1,855
Capital and reserves			
Combined share capitals	24	168	168
Combined share premium accounts		353	341
Combined reserves		1,609	1,346
Combined shareholders' funds		2,130	1,855

Source: Reed Elsevier Form 20-F.

Discussion Questions

1. Explain the major differences between the balance sheet and the income statement.
2. Define an asset.
3. Give examples of probable future resources that are *not* treated as assets under GAAP.
4. Define a liability.
5. Explain how the concepts of relevance and reliability apply to assets and liabilities.
6. What does it mean to characterize shareholders' equity as a residual claim?
7. Describe the different GAAP methods for measuring balance sheet book value for assets. Give an example of each method.
8. Explain what is meant by capitalizing an expense. How does this treatment affect the income statement?
9. What does the term *current* mean with respect to assets and liabilities?
10. Explain why the use of original (or historical) cost may still provide useful information for users of financial statements.
11. Explain why the use of market values may *not* provide useful information in some cases for users of financial statements.
12. How are the balance sheet and income statement related?
13. Explain the GAAP treatment for events that occur subsequent to the balance sheet date.
14. What is meant by the term *financial leverage?* How is it related to risk?

Problems

1. The balance sheet shown below is from a U.S. public company. Given the assets and liabilities shown, is the company (a) a bank, (b) an Internet portal, or (c) a railroad?

Consolidated Balance Sheets
(in thousands, except par value)

	December 31	
	XXXX	XXXX
Assets		
Current assets		
Cash and cash equivalents	$125,474	$ 63,571
Short-term investments in marketable securities	308,025	27,772
Accounts receivable, net of allowance of $4,967 in XXXX and $2,598 in XXXX	24,831	11,163
Prepaid expenses and other current assets	8,909	5,982
Total current assets	467,239	108,488
Long-term investments in marketable securities	90,266	16,702
Property and equipment, net	15,189	7,364
Other assets	49,190	10,958
Total assets	$621,884	$143,512
Liabilities and Shareholders' Equity		
Current liabilities		
Accounts payable	$ 6,302	$ 5,256
Accrued expenses and other current liabilities	34,419	12,685
Deferred revenue	38,301	5,085
Due to related parties	961	1,412
Total current liabilities	79,983	24,438
Deferred tax liability	4,443	—
Commitments and contingencies (Note 9)		
Minority interests in consolidated subsidiaries	1,248	716
Shareholders' equity		
Preferred stock, $0.001 par value; 10,000 shares authorized; none issued or outstanding in XXXX and XXXX	—	—
Common stock, $0.00017 par value; 900,000 shares authorized; 199,019 issued and outstanding in XXXX and 180,408 issued and outstanding in XXXX	23	20
Additional paid-in capital	522,997	151,744
Accumulated deficit	(8,442)	(32,963)
Accumulated other comprehensive income (loss)	21,632	(443)
Total shareholders' equity	536,210	118,358
Total liabilities and shareholders' equity	$621,884	$143,512

2. The balance sheet shown below is from a U.S. public company. Given the assets and liabilities shown, is the company (a) a bank, (b) an internet portal, or (c) a railroad?

Consolidated Balance Sheets
(dollars in millions, shares in thousands)

	December 31	
	XXXX	**XXXX**
Assets		
Current assets		
Cash and cash equivalents	$ 26	$ 11
Accounts receivable, net	172	314
Materials and supplies	191	220
Current portion of deferred income taxes	306	299
Other current assets	28	132
Total current assets	723	976
Property and equipment, net	23,110	22,369
Other assets	888	1,030
Total assets	$24,721	$24,375
Liabilities and Stockholders' Equity		
Current liabilities		
Accounts payable and other current liabilities	$ 1,873	$ 1,954
Long-term debt due within one year	288	232
Total current liabilities	2,161	2,186
Long-term debt and commercial paper	6,363	6,614
Deferred income taxes	6,731	6,422
Casualty and environmental liabilities	423	430
Employee merger and separation costs	216	262
Other liabilities	978	981
Total liabilities	16,872	16,895
Commitments and contingencies (see Notes 3, 9 and 11)		
Stockholders' equity		
Common stock, $0.01 par value 600,000 shares authorized; 492,818 shares and 486,637 shares issued, respectively	5	5
Additional paid-in-capital	5,584	5,428
Retained earnings	5,048	4,505
Treasury stock, at cost, 107,041 shares and 95,045 shares, respectively	(2,745)	(2,413)
Unearned compensation	(34)	(35)
Accumulated other comprehensive loss	(9)	(10)
Total stockholders' equity	7,849	7,480
Total liabilities and shareholders' equity	$24,721	$24,375

3. The balance sheet shown below is from a U.S. public company. Given the assets and liabilities shown, is the company (a) a bank, (b) an internet portal, or (c) a railroad?

Consolidated Balance Sheet
(in millions)

	December 31	
	XXXX	XXXX
Assets		
Cash and due from banks	$ 8,169	$ 11,736
Federal funds sold and securities purchased under resale agreements	82	187
Investment securities at fair value	9,888	13,505
Loans	65,734	67,389
Allowance for loan losses	1,828	2,018
Net loans	63,906	65,371
Due from customers on acceptances	98	197
Accrued interest receivable	507	665
Premises and equipment, net	2,117	2,406
Core deposit intangible	1,709	2,038
Goodwill	7,031	7,322
Other assets	3,949	5,461
Total assets	$97,456	$108,888
Liabilities		
Noninterest-bearing deposits	$23,953	$ 29,073
Interest-bearing deposits	48,246	52,748
Total deposits	72,199	81,821
Federal funds purchased and securities sold under repurchase agreements	3,576	2,029
Commercial paper and other short-term borrowings	249	401
Acceptances outstanding	98	197
Accrued interest payable	175	171
Other liabilities	2,403	3,947
Senior debt	1,983	2,120
Subordinated debt	2,585	2,940
Guaranteed preferred beneficial interests in Company's subordinated debentures	1,299	1,150
Stockholders' Equity		
Preferred stock	275	600
Common stock—$5 par value, authorized 150,000,000 shares; issued and outstanding 86,152,779 shares and 91,474,425 shares	431	457
Additional paid-in capital	8,712	10,287
Retained earnings	3,416	2,749
Cumulative foreign currency translation adjustments	—	(4)
Investment securities valuation allowance	55	23
Total stockholders' equity	12,889	14,112
Total liabilities and shareholders' equity	$97,456	$108,888

4. A company has a balance sheet asset account called Prepaid Insurance.
   a. Why does this account represent probable future economic benefits?
   b. What transactions cause this account to increase or decrease?
   c. How is this account related to the income statement?
   d. How is this account related to cash receipts or disbursements?

5. A company has a balance sheet asset account called Supplies.

   a. Why does this account represent probable future economic benefits?

   b. What transactions cause this account to increase or decrease?

   c. How is this account related to the income statement?

   d. How is this account related to cash receipts or disbursements?

6. A company has a balance sheet liability account called Unearned Revenue.

   a. Why does this account represent a probable future transfer of economic benefits?

   b. What transactions cause this account to increase or decrease?

   c. How is this account related to the income statement?

   d. How is this account related to cash receipts or disbursements?

7. Use the beginning balance sheet and list of transactions for the year (shown below) to produce an ending balance sheet. (Ignore income taxes.)

Beginning Balance Sheet

Cash	$ 1,000
Accounts receivable	3,000
Supplies	41,600
Total assets	$ 45,600
Accounts payable	1,200
Bank loan	30,000
Common stock	10,000
Retained earnings	4,400
Total liabilities and shareholders' equity	$ 45,600

Transactions for the Year

Selling price of services performed during year	$350,000
Cash collected from customers during year	330,000
Cost of supplies received during year	170,000
Cash paid for supplies during year	165,000
Cost of supplies used up during year	160,000
Cash paid on bank loan principal during year	5,000
Cash borrowed from bank during year	12,000
Cash paid for bank loan interest during year	3,000
Cash wages paid for work performed during year	45,000

8. Use the beginning balance sheet and list of transactions for the year (shown below) to produce an ending balance sheet. (Ignore income taxes.)

Beginning Balance Sheet

Cash	$ 80,000
Accounts receivable	190,000
Supplies	23,000
Total assets	$293,000
Accounts payable	140,000
Bank loan	80,000
Common stock	15,000
Retained earnings	58,000
Total liabilities and shareholders' equity	$293,000

Transactions for the Year

Selling price of services performed during year	$800,000
Cash collected from customers during year	840,000
Cost of supplies received during year	390,000
Cash paid for supplies during year	410,000
Cost of supplies used up during year	400,000
Cash paid on bank loan principal during year	60,000
Cash borrowed from bank during year	11,000
Cash paid for bank loan interest during year	8,000
Cash wages paid for work performed during year	375,000

9. Use the beginning balance sheet and list of transactions for the year (shown below) to produce an ending balance sheet. (Ignore income taxes.)

Beginning Balance Sheet

Cash	$ 256,000
Supplies	1,200,000
Total assets	$1,456,000
Accounts payable	473,000
Unearned revenue	180,000
Common stock	250,000
Retained earnings	553,000
Total liabilities and shareholders' equity	$1,456,000

Transactions for the Year

Selling price of services performed during year	$1,185,000
Cash collected from customers during year	1,200,000
Cost of supplies received during year	230,000
Cash paid for supplies during year	220,000
Cost of supplies used up during year	215,000
Cash wages paid for work performed during year	623,000

Research Reports

1. Below is some information from the annual report of France Telecom showing the differences in balance sheet book values under French GAAP and U.S. GAAP. Notice that as of June 30, 2002, the total assets using French GAAP are 96,030 million euros, while the total assets using U.S. GAAP are 62,258 million euros.

Major Assets and Liabilities under U.S. GAAP
(in millions)

	December 31, 2001		June 30, 2002		
	As Reported (€)	U.S. GAAP (€)	As Reported (€)	U.S. GAAP (€)	U.S. GAAP ($)
Assets					
Goodwill, net	34,963	35,264	34,041	12,612	12,426
Other intangible assets	18,189	17,472	19,279	16,204	15,965
Property, plant, and equipment	31,728	32,977	37,128	31,410	30,946
Investment securities	3,240	3,283	1,720	1,882	1,854
Net deferred tax assets (current and long-term)	5,767	2,873	3,862	150	148
Total			96,030	62,258	

a. Since the same assets are owned by France Telecom regardless of the GAAP used, explain how such large differences in asset book values could occur. (*Note:* You may want to look at the annual report for France Telecom at **www.francetelecom.com/en** to help with this answer.)

b. Explain what sorts of decisions might be affected by differences in total assets such as those shown above.

c. How do the above differences affect the usefulness of France Telecom's financial statements?

d. Which set of GAAP provides asset numbers that are more relevant? More reliable?

e. Do the above differences imply anything about the relative quality of French and U.S. GAAP?

2. Obtain the most recent annual report, or Form 10-K, for Unocal Corporation (**www.unocal.com**). (Unocal is one of the world's leading independent natural gas and crude oil exploration and production companies.)

a. What is the total amount reported by Unocal for Properties—net on the most recent balance sheet? How much of this total represents oil and gas properties?

b. Locate the Standardized Measure of Discounted Future Net Cash Flows at the end of the notes to the financial statements. What is the standardized measure as of the most recent balance sheet date?

c. Explain why the balance sheet measure differs from the standardized measure.

d. Explain how the difference between the balance sheet measure and the standardized measure has changed over the most recent accounting period.

e. Discuss the relevance and reliability of both measures.

3. Obtain the 2001 annual report, or Form 10-K, of Amazon.com.

a. What is the balance sheet book value for total assets at December 31, 2001?

b. What is the balance sheet book value for total liabilities at December 31, 2001?

c. How is it possible for a corporation to have total liabilities that exceed total assets?

d. What does it mean for a corporation to have a negative shareholders' equity?

e. Find out the price per share of Amazon.com stock on December 31, 2001. How can the share price be positive when the shareholders' equity balance sheet book value is negative?

4. Obtain the quarterly report Form 10-Q for UAL Corp. for the quarter ended September 30, 2002, from the SEC's EDGAR website. (UAL is the parent company of United Airlines.)

a. Locate the balance sheet in the quarterly report. What were UAL's total assets at September 30, 2002?

b. What were UAL's total liabilities at September 30, 2002?

Below is the announcement of UAL's bankruptcy filing:

Chicago—December 9, 2002   UAL Corp. (NYSE: UAL), the parent company of United Airlines, today announced it and certain of its U.S. subsidiaries have filed for protection under Chapter 11 of the U.S. Bankruptcy Code in the U.S. Bankruptcy Court for the Northern District of Illinois, Eastern Division, in Chicago. The Chapter 11 process will facilitate UAL's restructuring which is designed to restore the company to long-term financial health while operating in the normal course of business.

---

c. Is there any information in UAL's balance sheet as of September 30, 2002, that would have indicated the company would be bankrupt by December?

d. Is there any information in other parts of UAL's quarterly financial statements that would have indicated the company would be bankrupt by December?

e. Based on your analysis of the third quarter 2002 financial statements, and knowing that UAL went bankrupt shortly after the end of the quarter, what, if anything, can you conclude about the usefulness of balance sheet information for decision making?

5. Below are the asset sections of the balance sheets of America Online as of June 30, 1996 and 1997. Notice that the asset called "Deferred subscriber acquisition costs, net" was reported in 1996 with a book value of $314,181,000, but the same asset is shown with no book value on the 1997 balance sheet.

Consolidated Balance Sheets
(amounts in thousands, except share data)

	June 30	
	1997	1996
Assets		
Current assets		
Cash and cash equivalents	$124,340	$118,421
Short-term investments	268	10,712
Trade accounts receivable	65,306	49,342
Other receivables	26,093	23,271
Prepaid expenses and other current assets	107,466	65,290
Total current assets	323,473	267,036
Property and equipment at cost, net	233,129	111,090
Other assets		
Restricted cash	50,000	—
Product development costs, net	72,498	44,330
Deferred subscriber acquisition costs, net	—	314,181
License rights, net	16,777	4,947
Other assets	84,618	29,607
Deferred income taxes	24,410	135,872
Goodwill, net	41,783	51,691
Total assets	$846,688	$958,754

a. What happened to the asset "Deferred subscriber acquisition costs"? (You may need to look at the Form 10-K for June 30, 1997.)

b. The balance sheets shown above make it appear that America Online's assets actually decreased from 1996 to 1997. Would that be a correct interpretation?

c. What does America Online's treatment of "Deferred subscriber acquisition costs" from 1996 to 1997 suggest about managers' ability to affect financial statement book values?

6. The following statements were made by Boston Chicken, Inc., in documents filed with the SEC early in 1999:

In the course of performing the 1998 year-end financial audit, management of the Company has determined it will be necessary to re-audit and restate 1997 fiscal year-end financial statements. PricewaterhouseCoopers, LLP ("PWC"), the Company's recently appointed independent auditors, had advised the Company that, absent sufficient competent evidential matter to support both the appropriateness of certain accounting methods and principles and the reasonableness of certain assumptions used by prior management in reporting certain estimates, PWC would likely be unable to opine on the Company's fiscal 1998 financial statements. While the Company's present management recognizes that such information and evidence was scrutinized by prior management and by the Company's former independent auditors, it has been unable to provide PWC sufficient information and evidence to permit PWC to opine on the Company's fiscal 1998 financial statements. Therefore, the Company must revise and restate 1997 fiscal year-end financial results based on information presently available to it, which will also result in restatements of interim period financial reports for fiscal 1998.

The Company expects to file amended reports on Form 10-Q for the quarterly periods ended April 19, 1998, July 12, 1998 and October 4, 1998. The amended reports are expected to contain restated financial statements and revised management's discussion and analysis reflecting, among other things, a substantial material increase in area developer loan loss reserves recognized in 1997. The Company is currently reviewing and evaluating the Company's historical accounting policies and practices, which could result in additional material adjustments to 1997 year-end and 1998 interim net losses.

The second paragraph above states that the revised financial statements are likely to contain "a substantial material increase in area developer loan loss reserves recognized."

a. Obtain the quarterly report Form 10-Q for Boston Chicken from the SEC's EDGAR website. Find the balance sheet asset item "Notes Receivable, net." What were the balances for this asset on December 28, 1997, and April 19, 1998?

b. Using information available in the Form 10-Q, explain the change in the Notes Receivable balance for the quarter. How would the "loan loss reserves recognized" mentioned above relate to this change? (*Hint:* "Loan loss reserves" are the same as "provision for loan losses.")

c. The Form 10-Q also shows an income statement for the quarter. The income statement has an item called "Provision for loan losses" in the amount of $202,000 thousand for the quarter ended April 19, 1998. Use this income statement item to explain how changes in balance sheet book values are related to the income statement.

d. Why would Boston Chicken's new auditors (PricewaterhouseCoopers) be unable to give an opinion on financial statements from prior periods? What does this suggest about the reliability of balance sheet book values?

AFP/CORBIS

Chapter Learning Objectives

After reading this chapter you should understand

1. The differences between net income and net cash flows.
2. The different activities represented by operating, financing, and investing cash flows.
3. The two alternative forms for presenting operating cash flows information.
4. Why changes in balance sheet accounts provide a starting point for the cash flows statement.
5. Why changes in current asset and current liability accounts are important in arriving at cash flows from operating activities.
6. How to construct a cash flows statement.
7. How accounting method differences can affect cash flows from operating activities.
8. What supplementary information is included with a cash flows statement.
9. Why information about cash flows is useful.

Chapter 4

The Cash Flows Statement and the Importance of Cash Flows

Focus Company: Microsoft

Introduction

Chapter 2 showed that Microsoft's net income for the year ended June 30, 2000, was $9,421 million. How does this number compare with Microsoft's cash flows—the cash receipts and cash disbursements for the year? Microsoft's net cash from operations for the year ended June 30, 2000, was $13,961 million, substantially more than net income. Yet despite this fact, Microsoft ended the year with less cash than it started with. (The beginning cash balance was $4,975 million, and the ending cash balance was $4,846 million—you can verify this by looking at Microsoft's balance sheets in Chapter 3.) What then is the relationship between accounting net income and operating cash flows, and how are both of these items related to the change in a company's cash balance?

This chapter answers these questions by demonstrating (1) how accrual accounting net income is related to operating cash flows, (2) how firms generate cash other than through operations, and (3) what firms do with their cash. All of the information to answer these questions is available in a firm's cash flows statement, one of the financial statements included in a company's annual report. Microsoft's cash flows statement for the year ended June 30, 2000, is presented on page 94. To provide additional examples, the cash flows statements of the Boeing Company, IBM Corporation, Kmart Corporation, and Chrysler Corporation are presented at the end of this chapter.

In Chapter 2 the argument was made that accrual accounting net income was more useful than cash flows as a performance measure and for predicting future earnings and cash flows. You might wonder then why information about cash flows is presented as one of the basic financial statements. The answer is that although accrual accounting information is more useful than cash flows for some types of decisions, there are certain decisions for which cash flows information is extremely useful. For example, in making a decision as to whether a company will be able to meet its debt obligations as they come due, cash flows information may be more important than accrual method net income. Such decisions are made by creditors deciding whether to loan money to a company, or by suppliers agreeing to sell to a company on credit.

EARNINGS AND CASH FLOWS

Accrual accounting uses accruals to modify cash flows to arrive at net income, and accruals are necessary because (1) companies enter into transactions that affect more than one accounting period, and (2) in many transactions the economic effect of the transaction takes place in a different accounting period from the cash flow effect.

MICROSOFT CORPORATION
Cash Flows Statements
(in millions)

	Year Ended June 30		
	1998	**1999**	**2000**
Operations			
Net income	$ 4,490	$ 7,785	$ 9,421
Depreciation, amortization, and other noncash items	1,024	926	748
Write-off of acquired in-process technology	296	—	—
Gain on sales	—	(160)	(156)
Stock option income tax benefits	1,553	3,107	5,535
Unearned revenue	3,268	5,877	6,177
Recognition of unearned revenue from prior periods	(1,798)	(4,526)	(5,600)
Other current liabilities	208	1,050	(445)
Accounts receivable	(520)	(687)	(944)
Other current assets	(88)	(235)	(775)
Net cash from operations	8,433	13,137	13,961
Financing			
Common stock issued	959	1,350	2,245
Common stock repurchased	(2,468)	(2,950)	(4,896)
Put warrant proceeds	538	766	472
Preferred stock dividends	(28)	(28)	(13)
Net cash used for financing	(999)	(862)	(2,192)
Investing			
Additions to property and equipment	(656)	(583)	(879)
Cash portion of WebTV purchase price	(190)	—	—
Cash proceeds from sale of Softimage, Inc.	—	79	—
Purchases of investments	(19,114)	(36,441)	(43,158)
Maturities of investments	1,890	4,674	4,025
Sales of investments	10,798	21,080	28,085
Net cash used for investing	(7,272)	(11,191)	(11,927)
Net change in cash and equivalents	162	1,084	(158)
Effect of exchange rates on cash and equivalents	(29)	52	29
Cash and equivalents, beginning of year	3,706	3,839	4,975
Cash and equivalents, end of year	$ 3,839	$ 4,975	$ 4,846

Source: Microsoft Corporation annual report.

What this means is that, for some companies, decisions people make based on accrual accounting earnings may be much different from those they make based on cash flows. For example, in 1996 Boston Chicken, Inc., was a profitable company, reporting net income of $67 million for the year. The company's net income had doubled each year for the past two years. Using accrual accounting net income as a measure of economic performance, the company appeared to be doing extremely well.

Look at the cash flows statement for Boston Chicken for the same year (presented on page 95). Notice that the third line from the bottom—Net Increase (Decrease) in Cash and Cash Equivalents—reports negative cash flows of $209 million. This negative cash flow occurred despite the fact that Boston Chicken received more than $200 million in cash for new stock and warrants issued during the year. If Boston Chicken was so profitable, why was it using up so much cash so quickly?

In 1997, the following year, Boston Chicken reported a net loss of approximately $224 million, and not long after that the company became insolvent and was forced into bankruptcy. Although the company had appeared to be profitable, much of its cash was being used to make loans to franchisees to finance the acquisition of new franchises. These loans are reflected in the cash flows statement as issuance of notes receivable under the heading Cash Flows from Investing Activities. Boston Chicken is a good example of a situation in which accrual method financial accounting earnings did not provide investors with a complete picture of the company's economic activities. To solve the information asymmetry problem with respect to Boston Chicken required additional information about the company's cash flows.

BOSTON CHICKEN, INC., AND SUBSIDIARIES
Consolidated Statement of Cash Flows
(in thousands)

	Fiscal Year Ended December 29, 1996
Cash flows from operating activities	
Net income	$ 66,958
Adjustments to reconcile net income to net cash provided by operating activities:	
Depreciation and amortization	22,887
Interest on liquid yield option notes	13,793
Gain on issuances of subsidiary's stock	(38,163)
Deferred income taxes	14,059
Minority interest	5,235
Provision for write-down of assets	14,550
Loss (gain) on disposal of assets	68
Changes in assets and liabilities, excluding effects from acquisitions:	
Accounts receivable and due from affiliates	(7,193)
Accounts payable and accrued expenses	48,674
Deferred franchise revenue	3,174
Other assets and liabilities	868
Net cash provided by operating activities	144,910
Cash flows from investing activities	
Purchase of property and equipment	(115,062)
Proceeds from the sale of assets	86,320
Acquisition of other assets	(22,370)
Issuance of notes receivable	(1,467,065)
Repayment of notes receivable	993,151
Net cash used in investing activities	(525,026)
Cash flows from financing activities:	
Proceeds from issuance of common stock and warrants	112,863
Proceeds from issuance of subsidiary's common stock	135,422
Increase in deferred financing costs	(3,799)
Proceeds from revolving credit facilities	43,250
Repayments of revolving credit facilities	(117,256)
Net cash provided by financing activities	170,480
Net increase (decrease) in cash and cash equivalents	(209,636)
Cash and Cash Equivalents, beginning of year	310,436
Cash and Cash Equivalents, end of year	$ 100,800

Source: Boston Chicken, Inc., Form 10-K.

Cash Flows and the Business Operating Cycle

A firm's operating cycle is the time it takes to convert cash into new inventory, sell the inventory, and collect the receivable from the sale. The reason the operating cycle is important from the standpoint of cash flows is because during the time the firm is waiting to sell products and collect cash from the sales, it is still responsible for paying its bills on time. If a firm has to pay its employees and suppliers weeks or even months prior to the time it collects cash from sales to customers, it must arrange some alternative source of cash with which to pay its bills. This cash may come from borrowing or from selling stock.

Over the entire economic life of a firm, accrual method earnings and cash flows will be equal. Also, for most firms, if we compare earnings and cash flows over very long time periods the two measures will be quite close. However, in a single accounting period, earnings and cash flows may differ by a large amount. For some firms, such as Boston Chicken, earnings in a particular year may be positive while cash flows are negative. In other cases, such as Amazon.com (discussed at the end of this chapter), earnings in a particular year may be negative while cash flows are positive.

THE CASH FLOWS STATEMENT

During the first year of operation, the hypothetical software company in Chapter 2 had negative cash flows of $2,000 and positive accrual net income of $1,650. Here are the details of net income and cash flow:

	Accrual Method	Cash Method
Sales revenue	$ 9,000	$12,000
Computer expense	(3,000)	(9,000)
Rent expense	(3,600)	(2,700)
Blank CD expense	(150)	(500)
Shipping boxes expense	(300)	(1,500)
Postage expense	(300)	(300)
Net income (loss)	$ 1,650	$ (2,000)

The company had cash receipts of $12,000 for the year, which represent positive cash flows, and cash disbursements of $14,000, which represent negative cash flows. A cash flows statement for this company based on this information would look like this:

Cash Flows Statement	
Cash receipts	
Sales	$12,000
Cash disbursements	
Computers	9,000
Rent	2,700
Blank CDs	500
Shipping boxes	1,500
Postage	300
Total	14,000
Net cash flows	$ (2,000)

This method of preparing a statement of cash flows, by listing all of the cash receipts and disbursements for the year, is known as the *direct method*. Although the direct method is allowed under GAAP (and in fact is the preferred method according to the Financial Accounting Standards Board), the vast majority[1] of U.S. public companies choose to use an alternative method of preparing the cash flows statement known as the *indirect method*.[2]

Under the indirect method, the cash flows statement begins with accrual net income. The accounting accruals representing the difference between accrual net income and cash flows are used to reconcile net income with net cash flows. A cash flows statement for the hypothetical software start-up company based on the indirect method would look like this:

Cash Flows Statement (Indirect Method)	
Accrual net income	$ 1,650
Accrual adjustments	
Increase in unearned revenue	3,000
Increase in rent payable	900
Depreciation of computer	3,000
Increase in raw materials inventory	(350)
Increase in supplies inventory	(1,200)
Subtotal: Cash from operations	7,000
Investment in new computers	(9,000)
Net cash flows	$(2,000)

Note something very important about all of the adjustments to net income shown in the table above. They all represent changes in balance sheet accounts: Unearned Revenue, Rent Payable, Computer Equipment (both the depreciation and the purchase of new computers), Raw Materials Inventory, and Supplies Inventory. This relationship between changes in balance sheet accounts and the adjustments needed to reconcile net income and cash flows will be useful in the construction of the statement of cash flows later in the chapter.[3] Before proceeding, however, each of the accrual adjustments shown on the above table is discussed in more detail.

Increase in Unearned Revenue   Unearned Revenue, a balance sheet liability account, had a balance of zero at the beginning of the year and $3,000 at the end of the year. This increase represents a difference between accrual net income and cash flows. The cash receipts for sales of $12,000 was $3,000 greater than the sales revenue of $9,000 recorded under the accrual method. This $3,000 difference is represented by the increase in the Unearned Revenue account. To reconcile net income (which was increased by the $9,000 sales revenue) with cash flows (which was increased by the $12,000 cash receipts), the increase in the Unearned Revenue account must be added to net income. For the same reason, a decrease in Unearned Revenue would be subtracted from net income to arrive at cash flows.

Increase in Rent Payable   Rent Payable, a balance sheet liability account, had a balance of zero at the beginning of the year and $900 at the end of the year. This increase represents a difference between accrual net income and cash flows. The cash disbursement for rent of $2,700 was $900 less than the rent expense of $3,600 recorded under the accrual method. This $900 difference is represented by the

---

[1] Some surveys find that more than 90 percent of large U.S. public firms use the indirect rather than the direct method to present their cash flows statements.

[2] Those companies that do use the direct method for their cash flows statement must also provide a reconciliation of net income and cash flows from operations using the indirect method.

[3] The relationship between cash flows and changes in balance sheet accounts is developed more formally in the appendix to this chapter.

increase in the Rent Payable account. To reconcile net income (which was decreased by the $3,600 rent expense) with cash flows (which was decreased by the $2,700 cash disbursement), the increase in the Rent Payable account must be added to net income. For the same reason, a decrease in Rent Payable would be subtracted from net income to arrive at cash flows. Changes in other current liability accounts, such as Accounts Payable, Wages Payable, and Income Taxes Payable, must also be considered in a reconciliation of net income with cash flows.

Depreciation of Computer Depreciation expense is an example of what is known as a *noncash expense.* Depreciation results in an expense that reduces net income but does not represent a cash disbursement for the year. Other examples of noncash expenses are amortization expense and deferred income tax expense. When depreciation expense is recorded, net income is reduced by the depreciation expense of $3,000, but there is no cash effect.[4] To reconcile net income (which was decreased by the $3,000 depreciation expense) with cash flows (which was not affected by depreciation), the depreciation expense for the year (as well as any other noncash expenses) must be added back to net income. The $900 increase in rent payable (discussed earlier) is also a noncash expense.

Increase in Raw Materials Inventory Raw Materials Inventory, a balance sheet asset account, had a balance of zero at the beginning of the year and $350 at the end of the year. This increase represents a difference between accrual net income and cash flows. The cash disbursement for CDs of $500 was $350 more than the CD expense of $150 recorded under the accrual method. This $350 difference is represented by the increase in the Raw Materials Inventory account. To reconcile net income (which was decreased by the $150 CD expense) with cash flows (which was decreased by the $500 cash disbursement), the increase in the Raw Materials Inventory account must be subtracted from net income. For the same reason, a decrease in Raw Materials Inventory would be added to net income to arrive at cash flows.

Changes in other current asset accounts, such as Accounts Receivable and Prepaid Expenses, must also be considered in a reconciliation of net income with cash flows. For example, if accounts receivable increase during the year, it means that accrual method sales revenue was more than cash receipts. Therefore, the increase in Accounts Receivable would be subtracted from net income to arrive at cash flows.

Increase in Supplies Inventory Supplies Inventory, a balance sheet asset account, had a balance of zero at the beginning of the year and $1,200 at the end of the year. This increase represents a difference between accrual net income and cash flows. The cash disbursement for shipping boxes of $1,500 was $1,200 less than the shipping boxes expense of $300 recorded under the accrual method. This $1,200 difference is represented by the increase in the Supplies Inventory account. To reconcile net income (which was decreased by the $300 shipping boxes expense) with cash flows (which was decreased by the $1,500 cash disbursement), the increase in the Supplies Inventory account must be subtracted from net income. For the same reason, a decrease in Supplies Inventory would be added to net income to arrive at cash flows.

Investment in New Computers The final adjustment on the indirect cash flows statement is the $9,000 that was paid for the new computers. Under accrual accounting, this cash disbursement was treated as an asset, since the computers would provide a future economic benefit. The cost of the computers was allocated to the three-year period over which the computers were expected to benefit the company. This cost, in the form of depreciation expense, will reduce net

---

[4] Cash is reduced when new equipment is purchased. However, the cash flow effect of equipment purchases is disclosed separately on the statement of cash flows, as shown in more detail later in the chapter.

income over the three-year period. An adjustment has already been made to add back depreciation expense to net income. However, the $9,000 cash disbursement for the purchase of the computers must be recognized as a negative cash flow. The only unusual treatment required on the cash flows statement for the purchase of the computers is to report the cash disbursement separately from the other items. This is because an investment in new assets, such as equipment, buildings, land, or other types of investments, is not considered part of the operating activities of the company. Under GAAP, cash flows relating to investments must be reported separately from cash flows related to operations. This concept will be discussed in more detail below.

CONSTRUCTING A CASH FLOWS STATEMENT

The same techniques used above to construct a simple cash flows statement for a hypothetical company can also be used to construct Microsoft's cash flows statement. The place to begin the construction of a cash flows statement is the balance sheet. As discussed earlier, changes in balance sheet accounts provide much of the information needed for the cash flows statement. Here are three steps to follow to construct a cash flows statement:

Step 1: Compute the change in each balance sheet account for the year. Record increases in asset accounts (other than cash) as negative numbers and increases in liability and shareholders' equity accounts as positive numbers. Record decreases in asset accounts (other than cash) as positive numbers and decreases in liability and shareholders' equity accounts as negative numbers.

Step 2: Separate the balance sheet changes into two types: (1) changes in cash accounts and (2) changes in all other noncash balance sheet accounts. Because the balance sheet is always in balance, the total of the changes in the noncash accounts for the year must equal the change in the cash accounts for the year. Make sure this is the case.

Shown on page 100 are the changes in Microsoft's balance sheet accounts for the year ended June 30, 2000. Notice that the change in the cash account[5] (column 3) of (129) is equal to the total of the changes in all of the noncash accounts (column 4) of (129). We will use these changes in noncash balance sheet accounts, along with some additional information about Microsoft's activities for the year, to reconstruct Microsoft's cash flows statement.

Step 3: Use whatever additional information is available to separate the changes in noncash balance sheet accounts into three different categories: (1) changes relating to cash flows, (2) changes that affect net income but not cash flows, and (3) all other changes. These are discussed in more detail below.

1. *Changes that represent increases or decreases in cash.* Examples of these changes are purchases and sales of investments, purchases and sales of property and equipment, borrowing, repayment of loans, issuing new stock, payment of dividends, and stock repurchases. Also, some changes in current assets and current liabilities may result in increases or decreases in cash. For example, a

---

[5] Under GAAP, the balance sheet term *cash* includes what are known as *cash equivalents*. Cash equivalents are short-term (i.e., original maturity of three months or less) highly liquid investments that are easily converted into known amounts of cash with very little risk. In Microsoft's case, cash equivalents include commercial paper, certificates of deposit, government securities, and corporate notes and bonds.

	MICROSOFT CORPORATION **Balance Sheet Changes**			
	(1) **Balance Sheets** **for Year Ended**		**(3)** **Change in** **Cash** **Account**	**(4)** **Change in** **Noncash** **Accounts**
	6/30/99	**(2)** **6/30/00**		
Assets				
Current assets				
Cash and equivalents	4,975	4,846	(129)	
Short-term investments	12,261	18,952		(6,691)
Total cash and short-term investments ..	17,236	23,798		
Accounts receivable	2,245	3,250		(1,005)
Deferred income taxes	1,469	1,708		(239)
Other	752	1,552		(800)
Total current assets	21,702	30,308		
Property and equipment, net	1,611	1,903		(292)
Equity and other investments	14,372	17,726		(3,354)
Other assets	940	2,213		(1,273)
Total assets	38,625	52,150		
Liabilities and stockholders' equity				
Current liabilities				
Accounts payable	874	1,083		209
Accrued compensation	396	557		161
Income taxes	1,691	585		(1,106)
Unearned revenue	4,239	4,816		577
Other	1,602	2,714		1,112
Total current liabilities	8,802	9,755		
Deferred income taxes	1,385	1,027		(358)
Stockholders' equity	28,438	41,368		12,930
Total liabilities and stockholders' equity	38,625	52,150	(129)	(129)

Increases in assets, other than cash, are shown as negative numbers.

decrease in accounts receivable usually represents cash receipts, a decrease in accounts payable usually represents cash disbursements, and an increase in unearned revenue usually represents cash receipts.

2. *Changes that do not represent increases or decreases in cash, but that affect accrual method revenues or expenses.* Increases in accounts receivable represent accrual method sales that do not affect cash; increases in wages payable represent accrual method expenses that do not affect cash. Other examples of revenue or expense items that do not affect cash are changes in deferred tax assets or liabilities (representing tax expense); changes in inventory (representing cost of goods sold); and depreciation and amortization expense. The reason these items are important is they affect net income but not cash flows, and are thus necessary to reconcile Microsoft's net income with its cash flows. Also include the company's net income for the year in this category.

3. *All other changes not affecting cash or net income.* These are items that do not represent cash receipts or disbursements and also do not affect revenues or expenses. Examples are acquiring property and equipment by issuing stock, repurchasing stock by issuing bonds, or recording an unrealized gain or loss on marketable securities as part of shareholders' equity (discussed in Chapter 11).

As an accountant preparing Microsoft's cash flows statement, you would have access to all of Microsoft's journal entries for the year, and these journal entries would explain all of the increases and decreases in Microsoft's balance sheet accounts. In the discussion that follows, you will be given hypothetical journal entries that can be used in place of Microsoft's actual journal entries to help with the construction of the cash flows statement.[6]

The worksheet on page 108 has allocated all of the changes in Microsoft's noncash balance sheet accounts to one of the following categories—changes relating to cash flows, changes that affect net income, and all other changes—based on the journal entries provided. In these journal entries, **balance sheet changes having a cash effect are shown in bold,** and *balance sheet changes having a net income effect are shown in italics.*

Increase in Short-Term Investments: The net increase of $6,691 million indicates that Microsoft was purchasing more short-term investments than it sold, and these net purchases would reduce cash.

	Journal Entry Representing Changes in Short-Term Investments		
+/−	**Accounts [description of account]**	**Debit**	**Credit**
+	Short-Term Investments [balance sheet asset account]	6,691	
−	**Cash [balance sheet asset account]**		**6,691**

Increase in Accounts Receivable Increases in accounts receivable represent accrual method revenue but not cash receipts. Although the total increase in the account was $1,005 million, only $944 million of this increase represents Microsoft's revenue. The rest of the increase, in the amount of $61 million, represents increases in accounts receivable that occurred when Microsoft acquired other companies in a transaction referred to as an immaterial pooling of interests.

	Journal Entry Representing Changes in Accounts Receivable		
+/−	**Accounts [description of account]**	**Debit**	**Credit**
+	Accounts Receivable [balance sheet asset account]	1,005	
+	*Sales Revenue [income statement revenue account]*		*944*
+	Immaterial Pooling of Interests [balance sheet shareholders' equity account]		61

Increase in Deferred Income Taxes (Asset) The increase in deferred income tax assets of $239 million represents a decrease in income tax expense, a component of net income, but does not affect cash flows.

	Journal Entry Representing Changes in Deferred Income Tax Asset		
+/−	**Accounts [description of account]**	**Debit**	**Credit**
+	Deferred Income Taxes [balance sheet asset account]	239	
−	*Income Tax Expense [income statement expense account]*		*239*

[6] Because there is no way of knowing what Microsoft's real journal entries were, the hypothetical journal entries given in this chapter are based on assumptions rather than on actual Microsoft information.

Increase in Other Current Assets   The increase in this account represents assets that required cash but did not result in an income statement expense. Examples would be prepaid rent or prepaid insurance. Only $775 million of the $800 million increase had a cash flow effect. The other $25 million represents an increase in other current assets that occurred when Microsoft acquired other companies in a transaction referred to as an immaterial pooling of interests.

+/−	Journal Entry Representing Changes in Other Current Assets	Debit	Credit
+	Other Current Assets [balance sheet asset account]	800	
−	**Cash [balance sheet asset account]**		**775**
+	Immaterial Pooling of Interests [balance sheet shareholders' equity account]		25

Increase in Property and Equipment   The numbers on the balance sheet represents the *net* property and equipment, where the term *net* refers to the fact that the property and equipment has been reduced by depreciation expense taken in prior years, called *accumulated depreciation.* Therefore, if Microsoft did not purchase new property and equipment during the year, the net balance in property and equipment would decrease by the amount of depreciation expense. Microsoft's depreciation expense for the year was $668 million, which reduced net income but not cash flows.

The cash payments for additions to property and equipment during the year were $879 million. The other $81 million represents an increase in property and equipment that occurred when Microsoft acquired other companies in a transaction referred to as an immaterial pooling of interests.

+/−	Journal Entry Representing Changes in Property and Equipment	Debit	Credit
+	Property and Equipment (net) [balance sheet asset account]	292	
+	*Depreciation Expense [income statement expense account]*	668	
+	Immaterial Pooling of Interests [balance sheet shareholders' equity account]		81
−	**Cash [balance sheet asset account]**		**879**

Increase in Equity and Other Investments   The investments increased by $3,354 million. This change is not necessarily the same as the change in Microsoft's cash for two reasons. First, this account includes $170 million of unrealized gains that did not affect cash or net income. Second, Microsoft sold investments that originally cost $100 million for cash equal to $256 million, resulting in a gain of $156 million. The amount of cash Microsoft spent on new investments was $3,624 million.

+/−	Journal Entries Representing Changes in Equity and Other Investments	Debit	Credit
+	**Cash [balance sheet asset account]**	256	
+	*Gains on Sales [income statement revenue account]*		156
−	Equity and Other Investments [balance sheet asset account]		100
+	Equity and Other Investments [balance sheet asset account]	3,454	
−	Unrealized Gains/Losses [balance sheet shareholders' equity account] . .	170	
−	**Cash [balance sheet asset account]**		**3,624**

The net change in Cash is a decrease of $3,624 − $256 = $3,368 million, and the net change in Equity and Other Investments is an increase of $3,454 − $100 = $3,354 million.

Increase in Other Assets   Of the total increase of $1,273 million, $989 million represents cash disbursements for new investments. In addition, the balance was reduced by amortization expense of $677 million, a noncash expense that reduced net income; there were $113 million of unrealized losses recorded, which do not affect cash or net income; $821 million of additions to this account were financed by Other Current Liabilities, a balance sheet liability account; and $253 million of additions came from acquisitions of other companies recorded as immaterial pooling of interests.

+/−	Journal Entry Representing Changes in Other Noncurrent Assets		
	Accounts [description of account]	Debit	Credit
+	Other Noncurrent Assets [balance sheet asset account]	1,273	
+	*Amortization Expense [income statement expense account]*	*677*	
−	Unrealized Gains/Losses [balance sheet shareholders' equity account] . .	113	
−	**Cash [balance sheet asset account]**		**989**
+	Other Current Liabilities [balance sheet liability account]		821
+	Immaterial Pooling of Interests [balance sheet shareholders' equity account]		253

Increase in Accounts Payable   The increase in this account of $209 million represents costs that Microsoft incurred during the year but has not paid for at year-end. This increase affects net income but not cash.

+/−	Journal Entry Representing Changes in Accounts Payable		
	Accounts [description of account]	Debit	Credit
+	*Cost of Revenue [income statement expense account]*	*209*	
+	Accounts Payable [balance sheet liability account]		209

Increase in Accrued Compensation   This increase of $161 million represents wages that Microsoft has not paid at year-end. This increase affects net income but not cash.

+/−	Journal Entry Representing Changes in Accrued Compensation		
	Accounts [description of account]	Debit	Credit
+	*Cost of Revenue [income statement expense account]*	*161*	
+	Accrued Compensation [balance sheet liability account]		161

Decrease in Income Taxes Payable   The decrease in this account of $1,106 million represents cash that Microsoft paid to the government. This decrease affects cash but not net income.

+/−	Journal Entry Representing Changes in Income Taxes Payable		
	Accounts [description of account]	Debit	Credit
−	Income Taxes Payable [balance sheet asset account]	1,106	
−	**Cash [balance sheet asset account]**		**1,106**

Increase in Unearned Revenue Unearned revenue represents cash that has been received prior to the time that revenue is recognized under accrual accounting rules. The increase in unearned revenue of $577 million represents cash receipts for Microsoft.

	Journal Entry Representing Changes in Unearned Revenue		
+/−	Accounts [description of account]	Debit	Credit
+	Cash [balance sheet asset account]	577	
+	Unearned Revenue [balance sheet liability account]		577

Increase in Other Current Liabilities The total change in the account is $1,112 million, of which $291 million represents costs that have been included in net income but not paid for at year-end, and $821 million represents an increase in the Other Noncurrent Assets account.

	Journal Entry Representing Changes in Other Current Liabilities		
+/−	Accounts [description of account]	Debit	Credit
+	Other Non current Assets {balance sheet asset account]	821	
+	*Cost of Revenue [income statement expense account]*	*291*	
+	Other Current Liabilities [balance sheet liability account]		1,112

Decrease in Deferred Income Taxes (Liability) The decrease in the Deferred Income Tax liability account represents a reduction in income tax expense, a noncash item that is reflected in net income.

	Journal Entry Representing Changes in Deferred Income Tax Liability		
+/−	Accounts [description of account]	Debit	Credit
−	Deferred Income Taxes [balance sheet liability account]	358	
−	*Income Tax Expense [income statement expense account]*		*358*

Increase in Stockholders' Equity Shown on page 105 are changes to all of Microsoft's stockholders' equity accounts for the year. Each of the changes is analyzed below.

Conversion of Preferred to Common Stock This account represents the conversion of preferred stock into common stock. There are no cash or net income effects.

	Journal Entry Representing Changes in Convertible Preferred Stock		
+/−	Accounts [description of account]	Debit	Credit
−	Convertible Preferred Stock [balance sheet shareholders' equity account] . .	980	
+	Common Stock Issued [balance sheet shareholders' equity account] . . .		980

MICROSOFT CORPORATION	
Changes in Stockholders' Equity	
Convertible preferred stock	
Conversion of preferred to common stock	(980)
Common stock and paid-in capital	
Common stock issued	3,554
Common stock repurchased	(210)
Proceeds from sale of put warrants	472
Stock option income tax benefits	5,535
Retained earnings	
Net income	9,421
Net unrealized investment gains and losses	(283)
Translation adjustments and other	23
Preferred stock dividends	(13)
Immaterial pooling of interests	97
Common stock repurchased	(4,686)
	12,930

Source: Microsoft Corporation annual report.

Common Stock Issued The $3,554 million in common stock issued represents several transactions. Of the increase, $980 million resulted from the conversion of preferred stock, and $329 million arose from acquisitions of other companies accounted for as immaterial pooling of interests. Cash received for common stock was $2,245 million.

	Journal Entry Representing Common Stock Issued		
+/−	**Accounts [description of account]**	**Debit**	**Credit**
+	**Cash [balance sheet asset account]**	**2,245**	
−	Convertible Preferred Stock [balance sheet shareholders' equity account]	980	
−	Immaterial Pooling of Interests [balance sheet shareholders' equity account	329	
+	Common Stock Issued [balance sheet shareholders' equity account] . .		3,554

Common Stock Repurchased This account, a shareholders' equity account, with a debit balance of $210 million represents a cash outflow.

	Journal Entry Representing Common Stock Repurchased		
+/−	**Accounts [description of account]**	**Debit**	**Credit**
+	Common Stock Repurchased [balance sheet equity account—debit balance]	210	
−	**Cash [balance sheet asset account]**		**210**

Proceeds from Sale of Put Warrants   This account represents cash received by Microsoft for the sale of put warrants (a type of option).

+/−	Journal Entry Representing Proceeds from Sale of Put Warrants		
	Accounts [description of account]	**Debit**	**Credit**
+	**Cash [balance sheet asset account]**	**472**	
+	Proceeds from Sale of Put Warrants [balance sheet shareholders' equity account]		472

Stock Option Income Tax Benefits   This account represents taxes that Microsoft saved as a result of a tax deduction associated with employees exercising stock options. Under GAAP, this tax savings does not affect income tax expense or net income. However, there is a cash savings to Microsoft.

+/−	Journal Entry Representing Stock Option Income Tax Benefits		
	Accounts [description of account]	**Debit**	**Credit**
+	**Cash [balance sheet asset account]**	**5,535**	
+	Stock Option Income Tax Benefits [balance sheet shareholders' equity account]		5,535

Net Income   Microsoft's retained earnings is increased by the net income for the year.

Net Unrealized Investment Gains and Losses   This account represents changes in the market value of Microsoft's investments accounted for at market value. These unrealized gains and losses are not part of net income and have no cash effect.

+/−	Journal Entry Representing Unrealized Investment Gains and Losses		
	Accounts [description of account]	**Debit**	**Credit**
−	Unrealized Gains/Losses [balance sheet shareholders' equity account] . .	283	
−	Equity and Other Investments [balance sheet asset account]		170
−	Other Noncurrent Assets [balance sheet asset account]		113

Translation Adjustments and Other   This account represents changes in the value of Microsoft's assets and liabilities denominated in currencies other than U.S. dollars. The translation adjustments do not affect net income. Of the adjustments, $29 million represents cash effects, and $6 million results from acquisitions of other companies accounted for as immaterial pooling of interests.

+/−	Journal Entry Representing Translation Adjustments		
	Accounts [description of account]	**Debit**	**Credit**
+	**Cash [balance sheet asset account]**	**29**	
+	Immaterial Pooling of Interests [balance sheet shareholders' equity account]		6
+	Translation Adjustments [balance sheet shareholders' equity account] .		23

Preferred Stock Dividends   This account represents cash paid as a dividend to holders of Microsoft's preferred stock.

Journal Entry Representing Preferred Stock Dividends			
+/−	**Accounts [description of account]**	**Debit**	**Credit**
+	Preferred Stock Dividends [balance sheet equity account—debit balance]	13	
−	**Cash [balance sheet asset account]**		**13**

Immaterial Pooling of Interests   This account represents acquisitions of other companies during the year. The account has no income statement or cash effects.

Journal Entry Representing Immaterial Pooling of Interests			
+/−	**Accounts [description of account]**	**Debit**	**Credit**
+	Accounts Receivable [balance sheet asset account]	61	
+	Other Current Assets [balance sheet asset account]	25	
+	Property and Equipment [balance sheet asset account]	81	
+	Other Noncurrent assets [balance sheet asset account]	253	
−	Translation Adjustment [balance sheet shareholders' equity account] ...	6	
+	Common Stock Issued [balance sheet shareholders' equity account] .		329
+	Immaterial Pooling of Interests [balance sheet shareholders' equity account]		97

Common Stock Repurchased   This account represents cash paid by Microsoft to repurchase common stock.

Journal Entry Representing Common Stock Repurchased			
+/−	**Accounts [description of account]**	**Debit**	**Credit**
+	Common Stock Repurchased [balance sheet equity account— debit balance]	4,686	
−	**Cash [balance sheet asset account]**		**4,686**

On page 108 is a worksheet that allocates all of the changes in Microsoft's non-cash balance sheet accounts for the year to one of three categories—changes relating to cash flows (column 5), changes that affect net income (column 6), and all other changes (column 7)—based on the analysis of the journal entries. Notice that the total of the three categories (9,859 − 9,730 + 0) is equal to 129, the change in Microsoft's cash balance for the year.

We are now ready to use this worksheet information to construct Microsoft's cash flows statement. To do so, we need to separate Microsoft's cash flows into three different activities: operating activities, financing activities, and investing activities. We discuss each of these activities, as well as their treatment on the cash flows statement, below.

Cash Flows from Operating Activities

Under GAAP, cash flows from operating activities—also known as *operating cash flows* or *cash flows from operations*—are cash flows associated with producing and delivering goods and providing services. In general, these are the cash effects of transactions and other events that enter into the determination of net income. However, under GAAP, operating activities are defined to be all transactions and events *other than those specifically defined as investing or financing activities.* Investing and financing activities are discussed in more detail below.

MICROSOFT CORPORATION
Balance Sheet Changes and Changes in Noncash Accounts

	(1) (2) Balance Sheets for Year Ended		(3) Change in Cash Account	(4) Change in Noncash Accounts	(5) Changes Relating to Cash Flows	(6) Changes That Affect Net Income	(7) All Other Changes
	6/30/99	6/30/00					
Assets							
Current assets							
Cash and equivalents	4,975	4,846	(129)				
Short-term investments	12,261	18,952		(6,691)	(6,691) n		
Total cash and short-term investments ...	17,236	23,798					
Accounts receivable	2,245	3,250		(1,005)		(944) g	(61)
Deferred income taxes	1,469	1,708		(239)		(239) b	
Other	752	1,552		(800)	(775) h		(25)
Total current assets	21,702	30,308					
Property and equipment, net	1,611	1,903		(292)	(879) m	668 b	(81)
Equity and other investments	14,372	17,726		(3,354)	(3,368) n	(156) c	170
Other assets	940	2,213		(1,273)	(989) n	677 b	(961)
Total assets	38,625	52,150					
Liabilities and stockholders' equity							
Current liabilities							
Accounts payable	874	1,083		209		209 f	
Accrued compensation	396	557		161		161 f	
Income taxes	1,691	585		(1,106)	(1,106) f		
Unearned revenue	4,239	4,816		577	577 e		
Other	1,602	2,714		1,112		291 f	821
Total current liabilities	8,802	9,755					
Deferred income taxes	1,385	1,027		(358)		(358) b	
Stockholders' equity (see below)	28,438	41,368		12,930	3,372	9,421	137
Total liabilities and stockholders' equity ...	38,625	52,150	(129)	(129)	(9,859)	9,730	0
Changes in Stockholders' Equity							
Convertible preferred stock							
Conversion of preferred to common stock				(980)			(980)
Common stock and paid-in capital							
Common stock issued				3,554	2,245 i		1,309
Common stock repurchased				(210)	(210) j		
Proceeds from sale of put warrants				472	472 k		
Stock option income tax benefits				5,535	5,535 d		
Retained earnings							
Net income				9,421		9,421 a	
Net unrealized investment gains and losses				(283)			(283)
Translation adjustments and other				23	29 o		(6)
Preferred stock dividends				(13)	(13) l		
Immaterial pooling of interests				97			97
Common stock repurchased				(4,686)	(4,686) j		
				12,930	3,372	9,421	137

Note 1: Letters for columns (5) and (6) refer to corresponding items on Statement of Cash Flows shown on page 111 of this text.

Note 2: Increases in asset accounts are shown as negative numbers.

As mentioned previously, there are two permitted methods for computing cash flows from operating activities: the direct method and the indirect method.[7] While the FASB prefers the direct method, well over 90 percent of large U.S. public companies report using the indirect method. Also, even if a company uses the direct method, a reconciliation of net income and cash flows from operating activities using the indirect method must still be provided in the financial statements. Therefore, only the indirect method of computing cash flows from operating activities will be discussed below.

Computing Cash Flows from Operating Activities

To compute cash flows from operating activities under the indirect method, first start with the company's net income for the accounting period. Net income is then adjusted for two general categories of accounting accruals: (1) changes in current assets and liabilities and (2) noncash expenses. Next, adjust net income for any gains and losses on sales of assets, since cash flows associated with gains and losses are properly included as part of investing activities. Finally, adjustments must be made for miscellaneous items that affect the firm's cash flows but are not included in net income.

Changes in Current Assets and Liabilities   Changes in current assets and liabilities represent accounting accruals that are necessary to adjust accrual net income to arrive at cash flows from operating activities. These accruals are of two types. First, some changes represent accrual method revenues and expenses that do not have a cash flow consequence. Examples of these are increases in accounts receivable (representing sales but not cash collections), decreases in inventory (representing cost of goods sold but not cash disbursements), and increases in wages payable (representing wages expense but not cash disbursements).

The second type of change in current asset and liability accounts represents cash receipts or disbursements that have no effect on net income. Examples of these are decreases in accounts receivable (representing cash collections but not sales), decreases in accounts payable (representing cash disbursements but not expenses), and increases in inventory (representing cash disbursements but not cost of goods sold).

(There is one exception to the rules discussed above that relates to changes in inventories and accounts payable. Changes in inventories and accounts payable are subject to special treatment and are discussed in more detail later in the chapter.)

Finally, there are some types of changes in current assets and liabilities that do not affect the cash flows statement. These are changes that do not affect either cash flows or net income. An example of this is an increase in accounts receivable that results from the acquisition of another company for stock.

We can go through the changes in each of Microsoft's current asset and liability accounts and see how each of these changes should be handled on the company's cash flows statement, shown on page 111. All of these changes come from columns (5) and (6) on the Balance Sheet Changes worksheet shown on page 108.

The increase in short-term investments is properly classified as an investing activity, so that change will be discussed later. The increase in accounts receivable of $944 million represents accrual method sales (a component of net income) but not cash receipts. The increase in deferred income taxes of $239 million represents a decrease in income tax expense (a component of net income) but is not a cash disbursement. The increase in other current assets of $775 million

---

[7] The presentation of cash flows from investing and financing activities is exactly the same under either the direct or indirect methods. Only the presentation of cash flows from operating activities is affected by the choice of method.

represents cash disbursements (for example, for prepaid insurance) that does not affect net income. The increases in accounts payable and accrued compensation of $209 million and $161 million represent accrual method expenses (components of net income) but not cash disbursements. The decrease in income taxes payable of $1,106 million represents a cash disbursement but does not affect net income. The increase in unearned revenue of $577 million represents cash receipts but not accrual method sales. Finally, the increase in other current liabilities of $291 million represents accrual method expenses (components of net income) but not cash disbursements.

On Microsoft's cash flows statement, the changes in unearned revenue, accounts receivable, and other current assets are all reported separately. The change in deferred income taxes is included with other noncash expenses, discussed below. The changes in accounts payable, accrued compensation, income taxes payable, and other current liabilities are combined and reported as a total in the amount of $445 million.

Noncash Expenses In addition to the changes in current assets and liabilities, adjustments to net income are also required for noncash expenses that are not reflected in current assets or liabilities. In Microsoft's cash flows statement, there is an adjustment for depreciation, amortization, and other noncash items in the amount of $748 million. This consists of the change in the deferred income taxes current asset account of $(239) million, depreciation expense of $668 million, amortization expense (part of the change in other assets) of $677 million, and the change in deferred income tax liabilities of $(358) million.

Gains and Losses An adjustment is necessary to remove the effect of gains or losses from net income, since cash flows relating to sales of assets are generally classified as investing activities. In Microsoft's case, the company reported a gain on sales of $156 million, which is removed from net income by subtracting the gain. (If Microsoft had reported a loss, the loss would be removed by adding it back to net income.) Note that the tax effect of the gain is *not* reclassified, since under GAAP taxes are always considered operating activities.

Miscellaneous Items An adjustment is required for the stock option income tax benefits of $5,535 million. This item increased Microsoft's cash flows, but under GAAP it was included in shareholders' equity rather than treated as a reduction in income tax expense. Therefore, the tax benefit was never included in Microsoft's net income for the year.

After making all of the above adjustments to net income, we arrive at Microsoft's cash flows from operating activities of $13,961 million.

Cash Flows from Financing Activities

Financing activities[8] relate to the liabilities and shareholders' equity portions of the balance sheet and reflect such activities as selling stock, repurchasing stock, paying dividends, borrowing money, and repaying loans. Note that, although dividend payments are considered a financing cash flow item, interest payments are considered part of operating cash flows. This is consistent with the treatment of interest expense and dividends in the computation of net income, and is another example of the view that shareholders are residual claimants, and that the payment of dividends is not part of operating activities. Note also that under GAAP, the stock option income tax benefits (a shareholders' equity account) are considered an operating activity rather than a financing activity.

---

[8] Most public companies report cash flows from financing activities *after* cash flows from investing activities. Microsoft reports them in the opposite order.

MICROSOFT CORPORATION
Reconstructed Statement of Cash Flows
For the Year Ended June 30, 2000

Cash flows from operations		
Net income	a	9,421
Depreciation, amortization, and other noncash items	b	748
Gain on sales	c	(156)
Stock option income tax benefits	d	5,535
Unearned revenue changes	e	577
Other current liabilities	f	(445)
Accounts receivable	g	(944)
Other current assets	h	(775)
Net cash from operations		13,961
Cash flows from financing		
Common stock issued	i	2,245
Common stock repurchased	j	(4,896)
Put warrant proceeds	k	472
Preferred stock dividends	l	(13)
Net cash used for financing		(2,192)
Cash flows from investing		
Additions to property and equipment	m	(879)
Purchase, maturity, and sale of investments	n	(11,048)
Net cash used for investing		(11,927)
Net change in cash and cash equivalents		(158)
Effect of exchange rates on cash and equivalents	o	29
Cash and equivalents, beginning of year		4,975
Cash and equivalents, end of year		4,846

Note: Letters refer to corresponding items on Balance Sheet Changes worksheet.

Microsoft has four types of cash flows from financing activities. First, $2,245 million of cash receipts resulted from issuing new stock, probably to employees as part of the exercise of employee stock options. Second, Microsoft paid $4,896 million to repurchasing stock during the year. Many companies use stock repurchases as an alternative to dividend distributions to distribute cash to shareholders. Also, companies that have employee stock options outstanding need to repurchase stock to provide the necessary shares to issue to employees as the options are exercised. Third, Microsoft received $472 million from the sale of put warrants (a type of option). Finally, Microsoft paid $13 million in dividends to preferred shareholders during the year.

The net effect of these items for Microsoft is negative cash flows from financing activities of $2,192 million for the year. Although Microsoft does not borrow money to finance its operations, borrowing and repayment of loans is another common type of financing activity. For example, Boeing reported new borrowings and debt repayments as financing activity items on its cash flows statement.

Cash Flows from Investing Activities

Investing activities relate to the assets portion of the balance sheet and reflect such activities as making loans, collecting loans, purchasing new property or equipment, selling old property or equipment, purchasing equity investments, and selling equity investments. Cash received from a sale of assets, rather than the gain or loss on the sale, is reflected as an investing cash flow. For example, if Microsoft sells an asset with a book value of $100 million for cash of $256 million, it reports a gain on the sale of $156 million, an increase in net income. However, the investing cash flows from the sale would be $256 million.

Microsoft has only two types of cash flows from investing activities. First, Microsoft paid $879 million for new property and equipment during the year. Second, Microsoft has cash flows associated with the purchase, maturity, and sale of investments.[9] The net effect of all of these items for Microsoft is negative cash flows from investing activities of $11,927 million for the year.

Additional Cash Flow Information

Companies sometimes engage in major transactions that do not have an immediate effect on cash flows. For example, property or equipment may be purchased by issuing notes, or bonds may be converted into common stock. In Microsoft's case, the conversion of preferred stock into common stock is an example of such a noncash transaction. Since these types of transactions do not directly affect the current year's cash flows, they are not required to be included as part of the cash flows statement. However, under GAAP, information about significant noncash transactions must be disclosed in the financial statements, and this is usually done in the notes section of the financial statement.

For example, Microsoft reported the conversion of the preferred stock in a note to its financial statements. For another example of information about noncash transactions, look at the cash flows statement of Amazon.com, Inc., for the year ended December 31, 2000, reproduced on page 113. Amazon.com reported the following noncash transactions for the year at the bottom of the cash flows statement: fixed assets acquired under capital leases, fixed assets acquired under financing agreements, stock issued in connection with business acquisitions, and equity securities received for commercial agreements.

Companies must also provide supplemental cash flow information about the cash paid for interest and income taxes for the year. Amazon.com reported the total amount of cash paid for interest at the bottom of the cash flows statement. In another example, shown at the end of the chapter, IBM Corporation reported the total amounts of cash paid for income taxes and interest during the year at the bottom of the cash flows statement.

Finally, companies must disclose the effect of changes in foreign currency exchange rates on the cash flows statement. Notice that Microsoft, Amazon.com, and IBM all reported a separate item for the effect of exchange rate changes on cash and cash equivalents.

Changes in Inventories and Accounts Payable

It was pointed out earlier that changes in current assets and current liabilities are of two types: changes that affect cash but not net income (for example, collecting accounts receivable or paying accounts payable), or changes that affect net income but not cash (for example, an increase in accounts receivable or an increase in taxes payable). An exception to this rule is the case of increases in inventories and accounts payable.

Assume that a firm purchases inventory and does not pay for the purchases in cash, resulting in an increase in both inventories and accounts payable. These increases do not affect cash flows or net income. However, both increases must be shown as reconciling items on the cash flows statement. Failure to disclose

---

[9] On Microsoft's actual cash flows statement, the cash flows related to purchases, maturity, and sale of investments are shown separately. They are presented as one net amount here because the detailed information necessary to separate them is not publicly available.

AMAZON.COM, INC.
Consolidated Statement of Cash Flows
Year Ended December 31, 2000
(in thousands)

Cash and cash equivalents, beginning of period	133,309
Operating activities	
Net loss	(1,411,273)
Adjustments to reconcile net loss to net cash provided by (used in) operating activities:	
Depreciation of fixed assets and other amortization	84,460
Amortization of deferred stock-based compensation	24,797
Equity in losses of equity-method investees, net	304,596
Amortization of goodwill and other intangibles	321,772
Impairment-related and other	200,311
Amortization of previously unearned revenue	(108,211)
Loss (gain) on sale of marketable securities, net	(280)
Noncash investment gains and losses, net	142,639
Noncash interest expense and other	24,766
Changes in operating assets and liabilities:	
Inventories	46,083
Prepaid expenses and other current assets	(8,585)
Accounts payable	22,357
Accrued expenses and other current liabilities	93,967
Unearned revenue	97,818
Interest payable	34,341
Net cash provided by (used in) operating activities	(130,442)
Investing activities	
Sales and maturities of marketable securities	545,724
Purchases of marketable securities	(184,455)
Purchases of fixed assets	(134,758)
Investments in equity-method investees and other investments .	(62,533)
Net cash provided by (used in) investing activities	163,978
Financing activities	
Proceeds from exercise of stock options	44,697
Proceeds from long-term debt	681,499
Repayment of long-term debt	(16,927)
Financing costs	(16,122)
Net cash provided by financing activities	693,147
Effect of exchange-rate changes on cash and cash equivalents . .	(37,557)
Net increase (decrease) in cash and cash equivalents	689,126
Cash and cash equivalents, end of period	822,435
Supplemental cash flow information	
Fixed assets acquired under capital leases	4,459
Fixed assets acquired under financing agreements	4,844
Stock issued in connection with business acquisitions	32,130
Equity securities received for commercial agreements	106,848
Cash paid for interest	92,253

Source: Amazon.com, Inc., Form 10-K.

increases in inventories and increases in accounts payable could cause users of financial statements to overlook important information about the firm's current assets and liabilities. Because of this, the two increases are never netted together on the cash flows statement.

To illustrate this treatment, here are some example journal entries showing changes to inventory and accounts payable:

	Journal Entry Representing Changes in Inventory and Accounts Payable		
+/−	Accounts [description of account]	Debit	Credit
+	Inventory [balance sheet asset account]	1,000	
+	Accounts Payable [balance sheet liability account]		1,000
−	Accounts Payable [balance sheet liability account]	1,000	
−	Cash [balance sheet asset account]		1,000
+	Cost of Goods Sold {income statement expense account]	1,000	
−	Inventory [balance sheet asset account]		1,000

Notice that decreases in accounts payable affect cash, and decreases in inventory affect net income (through cost of goods sold, an expense account). However, increases in accounts payable and inventory do not affect cash or net income.

On the cash flows statement, an increase in inventory is subtracted from net income, as though the increase was paid for in cash. Similarly, an increase in accounts payable is added to net income, as though the increase was a noncash expense. In effect, each account is viewed as being independent of the other account. Since the two accounts have opposite effects in the computation of cash flows, they offset each other, and the net effect is zero. The following journal entries show how increases in inventory and accounts payable are viewed for purposes of the cash flows statement:

	Journal Entry Representing Increases in Inventory and Accounts Payable		
+/−	Accounts [description of account]	Debit	Credit
+	Inventory [balance sheet asset account]	1,000	
−	Cash [balance sheet asset account]		1,000
+	Cost of Goods Sold [income statement expense account]	1,000	
+	Accounts Payable [balance sheet liability account]		1,000

The cash flows statement for Kmart Corporation at the end of this chapter is an example of increases in both inventory and accounts payable shown separately as offsetting items. On the statement of cash flows, these items would be shown as follows:

Net Income	200,000
Add: Increase in Accounts Payable	1,000
Subtract: Increase in Inventory	(1,000)
Cash Flows from Operating Activities	200,000

CASH FLOWS INFORMATION IN OTHER COUNTRIES

Because a company's net cash flows are the difference between the cash balances at the beginning and the end of the accounting period, cash flows are a very objective (or reliable) measure, and there is little room for differences between countries with respect to cash flows measurement.

The major international difference is whether or not a cash flows statement is required in financial statements of publicly traded companies. International differences may also exist with respect to the definition of cash equivalents.

To illustrate reporting of cash flow information in another country, the cash flows statement of Reed Elsevier is presented at the end of this chapter. As you can see from the statement, although some of the terminology is different from the usual U.S. terminology—for example, decrease/(increase) in stocks rather than decrease/(increase) in inventories—the basic statement is quite similar to a cash flows statement for a U.S. company, with net cash inflow from operating activities being reported in the top portion of the statement.

USING CASH FLOWS INFORMATION TO MAKE DECISIONS

Consider the cash flows statement of Amazon.com presented on page 113, and imagine that you were faced with a decision that required the answer to the following question: Will Amazon.com become bankrupt within the next three years?

Bankruptcy is a legal way for a firm to protect itself from creditor claims when the firm is unable to pay its bills as they come due. In some cases bankruptcy is voluntary, and the firm is often able to work out an arrangement with its creditors that allows it to ultimately recover its financial health and continue to operate. In other cases the firm is forced into bankruptcy by the creditors, and the assets of the firm are sold off, with the proceeds used to satisfy creditors' claims. In this situation, shareholders often receive nothing for their common stock investment.

In its 2000 cash flows statement, Amazon.com reported negative cash flows from operating activities of $130 million. This means that Amazon.com's cash receipts with respect to its business activities of selling products over the Internet were $130 million less than its cash disbursements with respect to these same activities.

For some types of businesses, negative cash flows from operating activities may reflect the time it takes to collect accounts receivable. Recall the discussion of the business operating cycle at the beginning of the chapter. A profitable firm may have to pay for its purchases of raw materials and labor prior to the time that it collects its accounts receivable. If the firm is constantly growing, the growing accounts receivable collections may not catch up with the growing cash disbursements for purchases and wages for several years.

However, in Amazon.com's case the company has no accounts receivable (since it sells only to customers using credit cards—you could verify the fact that there are no accounts receivable by looking at Amazon.com's balance sheet). Cash collection on a sale is therefore immediate. Also, since Amazon.com does not manufacture anything, there is no time delay during the production of inventory that would increase the operating cycle. Therefore, you might expect Amazon.com to have a very short operating cycle. Finally, notice that Amazon.com's accounts payable and accrued expenses are increasing, thus allowing the company to delay payment of expenses while collecting sales revenue immediately. Based on this analysis, it does not appear that the negative cash flows from operating activities is due to a long operating cycle.

Another thing to notice is that, although Amazon.com had a net *increase* in cash and cash equivalents of $689 million for the year, this amount is almost the same as the $681 million increase in cash flows due to proceeds from long-term debt. This means that the increase in Amazon.com's cash for the year came from borrowing. This additional borrowing will require larger payments for interest in the future, thus putting even more strain on Amazon.com's cash flows. Finally, notice that Amazon.com generated $546 million of cash flows from sales and maturities of marketable securities. Anyone interested in Amazon.com's future cash flows would want to look at the balance sheet to determine the amount of marketable securities remaining for future accounting periods.

The conclusion from this analysis might be as follows: Amazon.com is financing its operations by borrowing and by selling marketable securities. At some future date the company will run out of borrowing ability, and it will also run out of marketable securities to sell. At that point, it will need positive cash flow from operating activities to avoid bankruptcy.

This example points out one way that people can use cash flows statements in their decision making. Cash flow information may also be used as an input to stock price valuation models used by security analysts or investors. Finally, cash flows statements may be used for contracting purposes. For example, a lender may require a borrowing firm to maintain a certain level of cash flows from operating activities to avoid having the loan become due.

Summary

This chapter discusses the importance of cash flow information for certain types of decisions. Constructing a cash flows statement using the indirect method shows how accrual accounting net income is related to operating cash flows. Firms also generate and use cash other than through operations: through financing activities and investing activities.

A three-step approach is presented for constructing a cash flows statement for a real company based on balance sheet changes and analysis of journal entries. The cash flows statement for Microsoft is constructed using this approach. Cash flows statements from other countries are quite similar to a U.S. cash flows statement.

The example of Amazon.com's cash flows demonstrates how users of financial statements might use cash flow information to make decisions.

Appendix 4–1

Cash Flows and Changes in Balance Sheet Accounts

This appendix develops the relationship between cash flows and changes in balance sheet accounts in a more formal way. Here is the basic accounting equation representing the balance sheet:

$$\text{Assets} = \text{Liabilities} + \text{Owners' Equity}$$

The left side of this equation can be separated into Cash and all other Noncash Assets. Similarly Owners' Equity can be separated into Retained Earnings and Other Equity. This results in the following equation:

$$\text{Cash} + \text{Noncash Assets} = \text{Liabilities} + \text{Retained Earnings} + \text{Other Equity}$$

Taking the balances in each of these accounts at the end of the year and subtracting the balances at the beginning of the year results in the change in the balance of each account for the year. Let the Greek letter delta (Δ) represent the change in an account balance from the beginning to the end of the year. For example, ΔCash represents the change in the cash balance from the beginning to the end of the year. The accounting equation representing these changes would look like this:

$$\Delta\text{Cash} + \Delta\text{Noncash Assets} = \Delta\text{Liabilities} + \Delta\text{Retained Earnings} + \Delta\text{Other Equity}$$

Since retained earnings is increased by net income and decreased by dividends, the change in retained earnings for any company for the year is equal to net income minus dividends. For simplicity, assume that a company does not pay dividends and that there are no other changes to retained earnings except net income (ΔRetained Earnings = Net Income). Incorporating this into the accounting equation results in:

$$\Delta\text{Cash} + \Delta\text{Noncash Assets} = \Delta\text{Liabilities} + \text{Net Income} + \Delta\text{Other Equity}$$

Moving the change in Noncash Assets to the right side of this equation demonstrates that the change in the Cash account for the year is equal to the change in all of the other balance sheet accounts for the year (keeping in mind that Net Income represents the change in Retained Earnings).

$$\Delta\text{Cash} = \Delta\text{Liabilities} - \Delta\text{Noncash Assets} + \text{Net Income} + \Delta\text{Other Equity}$$

This demonstrates why the starting point for constructing the cash flows statement is to compute the changes in all of the noncash balance sheet accounts, and why the changes in the noncash balance sheet accounts must equal the change in the Cash account.

When constructing a cash flows statement using the indirect method, the goal is to reconcile cash flows with net income. Alternatively, the goal is to explain the difference between the change in cash and net income for the year (ΔCash − Net Income). Moving the Net Income term to the left side of the equation results in the following:

$$\Delta\text{Cash} - \text{Net Income} = \Delta\text{Liabilities} + \Delta\text{Other Equity} - \Delta\text{Noncash Assets}$$

The left side of this equation (ΔCash − Net Income) is the difference between net income and the change in cash for the year. This is the amount that is reconciled on the statement of cash flows using the indirect method. The equation demonstrates that this amount is equal to the changes in all of the other balance sheet accounts.

Expressing the balance sheet changes in this way illustrates three points that will help to explain the construction of the cash flows statement.

1. Any cash receipt or cash disbursement (ΔCash) that does not affect net income (Net Income) results in a change in a noncash balance sheet account (ΔLiabilities + ΔOther Equity − ΔNoncash Assets). Examples are payment of accounts payable, receipt of cash from accounts receivable, cash payment for inventory, and cash payment for equipment.

2. Any transaction that affects net income (Net Income) but does not result in a cash receipt or cash disbursement (ΔCash) results in a change in a noncash balance sheet account (ΔLiabilities + ΔOther Equity − ΔNoncash Assets). Examples are depreciation expense, sale of merchandise for an account receivable, and recording rent expense for accrued rent.

3. Any transaction that only affects two noncash balance sheet accounts (ΔLiabilities + ΔOther Equity − ΔNoncash Assets) will not be taken into account in the reconciliation of cash flows and net income. Examples are acquiring a building in exchange for common stock, acquiring equipment in exchange for a note payable, and paying off a note payable using land.

THE BOEING COMPANY AND SUBSIDIARIES
Consolidated Statements of Cash Flows
(dollars in millions)

	Year Ended December 31		
	1999	**1998**	**1997**
Cash flows—operating activities			
Net earnings (loss)	$ 2,309	$ 1,120	$ (178)
Adjustments to reconcile net earnings (loss) to net cash provided by operating activities:			
Share-based plans	209	153	(99)
Depreciation	1,538	1,517	1,354
Amortization of goodwill and intangibles	107	105	104
Customer and commercial financing valuation provision	72	61	64
Gain on dispositions, net	(87)	(13)	
Changes in assets and liabilities			
Short-term investments	179	450	154
Accounts receivable	(225)	(167)	(240)
Inventories, net of advances and progress billings	2,030	652	(96)
Accounts payable and other liabilities	217	(840)	1,908
Advances in excess of related costs	(36)	(324)	(139)
Income taxes payable and deferred	462	145	(451)
Other	(597)	(479)	(272)
Accrued retiree health care	46	35	(4)
Net cash provided by operating activities	6,224	2,415	2,105
Cash flows—investing activities			
Customer and commercial financing—additions	(2,398)	(2,603)	(1,889)
Customer and commercial financing—reductions	1,842	1,357	1,025
Property, plant and equipment, net additions	(1,236)	(1,665)	(1,391)
Proceeds from dispositions	359	37	
Net cash used by investing activities	(1,433)	(2,874)	(2,255)
Cash flows—financing activities			
New borrowings	437	811	232
Debt repayments	(676)	(693)	(867)
Common shares purchased	(2,937)	(1,397)	(141)
Common shares issued			268
Stock options exercised, other	93	65	166
Dividends paid	(537)	(564)	(557)
Net cash used by financing activities	(3,620)	(1,778)	(899)
Net increase (decrease) in cash and cash equivalents	1,171	(2,237)	(1,049)
Cash and cash equivalents at beginning of year	2,183	4,420	5,469
Cash and cash equivalents at end of year	$ 3,354	$ 2,183	$ 4,420

Source: The Boeing Company Form 10-K.

INTERNATIONAL BUSINESS MACHINES CORPORATION AND SUBSIDIARY COMPANIES
Consolidated Statement of Cash Flows
(dollars in millions)

	At December 31		
	1999	**1998**	**1997**
Cash flow from operating activities			
Net income	$7,712	$6,328	$6,093
Adjustments to reconcile net income to cash provided from operating activities:			
Depreciation	6,159	4,475	4,018
Amortization of software	426	517	983
Deferred income taxes	(713)	(606)	358
Gain on disposition of fixed and other assets	(4,791)	(261)	(273)
Other changes that (used) provided cash:			
Receivables	(1,677)	(2,736)	(3,727)
Inventories	301	73	432
Other assets	(130)	219	(378)
Accounts payable	(3)	362	699
Other liabilities	2,827	902	660
Net cash provided from operating activities	10,111	9,273	8,865
Cash flow from investing activities			
Payments for plant, rental machines and other property	(5,959)	(6,520)	(6,793)
Proceeds from disposition of plant, rental machines and other property	1,207	905	1,130
Investment in software	(464)	(250)	(314)
Purchases of marketable securities and other investments	(3,949)	(4,211)	(1,617)
Proceeds from marketable securities and other investments	2,616	3,945	1,439
Proceeds from sale of the Global Network	4,880	—	—
Net cash used in investing activities	(1,669)	(6,131)	(6,155)
Cash flow from financing activities			
Proceeds from new debt	6,133	7,567	9,142
Short-term borrowings less than 90 days—net	276	499	(668)
Payments to settle debt	(7,510)	(5,942)	(4,530)
Preferred stock transactions—net	—	(5)	(1)
Common stock transactions—net	(6,645)	(6,278)	(6,250)
Cash dividends paid	(879)	(834)	(783)
Net cash used in financing activities	(8,625)	(4,993)	(3,090)
Effect of exchange rate changes on cash and cash equivalents	(149)	120	(201)
Net change in cash and cash equivalents	(332)	(1,731)	(581)
Cash and cash equivalents at January 1	5,375	7,106	7,687
Cash and cash equivalents at December 31	$5,043	$5,375	$7,106
Supplemental data			
Cash paid during the year for:			
Income taxes	$1,904	$1,929	$2,472
Interest	$1,574	$1,605	$1,475

Source: IBM Corporation Form 10-K.

KMART CORPORATION
Consolidated Statements of Cash Flows
(dollars in millions)

	Years Ended January 26, 2000, January 27, 1999 And January 28, 1998		
	1999	**1998**	**1997**
Cash flow from operating activities			
Net income from continuing operations	$ 633	$ 518	$ 249
Adjustments to reconcile net income from continuing operations to net cash provided by operating activities:			
Depreciation and amortization	770	671	660
Cash used for store restructuring and other charges	(80)	(94)	(105)
Increase in inventories	(565)	(169)	(31)
(Increase) decrease in accounts receivable	(62)	(76)	18
Increase (decrease) in trade accounts payable	157	124	(86)
Deferred income taxes and taxes payable	258	308	72
Decrease in other long-term liabilities	(116)	(64)	(27)
Changes in other assets and liabilities	92	60	15
Voluntary early retirement programs	—	19	114
Net cash provided by continuing operations	1,087	1,297	879
Net cash used for discontinued operations	(83)	(60)	(38)
Net cash provided by operating activities	1,004	1,237	841
Cash flow from investing activities			
Capital expenditures	(1,277)	(981)	(678)
Acquisition of Caldor leases	(86)	—	—
Proceeds from divestitures	—	87	133
Decrease in property held for sale or financing and other	—	99	420
Other, net	—	—	(60)
Net cash used for investing activities	(1,363)	(795)	(185)
Cash flow from financing activities			
Proceeds from issuance of long-term debt and notes payable . . .	297	—	337
Purchase of common shares	(200)	(30)	—
Issuance of common shares	63	76	37
Payments on long-term debt	(90)	(188)	(811)
Payments on capital lease obligations	(77)	(88)	(112)
Refinancing costs related to long-term debt and notes payable . . .	—	—	(15)
Net cash used for financing activities	(7)	(230)	(564)
Net (decrease) increase in cash and cash equivalents	(366)	212	92
Cash and cash equivalents, beginning of year	710	498	406
Cash and cash equivalents, end of year	$ 344	$ 710	$ 498

Source: Kmart Corporation Form 10-K.

CHRYSLER CORPORATION AND CONSOLIDATED SUBSIDIARIES
Consolidated Statement of Cash Flows
(in millions of dollars)

	Year Ended December 31		
	1997	**1996**	**1995**
Cash flows from Operating Activities			
Net earnings	$ 2,805	$ 3,529	$ 2,025
Adjustments to reconcile to net cash provided by operating activities:			
Depreciation and special tools amortization	2,696	2,312	2,220
Provision for credit losses	444	373	372
Deferred income taxes	279	1,120	186
Extraordinary item—Loss on early extinguishment of debt (Note 7)	—	191	—
Cumulative effect of a change in accounting principle (Note 1)	—	—	96
Change in receivables	(364)	(224)	848
Change in inventories	(706)	(691)	(435)
Change in prepaid expenses and other assets	(1,249)	(1,394)	(681)
Change in accounts payable and accrued and other liabilities	2,119	2,143	2,092
Other	404	(58)	231
Net cash provided by operating activities	6,428	7,301	6,954
Cash flows from investing activities			
Purchases of marketable securities	(2,778)	(4,346)	(5,160)
Sales and maturities of marketable securities	3,350	5,294	6,122
Finance receivables acquired	(28,335)	(19,906)	(24,437)
Finance receivables collected	9,089	3,062	3,795
Proceeds from sales of finance receivables	18,967	16,809	17,602
Proceeds from sales of nonautomotive assets	—	701	94
Expenditures for property and equipment	(3,419)	(3,271)	(2,597)
Expenditures for special tools	(1,703)	(1,364)	(1,049)
Purchases of vehicle operating leases	(2,028)	(794)	(460)
Other	652	248	179
Net cash used in investing activities	(6,205)	(3,567)	(5,911)
Cash flows from financing activities			
Change in short-term debt	627	410	(1,971)
Proceeds under long-term borrowings and revolving lines of credit	5,868	1,390	4,731
Payments on long-term borrowings and revolving lines of credit	(3,897)	(2,167)	(1,687)
Payment for early extinguishment of debt	—	(853)	—
Repurchases of common stock (Note 11)	(2,130)	(2,041)	(1,047)
Dividends paid	(1,096)	(963)	(710)
Other	145	105	39
Net cash used in financing activities	(483)	(4,119)	(645)
Change in cash and cash equivalents	(260)	(385)	398
Cash and cash equivalents at beginning of year	5,158	5,543	5,145
Cash and cash equivalents at end of Year	$ 4,898	$ 5,158	$ 5,543

Source: Chrysler Corporation Form 10-K.

REED ELSEVIER
Combined Statements of Cash Flows
(in pound millions)

	Notes	Year Ended December 31		
		1997	1998	1999
Operating profit (before joint ventures)		78	393	177
Exceptional charges to operating profit		502	79	239
Operating profit before exceptional items		580	472	416
Amortisation of goodwill and intangible assets (excluding joint ventures)		278	323	369
Depreciation charges		96	97	117
Net SSAP 24 pension credit	27	(1)	(4)	(3)
Total non-cash items		373	416	483
Decrease/(increase) in stocks		5	0	(9)
(Increase)/decrease in debtors		(25)	17	(8)
Increase in creditors		23	32	16
Movement in working capital		3	49	(1)
Net cash inflow from operating activities before exceptional items		956	937	898
Payments relating to exceptional items charged to operating profit	6	(26)	(258)	(138)
Net cash inflow from operating activities		930	679	760
Dividends received from joint ventures		17	11	4
Interest received		46	61	33
Interest paid		(105)	(106)	(114)
Returns on investments and servicing of finance		(59)	(45)	(81)
Taxation (including(pound) 74 million (1998: (pound)nil) exceptional repayments)		(180)	(144)	(99)
Purchase of tangible fixed assets		(121)	(151)	(137)
Proceeds from sale of fixed assets		10	11	15
Exceptional net payments from sale of fixed assets	6	(21)	0	0
Capital expenditure		(132)	(140)	(122)
Acquisitions	28	(726)	(1,232)	(166)
Payments against acquisition provisions		(5)	(11)	(1)
Exceptional net proceeds from sale of fixed asset investments and businesses	6,28	104	913	3
Merger expenses	6	(3)	(8)	0
Acquisitions and disposals		(630)	(338)	(164)
Equity dividends paid to the shareholders of the parent companies		(336)	(362)	(339)
Cash outflow before changes in short term investments and financing		(390)	(339)	(41)
Decrease in short term investments	28	299	63	297
Financing	28	120	192	(197)
Increase/(decrease) in cash	28	29	(84)	59
Adjusted figures				
Adjusted operating cash flow	10	862	808	780
Adjusted operating cash flow conversion		97%	99%	98%

Source: Reed Elsevier Form 20-F.

Discussion Questions

1. Explain why net income will in general not be the same as net cash flows for a year.

2. If cash flow information is useful, why report accrual accounting information?

3. What is the difference between a direct and an indirect statement of cash flows? Which type is used by most public companies.

4. Name the three parts of a cash flows statement. Give an example of a type of cash flow that would be found in each part.

5. Explain why changes in balance sheet accounts for the year provide the starting point for constructing a cash flows statement.

6. How are gains and losses treated on the cash flows statement?

7. How is depreciation treated on the cash flows statement?

8. Is depreciation a source of cash for a company? In other words, will more depreciation expense result in a higher cash flow?

9. Explain the difference in treatment on the cash flows statement for dividends paid and interest paid.

10. Why are changes in current asset and current liability accounts important in arriving at cash flows from operating activities?

11. Can accounting method differences ever affect cash flows from operating activities?

12. Which is more useful, cash flow information or accrual accounting information? Why?

13. In addition to net cash flows, what additional information is included with a cash flows statement (or in the accompanying notes)?

Problems

Here are some example journal entries that may be useful in completing the problems that follow:

+ Accounts Receivable [balance sheet asset account]	XXXX	
+ Sales [income statement revenue account]		XXXX
+ Cash [balance sheet asset account]	XXXX	
− Accounts Receivable [balance sheet asset account]		XXXX
+ Equipment [balance sheet asset account]	XXXX	
− Cash [balance sheet asset account]		XXXX
+ Depreciation Expense [income statement expense account]	XXXX	
+ Accumulated Depreciation [balance sheet contra-asset account]		XXXX
+ Cash [balance sheet asset account]	XXXX	
− Accumulated Depreciation [balance sheet contra-asset account]	XXXX	
− Equipment [balance sheet asset account]		XXXX
+ Gain [income statement gain account]		XXXX
+ Cash [balance sheet asset account]	XXXX	
− Accumulated Depreciation [balance sheet contra-asset account]	XXXX	
+ Loss [income statement loss account]	XXXX	
− Equipment [balance sheet asset account]		XXXX
+ Wages Expense [income statement expense account]	XXXX	
+ Wages Payable [balance sheet liability account]		XXXX
− Wages Payable [balance sheet liability account]	XXXX	
− Cash [balance sheet asset account]		XXXX
+ Cash [balance sheet asset account]	XXXX	
+ Bank Loan [balance sheet liability account]		XXXX
− Bank Loan [balance sheet liability account]	XXXX	
− Cash [balance sheet asset account]		XXXX
+ Cash [balance sheet asset account]	XXXX	
+ Common Stock [balance sheet equity account]		XXXX

1. Use the two balance sheets and additional information shown below to construct a cash flows statement for this company:

Balance Sheets	12/31/02	12/31/01
Cash	10,000	7,000
Accounts Receivable	6,000	4,000
Equipment	45,000	40,000
Less: Accumulated Depreciation	(8,000)	(6,000)
Total Assets	53,000	45,000
Wages Payable	11,000	8,500
Bank Loan	20,000	17,000
Common Stock	10,000	9,000
Retained Earnings	12,000	10,500
Total Liabilities and Shareholders' Equity	53,000	45,000

Net income	1,500
Depreciation expense	2,000
Equipment purchased	5,000
Sale of common stock	1,000
Bank loan repayments	2,000
New borrowings	5,000

2. Use the two balance sheets and additional information shown below to construct a cash flows statement for this company:

Balance Sheets	12/31/02	12/31/01
Cash	6,000	7,000
Accounts Receivable	3,500	4,000
Equipment	34,000	40,000
Less: Accumulated Depreciation	(5,000)	(6,000)
Total Assets	38,500	45,000
Wages Payable	7,000	8,500
Bank Loan	15,000	17,000
Common Stock	9,000	9,000
Retained Earnings	7,500	10,500
Total Liabilities and Shareholders' Equity	38,500	45,000

Gain from selling equipment	500
Net income	(3,000)
Depreciation expense	1,000
Original cost of equipment sold	6,000
Accumulated depreciation of equipment sold	2,000
Proceeds from selling equipment	4,500
Bank loan repayments	2,000

3. Use the two balance sheets and additional information shown below to construct a cash flows statement for this company:

Balance Sheets	12/31/02	12/31/01
Cash	8,600	7,000
Accounts Receivable	3,000	4,000
Equipment	42,000	40,000
Less: Accumulated Depreciation	(7,000)	(6,000)
Total Assets	46,600	45,000
Wages Payable	9,200	8,500
Bank Loan	17,000	17,000
Common Stock	9,500	9,000
Retained Earnings	10,900	10,500
Total Liabilities and Shareholders' Equity	46,600	45,000

Loss from selling equipment	1,200
Net income	400
Depreciation expense	3,000
Equipment purchased	6,000
Original cost of equipment sold	4,000
Accumulated depreciation of equipment sold	2,000
Proceeds from selling equipment	800
Sale of common stock	500

Here are some additional example journal entries that may be useful in completing the problems that follow:

+	Income Tax Expense [income statement expense account]	XXXX	
+	Taxes Payable [balance sheet liability account]		XXXX
−	Taxes Payable [balance sheet liability account]	XXXX	
−	Cash [balance sheet asset account]		XXXX
+	Inventory [balance sheet asset account]	XXXX	
−	Cash [balance sheet asset account]		XXXX
+	Cost of Goods Sold [income statement expense account]	XXXX	
−	Inventory [balance sheet asset account]		XXXX
+	Cost of Goods Sold [income statement expense account]	XXXX	
+	Accounts Payable [balance sheet liability account]		XXXX
−	Accounts Payable [balance sheet liability account]	XXXX	
−	Cash [balance sheet asset account]		XXXX

4. Use the two balance sheets and additional information shown below to construct a cash flows statement for this company:

Balance Sheets	12/31/02	12/31/01
Cash	285,000	150,000
Accounts Receivable	237,000	205,000
Inventory	302,000	357,000
Equipment	1,500,000	1,480,000
Less: Accumulated Depreciation	(300,000)	(260,000)
Total Assets	2,024,000	1,932,000
Accounts Payable	128,000	132,000
Taxes Payable	62,000	84,000
Wages Payable	240,000	225,000
Bank Loan	1,250,000	1,200,000
Common Stock	100,000	100,000
Retained Earnings	244,000	191,000
Total Liabilities and Shareholders' Equity	2,024,000	1,932,000

Net income	53,000
Depreciation expense	40,000
Equipment purchased	20,000
New bank loan	80,000
Repay bank loan	30,000

5. Use the two balance sheets and additional information shown below to construct a cash flows statement for this company:

Balance Sheets	12/31/02	12/31/01
Cash	142,000	150,000
Accounts Receivable	290,000	205,000
Inventory	380,000	357,000
Equipment	1,450,000	1,480,000
Less: Accumulated Depreciation	(280,000)	(260,000)
Total Assets	1,982,000	1,932,000
Accounts Payable	145,000	132,000
Taxes Payable	93,000	84,000
Wages Payable	210,000	225,000
Bank Loan	1,340,000	1,200,000
Common Stock	120,000	100,000
Retained Earnings	74,000	191,000
Total Liabilities and Shareholders' Equity	1,982,000	1,932,000

Net income	(117,000)
Depreciation expense	40,000
Gain on sale of equipment	35,000
Original cost of equipment sold	30,000
Accumulated depreciation of equipment sold	20,000
Proceeds from selling equipment	45,000
New bank loan	140,000
Sale of common stock	20,000

6. Use the two balance sheets and additional information shown below to construct a cash flows statement for this company:

Balance Sheets	12/31/02	12/31/01
Cash	177,000	150,000
Accounts Receivable	200,000	205,000
Inventory	375,000	357,000
Equipment	1,480,000	1,480,000
Less: Accumulated Depreciation	(260,000)	(260,000)
Total Assets	1,972,000	1,932,000
Accounts Payable	108,000	132,000
Taxes Payable	53,000	84,000
Wages Payable	230,000	225,000
Bank Loan	1,180,000	1,200,000
Common Stock	100,000	100,000
Retained Earnings	301,000	191,000
Total Liabilities and Shareholders' Equity	1,972,000	1,932,000

Net income	110,000
Depreciation expense	30,000
Loss on sale of equipment	15,000
Equipment purchased	80,000
Original cost of equipment sold	80,000
Accumulated depreciation of equipment sold	30,000
Proceeds from selling equipment	35,000
Repay bank loan	20,000

7. Use the two balance sheets and additional information shown below to construct a cash flows statement for this company:

Balance Sheets	12/31/02	12/31/01
Cash	177,000	218,000
Accounts Receivable	200,000	186,000
Inventory	375,000	300,000
Equipment	1,480,000	1,370,000
Less: Accumulated Depreciation	(260,000)	(210,000)
Total Assets	1,972,000	1,864,000
Accounts Payable	108,000	95,000
Taxes Payable	53,000	55,000
Wages Payable	230,000	193,000
Bank Loan	1,180,000	1,400,000
Common Stock	100,000	90,000
Retained Earnings	301,000	31,000
Total Liabilities and Shareholders' Equity	1,972,000	1,864,000

Net income	270,000
Depreciation expense	60,000
Gain on sale of equipment	60,000
Equipment purchased	140,000
Original cost of equipment sold	30,000
Accumulated depreciation of equipment sold	10,000
Proceeds from selling equipment	80,000
Repay bank loan	220,000
Sale of common stock	10,000

8. Use the two balance sheets and additional information shown below to construct a cash flows statement for this company:

Balance Sheets	12/31/02	12/31/01
Cash	280,000	218,000
Accounts Receivable	180,000	186,000
Inventory	296,000	300,000
Equipment	1,560,000	1,370,000
Less: Accumulated Depreciation	(280,000)	(210,000)
Total Assets	2,036,000	1,864,000
Accounts Payable	91,000	95,000
Taxes Payable	40,000	55,000
Wages Payable	190,000	193,000
Bank Loan	1,600,000	1,400,000
Common Stock	90,000	90,000
Retained Earnings	25,000	31,000
Total Liabilities and Shareholders' Equity	2,036,000	1,864,000

Net income	(6,000)
Depreciation expense	95,000
Loss on sale of equipment	5,000
Equipment purchased	220,000
Original cost of equipment sold	30,000
Accumulated depreciation of equipment sold	25,000
Proceeds from selling equipment	0
New bank loan	200,000

9. Use the two balance sheets and additional information shown below to construct a cash flows statement for this company:

Balance Sheets	12/31/02	12/31/01
Cash	218,000	218,000
Accounts Receivable	225,000	186,000
Inventory	240,000	300,000
Equipment	1,300,000	1,370,000
Less: Accumulated Depreciation	(200,000)	(210,000)
Total Assets	1,783,000	1,864,000
Accounts Payable	140,000	95,000
Taxes Payable	61,000	55,000
Wages Payable	178,000	193,000
Bank Loan	1,250,000	1,400,000
Common Stock	92,000	90,000
Retained Earnings	62,000	31,000
Total Liabilities and Shareholders' Equity	1,783,000	1,864,000

Net income	31,000
Depreciation expense	60,000
Gain on sale of equipment	18,000
Equipment sold	70,000
Accumulated depreciation of equipment sold	70,000
Proceeds from sale of equipment	18,000
Repay bank loan	150,000
Sale of common stock	2,000

Research Reports

1. Locate the 2001 annual report of The Rowe Companies. This is available from the SEC EDGAR database, as part of the Form 10-K, or from the company's website (**www.therowecompanies.com**). Find the cash flows statement in the annual report.

   a. What method does The Rowe Companies use to prepare its cash flows statement?

   b. Discuss how this method compares with the indirect method used by most companies. Is the information provided more useful?

   c. Discuss the two formats for the cash flows statement in terms of relevance and reliability.

   d. Discuss the two formats for the cash flows statement in terms of costs and benefits.

2. Locate the documents for Enron Corp. on the SEC EDGAR database website. On EDGAR, Enron is called ENRON CORP/OR. The SEC's central index key for Enron is 0001024401.

   a. Locate the cash flows statement in the following reports:

      10-K (annual report) for year ended 12/31/2000

      10-Q (quarterly report) for quarter ended 9/30/2000

      10-Q (quarterly report) for quarter ended 6/30/2000

      10-Q (quarterly report) for quarter ended 3/31/2000

   b. Compute Enron's quarterly cash flows from operating activities for each quarter for 2000. (You will have to compute these yourself, since the cash flows statements in the quarterly and annual reports only give cumulative year-to-date cash flows information. In other words, the cash flows from operating activities reported in the second quarter financial statement is the cash flows for the six-month period ended June 30, 2000. To compute the cash flows for the second quarter you have to subtract the cash flows reported for the first quarter. You must do this for quarters 2, 3, and 4.)

   c. The 10-K also reports unaudited quarterly information on revenues and net income. (You can find this by searching the document for the word *quarterly.*) Find Enron's net income for each quarter for 2000.

   d. On a graph, plot Enron's quarterly net income and quarterly cash flows from operating activities.

   e. What can you conclude from the patterns of cash flows and net income? In view of Enron's subsequent bankruptcy and the information that you know about Enron, discuss how useful this quarterly financial statement information would have been to investors.

3. Obtain the 2000 annual report of USAirways from the investor relations section of the company's website (**www.investor.usairways.com**) or the SEC EDGAR database.

   a. Explain why USAirways' cash flows from operating activities for 2000 were positive even though the company had a net loss for the year.

   b. USAirways spent $2,001 million of cash on new investments in 2000, which was more than their cash flows from operating activities plus its beginning cash balance. How did the company get the cash for this large investment in new assets?

   c. Comment on how USAirways' 2000 cash flows statement provides information about how risky the company was.

4. Obtain the financial statements for The Walt Disney Company. Find cash flows statements for the years ended September 30, 2002, and September 30, 2001.

   a. Explain why Disney's cash flows from operating activities were positive for 2001 despite the fact that net income was negative.

    b. Explain why Disney's total cash flows for 2001 were negative despite the fact that cash flows from operating activities were positive.

    c. Explain why cash flows from financing activities was positive in 2002 and negative in 2001.

    d. Explain the effects of changes in balance sheet balances for accounts receivable and accounts payable for 2002 and 2001.

5. Obtain the most recent financial statements for a U.S. public company.

    a. Compare the changes in balance sheet accounts using the beginning and ending balance sheets with the amounts reported on the cash flows statement. Do the changes agree? If not, try to determine the cause of the differences.

    b. Identify items on the cash flows statement that are also reported elsewhere on the financial statements. (For example, if depreciation and amortization are added back to net income, are these same amounts reported elsewhere in the financial statements?) Try to identify as many items as possible.

    c. Make a list of what additional information you would need to obtain to allow you to prepare the company's cash flows statement using changes in balance sheet accounts.

Chapter Learning Objectives

After reading this chapter you should understand

1. What the term *present value* means, and what factors determine present value.
2. The characteristics of a note, and how notes are accounted for.
3. How to account for notes with no interest, or interest rates below market.
4. What a discount or premium on a note represents.
5. What an annuity represents, and how annuities are used in computing present values.
6. The characteristics of a bond, and how the present value of a bond is computed.
7. How bonds payable are recorded under GAAP.
8. How bond premium and discount are amortized as part of interest expense.
9. The accounting treatment for bonds that are retired early.

Chapter 5

Notes Receivable, Notes Payable, and the Time Value of Money

Focus Company: The Boeing Company

Introduction

Until now, the focus of this book has been on three major financial statements: the income statement, the balance sheet, and the cash flows statement.[1] This chapter begins a more detailed study of financial reporting rules by focusing on the individual items that make up these financial statements.

The chapter begins by introducing one of the most basic types of assets or liabilities: a note. A *note* is a written promise to pay a certain amount of money at some future date. The note may or may not require the borrower to make interest payments.[2] Notes may be secured—that is, the lender has a claim on the borrower's assets as collateral—or they may be unsecured. Some notes are publicly traded, which are usually called *bonds* or *debentures*;[3] others are not. Notes are routinely issued by corporations to finance business activities, but they are also used by not-for-profit organizations, such as hospitals, as well as by local, state, and federal government agencies.

As an example, here is part of the note that Tandy Corporation received from CompUSA Inc. on the sale of Computer City, Inc. As you can see, this note is a written promise to pay a certain amount of cash (in this case, $136 million) at a certain date in the future (in this case, 14 semiannual payments of $9,714,285.71, beginning December 31, 2001). The note bears interest at the rate of 9.48 percent and is not publicly traded.

Subordinated Promissory Note

$136,000,000   August 31, 1998

FOR VALUE RECEIVED, CompUSA Inc., a Delaware corporation (the "MAKER"), promises to pay Tandy Corporation, a Delaware corporation (the "SELLER"), the principal sum of One Hundred Thirty Six Million Dollars ($136,000,000).

1. PRINCIPAL PAYMENTS. The principal amount of this Note shall be due and payable to the Seller in fourteen (14) equal semiannual installments of $9,714,285.71, the first payment to be made on December 31, 2001, and each subsequent payment to be made on each June 30 and December 31 [. . .] until the payment of this Note in full.

2. INTEREST. Interest on the unpaid principal balance of this Note shall accrue at a rate of nine and forty-eight/one hundredths percent (9.48%) per annum from the date hereof, calculated on the basis of a 365-day or 366-day year and for the actual days elapsed, and shall be payable semiannually in arrears, with the first interest payment due December 31, 1998, and subsequent payments due each June 30 and December 31 thereafter, until the payment of this Note in full.

Source: Tandy Corporation Form 10-K.

---

[1] A fourth financial statement—the statement of shareholders' equity—is discussed in Chapter 15.

[2] Even when a note does not explicitly require interest payments, the borrower may still be charged interest in the form of higher principal payments. This subject is discussed in more detail later in the chapter.

[3] According to *Black's Law Dictionary,* a debenture is an unsecured corporate obligation, whereas a bond is secured by a lien or mortgage on corporate property. Also, a bond is a long-term debt security, whereas a note is usually a shorter-term obligation.

This chapter will also introduce an important concept called the *time value of money*. Time value of money principles will be applied to compute the present value of future cash flows associated with notes. This present value approach will also be used to record notes receivable and notes payable on the balance sheet, as well as to recognize interest revenue and interest expense associated with notes.

NOTES AS ASSETS AND LIABILITIES

An *asset* is a probable future economic benefit owned by the company. A *liability* is a probable future transfer of economic benefits. The contractual right to future cash receipts evidenced by a note represents an asset to the holder of a note receivable, that is, the lender. The contractual obligation to make future cash payments required by a note represents a liability to the issuer of a note, or bond, payable—that is, the borrower. Since notes are frequently used in business transactions and as a way to lend and borrow money, they are often found on the balance sheets of publicly traded corporations. Often, notes receivable are included in asset categories such as investments or marketable securities, whereas notes payable are included in liability categories such as long-term debt, bonds, or debentures.

Reproduced below are portions of the balance sheets and financial statement notes[4] from The Boeing Company's annual report for 2000. Boeing reported a current asset called *current portion of customer and commercial financing* as well as a noncurrent asset called *customer and commercial financing*.

THE BOEING COMPANY AND SUBSIDIARIES Consolidated Statements of Financial Position (dollars in millions except per share data)		
	December 31	
	2000	**1999**
Assets		
Current portion of customer and commercial financing	995	799
Customer and commercial financing	5,964	5,205
Liabilities and Shareholders' Equity		
Short-term debt and current portion of long-term debt	1,232	752
Long-term debt	7,567	5,980

Source: The Boeing Company Form 10-K.

Note 10 to Boeing's financial statements (reproduced on page 135) indicates that customer and commercial financing at December 31, 2000, included $593 million of aircraft financing notes receivable and $915 million of commercial equipment financing notes receivable, for total notes receivable of $1,508 million. Note 10 also indicates when the principal payments on the notes receivable are due to be collected: $459 million in 2001, $106 million in 2002, and so forth. The principal payments due to be collected within one year are shown as current

---

[4] Companies' annual reports contain financial statement notes that provide information about the numbers appearing on the financial statements. This terminology is confusing, since financial statement notes are not the same thing as notes receivable and notes payable, which are the subject of this chapter.

assets (part of current portion of customer and commercial financing), and the principal payments due to be collected after one year are shown as noncurrent assets (part of customer and commercial financing) on Boeing's balance sheet. Finally, Note 10 provides information about the interest rates associated with Boeing's notes receivable: between 7.17 and 15.01 percent for fixed-rate notes.

Note 10 Customer and Commercial Financing		
Customer and commercial financing at December 31 consisted of the following:		
	2000	**1999**
Aircraft financing		
Notes receivable	$593	$781
Commercial equipment financing		
Notes receivable	915	730

Scheduled payments on customer and commercial financing are as follows:

Year	Principal Payments on Notes Receivable
2001	$ 459
2002	106
2003	95
2004	150
2005	229
Beyond 2005	469
Total	$1,508

Interest rates on fixed-rate notes ranged from 7.17% to 15.01%, and effective interest rates on variable-rate notes ranged from .81% to 5.5% above the London Interbank Offered Rate (LIBOR).

Source: The Boeing Company Form 10-K.

    Boeing's balance sheet also reports short-term debt and current portion of long-term debt of $1,232 million and long-term debt of $7,567 million for 2000, for total debt of $8,799 million. The details of the composition of the $8,799 million of debt are presented in Boeing's Note 15, shown on page 136. The majority of this debt consists of unsecured debentures and notes, senior medium-term notes, subordinated medium-term notes, and other notes. The principal amounts, interest rates, maturity dates, and book values associated with the various debt instruments are given. For example, the fifth note on the list has a principal amount of $300 million, a 6 3/4 percent interest rate, a maturity date of September 15, 2002, and a book value on Boeing's balance sheet of $299 million. (As discussed later in the chapter, notes often have a book value that differs from their principal amount.) Boeing also presents the details of principal payments due in the next five years: $538 million in 2001, $1,176 million in 2002, and so forth. On Boeing's balance sheet, the principal payments due within one year are shown as part of current liabilities, and the principal payments due after one year are shown as noncurrent liabilities.

Note 15 Debt		
Debt at December 31 consisted of the following:	**2000**	**1999**
Unsecured debentures and notes:		
$200, 8.25% due Jul. 1, 2000 . . . . $	—	$ 200
$174, 8 3/8% due Feb. 15, 2001	174	177
$49, 7.565% due Mar. 30, 2002	49	52
$120, 9.25% due Apr. 1, 2002	120	120
$300, 6 3/4% due Sep. 15, 2002	299	298
$300, 6.35% due Jun. 15, 2003	300	300
$200, 7 7/8% due Feb. 15, 2005	206	207
$300, 6 5/8% due Jun. 1, 2005	294	293
$250, 6.875% due Nov. 1, 2006	248	248
$175, 8 1/10% due Nov. 15, 2006	175	175
$350, 9.75% due Apr. 1, 2012	348	348
$400, 8 3/4% due Aug. 15, 2021	398	398
$300, 7.95% due Aug. 15, 2024	300	300
$250, 7 1/4% due Jun. 15, 2025	247	247
$250, 8 3/4% due Sep. 15, 2031	248	248
$175, 8 5/8% due Nov. 15, 2031	173	173
$300, 6 5/8% due Feb. 15, 2038	300	300
$100, 7.50% due Aug. 15, 2042	100	100
$175, 7 7/8% due Apr. 15, 2043	173	173
$125, 6 7/8% due Oct. 15, 2043	125	125
Senior debt securities 6.0%–9.4% due through 2011	1,563	30
Senior medium-term notes, 5.6%–10.0% due through 2017	1,775	1,426
Subordinated medium-term notes 6.4%–8.3% due through 2004	25	45
Capital lease obligations due through 2008	380	386
Other notes	779	363
	$8,799	$6,732

Maturities of long-term debt for the next five years are as follows:

2001	2002	2003	2004	2005
$538	$1,176	$832	$202	$1,209

Source: The Boeing Company Form 10-K.

THE TIME VALUE OF MONEY

Before presenting the financial reporting rules for notes receivable and notes payable, this section first develops the principle known as the *time value of money*. You may already be familiar with this principle from your finance courses. If so, the material below will be a refresher. If you are not familiar with time value of money principles, the material below will provide you with the basic rules necessary to understand how notes receivable and notes payable are recorded under GAAP.

The time value of money principle simply says that any cash you receive today is worth more than the same amount of cash received in the future. Conversely, the principle says that any cash payments you make today cost you more than the same amount of cash paid in the future.

Here is an example to illustrate why this is the case. Assume you live in a world with only one interest rate—say 10 percent. Everyone can borrow money from the bank at a 10 percent interest rate, and everyone can invest their money in a savings account and earn interest at 10 percent. Also, to keep things simple, assume that there is no risk. In other words, everyone always repays their loans, and banks never go out of business.

In this assumed world, receiving $1.00 today is the same as receiving $1.10 one year from today. That's because you could put the $1.00 in the savings account and earn interest of 10% × 1.00 = 0.10, so at the end of the year you would have $1.10 in your savings account. Similarly, receiving $1.00 at the end of one year is the same as receiving $0.91 today, since if you received $0.91 today you could put it in the savings account and earn interest of 10% × 0.91 = 0.09, so at the end of the year you would have $1.00 in your savings account. Therefore, the $1.00 you receive in the future is worth less to you than the $1.00 you receive today. The $1.00 received today is worth $1.00 today, whereas the $1.00 received at the end of one year is worth only $0.91 today.

But suppose you are not receiving $1.00; suppose instead that you want to spend $1.00 today. No problem. You can borrow $1.00 from the bank, spend it, and repay the bank at the end of the year. However, you will have to repay the bank $1.10, since the bank will charge you 10 percent interest on the loan. Similarly, if you spend $0.91 today, you will have to repay the bank $1.00—that is, $0.91 principal and $0.09 interest—at the end of one year. This means that $1.00 paid today is worth $1.00 today, whereas $1.00 paid at the end of one year is worth only $0.91 today.

Although this example has used an amount of $1.00, the principle works the same for any amount of cash received or paid. The general principle always holds: Cash received today is worth more than the same amount of cash received in the future, and cash paid today is worth more than the same amount of cash paid in the future.

Also, the principle holds for periods longer than one year. For example, if you receive $1.00 today and put it in the savings account for two years, at the end of two years you will have a balance of $1.21 in the savings account, determined as follows:

Initial principal	$1.00
First-year interest (10%)	0.10
Balance at end of first year	1.10
Second-year interest (10%)	0.11
Balance at end of second year	$1.21

This means that $1.00 received today is worth the same as $1.21 received at the end of two years. Alternatively, it means that $1.00 received at the end of two years is worth only $0.83 today, since you could put $0.83 in the savings account today and end up with $1.00 at the end of two years as follows:

Initial principal	$0.83
First-year interest (10%)	0.08
Balance at end of first year	0.91
Second-year interest (10%)	0.09
Balance at end of second year	$1.00

Notice something else that is important. While $1.00 received at the end of one year was worth $0.91 today, that same $1.00 received at the end of two years is worth only $0.83 today. This illustrates another principle about the time value of money: The longer the time period until cash is received in the future, the smaller is the value of the cash today. Similarly, the longer the time period until cash is paid in the future, the smaller is the value of the cash today.

Now consider what happens if the interest rate changes. Suppose that, instead of a 10 percent interest rate, the interest rate for borrowing and savings accounts is 15 percent. This means that $1.00 received today and deposited in the savings account will be worth $1.15 at the end of one year and $1.32 at the end of two years. Similarly, $1.00 received at the end of one year is only worth $0.87 today, and $1.00 received at the end of two years is only worth $0.76 today, as demonstrated below:

	One Year	Two Years
Initial principal	$0.87	$0.76
First-year interest (15%)	0.13	0.11
Balance at end of first year	$1.00	0.87
Second-year interest (15%)		0.13
Balance at end of second year		$1.00

With a 10 percent interest rate, the value today of $1.00 received at the end of one year was $0.91, and the value today of $1.00 received at the end of two years was $0.83. The corresponding values at a 15 percent interest rate are $0.87 and $0.76, respectively. This result illustrates still another principle about the time value of money: The higher the interest rate, the smaller is the value of cash received in the future relative to the same amount of cash received today. Similarly, the higher the interest rate, the smaller is the value of cash paid in the future relative to the same amount of cash paid today. The table below summarizes the results to this point:

THE VALUE TODAY OF $1.00 RECEIVED OR PAID IN THE FUTURE		
	Interest Rate	
Time Period	10%	15%
1 year	0.91	0.87
2 years	0.83	0.76

The value *today* of cash received or paid at any time is called the *present value* of the cash. Using this terminology, the present value of $1.00 received or paid today is simply $1.00. The present value of $1.00 received or paid *at the end of one year* (with a 10 percent interest rate) is $0.91, and the present value of $1.00 received or paid *at the end of two years* is $0.83.[5]

You can see that the present value of an amount of cash depends on three factors: (1) the amount of cash received or paid, (2) the length of time until the cash is received or paid, and (3) the interest rate.[6]

---

[5] We call the value *in the future* of cash received or paid at any time the *future value* of the cash. Using this terminology, the future value of $1.00 received or paid at the end of one year is simply $1.00, and the future value of $1.00 received or paid at the end of two years is also $1.00. The future value *at the end of one year* of $1.00 received or paid today (with a 10 percent interest rate) is $1.10, and the future value *at the end of two years* of $1.00 received or paid today is $1.21.

[6] In present value computations, the interest rate is referred to as the *discount rate*.

The concept of present value can be expressed mathematically. Let n be the *number* of time periods from today until the future cash receipt or payment. For example, if cash is to be received in one year then $n = 1$, and if cash is to be received in 10 years $n = 10$. Also, n can be expressed in time periods of any length. For example, n can be expressed as a number of days, weeks, months, or semiannual periods. If n is expressed in semiannual periods, then, for cash received at the end of one year, $n = 2$ (that is, two semiannual periods equal one year).

Let i be the *interest rate* that is used in the present value computation. Unlike the earlier example, in the real world there is not one single interest rate but many rates for many different types of loans and borrowers. In present value computations, the interest rate that is used is the interest rate applicable to the particular borrower at the time the loan is entered into. For loans or borrowers with more risk, the interest rate will be higher than for loans or borrowers with less risk.

There is a very important relationship between the interest rate and the length of the time periods (that is, the length of each n) used in present value computations. This is because interest rates are dependent on the length of time over which the interest is calculated. For example, in the earlier computations using the 10 percent interest rate, it was assumed that the 10 percent rate was an *annual interest rate*—that is, the rate of interest earned or paid for one year. However, suppose interest is required to be paid twice a year rather than once a year. Then the interest rate for each semiannual period would be equal to 1/2 of 10 percent, or 5 percent, and n would represent a time period of six months, that is, half of a year. Similarly, if interest is required to be paid each month, then the interest rate for each monthly period would be equal to 1/12 of 10 percent, or 0.83 percent, and n would represent a time period of one month, that is, one-twelfth of a year.

Here are two important rules to remember: (1) in present value computations, *the annual interest rate must always be adjusted to reflect the length of each time period;* (2) in present value computations you should *always express interest rates as decimals rather than percents* (in other words, use 0.08 rather than 8 percent). The following table demonstrates how to convert annual interest rates for use in present value computations:

MATCHING THE INTEREST RATE WITH THE TIME PERIOD IN PRESENT VALUE COMPUTATIONS			
Assume an Annual Interest Rate of:	If Interest Is Paid or Received Every:	Then Divide the Annual Interest Rate by:	To Arrive at the Correct Interest Rate in the Present Value Computation
0.10	Day	365	0.00027
0.10	Week	52	0.00192
0.10	Month	12	0.00833
0.10	Six months	2	0.05000
0.10	Year	1	0.10000

To calculate the present value of any future cash payment or cash receipt, use the following formula:

$$\text{Present value} = (\text{Future cash payment or receipt}) \times \frac{1}{(1 + i)^n}$$

Here are some examples:

EXAMPLES OF THE PRESENT VALUE OF A FUTURE CASH PAYMENT OR RECEIPT				
Future Cash Payment or Receipt	Number of Time Periods	Interest Rate (as a decimal)	Value of $\dfrac{1}{(1 + i)^n}$	Present Value
$ 200	1	0.10	0.909091	$ 181.82
200	1	0.05	0.952381	190.48
200	1	0.15	0.869565	173.91
200	2	0.10	0.826446	165.29
200	3	0.10	0.751315	150.26
200	4	0.10	0.683013	136.60
200	10	0.10	0.385543	77.11
500	12	0.08	0.397114	198.56
1,000	12	0.06	0.496969	496.97
2,000	12	0.05	0.556837	1,113.67
50,000	20	0.11	0.124034	6,201.70
100,000	30	0.12	0.033378	3,337.79
200,000	40	0.13	0.007531	1,506.23
1,000,000	50	0.20	0.000110	109.88

To make the computation of present values easier, many textbooks present tables showing different values for $1/(1 + i)^n$. These tables are usually referred to as present value tables or tables of present value factors. To use the table, simply find the value from the table that corresponds to the interest rate and number of periods you are using, and multiply the table amount by the future cash payment or future cash receipt to get the present value of the payment or receipt.

Present Value of an Annuity

Look at the sample note between CompUSA Inc. and Tandy Corporation shown at the beginning of this chapter. The note calls for 14 semiannual principal payments of $9,714,285.71 each. Suppose you wanted to compute the present value of all of these payments. One approach would be to compute 14 separate present value amounts (that is, one for each payment) and then add them all up. Present values have the property that they can be added together, since they all represent the value *today* of cash received or paid at any time in the future. The present value of a series of payments is simply the sum of the present values of each payment.

There is an easier way to compute present values of a certain kind of payment series called an *annuity*. To be considered an annuity a series of two or more payments must have two characteristics. First, *each payment in the series must be exactly the same amount as all the other payments.* Second, *the length of time between each payment in the series must be the same.*

Let's look at the payments in the CompUSA/Tandy note. First, each payment is exactly the same amount, since all the payments are $9,714,285.71. Second, since the payments are made semiannually (that is, twice a year on June 30 and December 31), the length of time between each payment is the same.[7] Therefore, we can treat this series of payments as an annuity.

The table below computes the present value of the 14 semiannual payments on the CompUSA/Tandy note, using a 10 percent annual interest rate, which corresponds to a 5 percent semiannual interest rate. The present value is equal to $96,158,226.23.

---

[7] The astute reader will notice that there are not exactly the same number of days in each semiannual period, so technically, if interest is computed on a daily basis, rather than a monthly or semiannual basis, the payments on the note are not strictly an annuity. We ignore this small difference in the example.

PRESENT VALUE OF 14 SEMIANNUAL NOTE PAYMENTS AT 10 PERCENT INTEREST

Payment Number	Amount of Payment	n	i	$\dfrac{1}{(1+i)^n}$	Present Value
1	$ 9,714,285.71	1	0.05	0.95238	$ 9,251,700.68
2	9,714,285.71	2	0.05	0.90703	8,811,143.50
3	9,714,285.71	3	0.05	0.86384	8,391,565.24
4	9,714,285.71	4	0.05	0.82270	7,991,966.89
5	9,714,285.71	5	0.05	0.78353	7,611,397.04
6	9,714,285.71	6	0.05	0.74622	7,248,949.56
7	9,714,285.71	7	0.05	0.71068	6,903,761.49
8	9,714,285.71	8	0.05	0.67684	6,575,010.94
9	9,714,285.71	9	0.05	0.64461	6,261,915.18
10	9,714,285.71	10	0.05	0.61391	5,963,728.75
11	9,714,285.71	11	0.05	0.58468	5,679,741.66
12	9,714,285.71	12	0.05	0.55684	5,409,277.77
13	9,714,285.71	13	0.05	0.53032	5,151,693.12
14	9,714,285.71	14	0.05	0.50507	4,906,374.40
Total	$135,999,999.94				$96,158,226.23

That same present value can be computed using the mathematical formula for the present value of an annuity[8] as follows:

$$\text{Present value of ordinary annuity} = \text{Amount of one payment} \times \left[\frac{1 - \dfrac{1}{(1+i)^n}}{i}\right]$$

Using this formula and the facts from the previous example, the present value of the annuity is as follows:

$$\$96,158,226.23 = \$9,714,285.71 \times 9.89864094$$

where

$$\left[\frac{1 - \dfrac{1}{(1+.05)^{14}}}{.05}\right] = 9.89864094$$

As you can see from this example, the present value of an annuity computed using the formula is the same as the sum of the separate present values for each payment.

To make the computation of present values of annuities easier, many textbooks present tables showing different values for

$$\left[\frac{1 - \dfrac{1}{(1+i)^n}}{i}\right]$$

These tables are usually referred to as *present values of ordinary annuities.* To use the table, simply find the value from the table that corresponds to the interest rate and number of periods you are using, and multiply the table amount by the amount of *one* of the annuity payments to get the present value of the annuity.

---

[8] Technically, this is the present value formula for an ordinary annuity in which payments are made or received at the *end* of each period. An alternative type of annuity, called an *annuity due,* has payments made or received at the *beginning* of each period. The formula for an annuity due will be discussed in Chapter 12 in connection with leases.

RECORDING NOTES RECEIVABLE AND PAYABLE

This section investigates the financial reporting treatment of notes receivable and notes payable. For an example, assume that Boeing sells a new airplane to United Airlines on January 1, 2001. The airplane costs $5,000,000, and United gives Boeing a note for the purchase price. This note is represented on Boeing's balance sheet as a note receivable (an asset) and on United's balance sheet as a note payable (a liability).

Here are the terms of the note: principal payments of $1,000,000 each year on December 31, together with interest at a rate of 8 percent. Assume for now that the 8 percent rate is the market interest rate for this type of note. In other words, assume that any other lender would charge United 8 percent for this type of loan.[9] The following schedule shows the payments that Boeing will receive, and United will pay, on the note:

CASH PAYMENTS/COLLECTIONS ON UNITED/BOEING NOTE—8 PERCENT INTEREST				
Payment Number	Date	Principal Payment	Interest Payment	Note Balance
	1/1/2001			$5,000,000
1	12/31/2001	$1,000,000	$ 400,000	4,000,000
2	12/31/2002	1,000,000	320,000	3,000,000
3	12/31/2003	1,000,000	240,000	2,000,000
4	12/31/2004	1,000,000	160,000	1,000,000
5	12/31/2005	1,000,000	80,000	$ —
Total		$5,000,000	$1,200,000	

The interest payments are equal to 8 percent of the outstanding note balance at the beginning of the year. For the first year, interest is equal to $0.08 \times \$5$ million = $400,000. After the first principal payment of $1 million, the note balance decreases to $4 million, so the interest for the second year is equal to $0.08 \times \$4$ million = $320,000.

Here are the entries made by Boeing and United to record the note:

Boeing: Journal Entry to Record Note Receivable			
+/−	Accounts [description of account]	Debit	Credit
+	Note Receivable [balance sheet asset account]	5,000,000	
+	Sales Revenue [income statement revenue account]		5,000,000

United: Journal Entry to Record Note Payable			
+/−	Accounts [description of account]	Debit	Credit
+	Airplane [balance sheet asset account]	5,000,000	
+	Note Payable [balance sheet liability account]		5,000,000

[9] The concept of a market interest rate is an important one for recording notes. You can think of the market rate as the rate that a bank or other commercial lender would normally charge for a loan to a customer with a particular level of risk. Thus, the market rate for a high-risk borrower would be higher than that for a low-risk borrower. For borrowers with very low risk the market rate is sometimes called the *prime rate*. For publicly traded debt, such as corporate bonds, the market rate is set by the buying and selling that occurs in the bond market.

The Note Receivable will be shown as an asset on Boeing's balance sheet. The payments due within one year ($1 million) will be a current asset, while the remaining payments ($4 million) will be a noncurrent asset. The Note Payable will be shown as a liability on United's balance sheet. The payments due within one year ($1 million) will be a current liability, while the remaining payments ($4 million) will be a noncurrent liability.

Here are the entries to record the first payment on the note by United and the receipt of the first payment by Boeing:

	United: Journal Entry to Record First Note Payment		
+/−	**Accounts [description of account]**	**Debit**	**Credit**
−	Note Payable [balance sheet liability account]	1,000,000	
+	Interest Expense [income statement expense account]	400,000	
−	Cash [balance sheet asset account]		1,400,000

	Boeing: Journal Entry to Record Receipt of First Note Payment		
+/−	**Accounts [description of account]**	**Debit**	**Credit**
+	Cash [balance sheet asset account]	1,400,000	
+	Interest Revenue [income statement revenue account]		400,000
−	Note Receivable [balance sheet asset account]		1,000,000

Similar entries would be made each year to record the note payments, interest expense for United, and interest revenue for Boeing. Notice that, although Boeing will receive total payments under the note of $6,200,000 (the principal of $5 million plus interest of $1.2 million), the selling price of the airplane was recorded at only $5,000,000, with the other $1,200,000 recorded as interest revenue. Similarly, although United will actually pay $6,200,000 in cash for the airplane, it records the airplane at the $5,000,000 purchase price, with the other $1,200,000 recorded as interest expense.

You might wonder what difference it makes whether a payment is recorded as interest revenue or sales revenue. The answer is that both the *timing* of revenue or expense as well as the *character* of revenue or expense are affected by how the note is recorded. Notice that Boeing records the principal amount of the note, that is, $5 million, as revenue all in the year 2001, while the interest revenue is recognized over the five-year term of the note in unequal amounts as the principal balance of the note is paid down. On United's side, the principal amount of the note is recorded as an asset, an airplane, that will be depreciated over the estimated useful life of the airplane. If the airplane is expected to be used by United for 10 years, United will recognize depreciation expense over that 10-year period. The interest expense is recognized over the five-year term of the note in unequal amounts that reflect the outstanding principal balance of the note. Thus, the proper treatment between principal and interest affects the timing of the recognition of revenue and expenses.

With respect to the character of the revenue or expense, Boeing will report sales revenue on the first line on its income statement, while interest revenue will be reported under the heading "other income." Also note that the number reported for sales revenue enters into the determination of Boeing's gross profit from selling airplanes, information that is very useful to investors. Information about interest revenue is also useful, but it should not be combined with sales revenue. Similarly, United reports interest expense separately from depreciation expense (which would be included as part of cost of operations) on its income statement.

Here is a computation of the present value of the cash flows associated with the Boeing/United note. Although the principal payments represent an annuity, the interest payments are all of different amounts. Therefore, the present value of each payment must be computed separately. The table below computes the present value of the cash flows assuming an 8 percent annual interest rate.

PRESENT VALUE OF FIVE ANNUAL NOTE PAYMENTS AT 8 PERCENT INTEREST

Payment Number	Amount of Payment	n	i	$\dfrac{1}{(1 + i)^n}$	Present Value
1	$1,400,000.00	1	0.08	0.9259	$1,296,296.30
2	1,320,000.00	2	0.08	0.8573	1,131,687.24
3	1,240,000.00	3	0.08	0.7938	984,351.98
4	1,160,000.00	4	0.08	0.7350	852,634.63
5	1,080,000.00	5	0.08	0.6806	735,029.85
Total	$6,200,000.00				$5,000,000.00

Notice something interesting: The present value of all of the note payments (principal plus interest) is equal to the principal amount of the note (that is, $5 million). This is not a coincidence. Any time the stated interest rate in a note is equal to the interest rate used to compute the present value of note payments, the present value of the payments will equal the principal amount of the note.

This means that when the note receivable is recorded on the balance sheet at $5,000,000, the note is also recorded at its present value. Consider what happens to the book value of the note at the end of the first year. When Boeing received the first annual payment, it recorded interest revenue and also reduced the book value of the note receivable. The book value on Boeing's books, as well as the book value of the note payable on United's books, after the first payment, was $4,000,000. Compare that amount with the present value, at the end of 2001, of the remaining four payments. Here is the computation:

PRESENT VALUE OF FOUR REMAINING NOTE PAYMENTS AT 8 PERCENT INTEREST

Payment Number	Amount of Payment	n	i	$\dfrac{1}{(1 + i)^n}$	Present Value
2	$1,320,000.00	1	0.08	0.9259	$1,222,222.22
3	1,240,000.00	2	0.08	0.8573	1,063,100.14
4	1,160,000.00	3	0.08	0.7938	920,845.40
5	1,080,000.00	4	0.08	0.7350	793,832.24
Total	$4,800,000.00				$4,000,000.00

Notice that the present value of the remaining note payments is equal to $4,000,000, the book value of the note after the first payment. As long as the present value is computed using the same interest rate as that stated in the note, the book value will always equal the present value.

Notes Issued at a Discount

What happens if the two interest rates—the rate stated in the note and the market rate—are not equal? Suppose that, in order to make the sale to United, Boeing offers to finance the purchase with a note at 3 percent interest rather than the market rate of 8 percent. If the note has a stated rate of 3 percent here are the payments:

CASH PAYMENTS/COLLECTIONS ON UNITED/BOEING NOTE—3 PERCENT INTEREST				
Payment Number	Date	Principal Payment	Interest Payment	Note Balance
	1/1/2001			$5,000,000
1	12/31/2001	$1,000,000	$150,000	4,000,000
2	12/31/2002	1,000,000	120,000	3,000,000
3	12/31/2003	1,000,000	90,000	2,000,000
4	12/31/2004	1,000,000	60,000	1,000,000
5	12/31/2005	1,000,000	30,000	0
Total		$5,000,000	$450,000	

The present value of the future cash flows associated with this note can be computed. However, the computation will use an interest rate of 8 percent—the market rate at the time the note is issued—to compute the present value. Notice that this is a different rate from the 3 percent interest rate stated in the note. Here is the present value of the note payments using an 8 percent interest rate in the computation:

PRESENT VALUE OF FIVE ANNUAL NOTE PAYMENTS					
Payment Number	Amount of Payment	n	i	$\dfrac{1}{(1+i)^n}$	Present Value
1	$1,150,000.00	1	0.08	0.9259	$1,064,814.81
2	1,120,000.00	2	0.08	0.8573	960,219.48
3	1,090,000.00	3	0.08	0.7938	865,277.14
4	1,060,000.00	4	0.08	0.7350	779,131.64
5	1,030,000.00	5	0.08	0.6806	701,000.69
Total	$5,450,000.00				$4,370,443.77

Notice that the total of all the payments is now $5,450,000 rather than $6,200,000, reflecting the lower interest rate. Also notice that the present value of these payments ($4,370,443.77) is no longer equal to the principal amount of the note. This means that the value *today* of the total future cash flows associated with the note is less than the $5,000,000 face amount of the note. In other words, if 8 percent is the correct market rate of interest, this note is not really worth $5,000,000; rather, it is worth only $4,370,443.77.

This difference between the principal amount of the note and its present value is called a *discount*. Discounts may arise with respect to both notes receivable and notes payable. A discount will arise whenever the stated interest rate in a note is *less than* the market interest rate, and the market interest rate is used to compute the present value of the note payments. In some cases, notes have no stated interest rate and are referred to as *zero coupon* notes or bonds. Zero coupon notes always have a discount since the market interest rate is always greater than zero.

If the stated interest rate in a note is *greater than* the market interest rate used to compute the present value of the note payments, the present value will be greater than the principal amount of the note, and this difference is referred to as a *premium*. Notes and bonds often have discounts or premiums associated with them, and these discounts and premiums are reflected in the financial accounting treatment of the note.

Under GAAP, a discount on a note receivable is recorded in a contra-asset account called Discount on Notes Receivable. A contra-asset account is an asset account with a credit balance.[10] The contra-asset account for the discount is netted against the Note Receivable asset account balance when the note is presented on the balance sheet. This netting allows the Note Receivable account to record the principal amount of the note, while at the same time allowing the note to be reflected on the balance sheet net of the discount. For notes payable, the discount is a contra-liability (with a debit balance) account called Discount on Notes Payable that is netted against the Note Payable liability account on the balance sheet.

A premium on a note receivable is recorded in an asset account called Premium on Notes Receivable. This account is added to the Note Receivable asset account balance when the note is presented on the balance sheet.[11] For notes payable, the premium is recorded in a liability account called Premium on Notes Payable that is added to the Note Payable liability account balance on the balance sheet.

To illustrate the use of a note discount account, here is how Boeing would record the note receivable if the stated interest rate in the note was 3 percent while the market interest rate at the time the note was issued was 8 percent:

	Boeing: Journal Entry to Record Discount Note Receivable		
+/−	**Accounts [description of account]**	**Debit**	**Credit**
+	Note Receivable [balance sheet asset account]	5,000,000	
+	Sales Revenue [income statement revenue account]		4,370,444
+	Discount [balance sheet contra-asset account—credit balance] ...		629,556

Under GAAP, if the stated interest rate in the note receivable is less than the market interest rate for the note at the time the note is issued, the note must be recorded at the present value of the future cash flows rather than at the principal or face amount. In the above example, the note receivable will be reported on Boeing's balance sheet at an amount equal to the balance in the Note Receivable account ($5,000,000) minus the balance in the Discount account ($629,556). The net of these two amounts is equal to $4,370,444, the present value of the note payments computed using the market interest rate of 8 percent.

Recording notes receivable in this way (using the present value of the future payments rather than the principal or face amount) is an attempt by accountants to report the substance of the transaction rather than its form. By accepting an interest rate on the note that is less than the market rate, Boeing is not really receiving $5,000,000 of *value* from United, and it would be misleading to users of Boeing's financial statements to record the sales price of the airplane at $5,000,000. Recording the note at its present value results in a sales price of $4,370,444, which is the present value of the future note payments at the market interest rate of 8 percent.

In addition to recording the correct sales revenue for Boeing (and the correct airplane cost for United), recording the present value of the note also results in Boeing recognizing interest revenue (as well as United recognizing interest expense) at the market rate of 8 percent. Recognizing interest revenue and expense in this manner is called the *effective interest rate method*. Under GAAP, interest revenue and expense on discount notes must be recognized using this method.

---

[10] One helpful way to think of a contra-asset account is as a negative asset, although there is really no such thing as a negative asset in the real world, just as there is no such thing as a negative number.

[11] This type of account is known as an *adjunct account.*

Here is how Boeing would recognize interest and principal payments on the collection of the 3 percent note receivable where the book value is equal to the principal amount less the discount:

RECORDING INTEREST ON 3 PERCENT NOTE AT 8 PERCENT MARKET INTEREST RATE

Payment Number	Date	Total Payment	8 Percent Interest	Reduction in Book Value	Book Value
	1/1/01				$4,370,443.77
1	12/31/01	$1,150,000.00	$ 349,635.50	$ 800,364.50	3,570,079.28
2	12/31/02	1,120,000.00	285,606.34	834,393.66	2,735,685.62
3	12/31/03	1,090,000.00	218,854.85	871,145.15	1,864,540.47
4	12/31/04	1,060,000.00	149,163.24	910,836.76	953,703.70
5	12/31/05	1,030,000.00	76,296.30	953,703.70	0.00
Total		$5,450,000.00	$1,079,556.23	$4,370,443.77	

Under the effective interest rate method, interest revenue for Boeing (or interest expense for United) is computed by multiplying the book value of the note at the beginning of the period by the interest rate that was used to compute the present value—in this case, 8 percent. The interest revenue (and expense) for the first year is therefore $0.08 \times \$4,370,443.77 = \$349,635.50$. Here is how the interest would be recorded by Boeing:

Boeing: Journal Entry to Record Receipt of First Note Payment

+/−	Accounts [description of account]	Debit	Credit
+	Cash [balance sheet asset account]	1,150,000	
−	Discount [balance sheet contra-asset account—credit balance]	199,635	
+	Interest Revenue [income statement revenue account]		349,635
−	Note Receivable [balance sheet asset account]		1,000,000

Notice that the Note Receivable account is reduced by the $1,000,000 principal payment required under the terms of the note, so that the balance in the Note Receivable account is $4,000,000 after the payment. The Discount account is debited (reduced) by the difference between the cash interest received by Boeing ($150,000) and the interest revenue computed under the effective interest rate method ($349,635), or $199,635. The balance in the Discount account is now $629,556 − $199,635 = $429,921. When the debit-balance asset account Note Receivable is netted against the credit-balance contra-asset Discount account, the net balance is $4,000,000 − $429,921 = $3,570,079. This is the same as the book value of the note in the interest amortization schedule above.

Notice that Boeing only received $150,000 of interest in cash, but it recorded interest revenue of $349,635. The use of a discount allows the recognition of more interest revenue than the interest stated in the note. Recall that the value of the note that Boeing received was only $4,370,444. However, by the time the note is paid off, Boeing will have received $5,000,000 in principal payments. The excess of these principal payments over the present value of the note represents additional interest to Boeing and is recognized through the use of the effective interest rate method.

Here is a schedule showing the collection of the rest of the interest payments, the reduction of the Discount account (called *amortization* of the Discount), and the net book value of the note on Boeing's balance sheet:

	AMORTIZATION OF DISCOUNT ON NOTE RECEIVABLE				
Payment Number	Date	Total Interest	Cash Interest	Discount Amortized	Discount Balance
	1/1/01				$629,556
1	12/31/01	$ 349,635	$150,000	$199,635	429,921
2	12/31/02	285,606	120,000	165,606	264,315
3	12/31/03	218,855	90,000	128,855	135,460
4	12/31/04	149,163	60,000	89,163	46,297
5	12/31/05	76,297	30,000	46,297	0
Total		$1,079,556	$450,000	$629,556	

Here is a schedule showing how the book value of the note—that is, the Note Receivable minus the Discount—changes over the term of the note:

	NET BOOK VALUE OF NOTE RECEIVABLE			
Payment Number	Date	Note Receivable (debit)	Discount (credit)	Net Book Value
	1/1/01	$5,000,000	$629,556	$4,370,444
1	12/31/01	4,000,000	429,921	3,570,079
2	12/31/02	3,000,000	264,315	2,735,685
3	12/31/03	2,000,000	135,460	1,864,540
4	12/31/04	1,000,000	46,297	953,703
5	12/31/05	0	0	0

Notice that the net book value resulting from the amortization of the Discount is the same (except for rounding differences) as the book value in the interest computation table.

A Real-Life Example

The present value principles and financial reporting rules discussed above can be applied to a real-life example. Presented below is some information from the financial statements of Intercel, Inc., a wireless telecommunications company. On April 16, 1996, Intercel issued notes payable that had a maturity date of May 1, 2006, and a principal amount of $360 million. The notes paid no interest until May 1, 2001, at which time they began to pay interest each November 1 and May 1, with the first interest payment on November 1, 2001. Intercel received a total of $200 million on the sale of the notes. Since $200 million is the amount that investors were willing to pay for these notes, this amount represents the present value of the future cash flows represented by the notes. The difference between the $360 million face amount and the $200 million present value of the notes represents a discount.

INTERCEL, INC. 4. Long-Term Obligations		
	December 31, 1996	December 31, 1995
12% Senior Discount Notes due May 2006	217.3	0.0

On April 16, 1996, the Company issued $360 million aggregate principal amount at maturity of the Company's 12% Senior Discount Notes due 2006 (the "April Notes") for approximately $200 million gross proceeds in a public offering.

The April Notes will fully accrete to face value on May 1, 2001, at which time they will bear interest, payable in cash, at a rate of 12% per annum on each May 1 and November 1, commencing November 1, 2001.

Unamortized original issue discount on the April Notes is being amortized using an effective interest rate of 12%.

Source: Intercel, Inc. Form 10-K.

The reason a discount is necessary for these notes is they do not pay interest for the first five years (from 1996 to 2001). Therefore, the present value of the future cash flows represented by the notes is less than the principal amount of $360 million. The statement that "the April Notes will fully accrete to face value on May 1, 2001" means that the discount is being amortized.[12] The amortization of the discount is based on an effective interest rate of 12 percent, which represents the market interest rate at the time the notes were issued.

Here is how the present value of the notes is computed. Since the notes will eventually pay interest each May 1 and November 1, we use a semiannual (that is, twice a year) interest rate of 6 percent (1/2 × 12 percent annual rate) and a present value period six months in length. According to Intercel, the discount will be fully amortized and the book value of the notes will be equal to the face amount of $360 million by May 1, 2001. From May 1, 1996, to May 1, 2001, is a period of five years, or 10 semiannual periods. Therefore, to compute the present value of the notes on May 1, 1996, we would use $i = 0.06$ and $n = 10$ in the present value formula.

There is one additional adjustment that is necessary before the present value of the notes can be computed. The notes were issued on April 16 rather than May 1, and the additional half-month time period must be accounted for in the computation. Since the time period for the computation is six months, the additional half-month represents 1/12 of a six-month time period, or 0.0833. Therefore, the present value will be computed for $360 million at $i = 0.06$ and $n = 10.0833$. Putting these values into the formula results in a present value of the notes of

$$\$360 \text{ million} \times \frac{1}{(1 + .06)^{10.0833}} = \$200 \text{ million}$$

This is the amount of cash that investors would be willing to pay on April 16, 1996, to purchase notes that had a value of $360 million on May 1, 2001, using a 12 percent annual interest rate with interest computed semiannually.

Thus when Intercel issued the notes it would have made the following journal entry:

	Intercel: Journal Entry to Record Discount Note Payable (in millions)		
+/−	**Accounts [description of account]**	**Debit**	**Credit**
+	Cash [balance sheet asset account]	200	
+	Discount [balance sheet contra-liability account—debit balance]	160	
+	Notes Payable [balance sheet liability account]		360

Notice that in the Intercel financial statement information presented above the book value of these notes on December 31, 1996, is $217.3 million rather than the $200 million issue price. This is because a portion of the discount has been amortized from April 16, 1996, through December 31, 1996. This discount amortization represents interest (at 12 percent) on the notes over that time period, even though no interest will actually be paid until the notes begin to bear interest in 2001. Here is how the discount amortization for 1996 would be computed:

---

[12] The term *accretion* means the gradual increase in the book value of the notes due to the amortization of the discount.

AMORTIZATION OF DISCOUNT ON INTERCEL, INC., NOTES (IN MILLIONS)					
Time Period	Number of Semiannual Periods	Semiannual Interest Rate	Amount of Interest Expense	Discount	Book Value
At issue date				160.0	200.0
Apr. 16–May 1	0.083	0.06	1.0	159.0	201.0
May 1–Nov. 1	1.000	0.06	12.1	146.9	213.1
Nov. 1–Dec. 31	0.333	0.06	4.3	142.7	217.3

The numbers on the table have been rounded to one decimal place. Intercel would make the following entry to recognize interest expense and discount amortization at December 31, 1996:

Journal Entry to Record Interest Expense and Discount Amortization (in millions)			
+/−	Accounts [description of account]	Debit	Credit
+	Interest Expense [income statement expense account]	17.3	
−	Discount [balance sheet contra-liability account—debit balance] . . .		17.3

The balance in the Discount account at the end of 1996 is $160 − $17.3 = $142.7, and the book value of the notes payable is equal to $360 − $142.7 = $217.3.

Here is a table showing the amortization of the entire $160 million of the Discount over the time period April 16, 1996, to May 1, 2001. As you can see from this table, the book value of the notes will equal $360 million on May 1, 2001, when the notes will begin to pay interest at 12 percent. Notice that the total of all the interest expense recorded from the amortization ($160 million) is equal to the total amount of the Discount.

AMORTIZATION OF DISCOUNT ON INTERCEL, INC., NOTES (IN MILLIONS)						
Year	Time Period	Number of Semiannual Periods	Semiannual Interest Rate	Amount of Interest Expense	Discount	Book Value
1996	At issue date				160.0	200.0
1996	Apr. 16–May 1	0.083	0.06	1.0	159.0	201.0
1996	May 1–Nov. 1	1.000	0.06	12.1	146.9	213.1
1996–97	Nov. 1–May 1	1.000	0.06	12.8	134.2	225.8
1997	May 1–Nov. 1	1.000	0.06	13.6	120.6	239.4
1997–98	Nov. 1–May 1	1.000	0.06	14.4	106.2	253.8
1998	May 1–Nov. 1	1.000	0.06	15.2	91.0	269.0
1998–99	Nov. 1–May 1	1.000	0.06	16.1	74.9	285.1
1999	May 1–Nov. 1	1.000	0.06	17.1	57.8	302.2
1999–00	Nov. 1–May 1	1.000	0.06	18.1	39.6	320.4
2000	May 1–Nov. 1	1.000	0.06	19.2	20.4	339.6
2000–01	Nov. 1–May 1	1.000	0.06	20.4	0.0	360.0
Total				160.0		

The Intercel note discussed above is an example of a zero coupon note. The term *zero coupon* refers to the fact that the stated, or coupon, interest rate on the notes is zero. (In the case in the Intercel note, the zero interest rate applies until May 1, 2001, at which time the notes will begin to pay interest at 12 percent.) As you can see from the above table, despite the fact that the notes pay no interest, investors still earn interest on the notes, and the issuing company still incurs interest expense. However, with zero coupon notes all of the interest comes in the form of the discount. The investors pay $200 million for the notes initially, but will receive $360 million at the maturity date. The additional $160 million (the discount) represents interest on the notes.

Notes Issued at a Premium

A discount on a note arises in cases where the stated interest rate on the note is less than the market interest rate at the time the note is issued. However, it is also possible for the stated interest rate on the note to be *greater* than the market interest rate at the time the note is issued. In that case, a premium would result. With a note premium, the book value of the note is greater than the face amount of the note.

Just as a note discount represents additional interest expense to the issuer (and additional interest revenue to the purchaser), a note premium represents a *reduction* in interest expense or interest revenue. For example, Boeing reports an 8 3/8 percent note with a face amount of $174 million due February 15, 2001, with a book value at December 31, 1999, of $177 million. This means that the balance in the Premium account at December 31, 1999, was $3 million. This $3 million balance in the Premium account was completely amortized during 2000, so that the book value of this particular note at December 31, 2000, was equal to the face amount of $174 million.

Assume that Boeing made two semiannual interest payments on this note during the year 2000. Each interest payment would be equal to half the stated annual interest rate (1/2 × 8 3/8 percent = 4.1875 percent) times the face amount of the note, or 0.041875 × $174 million = $7.3 million. Thus, the total payments for interest for 2000 would be 2 × $7.3 million, or $14.6 million. However, Boeing will not recognize $14.6 million of interest expense for the year, because the $3 million amortization of the premium reduces the interest expense to $11.6 million.[13]

Accrual of Interest Receivable or Payable

Up to this point the discussion has been simplified by assuming that interest paid on notes is paid at the end of the accounting period. However, it is usually the case that interest on notes is payable at some date other than year-end. In that case, an accounting accrual is necessary to record interest receivable or interest payable at the end of the year.

To illustrate, consider the Intercel notes discussed above. On May 1, 2001, the notes begin to accrue interest at the 12 percent stated interest rate. This means that every six months on November 1 and May 1, Intercel must make an interest payment equal to $360 million × 0.06 = $21.6 million. Since Intercel's year-end is December 31, the interest that accrues on the notes from November 1 until December 31 each year must be recorded as interest payable at year-end. The interest expense from November 1 through December 31 represents two months of the six-month interest payment that is due the following May 1. Since the interest due May 1 is $21.6 million, Intercel needs to accrue 2/6 × $21.6 million = $7.2 million at year-end. Here is the entry:

+/−	Journal Entry to Record Interest Expense and Interest Payable (in millions)		
	Accounts [description of account]	**Debit**	**Credit**
+	Interest Expense [income statement expense account]	7.2	
+	Interest Payable [balance sheet liability account]		7.2

[13] The entry to record the amortization of the premium would be to debit (reduce) the Premium account and credit (reduce) Interest Expense.

On the following May 1, when Intercel makes its normal semiannual interest payment, it will make the following entry:

	Journal Entry to Record Semiannual Interest Payment (in millions)		
+/−	**Accounts [description of account]**	**Debit**	**Credit**
+	Interest Expense [income statement expense account]	14.4	
−	Interest Payable [balance sheet liability account]	7.2	
−	Cash [balance sheet asset account]		21.6

RECORDING BONDS PAYABLE

The rest of this chapter focuses on financial reporting for a particular type of note called a *bond payable*. Large publicly traded companies, exempt organizations, and government entities sell bonds to the public as a way to finance their activities, and the bonds are often traded on secondary markets such as the New York Bond Exchange. This section examines in more detail the financial reporting rules relating to corporate bonds payable.

Characteristics of Bonds

There are many different types of bonds with different characteristics. To make it easier to learn the financial reporting rules for bonds, it is assumed for purposes of this section that bonds have the following characteristics:

1. Bonds have a face amount (that is, a principal or maturity value) of $1,000 each.
2. Bonds have a stated annual interest rate (called the *coupon rate*), which may be zero.
3. All of the principal is payable on the maturity date of the bond.
4. Bonds pay interest semiannually.
5. Each semiannual interest payment is equal to one-half of the stated interest rate times the face amount of the bond.

Consider the information about Boeing's debt presented at the beginning of this chapter. Notice that for each debt issue, the following information is given: the face amount, the stated interest rate, the maturity date, and the book value.

Cash Flows Associated with Bonds

Bonds have two different types of cash flows associated with them. First, bonds pay interest semiannually at the stated rate. This series of interest payments represents an annuity for purposes of computing the present value of the cash flows represented by the bond. Second, the repayment of the bond principal at the maturity date represents the payment of a single sum in the future to the holders of the bonds. Therefore, to compute the present value of a bond requires two computations: one for the present value of the interest payments and another for the present value of the principal. The present value of the bond is the sum of these present values.

Consider as an example the Boeing $250 million 7.25 percent debt due June 15, 2025, with a book value of $247 million at December 31, 2000, and 1999 (refer to the schedule of Boeing's debt at the beginning of this chapter). Assume that these are bonds issued June 15, 1995, with a 30-year maturity. Also, assume that when the bonds were issued the market rate of interest for Boeing's debt was 7.35

percent, which is higher than the bonds' stated interest rate of 7.25 percent. This means that, if investors required a return of 7.35 percent for an investment in Boeing's debt, they would be unwilling to buy Boeing's bonds and only receive interest of 7.25 percent. To sell the bonds, Boeing had to lower the issue price of the bonds below the face amount of $1,000 per bond, resulting in a discount. We can compute the selling price of the bonds (and therefore, the bond discount) by computing the present value of the cash flows reflected by Boeing's bonds. In making this present value computation, here is an important point: *Always use the market rate of interest,* rather than the stated rate.

The cash flows associated with the Boeing bonds are as follows. First, investors will receive 60 semiannual interest payments equal to half the *stated interest rate* times the face amount of the bonds. Half the stated interest rate is 1/2 × 0.0725, or 0.03625. Multiplying this by the face amount of a single bond means each bond will pay semiannual interest payments of $36.25. Since Boeing sold 250,000 bonds, the total cash interest payments for all of the bonds is 250,000 × $36.25 = $9,062,500. (This can also be computed as $250,000,000 face amount × 0.03625 interest rate = $9,062,500 total interest payments.)

Since the 60 semiannual interest payments are all the same amount, their present value can be computed by using the formula for the present value of an annuity. The number of periods is 60, and the interest rate is half of the *market interest rate* (1/2 × 0.0735), or 0.03675. Using these values in the formula and multiplying by the total amount of one interest payment ($9,062,500) results in the present value of the interest payments equal to

$$\$9{,}062{,}500 \times \left[\frac{1 - \frac{1}{(1 + 0.03675)^{60}}}{0.03675} \right] = \$218{,}314{,}170$$

At the maturity date of June 15, 2025, Boeing will repay the principal amount of $250,000,000 to the bondholders. The present value of this principal payment at the end of 60 semiannual periods using a semiannual interest rate of 0.03675 is equal to

$$\$250{,}000{,}000 \times \frac{1}{(1 + 0.03675)^{60}} = \$28{,}674{,}600$$

Adding together the present values of the interest payments and the principal payment gives the present value of the Boeing bond ($246,988,770), assuming an annual market interest rate of 7.35 percent and interest computed semiannually. This is the amount that investors would be willing to pay for the bonds. If investors paid $246,988,770 for the $250,000,000 face amount of Boeing bonds, they will earn an interest rate of 7.35 percent over the 30-year life of the bonds.

Here is how Boeing would record the sale of the bonds:

	Boeing: Journal Entry to Record Discount Bonds Payable		
+/−	**Accounts [description of account]**	**Debit**	**Credit**
+	Cash [balance sheet asset account]	246,988,770	
+	Discount [balance sheet contra-liability account—debit balance]	3,011,230	
+	Bonds Payable [balance sheet liability account]		250,000,000

To record interest expense for the first interest payment (December 15, 1995), Boeing would use the effective interest rate method. Interest expense is equal to the market interest rate *at the time the bonds are issued*[14] times the book value of the bonds at the beginning of the period. Therefore, for the first interest payment, the interest expense is $0.03675 \times \$246,988,770 = \$9,076,837$.

Boeing would record this interest expense with the following journal entry. (Recall that the cash payments for interest total $9,062,500 semiannually.)

+/−	Journal Entry to Record Interest Expense and Discount Amortization		
	Accounts [description of account]	Debit	Credit
+	Interest Expense [income statement expense account]	9,076,837	
−	Discount [balance sheet contra-liability account—debit balance]		14,337
−	Cash [balance sheet asset account]		9,062,500

Boeing will continue to pay interest in the amount of $9,062,500 each six months and will continue to record interest expense and discount amortization. As the discount is amortized, the book value of the bonds gradually increases, which means the amount of interest expense recorded under the effective interest rate method will also gradually increase. At the maturity date, the discount will be fully amortized, meaning the balance in the Discount account will be zero, and the book value of the bonds will equal their face value of $250,000,000.

Here is a table showing the interest expense and discount amortization from the issuance of the bonds through December 31, 2000:

	INTEREST EXPENSE AND DISCOUNT AMORTIZATION FOR BOEING BONDS				
Date	Interest Expense 3.675%	Cash Interest	Amortize Discount	Book Value of Discount	Book Value of Bonds
Jun-95				$3,011,230	$246,988,770
Dec-95	$9,076,837	$9,062,500	$14,337	2,996,893	247,003,107
Jun-96	9,077,364	9,062,500	14,864	2,982,029	247,017,971
Dec-96	9,077,910	9,062,500	15,410	2,966,618	247,033,382
Jun-97	9,078,477	9,062,500	15,977	2,950,641	247,049,359
Dec-97	9,079,064	9,062,500	16,564	2,934,077	247,065,923
Jun-98	9,079,673	9,062,500	17,173	2,916,905	247,083,095
Dec-98	9,080,304	9,062,500	17,804	2,899,101	247,100,899
Jun-99	9,080,958	9,062,500	18,458	2,880,643	247,119,357
Dec-99	9,081,636	9,062,500	19,136	2,861,507	247,138,493
Jun-00	9,082,340	9,062,500	19,840	2,841,667	247,158,333
Dec-00	9,083,069	9,062,500	20,569	2,821,098	247,178,902

In many cases, bonds are sold between interest payment dates. Because every semiannual interest payment, including the first one, is exactly the same amount (in the Boeing example, each payment is $9,062,500) and represents six months of interest, the initial purchaser who buys a bond between interest payment dates will receive too much interest on the first interest payment date. To counter this effect, the price that the purchaser pays to the company for a bond sold between

---

[14] This is an important point. Market interest rates change daily, but under GAAP, interest expense continues to be computed based on the market interest rate at the time the bonds were issued.

interest dates also includes a payment that represents accrued interest at the purchase date. In effect, a portion of the cash the issuing company receives from the purchaser represents interest payable, which is returned to the purchaser as part of the initial semiannual interest payment.

EARLY RETIREMENT OF BONDS

Since bonds are usually traded on secondary markets, it is possible for companies to buy back their bonds prior to the maturity date. Buying back bonds is simply a way for the company to repay the debt early. However, it is usually the case that when a company buys back its own bonds, the price it pays is not the same as the book value of the bonds on the company's balance sheet. This is because the current price of the company's bonds is based on the *current* market interest rate, whereas the book value of the bonds is based on the amortization of bond discount or premium using the market interest rate *at the time the bonds were issued*.

The effective interest rate method of recognizing interest expense ensures that the book value of the bonds will always equal the present value of the remaining cash flows from the bonds, but only using an interest rate equal to the market interest rate at the time the bonds were issued. Therefore, if interest rates change from the time the bonds are issued until the time they are repurchased by the company, the book value of the bonds will no longer equal the present value of future cash flows from the bonds based on the current market interest rate.

For example, consider the Intercel notes discussed earlier in the chapter. Recall that on May 1, 2001, the notes had a book value of $360 million. The stated interest rate from that point was 12 percent, payable semiannually on November 1 and May 1. However, assume that the market interest rate for notes of this type increases to 13 percent by May 1, 2001. (This increase could be caused by macroeconomic factors affecting overall interest rates in the economy, or it could represent investors' perceptions that Intercel was more risky and therefore required a higher interest rate.)

Since investors will require an interest rate of 13 percent from Intercel notes, while the notes pay interest only at the stated rate of 12 percent, investors will pay less for the notes, resulting in a decrease in the market price below the book value of $360 million. Therefore, if Intercel repurchased its bonds in the market, it could repurchase the bonds for less than $360 million. Repurchasing the bonds for less than their book value results in a gain on the repurchase. Similarly, repurchasing bonds for an amount in excess of book value (which would occur if market interest rates had decreased since the bonds were issued) would result in a loss on the repurchase. Prior to 2003, this gain or loss on the repurchase of bonds was treated as an extraordinary item under GAAP.

REPORTING NOTES IN OTHER COUNTRIES

The financial reporting rules in other countries are similar to the U.S. rules for notes receivable and notes payable. In most cases, notes with stated interest rates below or above market rates are recorded at a discount or premium, and the discount or premium is amortized as part of interest expense. The main difference between U.S. financial reporting and reporting in other countries has to do with the amount of information provided about the notes.

For example, here is the information disclosed by Reed Elsevier with respect to long-term debt:

23. Creditors: Amounts Falling Due after More than One Year

	2000	1999
Other loans repayable		
Within one to two years	4	3
Within two to five years	205	81
After five years	402	279
Obligations under finance leases (see note 25)	12	14
	623	377
Other creditors	27	14
Taxation	197	208
Accruals and deferred income	26	21
Total	873	620

Source: Reed Elsevier Form 20-F.

Compare this with the details provided by Boeing with respect to its notes payable, shown at the beginning of this chapter. The Reed Elsevier disclosure provides much less information. As part of its Form 20-F filed with the U.S. Securities and Exchange Commission, Reed Elsevier included additional disclosures to comply with U.S. reporting standards. Here is the additional U.S. disclosure related to long-term debt:

30. **U.S. Accounting Information (continued)**
Borrowings

	Currency	Year-end Interest Rates	2000	1999
Other loans and finance leases				
Private placement, 2000	U.S. dollar	9.71%	—	62
Public notes, 2000	U.S. dollar	6.63	—	93
Private placement, 2003	U.S. dollar	8.50	84	77
Public notes, 2005	U.S. dollar	7.00	101	93
Loans notes, 2005	Sterling	6.05	20	—
Swiss domestic bond, 2007	U.S. dollar	7.05	201	—
Private placement, 2023	U.S. dollar	6.63	101	93
Public debentures, 2025	U.S. dollar	7.50	101	93
Finance leases	Various	Various	17	18
Miscellaneous	Euro	Various	7	10
Total			632	539

Source: Reed Elsevier Form 20-F.

Here is some information about long-term liabilities from the annual report of Nokia Corporation, a Finnish maker of cellular telephones. Nokia prepares its financial statements using International Accounting Standards (IAS) and presents its results in millions of euros (EURm). The principal amounts of bonds are given in British pounds (GBP) or Finnish marks (FIM). The bond information provided by Nokia is quite similar to that provided by U.S. firms.

18.   **Long-Term Liabilities**

	Outstanding Dec. 31, 2000 (EURm)	Repayment Date beyond Five Years (EURm)
Long-term loans are repayable as follows:		
Loans from financial institutions	62	—
Pension loans	12	12
Other long-term finance loans	99	—
Deferred tax liabilities	69	—
Other long-term liabilities	69	58
	311	70

The long-term liabilities as of December 31, 2000 mature as follows:

	(EURm)	
2001	47	13.1%
2002	64	17.9
2003	31	8.7
2004	66	18.4
2005	—	—
Thereafter	150	41.9
	358	100.0%

Bonds	Million	Interest	2000 (EURm)	1999 (EURm)
1989–2004	40.0 GBP	11.375%	66	79
1993–2003	150.0 FIM	Floating	25	25
1996–2001	280.0 FIM	7.000%	—	47
			91	151

Source: Nokia annual report.

USING INFORMATION ABOUT NOTES TO MAKE DECISIONS

People use information about notes in two basic ways. First, information about notes payable is useful in making decisions about the riskiness of a firm. Too much debt increases the likelihood that the firm will at some point be unable to make required interest or principal payments, or both, which could result in bankruptcy. For example, the Boeing $174 million 8 3/8 percent note that was discussed earlier required the repayment of principal on February 15, 2001. Failure to make this payment on time could have possibly resulted in Boeing's bankruptcy.

The second main use of information about notes receivable and notes payable is in estimating future cash flows of a company. This chapter began by arguing that, since notes represent contractual rights or obligations to receive or make future cash flows at specified times, they are the most basic types of assets and liabilities. With enough information about a company's notes, users can make accurate projections of the amount and timing of future cash flows related to principal and interest payments. Thus, information about notes has the desirable feature of being both relevant and reliable.

Summary

This chapter focuses on financial reporting rules for one of the most basic types of assets or liabilities: a note receivable or note payable. Notes are reported as assets on the balance sheet of the lender and liabilities on the balance sheet of the borrower, and notes can be current, noncurrent, or partly current and partly noncurrent. Notes usually have a stated interest rate, but some notes do not pay interest and are known as zero coupon notes. Debentures and bonds are types of notes that are publicly traded on secondary markets and tend to be long term. Notes are used by corporations and also by not-for-profit organizations and governmental entities.

The basic accounting treatment for notes depends on whether the stated interest rate in the note is equivalent to the market interest rate of the borrower at the time the note is issued. If it is, then the note is recorded at its principal (face) amount. If the stated interest rate is different from the market interest rate of the borrower at the time the note is issued, a discount or premium must be recorded so that the net book value of the note reflects the present value of the future cash payments required under the note.

When a note is recorded with a discount or premium, interest revenue or interest expense is computed using the effective interest rate method. Under this method, interest expense (or revenue) for a period is equal to the market interest rate at the time the note was issued multiplied by the net book value of the note at the beginning of the period. Recording interest in this way requires amortization of the discount or premium, and this amortization results in the net book value of the note (computed using the original market interest rate) always being equal to the present value of the remaining cash flows.

The present value of a bond consists of the present value of the interest payments (an annuity) plus the present value of the principal payment due at the maturity date. Like other types of notes, bonds require a discount or premium if the stated interest rate in the bond differs from the market interest rate at the time the bonds are issued.

Since market interest rates change over time, and since the book value of a bond always reflects the present value of future cash flows using the market interest rate in effect when the bond was issued, the current market value of a bond will usually differ from its book value. When corporations repurchase their bonds in the bond market, this results in a gain or loss, and prior to 2003 this gain or loss was treated as an extraordinary item.

Appendix 5–1

Transfers of Notes and Accounts Receivable

A company may not want to wait until the operating cycle is complete to receive cash from its customers. In such a case, the company is able to convert notes or accounts receivable into immediate cash by transferring the receivables to a lender. The lender provides immediate cash for the receivables and charges the company a fee (or finance charge) that is similar to interest.

There are two main reasons why companies transfer their receivables and incur the additional expense. First, the company may simply need cash immediately, and transferring receivables may be the lowest cost way of obtaining cash. Second, the company may lack expertise in managing and collecting receivables and be willing to pay a fee to transfer this collection responsibility to someone better able to manage it.

Transfers of receivables take two general forms: a *sale* transaction, also called *factoring*; or a *borrowing* transaction, also called an *assignment*. In a sale transaction, the lender agrees to buy the receivables from the selling company. In a borrowing transaction, the lender agrees to make a loan to the borrowing company, with the receivable providing security, or collateral, for the loan.

In addition to these two different legal forms of transfer, that is, sale or borrowing, transfers of receivables also have one of two characteristics: They are either *with recourse* or *without recourse*. A transfer with recourse means that the transferring company remains liable to the lender in the event the lender is unable to collect the transferred receivables. This means that the transferring company retains the risk that the receivables will not be collected. A transfer without recourse, on the other hand, means that the lender assumes the responsibility, and risk, for collection of the transferred receivables.

The accounting treatment for sales and borrowing transactions is quite different. Assume a company transfers $100,000 of notes receivable to a lender for $95,000 cash, and that the lender charges a fee equal to 5 percent of the face amount of the transferred receivables. For a transfer treated as a sale, the journal entry to record this transaction would look like this:

	Journal Entry to Record Sale of Notes Receivable		
+/−	**Accounts [description of account]**	**Debit**	**Credit**
+	Cash [balance sheet asset account]	95,000	
+	Loss on Sale [income statement expense account]	5,000	
−	Notes Receivable [balance sheet asset account]		100,000

For the same transfer treated as a borrowing transaction, the journal entry would look like this:

	Journal Entry to Record Borrowing against Notes Receivable		
+/−	**Accounts [description of account]**	**Debit**	**Credit**
+	Cash [balance sheet asset account]	95,000	
+	Finance Charge [income statement expense account]	5,000	
+	Notes Payable [balance sheet liability account]		100,000

Notice the difference in these two entries. In the first entry, an asset (cash) is increased and an asset (notes receivable) is decreased. In the second entry, an asset (cash) is increased and a liability (notes payable) is also increased. While economically there may be little difference in these transactions, the financial statement effect can be important. The second entry, by increasing a current liability of the firm (notes payable), makes the firm's balance sheet look more risky. The ratio of current assets to current liabilities may decrease, and the ratio of debt to equity may increase. Therefore, managers who are concerned with the amount of liabilities reported on the firm's balance sheet would prefer to have the transfer of accounts receivable recorded as a sale transaction.

However, a sale of receivables *with recourse* is economically very similar to a borrowing transaction, since the transferor company remains at risk with respect to the transferred receivables. One desirable feature of a set of financial reporting standards is that transactions that are economically similar should be reported in a similar way on companies' financial statements. Therefore, under GAAP a sale of receivables with recourse will be recorded as a borrowing transaction *unless* all of the following conditions are met:

1. The transferor surrenders control of the future economic benefits embodied in the receivables.
2. The transferor's obligation under the recourse provisions can be reasonably estimated.

3. The transferee cannot require the transferor to repurchase the receivables except pursuant to the recourse provisions.

If all three of these conditions are met, a sale of accounts receivable with recourse may be accounted for as a sale. However, if the three conditions are not met, the sale must be accounted for as a borrowing transaction and a liability recorded for the note payable to the lender.

Discussion Questions

1. Explain the characteristics of a note. Are all of these necessary in every note? Which features are essential?
2. How can the same note be recorded on the balance sheets of two different companies at the same time?
3. What is meant by the *present value* of a cash payment?
4. What factors determine a payment's present value?
5. Explain how the interest rate used in a present value computation is related to the length of the time period between interest payments.
6. Explain how the present value of a payment changes as the length of time until payment changes.
7. Explain how the present value of a payment changes as the interest rate changes.
8. Give the formula for computing the present value of $1.
9. What is an annuity? Give the formula for computing the present value of an annuity of $1.
10. Explain how notes are recorded under GAAP.
11. Explain the accounting treatment for notes with no interest or interest rates below market.
12. Explain how interest income or interest expense on notes are recorded under GAAP.
13. What is a discount? What is the accounting treatment for discounts?
14. What is a premium? What is the accounting treatment for premiums?
15. How is the present value of a bond computed?
16. How are bonds payable recorded under GAAP?
17. Explain what is meant by the amortization of a discount or premium. What method is used to compute the amortization under GAAP?
18. Explain the accounting treatment for bonds that are retired early.

Problems

1. On January 1, a company borrows $400,000 and gives a note with an interest rate of 6 percent (equal to the current market rate). The note will be repaid in eight *equal annual principal payments, plus interest,* with each payment due on December 31 each year.
   a. What is the interest expense each year?
   b. Assume the note will be paid off in eight equal annual payments, including interest. What is the amount of each payment?
   c. Assume the note will be paid off in eight equal annual payments, including interest. What is the interest expense each year?

2. On January 1, a company borrows $750,000 and gives a note with an interest rate of 8.5 percent (equal to the current market rate). The note will be repaid in three *equal annual principal payments, plus interest,* with each payment due on December 31 each year.
   a. What is the interest expense each year?

   b. Assume the note will be paid off in three equal annual payments, including interest. What is the amount of each payment?

   c. Assume the note will be paid off in three equal annual payments, including interest. What is the interest expense each year?

3. On January 1, a company borrows $1,000,000 and gives a note with an interest rate of 5 percent (equal to the current market rate). The note will be repaid in 10 *equal annual principal payments, plus interest,* with each payment due on December 31 each year.

   a. What is the interest expense each year?

   b. Assume the note will be paid off in 10 equal annual payments, including interest. What is the amount of each payment?

   c. Assume the note will be paid off in 10 equal annual payments, including interest. What is the interest expense each year?

4. On January 1, a company borrows $400,000 and gives a note with an interest rate of 6 percent when the market interest rate for this type of loan is 9 percent. The note will be repaid in eight *equal annual principal payments, plus interest,* with each payment due on December 31 each year.

   a. Give the journal entry for the first payment.

   b. What is the interest expense each year?

   c. Assume the note will be paid off in eight equal annual payments, including interest. Give the journal entry for the first payment.

   d. Assume the note will be paid off in eight equal annual payments, including interest. What is the interest expense each year?

5. On January 1, a company borrows $750,000 and gives a note with an interest rate of 8.5 percent when the market interest rate for this type of loan is 10 percent. The note will be repaid in three *equal annual principal payments, plus interest,* with each payment due on December 31 each year.

   a. Give the journal entry for the first payment.

   b. What is the interest expense each year?

   c. Assume the note will be paid off in three equal annual payments, including interest. Give the journal entry for the first payment.

   d. Assume the note will be paid off in three equal annual payments, including interest. What is the interest expense each year?

6. On January 1, a company borrows $1,000,000 and gives a note with an interest rate of 5 percent when the market interest rate for this type of loan is 7.5 percent. The note will be repaid in 10 *equal annual principal payments, plus interest,* with each payment due on December 31 each year.

   a. Give the journal entry for the first payment.

   b. What is the interest expense each year?

   c. Assume the note will be paid off in 10 equal annual payments, including interest. Give the journal entry for the first payment.

   d. Assume the note will be paid off in 10 equal annual payments, including interest. What is the interest expense each year?

7. On July 1, a company sells 100 bonds. The bonds have a par value of $1,000, a coupon rate of 8 percent, and a maturity of five years, and they pay interest semiannually on June 30 and December 31. The market interest rate for bonds of similar risk is 8 percent.

   a. What is the interest expense each year?

   b. Give the journal entries to record the first two payments on June 30 and December 31.

8. On July 1, a company sells 100 bonds. The bonds have a par value of $1,000, a coupon rate of 6.5 percent, and a maturity of seven years, and they pay interest semiannually on June 30 and December 31. The market interest rate for bonds of similar risk is 6.5 percent.

   a. What is the interest expense each year?

   b. Give the journal entries to record the first two payments on June 30 and December 31.

9. On July 1, a company sells 100 bonds. The bonds have a par value of $1,000, a coupon rate of 11 percent, and a maturity of 10 years, and they pay interest semiannually on June 30 and December 31. The market interest rate for bonds of similar risk is 11 percent.

   a. What is the interest expense each year?

   b. Give the journal entries to record the first two payments on June 30 and December 31.

10. On July 1, a company sells 100 bonds. The bonds have a par value of $1,000, a coupon rate of 7 percent, and a maturity of five years, and they pay interest semiannually on June 30 and December 31. The market interest rate for bonds of similar risk is 9 percent.

    a. What is the interest expense each year?

    b. Give the journal entries to record the first two payments on June 30 and December 31.

11. On July 1, a company sells 100 bonds. The bonds have a par value of $1,000, a coupon rate of 9 percent, and a maturity of seven years, and they pay interest semiannually on June 30 and December 31. The market interest rate for bonds of similar risk is 7 percent.

    a. What is the interest expense each year?

    b. Give the journal entries to record the first two payments on June 30 and December 31.

12. On July 1, a company sells 100 bonds. The bonds have a par value of $1,000, a coupon rate of 3 percent, and a maturity of 10 years, and they pay interest semiannually on June 30 and December 31. The market interest rate for bonds of similar risk is 8 percent.

    a. What is the interest expense each year?

    b. Give the journal entries to record the first two payments on June 30 and December 31.

13. A company issues a $1,000 par zero coupon bond that matures in 20 years. The bond is sold to yield an interest rate of 6 percent. (Assume semiannual interest computations.)

    a. What is the selling price of the bond?

    b. Give the journal entries to record interest expense for the first two semiannual periods.

14. A company issues a $1,000 par zero coupon bond that matures in 10 years. The bond is sold to yield an interest rate of 8 percent. (Assume semiannual interest computations.)

    a. What is the selling price of the bond?

    b. Give the journal entries to record interest expense for the first two semiannual periods.

15. A company issues a $1,000 par zero coupon bond that matures in 12 years. The bond is sold to yield an interest rate of 12 percent. (Assume semiannual interest computations.)

   a. What is the selling price of the bond?

   b. Give the journal entries to record interest expense for the first two semi-annual periods.

Research Reports

1. Identify a U.S. corporation with publicly traded debt. Find the face amount, coupon rate, maturity date, current yield, and market value of the debt. You can find this information in *The Wall Street Journal* or the financial pages of other major newspapers. Find this information for the most current date you can.

   a. Find a copy of the most recent financial statements available for this company. You can find financial statements on the company website or using the SEC EDGAR database.

   b. From the notes to the financial statement, find the book value of the bond you identified. Remember, book value is face amount less discount (or plus premium).

   c. From the information in the note, compute the market interest rate in effect at the time the bond was issued. (*Hint:* This is the interest rate that makes the present value of the remaining cash flows equal to the book value of the bond).

   d. Compute the book value of the bond at the most recent interest payment date. This will require you to amortize any discount or principal from the date of the financial statement to the most recent interest date.

   e. Compute the gain/loss that the firm would realize if it repurchased the bond now. This will be the difference between the current book value and the current market value.

2. Locate the 2001 financial statements for Vertex Pharmaceuticals Incorporated from the SEC's EDGAR database or the company website (**www.vrtx.com**).

   a. Read Note K of Vertex's notes to the financial statements. In 2000 Vertex issued convertible subordinated notes on two different dates. What was the principal amount, interest rate, and due date of these notes?

   b. Find the cash flows statement for Vertex. Find the cash flows associated with the issuance of the 2000 notes. Is the amount on the cash flows statement the same as the principal of the notes? If not, why not?

   c. Find the income statement for Vertex. In 2001, Vertex reported a gain on the early extinguishment of debt. What was the amount of the gain? Is this gain net of income taxes? If not, why not?

   d. Explain how the gain on early extinguishment was computed. Trace the cash flow consequences of the early extinguishment to Vertex's cash flows statement for 2001. Was the cash flow positive or negative?

   e. Using the information about the early extinguishment, compute the market interest rate for these notes at the date of the extinguishment.

3. Here is some information from the annual report of General Mills, Inc.:

(in millions)	May 26, 2002	May 27, 2001
6% notes due 2012	$2,000	$ —
5 1/8% notes due 2007	1,500	—
Medium-term notes, 4.8% to 9.1%, due 2003 to 2078	922	1,274
7.0% notes due Sept. 15, 2004	150	157
Zero coupon notes, yield 11.1%, $261 due Aug. 15, 2013	78	70
Zero coupon notes, yield 11.7%, $54 due Aug. 15, 2004	42	38
8.2% ESOP loan guaranty, due through June 30, 2007	21	30
Notes payable, reclassified	1,050	1,000
Other	76	1
	5,839	2,570
Less amounts due within one year	(248)	(349)
Total long-term debt	$5,591	$2,221

a. Demonstrate that the book value of the $261 zero coupon note due August 15, 2013, is 70 at May 27, 2001. For purposes of this computation assume that the interest computation is made semiannually. Also, assume that the time period from May 27, 2001, to August 15, 2001, is 2 1/2 months. (Your answer may differ slightly due to rounding.)

b. Demonstrate that the book value of this same note increases to 78 on May 26, 2002. (Your answer may differ slightly due to rounding.)

c. Compute what the book value of this note will be in May 2003. Verify your computation by obtaining the company's annual report for that year.

d. Demonstrate that the book value of the $54 zero coupon note due August 15, 2004, is 38 at May 27, 2001. For purposes of this computation assume that the interest computation is made semiannually. Also, assume that the time period from May 27, 2001, to August 15, 2001, is 2 1/2 months. (Your answer may differ slightly due to rounding.)

e. Demonstrate that the book value of this same note increases to 42 on May 26, 2002. (Your answer may differ slightly due to rounding.)

f. Compute what the book value of this note will be in May 2003. Verify your computation by obtaining the company's annual report for that year.

4. Here is some information from the quarterly report of General Mills, Inc. for November, 2002.

On October 28, 2002, we completed a private placement of zero coupon convertible debentures with a face value of approximately $2.23 billion for gross proceeds of approximately $1.50 billion. The issue price of the debentures was $671.65 for each $1,000 in face value, which represents a yield to maturity of 2.00%. The debentures cannot be called by General Mills for three years after issuance and will mature in 20 years.

a. Demonstrate that the issue price of each debenture will be $671.65. For purposes of this computation assume that the interest computation is made semiannually. (Your answer may differ slightly due to rounding.)

b. Compute the interest expense for each debenture for each year over the 20-year term.

5. Here is a note from the financial statements of Dole Food Company Inc. relating to the company's long-term debt:

In July 2000, the Company repaid its $225 million, 6.75% notes, which matured on July 15, 2000. As of January 1, 2000, these notes had been classified as long-term due to the Company's ability and intent as of that date to refinance the maturity using a long-term instrument. The Company financed $40 million of this maturity under its 364-day Facility, which was subsequently repaid. The remaining $185 million was financed under the Company's Long-term Facility, which was also subsequently repaid.

---

a. Explain why the notes were classified as "long-term" on January 1, 2000, despite the fact that the notes matured on July 15, 2000.

b. Financial statements are sometimes said to reflect "substance over form." Explain how the above treatment reflects the economic substance of the debt rather than the legal form.

c. Does this substance over form approach result in more relevant financial statements?

d. Does this substance over form approach result in more reliable financial statements?

© Vince Streano/CORBIS

Chapter Learning Objectives

After reading this chapter you should understand:

1. The concept of economic income and its relationship to financial accounting income.
2. The concept of conservatism as it relates to financial reporting.
3. How bad debt expense is recognized under the allowance method.
4. How the lower of cost or market method is used to reduce inventory values.
5. How the impairment rule is applied to reduce balance sheet asset values.
6. How to account for expected future costs associated with restructurings.
7. How contingent liabilities are accounted for.
8. How expected future warranty costs are accounted for.
9. How to account for expected losses from discontinued operations.

Chapter 6

Timely Reporting: Recognizing Future Bad News Early

Focus Company: Chevron Corporation

Introduction

The financial statements for Chevron Corporation for the year ended December 31, 2000, provide the following information about write-offs of certain assets:

Asset write-offs and revaluations (in millions)

Exploration and production

    Oil and gas property impairments—U.S. . . . . $ (50)

Refining, marketing and transportation

    Pipeline asset impairments—U.S. . . . . (30)

Chemicals

    Manufacturing facility impairment—U.S. . . . . (90)

    (170)

In accordance with its policy, the company recorded impairments of assets to be held and used when changes in circumstances—primarily related to lower oil and gas prices, downward revisions of reserves and changes in the use of the assets—indicated that the carrying values of the assets could not be recovered through estimated future before-tax undiscounted cash flows.

Source: Chevron Form 10-K.

What this means is that Chevron's management determined that $170 million of assets—oil and gas properties, pipelines, and manufacturing facilities—would be unlikely to provide future economic benefits to the company equal to the assets' book values, and that these assets were therefore written off (that is, their book values were reduced) on the company's balance sheet. This does not mean that anything happened to the physical assets; the oil fields, pipelines, and refineries were all still intact and being used by Chevron. However, in the opinion of Chevron's management the book value of these assets on Chevron's balance sheet was greater than the future cash flows that the assets would generate. This results in an *impairment*[1] of the assets under GAAP and requires the write-off.

Why does GAAP require this treatment? These assets will continue to be used by Chevron and will produce revenues in the future. However, because their balance sheet book value exceeds the expected future cash flows from the assets, continued use of the assets will result in an accounting loss for Chevron. Under GAAP, if Chevron's management expects a future loss from the use of an asset, they must recognize the loss immediately and may not wait until it is actually incurred in the future.

[1]The GAAP rules for impairments of assets are discussed in more detail later in the chapter.

This characteristic of GAAP—that expected future losses are recognized immediately, whereas expected future gains are deferred until they are realized—is a fundamental concept underlying financial reporting and is known as *conservatism*. This chapter presents a conceptual overview of the concept of conservatism, as well as presenting detailed financial reporting rules that incorporate conservatism.

ECONOMIC INCOME AND TIMELY REPORTING

To understand accounting conservatism, it is necessary to first understand the relationship between accounting income and something known as *economic income*. Economic income is equal to the increase (or decrease) in an individual's wealth for the year, plus the individual's consumption during that same year. For example, if your savings account balance was $2,000 at the beginning of the year, $3,500 at the end of the year, and during the year you consumed (that is, used up) $8,000 worth of things like food, clothing, housing, transportation, entertainment, and education, your economic income would be

$$(\$3,500 - \$2,000) = \$1,500 + \$8,000 = \$9,500$$

Change in wealth + Consumption = Income

A similar definition can be applied to the income reported in the income statement of a publicly traded corporation. Economic income for a public corporation would consist of two parts. The first part is the change in the market value of shareholders' equity for the year, which is equal to the change in the stock price multiplied by the number of shares of stock outstanding. This is similar to the change in wealth in the case of an individual. The second part of economic income for a public corporation is the dividends paid during the year. This is similar to consumption in the case of an individual.

Here is a computation of economic income for Chevron for the year 2000 based on this definition. The change in the market value of Chevron's shareholders' equity was a *decrease* of $2,703 million. When this decrease is combined with the dividends paid by Chevron of $1,688 million, the result is Chevron's economic income: a loss of $1,015 million. Comparing this with Chevron's reported accounting net income of $5,185 million points out how different economic income and accounting income can be.

COMPUTATION OF ECONOMIC INCOME FOR 2000		
	December 31	
	2000	**1999**
Number of shares outstanding (millions)	641	656
Price per share ($)	84.44	86.63
Market value of shareholders' equity (millions of $)	54,126	56,829
Change in market value (2000–1999)		(2,703)
Plus dividends (millions of $)		1,688
Economic income for 2000 (millions of $)		(1,015)
Accounting net income for 2000 (millions of $)		5,185

What causes this difference between economic income and accounting income? Two major reasons are (1) the GAAP revenue recognition rule that says revenue cannot be recognized for accounting purposes until it is earned, and (2) the GAAP matching principle that says expenses should be matched against revenue. The effect of these rules is to delay the recognition of revenue until a date that is near the time the revenue will be received in cash, and to also delay the recognition of expenses, such as inventory or depreciation, until the time of future revenue recognition.

By way of contrast, economic income has no such rules. Economic income represents changes in investors' expectations about what will happen to the firm's cash flows in future years. These expected future cash flows are taken into account by investors in setting stock prices regardless of when they are actually recognized for financial reporting purposes. If investors receive information that causes them to revise their beliefs about the firm's future cash flows, the firm's stock price will change.

Here is an example. Assume that the price of oil decreased in 1999. This means that in future years when Chevron purchases oil to refine into gasoline, its future costs will be less than they would have been if the price of oil had remained constant. Investors use this information in determining the price they are willing to pay for Chevron's stock. The decrease in expected future costs due to the oil price decrease will result in an increase in the price of Chevron's stock, which in turn will increase Chevron's economic income for 1999 (the year of the oil price decrease) even though the lower future costs will not be realized by Chevron for many years. In effect, the decrease in oil price represents good news for Chevron's shareholders, and this good news is incorporated into Chevron's stock price immediately, regardless of when the accounting impact occurs.

Similarly, if we assume that oil prices increased in 2000, investors would expect future costs of purchasing oil to increase, and this would lead to a decline in Chevron's stock price. The decline in the stock price will result in negative economic income for 2000, which is contrary to the positive accounting income reported by Chevron in 2000. The positive accounting income results from refining and selling gasoline during 2000. The costs associated with these sales of gasoline in 2000 were already anticipated by investors prior to the start of 2000, but the investors based their estimate on the old price of oil, which was lower. When the sales of gasoline in 2000 are actually realized, the result is positive accounting income, but the higher-than-expected costs caused by the increase in oil prices in 2000 results in negative economic income for 2000.

What this example illustrates is that economic income is more timely than accounting income, because economic income does not wait for revenue recognition, or matching, to occur. By waiting for revenue to be realized, and by matching expenses with revenue, accounting income is less timely than economic income.

Conservative Accounting and Timely Reporting

There is an important exception to the rule that accounting income is recognized later than economic income, and it has to do with cases of expected future losses. In a number of situations discussed in this chapter, accounting rules require the write-off of assets (or the recording of liabilities) in cases where there is an expected future *decrease* in cash flows (or some other type of future loss) without waiting for the future realization event to occur. This is consistent with the accounting concept of conservatism. Under this conservative approach, unrealized expected future *increases* in cash flows are not recognized in accounting income in a timely manner, but unrealized expected future *decreases* in cash flows are recognized in accounting income in a timely manner.

Under accounting conservatism, bad news is likely to be incorporated quickly into both economic income and accounting income. However, good news, while quickly incorporated into economic income in the form of stock price increases, will not be recognized in accounting income until some future accounting period when the cash flows associated with the good news are realized.

Understanding this treatment of expected future losses helps explain Chevron's asset write-offs discussed at the beginning of this chapter. The management of Chevron identified certain assets for which the book value of the assets on

Chevron's balance sheet exceeded the expected future cash flows from the assets, which would lead to a future loss when the cash flows were realized and the assets depreciated. Therefore, under conservative accounting as reflected in the impairment rule, Chevron is required to recognize the future losses in the current accounting period, that is, in a timely manner, by writing down the book values of the assets.

Note that Chevron was not allowed to write *up* the values of those assets that have appreciated in value. Also note that if the values of the assets that have been written down later increase, Chevron will *not* be allowed to reverse the write-downs and restore the assets to their original value.

The rest of this chapter explores a series of GAAP rules that all have the same objective: to recognize expected future losses in the current accounting period. As you read through the rest of the chapter, it may seem that the accounting rules being discussed are unrelated to each other. For example, the rules cover such seemingly unrelated items as uncollectible receivables, inventory write-downs, and liabilities for future lawsuit settlements. However, keep in mind that all of these items are similar in that they all require a current year accounting recognition for losses that are expected to arise in the future. The items discussed in this chapter are all covered by the accounting concept of conservatism.

BAD DEBTS

When a firm records revenue under the accrual method and cash is not collected at the time of the sale, an account receivable is also recorded as an asset. Sometimes the firm will be unable to collect an account receivable because the buyer becomes insolvent after the sale. In accounting terminology, the failure to collect an account receivable results in what is known as a bad debt.[2]

GAAP rules for recognizing bad debts associated with accounts receivable follow what is known as the *allowance method*. Under the allowance method, expected future bad debts are recognized in the accounting period in which the original sale was recorded rather than in a future period when it becomes known that the buyer will be unable to pay the amount owed.

For example, at December 31, 2000, Chevron reported accounts and notes receivable on its balance sheet in the amount of $3,837 million. However, on the basis of past experience, Chevron's managers know that not all of these receivables will ultimately be collected. Those that prove to be uncollectible will ultimately have to be written off as bad debts, an income statement expense that reduces net income.[3]

Since the revenue associated with the $3,837 million of accounts receivable was recognized in 2000, waiting to recognize some of those same receivables as bad debts in a future year would be a violation of the matching principle. Under the matching principle, Chevron should recognize the expense for bad debts in the same accounting period that it recognizes the related sales revenue represented by the receivable. The allowance method accomplishes this by recognizing *expected future uncollectible receivables* as bad debts in the current year.

The allowance method requires the use of a contra-asset account (that is, an asset account with a credit balance) called the Allowance for Doubtful Accounts.[4] When bad debt expense is recorded for the current year, by a debit to Bad Debt Expense, the credit portion of the entry is made to the Allowance for Doubtful Accounts as follows:

---

[2] Managing bad debts for a publicly traded company is an important management task. All large companies that sell on credit have credit managers responsible for managing the level of bad debts that the firm incurs.

[3] It could be argued that bad debts are a reduction in revenue rather than an expense. Nevertheless, the term *bad debt expense* is commonly used.

[4] The Allowance for Doubtful Accounts is also called the Allowance for Bad Debts, the Allowance for Uncollectibles, or sometimes simply the Allowance.

	Journal Entry to Record Bad Debt Expense		
+/−	Accounts [description of account]	Debit	Credit
+	Bad Debt Expense [income statement expense account]	800	
+	Allowance for Doubtful Accounts [balance sheet contra-asset account] . .		800

The contra-asset account Allowance for Doubtful Accounts is combined with accounts receivable on the balance sheet, so that only the net receivables are reported. Here is the accounts receivable portion of Chevron's balance sheet:

Consolidated Balance Sheet (in millions)		
	At December 31	
	2000	1999
Assets		
Accounts and notes receivable (less allowance: 2000—$30; 1999—$36)	$3,837	$3,688

Source: Chevron Form 10-K.

At December 31, 2000, Chevron reported $3,837 million of accounts and notes receivable, but this amount was reduced by an allowance of $30 million. Therefore, Chevron's account balances related to receivables would look like this:

ACCOUNTS RECEIVABLE (IN MILLIONS)		
	December 31	
	2000	1999
Accounts and notes receivable	$3,867	$3,724
Less: Allowance for doubtful accounts	(30)	(36)
Net receivables reported on balance sheet	$3,837	$3,688

Writing Off an Uncollectible Account

When bad debt expense is recorded through the use of the Allowance for Doubtful Accounts, it is not known with certainty exactly which accounts receivable will ultimately become uncollectible. For example, the Chevron statement above shows an allowance for doubtful accounts of $30 million at the end of 2000, but the managers of Chevron don't know exactly which of their $3,867 million of gross receivables will ultimately prove to be uncollectible. The $30 million is the managers' best estimate of expected future uncollectibles based on past experience and current economic conditions.

Over time, however, as customers fail to pay their accounts, it becomes apparent which accounts are uncollectible, and at some point managers will determine that collection efforts should cease and the accounts are written off. At that time, the specific account receivable is written off by reducing both Accounts Receivable and the Allowance for Doubtful Accounts. For example, if Chevron was owed $5,000 by the XYZ Fuel Company at the end of 2000, and sometime in 2001 XYZ Fuel declared bankruptcy and was unable to pay any of its creditors, Chevron would write off the XYZ receivable in 2001 as follows:

	Journal Entry to Write Off Uncollectible Account		
+/−	Accounts [description of account]	Debit	Credit
−	Allowance for Doubtful Accounts [balance sheet contra-asset account] . .	5,000	
−	Accounts Receivable [balance sheet asset account]		5,000

Notice two important things about the entry to write off an uncollectible account under the allowance method. First, there is no effect on net income in the year of the write-off, since neither Allowance for Doubtful Accounts nor Accounts Receivable are income statement accounts. Under the allowance method, all of the income statement effect occurs in the year that the bad debt expense is recorded. Second, since an asset account (Accounts Receivable) and a contra-asset account (Allowance for Doubtful Accounts) are both reduced by the same amount, there is no effect on Chevron's reported total assets due to this journal entry. The result is that neither net income nor total assets are affected in the year of the write-off. This is an important feature of the allowance method: All of the financial statement impact of a bad debt, both on the income statement and balance sheet, occurs in the year that the estimated bad debt expense is recorded.

Estimating Bad Debt Expense under the Allowance Method

This section illustrates two methods for determining bad debt expense under the allowance method: the percentage of sales method and the percentage of receivables method. The percentage of receivables method is often called the *aging method,* for reasons that will become apparent.

Percentage of Sales Method

Under the percentage of sales method, bad debt expense is based on a percentage of the firm's total credit sales for the year. For example, if managers of Chevron determine, based on prior experience, that on average 0.061 percent of all sales result in uncollectible accounts, then the 2000 bad debt expense for Chevron would be computed as follows: sales of \$50,592 million $\times$ 0.00061 = \$31 million bad debt expense for 2000. (Chevron's actual bad debt expense for 2000 was \$31 million.)

Here is the entry Chevron would make to record bad debt expense for 2000:

+/−	Journal Entry to Record Chevron Bad Debt Expense for 2000 (in millions)		
	Accounts [description of account]	**Debit**	**Credit**
+	Bad Debt Expense [income statement expense account]	31	
+	Allowance for Doubtful Accounts [balance sheet contra-asset account] . .		31

The activity in the Allowance for Doubtful Accounts for Chevron for 2000 can be summarized as follows:

ALLOWANCE FOR DOUBTFUL ACCOUNTS (IN MILLIONS)	
Balance, 12/31/1999	\$36
Write-off of uncollectible accounts	(37)
Bad debt expense	31
Balance, 12/31/2000	\$30

The Allowance for Doubtful Accounts is decreased by the write-off of uncollectible accounts and increased by the bad debt expense. Notice that prior to the time that the bad debt expense is recorded, the balance in the Allowance account could be negative, that is, a debit balance, since the write-offs for the year of \$37 million exceeded the beginning balance in the account of \$36 million. This is not unusual and causes no problems, since bad debt expense would always be recorded prior to the preparation of a firm's financial statements.

Notice that under the percentage of sales method, the ending balance in the Allowance for Doubtful Accounts is not considered in the computation of bad debt expense. This means that, theoretically, the balance could shrink to zero or, alternatively, could continue to grow until it became larger than the Accounts Receivable balance. Although this could happen in theory, in reality the percentage used to record bad debt expense must be based on the firm's actual write-off experience. Therefore, if the balance in the Allowance for Doubtful Accounts either grew or shrank by a large amount over time, this would be an indication that the percentage being used to estimate bad debts should be revised to correspond more closely to actual experience.

Percentage of Receivables Method

The percentage of receivables method is based on managers' estimation of the correct ending balance in the Allowance for Doubtful Accounts. For example, assume that Chevron's managers determined that, based on past experience, an Allowance for Doubtful Accounts equal to 0.776 percent of accounts receivable was necessary at the end of 2000. Since the ending balance of accounts receivable (before reduction for the Allowance for Doubtful Accounts) was $3,867 million, the balance required would be 0.00776 × $3,867 million = $30 million.

Notice that, unlike the percentage of sales method, *we have not computed Chevron's bad debt expense.* Instead, we have computed the ending balance that is required in the Allowance for Doubtful Accounts. To compute bad debt expense under the percentage of receivables method requires two steps: First, compute the required ending balance in the Allowance for Doubtful Accounts; second, compare that balance with the actual balance in the account after all write-offs of uncollectible accounts have been made. The bad debt expense for the year is the amount necessary to adjust the actual balance to the computed balance.

In the case of Chevron, here is how the computation of bad debt expense would be made under the percentage of receivables method:

COMPUTATION OF BAD DEBT EXPENSE (IN MILLIONS)	
Allowance for Doubtful Accounts	
Balance, 12/31/1999	$36
Write-off of uncollectible accounts	(37)
Subtotal: balance after write-offs	(1)
Balance required at 12/31/2000	30
Bad Debt Expense	$31

After the write-offs of uncollectible accounts, Chevron's Allowance for Doubtful Accounts has a debit balance of $1 million, whereas the required balance is a credit balance of $30 million. The necessary entry to adjust the balance from a debit of $1 million to a credit of $30 million is therefore

Journal Entry to Record Chevron Bad Debt Expense for 2000 (in millions)			
+/−	Accounts [description of account]	Debit	Credit
+	Bad Debt Expense [income statement expense account]	31	
+	Allowance for Doubtful Accounts [balance sheet contra-asset account] . .		31

Often, the percentage of receivables that are expected to become uncollectible is a weighted average based on how old the year-end receivables are—that is, how long a time has passed since the due date of the receivable. Basing the percentage of receivables on the age of the receivables is known as the *aging method*. The computation requires an aging schedule of receivables that looks like this:

AGING OF ACCOUNTS RECEIVABLE (IN MILLIONS)	
Age of Receivables	**Amount**
Over 90 days past due	$ 28
61 to 90 days past due	87
31 to 60 days past due	187
Less than 31 days past due	633
Current receivables not yet due	2,932
Total	$3,867

Since receivables that are past due are less likely to be collected than are current receivables, a higher percentage of uncollectibles is expected for these past due balances. Similarly, the longer a receivable is past due, the more likely it is that the receivable will ultimately become uncollectible. When the balance in accounts receivable is aged in this way, the percentage applied to each amount on the schedule will increase with the age of the receivables. Here is an example of how an aging schedule could be used to compute the required ending balance in the Allowance for Doubtful Accounts for Chevron:

AGING OF ACCOUNTS RECEIVABLE (IN MILLIONS)			
Age of Receivables	**Receivable Balance**	**Estimated Uncollectibles**	**Allowance Balance**
Over 90 days past due	$ 28	25.000%	$ 7.00
61 to 90 days past due	87	10.000	8.70
31 to 60 days past due	187	5.000	9.35
Less than 31 days past due	633	0.500	3.17
Current receivables	2,932	0.061	1.78
Total	$3,867		$30.00

Just as when a single percentage is used, the aging schedule is only the first step in the computation of the bad debt expense for the year. The computed balance required in the Allowance for Doubtful Accounts must then be compared with the actual balance in the account after all write-offs for the year, and the amount necessary to adjust the actual balance to equal the required balance is the bad debt expense for the year.

Conservatism and the Matching Principle

The allowance method for recording bad debts is an example of conservative accounting in that it records estimated future bad debts as an expense in the current year rather than waiting for the bad debts to be realized in a future year. However, when applied to accounts receivable, the allowance method is also an example of the matching principle, since it results in a matching of an expense (bad debts) with the revenue related to the expense (sales revenue) in the same accounting period.

The allowance method must be applied to all receivables, even those for which the matching principle is not applicable. For example, a company that makes loans (such as a bank or savings and loan) must record a loan-loss reserve for expected future bad debts. The loan-loss reserve is similar to the allowance for doubtful accounts. In this situation, since the loans do not represent revenue to the lender, recording expected future bad debts in the current year is *not* an application of the matching principle.

LOWER OF COST OR MARKET

The allowance method of recording bad debt expense is an example of conservative accounting. Managers must estimate the amount of future uncollectible accounts, and they must record estimated future bad debts as an expense in the current accounting period. Managers are not allowed to delay the recognition of the bad debt expense until some future accounting period when the bad debt is actually realized.

A second example of conservative accounting relates to the cost of inventories on the balance sheet. Under GAAP, inventories are normally valued at original cost. However, whenever the current value of the inventory is less than its original cost, it is likely that a future sale of the inventory will result in a loss, since the future selling price (that is, the current value of the inventory) will be less than the future cost of goods sold (that is, the original cost of the inventory). Therefore, consistent with conservative accounting, if the current value of inventory is less than the inventory's original cost, the book value of the inventory must be written down (that is, reduced) to current value. This accounting treatment is called the *lower of cost or market method*, since the current value of the inventory is referred to as its *market value*.

To illustrate this, assume that the market value of Chevron's inventory is determined to be $50 million less than book value. Here is the journal entry to record this hypothetical write-down:

Journal Entry to Record Write-Down of Inventory to Market Value (in millions)			
+/–	Accounts [description of account]	Debit	Credit
+	Loss on Inventory Write-down [income statement expense account]	50	
–	Inventory [balance sheet asset account]		50

There are two ways that the lower of cost or market method can be applied: (1) at the aggregate level or (2) on an item-by-item basis. To illustrate each of these methods, assume a firm has the following items in inventory at the end of 2000:

LOWER OF COST OR MARKET EXAMPLE							
Item Number	Number of Units	Unit Cost	Total Cost	Unit Market Value	Total Market Value	Lower of Cost or Market	Total LCM
1	1,000	$1.00	$ 1,000	$2.00	$ 2,000	$1.00	$ 1,000
2	2,400	2.15	5,160	4.00	9,600	2.15	5,160
3	3,200	4.30	13,760	2.15	6,880	2.15	6,880
4	1,800	1.75	3,150	2.10	3,780	1.75	3,150
5	4,600	0.60	2,760	1.70	7,820	0.60	2,760
6	3,300	2.90	9,570	1.10	3,630	1.10	3,630
Total	16,300		$35,400		$33,710		$22,580

For inventory item numbers 1, 2, 4, and 5, the cost of the units is lower than the market value, whereas for units 3 and 6 the market value is lower than the cost. At the aggregate level, the total market value of the inventory ($33,710) is less than the total cost of the inventory ($35,400). This means that under GAAP, the book value of inventory would be written down from $35,400 to $33,710. However, if the lower of cost or market rule is applied on an item-by-item basis, the total inventory value is $22,580, and the book value of inventory would be written down to that amount.

Applying lower of cost or market on an item-by-item basis will always give a lower inventory amount than the aggregate method, since under the aggregate method any increases in market values for some inventory items will offset decreases in market values for other items. Therefore, the item-by-item approach is more conservative. While both methods are allowed under GAAP, the item-by-item approach is the one most commonly used.

When applying the lower of cost or market rule, it is necessary to correctly compute the market value of an inventory item. Under GAAP, there is a special procedure for computing market value. In general, market value means the replacement cost of the inventory item. However, there are two additional constraints on market value: a ceiling amount and a floor amount. If the replacement cost of an inventory item is greater than the ceiling amount, the ceiling amount is used as the market value. Similarly, if the replacement cost of an inventory item is less than the floor amount, the floor amount is used as the market value.

The ceiling amount is equal to the *net realizable value* of the inventory item. Net realizable value is the expected selling price reduced by expected costs of disposition. In other words, net realizable value is the greatest amount of cash that the inventory is expected to generate upon a future sale. For example, assume that inventory cost is $100, replacement cost is $80, and net realizable value is $70. The inventory book value must be written down to $70, the ceiling amount.

The rationale for this rule is as follows: If the future cost of goods sold exceeds the net cash generated from selling the inventory, the firm will realize a future loss on the sale. Continuing the above example, if the inventory book value was only written down to the $80 replacement cost, a future sale for $70 (the net realizable value) would result in a loss of $10 ($70 selling price less $80 cost of goods sold). Since the reason for employing the lower of cost or market rule is to recognize expected future losses in the current accounting period, the lower of cost or market rule requires market value (and thus future cost of goods sold) to be less than or equal to net realizable value.

The floor amount is equal to the net realizable value *reduced by the normal profit margin* for the inventory item. If managers were allowed to write down the cost of inventory to an amount that was less than the net realizable value reduced by the normal profit margin, a subsequent sale of the inventory at net realizable value would result in a profit that exceeds the firm's normal profit from the inventory item. This would potentially allow managers to take write-downs in one year but report abnormally large profits in future years. For example, assume that a firm has an inventory item that normally sells for $10 and that the firm's normal markup is 40 percent of selling price. This means that the firm normally earns a profit of $4 on each sale of this item. If managers were allowed to use the lower of cost or market rule to reduce the balance sheet book value of the inventory item below $6 (that is, the net realizable value of $10 reduced by the normal profit margin of $4), then a future sale of the item for $10 would result in the firm recognizing more than the normal $4 profit.

Here are some examples to illustrate the use of the ceiling and floor constraints together with the lower of cost or market rule. A simple way to remember which measure of market value to use is to rank the three measures (replacement cost, ceiling amount, and floor amount) from highest to lowest and then choose the number in the middle as the market value.

EXAMPLES OF LOWER OF COST OR MARKET CONSTRAINTS					
	Case 1	Case 2	Case 3	Case 4	Case 5
Replacement cost	$4.00	$4.00	$4.00	$2.00	$6.00
Net realizable value	7.00	7.00	3.00	5.00	7.00
Net realizable value minus profit margin	6.00	3.00	2.00	3.00	5.00
Value for market	6.00	4.00	3.00	3.00	6.00
Original cost	5.00	5.00	5.00	5.00	5.00
Lower of cost or market	5.00	4.00	3.00	3.00	5.00

In case 1, market cannot be less than the floor amount of $6.00. Since the original cost of $5.00 is less than market, cost is used. In case 2, market is simply replacement cost. Since the market of $4.00 is less than original cost of $5.00 the inventory is written down to $4.00. In case 3, market cannot be greater than the ceiling amount of $3.00. Since the market of $3.00 is less than the original cost, the inventory is written down to $3.00. In case 4, market cannot be less than the floor amount of $3.00. Since the market of $3.00 is less than the original cost, the inventory is written down to $3.00. In case 5, market is simply replacement cost. Since the original cost of $5.00 is less than market, cost is used.

ASSET IMPAIRMENTS

A third example of accounting conservatism is the impairment of Chevron's assets that was illustrated in the introduction to this chapter. An impairment occurs whenever the balance sheet book value of a noncurrent asset exceeds the future cash flows that management expects the asset to generate. Under GAAP, assets that have become impaired must be written down to their fair market value. An impairment test is necessary any time an event occurs that management believes may have decreased the fair market value of an asset. For example, a decline in oil and gas prices will decrease the market value of Chevron's oil and gas reserves, thus requiring an impairment test.

The impairment test requires the following procedure. First, management must estimate the future net cash flows that the asset will generate over its lifetime. (Even though these cash flows will be received in the future, and thus their present value is less than their future value, present values are *not* used for the impairment test.) If the book value of the asset is greater than the expected future cash flows, the asset is considered to be impaired. In this case, continuing to depreciate the asset on the basis of its book value would result in future accounting losses from the asset, since the future depreciation would exceed the future cash flows from the asset. Consistent with conservative accounting, these future expected losses must be recognized in the current accounting period by writing down the book value of the asset.

If the asset is found to be impaired, its book value is reduced to equal the fair market value of the asset. The fair market value of the asset is unlikely to be the same as the future cash flows that were used in the impairment test. For example, if an asset with a book value of $100,000 has future expected cash flows of $80,000 and a fair market value of $65,000, the asset is considered to be impaired because the $80,000 cash flows are less than the $100,000 book value, and the asset must be written down to its $65,000 fair market value.

An asset that has been written down as impaired may not later be written back up if the market value increases. For example, if Chevron determines that some of its oil and gas reserves are impaired because of a decline in oil and gas prices, and prices later increase, the company may not write up the asset book values to reflect the later increase in market value. Writing down asset values is consistent with conservative accounting. However, increases in asset values requires a realization event, such as a sale, before the market value increase may be recognized for accounting purposes.

RESTRUCTURING CHARGES

It is a common practice for companies to periodically restructure their business operations, and these restructurings frequently result in the company committing to incur significant future costs. For example, management may decide to close a number of unprofitable factories or stores, resulting in future losses on disposal of these assets. Inventories that are no longer part of the new business plan may be disposed of in the future at a loss. Employees' jobs may be eliminated, requiring costly future severance payments or early retirement incentives.

Although these costs may be incurred over several future accounting periods, because they relate to the restructuring decision, and because management can reasonably estimate these costs, prior to 2003 future restructuring costs were treated as an expense in the current accounting period. Since these costs do not meet the definition of an extraordinary item—that is, they are not both infrequent and unusual—they must be reported before income tax expense on the income statement, although they are usually labeled as nonoperating items.

One potential concern that users of financial statements should have regarding restructuring charges is whether management is overestimating the future costs associated with the restructuring. If this occurs there will be a large restructuring charge in the current accounting period, but earnings in future accounting periods will be unusually high since many future expenses will have already been recorded as part of the restructuring charge. If a company reports a large restructuring charge in one year and then reports unusually high net income in the subsequent year, the high net income may be a result of a successful business restructuring, but it may also be due to recognizing future costs in an earlier accounting period.

Here is an example of how an overstatement of a restructuring charge would increase future earnings. Assume that XYZ Company normally has $2,000,000 of expenses each year relating to employee terminations. These expenses might include severance pay, continuation of medical benefits, job training, or similar types of costs. Assume that in 2000 the management of XYZ decided to restructure part of the company's operations, and that because of the restructuring they expected employee termination expenses in 2001 to be to $7,000,000 rather than the usual $2,000,000. Assume the company recorded a restructuring charge in 2000 for these expected future costs as follows:

	Journal Entry to Record Restructuring Charge for 2000		
+/−	Accounts [description of account]	Debit	Credit
+	Restructuring Charge [income statement expense account]	7,000,000	
+	Restructuring Liability [balance sheet liability account]		7,000,000

The above entry records a $7,000,000 expense in 2000 related to costs expected to be incurred in 2001. During 2001, when XYZ actually paid $7,000,000 in termination expenses, it made the following entry:

Journal Entry to Record Payment of Employee Termination Expenses in 2001			
+/−	Accounts [description of account]	Debit	Credit
−	Restructuring Liability [balance sheet liability account]	7,000,000	
−	Cash [balance sheet asset account]		7,000,000

Notice what happened to net income in 2001. Normally, XYZ would recognize $2,000,000 of employee termination expense in 2001. However, because of the restructuring charge, all of the employee termination expenses from 2001 were recognized in 2000. This means that the pretax earnings of XYZ were $2,000,000 higher in 2001 than they would have been without the restructuring charge in 2000. The FASB became concerned that restructuring costs were being improperly recorded. As a result, GAAP was changed so that, beginning in 2003, restructuring charges may only be recorded in the year that a liability is actually incurred, rather than in the year management adopts a restructuring plan.

CONTINGENT LIABILITIES

Often a firm will expect negative future cash flows based on the outcome of some uncertain future event. An example is a firm that is a defendant in a lawsuit, where, depending on the outcome of the lawsuit, the firm may have to pay a future judgment. A liability that is dependent upon some uncertain future event, such as a lawsuit outcome, is known as a *contingent liability*. The GAAP rules governing reporting of contingent liabilities are discussed in this section.

The financial reporting treatment for a contingent liability depends on how likely it is that the outcome of the uncertain future event will result in negative future cash flows for the firm. For this purpose, there are three levels of certainty with respect to the future negative cash flows:

- The likelihood of future negative cash flows is *probable.*
- The likelihood of future negative cash flows is *reasonably possible.*
- The likelihood of future negative cash flows is *remote.*

If the likelihood of future negative cash flows is probable a*nd the amount of the expected future negative cash flows can be estimated with reasonable accuracy*, then the expected future negative cash flows should be reported as a liability on the balance sheet as well as a loss or expense on the income statement. If the amount of future negative cash flows cannot be estimated, but a range of expected negative cash flows can be estimated, then the lower amount of the range should be recorded as a liability and loss, and the upper amount of the range should be disclosed in a note to the financial statements.

If the likelihood of future negative cash flows is probable, but the amount of the expected future negative cash flows *cannot* be estimated with reasonable accuracy, or if the likelihood of future negative cash flows is *reasonably possible,* then the details of the contingent liability should be disclosed in a note to the financial statements.

If the likelihood of future negative cash flows is *remote,* then no disclosure is necessary in the financial statements. Also, as with all other GAAP rules, no special accounting treatment is required for amounts that are not material.

Notice how much influence managers have on the recording of contingent liabilities. First, managers must determine whether the likelihood of negative future cash flows is probable, reasonably possible, or remote. Unless the likelihood is probable, no liability will be recorded. Second, even if the likelihood is probable, managers must be able to estimate the amount of the future cash flow effect. If the amount cannot be estimated, or if the range of estimated future amounts includes zero, no contingent liability (or loss) will be recorded. Since the more liabilities a company reports on its balance sheet, the riskier it looks to investors, managers may have incentives to keep contingent liabilities from being recorded.

To illustrate the application of the contingent liability rules, here is some information from the notes to Chevron's 1996 financial statements:

> OXY U.S.A. brought a lawsuit in its capacity as successor in interest to Cities Service Company, which involved claims for damages resulting from the allegedly improper termination of a tender offer to purchase Cities' stock in 1982 made by Gulf Oil Corporation, acquired by Chevron in 1984. A trial with respect to the claims ended in July 1996 with a judgment against the company of $742, including interest, which continues to accrue. The company has filed an appeal. While the ultimate outcome of this matter cannot be determined presently with certainty, the company believes that errors were committed by the trial court that should result in the judgment being reversed on appeal.
>
> Source: Chevron 1996 Form 10-K.

This is an example of a contingent liability. Chevron filed an appeal with respect to this lawsuit, and depending on the outcome of the appeal, Chevron may have to pay up to $742 million, plus interest, in the future. Since, in the opinion of Chevron's management, "the company believes that errors were committed by the trial court that should result in the judgment being reversed on appeal," management believes that the likelihood of future negative cash flows with respect to this lawsuit are reasonably possible but not probable. Therefore, disclosure is made in the notes to the financial statements, but no amount is recorded as a liability on the balance sheet or as a loss or expense on the income statement. Chevron had a similar note in its 1997 financial statements.

Here is the financial statement note from Chevron's 1998 financial statements regarding this lawsuit:

> The company is a defendant in a lawsuit that OXY U.S.A. brought in its capacity as successor in interest to Cities Service Company. The lawsuit claims damages resulting from the allegedly improper termination of a tender offer made by Gulf Oil Corporation, acquired by Chevron in 1984, to purchase Cities Service in 1982. A 1996 trial resulted in a judgment against the company of $742 million, including interest that continues to accrue at 9.55 percent per year while this matter is pending. The Oklahoma Supreme Court affirmed the lower court's decision in March 1999, and accordingly, the company recorded in 1998 results a litigation reserve of $637 million, substantially all of which pertained to this lawsuit. The ultimate outcome of this matter cannot be determined presently with certainty, and the company will seek further review of this case in the appropriate courts.
>
> Source: Chevron 1998 Form 10-K.

Since Chevron's management knew in March 1999 that the company had lost its appeal, the likelihood of future negative cash flows relating to this lawsuit increased from reasonably possible to probable. Therefore, in accordance with GAAP, "the company recorded in 1998 results a litigation reserve of $637 million, substantially all of which pertained to this lawsuit." This means that Chevron recorded in its 1998 financial statements a balance sheet liability as well as an income statement expense for $637 million.

Notice that the appeals court judgment was not entered until March 1999, but Chevron recorded the liability at December 31, 1998. This is because, based on information that was available to management at the time the 1998 financial statements were being prepared, it was probable that Chevron would have to pay the judgment from the lawsuit. Under conservative accounting rules, Chevron recorded the liability and the expense in 1998.

Listed below are categories of special items and their net increase (decrease) to net income, after related tax effects:

	Year Ended December 31		
	1998	**1997**	**1996**
Other, net			
Settlement of insurance claims	105	7	—
Caltex write-off of start-up costs (SOP 98-5)	(25)	—	—
Litigation and regulatory issues*	**(682)**	**(24)**	**(90)**
Performance stock options	—	(66)	—
Federal lease cost refund	—	—	12
	(602)	(83)	(78)
Total special items, after tax	$(606)	$ 76	$(44)

*1998 includes provision related to Cities Service litigation.

Source: Chevron 1998 Form 10-K.

Interestingly enough, the plaintiff in the lawsuit (Occidental Petroleum) did not record the additional income from the lawsuit settlement until 1999, the year *after* Chevron recorded the liability and expense. Here is the note from Occidental Petroleum's 1999 financial statements reporting the lawsuit settlement:

In December 1999, OXY USA settled its long-standing litigation with Chevron U.S.A. Inc. (Chevron) for a cash payment of $775 million from Chevron. The related pre-tax income of $775 million is reported as interest, dividends and other income in the accompanying consolidated statements of operations.

Source: Occidental Petroleum 1999 Form 10-K.

Here is the Occidental Petroleum income statement for 1999 showing the lawsuit settlement as part of interest, dividends, and other income for 1999:

OCCIDENTAL PETROLEUM CORPORATION AND SUBSIDIARIES
Consolidated Statements of Operations
For the Years Ended December 31
(in millions, except per-share amounts)

	1999	**1998**	**1997**
Revenues			
Net sales and operating revenues			
Oil and gas operations	$4,572	$3,621	$3,667
Chemical operations	3,038	2,975	4,349
	7,610	6,596	8,016
Interest, dividends, and other income	**913**	**261**	**88**

Source: Occidental Petroleum 1999 Form 10-K.

Why did Chevron report the liability and expense from the lawsuit settlement in its 1998 financial statements while Occidental Petroleum reported the income from the settlement in 1999? The answer is conservative accounting. Since Chevron's management realized at the time the 1998 financial statements were filed that it was probable that the company would have to make the payment, they were required under GAAP to record the liability and expense in 1998, even though the lawsuit was not settled until 1999. In contrast, GAAP rules do not allow for the recognition of contingent assets, so Occidental Petroleum could not recognize the income from the settlement until 1999, the year that the settlement was finally agreed to by Chevron.

WARRANTIES

A warranty is an example of a specific type of contingent liability. Any time a firm sells a product that includes a warranty, there is some probability that future repairs will have to be made. For example, if DaimlerChrysler sells a new vehicle with a three-year warranty, there is some probability that during the next three years the vehicle will require some repairs and that DaimlerChrysler will incur costs in connection with the repairs. At the time the vehicle is sold there is no actual liability, since the vehicle does not need any repairs; in fact, it may never need repairs under the warranty. Nevertheless, DaimlerChrysler knows from prior experience that it is *probable* that at least some of the vehicles it sells will require future repairs that will result in future negative cash flows for the company. Therefore, under the contingent liability rules the company must record a liability and an expense for the future warranty costs it expects to incur.

For example, assume that DaimlerChrysler estimates, based on prior experience, that on average it incurs $50 in future warranty costs for every vehicle it sells. Assume that it sells 200,000 vehicles during 2000. At the end of 2000, the company would make the following accounting entry to account for the expected warranty expense of 200,000 × $50 = $10 million:

	Example of Recording Expected Future Warranty Costs (in millions)		
+/−	Accounts [description of account]	Debit	Credit
+	Warranty Expense [income statement expense account	10	
+	Warranty Liability [balance sheet liability account]		10

Assume that in the following year DaimlerChrysler actually spends $8 million on warranty repairs. Here is the entry that is made to record the cost of the warranty repairs:

	Example of Recording Amounts Spent on Warranty Repairs (in millions)		
+/−	Accounts [description of account]	Debit	Credit
−	Warranty Liability [balance sheet liability account]	8	
−	Cash [balance sheet asset account]		8

Notice that, just as with the allowance method for recording bad debt expense, all of the income statement effect of the warranty repairs is recorded in the prior year, the same year in which the revenue from vehicle sales is recorded.

DISCONTINUED OPERATIONS

Recall from Chapter 2 that the disposition of a component of an entity by a company results in an income statement item called *discontinued operations*. Income or loss from discontinued operations is reported at the bottom of the income statement after income tax expense but before extraordinary items. Income or loss from discontinued operations consists of two components: the income or loss from the operations of the disposed component, and the gain or loss on the sale of the component.

It is common in dispositions for some period of time to pass between the decision of the company's board of directors to sell the business segment and the date of the actual sale. For example, Chevron's board of directors might have decided in October 2000 to dispose of the company's chemicals business, but the sale of all of the chemicals operations may not have occurred until May 2001. In this case, consistent with conservative accounting, and recognizing bad news early, the accounting treatment for the disposal in 2000 depends on whether the assets of the component to be disposed of have suffered an impairment loss.

If the future disposition is expected to result in a gain, the gain is not reported until the year that the segment is disposed of (2001 in the above example). However, if the assets of the component to be disposed of have a book value that is greater than the undiscounted expected future cash flows related to the assets, then an impairment loss has been incurred. In this case the general impairment loss rules require that the book value of the assets be reduced to reflect their fair market value, and that an impairment loss be recorded. The lower book value is then used for purposes of computing future gain or loss on disposition.

DIFFERENT DEFINITIONS OF CONSERVATISM

In this book the term *conservatism* is used very broadly to mean that accountants estimate and record expected future losses or expenses in the current accounting period rather than waiting for these losses or expenses to be realized in the future. The Financial Accounting Standards Board, in its "Statement of Financial Accounting Concepts No. 2: Qualitative Characteristics of Accounting Information," addresses the issue of conservatism, but the FASB's notion of conservatism is somewhat different than that used in this book.

The FASB states that at one time the idea of conservatism could be expressed as follows: "anticipate no profits but anticipate all losses." However, the FASB's view is that such a definition of conservatism has led in the past to consistent underreporting of asset values on balance sheets, which in turn led to overstatement of subsequent year net income. Therefore, the FASB rejects this notion of conservatism.

In "Statement of Financial Accounting Concepts No. 2," the FASB defines *conservatism* as follows: "A prudent reaction to uncertainty to try to ensure that uncertainty and risks inherent in business situations are adequately considered." Unfortunately, this definition is not very helpful in trying to define what the FASB means by conservatism. To help clarify what it means, the FASB gives the following example of conservatism: "if two estimates of amounts to be received or paid in the future are about equally likely, conservatism dictates using the less optimistic estimate; however, if two amounts are not equally likely, conservatism does not necessarily dictate using the more pessimistic amount rather than the more likely one. Conservatism no longer . . . justifies recognizing losses before there is adequate evidence that they have been incurred."

From the above discussion, it is apparent that the FASB views conservatism as applying to decisions about the correct amount to record for specific revenues or expenses. When two amounts are equally likely, the FASB concept of conservatism requires that the less optimistic estimate be used. The way this is commonly applied in practice is as follows: Whenever there is doubt about an amount to record in the financial statements, conservatism dictates that the amount used should *not* overstate assets or net income. However, in no case should assets or net income be intentionally understated.

TIMELY REPORTING IN OTHER COUNTRIES

Financial reporting rules in other countries often contain provisions similar to those discussed in this chapter. Here are some examples from the financial statements of Reed Elsevier (based on Dutch/U.K. GAAP), Nestlé (based on International Accounting Standards), and Akzo Nobel (based on Dutch GAAP).

Lower of Cost or Market for Inventory Valuation

Here are some financial statement notes describing the accounting treatment of inventory, called *stocks* in U.K. terminology. You can see that all three of these companies used some form of the lower of cost or market valuation method.

Reed Elsevier

Stocks and work in progress are stated at the lower of cost, including appropriate attributable overheads, and estimated net realisable value.

Nestlé

A provision is established when the net realisable value of any inventory item is lower than the value calculated above.

Akzo Nobel

Inventories are stated at the lower of cost or net realizable value.

Restructuring Charges

Here is information from the financial statements notes of Reed Elsevier related to what the company calls *exceptional items:*

8.	Exceptional Items (millions of pounds)		
	2000	**1999**	**1998**
Reorganisation costs (i)	**(77)**	**(161)**	—

(i) Reorganisation costs related to a major programme of reorganisation across the Reed Elsevier businesses, commenced in 1999. Costs include employee severance, surplus leasehold property obligations and fixed asset write offs.

Source: Reed Elsevier Form 20-F.

Here is a portion of the 2000 income statement of Nestlé showing restructuring costs for both 2000 and 1999:

Consolidated Income Statement Year Ended December 31, 2000 (in millions of CHF)			
	Notes	**2000**	**1999**
Sales to customers	1	81,422	74,660
Cost of goods sold		(38,121)	(35,912)
Distribution expenses		(5,884)	(5,268)
Marketing and administration expenses		(26,467)	(23,887)
Research and development costs		(1,038)	(893)
Restructuring costs		**(312)**	**(402)**
Amortisation of goodwill		(414)	(384)
Trading profit	1	9,186	7,914

Source: Nestlé annual report.

Impairment of Noncurrent Assets

Here is a portion of the cash flows statement of Nestlé showing the add-back to net income for the noncash impairment of tangible fixed assets. Notice that there is also an add-back for the noncash impairment of goodwill, an intangible asset.

Consolidated Cash Flow Statement Year Ended December 31, 2000 (in millions of CHF)			
	Notes	**2000**	**1999**
Operating activities			
Net profit of consolidated companies		5,580	4,545
Depreciation of tangible fixed assets	11	2,737	2,597
Impairment of tangible fixed assets	**11**	**223**	**373**
Amortisation of goodwill	14	414	384
Depreciation of intangible assets	15	179	92
Impairment of goodwill	14	230	212
Increase/(decrease) in provisions and deferred taxes		(4)	101
Decrease/(increase) in working capital	25	(368)	235
Other movements		(140)	(352)
Operating cash flow		8,851	8,187

Source: Nestlé annual report.

Here are examples from the notes to the financial statements of Nestlé and Akzo Nobel discussing the accounting principles applied to impairments. Notice that in the Nestlé note the impairment test is based on the *present value* of future cash flows. This is different than the U.S. GAAP impairment test, which is based on undiscounted future cash flows.

Nestlé

Impairment of assets

Consideration is given at each balance sheet date to determine whether there is any indication of impairment of the carrying amounts of the Group's assets. If any indication exists, an asset's recoverable amount is estimated. An impairment loss is recognised whenever the carrying amount of an asset exceeds its recoverable amount. The recoverable amount is the greater of the net selling price and value in use. In assessing value in use, the estimated future cash flows are discounted to their present value based on the average borrowing rate of the country where the assets are located, adjusted for risks specific to the asset.

Akzo Nobel

Property, Plant and Equipment

Depreciation is computed by the straight-line method based on estimated useful life, which in the majority of cases is 10 years for plant equipment and machinery, and which ranges from 20 to 30 years for buildings. **In cases where the book value so computed permanently exceeds the value to the business additional write-downs are made.**

Contingent Liabilities

The Nestlé annual report contains a note (see page 186) regarding contingent liabilities. Notice two things about this accounting treatment relative to U.S. GAAP. First, there can be contingent *assets* as well as liabilities. Contingent assets are not allowed under U.S. GAAP. Second, the contingent liabilities are disclosed in the notes to the accounts. Under U.S. GAAP, they would be recorded in the financial statements if they were both probable and able to be estimated.

Contingent Assets and Liabilities

Contingent assets and liabilities arise from conditions or situations, the outcome of which depends on future events. They are disclosed in the notes to the accounts.

Provisions

These include liabilities of uncertain timing or amounts that arise from restructuring, environment, litigation and other risks. Provisions are recognised when there exists a legal or constructive obligation stemming from a past event and when the future cash outflows can be reliably estimated. Obligations arising from restructuring plans are recognised only upon their announcement.

Source: Nestlé annual report.

The above note also reports a second category called *provisions* that include liabilities of uncertain timing or amounts. These appear to be similar to the U.S. GAAP concept of contingent liabilities.

Reed Elsevier reported the following contingent liability in the notes to its financial statements. (The notation "'L'm" stands for millions of British pounds.)

27.	Contingent Liabilities

There are contingent liabilities amounting to 'L'10m (1999 'L'23m) in respect of borrowings of former subsidiaries.

Source: Reed Elsevier Form 20-F.

EFFECTS OF EARLY RECOGNITION ON THE CASH FLOWS STATEMENT

All of the accounting rules discussed in this chapter deal with recognition of a current-year expense related to either an expected future negative cash flow or an expected future loss. When the expense is recognized in the current accounting period, the result is either the creation of a liability or the writing down of the book value of an asset. This means that all of the expenses are noncash expenses. Since these expenses reduce net income in the current year, but do not affect cash flows, they must be added back to net income in the computation of cash flows from operating activities.

Chevron's explanation of the lawsuit settlement liability and expense in its 1998 statement of cash flows is shown on the top of page 187. In the subsequent year (1999) when Chevron paid the lawsuit settlement, cash flows would be reduced. Chevron's 1999 cash flows statement, showing both the cash flow impact of the 1998 expense (added back to net income as a noncash expense) and the 1999 reduction in cash flows due to the cash payment, is also shown on page 187.

"Other, net" operating activities in 1998 include a noncurrent provision for the Cities Service litigation.

Consolidated Statement of Cash Flows
(in millions)

	Year Ended December 31		
	1998	**1997**	**1996**
Operating Activities			
Net income	$1,339	$3,256	$2,607
Adjustments			
Depreciation, depletion and amortization	2,320	2,300	2,216
Dry hole expense related to prior years' expenditures	40	31	55
Distributions greater than (less than) income from equity affiliates . .	25	(353)	83
Net before-tax (gains) losses on asset retirements and sales	(45)	(344)	207
Net foreign exchange gains	(20)	(69)	(10)
Deferred income tax provision	266	622	359
Net (increase) decrease in operating working capital	(809)	(253)	649
Other, net	**615**	**(310)**	**(219)**
Net cash provided by operating activities	$3,731	$4,880	$5,947

Source: Chevron 1998 Form 10-K.

	Year Ended December 31		
(in millions)	**1999**	**1998**	**1997**
Operating Activities			
Net income	$2,070	$1,339	$3,256
Adjustments			
Depreciation, depletion and amortization	2,866	2,320	2,300
Dry hole expense related to prior years' expenditures	126	40	31
Distributions (less than) greater than income from equity affiliates . .	(258)	25	(353)
Net before-tax gains on asset retirements and sales	(471)	(45)	(344)
Net foreign currency losses (gains)	23	(20)	(69)
Deferred income tax provision	226	266	622
Net decrease (increase) in operating working capital	636	(809)	(253)
(Decrease) increase in Cities Service provision	**(149)**	**924**	**—**
Cash settlement of Cities Service litigation	**(775)**	**—**	**—**
Other, net	187	(309)	(310)
Net cash provided by operating activities	$4,481	$3,731	$4,880

Source: Chevron 1999 Form 10-K.

USING INFORMATION ABOUT FUTURE LOSSES TO MAKE DECISIONS

Information about expected future negative cash flows is very useful information to the extent that it allows investors and other interested users to quickly incorporate the bad news into a company's stock price. However, in some cases, such as inventory write-downs, restructuring charges, or asset impairments, this bad news may have already been anticipated or expected by investors. Therefore, there may be little new information in these financial statement write-downs.

One important use of information about the allowance for doubtful accounts is to determine if write-offs of receivables are increasing or decreasing as a percentage of sales, thus providing information about changes in the company's credit or collection policies. In addition, it is often useful to compare the balance in the allowance for doubtful accounts with the balance in accounts receivable. If the allowance account is increasing or decreasing as a percentage of accounts receivable, it may be an indication that the company's credit and collection experience is changing. It may also indicate that management is recording either too large or too small an amount for bad debt expense.

Finally, it should be noted that many of the items discussed in this chapter are onetime or transitory items, and therefore their impact on future earnings may be minimal. In many cases, securities analysts disregard these nonrecurring items in their forecast of future earnings. However, large companies like Chevron may have such nonrecurring items every year, making it difficult to see how these items should be ignored. For example, here is the financial statement note disclosing Chevron's special items for the years 2000, 1999, and 1998:

Note 3.	Special Items and Other Financial Information

Net income is affected by transactions that are unrelated to or are not necessarily representative of the company's ongoing operations for the periods presented. These transactions, defined by management and designated "special items," can obscure the underlying results of operations for a year as well as affect comparability of results between years.

Listed below are categories of special items and their net increase (decrease) to net income, after related tax effects.

	Year Ended December 31		
	2000	**1999**	**1998**
Asset write-offs and revaluations			
Exploration and production			
Oil and gas property impairments			
U.S	$ (50)	$ (204)	$ (44)
International	—	—	(6)
Other asset write-offs	—	(37)	—
Refining, marketing and transportation			
Pipeline asset impairments—U.S	(30)	—	(18)
Marketing asset impairments—U.S.	—	—	(4)
Chemicals			
Manufacturing facility impairment—U.S.	(90)	—	—
Other asset write-offs	—	(43)	(19)
All other			
Coal mining asset impairment—U.S.	—	(34)	—
Information technology and other asset write-offs	—	(28)	(68)
	(170)	(346)	(159)
Asset dispositions, net			
Marketable securities	99	30	—
Pipeline interests	—	75	—
Real estate	—	60	—
Coal assets	—	60	–
Oil and gas assets	—	17	(9)
Caltex interest in equity affiliate	—	(31)	—
	99	211	(9)
Prior-year tax adjustments	(77)	109	271
Environmental remediation provisions, net	(208)	(123)	(39)

(continued)

	Year Ended December 31		
	2000	**1999**	**1998**
Restructurings and reorganizations			
Corporate	—	(158)	—
Caltex affiliate	—	(25)	(43)
	—	(183)	(43)
LIFO inventory gains (losses)	23	38	(25)
Other, net			
Dynegy equity adjustment	104	—	—
Insurance recovery gain	23	—	—
Pension/OPEB curtailment gains	16	—	—
Litigation and regulatory issues	(62)	78	(682)
Settlement of insurance claims for environmental remediation costs and damages	—	—	105
Caltex write-off of start-up costs (SOP98-5	—	—	(25)
	81	78	(602)
Total special items, after tax	$(252)	$(216)	$(606)

Source: Chevron Form 10-K.

As you can see from the above note, Chevron has reported special items of $252 million, $216 million, and $606 million over the three-year period. It is not apparent why users of Chevron's financial statements would want to ignore these types of items in the forecasting of Chevron's future earnings.

Summary

This chapter discusses one of the differences between economic income and accounting income—the fact that economic income usually recognizes expected future events more quickly than does accounting income, which usually delays recognition until some realization event that may be verified by an independent third party. However, for certain types of expected future losses or negative cash flows, GAAP requires immediate recognition of a loss or an expense in the current accounting period. This treatment is referred to as conservatism.

Examples of this treatment are (1) the allowance method for bad debts, (2) the lower of cost or market method for inventories, (3) impairment of noncurrent assets, (4) restructuring charges, (5) contingent liabilities, (6) warranty expenses, and (7) losses from discontinued operations. For each of these situations, the GAAP accounting treatment is discussed and illustrated with examples in the chapter. In addition, examples from financial statement of non-U.S. companies are given to illustrate similarities and differences between U.S. GAAP and GAAP from other countries.

Since the items discussed in this chapter all result in current-period expenses or losses but no current cash flow effects, the impact of these items on the cash flows statement is explained. In the year that the expense is recorded, an adjustment to net income for the noncash expense is necessary to compute cash flows from operating activities. In a future accounting period, when a cash payment is made with no income statement effect, an adjustment is also necessary to arrive at cash flows from operating activities.

When using the items discussed in this chapter to make decisions, users of financial statements must exercise caution. Some types of expenses, such as bad debts and warranty costs, are common recurring expenses that should be considered in any forecast of future earnings. Other expenses, such as restructuring charges, impairments, or contingent liabilities, may represent transitory, nonrecurring items that are not expected to persist into the future. However, many large companies have these types of nonrecurring expenses every year.

Discussion Questions

1. Explain the concept of *economic income,* and compare it with financial accounting income. Which is more relevant? Which is more reliable?

2. Conservatism in accounting is often described as recognizing bad news early but waiting to recognize good news until it is realized. Discuss the costs and benefits associated with this view, and contrast this view with the more narrow view expressed by the FASB.

3. Explain when bad debt expense is recognized under the allowance method. Discuss the relevance and reliability of this method.

4. Under the allowance method for bad debts, what are the income statement and balance sheet effects of writing off an uncollectible account?

5. Under the allowance method, can the amount of uncollectible accounts written off during a year ever be more than the beginning balance in the allowance for doubtful accounts? Explain.

6. The percentage of sales method and the percentage of accounts receivable method of computing bad debt expense each apply a percentage to compute an amount. What does the computed amount represent in each method?

7. Explain what an aging schedule is and how it is used to compute bad debt expense.

8. Explain the lower of cost or market method of inventory valuation. How is this method an example of conservatism?

9. Explain the different measures of *market* used in the lower of cost or market valuation method.

10. What is the difference between the aggregate and the item-by-item approach to the lower of cost or market method?

11. What are the costs and benefits of the lower of cost or market method?

12. Explain the impairment rules, including the role of expected future cash flows and market values. How do these rules provide information useful to investors?

13. What is the reason for not considering the present value of future expected cash flows when applying the impairment rules?

14. Explain the accounting rules for a restructuring.

15. Recording a restructuring charge in one year may result in higher profits in following years. Explain how this might occur.

16. What is a contingent liability? How is it different from an actual liability?

17. Explain the accounting rules for recording contingent liabilities.

18. Explain the accounting rules for recording expected future warranty costs.

19. How do the warranty accounting rules reflect the matching principle?

20. Discuss the warranty accounting rules in terms of relevance and reliability.

21. Explain the accounting rules for discontinued operations.

22. What is the difference between (*a*) income or loss from discontinued operations, and (*b*) gain or loss from disposal of discontinued operations?

23. How do the accounting rules for discontinued operations provide useful information to investors?

Problems

1. Here is some information about the accounts receivable and allowance for doubtful accounts for a company:

Accounts receivable balance at end of year	$ 200,000
Allowance for doubtful accounts balance at beginning of year	$ 25,000
Accounts written off during the year	$ 13,000
Credit sales during the year	$1,000,000

a. Assume the company uses the percent of sales method to compute bad debt expense. Based on experience, management estimates that 1.5 percent of credit sales will be uncollectible. Compute (*i*) the bad debt expense for the year and (*ii*) the balance in the allowance for doubtful accounts at the end of the year.

b. Assume the company uses the percent of receivables method to compute bad debt expense. Based on experience, management estimates that 14 percent of accounts receivable will be uncollectible. Compute (*i*) the bad debt expense for the year and (*ii*) the balance in the allowance for doubtful accounts at the end of the year.

2. Here is some information about the accounts receivable and allowance for doubtful accounts for a company:

Accounts receivable balance at end of year	$100,000
Allowance for doubtful accounts balance at beginning of year	$ 30,000
Accounts written off during the year	$ 15,000
Credit sales during the year	$800,000

a. Assume the company uses the percent of sales method to compute bad debt expense. Based on experience, management estimates that 2 percent of credit sales will be uncollectible. Compute (*i*) the bad debt expense for the year and (*ii*) the balance in the allowance for doubtful accounts at the end of the year.

b. Assume the company uses the percent of receivables method to compute bad debt expense. Based on experience, management estimates that 30 percent of accounts receivable will be uncollectible. Compute (*i*) the bad debt expense for the year and (*ii*) the balance in the allowance for doubtful accounts at the end of the year.

3. Here is some information about the accounts receivable and allowance for doubtful accounts for a company:

Accounts receivable balance at end of year	$ 90,000
Allowance for doubtful accounts balance at beginning of year	$ 15,000
Accounts written off during the year	$ 16,000
Credit sales during the year	$650,000

a. Assume the company uses the percent of sales method to compute bad debt expense. Based on experience, management estimates that 1.75 percent of credit sales will be uncollectible. Compute (*i*) the bad debt expense for the year and (*ii*) the balance in the allowance for doubtful accounts at the end of the year.

b. Assume the company uses the percent of receivables method to compute bad debt expense. Based on experience, management estimates that 17 percent of accounts receivable will be uncollectible. Compute (*i*) the bad debt expense for the year and (*ii*) the balance in the allowance for doubtful accounts at the end of the year.

4. Here is some information about the accounts receivable and allowance for doubtful accounts for a company:

Accounts receivable balance at end of year	$ 80,000
Allowance for doubtful accounts balance at beginning of year	$ 20,000
Accounts written off during the year	$ 22,000
Credit sales during the year	$975,000

a. Assume the company uses the percent of sales method to compute bad debt expense. Based on experience, management estimates that 2 percent of credit sales will be uncollectible. Compute (*i*) the bad debt expense for the year and (*i*) the balance in the allowance for doubtful accounts at the end of the year.

b. Assume the company uses the percent of receivables method to compute bad debt expense. Based on experience, management estimates that 25 percent of accounts receivable will be uncollectible. Compute (*i*) the bad debt expense for the year and (*ii*) the balance in the allowance for doubtful accounts at the end of the year.

5. Here is some information about the accounts receivable and allowance for doubtful accounts for a company:

Accounts receivable balance at end of year	$ 300,000
Allowance for doubtful accounts balance at beginning of year	$ 40,000
Accounts written off during the year	$ 15,000
Credit sales during the year	$3,500,000

a. Assume the company uses the percent of sales method to compute bad debt expense. Based on experience, management estimates that 0.5 percent of credit sales will be uncollectible. Compute (*i*) the bad debt expense for the year and (*ii*) the balance in the allowance for doubtful accounts at the end of the year.

b. Assume the company uses the percent of receivables method to compute bad debt expense. Based on experience, management estimates that 15 percent of accounts receivable will be uncollectible. Compute (*i*) the bad debt expense for the year and (*ii*) the balance in the allowance for doubtful accounts at the end of the year.

6. Here is some information about the accounts receivable and allowance for doubtful accounts for a company:

Accounts receivable balance at end of year	$ 200,000
Allowance for doubtful accounts balance at beginning of year	$ 45,000
Accounts written off during the year	$ 30,000
Credit sales during the year	$2,750,000

a. Assume the company uses the percent of sales method to compute bad debt expense. Based on experience management estimates that 1 percent of credit sales will be uncollectible. Compute (*i*) the bad debt expense for the year and (*ii*) the balance in the allowance for doubtful accounts at the end of the year.

b. Assume the company uses the percent of receivables method to compute bad debt expense. Based on experience management estimates that 20 percent of accounts receivable will be uncollectible. Compute (*i*) the bad debt expense for the year and (*ii*) the balance in the allowance for doubtful accounts at the end of the year.

7. A company has accounts receivable at the end of the year of $200,000, as shown in the aging schedule below. Management's estimate of the percentage of uncollectible receivables for each aging group is also shown below.

	Receivable Balance	Estimated Uncollectible
Over 90 days past due	$ 1,000	50%
61 to 90 days past due	3,000	20
31 to 60 days past due	5,000	10
Less than 31 days past due	11,000	5
Current receivables	180,000	2
Total	$200,000	

The balance in the allowance for doubtful accounts at the beginning of the year is $5,000, and the amount of accounts written off during the year is $4,500.

Using the aging schedule, compute (*a*) the bad debt expense for the year and (*b*) the ending balance in the allowance for doubtful accounts.

8. A company has accounts receivable at the end of the year of $1,000,000, as shown in the aging schedule below. Management's estimate of the percentage of uncollectible receivables for each aging group is also shown below.

	Receivable Balance	Estimated Uncollectible
Over 90 days past due	$ 12,000	40%
61 to 90 days past due	28,000	25
31 to 60 days past due	40,000	8
Less than 31 days past due	120,000	4
Current receivables	800,000	1
Total	$1,000,000	

The balance in the allowance for doubtful accounts at the beginning of the year is $30,000, and the amount of accounts written off during the year is $28,000.

Using the aging schedule, compute (*a*) the bad debt expense for the year and (*b*) the ending balance in the allowance for doubtful accounts.

9. A company has accounts receivable at the end of the year of $450,000, as shown in the aging schedule below. Management's estimate of the percentage of uncollectible receivables for each aging group is also shown below.

	Receivable Balance	Estimated Uncollectible
Over 90 days past due	$ 5,000	30%
61 to 90 days past due	8,000	15
31 to 60 days past due	20,000	7
Less than 31 days past due	37,000	3
Current receivables	380,000	0.5
Total	$450,000	

The balance in the allowance for doubtful accounts at the beginning of the year is $6,500, and the amount of accounts written off during the year is $7,000.

Using the aging schedule, compute (*a*) the bad debt expense for the year and (*b*) the ending balance in the allowance for doubtful accounts.

10. The following information relates to an item of inventory:

Original cost	10
Replacement cost	8
Net realizable value	11
Normal profit margin	2

    Compute the inventory value for this item under lower of cost or market method.

11. The following information relates to an item of inventory:

Original cost	15
Replacement cost	14
Net realizable value	12
Normal profit margin	4

    Compute the inventory value for this item under lower of cost or market method.

12. The following information relates to an item of inventory:

Original cost	20
Replacement cost	22
Net realizable value	23
Normal profit margin	6

    Compute the inventory value for this item under lower of cost or market method.

13. The following information relates to an item of inventory:

Original cost	12
Replacement cost	6
Net realizable value	12
Normal profit margin	2

    Compute the inventory value for this item under lower of cost or market method.

14. The following information relates to an item of inventory:

Original cost	30
Replacement cost	34
Net realizable value	35
Normal profit margin	5

    Compute the inventory value for this item under lower of cost or market method.

15. The following information relates to an item of inventory:

Original cost	5
Replacement cost	6
Net realizable value	4
Normal profit margin	1

    Compute the inventory value for this item under lower of cost or market method.

16. The table below shows the number of units, the unit cost, and the market value for items in a firm's inventory.

Item Number	Number of Units	Unit Cost	Unit Market Value
1	3,000	2.00	1.80
2	4,000	3.00	3.20
3	1,500	4.00	3.90
4	4,500	2.50	2.75

a. Compute the value of the inventory under the lower of cost or market method applied at the aggregate level.

b. Compute the value of the inventory under the lower of cost or market method applied on an item-by-item basis.

17. The table below shows the number of units, the unit cost, and the market value for items in a firm's inventory.

Item Number	Number of Units	Unit Cost	Unit Market Value
A	20,000	17.00	16.00
B	28,000	19.00	22.00
C	32,000	15.00	12.00
D	19,000	12.00	13.00

a. Compute the value of the inventory under the lower of cost or market method applied at the aggregate level.

b. Compute the value of the inventory under the lower of cost or market method applied on an item-by-item basis.

18. The table below shows the number of units, the unit cost, and the market value for items in a firm's inventory.

Item Number	Number of Units	Unit Cost	Unit Market Value
101	400	56.00	58.00
102	600	52.00	48.00
103	300	68.00	65.00
104	500	44.00	45.00

a. Compute the value of the inventory under the lower of cost or market method applied at the aggregate level.

b. Compute the value of the inventory under the lower of cost or market method applied on an item-by-item basis.

19. A corporation has an asset with a book value of $250,000. Managers estimate that the expected future cash flows from this asset are $225,000. The market value of the asset is estimated to be $210,000.

a. Is the asset considered impaired under GAAP?

b. If the asset is impaired, at what amount should the asset be recorded?

20. A corporation has an asset with a book value of $1,800,000. Managers estimate that the expected future cash flows from this asset are $2,000,000. The market value of the asset is estimated to be $1,500,000.

a. Is the asset considered impaired under GAAP?

b. If the asset is impaired, at what amount should the asset be recorded?

21. A corporation has an asset with a book value of $850,000. Managers estimate that the expected future cash flows from this asset are $800,000. The market value of the asset is estimated to be $700,000.

    a. Is the asset considered impaired under GAAP?

    b. If the asset is impaired, at what amount should the asset be recorded?

22. A corporation is a defendant in a lawsuit. Management estimates that, if the corporation loses the lawsuit, it will have to pay $1,000,000. How should this contingent liability be reflected in the financial statements if the likelihood the corporation will lose the lawsuit is probable?

23. A corporation is a defendant in a lawsuit. Management estimates that, if the corporation loses the lawsuit, it will have to pay $800,000. How should this contingent liability be reflected in the financial statements if the likelihood the corporation will lose the lawsuit is reasonably possible?

24. A corporation is a defendant in a lawsuit. Management estimates that, if the corporation loses the lawsuit, it will have to pay $2,500,000. How should this contingent liability be reflected in the financial statements if the likelihood the corporation will lose the lawsuit is remote?

Research Reports

1. Using library research, locate an article in the financial press that discusses the concept of *conservatism* as it relates to accounting.

    a. Relate the discussion of conservatism in your article to the way conservatism is presented in this chapter.

    b. Relate the discussion of conservatism in your article to the view of conservatism expressed by the FASB.

2. Obtain a copy of the Financial Accounting Standards Board's "Statement of Financial Accounting Concepts No. 2: Qualitative Characteristics of Accounting Information."

    a. In your own words, summarize the FASB's views of conservatism.

    b. Explain why the FASB is trying to narrow the definition of conservatism. What problems is the FASB concerned with if a broader definition of conservatism is allowed?

    c. Discuss the relevance and reliability of the FASB's approach to conservatism relative to other views of conservatism.

3. Find the annual report for a public company of your choice for any recent year.

    a. What is the financial accounting net income for the year?

    b. Compute the company's economic income for the same year.

    c. Explain the major differences between reported net income and the economic income you computed.

4. Shown below is some information from Chevron's 2000 Form 10-K.

Schedule II—Valuation and Qualifying Accounts (in millions)			
	Year Ended December 31		
	2000	1999	1998
Employee Termination Benefits			
Balance at January 1	$ 85	$ —	$—
Additions charged to costs and expenses	—	220	—
Expenditures	(85)	(135)	—
Balance at December 31	$ —	$ 85	$—

a. Explain what the account Employee Termination Benefits represents.

b. Explain how the $220 million amount for 1999 will affect the financial statements.

c. Explain how the $85 million amount for 2000 will affect the financial statements.

Here is some additional information from the same Form 10-K.

Schedule II—Valuation and Qualifying Accounts
(in millions)

	Year Ended December 31		
	2000	**1999**	**1998**
Allowance for Doubtful Accounts			
Balance at January 1	$ 43	$ 31	$33
Additions to allowance	31	66	3
Bad debt write-offs	(23)	(54)	(5)
Balance at December 31	$ 51	$ 43	$31

d. What is the amount of Chevron's bad debt expense each year?

e. Obtain Chevron's financial statements for these three years.

    i. Compute the bad debt expense as a percentage of Chevron's sales each year.

    ii. Compute the ending balance in the allowance for doubtful accounts as a percentage of the ending accounts receivable each year.

    iii. Comment on any changes in these percentages.

    iv. Provide an explanation for why the balances in the above table do not agree with the amounts reported on Chevron's balance sheet. (Hint: does Chevron have any other receivables on the balance sheet?)

5. Obtain the 2002 financial statements for the Kellogg Company. Locate Note 3 in the notes to the financial statements. The note is titled "Restructuring and Other Charges."

a. Kellogg recorded an impairment loss of $5 million in 2002. Explain the nature of this loss and how it was accounted for in Kellogg's financial statements.

b. Kellogg recognized restructuring charges in 2001 and 2000.

    i. What was the amount of the restructuring charges in each of these years?

    ii. Describe the general types of restructuring costs that Kellogg incurred.

    iii. What was the amount of cash outlays incurred for restructuring programs for 2001 and 2000?

    iv. Explain why the restructuring charges each year are different from the cash outlays.

    v. Kellogg reduced the 2001 restructuring charge by "credits for reserve adjustments" of $15 million. Explain what this credit represents.

    vi. What is the amount of the restructuring liability remaining at the end of 2002?

Courtesy of The Goodyear Tire & Rubber Company

Chapter Learning Objectives

After reading this chapter you should understand

1. The relationship between ending inventory and cost of goods sold.
2. The difference between a period cost and a product cost.
3. How accounting for inventory costs of manufacturers differs from retailers.
4. The difference between the periodic and perpetual inventory systems.
5. What is meant by a cost flow assumption.
6. The average cost, last-in, first-out (LIFO), and first-in, first-out (FIFO) cost flow assumptions.
7. How different cost flow assumptions affect the balance sheet and income statement.
8. The dollar value LIFO method.
9. The disclosures required under LIFO.

Chapter 7

Product Costs: Inventories and Cost of Goods Sold

Focus Company: The Goodyear Tire & Rubber Company

Introduction

Presented below is some income statement information from The Goodyear Tire & Rubber Company. Notice that the cost of goods sold for 1999 of $10,351.4 million is equal to 80 percent of net sales. By way of contrast, Microsoft's cost of goods sold for 2000 was 13 percent of sales. Because cost of goods sold is such a large percentage of Goodyear's sales, measuring cost of goods sold accurately can have an important effect on the computation of net income. Also, information about Goodyear's cost of goods sold would be extremely useful for anyone trying to forecast Goodyear's future earnings.

Consolidated Statement of Income (in millions)			
	Year Ended December 31		
	1999	**1998**	**1997**
Net Sales	$12,880.6	$12,626.3	$13,065.3
Cost of goods sold	10,351.4	9,672.9	10,015.6

Source: Goodyear Form 10-K.

Where does the cost of goods sold number come from? In Goodyear's case, here is the composition of 1999 cost of goods sold:

GOODYEAR Cost of Goods Sold for 1999 (in millions)	
Beginning inventory from prior year (1998)	$ 2,164.5
Plus: Purchases and other costs incurred in 1999	10,474.1
Goods available for sale during 1999	12,638.6
Less: Ending inventory (1999)	(2,287.2)
Cost of goods sold	$10,351.4

Notice two important things. First, the total amount of products Goodyear had available for sale in 1999 is equal to $12,638.6 million, and this total is composed partly of items that were included in the prior year's (1998) ending inventory (equal to $2,164.5 million) and partly of items that were purchased or manufactured during 1999 (equal to $10,474.1 million). Second, the total of goods available for sale in 1999 is reclassified into one of two different categories:

- Ending inventory, which appears on Goodyear's 1999 balance sheet.
- Cost of goods sold, which appears on Goodyear's 1999 income statement.

The above analysis illustrates an important relationship between ending inventory and cost of goods sold: When one is higher, the other must be lower. For example, if Goodyear's 1999 ending inventory was $1,000 million higher (that is, $3,287.2 million rather than $2,287.2 million), the cost of goods sold would, of necessity, be $1,000 million lower (that is, $9,351.4 million rather than $10,351.4 million).

This chapter discusses two major accounting issues relating to cost of goods sold and inventories. First, we discuss what costs are included as part of goods available for sale. This will involve the identification of costs that are product costs rather than period costs. Second, we discuss the accounting rules, called *cost flow assumptions*, that separate goods available for sale into two components: cost of goods sold and ending inventory.

PRODUCT AND PERIOD COSTS

As was discussed in Chapter 2, accountants usually refer to a cost as being one of two types: product costs and period costs. Before proceeding, however, it is important to understand exactly what we mean by the term *cost* in this context.

First, cost does not necessarily mean the same thing as expense, although usually the terms *period cost* and *expense* have the same meaning: a reduction in net income in the current accounting period. A good way to think about the definition of *cost* is how much you paid, or will pay, for something. It is in this sense of the word that we speak of original cost, historical cost, or amortized cost for balance sheet book values.

If the thing that we paid (or will pay) for provides a benefit to the firm that relates only to the current accounting period, then the cost is treated as a current period expense. Thus, the cost of insurance on the company headquarters building for the year and the cost of the annual financial statement audit are both treated as an expense. If the thing that we paid (or will pay) for provides a benefit beyond the current accounting period, then we capitalize the cost as an asset on the firm's balance sheet. Thus, the cost of a truck or a factory is not expensed currently; instead, it is recorded as an asset on the firm's balance sheet. The cost of the asset is recovered through depreciation over the future accounting periods in which the asset provides a benefit to the firm.

In addition to costs that provide a benefit to only the current accounting period and those that provide a benefit over several accounting periods, there is a third type of cost a firm incurs: the cost of the products or services the firm sells to customers. If the firm is a retailer, this cost is simply the cost of purchasing the items sold to customers. If the firm is a manufacturer, this cost is the total cost of manufacturing the products that are sold. If the firm provides services to customers, such as an accounting, law, or engineering firm, this cost is the cost of the services that have been provided during the period. These costs are what accountants mean by product costs.

To be recorded under accrual accounting, a cost must have been incurred during the current accounting period. In this context, incurring a cost means that the products or services that the firm is purchasing were received during the current accounting period, regardless of whether the cost is paid in cash or is recorded as a liability. Thus, wages paid during the year to factory workers for work performed during the year are costs of the current year. Also, wages that are owed to factory workers at the end of the current year, but that will be paid next year, are also costs of the current year. However, wages paid in this year to factory workers for work that was performed in the previous year do not represent a cost of the current year.

One final word about costs: For this purpose, accountants regard depreciation as a cost. Thus, the depreciation recorded for the current year on the factory building and manufacturing equipment is considered a cost of the products that are manufactured during the year. Depreciation is an allocation of the total cost of an asset to two or more accounting periods. If we purchase a manufacturing machine for $100,000 and expect it to last five years, the cost of the products manufactured with the machine should include $20,000 per year of depreciation expense.

Now that we understand what is meant by the term *cost*, the next step is to identify which costs for the current year relate to the products or services we sell. These are considered product costs. All of the product costs for the current year, together with the prior year's ending inventory, make up goods available for sale for the current year and will be allocated to either cost of goods sold or ending inventory at the end of the year.

WHAT COSTS ARE INCLUDED IN INVENTORY COSTS?

In this section we discuss different categories of product costs for three types of industries: manufacturers, retailers, and service industries. These costs are classified into one of three categories: raw materials, direct labor, and overhead. Each of these categories is discussed in more detail below.

Raw Materials

For a retailer, the cost of goods available for sale consists simply of the cost of the goods themselves, plus any freight or shipping costs to get the goods to the seller. For a manufacturer, part of the cost of manufacturing products is the cost of raw materials that go into the product. For example, Goodyear's raw materials would consist of rubber and other components, such as steel or nylon, that go into making tires and other rubber products. For a company like Apple Computer, raw materials would consist of the basic components of its computers, such as monitor screens, hard drives, memory chips, plastic, and wire. Boeing's raw materials would be extensive: aluminum, plastic, lubricants, tubing, cables, wires, airplane seats, oxygen masks, and small ovens for heating up airplane meals. For Microsoft, raw materials would be blank CDs, cardboard, and paper.

Direct Labor

Retailers have no direct labor. This does not mean that retailers do not pay wages, just that the wages paid by retailers are not considered part of the cost of the products they sell. For manufacturers, direct labor includes the wages paid to factory workers who manufacture the firm's products, as well as managers and supervisory personnel who are also directly involved in the manufacturing process. For companies engaged in providing services, such as engineering, medical, legal, or business consulting, direct labor costs represent the majority of the firm's product costs. The cost of direct labor includes not only the wages paid, but also payroll taxes, pensions, and other fringe benefits.

Overhead

Overhead may be thought of as all other costs related to a product other than raw materials and direct labor. Examples are rent on factory buildings and manufacturing equipment; depreciation of factory buildings and manufacturing equipment; utilities related to manufacturing; insurance for factory buildings and manufacturing equipment; and maintenance of factory buildings and manufacturing equipment. Including overhead as part of the cost of a product is known as *full-absorption costing* and is required under GAAP.

The classification of a cost as manufacturing overhead, and thus a product cost, rather than a period cost has important implications for reported net income. Consider a company that manufactures 1,000 units of a product during the year. It sells 800 units and has 200 units remaining in ending inventory. Assume that the company incurs $2,000 of utility costs during the year. If the utilities are classified as a period cost, they reduce pretax income by $2,000 for the year. However, if the utilities are classified as related to manufacturing, and therefore a product cost, the cost of the units manufactured is increased by $2.00 per unit—that is, $2,000 of utility costs divided by 1,000 units manufactured. Since 800 units were sold during the year, only 800 × $2.00, or $1,600, of the utility cost will be treated as an expense for the current year, as part of cost of goods sold. The remaining 200 × $2.00, or $400, will be included as part of the cost of ending inventory, a balance sheet asset account. Thus, the classification of manufacturing overhead affects reported net income for the period.

Another way that manufacturing overhead can affect net income is in cases where the scale of manufacturing activity changes from the prior year. Consider the example discussed in the previous paragraph. Assume that, instead of manufacturing 1,000 units during the year, the firm manufactured 4,000 units, with 200 units still in ending inventory. Under these assumptions, the cost of the units manufactured is increased by $0.50 per unit—that is, $2,000 of utility costs divided by 4,000 units manufactured. Since 3,800 units were sold during the year, 3,800 × $0.50, or $1,900, of the utility cost will be treated as an expense for the current year, as part of cost of goods sold. The remaining 200 × $0.50, or $100, will be included as part of the cost of ending inventory. Thus, a change in the scale of manufacturing activity from 1,000 units to 4,000 units causes an increase in the amount of utility costs treated as a current period expense.

Manufacturers

Inventories of manufacturers generally consist of three distinct inventory accounts: raw materials inventory, work in process (WIP) inventory, and finished goods (or finished products) inventory. To illustrate this concept, here is the inventory information from the notes to Goodyear's 1999 financial statements:

Note 6—Inventories (in millions)		
	1999	**1998**
Raw materials	$ 389.7	$ 369.9
Work in process	99.2	87.5
Finished product	1,798.3	1,707.1
	$2,287.2	$2,164.5

Source: Goodyear Form 10-K.

The raw materials inventory account keeps track of the cost of raw materials on hand at the end of the year. When the manufacturing process is begun and raw materials are used in the production process, these costs are transferred out of the raw materials inventory account and into the work in process inventory account. The work in process inventory account accumulates not only the raw materials costs, but also direct labor and overhead costs as well. When the goods complete the production process, their costs are transferred out of the work in process account and into the finished goods inventory account.

Here are some numbers to illustrate these transfers for Goodyear for 1999:[1]

---

[1] The details of the work in process inventory in this example are made up.

ANALYSIS OF INVENTORY ACCOUNTS FOR 1999
(in millions)

	Raw Materials	Work in Process	Finished Goods
Beginning balance, 1/1/1999	$ 369.9	$ 87.5	$ 1,707.1
Purchase of raw materials	3,678.8		
Transfers to work in process	(3,659.0)	3,659.0	
Direct labor costs		4,181.7	
Overhead costs			
Depreciation		1,214.2	
Utilities		983.6	
Rent		415.8	
Transfers to finished goods		(10,442.6)	10,442.6
Cost of goods sold			(10,351.4)
Ending balance, 12/31/1999	$ 389.7	$ 99.2	$ 1,798.3

Assume that Goodyear purchased $3,678.8 million of raw materials during 1999. These purchases increased the raw materials inventory account. Raw materials inventory was decreased by transfers of raw materials into the production process, equal to $3,659.0 million for 1999. This transfer reduced raw materials inventory and increased work in process inventory. In addition, the work in process inventory account also accumulated direct labor costs incurred during the year, assumed to equal $4,181.7 million for 1999. Overhead costs, such as depreciation, utilities, and rent relating to 1999 manufacturing activities were also added to the work in process inventory, equal to $2,613.6 million for 1999. During 1999, Goodyear completed production of products costing $10,442.6 million, which were transferred to finished goods inventory. Finally, products costing $10,351.4 million were sold during 1999, and this amount was transferred out of finished goods inventory and recorded as cost of goods sold, an income statement expense account.

Here are the journal entries to record all of these costs and transfers for the year:

Journal Entry to Record Purchase of Raw Materials

+/−	Accounts [description of account]	Debit	Credit
+	Raw Materials Inventory [balance sheet asset account]	3,678.8	
+	Accounts Payable [balance sheet liability account]		3,678.8

Journal Entry to Record Transfer of Raw Materials to Work in Process

+/−	Accounts [description of account]	Debit	Credit
+	Work in Process Inventory [balance sheet asset account]	3,659.0	
−	Raw Materials Inventory [balance sheet asset account]		3,659.0

Journal Entry to Record Direct Labor Costs

+/−	Accounts [description of account]	Debit	Credit
+	Work in Process Inventory [balance sheet asset account]	4,181.7	
+	Wages Payable [balance sheet liability account]		4,181.7

Journal Entry to Record Overhead			
+/−	Accounts [description of account]	Debit	Credit
+	Work in Process Inventory [balance sheet asset account]	2,613.6	
+	Accumulated Depreciation [balance sheet contra-asset account] ...		1,214.2
+	Utilities Payable [balance sheet liability account]		983.6
+	Rent Payable [balance sheet liability account]		415.8

Journal Entry to Record Transfer of Work in Process to Finished Goods			
+/−	Accounts [description of account]	Debit	Credit
+	Finished Goods Inventory [balance sheet asset account]	10,442.6	
−	Work in Process Inventory [balance sheet asset account]		10,442.6

Journal Entry to Record Cost of Goods Sold			
+/−	Accounts [description of account]	Debit	Credit
+	Cost of Goods Sold [income statement expense account]	10,351.4	
−	Finished Goods Inventory [balance sheet asset account]		10,351.4

Alternatively, the entries may all be combined into a single entry, with only the *changes* in the inventory accounts being recorded, as follows:

Journal Entry to Record Changes in Inventory Balances			
+/−	Accounts [description of account]	Debit	Credit
+	Raw Materials Inventory [balance sheet asset account]	19.8	
+	Work in Process Inventory [balance sheet asset account]	11.7	
+	Finished Goods Inventory [balance sheet asset account]	91.2	
+	Cost of Goods Sold [income statement expense account]	10,351.4	
+	Accounts Payable [balance sheet liability account]		3,678.8
+	Wages Payable [balance sheet liability account]		4,181.7
+	Accumulated Depreciation [balance sheet contra-asset account] ...		1,214.2
+	Utilities Payable [balance sheet liability account]		983.6
+	Rent Payable [balance sheet liability account]		415.8

Retailers

Unlike manufacturers, retailers have only a single inventory account that represents the merchandise they have available for sale at year-end. Rather than reporting raw materials, direct labor, and overhead, retailers record only the cost, together with any transportation charges, of merchandise purchased for resale.

Service Industries

Although it may at first seem that firms in service industries, such as law, engineering, and consulting, would not have inventories, in fact these types of firms do have work in process inventories, but not raw materials or finished goods. The reason is that these types of firms often enter into contracts to complete a specific project for a client. As the work is performed by employees of the firm, their wages, as well as other types of costs such as travel, data processing, or photocopying, are treated as a product cost and accumulated in a work in process inventory account. At the end of the engagement, when the project is completed, the client is billed for the work, and the work in process inventory account is transferred to cost of revenue, similar to cost of goods sold, on the income statement.

WHEN COST OF GOODS SOLD IS MEASURED: PERIODIC VERSUS PERPETUAL SYSTEMS

In the example journal entries shown in the preceding section, the simplifying assumption was made that all of Goodyear's 1999 inventory activity was recorded at the end of the year. In fact, firms are constantly purchasing raw materials, transferring materials into production, incurring labor and utility costs, and selling products. How are these costs dealt with by real companies throughout the year?

The answer depends on which of two different inventory accounting methods the firm is using: the periodic method or the perpetual method. Each of these methods is discussed below.

The Periodic Method

Under the periodic method, inventory balances are only adjusted once at the end of the accounting period. Also, cost of goods sold is only recorded at the end of the accounting period. During the accounting period, any purchases of new inventory items are recorded in a temporary account called Purchases. This account is used during the accounting period to accumulate costs, but it is eliminated at the end of the accounting period and does not appear on either the income statement or the balance sheet. During the year, the Purchases account has a debit balance.

For example, assume that on January 5, 1999, Goodyear purchased $2 million of rubber for use in making tires. Here is the entry to record this purchase under a periodic inventory system:

	Journal Entry to Record Purchases (Periodic Method)		
+/−	**Accounts [description of account]**	**Debit**	**Credit**
+	Purchases [temporary account]	2	
+	Accounts Payable [balance sheet liability account]		2

Similar entries would be made for other purchases, as well as for direct labor and overhead during the year. At the end of 1999, the balance in Goodyear's Purchases account would be equal to $10,474.1 million, composed of the following costs:

PRODUCT COSTS (in millions)	
Purchase of raw materials	$ 3,678.8
Direct labor costs	4,181.7
Overhead costs	
Depreciation	1,214.2
Utilities	983.6
Rent	415.8
Total product costs for 1999	$10,474.1

At December 31, 1999, Goodyear would take a physical inventory, which means it would count, and determine the cost of, all the raw materials, work in process, and finished goods on hand at the end of the year. The following entry would be made to adjust the balances in the inventory accounts and to eliminate the Purchases account.

	Journal Entry to Record Changes in Inventory Balances (Periodic Method)		
+/−	Accounts [description of account]	Debit	Credit
+	Raw Materials Inventory [balance sheet asset account]	19.8	
+	Work in Process Inventory [balance sheet asset account]	11.7	
+	Finished Goods Inventory [balance sheet asset account]	91.2	
+	Cost of Goods Sold [income statement expense account]	10,351.4	
−	Purchases [temporary account]		10,474.1

The Perpetual Method

Under the perpetual inventory method, all product costs are debited directly to the respective inventory accounts (raw materials or work in process) as they are incurred. For example, the same $2 million purchase of rubber used in the previous example would be recorded as follows:

	Journal Entry to Record Purchases (Perpetual Method)		
+/−	Accounts [description of account]	Debit	Credit
+	Raw Materials Inventory [balance sheet asset account]	2	
+	Accounts Payable [balance sheet liability account]		2

Any time products are transferred between production processes, additional entries are made to record transfers of raw materials to work in process, or to record transfers of work in process to finished goods. Finally, any time a sale is made during the year, finished goods inventory is reduced and cost of goods sold is increased.

Obviously, the perpetual inventory method requires a much more sophisticated accounting information system and much more data processing during the year than does the periodic method. Because of this, the periodic method was the primary method used by large corporations in the past. However, with the increase in information and data-processing technologies, most large companies today use a perpetual system.

Even if a perpetual system is used, it is often necessary to take a periodic physical inventory to control for stolen or damaged merchandise that would not normally be recorded under the company's accounting system. For example, if Goodyear's perpetual inventory records indicate an ending finished goods inventory of $1,800 million, but a physical inventory indicates only $1,798.3 million of finished goods are actually on hand at year-end (a difference of $1.7 million), the following entry would be made:

	Journal Entry to Record Inventory Shortages (Perpetual Method)		
+/−	Accounts [description of account]	Debit	Credit
+	Inventory Shortages [income statement expense account]	1.7	
−	Finished Goods Inventory [balance sheet asset account]		1.7

Inventory Shortages would most likely be combined with Cost of Goods Sold on the income statement. Notice that with a periodic inventory system this entry is not necessary, since the ending balance in Finished Goods Inventory under a periodic system would be determined by a physical count at year-end. Any difference between the beginning and ending inventory balances would be recorded as part of cost of goods sold.

COST FLOW ASSUMPTIONS FOR CHANGING PRICES

Up to this point, we have assumed that managers know the cost of a particular item of inventory. For example, assume that the total cost for a tire, including raw materials, direct labor, and overhead, is $29.95 per tire. If managers know that there are 57 million tires in inventory at year-end, it is easy to compute the value of ending inventory at 57 million × $29.95 = $1,707 million.

However, for most companies the costs of their products do not remain constant but change over time. For example, Goodyear's 1999 annual report has the following discussion by management of changes in product costs:

> Raw material costs decreased during 1999 and 1998, but are expected to increase in 2000. Labor costs increased in both 1999 and 1998, due in part to United States wage agreements, which provided for significant wage and benefit improvements. The impact of increased labor costs was somewhat mitigated by the reduction of manufacturing personnel throughout the world resulting from the Company's rationalization programs. Manufacturing costs were adversely affected in 1998 by the transition to seven-day operations at certain U.S. and European production facilities. Costs in both 1999 and 1998 benefited from efficiencies achieved as a result of ongoing cost containment measures.
>
> Source: Goodyear annual report.

If Goodyear's costs are constantly changing, as the above paragraph suggests, how do managers know the cost of any particular tire in their ending inventory? For example, if bulk rubber costs change, how can Goodyear keep track of which rubber ends up in which tires? Or imagine a grocery store with thousands of items on its shelves at year-end, all of them with changing costs during the year. How do the store managers know what the cost of a particular can of green beans is at year-end unless they can identify exactly when that can was purchased and what the cost was?

To deal with this problem of changing inventory costs, accountants have developed what are called *cost flow assumptions*. A cost flow assumption simply says that we *assume* that we know the *order* in which product costs enter into the company's inventory, and also the order in which costs leave the company's inventory. To illustrate the need for a cost flow assumption, consider the following simplified example.

Assume that, rather than having millions of tires in inventory, Goodyear had only two tires in its 1998 ending inventory and that these tires had a cost of $40 each. Assume further that Goodyear manufactured four tires during 1999. Because of increasing costs, the first two tires manufactured had a cost of $50 each, and the next two tires manufactured had a cost of $60 each. During 1999, assume Goodyear sold four tires for $100 each and had two tires remaining in ending inventory. All six tires are identical in every way except for their cost to manufacture.

Under these facts, what is Goodyear's gross profit for 1999? Obviously, the answer to this question depends on which tires were sold and which tires remained in ending inventory. Here are some possibilities.

Assumptions about Which Two Tires Were in Ending Inventory			
	2 @ 60	2 @ 50	2 @ 40
Ending inventory	120	100	80

Assumptions about Which Four Tires Were Sold			
	2 @ 40	2 @ 40	2 @ 50
	2 @ 50	2 @ 60	2 @ 60
Sales	400	400	400
Cost of goods sold	(180)	(200)	(220)
Gross profit	220	200	180

Alternative Computation of Cost of Goods Sold			
Beginning inventory	80	80	80
Plus purchases	220	220	220
Goods available for sale	300	300	300
Less ending inventory	(120)	(100)	(80)
Cost of goods sold	180	200	220

The first column assumes that the two tires remaining in ending inventory cost $60, while the four tires that were sold cost $40 and $50. Under these assumptions, the ending inventory is $120, the cost of goods sold is $180, and the gross profit is $220.

The second column assumes that the two tires remaining in ending inventory cost $50, while the four tires that were sold cost $40 and $60. Under these assumptions, the ending inventory is $100, the cost of goods sold is $200, and the gross profit is $200.

The third column assumes that the two tires remaining in ending inventory cost $40, while the four tires that were sold cost $50 and $60. Under these assumptions, the ending inventory is $80, the cost of goods sold is $220, and the gross profit is $180.

Notice that in all three of these cases, the cost of goods available for sale is always $300. Therefore, the problem of changing product costs only affects the allocation of goods available for sale between cost of goods sold and ending inventory.

Also notice that we are constrained in what we can assume about the costs of the tires. We cannot assume that all six of the tires cost $60 because there were only two tires manufactured at that price. Likewise, we cannot assume that the two tires that cost $40 were both sold and also remained in ending inventory. In the end, our cost assumptions must correspond with the actual costs the company incurred.

Finally, note that over the entire economic life of a company the total net income will be the same regardless of which assumption is made about inventory costs. Assigning higher costs to ending inventory results in a lower cost of goods sold in the current year but will result in a higher cost of goods sold in a future year when the inventory is liquidated.

An extremely important point to notice about the above example is this: *The company's earnings are different based on which tires we assume were sold.* In other words, Goodyear's managers could affect the company's net income by their selection of which tires to sell and which tires to keep in ending inventory. Obviously, since all six tires are identical, Goodyear's net income should not depend on which tires managers decide to sell.

The solution to this problem is to apply a cost flow assumption and to assume that we know the order in which the costs that Goodyear incurred during the year enter into cost of goods sold. The three choices available under GAAP are

- Average cost
- First-in, first-out (FIFO)
- Last-in, first-out (LIFO)

Each of these cost flow assumptions is explained in detail below.

Average Cost

The average cost assumption assumes that each item that makes up goods available for sale has the *same cost* and that this cost is equal to the average cost of all of the items combined. In the tire example used above, Goodyear's goods available for sale consists of six tires. Under the average cost method, first compute the average cost of all of the tires, and then assume that each tire has a cost equal to the average cost.

The total cost of goods available for sale in the tire example is $300. Dividing the total goods available for sale by the six tires available to sell results in an average cost per tire equal to $300/6 = $50. The average cost method assumes that the six tires representing goods available for sale have a cost of $50 each. This means that the ending inventory of two tires has a cost of $100, and the cost of goods sold for the four tires sold is equal to $200.

This method of computing average cost is a *weighted average*, where the weights are the number of units produced, or purchased, at a particular cost. To illustrate, assume that, instead of producing two tires at a cost of $60 each, Goodyear produces 200 tires at a cost of $60 each. Now there are 204 tires available for sale, with goods available for sale equal to $12,180, computed as follows:

Weighted Average Cost		
Number of Tires	Cost per Tire	Total Cost
2	$40	$ 80
2	50	100
200	60	12,000
204		$12,180

The average cost in this example is $12,180/204 = $59.71.[2]

First-in, First-out (FIFO)

The first-in, first-out (FIFO) assumption assumes that the *oldest* units purchased or produced—that is, the first in—are the first units sold—that is, the first out. Consequently, the *newest* units purchased or produced are assumed to be those that remain in ending inventory.

Continuing with the tire example, the cost of goods sold represents four tires sold, and under a FIFO cost flow assumption these are assumed to be the four oldest tires. The four oldest tires produced are the two tires costing $40 that were included in beginning inventory and the two costing $50 that were produced first during the year. Therefore, these four tires are considered to make up cost of goods sold, and the amount of the cost of goods sold is 2 × $40 + 2 × $50 = $180.

---

[2] Notice that the weighted average cost is *not* equal to (40 + 50 + 60)/3 = 50. This only works if the number of units produced at each price is exactly the same.

The ending inventory represents two tires still in inventory at year-end, and under a FIFO cost flow assumption these are assumed to be the two newest tires. The two newest tires are the two tires produced later in the year costing $60. Therefore, these two tires are assumed to make up ending inventory, and the cost of ending inventory is 2 × $60 = $120.

FIFO COST OF GOODS SOLD	
Beginning inventory	$ 80
Plus purchases	220
Goods available for sale	300
Less ending inventory	(120)
Cost of goods sold	$ 180

Under GAAP, there is no requirement that the physical flow of inventory match the cost flow assumption adopted for financial reporting purposes. For example, Goodyear could adopt the FIFO cost flow assumption even though it does not sell the oldest tires first. However, when working inventory problems it is often useful to have a mental image of a cost flow assumption, and a good mental image of a FIFO flow of products is a grocery store. In a grocery store, it is important that products not be allowed to sit on the shelves too long. Therefore, when the grocery store employees restock the shelves, they move the oldest products to the front of the shelf, and they restock the new products at the back of the shelf. In this way, a grocery store attempts to get customers to purchase the oldest products first, leaving the newest products in ending inventory. Keep in mind, however, that even though the flow of products in a grocery store tend to move in a FIFO manner, a grocery store can adopt a different inventory cost flow assumption for financial reporting purposes.

Last-in, First-out (LIFO)

The last-in, first-out (LIFO) assumption assumes that the *newest* units purchased or produced—that is, the last in—are the first units sold—that is, the first out. Consequently, the *oldest* units purchased or produced are assumed to be those that remain in ending inventory.

Continuing with the tire example, the cost of goods sold represents four tires sold, and under a LIFO cost flow assumption these are assumed to be the four newest tires. The four newest tires produced are the two tires costing $60 that were produced at the end of the year and the two costing $50 that were produced first during the year. Therefore, these four tires are considered to make up cost of goods sold, and the amount of the cost of goods sold is 2 × $60 + 2 × $50 = $220.

The ending inventory represents two tires still in inventory at year end, and under a LIFO cost flow assumption these are assumed to be the two oldest tires. The two oldest tires are the two tires that were in the beginning inventory costing $40. Therefore, these two tires are assumed to make up ending inventory, and the cost of ending inventory is 2 × $40 = $80.

LIFO COST OF GOODS SOLD	
Beginning inventory	$ 80
Plus purchases	220
Goods available for sale	300
Less ending inventory	(80)
Cost of goods sold	$ 220

A good mental image for a LIFO physical flow of products is a coal pile. As new coal is purchased, it is placed on the top of the pile. As customers buy the coal, it is taken off of the top of the pile. Therefore, the coal that customers are buying is the newest coal on the pile, while the coal at the bottom of the pile is the oldest in the pile and may have been in inventory since the coal pile was first started. However, keep in mind that, as with the other cost flow assumptions, a physical LIFO flow of products is not necessary to adopt the LIFO method for financial reporting purposes.

One important difference between the LIFO and FIFO cost flow assumptions is that under the LIFO method, year-end purchasing or manufacturing decisions may affect reported net income for the year. Here are some examples to illustrate this point.

First, assume in the tire example that management decides to produce one additional tire at year end, so that there are three tires produced at a cost of $60 each rather than the two in the original example. If four tires are sold during the year (as in the original example), there will be three tires left in ending inventory. Under the FIFO assumption, there is no change in cost of goods sold, as shown in the computation below. However, under the LIFO assumption the cost of goods sold increases from $220 in the original example to $230. This is because the extra unit produced at year-end costing $60 is assumed under LIFO to have been sold during the year. Under FIFO, this extra unit simply increases the balance in ending inventory.

HOW YEAR-END INVENTORY DECISIONS AFFECT LIFO COST OF GOODS SOLD

Case 1: Produce an Extra Tire Costing $60

	LIFO Assumption		FIFO Assumption	
Beginning inventory	$ 80	2 × $40	$ 80	2 × $40
Plus purchases	280	2 × $50 + 3 × $60	280	2 × $50 + 3 × $60
Goods available for sale	360		360	
Less ending inventory	(130)	2 × $40 + 1 × $50	(180)	3 × $60
Cost of goods sold	$ 230	1 × $50 + 3 × $60	$ 180	2 × $40 + 2 × $50

Case 2: Allow Inventory to Decrease from Two Tires to One Tire

	LIFO Assumption		FIFO Assumption	
Beginning inventory	$ 80	2 × $40	$ 80	2 × $40
Plus purchases	160	2 × $50 + 1 × $60	160	2 × $50 + 1 × $60
Goods available for sale	240		240	
Less ending inventory	(40)	1 × $40	(60)	1 × $60
Cost of goods sold	$ 200	1 × $40 + 2 × $50 + 1 × $60	$ 180	2 × $40 + 2 × $50

Now consider what happens if managers decide to let inventory levels decline at year-end by decreasing production from four tires during the year to three tires, with only one tire produced at a cost of $60. As shown in case 2 above, the FIFO cost of goods sold remains unchanged. However, the LIFO cost of goods sold decreases from $220 to $200. This lower cost of goods sold, which would result in higher reported net income for the company, is known as a *LIFO liquidation* and is discussed later in the chapter.

To summarize, under the FIFO assumption managers' year-end inventory or production decisions do not affect net income or cost of goods sold. However, under the LIFO assumption both net income and cost of goods sold may be affected by year-end inventory or production decisions. Therefore, LIFO allows managers the ability to affect reported earnings through their year-end production or purchasing decisions.

Dollar Value LIFO

The method of computing LIFO inventories and cost of goods sold illustrated above is known as *unit LIFO* since each unit in inventory is assigned a cost based on a LIFO cost flow assumption. Although conceptually easy to comprehend, unit LIFO is not typically used in practice. Instead, firms using the LIFO cost flow assumption often use a procedure known as *dollar value LIFO*, which is explained in this section.

Before going through the procedure for computing dollar value LIFO, it is helpful to understand the purpose of the computations. Notice from the tire example used above that when the quantity of units in ending inventory is equal to the quantity of units in beginning inventory, the ending LIFO inventory is exactly the same as the beginning LIFO inventory. In the above example, when there are two tires in beginning and ending inventory, the LIFO beginning and ending inventories are both $80. The reason for this is that, under a LIFO cost flow assumption, the units in ending inventory are considered to be the *oldest* units, and these oldest units would come from the beginning inventory. Therefore, under LIFO, unless there is a *quantity* increase or decrease in the inventory over the year, the ending inventory will be exactly the same as the beginning inventory.

However, if we compare the beginning and ending inventories under FIFO, the ending inventory is $120 while the beginning inventory was $80, despite the fact that there are only two units in inventory at the beginning and the end of the year. This $40 increase represents a *price* increase for the year. What this means is that, using a FIFO cost flow assumption, there are two ways that inventory values can increase during a year: a *quantity* increase and a *price* increase. However, under LIFO there is only one way that inventory values can increase during a year: a *quantity* increase. The goal of the dollar value LIFO computation is to *separate quantity increases from price increases*.

Rather than using the number of units in ending inventory to compute the year-end LIFO inventory amount, dollar value LIFO starts with the *dollar amount* of ending inventory based on a FIFO cost flow assumption. This makes record keeping much easier, since for internal management purposes companies usually keep their inventory records on a FIFO basis. Using dollar value LIFO, the firm simply makes a single LIFO adjustment to inventory at the end of the accounting period to prepare the financial statements.

This can be illustrated using the previous tire example, where management produced a third tire costing $60 at the end of the year, so that there are three tires in ending inventory. A dollar value LIFO computation would *not* begin with the fact that there are three tires in ending inventory. Rather, it would begin with the fact that the dollar value of the ending inventory (at current FIFO cost) is $180. The dollar value LIFO procedure then converts this $180 from a FIFO to a LIFO amount through the use of a price index.

The price index is a key concept in dollar value LIFO. The price index is computed using the following ratio:

$$\frac{\text{Ending inventory at current year cost}}{\text{Ending inventory at base year cost}}$$

The base year is the first year that the company adopted the LIFO cost flow assumption. Therefore, the price index is a measure of how much the company's inventory costs have increased, in percentage terms, since the adoption of LIFO.

Assume that Goodyear adopted LIFO in 1975 when the cost of manufacturing a tire was $17.50. The current year cost of manufacturing a tire at year-end is $60. Here is the computation of Goodyear's price index based on this example:

$$\text{Price index} = \frac{3 \times \$60 = \$180}{3 \times \$17.50 = \$52.50} = 3.4286$$

The reason this index approach is easier than unit LIFO is because the index can be developed using only a *sample* of the company's inventory. Goodyear actually has thousands of different products in ending inventory, and keeping cost records on all of them since 1975 would be burdensome. Using the index approach of dollar value LIFO, Goodyear can compute the index using only a small sample of actual inventory. If the sample is determined randomly following proper statistical procedures, the index developed using just the sample of inventory items can then be applied to price Goodyear's entire inventory.

Once the price index is computed it is then used to convert the ending inventory at current cost to a base-year amount. This is done by dividing the ending inventory at current cost by the price index for the year. Here is the computation using the tire example:

$$\text{Ending inventory at base-year cost} = \frac{\$180}{3.4286} = \$52.50$$

Once again, the reason this procedure is much easier than simply computing the base-year cost of the entire inventory directly is that the price index can be based on only a small sample of the actual inventory. For example, if Goodyear's ending inventory consists of thousands of items with a total current year cost of $180,000,000, the same procedure can be applied to arrive at the base-year cost of the entire inventory: $180,000,000/3.4286 = $52,499,563.

Once the ending inventory at base-year cost is computed, the next step is to compare this amount with the *beginning inventory at base-year cost*. Since both the ending and beginning inventories have been stated at base-year cost, this procedure *removes any price increases from the ending inventory*. This means that any increase in the ending inventory over the beginning inventory when both are stated at base-year cost *must* be due to a *quantity increase*.

First compute the beginning inventory at base-year cost. For a real company, this information would be contained in the company's permanent inventory accounting records and would be carried forward from year to year. However, it is easy to compute the beginning inventory at base-year cost in our tire example—it's just the two units in beginning inventory times the $17.50 base year cost, or $35.00.

Here is the computation of the quantity increase for the year:

Ending inventory at base-year cost	$52.50
Less: Beginning inventory at base-year cost	($35.00)
Quantity increase for the year	$17.50

This computation demonstrates there is a *quantity increase* for the year of $17.50, which is equal to the cost of one additional unit at base-year cost. This represents the third tire that was added in the example. The reason we know it is a quantity increase and not a price increase is because the price increase has been removed through the use of the price index.

In LIFO terminology, this quantity increase is referred to as a *layer*. Under the dollar value LIFO approach, a company's inventory consists of a base-year layer, and new layers representing quantity increases after the base year. A good mental image of this concept is a wedding cake, with several layers of cake stacked on top of one another.

Since this quantity increase was added during the current year, it is not appropriate to use a base-year cost of $17.50 for the third tire in the inventory. The third tire should have a cost equal to the current-year cost, since it was added to inventory during the current year. To convert the quantity increase from base-year cost to current-year cost, multiply the quantity increase (that is, the layer) by the price index for the current year.

Current-year layer at base-year cost	$17.50
Times: Current-year price index	× 3.4286
Current-year layer at current cost	$60.00

The final step is to add the current layer, at current cost, to the beginning LIFO inventory amount to compute the ending LIFO inventory. Here is the computation using the example:

Current-year layer at current cost	$ 60.00
Plus: Beginning LIFO inventory	$ 80.00
Ending LIFO inventory	$140.00

Notice that this ending LIFO inventory amount of $140.00 is *not* equal to the ending inventory of $130.00 computed under unit LIFO. The difference of $10.00 is due to the fact that dollar value LIFO prices the current-year layer at the end-of-year cost of $60, whereas unit LIFO used a cost of $50.00 for the third tire added to inventory.[3]

Here is a summary of the steps for computing LIFO inventory using the dollar value method:

Step 1. Convert the end-of-year dollar amount of ending inventory, at current cost, to base-year cost by dividing by a price index. The price index (reflecting current-year and base-year costs for a sample of inventory items) represents the relative increase in inventory costs from the base year to the end of the current year.

Step 2. Compare ending inventory at base-year cost with beginning inventory at base-year cost. Since price increases have been removed through the use of the price index, any increase represents a *quantity* difference, called a *layer*.

Step 3. Price any quantity increase by multiplying the current-year layer by the price index for the current year. Add this layer, priced at current cost, to the beginning inventory. If there is a quantity decrease rather than an increase, reduce prior year layers in reverse order (newest first).

Here is a comprehensive example of dollar value LIFO over multiple years, with inventory decreases as well as increases. In this example, the company adopts LIFO for 2001. The inventory value at January 1, 2001, of $2,500 becomes the base-year layer. Any future increases in inventory values due to cost increases are removed by the use of the price index. Any future increases in inventory quantities result in a new layer being added for the year of the increase. The new layer is priced at current cost using the current-year index.

---

[3] In actual practice, some companies avoid this difference by using two different price indexes: one to convert the ending inventory to base-year cost, and a second, based on costs at the beginning of the year, to reprice the current layer at current cost.

COMPREHENSIVE DOLLAR VALUE LIFO INVENTORY EXAMPLE (2000 IS BASE YEAR)					
	2000	**2001**	**2002**	**2003**	**2004**
Ending inventory at current cost	$2,500	$3,400	$4,600	$3,900	$5,200
Divide by price index	÷ 1.00	÷ 1.12	÷ 1.23	÷ 1.31	÷ 1.47
Ending inventory at base-year cost (see (1) below)	$2,500	$3,036	$3,740	$2,977	$3,537
Less: Beginning inventory at base-year cost		2,500	3,036	3,740	2,977
New layer at base-year cost	$2,500	$536	$704	$*(763)	$560
Multiply by price index	× 1.00	× 1.12	× 1.23		× 1.47
New layer at current cost	$2,500	$600	$866	$(932)	$824
Plus: Beginning LIFO inventory		2,500	3,100	3,966	3,034
Ending LIFO inventory (see (2) below)	$2,500	$3,100	$3,966	$3,034	$3,858
*Reduction in layers in 2003	2002	$ 704	× 1.23	$ 866	
	2001	59	× 1.12	66	
		$ 763		$ 932	

Recap of Inventory Layers by Year				
	Layer	(1) Base-Year Cost	Price Index	(2) LIFO Cost
Base-year (2000) inventory	2000	$2,500	× 1.00	$2,500
	2000	$2,500	× 1.00	$2,500
	2001	536	× 1.12	600
2001 inventory		$3,036		$3,100
	2000	$2,500	× 1.00	$2,500
	2001	536	× 1.12	600
	2002	704	× 1.23	866
2002 inventory		$3,740		$3,966
	2000	$2,500	× 1.00	$2,500
	2001	477	× 1.12	534
2003 inventory		$2,977		$3,034
	2000	$2,500	× 1.00	$2,500
	2001	477	× 1.12	534
	2004	560	× 1.47	824
2004 inventory		$3,537		$3,858

In 2003 there is a decrease in the quantity of inventory equal to $763 at base-year cost. This means that prior-year layers equal to $763, at base-year cost, must be removed from the prior-year inventory. Of this total, $704 completely eliminates the 2002 layer, leaving an additional $59 to reduce the 2001 layer. The 2001 layer is reduced from $536 to $477, at base-year cost.

Pooling and LIFO

A basic assumption of LIFO is that items in ending inventory are the same as those in beginning inventory. Under a LIFO cost flow assumption, if there is no quantity increase during a year the ending inventory cost is exactly the same as the beginning inventory cost. Although a physical LIFO flow of units through the inventory is not necessary to adopt a LIFO cost flow assumption, a problem arises if the items in ending inventory are not of the same *type* as those in beginning inventory.

For example, assume that Goodyear's beginning inventory consists solely of automobile tires, and that during the year Goodyear stops producing automobile tires and begins producing rubber boots and raincoats. If Goodyear's ending inventory consists exclusively of boots and raincoats, and the beginning inventory consists exclusively of automobile tires, how can LIFO be applied?

The answer is that LIFO is applied *separately* for groups of similar inventory items, called *pools*. For purposes of computing LIFO inventories, all items within an inventory pool are treated as though they are the same type of item, regardless of any differences between the items that may exist. For example, Goodyear may have one inventory pool consisting of automobile tires, one of truck tires, one of airplane tires, one of boots and raincoats, and so forth. A separate LIFO computation would be made for each pool. DaimlerChrysler may have separate inventory pools for automobiles, trucks, minivans, and parts. Under this view, a 2001 Dodge Caravan minivan is considered to be the same as a 1990 Dodge Caravan, and under LIFO the 1990 cost will be applied to the 2001 Caravans in ending inventory.

As long as items are within the same LIFO pool, they are considered to be the same item for purposes of the LIFO computation. For example, when Goodyear began producing steel belted tires rather than nylon belted tires, an ending inventory of steel belted tires would be treated as though they were the same tires as a beginning inventory of nylon belted tires, as long as the two tire types were part of the same LIFO pool.

Here is an example of the difference in inventory values that can result depending on how LIFO inventory pools are applied. Assume that in 1980 Goodyear's inventory consisted solely of 1,000 rubber tires costing $20 per tire. Assume that over time Goodyear gradually shifted production from rubber tires to nylon belted tires (which cost $30 per tire), so that by 1990 the ending inventory consisted of 500 rubber tires and 500 nylon belted tires. Later, production shifted again to steel belted tires (which cost $40 per tire), so that by 2000 the ending inventory consisted of 100 rubber tires, 400 nylon belted tires, and 500 steel belted tires. Here is how Goodyear's ending inventory in 2000 would differ based on their LIFO pooling choices:

EXAMPLE OF EFFECT OF LIFO POOLS

Separate LIFO Pools				Single LIFO Pool	
1980	**Rubber Tires**			**1980**	**Tires**
Units	1,000			Units	1,000
Cost	$ 20			Cost	$ 20
Total	$20,000			Total	$20,000
1990	**Rubber Tires**	**Nylon Belted**		**1990**	**Tires**
Units	500	500		Units	1,000
Cost	$ 20	$ 30		Cost	$ 20
Total	$10,000	$15,000		Total	$20,000
Total inventory		$25,000			
2000	**Rubber Tires**	**Nylon Belted**	**Steel Belted**	**2000**	**Tires**
Units	100	400	500	Units	1,000
Cost	$ 20	$ 30	$ 40	Cost	$ 20
Total	$ 2,000	$12,000	$20,000	Total	$20,000
Total inventory			$34,000		

With multiple pools, the change in the type of tires results in a new inventory cost for the new types of tires, causing an increase in ending inventory from $20,000 in 1980 to $34,000 in 2000, despite the fact that the number of units has remained constant at 1,000. However, if a single inventory pool for tires is used, the tires in the 2000 ending inventory are assumed to have the same cost (that is, $20) as the tires in the 1980 inventory. Since there has not been a quantity increase, the ending inventory remains at $20,000.

EFFECTS OF COST FLOW ASSUMPTIONS ON EARNINGS AND ASSETS

The different inventory cost flow assumptions affect cost of goods sold in a predictable way. If inventory costs are *increasing,* LIFO results in a larger cost of goods sold (and consequently smaller gross profit and net income) than FIFO. If inventory costs are *decreasing* just the opposite effect occurs—LIFO results in a smaller cost of goods sold (and consequently larger gross profit and net income) than FIFO.

With respect to balance sheet book values for inventories, if inventory costs are *increasing* LIFO results in a smaller inventory book value than FIFO. When inventory costs are *decreasing* LIFO results in a larger inventory book value than FIFO.

Here is a table that summarizes the effects of inventory cost flow assumptions on earnings and asset values. Only the effects for the LIFO and FIFO assumptions are shown in the table. The effects of the average cost assumption are between the LIFO and FIFO effects.

	EFFECT OF LIFO RELATIVE TO FIFO	
	Inventory Costs Increasing	**Inventory Costs Decreasing**
Cost of goods sold	LIFO higher	LIFO lower
Gross profit	LIFO lower	LIFO higher
Net income	LIFO lower	LIFO higher
Inventory book value	LIFO lower	LIFO higher

If over time the costs of a firm's products tend to increase, then it is clear that the use of the LIFO cost flow assumption would result in lower net income. Why then would managers adopt LIFO?

There are two answers to this question. The first answer is a theoretical justification for LIFO based on an argument that goes as follows: Under LIFO, the cost of goods sold for the current year reflects current-year costs of products, even though these products may still be in inventory at year-end. This means that LIFO matches current inventory costs with current sales revenue, resulting in a better matching of costs and revenues. Under FIFO, current-year cost of goods sold reflects the costs of goods that were purchased or produced in the prior year when costs were lower. Therefore, FIFO results in a matching of prior-year costs with current-year revenues and overstates net income. The additional gross profit that firms report when their cost of goods sold reflects lower prior-year costs is known as an *inventory holding gain.* Many accountants argue that LIFO is a preferable accounting method because it removes inventory holding gains from income.

The second answer to the question, Why do managers adopt LIFO? is a simpler one: It saves the firm taxes. In periods of rising prices, LIFO not only results in lower net income, but it results in *lower taxable income* as well.[4] This

---

[4] This result assumes that inventory quantities do not decrease. If inventory quantities decrease, then the tax benefits of LIFO reverse and the company's taxable income is higher under LIFO. This is discussed later in the chapter.

lower taxable income means that firms pay less in income taxes each year, thus increasing their cash flows. Since the LIFO cost flow assumption does not have a direct cash flow effect, this tax-related cash flow increase means that firms that use LIFO realize higher cash flows than those that do not use LIFO, despite the fact that the net income of the LIFO firms is lower.

THE LIFO TAX CONFORMITY REQUIREMENT

The U.S. tax law contains a requirement, known as the *LIFO conformity requirement,* that applies to all corporations that use the LIFO method for income tax purposes. Under the conformity requirement, a firm may only use LIFO for income tax purposes if the firm also uses LIFO for financial reporting purposes.

This requirement does not apply to foreign subsidiaries of U.S. parent firms where the foreign subsidiary does not do business in the United States. Also, the rule does not apply to foreign parents of U.S. subsidiaries. Therefore, it is common to see multinational firms reporting U.S. inventories on LIFO, to obtain the U.S. tax savings, and non-U.S. inventories using FIFO or average cost.

Sometimes firms stop realizing an income tax benefit from the use of LIFO. This could be because inventory costs are no longer increasing, or because inventory quantities are decreasing. Also, companies with U.S. tax losses may get no tax benefit for lower LIFO taxable income. When this happens, managers may decide that, without the U.S. tax benefits, there is no reason to continue to use LIFO. In these cases, the firm may change back to FIFO or average cost. For example, in 2000 Goodyear switched inventory methods from LIFO to FIFO. Here is the financial statement note explaining this change:

> During the fourth quarter of 2000, the Company changed its method of inventory costing from last-in, first-out (LIFO) to first-in, first-out (FIFO) for domestic inventories. Prior periods have been restated to reflect this change. The method was changed in part to achieve a better matching of revenues and expenses. The change increased net income in 2000 by $44.4 million.
>
> Source: Goodyear Form 10-K.

It is interesting that the reason given for the inventory method change—to achieve a better matching of revenues and expenses—is the same reason often used by companies changing *from* FIFO *to* LIFO! Without additional information about management's expectations concerning future inventory levels and costs it is difficult to determine exactly why Goodyear changed its inventory cost flow assumption.

LIFO DISCLOSURE REQUIREMENTS

For a company using LIFO, in the absence of a quantity increase the ending inventory has the same cost as the beginning inventory. When a company uses LIFO for several years, the book value of ending inventory begins to reflect very old costs, and these old costs are often much lower than the current costs of purchasing or producing inventory.

Accounting standard setters in the United States were concerned that the old costs reflected in LIFO balance sheet book value numbers would not provide users of financial statements with useful information about the company's current investment in inventory. Therefore, any firm that uses LIFO must disclose in the notes to the financial statements what the inventory book value *would have been* if the inventory were valued at current cost. In most cases, the firm discloses what inventory book values would have been if it had used the FIFO method, since FIFO cost is usually not materially different from current cost.

There are two approaches that firms use to provide this information. First, firms may disclose what the book value would have been under FIFO or current cost. Second, they may disclose the *difference* between the book value of LIFO inventories and what the book value would have been under FIFO or current cost.

This difference between the book value of LIFO inventories and what the book value would have been under FIFO or current cost is called the *LIFO reserve.* Here is an example of Goodyear's LIFO reserve disclosure in the notes to its financial statements.

The cost of inventories using the last-in, first-out (LIFO) method (approximately 37.4% of consolidated inventories in 1999 and 39.7% in 1998) was less than the approximate current cost of inventories by $306.2 million at December 31, 1999 and $322.4 million at December 31, 1998.

Source: Goodyear Form 10-K.

In other words, Goodyear's LIFO reserve was $306.2 million at the end of 1999 and $322.4 million at the end of 1998.

Using the LIFO Reserve Information

There are two main uses of LIFO reserve information. First, by adding the amount of the LIFO reserve back to the LIFO ending inventory it is possible to obtain a measure of the book value of inventories at current (or FIFO) cost. For example, here are Goodyear's inventory book values based on current cost:

INVENTORY AT CURRENT COST		
	1999	1998
Raw materials	$ 389.7	$ 369.9
Work in process	99.2	87.5
Finished goods	1,798.3	1,707.1
LIFO inventory	$2,287.2	$2,164.5
Plus: LIFO reserve	306.2	322.4
Inventory at current cost	$2,593.4	$2,486.9

This information allows users of Goodyear's financial statements to replace the less relevant LIFO balance sheet book values with more relevant current cost information. The second way LIFO reserve information may be used is to convert LIFO cost of goods sold to an estimate of FIFO cost of goods sold. In this way, users of financial statements of a LIFO firm can adjust the pretax income and net income of the LIFO firm to make these numbers more consistent, from an accounting method standpoint, with those of a FIFO firm. The information necessary to make this adjustment is the *change* in the LIFO reserve from the previous year. Here is an example using Goodyear's LIFO reserve information for 1999:

APPROXIMATE FIFO COST OF GOODS SOLD FOR 1999			
	As Reported LIFO	LIFO Reserve	Approximate FIFO
Beginning inventory from prior year (1998)	$ 2,164.5	$ 322.4	$ 2,486.9
Plus: Purchases and other costs incurred in 1999	10,474.1		10,474.1
Goods available for sale during 1999	$12,638.6		$12,961.0
Less: Ending inventory (1999)	(2,287.2)	(306.2)	(2,593.4)
Cost of goods sold	$10,351.4	$ 16.2	$10,367.6

As you can see from this computation, the $16.2 million decrease in Goodyear's LIFO reserve results in an increase in FIFO cost of goods sold over LIFO cost of goods sold. This higher FIFO cost of goods sold would result in $16.2 million lower pretax income under FIFO. To compute the effect on net income, the tax effect of the $16.2 million would need to be included. For example, if Goodyear's 1999 income tax rate was 35 percent, then Goodyear's net income under FIFO would have been lower than reported LIFO net income by approximately $16.2 million $\times$ (1 − 35%) = $10.53 million.

Notice that the balance in Goodyear's LIFO reserve *decreased* from $322.4 million in 1998 to $306.2 million in 1999. This decrease in the LIFO reserve means that the difference between the LIFO and FIFO cost of inventory is getting smaller. Because of this decrease, the usual expectation that LIFO cost of goods sold is higher than FIFO cost of goods sold does not hold. With a decrease in the LIFO reserve, the cost of goods sold is higher under FIFO; consequently, the net income is lower under FIFO.

There are two possible causes of a decrease in the LIFO reserve. The first cause is decreasing product costs. If product costs decrease during the year, then the FIFO cost of goods sold will be larger than the LIFO cost of goods sold, and the FIFO inventory book value will decrease relative to the LIFO inventory book value. The second cause of a decrease in the LIFO reserve is a decrease in inventory quantities resulting in a reduction of prior year LIFO layers. The effect of such a reduction is discussed in the next section.

LIQUIDATIONS OF LIFO INVENTORY LAYERS

If inventory costs are increasing, then LIFO cost of goods sold is higher than FIFO and LIFO net income is lower than FIFO. There is an important exception to this rule, and that is in a case where inventory quantities are decreasing. A quantity decrease under LIFO results in the removal of prior years' inventory layers. This reduction in prior layers, known as a *LIFO liquidation*, causes very old LIFO inventory costs to be removed from the inventory balance sheet book value. Recall that the total goods available for sale for a year must all be allocated to either ending inventory or cost of goods sold. If old LIFO costs are removed from ending inventory, they must flow through current-year cost of goods sold, resulting in a lower cost of goods sold and a corresponding higher net income under LIFO.

To summarize: (1) A reduction in inventory quantities under LIFO results in (2) a liquidation of old LIFO layers, which results in (3) a decrease in LIFO cost of goods sold relative to FIFO, which results in (4) an increase in LIFO net income relative to FIFO.

This means that in years in which inventory quantities decrease, a LIFO firm will report higher net income than it would have if inventory levels had remained constant or increased. Also, the firm will pay more income taxes in the year of a LIFO liquidation, since its taxable income will also be higher. This can cause a problem for users of financial statement information since the firm looks more profitable because net income is higher, when in fact the firm is worse off because cash flows have been reduced for additional tax payments.

Keep in mind that most multinational firms use LIFO for only a portion of their inventories. For example, Goodyear used LIFO for 37.4 percent of its inventories in 1999. Therefore, a LIFO liquidation may occur even though the overall inventory book value increases for the year.

Because of the additional income taxes associated with a LIFO liquidation, managers usually try to avoid such liquidations if possible. However, there are some cases in which LIFO liquidations will occur. First, shortages or strikes may prevent the acquisition of the usual inventory quantities at year-end, resulting in an unintentional decrease in ending inventories. This occurred during the early 1970s to oil companies when many oil exporting countries refused to sell oil to

U.S. firms. Second, managers may make a conscious decision to reduce inventory levels as firms move to just-in-time (JIT) inventory systems. This decision trades off the cost savings associated with the JIT inventory system with the additional income taxes that result from the LIFO liquidation. Third, managers may deliberately reduce year-end inventory levels to increase reported earnings.

INVENTORY ACCOUNTING IN OTHER COUNTRIES

Because of U.S. tax benefits, the LIFO inventory method is primarily used in the United States. Multinational corporations, as well as non-U.S. corporations, tend to use FIFO or average cost for their non-U.S. inventories. Germany changed its tax law in the 1990s to allow the use of LIFO, and some German corporations (for example, BASF) switched their inventory accounting method to LIFO. Also, the Netherlands allows companies to use LIFO for income tax purposes but FIFO or average cost for financial reporting purposes, so that Dutch companies can achieve LIFO tax benefits without reporting their inventory costs under LIFO.

While LIFO is primarily used in the United States, almost all countries require the use of the lower of cost or market method for valuing inventories. (The lower of cost or market method was discussed in Chapter 6.) When the lower of cost or market method is applied, the amount used for the cost computation will be either LIFO cost, FIFO cost, or average cost. Since LIFO usually results in lower inventory costs, it is unusual to see a LIFO firm writing inventories down to market value.

Here are some examples of accounting method disclosures regarding inventory (called *stocks* in the U.K.) accounting from non-U.S. firms:

Stocks and work in progress are stated at the lower of cost, including appropriate attributable overheads, and estimated net realisable value.

Source: Reed Elsevier annual report.

Raw materials and purchased finished goods are valued at purchase cost. Work in progress and manufactured finished goods are valued at production cost. Production cost includes direct production costs and an appropriate proportion of production overheads and factory depreciation. Movements in raw materials inventories and purchased finished goods are accounted for using the FIFO (first-in, first-out) method. The weighted average cost method is used for other inventories. A provision is established when the net realisable value of any inventory item is lower than the value calculated above.

Source: Nestlé annual report.

Inventories are stated at the lower of cost and net realizable value. Cost is determined on a first-in, first-out (FIFO) basis. Net realizable value is the amount that can be realized from the sale of the inventory in the normal course of business after allowing for the costs of realization. In addition to the cost of materials and direct labor, an appropriate proportion of production overheads is included in the inventory values.

Source: Nokia annual report.

Inventories are stated at the lower of cost or net realizable value. Cost, defined as the full manufacturing cost related to the stage of processing, is determined by the first-in, first-out (FIFO) method. Provisions are made for obsolescence.

Source: Akzo Nobel annual report.

Inventories are valued at the lower of acquisition or manufacturing cost or market, cost being generally determined on the basis of an average or first-in, first-out method ("FIFO"). Certain of the Group's U.S. inventories are valued using the last-in, first-out method ("LIFO"). Manufacturing costs comprise direct material and labor and applicable manufacturing overheads, including depreciation charges. If the FIFO method had been used instead of the LIFO method, inventories would have been higher by [EURO]1,058.

Source: DaimlerChrysler Form 20-F.

Notice that in the case of Reed Elsevier there is no disclosure of the cost flow assumption used to value the inventory. Nestlé uses the FIFO and average cost methods, whereas Nokia and Akzo Nobel use FIFO. In the case of Daimler-Chrysler, non-U.S. inventories are valued using FIFO or average cost; however, U.S. inventories are valued using LIFO, and information about the LIFO reserve is also presented. Finally, all of these companies value manufactured inventories using the full cost method, which means they include overhead as well as raw materials and direct labor in determining product costs.

INVENTORIES AND THE CASH FLOWS STATEMENT

Inventories and the accounts payable that result from inventory purchases affect the statement of cash flows in many ways. First, to the extent that inventories are written down under the lower of cost or market valuation method, the write-down results in a noncash expense that must be added back to net income to arrive at cash flows from operating activities under the indirect method. Second, to the extent that depreciation of factory buildings and equipment is added to the cost of ending inventory as part of overhead, the depreciation does not represent a noncash expense, since it is not reported as an expense on the income statement.

Third, if a company increases inventory levels, this represents a cash outflow but does not reduce net income. Fourth, if a company decreases inventory levels, this represents a noncash expense for cost of goods sold. Fifth, if a company increases accounts payable for products purchased during the year, this represents a noncash expense to the extent the purchases increase cost of goods sold. Finally, to the extent that a company pays off accounts payable, this represents a cash outflow without an effect on net income.

USING INFORMATION ABOUT PRODUCT COSTS TO MAKE DECISIONS

Product cost information can be used in several basic ways to make decisions. Expressing cost of goods sold as a percentage of sales allows comparisons across time and across different companies and provides important information about gross margins. Also, the inventory turnover ratio, equal to cost of goods sold divided by average inventory, is an important measure of how efficiently the company is utilizing inventories.

However, even sophisticated users of financial statements may find that information about product costs is difficult to interpret accurately. Here are some examples of problems faced by users of financial statements.

Changes in Overhead Allocation Rates

Factory overhead is treated as a product cost and allocated to all units produced during the year. To the extent that these overhead costs are fixed (such as depreciation on the factory building), changes in the level of production will change the per-unit overhead cost of production. To illustrate, for a given amount of depreciation, if a firm doubles its production the depreciation overhead cost per unit will be cut in half.

If the same percentage of units produced ends up in ending inventory, this change in the overhead rate will not affect net income. However, assume that a firm doubles production but sells the same number of units as before. In this situation, the amount of factory depreciation that gets expensed as part of cost of goods sold will be only half as much as it would under the previous level of production. Therefore, the firm will appear to be more profitable when in fact there has been no change in profitability.

Determining Optimal Inventory Quantities

It is not clear how users of financial statements can tell whether the firm's ending inventory is the optimal amount. In general, less inventory is better than more inventory, since more inventory increases costs such as storage, insurance, and handling as well as increasing the probability of losses from obsolescence. Also, inventory represents an investment by the firm, and to the extent that the firm could invest the same amount in more productive assets, firm value is not being maximized.

However, there are also costs associated with not having enough inventory. Firms that run out of stock may be unable to fill customer orders and may lose business. Also, running short of inventory may result in costly and inefficient production runs in an attempt to keep up with customer demand. Finally, a buildup of inventories at year-end may be a signal that managers are expecting increased sales in the coming year, and a decrease in inventories may signal managers' expectations of a downturn in sales. Therefore, determining whether less inventory is a good or bad sign really depends on understanding a great deal about the underlying business being analyzed.

LIFO Liquidations

If a LIFO firm's LIFO reserve decreases, is this good or bad news? A decrease in the LIFO reserve could mean management has been successful in reducing inventory quantities, which may signal lower costs for the firm in the future. However, such efficiencies come at the expense of higher tax payments in the current year. Also, a decrease as a result of falling input costs is a strong positive signal about firm value. Finally, a decrease due to manager manipulation of year-end inventory levels in an effort to increase reported net income is a bad signal, since tax payments will increase with no corresponding benefits to the firm.

LIFO-FIFO Comparisons

Using the change in the LIFO reserve allows a computation of an approximate FIFO cost of goods sold for LIFO firms, and this allows users to convert LIFO income statements to FIFO income statements. At first glance, it may appear that this is a highly useful exercise that will allow a direct comparison of net income of LIFO and FIFO firms.

However, there are some more subtle issues that should be considered before making such comparisons. For example, firms using LIFO differ in fundamental and systematic ways from those that use FIFO. It is not clear that simply making a mechanical adjustment based on the change in the LIFO reserve allows a comparison of LIFO and FIFO firms. The analyst may still be comparing apples and oranges even after such a conversion. Second, current-year LIFO net income may more accurately reflect a LIFO firm's future earnings, particularly in an inflationary economy. Although it is possible to use LIFO reserve information to convert a LIFO firm's net income into FIFO net income, it is not clear that this converted net income number would be useful for decision making.

Summary

This chapter presents GAAP rules relating to inventories and cost of good sold. The concept of product costs and period costs is reviewed, and it is shown that, for manufacturers, product costs consist of raw materials, direct labor, and overhead. In addition, manufacturers utilize three types of inventory accounts—raw materials, work in process, and finished goods—to accumulate manufacturing costs, whereas retailers and service providers use a single inventory account. The two basic approaches to recording purchases and cost of goods sold—periodic inventory method and perpetual inventory method—are also discussed.

When product costs are changing over time, it is necessary for a firm to adopt an inventory cost flow assumption to allocate total goods available for sale between ending inventory and cost of goods sold. Three methods are available under GAAP. The average cost assumption assumes that all items in goods available for sale have the same cost, and that this cost is the weighted average cost for all units. The first-in, first-out (FIFO) method assumes that ending inventory consists of the newest costs while cost of goods sold consists of the oldest costs. The last-in, first-out (LIFO) method assumes that ending inventory consists of the oldest costs while cost of goods sold consists of the newest costs. The dollar value LIFO method uses a price index to remove price changes from inventory costs, thus simplifying the record-keeping and computational requirements of using LIFO.

When costs are increasing, the LIFO method results in higher cost of goods sold and lower net income and inventory values relative to FIFO. The use of the LIFO method for tax purposes results in lower taxable income, thus reducing a LIFO firm's income tax expense. When inventory levels decrease, known as a LIFO liquidation, LIFO firms report lower cost of goods sold and higher net income.

Because of the U.S. tax conformity rule, firms using LIFO for tax purposes are required to use the same cost flow assumption for financial reporting purposes. Also, GAAP rules require LIFO firms to disclose the current cost of ending inventories. This information allows users of financial statements to convert LIFO balance sheets and income statements into approximate FIFO statements.

Discussion Questions

1. What is the relationship between ending inventory and cost of goods sold?
2. Explain the difference between a *period cost* and a *product cost*. Give examples of each type.
3. What is meant by the term *overhead* for purposes of inventory valuation? Give some examples.
4. Explain how accounting for inventory costs of manufacturers differs from retailers. What additional accounts are required?
5. Explain the difference between the periodic and perpetual inventory systems. What are the costs and benefits of each method?
6. What is meant by a cost flow assumption? Why is a cost flow assumption necessary?
7. Explain the assumptions underlying the first-in, first-out (FIFO) cost flow assumption.
8. Explain the assumptions underlying the last-in, first-out (LIFO) cost flow assumption.
9. Explain the assumptions underlying the average cost cost flow assumption.
10. What is the relationship between the inventory cost flow assumption a firm uses and the physical flow of goods through the inventory?
11. How do year-end purchasing decisions affect cost of goods sold?
12. Assume input prices are increasing for a firm. Will the cost of goods sold under the LIFO method be higher or lower than under the FIFO method?

13. What is meant by the term *LIFO reserve?*

14. Assume input prices and inventory quantities are increasing for a firm using LIFO. Will the LIFO reserve decrease or increase for the year?

15. How does the LIFO reserve provide useful information to investors?

16. Explain what is meant by *dollar value LIFO*. How does this differ from the unit LIFO approach?

17. What is a price index, and how is it used in the dollar value LIFO computation?

18. Why would managers prefer to use dollar value LIFO rather than unit LIFO?

19. Explain the concept of an inventory pool. Why is it important?

20. What effect does the number of inventory pools have on cost of goods sold under dollar value LIFO?

21. What is a base year for purposes of dollar value LIFO? What role does it play in the computation?

22. Explain the concept of an inventory layer under dollar value LIFO.

23. What is a LIFO liquidation? How does it affect cost of goods sold?

24. Explain the LIFO income tax conformity requirement.

25. Explain the disclosures required under LIFO.

26. Discuss the costs and benefits of the different inventory cost flow assumptions.

27. Why isn't the LIFO cost flow assumption used in most countries (other than the United States)?

28. How do inventories affect the computation of cash flows from operating activities?

Problems

1. The beginning and ending inventory balances for a manufacturing company are shown in the table below:

	Raw Materials	Work in Process	Finished Goods
Beginning inventory	250,000	180,000	210,000
Ending inventory	270,000	205,000	280,000

In addition, the company purchased $450,000 of raw materials and incurred $280,000 in direct labor and $160,000 in overhead during the year. Compute the cost of goods sold for the year.

2. The beginning and ending inventory balances for a manufacturing company are shown in the table below:

	Raw Materials	Work in Process	Finished Goods
Beginning inventory	1,680,000	850,000	670,000
Ending inventory	1,780,000	1,460,000	400,000

In addition, the company purchased $3,100,000 of raw materials and incurred $2,200,000 in direct labor and $1,960,000 in overhead during the year. Compute the cost of goods sold for the year.

3. The beginning and ending inventory balances for a manufacturing company are shown in the table below:

	Raw Materials	Work in Process	Finished Goods
Beginning inventory	750,000	580,000	490,000
Ending inventory	900,000	1,090,000	1,040,000

In addition, the company purchased $2,800,000 of raw materials and incurred $2,200,000 in direct labor and $1,960,000 in overhead during the year. Compute the cost of goods sold for the year.

4. The table below contains information about the number of units and cost per unit for a company's beginning inventory and purchases made during the year. The company sold 850 units during the year.

Date	Number of Units	Cost per Unit
Beginning	80	10
1/10	100	11
3/8	50	12
7/23	380	16
9/3	150	17
12/18	200	18

a. Compute the ending inventory and cost of goods sold using the average cost inventory cost flow assumption.

b. Compute the ending inventory and cost of goods sold using the first-in, first-out (FIFO) inventory cost flow assumption.

c. Compute the ending inventory and cost of goods sold using the last-in, first-out (LIFO) inventory cost flow assumption.

5. The table below contains information about the number of units and cost per unit for a company's beginning inventory and purchases made during the year. The company sold 14,500 units during the year.

Date	Number of Units	Cost per Unit
Beginning	3,000	2.30
1/31	2,000	2.50
2/28	1,000	3.00
4/30	7,000	2.80
8/31	2,500	3.10
11/30	3,500	3.50

a. Compute the ending inventory and cost of goods sold using the average cost inventory cost flow assumption.

b. Compute the ending inventory and cost of goods sold using the first-in, first-out (FIFO) inventory cost flow assumption.

c. Compute the ending inventory and cost of goods sold using the last-in, first-out (LIFO) inventory cost flow assumption.

6. The table below contains information about the number of units and cost per unit for a company's beginning inventory and purchases made during the year. The company sold 55 units during the year.

Date	Number of Units	Cost per Unit
Beginning	15	310
3/1	10	360
5/1	12	390
9/1	15	380
10/1	10	370
12/1	12	410

a. Compute the ending inventory and cost of goods sold using the average cost inventory cost flow assumption.

b. Compute the ending inventory and cost of goods sold using the first-in, first-out (FIFO) inventory cost flow assumption.

c. Compute the ending inventory and cost of goods sold using the last-in, first-out (LIFO) inventory cost flow assumption.

7. The table below contains information about the number of units and cost per unit for a company's beginning inventory and purchases made during the year. The company sold 110 units during the year.

Date	Number of Units	Cost per Unit
Beginning	150	35
3/15	30	38
6/15	20	39
7/15	40	40
10/15	30	43
12/15	40	44

a. Compute the ending inventory and cost of goods sold using the average cost inventory cost flow assumption.

b. Compute the ending inventory and cost of goods sold using the first-in, first-out (FIFO) inventory cost flow assumption.

c. Compute the ending inventory and cost of goods sold using the last-in, first-out (LIFO) inventory cost flow assumption.

8. The table below contains information about the number of units and cost per unit for a company's beginning inventory and purchases made during the year. The company sold 120 units during the year.

Date	Number of Units	Cost per Unit
Beginning	10	4.50
2/6	60	5.00
4/8	50	5.20
6/3	80	5.40
9/12	20	5.80
10/25	400	6.00

a. Compute the ending inventory and cost of goods sold using the average cost inventory cost flow assumption.

b. Compute the ending inventory and cost of goods sold using the first-in, first-out (FIFO) inventory cost flow assumption.

c. Compute the ending inventory and cost of goods sold using the last-in, first-out (LIFO) inventory cost flow assumption.

9. The table below contains information about the number of units and cost per unit for a company's beginning inventory and purchases made during the year. The company sold 310 units during the year.

Date	Number of Units	Cost per Unit
Beginning	20	200
4/20	30	210
5/28	400	220
6/15	30	230
8/25	20	240
12/20	10	250

a. Compute the ending inventory and cost of goods sold using the average cost inventory cost flow assumption.

b. Compute the ending inventory and cost of goods sold using the first-in, first-out (FIFO) inventory cost flow assumption.

c. Compute the ending inventory and cost of goods sold using the last-in, first-out (LIFO) inventory cost flow assumption.

10. A company adopts the dollar value LIFO inventory cost flow assumption for 2001 (the base year), when the ending LIFO inventory is $160,000. For 2002, the ending inventory at current cost is $200,000 and the price index for 2002 is 1.15.

a. Compute the ending LIFO inventory at the end of 2002 using the dollar value method.

b. Compute the LIFO reserve at the end of 2002.

11. A company adopts the dollar value LIFO inventory cost flow assumption for 2001 (the base year), when the ending LIFO inventory is $1,200,000. For 2002, the ending inventory at current cost is $1,400,000 and the price index for 2002 is 1.10.

    a. Compute the ending LIFO inventory at the end of 2002 using the dollar value method.

    b. Compute the LIFO reserve at the end of 2002.

12. A company adopts the dollar value LIFO inventory cost flow assumption for 2001 (the base year), when the ending LIFO inventory is $800,000. For 2002, the ending inventory at current cost is $875,000 and the price index for 2002 is 1.03.

    a. Compute the ending LIFO inventory at the end of 2002 using the dollar value method.

    b. Compute the LIFO reserve at the end of 2002.

13. The table below shows the ending inventory amount, at current cost, and price index each year for a five-year period beginning with the year 2000, the base year. Use this information to compute the ending inventory each year under dollar value LIFO.

	2000	2001	2002	2003	2004
Ending inventory at current cost	$80,000	$97,000	$108,000	$123,000	$134,000
Price index	1.00	1.05	1.08	1.12	1.15

14. The table below shows the ending inventory amount, at current cost, and price index each year for a five-year period beginning with the year 2000, the base year. Use this information to compute the ending inventory each year under dollar value LIFO.

	2000	2001	2002	2003	2004
Ending inventory at current cost	$450,000	$480,000	$470,000	$520,000	$555,000
Price index	1.00	1.03	1.09	1.14	1.16

15. The table below shows the ending inventory amount, at current cost, and price index each year for a five-year period beginning with the year 2000, the base year. Use this information to compute the ending inventory each year under dollar value LIFO.

	2000	2001	2002	2003	2004
Ending inventory at current cost	$160,000	$195,000	$234,000	$268,000	$210,000
Price index	1.00	1.08	1.15	1.19	1.24

Research Reports

1. Locate the annual report for a public company that uses the LIFO inventory method.

    a. Does the company use LIFO for 100 percent of its inventories?

        i. If yes, why do you think the company uses LIFO for 100 percent of its inventories? In other words, what are the benefits of LIFO?

        ii. If no, what inventories are valued using LIFO? What other inventory cost flow assumptions are used? Why aren't 100 percent of the inventories valued using LIFO? In other words, what are the costs of using LIFO?

    b. What is the balance sheet inventory amount at the end of the current year and prior year?

    c. What is the amount of the LIFO reserve at the end of the current year and prior year?

d. What is the cost of goods sold for the current year?

e. Use the LIFO reserve information to compute what the ending inventory would have been in the current year under FIFO.

f. Use the LIFO reserve to compute what the cost of goods sold for the current year would have been under FIFO.

g. Is the company saving U.S. income taxes by using the LIFO method?

2. For 1999, the Form 10-K of R. R. Donnelley & Sons Company reports: "The company recognized a LIFO benefit of $5.2 million in 1999 due to declining prices and lower inventories subject to LIFO, which reduced 1999 cost of sales."

a. Locate the 1999 financial statements of R. R. Donnelley & Sons Company.

b. Locate the LIFO reserve information in the financial statements.

c. Recompute the $5.2 million reduction in cost of sales for 1999 using the LIFO reserve information.

3. For 2001, the Form 10-K of Sears, Roebuck and Co. reports: "The LIFO adjustment to cost of sales was a charge of $25 million in 2001."

a. Locate the 2001 financial statements of Sears, Roebuck and Co.

b. Locate the LIFO reserve information in the financial statements.

c. Recompute the $25 million charge to cost of sales for 2001 using the LIFO reserve information.

4. In the Form 10-K for Jo-Ann Stores, Inc., for the year ended February 3, 2001, the company reports: "The Company has changed its method of valuing inventory and cost of sales from the last-in, first-out method ("LIFO") to the FIFO method in fiscal 2001."

a. Locate the financial statements of Jo-Ann Stores, Inc., for the year ended February 3, 2001.

b. Locate the financial statement note that describes the change in accounting method.

c. What are the reasons given by Jo-Ann Stores, Inc., for changing accounting methods?

d. Analyze each of these reasons in terms of the costs and benefits of the LIFO and FIFO methods.

e. Based on the information in the financial statement note, was the use of the LIFO method increasing or decreasing the earnings of Jo-Ann Stores, Inc.?

f. Do you think the use of the LIFO method was causing Jo-Ann Stores, Inc., to pay less U.S. income taxes? How do you think this might have affected the company's decision to change accounting methods?

g. Under GAAP, when a company changes from the LIFO inventory method, the prior-year financial statements are restated to reflect the new accounting method. This is different from the usual treatment for a change in accounting principle, which requires a cumulative effect computation in the year of the change. Discuss why U.S. standard setters would require a different treatment for a change from the LIFO inventory method.

5. In the Form 10-K for the E. W. Scripps Company for the year ended December 31, 2000, the company reports: "Effective July 1, 2000, the Company began accounting for newsprint inventories by the first in, first out ("FIFO") method. Newsprint inventories were previously valued using the last in, first out ("LIFO") method."

a. Locate the financial statements of the E. W. Scripps Company for 2000.

b. Locate the financial statement note that describes the change in accounting method.

c. What is the reason given by the E. W. Scripps Company for changing accounting methods?

d. Analyze this reason in terms of the costs and benefits of the LIFO and FIFO methods.

e. Based on the information in the financial statement note, was the use of the LIFO method increasing or decreasing the earnings of the E. W. Scripps Company?

f. Do you think the use of the LIFO method was causing the E. W. Scripps Company to pay less U.S. income taxes? How do you think this might have affected the company's decision to change accounting methods?

g. Under GAAP, when a company changes from the LIFO inventory method, the prior-year financial statements are restated to reflect the new accounting method. This is different from the usual treatment for a change in accounting principle, which requires a cumulative effect computation in the year of the change. Discuss why U.S. standard setters would require a different treatment for a change from the LIFO inventory method.

Tim Boyle/Getty Images

Chapter Learning Objectives

After reading this chapter you should understand

1. Why depreciation information is useful.
2. What items are included in the cost of an asset.
3. How the cost of a self-constructed asset is determined.
4. The accounting treatment of expenditures on repairs and maintenance.
5. The role of estimated useful life and salvage value in computing depreciation.
6. Straight-line and accelerated depreciation methods.
7. How different depreciation methods affect the balance sheet and income statement.
8. The relationship between depreciation and gains and losses.
9. The accounting treatment of exchanges of assets.

Chapter 8

Allocating the Cost of Property and Equipment

Focus Company: AMR Corporation

Introduction

AMR Corporation, the parent company of American Airlines, provided the following financial statement information about the effect of aircraft depreciation on the company's 1999 net income.

Effective January 1, 1999, in order to more accurately reflect the expected useful life of its aircraft, the Company changed its estimate of the depreciable lives of certain aircraft types from 20 to 25 years and increased the residual value from five to 10 percent. It also established a 30-year life for its new Boeing 777 aircraft, first delivered in the first quarter of 1999. As a result of this change, depreciation and amortization expense was reduced by approximately $158 million and net earnings were increased by approximately $99 million, or $0.63 per common share diluted, for the year ended December 31, 1999.

Source: AMR Corporation Form 10-K.

According to this information, the managers of AMR changed their estimates of (1) the depreciable lives of aircraft and (2) the residual value of aircraft, and these changes increased 1999 net income by approximately $99 million. AMR's reported income from continuing operations after tax for 1999 (after the change in the estimates) was $656 million. This means that the change in estimates increased income from continuing operations from $557 million to $656 million, an increase of 18 percent.

This illustrates two important concepts. First, for many industries depreciation expense is a major component of net income, and understanding the pattern of a company's depreciation is extremely important for understanding past earnings and forecasting future earnings. Second, managers' estimates and assumptions can have a big impact on the amount of depreciation expense a company records. Understanding how managers can affect depreciation expense is important for anyone using financial accounting information to make decisions.

This chapter focuses on GAAP rules related to depreciation. Since depreciation is an allocation of the cost of an asset to future accounting periods, an important part of understanding depreciation is understanding what constitutes the cost of a depreciable asset. Also, how an asset is depreciated affects the gain or loss realized on the eventual disposal or write-off of the asset. The discussion begins by addressing a fundamental issue about depreciation: Why is it necessary?

WHY IS DEPRECIATION NECESSARY?

Depreciation is simply a way of allocating the cost of an asset in a systematic and rational manner to the different accounting periods that will benefit from the asset's use. For example, if American Airlines purchases a new Boeing 777 aircraft, the managers of AMR expect the aircraft to provide transportation services for

233

30 years. It therefore seems reasonable to allocate a portion of the cost of the aircraft to each of the 30 years during which it will be used by AMR.

Consider for a moment two likely alternatives to depreciating the aircraft. First, AMR could capitalize the cost of the aircraft as an asset and leave the cost on the balance sheet until the aircraft is disposed of, or scrapped, 30 years in the future. The second alternative would be to treat the cost of the aircraft as an expense in the year purchased. Each of these possibilities is discussed in turn.[1]

Capitalizing the Cost

What would happen if AMR simply kept the new aircraft as an asset on its balance sheet for 30 years, without recording any annual depreciation? At some time in the future when AMR disposed of the aircraft, the asset amount would be written off as a reduction of retained earnings. In fact, up until the middle of the nineteenth century this is how corporations accounted for their noncurrent assets, such as sailing ships. It was not thought necessary to record an annual expense for depreciation. The main concerns of shareholders and lenders at that time were that dividends not be paid in excess of retained earnings. Provided there were sufficient retained earnings from prior years to absorb write-offs of noncurrent assets as they were disposed of, there was no demand by shareholders or lenders that depreciation be treated as an annual expense.

What apparently changed this view was the rise of railroad corporations in the mid-nineteenth century. There are several views as to why railroad corporations led accountants to treat depreciation as an annual expense in the determination of net income, and we present two as examples. One view is that the nature of railroad assets themselves and the rapid wearing-out of steam engines, tracks, bridges, and rolling stock caused accountants to focus their attention on how best to account for these costs. This intellectual attention by accountants eventually led to the practice of recording depreciation expense on an annual basis.

An alternative view of depreciation is based on the interaction of government regulation and the need to measure annual profits. Two types of government regulation were imposed on railroad corporations. First, governments began to regulate the rates that railroads could charge their customers, and these rates were often based on the profits of the railroad corporation. For example, railroads might be allowed to charge rates that did not result in annual profits in excess of ten percent of capital. By recording annual depreciation expense, railroads could reduce their reported profits, without changing cash flows, and charge higher rates. Second, governments began to tax the profits of railroad corporations, and in the case of income taxes, the amount of tax a railroad paid was directly related to the accounting profits it earned. By recording annual depreciation expense, railroads could lower their taxable income and the amount of income tax they paid.

Several things should be apparent from this discussion. First, whether firms record depreciation or not has no direct cash flow effect, since depreciation is a noncash expense. Since there is no cash flow effect, depreciation expense in and of itself cannot affect the value of a corporation's stock. Whether AMR records depreciation or not, the stock of AMR Corporation should have the same value.

Second, depreciation appears to be useful in situations where (1) an annual measure of profitability is needed (such as net income) rather than a cumulative measure of profitability (such as retained earnings), and (2) it is advantageous to report an annual measure of profitability that is as low as possible (for example, to reduce the impact of government regulation or taxation).

---

[1] Much of the discussion that follows in this section is based on Ross Watts and Jerold Zimmerman, "The Demand for and Supply of Accounting Theories: The Market for Excuses," *Accounting Review* 54 (1979), pp. 273–304.

Third, depreciation might be useful in industries in which revenues depend on expensive equipment that wears out rapidly if not maintained, such as railroads or airlines. The information contained in annual depreciation expense may provide useful information about how rapidly equipment is wearing out and how well managers are maintaining the equipment.

Immediate Expensing of Equipment

What if, rather than capitalizing the cost of a new aircraft as a balance sheet asset, AMR simply treated the cost of the aircraft as an expense in the year it is purchased? In effect, this would place AMR on a cash method of accounting. As we saw in Chapter 2, the cash method of accounting is lumpy in that it tends to bunch expenses into one year. AMR would show losses in years when new aircraft were purchased, but it would appear to be highly profitable in years without aircraft purchases. Although these measures of net income would closely reflect AMR's cash flows, users of financial statements are already provided with cash flow information through the cash flows statement. Therefore, it is not clear what additional information would be provided by reporting acquisitions of noncurrent assets as an expense.

WHAT IS INCLUDED IN THE COST OF AN ASSET?

In many cases, the cost recorded on the balance sheet for an asset is more than simply the amount the company paid to purchase the asset. Under GAAP, the cost of an asset includes all of the costs necessary to place the asset in a condition where it is ready to be used by the company. For example, transportation, special electrical wiring, and reinforced concrete floors would all be part of the cost of a new machine. In the case of a new aircraft, there may be costs associated with testing the aircraft before it is certified as ready to fly. In the case of an underground oil or natural gas reserve, the cost of the asset includes the cost of drilling wells necessary to extract the minerals.

When land with an existing building is purchased with the intention of demolishing the old building and constructing a new one, the cost of the old building, as well as the demolition cost, are added to the cost of the land. In other words, in order to get the land in a state of readiness to build, the additional costs had to be incurred.

Often a group of assets are acquired together for one single purchase price. For example, when a building is purchased, usually the land on which it is located is also purchased, and there is a single price paid for both the land and the building. Similarly, an entire shopping center consisting of multiple buildings may be purchased for a single price. Finally, when a business is acquired, the acquiring company pays a single price for all of the target company's assets, such as buildings, equipment, patents, furniture, inventory, and accounts receivable.

In the case of a group purchase of assets, the total purchase price must be allocated among all of the individual assets. This is necessary because (1) the assets may have different useful lives for depreciation purposes (or, in the case of land, may not be depreciable at all), and (2) if the assets are disposed of or otherwise converted into cash in the future (such as inventory), the cost of the asset must be used in calculating any gain or loss on the disposition. The allocation of the purchase price to each asset is done by multiplying the total purchase price by a fraction. The numerator of the fraction is the fair market value of the individual asset, and the denominator is the sum of the fair market values of all of the assets purchased. In this situation, it is not necessary for the sum of the individual fair market values to equal the group purchase price, since an individual asset will often have a different price than a corresponding asset sold as part of a group.

The Cost of Self-Constructed Assets

Sometimes companies build their own assets rather than purchasing them. Examples are factory buildings, oil refineries, pipelines, and cellular phone towers. In the case of self-constructed assets, the cost of the asset is computed in a manner similar to the cost of manufactured inventory, by including the cost of raw materials, direct labor, and any overhead related to the construction. In addition, as discussed below, interest incurred during the construction period is sometimes treated as a cost of a self-constructed asset.

Capitalized Interest

An unusual feature of GAAP rules is that they require the capitalization of interest incurred during the construction period as part of the cost of self-constructed assets. For example, assume that AMR decides to build a new aircraft hanger in Dallas, it takes six months to construct the hanger, and the cost of the construction is $100,000. AMR finances the construction by taking out a construction loan for $100,000 and pays interest on the loan at an annual rate of 8 percent. During the six-month construction period, AMR will incur $0.04 \times \$100,000 = \$4,000$ of interest. Under GAAP, this $4,000 of interest is considered part of the cost of construction and is added to the book value of the hanger. The $4,000 will *not* be included as interest expense on the income statement.

Here is some income statement information about AMR's actual capitalized interest. For 2000, AMR incurred $467 million of interest, but it capitalized $151 million, leaving a net interest expense of $467 - $151 = $316 million. This means that without the interest capitalization rules, AMR's pretax income would have been $151 million lower.

	Year Ended December 31		
	2000	**1999**	**1998**
Other income (expense)			
Interest income	154	95	133
Interest expense	**(467)**	**(393)**	**(372)**
Interest capitalized . . .	**151**	**118**	**104**
Miscellaneous—net	68	30	(20)

Source: AMR Corporation Form 10-K.

The peculiar thing about capitalizing construction interest is that GAAP rules treat the cost of *debt* capital, that is, interest, as an asset cost, but they ignore the cost of *equity* capital, for example, dividends. To see how this is the case, assume that in the aircraft hanger example AMR had sold $100,000 worth of common stock to finance construction of the hanger, and that AMR had no interest-bearing debt outstanding. Under GAAP, no interest is capitalized since AMR incurred no interest, so the hanger would have a cost that is $4,000 less than if it were financed with debt. However, AMR still has a cost of capital associated with the new common stock issued, but the cost of capital for equity is ignored under GAAP.

Also, any *opportunity cost* associated with the construction is not treated as a cost. For example, suppose that, in the hanger example AMR had paid for the construction using $100,000 of cash that had been earning 8 percent interest in a savings account. During the six months of the construction period, AMR would have lost the $4,000 of interest income it would have earned had it not built the hanger. Under GAAP, this opportunity cost is not considered a cost of construction.

Here is a summary of the GAAP rules for capitalizing construction period interest:

1. Interest is only capitalized for (*a*) assets constructed for use by the company, or (*b*) assets constructed for sale or lease as discrete projects (such as a ship or

a real estate development). However, in no case will interest be capitalized for routine inventory items.

2. Interest capitalization begins when three conditions are present: (*a*) expenditures for the asset have been made; (*b*) activities are in progress to get the asset ready for its intended use; and (*c*) interest cost is being incurred. Interest capitalization ends when the asset is substantially complete and ready to be used by the company.

3. The amount capitalized is the *lower* of the actual interest incurred by the company for the year or the avoidable interest.

4. The avoidable interest is equal to the average accumulated expenditures multiplied by an interest rate.

5. The average accumulated expenditures are calculated by multiplying each expenditure related to the construction by a fraction. The numerator of the fraction is the number of months from the time the expenditure is made until the time the construction is completed (or until the end of the year, if sooner), and the denominator of the fraction is 12. The total of these weighted expenditures is the average accumulated expenditures during the year.

6. The interest rate used is determined as follows. If a specific construction loan is taken out, the interest rate associated with the construction loan may be used. However, if the average accumulated expenditures exceed the amount of any construction loan, a weighted average interest rate reflecting all of the company's outstanding debt is applied to the excess.

Here is an example to illustrate the application of these rules. Assume that AMR began construction of a hanger on February 1, 2001, and completed construction on December 31, 2001. Costs were incurred throughout the year according to the following schedule.

EXAMPLE COMPUTATION OF AVERAGE ACCUMULATED EXPENDITURES

Date of Expenditure	Amount of Expenditure	Number of Months to Year-End	Weight	Accumulated Average Expenditures
2/1/01	$ 5,000	11	11/12	$ 4,583
3/31/01	28,000	9	9/12	21,000
7/1/01	21,000	6	6/12	10,500
10/31/01	32,000	2	2/12	5,333
12/01/01	14,000	1	1/12	1,167
Total	$100,000			$42,583

Given these numbers, the average accumulated expenditures associated with the construction are $42,583. Assume that AMR took out a 7 percent construction loan for $30,000 to finance part of the construction. AMR had total interest-bearing debt at the end of 2001 of $4,720 million and total interest expense of $467 million. The weighted average interest rate for 2001 is therefore 467/4,720, or 9.9 percent. Here is the computation of AMR's capitalized interest based on this example.

COMPUTATION OF AVOIDABLE INTEREST

	Average Accumulated Expenditures	Interest Rate	Avoidable Interest
Amount of construction loan	$30,000	7%	$2,100
Excess of average accumulated expenditures over construction loan	12,583	9.9	1,246
	$42,583		$3,346

Since the avoidable interest of $3,346 is less than the actual interest incurred for the year ($467 million), the avoidable interest is capitalized as part of the cost of the hanger.

REPAIRS VERSUS IMPROVEMENTS

As you can see from the income statement information below, AMR typically spends about $1,000 million per year on maintenance and repairs. When dealing with repair and maintenance expenditures, managers must decide whether to expense the expenditure in the current accounting period, as AMR has done below, or to treat the expenditures as an additional cost of the asset.

| | Year Ended December 31 | | |
	2000	1999	1998
Expenses			
Wages, salaries, and benefits	$6,783	$6,120	$5,793
Aircraft fuel	2,495	1,696	1,604
Depreciation and amortization	1,202	1,092	1,040
Maintenance, materials, and repairs	**1,095**	**1,003**	**935**
Commissions to agents	1,037	1,162	1,226
Other rentals and landing fees	999	942	839
Food service	777	740	675
Aircraft rentals	607	630	569
Other operating expenses	3,327	3,189	2,847
Total operating expenses	$18,322	$16,574	$15,528

Source: AMR Corporation Form 10-K.

For example, if an engine on one of AMR's 757 aircraft breaks down and AMR's mechanics repair the engine, the expenditures associated with the repair (raw materials, direct labor, overhead) should properly be treated as a current period expense. However, what if the old engine is replaced with a brand new engine? Should the cost of the new engine be capitalized as a new asset? Or should it be treated as an expense just as the repair would be?

The answer to this question is not an easy one, and there are many examples of this type that managers, and accountants, encounter in different industries. Examples might be replacing a roof on a factory building for a manufacturer; rebuilding diesel engines for a trucking company; installing a new air-conditioning system for a retailer; and upgrading a clean-room facility for a chip maker. An additional complication is deciding what constitutes a separate asset for accounting purposes. For example, AMR treats aircraft engines as assets separate from the airframes. Therefore, a purchase of a new engine is treated as an asset addition rather than a repair of an existing asset.

As a general rule, one of the following must have occurred before a repair or maintenance expenditure should be capitalized as a new asset: (1) the useful life of the asset has been increased, (2) the quantity of units produced by the asset is increased, or (3) the quality of the units produced by the asset is increased. Under this rule, if the repair of an aircraft engine increases the useful life of the engine beyond its original useful life, or allows it to operate more quietly or use less fuel, the cost would be capitalized.

VALUATION VERSUS ALLOCATION

Before covering the details of depreciation, there is an important point that should be understood: Depreciation is a method of cost allocation, *not* a method of valuation. This means that when depreciation on an asset is recorded there is no attempt to arrive at a book value that approximates the market value of the asset. It is true that over time the market value of depreciable assets will decline, and that as depreciation is recorded each year the book value of the assets will also decline. However, at any particular time, the book value of a depreciable asset will rarely be equal to the market value of the asset.

ESTIMATING USEFUL LIVES AND SALVAGE VALUE

Three pieces of information are necessary to compute depreciation for an asset: (1) the cost of the asset, (2) the useful life of the asset, and (3) the asset's salvage value. The concept of an asset's cost was discussed earlier in the chapter. This section focuses on the estimated useful life and the salvage value estimate.

The useful life used for depreciation purposes is the economic life rather than the physical life. The *economic useful life* means how long the asset will be used by the current owner. For example, AMR's managers estimate that a new 777 aircraft will have a useful life of 30 years. However, at the end of that time the aircraft is not expected to be scrap. AMR will sell the aircraft for whatever the value of a 30-year-old 777 is at that time. Keep in mind that there are still World War II–era airplanes that are capable of flying. However, it is unlikely that they would be useful to commercial airlines.

Sometimes the economic life of an asset ends because of some change in the economics of an industry. For example, increased fuel costs may make older aircraft obsolete even though they are still capable of flying, just because their fuel consumption is too high. Computers may be disposed of if they become technologically obsolete because of the introduction of some new software. Television broadcasting equipment may have to be retired in the switch to high-definition television. Cash registers must be discarded by supermarkets in favor of bar-code scanners.

How do managers know the useful life of an asset when it is acquired by a company? The straightforward answer is, they don't. The useful lives used in financial statement depreciation are simply estimates, and they may change over time as different circumstances cause managers to change their estimates. However, there are some general approaches that managers use to determine an asset's estimated useful life.

First, managers may base their estimate on previous experience with similar assets. If AMR adds 777 aircraft to its fleet, experience with 737 and 747 aircraft provides managers with information about the expected useful life of the new aircraft. Second, managers may look at the experiences of other firms in their industry. AMR will probably use the same useful lives for its aircraft as United and Delta. If AMR's lives are significantly longer or shorter than those of other airlines, users of financial statements will want an explanation. Third, managers may obtain information from the manufacturer as to how long similar assets have lasted in the past. However, in the end the correct useful life for a particular asset used in a particular activity by a particular corporation is often a matter of guesswork, with the estimate subject to revision as more accurate information becomes available.

Here is information about the estimated useful lives of assets presented in the notes to AMR Corporation's financial statements:

	Depreciable Life
Boeing 727-200 aircraft	2003 (1)
Other American jet aircraft	20–30 years
Regional aircraft and engines	16–20 years

(1) Approximate final aircraft retirement date.

Source: AMR Corporation Form 10-K.

Notice that the 727-200 aircraft are being depreciated through the year 2003. This is because AMR has stated it intends to completely phase out that aircraft type by the end of 2003. This is a good example of the difference between an asset's *physical life* and its *economic useful life* to its current owner. The 727 aircraft will still be capable of flying after 2003, but it will no longer be economical for AMR to operate them as part of its aircraft fleet.

In some cases, assets do not have an estimated useful life, since their usefulness is assumed to go on forever, or at least for a very long time. Land is an example. Since land continues to be used for an indefinite time into the future, there is no estimated useful life. This means that land is usually not depreciated. However, buildings are depreciated, as are other types of land improvements such as roads, drainage ditches, wells, and landscaping.

The second item of information that must be estimated before depreciation can be computed is *salvage value*, also called *residual value*. Salvage value is the estimate of the asset's market value at the end of the asset's useful life. Just as with useful life, salvage value is often a matter of guesswork, and the longer the estimate of the useful life, the more difficult estimating salvage value becomes. Often, a percentage of the original cost is used rather than a dollar amount. Here is the information that AMR provided about salvage value in the notes to its financial statements:

Residual values for aircraft, engines, major rotable parts, avionics and assemblies are generally five to 10 percent, except when a guaranteed residual value or other agreements exist to better estimate the residual value.

Source: AMR Corporation Form 10-K.

Salvage value is important to the depreciation computation because the cost to be allocated to future accounting periods is the asset's original cost less the estimated salvage value. Therefore, if a new 777 aircraft costs $20 million and has an estimated salvage value at the end of 30 years of 10 percent ($2 million), the cost that is depreciated over the 30-year life is $20 million − $2 million = $18 million.[2]

TYPES OF DEPRECIATION

This section discusses the rules for computing depreciation expense under different methods. In all cases, depreciation is recorded by a credit to a contra-asset account called Accumulated Depreciation. On the balance sheet, the asset accounts for Property and Equipment are offset against the contra-asset accounts for Accumulated Depreciation, and the net of these two amounts is the net book value of the depreciable assets. Here is an example from AMR's balance sheet:

---

[2] Notice that there is no application of time value of money principles in estimating salvage value. In other words, if managers estimate a salvage value of $2 million at the end of 30 years, the entire $2 million, rather than the present value, is taken into account in determining the depreciable cost.

	December 31	
	2000	**1999**
Equipment and property		
Flight equipment, at cost	$20,041	$16,912
Less accumulated depreciation	6,320	5,589
	13,721	11,323
Purchase deposits for flight equipment . . .	1,700	1,582
Other equipment and property, at cost . . .	3,639	3,247
Less accumulated depreciation	1,968	1,814
	1,671	1,433
	$17,092	$14,338

Source: AMR Corporation Form 10-K.

The debit portion of a depreciation entry may go to one of several accounts. For example, AMR's depreciation of aircraft would go directly to an expense account for depreciation expense. You can see AMR's depreciation and amortization of $1,202 million listed along with other expenses below. For a manufacturer, depreciation of factory equipment and buildings would be debited to work in process inventory and would end up as cost of goods sold or ending inventory. Depreciation of research equipment may be classified as research and development expense.

	Year Ended December 31		
	2000	**1999**	**1998**
Expenses			
Wages, salaries, and benefits	$ 6,783	$ 6,120	$ 5,793
Aircraft fuel	2,495	1,696	1,604
Depreciation and amortization	**1,202**	**1,092**	**1,040**
Maintenance, materials, and repairs . . .	1,095	1,003	935
Commissions to agents	1,037	1,162	1,226
Other rentals and landing fees	999	942	839
Food service	777	740	675
Aircraft rentals	607	630	569
Other operating expenses	3,327	3,189	2,847
Total operating expenses	$18,322	$16,574	$15,528

Source: AMR Corporation Form 10-K.

Presented below are the rules for four different depreciation methods: straight-line, declining balance, sum-of-the-years'-digits, and units of production.

Straight-Line

The straight-line method is the simplest type of depreciation and is used most frequently in practice. Under this method, depreciation for a year is computed as follows:

$$\frac{\text{Cost} - \text{Salvage value}}{\text{Useful life}}$$

Accelerated

Unlike straight-line depreciation, in which depreciation expense is the same each year, accelerated depreciation results in annual depreciation that is high in the early years of an asset's life and low in the later years. There are several reasons why managers may choose an accelerated method. First, it is a more conservative method in that it results in more depreciation expense, and consequently lower net income, in the early years of an asset's life. This may be useful in situations in which it is difficult to estimate an asset's life or when managers are concerned that an asset may become obsolete quickly.

A second reason that accelerated depreciation may be chosen is that repairs and maintenance expenses often increase with the age of an asset. If depreciation expense is decreasing with the age of the asset while repairs and maintenance are increasing, the total cost of owning the asset may remain relatively constant over time.

A third reason for selecting accelerated depreciation is that an asset's productivity may decline with age. If the goal of depreciation is to match an asset's cost with revenues generated by the asset, and if the asset is more productive in its early years, then accelerated depreciation may do a better job of matching revenues and expenses. Despite these theoretical arguments in favor of accelerated depreciation, most corporations in the United States, such as AMR Corporation, use straight-line depreciation.

The two common methods of accelerated depreciation are the declining balance method and the sum-of-the-years'-digits method.

Declining Balance Method

Depreciation expense under the declining balance method is equal to the book value of the asset at the beginning of the year multiplied by a constant rate. Here is how to compute depreciation expense using the declining balance method:

$$\text{Book value at beginning of year} \times \text{Constant rate} = \text{Depreciation expense}$$

Since book value is equal to the asset's original cost reduced by prior-year accumulated depreciation, the book value decreases each year as the asset is depreciated, resulting in a decline in depreciation expense over time. Under the declining balance method, the asset's salvage value is not taken into account in the computation. However, once the asset's book value reaches the estimated salvage value of the asset, no additional depreciation may be taken.

The rate used in the computation is a multiple of the straight-line rate. Typically companies use twice the straight-line rate, and this is referred to as double declining balance or 200 percent declining balance depreciation. For example, the straight-line rate for an asset with a 30-year life is 1/30, or 0.03333 per year. Doubling this rate results in a declining balance rate of $2 \times 0.033 = 0.06666$ per year.

Although double the straight-line rate is a commonly used method, other multiples are also possible, such as 175 percent, 150 percent, or 125 percent. The smaller the multiple, the less depreciation will be taken in early years relative to later years. The 125 percent declining balance rate used for a 30-year asset life is $1.25 \times 0.033 = 0.04125$.

Sum-of-the-Years'-Digits Method

Depreciation expense under the sum-of-the-years'-digits method is equal to the cost minus salvage value of the asset multiplied by a decreasing rate. Here is how to compute depreciation expense using the sum-of-the-years'-digits method:

$$(\text{Cost} - \text{Salvage value}) \times \text{Decreasing rate} = \text{Depreciation expense}$$

Since cost minus salvage value is constant, multiplying this by a decreasing rate each year results in a decline in depreciation expense over time.

The decreasing rate used in the computation is a fraction. The numerator of the fraction is the number of years *remaining* in the asset's estimated useful life at the beginning of the accounting period. For example, in the first year of the useful life of a 777 aircraft the numerator is 30, in the twenty-eighth year of the useful life the numerator is 3, and in the last year of the useful life the numerator is 1.

The denominator of the decreasing rate is the sum of all of the numbers in the numerators over the asset's entire estimated useful life. For example, with a 30-year life the denominator is equal to $30 + 29 + 28 + 27 + \ldots + 3 + 2 + 1 = 465$.[3] Therefore, in the first year of the 777 aircraft's life the depreciation rate is $30/465 = 0.064516$, and the depreciation rate in the last year of the aircraft's life is $1/465 = 0.002151$. For an asset with a five year life the denominator is equal to $5 + 4 + 3 + 2 + 1 = 15$. The rate in the first year is $5/15$, in the second year is $4/15$, in the third year is $3/15$, in the fourth year is $2/15$, and in the last year is $1/15$.

Units of Production

Under the units of production method, the useful life of an asset is expressed in units of production, such as number of units produced for a manufacturing machine or number of miles driven for a truck, rather than in years. This method results in a better matching of depreciation expense with revenue in cases in which the asset is not used at a constant rate over its life. For example, if a machine is used for three shifts per day for the first two years of its life, sits idle for the third year, and is used for one shift per day in its fourth and fifth years, depreciation based on a certain number of years will not reflect this usage.

To compute depreciation expense under the units of production method, first divide the cost minus salvage value of the asset by the estimated number of units that the asset is expected to produce over its entire life. This results in a depreciation rate per unit. The depreciation expense for a year is equal to this rate multiplied by the number of units produced in the year:

$$\frac{\text{Cost} - \text{Salvage value}}{\text{Expected total units}} \times \text{Units produced in year}$$

For example, if a 777 aircraft is expected to fly for 45,000 hours over its lifetime, the cost is $20 million, and the salvage value is $2 million, the depreciation rate per hour flown is $18million/45,000 == $400 per hour. If AMR flies one of its 777s for 2,000 hours during the year, depreciation expense will be $2,000 \times \$400 = \$800,000$ for the year.

Comparison of Methods

The table on page 244 shows a comprehensive example that compares the depreciation per year under each of the first three methods. (The units of production method is not illustrated.) The example assumes a purchase of an aircraft for $20 million with an estimated $2 million salvage value and a 30-year life. The straight-line rate is 1/30, or 0.03333, and the double declining balance rate is 0.06666. The sum of the years' digits is 465.

There are several things you should notice from this example. First, notice that the total depreciation expense over the entire life of the asset recorded under each of these methods is $18,000,000, equal to the cost of the asset minus the salvage value. This illustrates an important point about depreciation: *Over the life of an asset, the total depreciation expense taken will be the same regardless of the method used.* Second, notice that under both the sum-of-the-years'-digits method and the double declining balance methods, the depreciation in the early years of the asset's life is greater than the straight-line depreciation, and this relationship reverses in the later years.

Finally, notice that under the double declining balance method, the asset is not fully depreciated after 30 years. The exact number of years required to fully depreciate the asset depends on the salvage value, since the book value cannot be

[3] The mathematical formula to compute this sum is $n(n + 1)/2$ where n is the number of years in the asset's life.

reduced below salvage value. If the estimated salvage value were $3 million rather than $2 million, the asset would be fully depreciated after 28 years.[4]

DEPRECIATION EXAMPLES

Asset with $20 Million Cost, $2 Million Salvage Value, and 30-Year Life

Year	Straight-Line Depreciation	Sum-of-Years'-Digits		Double Declining Balance	
		Rate	Depreciation	Book Value	Depreciation
1	$ 600,000	0.064516	$ 1,161,290	$20,000,000	$ 1,333,333
2	600,000	0.062366	1,122,581	18,666,667	1,244,444
3	600,000	0.060215	1,083,871	17,422,222	1,161,481
4	600,000	0.058065	1,045,161	16,260,741	1,084,049
5	600,000	0.055914	1,006,452	15,176,691	1,011,779
6	600,000	0.053763	967,742	14,164,912	944,327
7	600,000	0.051613	929,032	13,220,585	881,372
8	600,000	0.049462	890,323	12,339,212	822,614
9	600,000	0.047312	851,613	11,516,598	767,773
10	600,000	0.045161	812,903	10,748,825	716,588
11	600,000	0.043011	774,194	10,032,237	668,816
12	600,000	0.040860	735,484	9,363,421	624,228
13	600,000	0.038710	696,774	8,739,193	582,613
14	600,000	0.036559	658,065	8,156,580	543,772
15	600,000	0.034409	619,355	7,612,808	507,521
16	600,000	0.032258	580,645	7,105,287	473,686
17	600,000	0.030108	541,935	6,631,602	442,107
18	600,000	0.027957	503,226	6,189,495	412,633
19	600,000	0.025806	464,516	5,776,862	385,124
20	600,000	0.023656	425,806	5,391,738	359,449
21	600,000	0.021505	387,097	5,032,289	335,486
22	600,000	0.019355	348,387	4,696,803	313,120
23	600,000	0.017204	309,677	4,383,682	292,245
24	600,000	0.015054	270,968	4,091,437	272,762
25	600,000	0.012903	232,258	3,818,675	254,578
26	600,000	0.010753	193,548	3,564,096	237,606
27	600,000	0.008602	154,839	3,326,490	221,766
28	600,000	0.006452	116,129	3,104,724	206,982
29	600,000	0.004301	77,419	2,897,742	193,183
30	600,000	0.002151	38,710	2,704,559	180,304
	$18,000,000	1.000000	$18,000,000	2,524,255	168,284
				2,355,972	157,065
				2,198,907	146,594
				2,052,313	52,313*
					$18,000,000

*Book value cannot be reduced below $2 million salvage value.

Part-Year Depreciation

In the example just discussed it is assumed that a complete year's worth of depreciation expense is recorded in the first year that an asset is acquired. However, in the year an asset is acquired depreciation expense should only be recorded for the portion of the year that the asset was used by the company. For example, if AMR acquires a new 777 on September 1, only four months of depreciation (September through December) should be recorded in the first year. This means that

[4] One practical approach to dealing with this problem is to switch depreciation methods to the straight-line method when the asset is nearing the end of its useful life. To compute straight-line depreciation for the remaining life of an asset, the book value of the asset at the time of the switch, less the estimated salvage value, is divided by the number of years remaining in the asset's useful life.

the first year's depreciation from the above example should be multiplied by 4/12 to obtain the correct depreciation for the first four months of the asset's life.

In subsequent years, straight-line depreciation will remain the same as that shown in the above example—that is, $600,000 per year. However, under one of the accelerated methods, subsequent-year depreciation is also affected. For example, the year 2 depreciation under sum-of-the-years'-digits would be equal to $8/12 \times \$1,161,290$ plus $4/12 \times \$1,122,581 = \$1,148,387$. For each subsequent year, 8/12 of the prior year's depreciation and 4/12 of the current year's depreciation would be taken.

HOW DEPRECIATION METHODS AND ESTIMATES AFFECT NET INCOME

As we saw at the beginning of this chapter, the estimates that managers make with respect to useful lives and salvage values can have a big impact on a company's reported net income. In general, the longer the estimated useful life used, the higher the company's net income, and the higher the estimated salvage value, the higher the company's net income. Finally, the use of accelerated depreciation will result in lower net income in the early years of an asset's life, and this difference will reverse in the later years.

It may be useful to think of managers having access to a portfolio of choices regarding asset depreciation, which gives them a great deal of freedom to make choices that can result in a broad range of possible depreciation expense amounts, all of them consistent with GAAP. Estimating short lives and low salvage values and using accelerated depreciation results in the lowest measure of net income. In contrast, estimating long lives and high salvage values and using straight-line depreciation results in the highest possible net income.

Other income statement depreciation effects may be more subtle. For example, capitalizing interest expense as part of the cost of an asset will increase current-year net income, because interest expense is reduced, but will decrease future net income since the higher cost of the asset will lead to more future depreciation expense. Similarly, the decision to capitalize repairs and maintenance can increase current-year net income but reduce future net income.

Changes in Estimates

Managers must constantly update their estimates of the useful lives and salvage values of assets on the basis of current information. This may lead to changes in estimates, as we saw earlier in the case of American Airlines. When managers change accounting *estimates* there is no impact on prior-year financial statements or retained earnings, nor is there any cumulative effect computation as is required for a change of accounting *method*. The new estimates are simply applied to compute the net income for the current year. However, as was seen with AMR, the effect of the change in estimates on current-year net income is disclosed in the notes to the financial statements if it is a material amount.

DEPRECIATION AND SUBSEQUENT GAINS AND LOSSES

If managers had perfect foresight, an asset would be sold at the end of its estimated useful life for an amount equal to its estimated salvage value. Since at the end of the asset's life the book value should equal the salvage value, no gain or loss would be reported on the sale.[5] However, as a practical matter this will rarely be the case.

---

[5] Gain or loss is the difference between the amount realized on a sale and the asset's book value.

An asset may be sold before or after the end of its estimated useful life, and it may be sold for an amount that differs from its estimated salvage value. Because of this, firms usually recognize gains or losses on sales of assets. When thought of in this way, a loss on a sale implies that the firm did not take enough depreciation on the asset in prior years—that is, the book value of the asset at the end of its actual useful life exceeded the actual salvage value. Here is an example:

EXAMPLE OF LOSS ON SALE OF ASSET		
Amount realized (selling price)		$1,000
Less: Book value		
Cost	$ 5,000	
Accumulated depreciation	(3,600)	1,400
Loss		$ (400)

The firm sells an asset that originally cost $5,000 for $1,000. At the time of the sale, the asset's accumulated depreciation is $3,600, meaning the book value is $5,000 − $3,600 = $1,400. Since the amount realized of $1,000 is less than the book value of $1,400, the firm records a loss of $400 on the sale. Here is what the journal entry would look like to record this loss:

+/−	Journal Entry to Record Loss on Sale of Asset		
	Accounts [description of account]	**Debit**	**Credit**
+	Loss on Sale [income statement loss account]	400	
+	Cash [balance sheet asset account]	1,000	
−	Accumulated Depreciation [balance sheet contra-asset account]	3,600	
−	Equipment [balance sheet asset account]		5,000

Notice that the $400 loss stems from the fact that the accumulated depreciation is not large enough. If the firm had taken $400 more depreciation in prior years, the book value at the time of the sale would have equaled $1,000, the amount realized, and there would have been no loss.

The implication of this is as follows. Any manager who, in estimating useful lives and salvage values for assets, estimates lives that are too long or salvage values that are too high faces the probability of future losses when the assets are disposed of. Managers who want to avoid reporting losses on sales of assets should use short estimated useful lives and low salvage values or should use accelerated depreciation methods.

The result for gains on sales of assets is not so straightforward, since gains can come from two different sources. First, a gain on disposition of an asset may indicate too much depreciation was taken in prior years. In the above example, if the accumulated depreciation was $4,600, rather than $3,600, the book value of the asset would be $400, and a sale for $1,000 would result in a gain of $600.

The second way a company can realize a gain on selling assets is if the asset has *increased* in value since the time it was purchased. In this case, a gain will result even if no depreciation is taken on the asset. In the above example, if the asset originally costing $5,000 increases in value and is later sold for $8,000, the company will report a $3,000 gain, even if no depreciation is taken on the asset. Therefore, the presence of a gain on an income statement may indicate the company is using a rapid depreciation method, resulting in too much depreciation being taken, or it may indicate that assets of the company have appreciated in value.

EXCHANGES OF ASSETS

Sometimes rather than selling assets, companies will exchange their assets for assets of another company. For example, AMR might exchange a 757 aircraft for some fuel trucks owned by United Airlines. AMR would transfer the title to the aircraft to United and receive from United the titles to the fuel trucks. An exchange of this type is called a *non monetary exchange*, because the consideration received in the exchange consists of assets other than monetary assets, like cash or accounts or notes receivable. If the asset being exchanged has a market value that is different from its net book value, a gain or loss will result from the exchange.

Continuing with the above example, assume that AMR's aircraft was worth $10 million if it were sold on the used-aircraft market. The aircraft originally cost $15 million, and AMR has taken $8 million of depreciation, so the book value is $7 million. Since AMR has received $10 million worth of fuel trucks from United in exchange for an aircraft with a book value of only $7 million, AMR has realized a $3 million gain on the exchange.

Similarly, if AMR had taken only $4 million of depreciation on the aircraft in the above example, its book value would have been $11 million. Since AMR has received $10 million worth of fuel trucks from United in exchange for an aircraft with a book value of $11 million, AMR has realized a $1 million loss on the exchange.

Notice in the above examples that the amount of gain or loss recognized is the difference between the *market value* of the asset given up and that asset's net book value. Usually, these two amounts will differ, since depreciation is not designed to reflect the decline in an asset's market value each year. In cases in which the market value of the asset being given up cannot be determined, but the market value of the asset being received can be determined, the value of the asset being given up is assumed to be equal to the value of the asset being received.

Under GAAP, the general rule for nonmonetary exchanges is to recognize in the income statement any gain or loss realized on the exchange. Applying this rule to the above examples, AMR would recognize a gain of $3 million on its income statement in the first example, and a loss of $1 million on its income statement in the second example. In both cases, the book value of the asset received would be equal to its market value, which is $10 million in these examples. Here are the journal entries to recognize the gain or loss from the above examples:

	Journal Entry to Record Gain on Exchange of Asset (in millions)		
+/−	Accounts [description of account]	Debit	Credit
+	Fuel Trucks [balance sheet asset account]	10	
−	Accumulated Depreciation [balance sheet contra-asset account]	8	
−	Aircraft [balance sheet asset account]		15
+	Gain [income statement gain account]		3

	Journal Entry to Record Loss on Exchange of Asset (in millions)		
+/−	Accounts [description of account]	Debit	Credit
+	Fuel Trucks [balance sheet asset account]	10	
−	Accumulated Depreciation [balance sheet contra-asset account]	4	
+	Loss [income statement loss account]	1	
−	Aircraft [balance sheet asset account]		15

There is an exception to the general rule in the case of an exchange of *similar* assets when the exchange results in a gain. In this special case, the gain is not recognized under GAAP.[6] Similar assets are assets that are of the same type, such as two buildings or two fork lifts. To see how this rule works, assume that in the above examples AMR is giving up a 757 aircraft to United in exchange for one of United's 747 aircraft. Assume that both aircraft have market values of $10 million. In this exchange, since both assets are aircraft, they are considered to be similar, and therefore the exception to the general rule will apply to any gains on the exchange.

If the net book value of the AMR aircraft given up is $7 million, AMR will realize a gain of $3 million on the exchange of aircraft. Under the exception for exchanges of similar assets at a gain, this gain is not recognized in the income statement of AMR. Instead, the book value of the new aircraft is reduced by the amount of the gain. The book value of the new aircraft would be its market value ($10 million) reduced by the gain that is not recognized on the exchange ($3 million). Here is the journal entry to record this transaction:

	Journal Entry to Record Exchange of Similar Asset (in millions)		
+/−	**Accounts [description of account]**	**Debit**	**Credit**
+	Aircraft (new) [balance sheet asset account]	7	
−	Accumulated Depreciation [balance sheet contra-asset account]	8	
−	Aircraft (old) [balance sheet asset account]		15

The reason for the exception is that appreciation in asset values is not recognized unless the asset is sold. If the asset is merely exchanged for a similar asset (for example, one aircraft for another aircraft), the firm ends up in essentially the same economic position as before the exchange. Therefore, to allow the recognition of a gain, and a subsequent increase in the book value of the new asset, under this situation would be inconsistent with GAAP's emphasis on reporting the economic substance, rather than the form, of transactions.

If the net book value of the aircraft given up in the above example had been $11 million, so that AMR realized a loss on the exchange, the loss would be recognized on the income statement in the current year, since the exception to the general rule only applies to gains. This is another example of the application of the conservatism rule discussed in Chapter 6. Even though the transactions might be otherwise identical, GAAP rules require the recognition of a loss on an exchange of similar assets but do not allow the recognition of a gain.

DEPRECIATION IN OTHER COUNTRIES

Depreciation rules in other countries are generally similar to those in the United States. However, the level of disclosure regarding property and equipment and accumulated depreciation is often greater in foreign financial statements. For example, AMR does not provide information about changes in property and equipment or accumulated depreciation in its financial statements. Presented on the next page is Goodyear's financial statement disclosure about properties and plants.

---

[6] It is common in exchanges for one party to receive cash in addition to the asset exchanged. This is done to equalize the values of the assets being exchanged. In the case of an exchange of similar assets at a gain where cash is received, it is possible to recognize gain in certain circumstances.

Note 9
Properties and Plant
(in millions)

	2000		
	Owned	**Capital Leases**	**Total**
Properties and plants, at cost			
Land and improvements	$ 390.3	$ 20.7	$ 411.0
Buildings and improvements ...	1,683.4	108.5	1,791.9
Machinery and equipment	8,537.5	92.3	8,629.8
Construction in progress	550.9	—	550.9
	11,162.1	221.5	11,383.6
Accumulated depreciation	(5,785.5)	(77.1)	(5,862.6)
	$ 5,376.6	$144.4	$ 5,521.0

	1999		
	Owned	**Capital Leases**	**Total**
Properties and plants, at cost			
Land and improvements	$ 445.4	$ 11.7	$ 457.1
Buildings and improvements	1,652.9	96.6	1,749.5
Machinery and equipment	8,234.8	148.3	8,383.1
Construction in progress	722.7	—	722.7
	11,055.8	256.6	11,312.4
Accumulated depreciation	(5,470.9)	(80.5)	(5,551.4)
	$ 5,584.9	$176.1	$ 5,761.0

The weighted average useful lives of property used in arriving at the annual amount of depreciation provided are as follows: buildings and improvements, approximately 18 years; machinery and equipment, approximately 10 years.

Source: Goodyear Form 10-K.

Compare Goodyear's disclosure above with that of Reed Elsevier presented below. Reed Elsevier provides more information about increases and decreases in the various asset and accumulated depreciation categories than Goodyear does.

16.	Tangible Fixed Assets (in 'L'm)		
	Land and Buildings	**Plant, Equipment, and Computer Systems**	**Total**
Cost			
At 1 January 2000	170	743	913
Acquisitions	4	20	24
Capital expenditure	5	139	144
Disposals	(21)	(116)	(137)
Exchange translation differences	10	40	50
At 31 December 2000	168	826	994
Accumulated depreciation			
At 1 January 2000	45	482	527
Acquisitions	—	10	10
Disposals	—	(104)	(104)
Charge for the year	7	111	118
Exchange translation differences	4	23	27
At 31 December 2000	56	522	578
Net book amount			
At 1 January 2000	125	261	386
At 31 December 2000	112	304	416

Source: Reed Elsevier Form 20-F.

Here is Reed Elsevier's disclosure regarding the useful lives and depreciation methods used. As you can see, this disclosure is similar to Goodyear's and AMR's.

Tangible fixed assets are stated in the balance sheet at cost less accumulated depreciation. No depreciation is provided on freehold land.

Freehold buildings and long leases are depreciated over their estimated useful lives. Plant and equipment is depreciated on a straight line basis at rates from 5%–33%. Short leases are written off over the duration of the lease.

Source: Reed Elsevier Form 20-F.

For another example of non-U.S. disclosure, here is the information about Michelin's depreciation policies under French GAAP:

c. Tangible Fixed Assets

Land, buildings and plants are valued at cost.

Depreciation is calculated on a straight line basis and the principal useful lives used are:

Buildings: 25 years,

Plant and machinery, fixtures and fittings: 7 to 12 years,

Other tangible fixed assets: 2 to 12 years.

Wherever there is evidence that an asset has lost value, its net book value is written down to its residual value and a charge is recorded.

Source: Michelin annual report.

Finally, for an example of extensive disclosure regarding changes in different asset categories and the related accumulated depreciation accounts, here is Nokia's financial statement disclosure related to depreciation:

11. Property, plant and equipment (in EURm)	2000	1999
Land and water areas		
Acquisition cost Jan. 1	111	67
Additions	33	48
Disposals	−3	−9
Translation differences	2	5
Net carrying amount Dec. 31	143	111
Buildings and constructions		
Acquisition cost Jan. 1	540	460
Additions	224	145
Disposals	−39	−85
Translation differences	14	20
Accumulated depreciation Dec. 31	−117	−104
Net carrying amount Dec. 31	622	436
Machinery and equipment		
Acquisition cost Jan. 1	2,382	1,685
Additions	1,089	863
Disposals	−178	−207
Translation differences	50	41
Accumulated depreciation Dec. 31	−1,718	−1,208
Net carrying amount Dec. 31	1,625	1,174
Other tangible assets		
Acquisition cost Jan. 1	53	86
Additions	34	12
Disposals	−15	−52
Translation differences	2	7
Accumulated depreciation Dec. 31	−46	−44
Net carrying amount Dec. 31	28	9
Advance payments and fixed assets under construction		
Acquisition cost Jan. 1	301	151
Additions	230	352
Disposals	−62	−32
Transfers		
Land and water areas	−4	−1
Buildings and constructions	−76	−13
Machinery and equipment	−91	−162
Translation differences	16	6
Net carrying amount Dec. 31	314	301

Source: Nokia annual report.

7.	Depreciation (in EURm)		
		2000	**1999**
Depreciation by asset category			
Intangible assets			
Capitalized development costs		118	110
Intangible rights		50	34
Goodwill		140	71
Other intangible assets		29	19
Property, plant and equipment			
Buildings and constructions		27	18
Machinery and equipment		615	405
Other tangible assets		30	8
Total		1,009	665
Depreciation by function			
Cost of sales		298	201
R&D		244	241
Selling, marketing and administration		230	101
Other operating expenses		97	51
Goodwill		140	71
Total		1,009	665

Source: Nokia annual report.

Property, plant and equipment

Property, plant and equipment are stated at cost less accumulated depreciation. Depreciation is recorded on a straight-line basis over the expected useful lives of the assets as follows:

    Buildings and constructions 20–33 years

    Machinery and equipment 3–10 years

Land and water areas are not depreciated. Maintenance, repairs and renewals are generally charged to expense during the financial period in which they are incurred. However, major renovations are capitalized and depreciated over their expected useful lives. Gains and losses on the disposal of fixed assets are included in operating profit/loss.

Source: Nokia annual report.

DEPRECIATION AND THE CASH FLOWS STATEMENT

Depreciation and other transactions relating to property and equipment can affect the cash flows statement in several ways, as illustrated by AMR Corporation's cash flows statement as shown on page 253. The first and most obvious effect is the add-back of depreciation expense to net income to arrive at cash flows from operating activities. In AMR's case, this add-back is equal to $928 million for 2000.

It is important to understand that, although depreciation expense is added to net income to arrive at cash flows, *depreciation is not a source of cash for a company.* In other words, if AMR had more depreciation expense, it would *not* have more cash flow. The reason is that the add-back simply reverses the reduction in net income caused by depreciation, a noncash expense. A better way to think about the relationship between depreciation and cash flows is to focus on the fact that depreciation is a noncash expense; no matter how much depreciation a firm has, its cash is not reduced by the depreciation.

AMR CORPORATION
Consolidated Statements of Cash Flows
(in millions)

	Year Ended December 31		
	2000	**1999**	**1998**
Cash flow from operating activities			
Income from continuing operations after extraordinary loss	$ 770	$ 656	$1,114
Adjustments to reconcile income from continuing operations after extraordinary loss to net cash provided by operating activities:			
Depreciation	**928**	**864**	**830**
Amortization	274	228	210
Deferred income taxes	461	183	268
Extraordinary loss on early extinguishment of debt	14	—	—
Gain on sale of other investments, net	(57)	(95)	—
Gain on disposition of equipment and property	**—**	**(15)**	**(19)**
Change in assets and liabilities:			
Decrease (increase) in receivables	(169)	261	(185)
Increase in inventories	(111)	(140)	(36)
Increase in accounts payable and accrued liabilities	579	42	343
Increase in air traffic liability	438	84	128
Other, net	15	196	144
Net cash provided by operating activities	3,142	2,264	2,797
Cash flow from investing activities			
Capital expenditures, including purchase deposits on flight equipment	**(3,678)**	**(3,539)**	**(2,342)**
Net decrease (increase) in short-term investments	(438)	(253)	348
Acquisitions and other investments	(50)	(99)	(137)
Proceeds from:			
Dividend from Sabre Holdings Corporation	559	—	—
Sale of equipment and property	**238**	**79**	**262**
Sale of other investments	94	85	—
Sale of discontinued operations	—	259	—
Other	—	18	—
Net cash used for investing activities	(3,275)	(3,450)	(1,869)
Cash flow from financing activities			
Payments on long-term debt and capital lease obligations	(766)	(280)	(547)
Proceeds from:			
Issuance of long-term debt	836	1,956	246
Exercise of stock options	67	25	85
Short-term loan from Sabre Holdings Corporation	—	300	—
Sale-leaseback transactions	**—**	**54**	**270**
Repurchase of common stock	—	(871)	(945)
Net cash provided by (used for) financing activities	137	1,184	(891)
Net increase (decrease) in cash	4	(2)	37
Cash at beginning of year	85	87	50
Cash at end of year	$ 89	$ 85	$ 87

Source: AMR Corporation Form 10-K.

The second effect of property and equipment on the cash flows statement is the subtraction from net income of the gain on disposition of equipment and property for $15 million in 1999 and $19 million in 1998. The reason these are subtracted is to remove the effect of the gains, which originally increased net income on the income statement. Under GAAP, cash flows related to selling property and equipment are properly classified as investing activities. Since gains and losses enter into the computation of net income, but are not considered part of cash flows from operating activities, all gains must be subtracted from net income, and all losses must be added back to net income in the operating cash flows portion of the cash flows statement.

The third effect of property and equipment on AMR's cash flows statement is the subtraction of $3,678 million from cash flows from investing activities for capital expenditures, including purchase deposits on flight equipment. This represents cash that AMR spent to acquire new property and equipment during the year.

The fourth effect on the cash flows statement is the increase in cash flows from investing activities for sale of equipment and property for $238 million in 2000. This represents the cash received by AMR for dispositions of old property and equipment. Notice that in 1999 the amount of cash received for dispositions ($79 million) is *not* the same as the amount of gain added back to net income ($15 million). These two amounts are also different for 1998, when gains of $19 million were added back to net income but proceeds from sales of equipment and property were $262 million. This is because the gain or loss reflects the difference between the amount realized on the sale and the book value of the asset disposed of, whereas the cash proceeds from the sale reflects only the cash realized. For example, in 1999 AMR received $79 million from asset sales but added back a gain of only $15 million. This implies that the book value of assets disposed of in 1999 was equal to $79 million − $15 million = $64 million. Even assets that are sold at a loss will generate a positive cash flow.

The final effect on the cash flows statement is the increase in cash flows from financing activities for sale-leaseback transactions, an increase of $54 million in 1999. A sale-leaseback is a financing device similar to borrowing and using property as collateral. Under a sale-leaseback, AMR sells assets to a financial institution, such as a bank or insurance company, and then leases these same assets back from the financial institution. AMR receives cash from the sale but incurs a liability for future lease payments. Since this transaction is essentially a way for AMR to borrow money, it is treated as financing cash flows rather than as a sale of assets.

USING INFORMATION ABOUT DEPRECIATION TO MAKE DECISIONS

To those users of financial statement information who are concerned with firm valuation, depreciation may appear to provide little useful information since it is a noncash expense. To some extent, depreciation represents a sunk cost since future depreciation charges are determined by prior decisions to purchase buildings and equipment that have already been made. For this reason some analysts focus on a measure called *EBITDA*, which stands for earnings before interest, taxes, depreciation, and amortization.

However, depreciation can provide a great deal of useful information about a firm that can help with valuation decisions. For example, dividing the amount of accumulated depreciation by the cost of assets gives a measure of the age of the assets. The closer the assets are to being fully depreciated, the more likely it is that the firm will have to replace the assets. Also, older assets may be less productive than newer assets.

AMR provides information in its Form 10-K about the ages of their aircraft, an indication that such information is useful to users of financial statements, at least for industries such as airlines, in which the age of equipment is an important factor in profitability. On the following schedule, AMR indicates that its average age for aircraft is 11 years. Based on a 30-year life, this means that, on average, 11/30, or 37 percent, of the aircraft life has been used. Dividing AMR's accumulated depreciation on flight equipment (from the balance sheet) of $6,320 million by the cost of flight equipment of $20,041 million results in an estimated age of 32 percent of aircraft life.

Flight Equipment

Owned and leased aircraft operated by American at December 31, 2000:

Equipment Type	Current Seating Capacity (1)	Total	Weighted Average Age (years)
Airbus A300-600R	192/250/251	35	11
Boeing 727-200	138	60	24
Boeing 737-800 (2)	134	51	1
Boeing 757-200	176	102	8
Boeing 767-200	165	8	18
Boeing 767-200 Extended Range	158	22	14
Boeing 767-300 Extended Range	190/207/228	49	8
Boeing 777-200 Extended Range	230/237/252/254	27	1
Fokker 100	56/87	75	8
McDonnell Douglas MD-11	238	7	8
McDonnell Douglas MD-80	112/125/127/129	276	13
McDonnell Douglas MD-90	135	5	4
Total		717	11

(1) American's current seating capacity includes the effect of aircraft reconfigured under the Company's More Room Throughout Coach program.
(2) The Boeing 727-200 fleet will be removed from service by the end of 2003.

Source: AMR Corporation Form 10-K.

The type of depreciation (accelerated or straight-line) and the estimated useful lives (short or long) also provide information about managers' expectations regarding equipment. If managers use accelerated depreciation, it may signal they are uncertain as to the actual useful life of the assets, and they are taking a conservative view to avoid future losses if the assets become obsolete.

Short estimated useful lives, relative to other companies in the same industry, may indicate that managers expect to use the assets in a way that will wear them out quickly. For example, operating a commuter airline that has many short routes with frequent takeoffs and landings may wear out aircraft more quickly than using the same aircraft to fly internationally. Short estimated useful lives may also indicate a lack of maintenance.

Information about depreciation is also useful in attempting to forecast future cost of goods sold and gross profit, since depreciation is an overhead item that must be allocated to inventory and cost of goods sold. Therefore, if the scale of production is expected to change in the future, fixed costs such as depreciation will be allocated over more units, resulting in a smaller cost per unit and a change in the company's gross profit percentage.

Finally, information about capitalized interest can be important for estimating future earnings. Since capitalized interest represents a cash outflow that is not recorded as an expense, future interest expense may be higher than current interest expense once the construction period ends and interest stops being capitalized.

Summary

This chapter discusses depreciation as an allocation of the cost of noncurrent assets to future accounting periods. The cost of a noncurrent asset includes all costs necessary to bring the asset to a state where it can be used by the company. A lump-sum purchase price must be allocated among a group of purchased assets on the basis of relative fair market values. The cost of self-constructed assets includes overhead costs as well as interest incurred during the construction period.

Costs subsequent to acquisition are also discussed. Managers must make a determination as to whether these costs should be expensed in the current accounting period as repairs and maintenance, or capitalized as assets with their cost recovered through depreciation.

Depreciation expense is affected by managers' estimates of (1) the expected useful life of the asset and (2) the expected salvage value. To the extent that these estimates prove to be wrong, a gain or loss on disposition will occur. Also, if assets are disposed of by exchanging them for similar assets, gains are not recognized under GAAP.

Four methods of depreciation are illustrated: straight-line, declining balance, sum-of-the-years'-digits, and units of production. The choice of depreciation method, as well as the estimate of useful life and salvage value, can affect both net income and book value of assets.

Discussion Questions

1. Explain why depreciation information is useful.
2. Explain the costs and benefits of two alternatives to recording depreciation: (*a*) immediate expensing and (*b*) capitalizing until the asset is disposed of.
3. Explain what this statement means: Depreciation is a method of cost allocation, not a method of valuation.
4. To compute depreciation, what items must be estimated by managers?
5. Explain what items make up the *cost* of an asset for accounting purposes.
6. How is the cost of a self-constructed asset determined?
7. Explain the reasoning for capitalizing construction period interest. Does capitalizing interest provide relevant and reliable information?
8. Explain the GAAP rules for computing capitalized interest.
9. How are expenditures on repairs and maintenance treated under GAAP?
10. Discuss how you would decide whether to capitalize or expense a repair item, such as a new roof for a building.
11. Discuss some ways that managers could use to estimate useful lives and salvage values.
12. Explain the difference between physical useful life and economic useful life.
13. Explain the difference between straight-line and accelerated depreciation. Which is more reliable? Which is more relevant?
14. How do the sum-of-the-years'-digits and the declining balance methods differ?
15. Explain the units of production method of depreciation. In what circumstances is this method most likely to provide useful information?
16. Why might managers choose one method of depreciation over another?
17. What happens when managers' estimates of useful lives or salvage value change during an asset's life? What are the accounting consequences?
18. Explain how the amount of depreciation recorded on an asset is related to the gain or loss recorded when the asset is sold.
19. Discuss the total amount of depreciation expense recorded over an asset's useful life under different depreciation methods.

20. How is depreciation recorded for an asset that is owned for only part of an accounting period?
21. Explain how differences in estimated useful life or salvage value can affect reported net income.
22. Explain how depreciation expense is related to cash flows.
23. Is depreciation a source of cash for a firm?
24. Explain the accounting treatment of exchanges of assets.

Problems

1. On January 1, a company acquires an asset with the following cost, estimated useful life (in years), and estimated salvage value:

Cost	50,000
Salvage value	8,000
Useful life	10

   a. Compute the depreciation expense each year using the straight-line method.
   b. Compute the depreciation expense each year using the sum-of-the-years'-digits method.
   c. Compute the depreciation expense each year using the 200 percent (double) declining balance method.

2. On January 1, a company acquires an asset with the following cost, estimated useful life (in years), and estimated salvage value:

Cost	200,000
Salvage value	25,000
Useful life	8

   a. Compute the depreciation expense each year using the straight-line method.
   b. Compute the depreciation expense each year using the sum-of-the-years'-digits method.
   c. Compute the depreciation expense each year using the 200 percent (double) declining balance method.

3. On January 1, a company acquires an asset with the following cost, estimated useful life (in years), and estimated salvage value:

Cost	350,000
Salvage value	60,000
Useful life	6

   a. Compute the depreciation expense each year using the straight-line method.
   b. Compute the depreciation expense each year using the sum-of-the-years'-digits method.
   c. Compute the depreciation expense each year using the 200 percent (double) declining balance method.

4. On January 1, a company acquires an asset with the following cost, estimated useful life (in years), and estimated salvage value:

Cost	1,000,000
Salvage value	120,000
Useful life	9

   a. Compute the depreciation expense each year using the straight-line method.
   b. Compute the depreciation expense each year using the sum-of-the-years'-digits method.

   c. Compute the depreciation expense each year using the 200 percent (double) declining balance method.

5. On January 1, a company acquires an asset with the following cost, estimated useful life (in years), and estimated salvage value:

Cost	300,000
Salvage value	30,000
Useful life	7

   a. Compute the depreciation expense each year using the straight-line method.

   b. Compute the depreciation expense each year using the sum-of-the-years'-digits method.

   c. Compute the depreciation expense each year using the 200 percent (double) declining balance method.

6. On January 1, a company acquires an asset with the following cost, estimated useful life (in years), and estimated salvage value:

Cost	800,000
Salvage value	50,000
Useful life	4

   a. Compute the depreciation expense each year using the straight-line method.

   b. Compute the depreciation expense each year using the sum-of-the-years'-digits method.

   c. Compute the depreciation expense each year using the 200 percent (double) declining balance method.

7. A corporation purchases an machine that is expected to run for 1,000 hours before being scrapped. The machine cost $250,000 and is expected to have zero salvage value.

   a. Assume the machine is operated for 350 hours during the year. Compute the depreciation expense under the units of production method.

   b. Assume the machine is operated for 475 hours during the year. Compute the depreciation expense under the units of production method.

8. A corporation purchases a refinery that is expected to produce 80,000 barrels of chemicals before being scrapped. The refinery cost $1,380,000 and is expected to have zero salvage value.

   a. Assume the refinery produces 18,000 barrels of chemicals during the year. Compute the depreciation expense under the units of production method.

   b. Assume the refinery produces 12,000 barrels of chemicals during the year. Compute the depreciation expense under the units of production method.

9. A corporation purchases a truck that is expected to run for 125,000 miles before being scrapped. The truck cost $80,000 and is expected to have zero salvage value.

   a. Assume the truck is driven for 35,000 miles during the year. Compute the depreciation expense under the units of production method.

   b. Assume the truck is driven for 45,000 miles during the year. Compute the depreciation expense under the units of production method.

10. A corporation builds a new building during the year at a cost of $200,000. Construction begins January 31, and the building is completed and ready to be used on December 31. The payments for construction were made according to the following schedule:

Date of Expenditure	Amount of Expenditure
1/31	25,000
4/30	30,000
5/31	45,000
7/31	80,000
10/31	20,000

To finance part of the construction, the corporation took out a construction loan for $80,000 with an interest rate of 6 percent. The average interest rate on the corporation's other borrowings during the year was 8.5 percent. The total interest expense paid by the corporation during the year was $80,000.

Compute the amount of interest to be capitalized during the year.

11. A corporation builds a new building during the year at a cost of $500,000. Construction begins March 1, and the building is completed and ready to be used on December 31. The payments for construction were made according to the following schedule:

Date of Expenditure	Amount of Expenditure
3/1	100,000
4/1	100,000
5/1	100,000
6/1	100,000
7/1	100,000

To finance part of the construction, the corporation took out a construction loan for $100,000 with an interest rate of 7 percent. The average interest rate on the corporation's other borrowings during the year was 9 percent. The total interest expense paid by the corporation during the year was $50,000.

Compute the amount of interest to be capitalized during the year.

12. A corporation builds a new building during the year at a cost of $200,000. Construction begins April 30, and the building is completed and ready to be used on December 31. The payments for construction were made according to the following schedule:

Date of Expenditure	Amount of Expenditure
4/30	50,000
9/30	30,000
10/31	40,000
11/30	60,000
12/31	20,000

To finance part of the construction, the corporation took out a construction loan for $30,000 with an interest rate of 5 percent. The average interest rate on the corporation's other borrowings during the year was 7 percent. The total interest expense paid by the corporation during the year was $10,000.

Compute the amount of interest to be capitalized during the year.

13. A corporation exchanges an asset with an original cost of $150,000 and accumulated depreciation of $60,000 for an asset with a market value of $120,000.

a. Give the journal entry to record the exchange, assuming the assets are *not* similar.

b. Give the journal entry to record the exchange, assuming the assets are similar.

14. A corporation exchanges an asset with an original cost of $30 million and accumulated depreciation of $12 million for an asset with a market value of $22 million.

a. Give the journal entry to record the exchange, assuming the assets are *not* similar.

b. Give the journal entry to record the exchange, assuming the assets are similar.

15. A corporation exchanges an asset with an original cost of $900,000 and accumulated depreciation of $230,000 for an asset with a market value of $550,000.

a. Give the journal entry to record the exchange, assuming the assets are *not* similar.

b. Give the journal entry to record the exchange, assuming the assets are similar.

Research Reports

1. The journal *Accounting Today* reports the following in an article in its July 8, 2002 edition:

The audit committee of troubled communications carrier WorldCom Inc. has uncovered what may be the largest accounting fraud in U.S. history, with the discovery that the company had improperly booked some $3.8 billion in expenses as capital expenditures. The improper booking subsequently raised the company's cash flow—a key indicator on fiscal health—as well as profit for the past five quarters.

---

a. Explain what it means to book expenses as capital expenditures.

b. What effect does booking expenses as capital expenditures have on a company's net income?

c. If expenses are booked as capital expenditures, how will future year earnings be affected?

d. Explain how booking expenses as capital expenditures can affect a company's cash flow. (*Hint:* Focus on cash flows from operating activities rather than total cash flows.)

2. Obtain the financial statements for three airlines. For each airline explain the types of aircraft operated and the depreciation methods used for the aircraft. Explain the assumptions that are used for useful lives and salvage values. Comment on any differences that you note.

3. The Form 10-K for Movie Gallery, Inc., for the year ended January 6, 2002, contains the following description of how the Movie Gallery depreciates its rental video tapes. The rental library is called the "rental inventory," and the depreciation is called "amortization" in the financial statements.

Rental Inventory

Rental inventory is stated at cost and amortized over its economic useful life. Under the Company's policy, the cost of base stock movie inventory, consisting of two copies per title for each store, is amortized on an accelerated basis to a net book value of $8 over six months and to a $4 salvage value over the next thirty months. The cost of non-base stock movie inventory, consisting of the third and succeeding copies of each title per store, is amortized on an accelerated basis over six months to a net book value of $4 which is then amortized on a straight-line basis over the next 30 months or until the movie is sold, at which time the unamortized book value is charged to cost of sales.

---

a. Assume new videos cost Movie Gallery $10 each, and the company buys 5 copies of each title. Assume that in January it acquires 25 new titles. Compute the amortization expense for the year on the videos acquired in January. Assume none are sold during the year.

b. Obtain the financial statements of Blockbuster Inc. for 2001. On July 1, 2001, Blockbuster changed its method of amortizing its video rental library. Explain how Blockbuster's new amortization method differs from that of Movie Gallery.

c. Using the same assumptions as in *a* above, compute Blockbuster's amortization expense for the year on the videos acquired in January.

d. Obtain the Form 10-Q for Movie Gallery for the quarter ended October 6, 2002. What does Movie Gallery say about the difference between its method of amortization and that used by its competitors?

e. What are the costs and benefits if Movie Gallery continues to use an amortization method that is different from its competitors?

4. Obtain the financial statements for the Walt Disney Company for the years ended September 30, 1997, and September 30, 2001.

a. What is the original cost of the asset "Attractions, buildings and equipment" at 9/30/2001 and 9/30/1997?

b. What is the depreciation expense for the years ended 9/30/2001 and 9/30/1997? (*Hint:* You can find the depreciation expense on the cash flows statement.)

c. Divide the original cost of the assets by the depreciation expense for the year. If the Walt Disney Company is using straight-line depreciation, what does this number represent?

d. Why is the ratio of asset cost to depreciation expense different in 2001 and 1997? What might this imply about the depreciation expense for the Walt Disney Company?

5. Obtain the financial statements for Noble Energy, Inc., for 2002. The income statement reports the total amount of interest for the year, as well as the amount that has been capitalized.

a. Recompute Noble Energy's net income for 2001 and 2002 assuming that all of the interest had been expensed rather than capitalized. Remember to adjust the income tax expense as well in the computation of net income.

b. Based on your computations in *a* above, what incentives to managers of corporations have to capitalize interest?

c. Explain what effect the capitalized interest will have on Noble Energy's net income in future years.

d. Using the reported interest amounts on the income statement and the long-term debt, including current portion, on the balance sheet, compute Noble Energy's average interest rate for 2001 and 2002.

e. Using the interest rate in *d* above, compute the amount of Noble Energy's Average Accumulated Expenditures for 2001 and 2002.

f. Based on your computations in *e* above, has Noble Energy's construction activity varied much between the two years?

6. Shown below is some information from the Form 10-K of Qwest Communications International Inc. for 2001:

Optical Capacity Asset Sales

The Company sells optical capacity on its network primarily to other telecommunications service providers in the form of sales of specific channels on Qwest's "lit" network or sales of specific dark fiber strands. These arrangements have typically been structured as indefeasible rights of use, or IRUs, which are the exclusive right to use a specified amount of capacity or fiber for a specified period of time, usually 20 years or more. In some cases, Qwest enters into two transactions that occur at the same time: one to sell IRUs to companies and a second to acquire optical capacity from such companies. These arrangements are referred to as "contemporaneous transactions." These purchases allow the Company to expand its fiber optic network both domestically and internationally.

When Qwest acquires and sells optical capacity to a company in the same period in separate cash transactions, the Company generally applies the guidance in Accounting Principles Board ("ABP") Opinion No. 29, "Accounting for Nonmonetary Transactions," and Emerging Issues Task Force ("EITF") Issue No. 01-02, "Interpretations of APB Opinion No. 29," to those transactions. Qwest recognizes revenue based on fair value for these contemporaneous transactions principally based on the following factors: (1) whether the assets exchanged are dissimilar (assets held for sale in the ordinary course of business for assets to be used to provide telecommunication services), (2) whether fair value can be determined within reasonable limits and (3) whether from an accounting perspective, the earnings process is complete.

a. Explain how the sale of fiber-optic capacity to a company and the contemporaneous purchase of fiber-optic capacity from the same company should be viewed from a financial reporting standpoint. Is the transaction more like a sale and purchase, or is it more like an exchange of assets?

b. Obtain a copy of the SEC Form 8-K "Current Report" for Qwest Communications International dated November 14, 2002. Under the heading "Contemporaneous and Cash Sales of Optical Capacity Assets," what does Qwest say about its accounting treatment of the revenue recognition for optical capacity asset sales?

c. Locate one or more articles in the financial press discussing Qwest's accounting for fiber-optic capacity transactions. In your opinion, was Qwest's management correct in their original accounting treatment? Why or why not?

© Paul Conklin/PhotoEdit

Chapter Learning Objectives

After reading this chapter you should understand

1. Why taxable income and financial accounting income differ.
2. Why differences between taxable income and net income cause financial reporting problems.
3. The difference between the tax basis of an asset or liability and its book value.
4. How temporary differences affect future income tax payments.
5. How temporary differences result in deferred tax assets and liabilities.
6. How income tax expense is computed.
7. The difference between current and deferred income tax expense.
8. How permanent differences affect the computation of income tax expense.
9. What tax-related items must be disclosed in the financial statements.

Chapter 9

Accounting for Income Taxes

Focus Company: Campbell Soup Company

Introduction

The Campbell Soup Company does business in many U.S. states and in several foreign countries, and Campbell Soup files income tax returns and pays income taxes in all of these locations. If you added up all of the income taxes on all of Campbell Soup's various income tax returns for the year 1999, you would find that the company's income taxes totaled $295 million, consisting of $231 million in U.S. federal income tax, $31 million in state income tax, and $33 million in foreign income tax. However, as you can see below, the amount for income tax expense, called *taxes on earnings*, that appears on Campbell Soup's 1999 income statement is $373 million.

Consolidated Statements of Earnings (millions, except per share amounts)			
	1999	**1998**	**1997**
Earnings before taxes	$1,097	$1,073	$991
Taxes on earnings (Note 11)	373	384	357
Earnings from continuing operations . . .	$ 724	$ 689	$634

Source: Campbell Soup Company Form 10-K.

Why does Campbell Soup record an income tax expense of $373 million when its actual income taxes for 1999 were only $295 million? The answer is that, under GAAP, income tax expense is based on the pretax income reported on the income statement. Financial accounting pretax income will often be substantially different from taxable income reported on the company's tax returns.

For example, Campbell Soup's financial accounting depreciation expense for 1999 was $255 million. However, for 1999 Campbell Soup had income tax depreciation equal to $352 million, a difference of $97 million. This difference of $97 million between financial accounting pretax income and tax return taxable income results in a difference of $34 million between the income tax expense reported on Campbell Soup's 1999 income statement and the actual income taxes paid by Campbell Soup for 1999.

This chapter explains the GAAP rules for recording income tax expense, using what are called *deferred tax assets* and *deferred tax liabilities*. The chapter also covers the financial statement disclosures required for income taxes and discusses how information about a company's income taxes can be useful for making decisions.

THE PROBLEMS OF ACCOUNTING FOR INCOME TAX EXPENSE

Recording income tax expense causes problems for accountants, not only in the United States but also in many other countries. There are two basic problems that have to be dealt with when recording income tax expense. The first problem is that pretax financial accounting income is generally *not* the same as tax return taxable income. The second is that taxes actually paid may not be useful information for decision making. We address each of these problems in more detail below.

Pretax Financial Accounting Income Is Not the Same as Taxable Income

In the United States, a corporation's federal income tax is based on taxable income rather than financial accounting income. Taxable income is determined under accounting rules specified by the Internal Revenue Code, Treasury Department regulations, Internal Revenue Service revenue rulings, and decisions of various federal courts. Although there are many similarities between income tax rules and GAAP—for example, both use the accrual method of accounting—there are also many differences, and these differences cause financial accounting pretax income to differ from taxable income.

A good example is depreciation expense. Financial accounting depreciation expense is based on an asset's estimated useful life and expected salvage value after applying one of the depreciation methods outlined in Chapter 8: straight-line, declining balance, sum-of-the-years'-digits, or units of production. However, depreciation expense for U.S. income tax purposes is determined under a completely different set of rules, called the Modified Accelerated Cost Recovery System (MACRS). Under MACRS, an asset's expected useful life and salvage value are ignored, and depreciation is based on statutory recovery periods using the double declining balance method. Because of these differences, financial accounting depreciation expense and income tax depreciation expense will seldom be the same.

Here are some other examples of differences between financial accounting income and taxable income:

1. Under financial accounting rules, revenue received in advance is treated as a liability, that is, unearned revenue; for tax purposes, this revenue is usually taxable in the year it is received.

2. When certain types of assets are sold and the selling price is in the form of a note receivable this is known as an *installment sale* for income tax purposes. The taxable income from an installment sale is not recognized until the year that the principal payments on the note are received by the seller. For financial accounting purposes, the income from the sale is recognized in the year that the note is received.

3. Certain types of accrued expenses based on estimates of future events are routinely recorded under financial accounting rules. Examples are bad debt expense, warranty expense, expenses for retired employees, contingent liabilities, and restructuring charges. For income tax purposes, no tax deduction is allowed for these expenses until the year they are actually paid.

4. A company receives a tax deduction when it makes a cash contribution to an employee retirement plan. For financial accounting purposes, retirement plan expense is computed under a complex formula that ignores cash contributions to the plan.

5. Intangible assets purchased as part of a business acquisition are amortized for tax purposes over 15 years. For financial accounting purposes, these assets are amortized over their estimated useful life.

6. Under financial accounting rules, certain types of leased assets are treated as having been purchased by the lessee. These same assets are treated as being leased for tax purposes.

While this list is by no means exhaustive, it serves to illustrate an important point: There are many different ways in which financial accounting income and taxable income can differ.

Taxes Actually Incurred May Not Be a Useful Number

Even though financial accounting income and taxable income may differ, this does not in and of itself have to cause a problem for accountants. One solution to deal with the difference between financial accounting income and taxable income is simply to report the actual income taxes incurred during a particular year as the income tax expense for that year. For example, assume Campbell Soup's pretax accounting income is $2,000 million for a year, its taxable income is $3,000 million for the same year, and its tax rate is 35 percent. The company could simply report the $1,050 million of taxes actually incurred for the year as its income tax expense. In that case, its net income would be $2,000 million − $1,050 million = $950 million.

The problem with this approach is that the amount of income taxes actually incurred for a particular year may not be useful information for making decisions about a company. This is because reporting only the income taxes actually incurred for a particular year may overstate revenues or expenses, and it may also overstate assets or liabilities. Here is an example to show why this is the case.

Assume Campbell Soup has a 35 percent tax rate, and that the company expects pretax accounting income, and taxable income, of $3,000 in 2002 and 2003. Under these assumptions, Campbell Soup's net income is $1,950 per year, or $3,900 for the two-year period, as shown in the following table's first two columns:

EXAMPLE OF $1,000 RESTRUCTURING CHARGE RECORDED IN 2002 (TAX DEDUCTION ALLOWED IN 2003)

	Without Restructuring Charge		With Restructuring Charge	
	2002	2003	2002	2003
Income tax rules				
Taxable income	3,000	3,000	3,000	2,000
Actual tax paid (35%)	1,050	1,050	1,050	700
Financial accounting rules				
Pretax income	3,000	3,000	2,000	3,000
Actual tax paid	(1,050)	(1,050)	(1,050)	(700)
Net income	1,950	1,950	950	2,300
Net income over two years		3,900		3,250
Difference in net income				(650)
Composed of				
Restructuring charge				(1,000)
Tax savings				350
				(650)

Now assume that Campbell Soup records a $1,000 restructuring charge at the end of 2002 for expected costs of a restructuring that will take place in 2003. The restructuring charge reduces pretax accounting income by $1,000. However, the restructuring costs are not deductible under U.S. income tax rules until they are actually paid in 2003. Therefore, Campbell Soup's pretax income for 2002 is $2,000, but the income taxes paid remain at $1,050, resulting in net income of $950, a reduction of $1,000. However, in 2003 the company receives the tax deduction when the restructuring charges are paid, reducing income taxes paid in 2003 to $700. This reduction in income taxes results in net income of $2,300 for 2003, an increase of $350 due to the restructuring charge. Notice that with the restructuring charge, the net income for the two-year period is $3,250, a decrease of $650, meaning that the net cost to the company of the $1,000 restructuring charge was only $650.

Consider what happens if Campbell Soup provides this information to users of its financial statements. For 2002, the company has overstated the restructuring charge, reducing net income by $1,000 when the net-of-tax cost to the company is only $650. Similarly, it has overstated net income in 2003 by reporting the tax savings from the restructuring charge in that year. The company appears to be much less profitable than is actually the case in 2002, and much more profitable in 2003. Therefore, reporting the actual income taxes incurred during a year may not provide useful information to users and may overstate income in some years and understate income in other years.[1]

The same problem exists with respect to assets and liabilities. If Campbell Soup records a restructuring liability for $1,000 at the end of 2002, it will have overstated its liabilities, since the future restructuring will only cost the company $650 net of the income tax savings. Users of Campbell Soup's financial statements may expect a cash outflow of $1,000 in 2003, even though managers know that the net expected cash outflow is only $650.

Under GAAP, both of the problems illustrated in this example—overstating revenues or expenses, and overstating assets or liabilities—are overcome through the use of deferred tax assets and deferred tax liabilities. Deferred tax assets and liabilities result in a better matching of income tax expense with the revenues that generate the tax expense. Also, deferred tax assets and liabilities reduce the overstatement of assets and liabilities due to taxes and have the effect of reporting assets and liabilities at their net-of-tax amounts.

RECORDING INCOME TAX EXPENSE

Under GAAP, income tax expense is computed using what is known as the *liability method*. Under the liability method, deferred tax assets and liabilities are computed at the end of each year based on differences between (1) financial accounting assets and liabilities and (2) assets and liabilities determined under income tax rules.

To understand accounting for income taxes under GAAP, it is first necessary to understand the concept of a tax basis. Just as every asset (and liability) on the balance sheet has a book value, every asset (and liability) also has what is known as a *tax basis*. The tax basis of an asset (or liability) is the book value that would result from applying income tax rules, rather than financial accounting rules, in recording the asset (or liability). For example, if different depreciation expense amounts are used for financial accounting and income tax purposes, accumulated depreciation will also differ, which in turn results in a difference between the net book value and tax basis of the asset being depreciated.

Here is an example. Assume that Campbell Soup purchases new equipment for $1,000, and that financial accounting depreciation expense for the first year is $150. Assume that the first-year depreciation under income tax rules (MACRS) is $225. Under these assumptions, the equipment has a balance sheet book value of

---

[1] Another way to think about this issue is that reporting the restructuring charge in one year and the tax effect in a different year is a violation of the matching principle discussed in Chapter 2.

$850 at the end of the first year, as shown in the computation below. However, the equipment has a tax basis of $775 at the end of the first year. Notice that the difference between the book value and the tax basis (equal to $75) is the same as the difference in depreciation expense.

EXAMPLE OF DEPRECIATION DIFFERENCE		
	Financial Accounting Rules	**Income Tax Rules**
Original cost	$1,000	$1,000
Year 1 depreciation	(150)	(225)
Net book value	$ 850	
Tax basis		$ 775

This example demonstrates an important point about the liability method: Even though accountants are interested in the *income* difference between financial accounting income and taxable income, under the liability method they measure this income difference using the difference between book values and tax bases of assets and liabilities.

There are two major types of differences between financial accounting income and taxable income, and these differences are generally referred to as *book-tax differences*. The first type of book-tax difference—known as a *temporary difference*—is further divided into two types: taxable temporary differences and deductible temporary differences. Both of these are discussed below, along with the second type of book-tax difference, known as a *permanent difference*.

Temporary Differences

A temporary difference is a difference between the book value and tax basis of an asset (or liability) that will result in a *future* difference between taxable income and financial accounting income in the year when the asset is realized (or used up) or the liability is paid (or otherwise settled). This future difference in income is referred to as the reversal of the temporary difference. *All temporary differences will eventually reverse* in the future, and this future reversal will affect taxable income and financial accounting income differently. If future financial accounting income will be *less than* future taxable income, the temporary difference is called a *taxable* temporary difference. If future financial accounting income will be *greater than* future taxable income, the temporary difference is called a *deductible* temporary difference.

The table below shows that temporary differences arise for two basic reasons. First, differences may arise when income tax rules recognize an item of revenue or expense *sooner than* financial accounting rules. Second, differences may arise when income tax rules recognize an item of revenue or expense *later than* financial accounting rules.

ORIGINS OF TEMPORARY DIFFERENCES		
	Tax Recognition *before* Financial Accounting Recognition	**Tax Recognition *after* Financial Accounting Recognition**
Revenue Item	Revenue item included in taxable income but not financial accounting income (example 1 below)	Revenue item included in financial accounting income but not taxable income (example 2)
Expense Item	Expense item treated as a current tax deduction but not recognized for financial accounting purposes (example 3)	Expense item recognized for financial accounting purposes but not treated as a current tax deduction (example 4)

Here are examples of these four different types of temporary differences and how they affect the difference between book value and tax basis of assets and liabilities:

Example 1: *Revenue item included in taxable income but not financial accounting income (deductible temporary difference)* On December 31, a firm rents out some vacant office space and receives cash of $1,000 as advance payment of next year's rent. Under financial accounting rules, the firm records the cash received as unearned revenue, a liability. However, under income tax rules, the rent is considered revenue in the year the cash is received. Therefore, the firm records a liability (unearned revenue) with a book value of $1,000 and a tax basis of zero. This results in a deductible temporary difference.

In the following year, the firm reports $1,000 of rent revenue for financial accounting purposes. Since the rent was already recognized as income for tax purposes in the previous year, taxable income is not increased. Therefore, financial accounting income in the future year will be higher than taxable income.

Example 2: *Revenue item included in financial accounting income but not taxable income (taxable temporary difference)* A firm sells an asset and receives a note receivable for $1,000 payable in one year, plus interest. Under financial accounting rules, the $1,000 value of the note is included in revenue in the year of the sale. However, under income tax rules, the sale is considered an installment sale and the revenue is not included in taxable income until the principal on the note is collected in the following year. Therefore, the firm records an asset (note receivable) with a book value of $1,000 and a tax basis of zero. This results in a taxable temporary difference.

In the following year, the firm reports $1,000 of taxable income when the principal payment is received on the note. Since this note was already recognized as income for financial accounting purposes in the previous year, financial accounting income is not increased. Therefore, financial accounting income in the future year will be lower than taxable income.

Example 3: *Expense item treated as a current tax deduction but not recognized for financial accounting purposes (taxable temporary difference)* A firm purchases a new asset for $1,000 and records $150 of depreciation expense for financial accounting purposes but $225 of MACRS depreciation for income tax purposes. The firm reduces the book value of the depreciable asset by $150 for financial accounting purposes, resulting in a book value of $850. For income tax purposes, the firm reduces the tax basis of the depreciable asset by $225, resulting in a tax basis of $775. This results in a taxable temporary difference.

Assume the depreciable asset has zero salvage value. In future years, the firm will report $850 of depreciation expense over the remaining useful life of the asset for financial accounting purposes. However, the firm will report only $775 of depreciation expense over the remaining useful life of the asset for income tax purposes. Therefore, the financial accounting income in future years will be lower than taxable income.

Example 4: *Expense item recognized for financial accounting purposes but not treated as a current tax deduction (deductible temporary difference)* A firm records a liability for future restructuring charges of $1,000 at the end of the year. Under financial accounting rules, this results in an expense of $1,000 in the current year. However, under income tax rules, the expense is only deductible in the year it is paid. Therefore, the firm records a liability (restructuring charge) with a book value of $1,000 and a tax basis of zero. This results in a deductible temporary difference.

In the following year, when the restructuring liability is paid in cash, the firm will receive a $1,000 tax deduction, reducing taxable income. However, the expense was already recognized in the previous year for financial accounting purposes, so there is no effect on financial accounting income. Therefore, the financial accounting income in future years will be higher than taxable income.

The following table summarizes these four types of temporary differences from the above examples:

			End of First Year		Type of
Example	**Type of Revenue or Expense**	**Asset or Liability**	**Book Value**	**Tax Basis**	**Temporary Difference**
EXAMPLES OF TEMPORARY DIFFERENCES					
1	Rent revenue in advance	Unearned revenue (liability)	$1,000	$ 0	Deductible
2	Installment sale revenue	Note receivable (asset)	1,000	0	Taxable
3	Depreciation expense	Equipment (asset)	850	775	Taxable
4	Restructuring expense	Restructuring liability (liability)	1,000	0	Deductible

Deferred Tax Assets and Liabilities

Under GAAP, whenever a company has temporary book-tax differences at the end of the accounting period the company must also record deferred tax assets or liabilities on the balance sheet. The deferred tax assets and liabilities are equal to the temporary differences multiplied by the company's income tax rate. Thus, deferred tax assets and liabilities represent the *income tax effect* of the company's various temporary differences.

Deferred tax *assets* arise when there are deductible temporary differences for the year. The deferred tax asset is equal to the end-of-year deductible temporary differences multiplied by the company's tax rate. For example, if a company has $1,000 of deductible temporary differences at the end of the year and a 35 percent tax rate, the deferred tax asset is equal to $1,000 × 0.35 = $350.

Deferred tax *liabilities* arise when there are taxable temporary differences for the year. The deferred tax liability is equal to the end-of-year taxable temporary differences multiplied by the company's tax rate. For example, if a company has $2,000 of taxable temporary differences at the end of the year and a 35 percent tax rate, the deferred tax liability is equal to $2,000 × 0.35 = $700.

To summarize:

- Deductible temporary differences result in deferred tax assets.
- Taxable temporary differences result in deferred tax liabilities.

To illustrate this concept, here are the deferred tax assets and liabilities of Campbell Soup Company at the end of 1999 and 1998:

Deferred tax liabilities and assets are comprised of the following:	1999	1998
Depreciation	$176	$142
Pensions	122	112
Other	179	185
Deferred tax liabilities	477	439
Benefits and compensation	209	209
Restructuring accruals	31	50
Tax loss carryforwards	17	15
Other	50	71
Gross deferred tax assets	307	345
Deferred tax asset valuation allowance ...	(17)	(15)
Net deferred tax assets	290	330
Net deferred tax liability	$187	$109

Source: Campbell Soup Company Form 10-K.

Campbell Soup's statement reports deferred tax liabilities for depreciation, pensions, and other. The depreciation deferred tax liability represents the taxable temporary differences between the book value and tax basis of Campbell Soup's depreciable assets, multiplied by Campbell Soup's tax rate. For example, if Campbell Soup has a 35 percent tax rate, the deferred tax liability of $176 million for depreciation represents a taxable temporary difference of $502,857,143. Multiplying the taxable temporary difference by the tax rate results in the deferred tax liability, equal to $502,857,143 × 0.35 = $176 million.

The pension deferred tax liability represents the taxable temporary difference between the book value and tax basis of Campbell Soup's prepaid pension asset.[2] When Campbell Soup contributes cash to the employee pension trust, the cash contribution results in a current tax deduction. However, under financial accounting rules the contribution is treated as a prepaid pension expense, an asset on the balance sheet. For tax purposes, this prepaid pension asset has a zero tax basis. If Campbell Soup has a 35 percent tax rate, the deferred tax liability of $122 million represents a taxable temporary difference of $348,571,429. Multiplying the taxable temporary difference by the tax rate results in the deferred tax liability, equal to $348,571,429 × 0.35 = $122 million.

The company's statement also reports deferred tax assets for benefits and compensation, restructuring accruals, tax loss carryforwards, and other. The benefits and compensation deferred tax asset represents the deductible temporary difference between the book value and tax basis of Campbell Soup's liability for future postretirement benefits.[3] When Campbell Soup records a liability for future postretirement benefits, an expense is recognized for financial accounting purposes. However, for tax purposes this liability does not result in a tax deduction until it is actually paid in the future. Therefore, the liability has a zero basis for tax purposes. If Campbell Soup has a 35 percent tax rate, the deferred tax asset of $209 million represents a deductible temporary difference of $597,142,858. Multiplying the deductible temporary difference by the tax rate results in the deferred tax asset, equal to $597,142,858 × 0.35 = $209 million.

The restructuring accruals deferred tax asset represents the deductible temporary difference between the book value and tax basis of Campbell Soup's liability for future restructuring expenses. When Campbell Soup records a liability for future restructuring expenses, an expense is recognized for financial accounting purposes. However, for tax purposes this liability does not result in a tax deduction until it is actually paid in the future. Therefore, the liability has a zero basis for tax purposes. If Campbell Soup has a 35 percent tax rate, the deferred tax asset of $31 million represents a deductible temporary difference of $88,571,429. Multiplying the deductible temporary difference by the tax rate results in the deferred tax asset, equal to $88,571,429 × 0.35 = $31 million.

On the next page is a summary of Campbell Soup's deferred tax assets and liabilities for 1999, assuming a 35 percent tax rate. The company's statement also reports deferred tax assets relating to tax loss carryforwards and a deferred tax asset valuation allowance. Both of these items will be covered in more detail later in the chapter and are excluded from the analysis at this time.

---

[2] Pension accounting is discussed in Chapter 14.

[3] Postretirement benefits are discussed in Chapter 14.

ANALYSIS OF DEFERRED TAX ASSETS AND LIABILITIES

Temporary Difference Related to	Balance Sheet Account	(Taxable) Deductible Temporary Difference	Assumed Tax Rate	Deferred Tax (liability) Asset
Depreciation	Property and equipment	(502,857,143)	35%	(176)
Pensions	Prepaid pension asset	(348,571,429)	35	(122)
Other	Unknown	(511,428,571)	35	(179)
Total				(477)
Benefits and compensation	Postretirement liability	597,142,858	35	209
Restructuring accruals	Restructuring liability	88,571,429	35	31
Other	Unknown	142,857,143	35	50
Total				290
Net deferred tax liability (in millions)				(187)

Discounting of Deferred Tax Assets and Liabilities

Some accountants argue that deferred tax assets and liabilities should be reported at their net present value, that is, discounted, to reflect how long they are expected to remain on the balance sheet before reversing in the future. For example, assume that Campbell Soup records a $1,000 restructuring liability in 2002 but does not expect to actually pay the restructuring costs until 2005. The $1,000 liability represents a deductible temporary difference that, when multiplied by the 35 percent tax rate, results in a deferred tax asset of $350. This deferred tax asset will remain on the balance sheet until 2005, when the company receives a tax deduction for the $1,000 expenditure. An argument is sometimes made that the present value of the $350 should be recorded as the deferred tax asset.

To see why this argument is incorrect, notice that the $350 is based on the amount of the restructuring liability of $1,000. If the $1,000 reflects the present value of the future cash outflows expected to be paid for restructuring costs, then the $350 will also reflect the present value of the future tax savings. Therefore, no discounting is necessary. However, if the $1,000 does not reflect the present value of the future cash outflows, then the restructuring liability has been overstated. In that case, the fact that the deferred tax asset is also overstated is not a problem, but rather helps reduce the overstatement of the restructuring liability. Therefore, regardless of how the restructuring liability is recorded, there is no need to discount the deferred tax asset.

Income Tax Expense

This section explains how to compute Campbell Soup's income tax expense. Under GAAP, a firm's income tax expense consists of two components. One component is called the *current tax expense,* and the other is called the *deferred tax expense* or *deferred tax benefit.*

Income tax expense = Current tax expense + deferred tax expense − deferred tax benefit

Each of these items is discussed below.

Current Tax Expense

A firm's current tax expense is the amount of actual income tax reflected on the firm's various tax returns for the year. This usually consists of U.S. federal income tax, state income taxes, and foreign income taxes (for multinational firms). On the next page is Campbell Soup's current income tax expense for 1997 through 1999:

	1999	**1998**	**1997**
Income taxes			
Currently payable			
Federal	$231	$311	$330
State	31	44	32
Non-U.S.	33	50	28
	$295	$405	$390

Source: Campbell Soup Company Form 10-K.

Current tax expense is not the same as cash payments for taxes, since firms may owe taxes when their tax return is filed after year end, or they may be due refunds. Taxes payable or refunds receivable are recorded on the balance sheet just like other payables and receivables. Here are Campbell Soup's taxes payable, called *accrued income taxes,* for 1999 and 1998:

	1999	**1998**
Current Liabilities		
Notes payable	$1,987	$1,401
Payable to suppliers and others . .	511	506
Accrued liabilities	415	638
Dividend payable	97	95
Accrued income taxes	**136**	**163**
Total current liabilities	$3,146	$2,803

Source: Campbell Soup Company Form 10-K.

In other words, Campbell Soup's current tax expense for 1999 was $295 million, but only $159 million of this amount had actually been paid in cash by the end of the 1999 accounting period. The balance of $136 million, represented by the liability for accrued income taxes on the balance sheet, was paid to the taxing authorities after year-end.

Deferred Tax Expense or Deferred Tax Benefit

Under GAAP, a firm's deferred tax expense or deferred tax benefit is equal to the *change* in the net deferred tax liabilities or assets for the year. Increases in deferred tax liabilities (or decreases in deferred tax assets) result in deferred tax expense. A deferred tax benefit represents a *reduction* in tax expense for the year. Increases in deferred tax assets (or decreases in deferred tax liabilities) result in deferred tax benefits. Here is Campbell Soup's deferred income tax expense (benefit) for 1997 through 1999:

	1999	**1998**	**1997**
Income taxes			
Deferred			
Federal	64	(1)	(40)
State	2	(7)	2
Non-U.S.	12	(13)	5
	78	(21)	(33)

Source: Campbell Soup Company Form 10-K.

For 1999, Campbell Soup's deferred tax expense was $78 million. This is equal to the increase in the net deferred tax liability for the year. Net deferred tax liability was $187 million at the end of 1999 and $109 million at the end of 1998. Thus, the increase in deferred tax liabilities for 1999 was equal to $187 million − $109 million = $78 million.

Here is the journal entry to record Campbell Soup's 1999 income tax expense:

+/−	Accounts [description of account]	Debit	Credit
	Journal Entry to Record Income Tax Expense 1999		
+	Income Tax Expense [income statement expense account]	373	
−	Cash [balance sheet asset account]		159
+	Accrued Income Taxes [balance sheet liability account]		136
+	Deferred Tax Liability [balance sheet liability account]		78

The income tax expense of $373 million is the total of the current tax expense of $295 million and the deferred tax expense of $78 million. The credit to the Deferred Tax Liability account for $78 million will increase the balance in that account from $109 million (the balance at the end of 1998) to $187 million (the balance at the end of 1999).

For 1998, Campbell Soup had current tax expense of $405 million and a deferred tax benefit of $21 million. Here is how Campbell Soup's 1998 income tax expense would be recorded:

+/−	Accounts [description of account]	Debit	Credit
	Journal Entry to Record Income Tax Expense 1998		
+	Income Tax Expense [income statement expense account]	384	
−	Deferred Tax Liability [balance sheet liability account]	21	
+	Accrued Income Taxes [balance sheet liability account]		163
−	Cash [balance sheet asset account]		242

Notice that the $21 million debit for the deferred tax benefit is to the net Deferred Tax Liability account rather than a Deferred Tax Asset account, since Campbell Soup still had a net deferred tax liability (equal to $109 million) at the end of 1998.

Tax Rate

To compute total net deferred tax asset or liability, the individual deductible and taxable temporary differences are multiplied by the firm's tax rate. This is usually the tax rate the firm faces in the current year. However, if the future tax rate will be different from the current-year tax rate, the future tax rate should be used in the computation. Because the future tax rate is applied to all of the firm's temporary differences at the end of the year, regardless of when the temporary differences originated, a change in tax rate can have a large impact on income tax expense for the year of the change.

PERMANENT DIFFERENCES

Temporary differences represent future differences between financial accounting income and taxable income when the underlying assets are realized (or used up) or the underlying liabilities are paid (or otherwise settled). Another way to think of temporary differences is that they represent book-tax differences that will reverse in future years. In other words, the effect of the book-tax difference in the current year will be offset by a corresponding book-tax difference in a future year or years. For example, if tax depreciation expense exceeds financial accounting depreciation expense in the current year, it means that in a future year or years tax depreciation expense will be less than financial accounting depreciation expense.

There are some types of book-tax differences that will have *no* effect on future income. In other words, the current-year book-tax difference will never reverse in the future. These book-tax differences are known as *permanent differences*.

An example of a permanent difference is interest revenue received from investments in state and local government bonds, called *municipal bonds*. Under U.S. tax law, interest from municipal bonds is excluded from taxable income and will therefore never be subject to U.S. tax. This means that when a firm receives municipal bond interest, there is no difference between the book value and tax basis of any asset, and therefore there is no temporary difference. Since permanent differences will not result in future differences between financial accounting income and taxable income, no deferred tax assets or liabilities are recorded for permanent differences.

NET OPERATING LOSSES

When firms have negative taxable income for a year, the tax loss is referred to as a *net operating loss* (NOL). Because of temporary and permanent differences, the amount of the net operating loss will not be the same as the amount of the pretax loss reported on the income statement. Under U.S. tax law, and the tax laws of many states and foreign countries, tax net operating losses may be used to offset taxable income in prior years, resulting in a tax refund. Under current U.S. federal tax rules, net operating losses may be used to offset taxable income in the two years prior to the year of the loss. Offsetting prior year taxable income in this manner is referred to as a *carryback* of the loss. The tax refund from the loss carryback is recorded as a tax benefit on the income statement, reducing financial accounting income tax expense for the year of the tax loss. If pretax accounting income is also a loss, the financial accounting pretax loss will be reduced by the amount of the tax benefit from the net operating loss carryback. For an example of a tax benefit from a net operating loss carryback, consider Kmart's income statement for 2000, shown on the next page.

KMART CORPORATION
Consolidated Statements of Operations
Years Ended January 31, 2001, January 26, 2000 and January 27, 1999
(dollars in millions, except per share data)

	2000	1999	1998
Sales	$37,028	$35,925	$33,674
Cost of sales, buying and occupancy	29,658	28,111	26,319
Gross margin	7,370	7,814	7,355
Selling, general and administrative expenses	7,415	6,514	6,245
Voluntary early retirement programs	—	—	19
Continuing income (loss) before interest, income taxes and dividends on convertible preferred securities of subsidiary trust	(45)	1,300	1,091
Interest expense, net	287	280	293
Income tax provision (benefit)	**(134)**	**337**	**230**
Dividends on convertible preferred securities of subsidiary trust, net of income taxes of $25, $27 and $27, respectively	46	50	50
Net income (loss) from continuing operations	(244)	633	518
Discontinued operations, net of income taxes of $(124)	—	(230)	—
Net income (loss)	$ (244)	$ 403	$ 518

Source: Kmart Corporation Form 10-K.

Kmart's net loss of $244 million for 2000 has been reduced by an income tax benefit of $134 million due to a carryback of the tax loss. To see how the loss was carried back, here is some information from the notes to Kmart's financial statements for 2000:

Income Tax Provision (credit)

	2000	1999	1998
Current			
Federal	$(149)	$133	$ 70
State and local	2	17	21
Foreign	14	11	12
	(133)	161	103

Source: Kmart Corporation Form 10-K.

Notice that Kmart's current federal tax provision for 2000 is a credit, that is, a benefit, of $149 million. This benefit represents refunds of federal income taxes from 1999 and 1998, years in which total federal income taxes of $133 million and $70 million were paid. The tax benefit from the loss carryback in 2000 is off-set by state and local taxes of $2 million and foreign taxes of $14 million.

Here is the journal entry that Kmart would use to record the loss carryback:

	Journal Entry to Record Carryback of Net Operating Loss		
+/−	**Accounts [description of account]**	**Debit**	**Credit**
+	Income Tax Receivable [balance sheet asset account]	149	
−	Income Tax Expense [income statement expense account]		149

Sometimes a firm has such a large tax loss in a year that the loss exceeds taxable income in the prior two years. This means that, even after the loss carryback and the refund of taxes, there is still a portion of the tax loss that is not used to generate refunds. In this situation, the firm has what is called a *loss carryforward*, or *loss carryover*. A loss carryforward is used to offset future taxable income and will thus reduce future taxes paid. Under current U.S. tax law, the loss may be carried forward for up to 20 years.

Under GAAP, firms recognize the future tax benefit of the loss carryforward by recording a deferred tax asset. The deferred tax asset is equal to the loss carryforward multiplied by the firm's tax rate. Shown below is an example of a firm with a tax benefit from a net operating loss carryforward. Cannondale Corporation has a pretax loss for 2000 of $4,194 thousand. This pretax loss is reduced by a tax benefit of $1,902 thousand.

CANNONDALE CORPORATION AND SUBSIDIARIES
Consolidated Statements of Operations
(in thousands, except per share data)

	Year Ended July 1, 2000	Year Ended July 3, 1999	Year Ended June 27, 1998
Net sales	$160,519	$176,819	$171,496
Cost of sales	112,100	114,627	110,113
Gross profit	48,419	62,192	61,383
Expenses			
Selling, general and administrative	39,718	40,599	39,361
Research and development	8,470	10,222	6,750
	48,188	50,821	46,111
Operating income	231	11,371	15,272
Other income (expense)			
Interest expense	(6,308)	(4,557)	(1,995)
Other income	1,883	1,160	653
	(4,425)	(3,397)	(1,342)
Income (loss) before income taxes and extraordinary item	(4,194)	7,974	13,930
Income tax (expense) benefit	1,902	(2,051)	(4,578)
Income (loss) before extraordinary item	(2,292)	5,923	9,352
Extraordinary loss on early extinguishment of debt, net of $143 tax benefit	(234)	—	—
Net income (loss)	$ (2,526)	$ 5,923	$ 9,352

Source: Cannondale Corporation Form 10-K.

From examining Cannondale's income tax note in the financial statements (shown on the next page), it is clear that this $1,902 thousand tax benefit is due to a loss carryforward rather than a loss carryback. You can see this is the case because the amounts for current federal tax expense in the two preceding years (1999 and 1998) are both negative, indicating tax losses in those years as well. Without positive taxable income in these prior years, there is no way that Cannondale's 2000 loss can generate a tax refund. Therefore, the $2,978 thousand current federal tax benefit represents the expected future tax savings from carrying the tax loss forward.

CANNONDALE CORPORATION AND SUBSIDIARIES
Notes to Consolidated Financial Statements

The income tax (benefit) provision consists of the following (in thousands):

	Year Ended July 1, 2000	Year Ended July 3, 1999	Year Ended June 27, 1998
Current			
Federal	$(2,978)	$ (309)	$ (786)
Foreign	1,821	2,733	5,067
State	(497)	(244)	(128)
Total current	(1,654)	2,180	4,153
Deferred			
Federal	230	(52)	412
Foreign	(526)	(71)	(59)
State	48	(6)	72
Total deferred	(248)	(129)	425
Total	$(1,902)	$2,051	$4,578

Source: Cannondale Corporation Form 10-K.

In addition to tax loss carryforwards, firms also have other types of tax benefits, such as tax credits, that may be carried forward. In the United States, some common types of tax credits are the research and development tax credit, the foreign tax credit, and the alternative minimum tax (AMT) credit. Here is some additional information from Cannondale's financial statement notes discussing its tax benefit carryforwards:

Included in the deferred tax asset balance as of July 1, 2000, the Company has available for U.S. federal income tax purposes research and development credit, foreign tax credit and alternative minimum tax credit carryforwards of approximately $1,239,000, $2,839,000 and $180,000, respectively. The Company also has state net operating loss carryforwards of approximately $449,000. The research and development credit carryforwards expire in fiscal 2019 and 2020. The foreign tax credit carryforward expires in fiscal 2005. The alternative minimum tax credit carryforward has no expiration, and will be carried forward indefinitely until utilized. The state net operating loss carryforwards are related to a number of state jurisdictions and will expire at various times between fiscal 2003 and 2015.

Source: Cannondale Corporation Form 10-K.

Recall that when we examined the composition of Campbell Soup's deferred tax assets, the company reported a deferred tax asset in the amount of $17 million relating to tax loss carryforwards. Here is how Campbell Soup explained the tax loss carryforwards in the notes to its financial statements. Keep in mind that the amount of the loss carryforward (which is $55 million in Campbell Soup's case) differs from the amount of the deferred tax asset ($17 million) because the deferred tax asset is equal to the amount of the loss carryforward multiplied by the company's tax rate.

For income tax purposes, subsidiaries of the company have tax loss carryforwards of approximately $55. Of these carryforwards, $27 expire through 2011 and $28 may be carried forward indefinitely. The current statutory tax rates in these countries range from 28% to 53%.

Source: Campbell Soup Company Form 10-K.

You might wonder why Campbell Soup had tax loss carryforwards when it had a current U.S. tax expense for the year. The reason is that the loss carryforwards were from other countries and may only be used to offset taxable income in those same countries. For example, if Campbell Soup has a tax loss in France and taxable income in the United States, the U.S. taxable income cannot be offset with the French net operating loss carryforward. It is common to see profitable multinational corporations reporting tax loss carryforwards from foreign countries.

VALUATION ALLOWANCE

Deferred tax assets represent future tax benefits a company expects to receive related to deductible temporary differences and net operating loss carryforwards. However, these future tax benefits will only be realized to the extent the company generates positive taxable income in the future. A company that never generates taxable income will never receive any future benefits for loss carryforwards or other types of deferred tax assets.

Because there is some uncertainty as to the ultimate realization of deferred tax assets, there is a requirement under GAAP that managers assess the likelihood that the future tax benefits represented by deferred tax assets will actually be realized by the firm. To the extent it is more likely than not that the benefits will be realized, the deferred tax assets may be recorded by the firm.

If the realization of future tax benefits is not considered to be more likely than not, GAAP requires a valuation allowance be established to reduce the amount of deferred tax assets recorded. The valuation allowance is a contra-asset account that, when combined with the deferred tax asset balance, reduces the deferred tax asset to an amount that is likely to be realized in the future.

Campbell Soup has recorded a valuation allowance in connection with its deferred tax asset for the loss carryforward. Here are both the deferred tax asset and the valuation allowance:

Tax loss carryforwards	17	15
Deferred tax asset valuation allowance	(17)	(15)

Source: Campbell Soup Company Form 10-K.

In the case of Campbell Soup, managers have established a valuation allowance equal to the entire amount of the deferred tax asset. This means that managers do *not* believe that it is more likely than not that the future tax benefits of the loss carryforwards will be realized. Here is the journal entry to record the increase in the valuation allowance from $15 million to $17 million.

\+/−	**Journal Entry to Record Increase in Deferred Tax Asset Valuation Allowance**		
	Accounts [description of account]	**Debit**	**Credit**
+	Income Tax Expense [income statement expense account]	2	
+	Valuation Allowance [balance sheet contra-asset account]		2

The $2 million increase in income tax expense is necessary to offset the $2 million tax benefit recorded when the deferred tax asset was increased from $15 million to $17 million.

Not all companies establish valuation allowances for their loss carryforward deferred tax assets. Here is some information from Cannondale's financial statement notes discussing the likelihood that the deferred tax assets will actually be realized:

Realization of these tax carryforwards is dependent on generating sufficient taxable income prior to the expiration of the various credits. Approximately $13 million of future taxable income during the carryforward period will be necessary for the Company to utilize the entire credit carryforward amount. In the event that the Company does not realize such earnings, a charge would be required. Management believes the Company will obtain the full benefit of the entire deferred tax asset on the basis of its evaluation of the Company's anticipated future profitability from both its motorsports and bicycle operating segments. Based on management's assessment, it is more likely than not that the entire net deferred tax asset recorded as of July 1, 2000 will be realized through future taxable earnings and/or implementation of tax planning strategies.

Source: Cannondale Corporation Form 10-K.

COMPREHENSIVE EXAMPLE

Here is some information about Campbell Soup Company's temporary differences, deferred tax assets, and deferred tax liabilities at the end of 1999 (all dollar amounts are in millions of dollars):

TEMPORARY DIFFERENCES AND DEFERRED TAX ASSETS AND LIABILITIES AT END OF 1999

Temporary Difference Related to	Balance Sheet Account	(Taxable) Deductible Temporary Difference	Tax Rate	Deferred Tax (liability) Asset
Depreciation	Property and equipment	(503)	35%	(176)
Pensions	Prepaid pension asset	(349)	35	(122)
Other	Unknown	(511)	35	(179)
Deferred tax liabilities				(477)
Benefits and compensation	Postretirement liability	597	35	209
Restructuring accruals	Restructuring liability	89	35	31
Tax loss carryforwards	None	49	35	17
Other	Unknown	143	35	50
Gross deferred tax assets				307
Valuation allowance				(17)
Net deferred tax assets				290
Net deferred tax liability				(187)

Assume that during 2000 the company had income tax depreciation in excess of financial accounting depreciation of $80, and the balance sheet liability for restructuring accruals increased by $20. Also, during 2000 the company received $30 of advance rental income related to the year 2001. This was recorded as unearned revenue (a current liability) on the balance sheet but is taxable in 2000. All other temporary differences remained the same as the prior year.

Also during 2000 the corporate tax rate increased from 35 percent to 36 percent. Finally, the company incurred a net operating loss carryforward of $10 in 2000 that will be carried forward to future years. Management expects that it is more likely than not that 10 percent of deferred tax assets related to net operating loss carryforwards will be realized in the future. The current tax expense for 2000 is $280, of which $190 has already been paid in cash (reflected in an account called Prepaid Income Tax).

Under these assumptions, what is Campbell Soup's income tax expense for 2000?

Step 1:   Compute the temporary differences at the end of the year. In this case, the taxable temporary difference for depreciation increased by $80 due to the excess of income tax depreciation over financial accounting depreciation. The deductible temporary difference for restructuring accruals increased by $20 due to the increase in the balance sheet liability. There is a new deductible temporary difference for the unearned rent liability equal to $30.

Step 2:   Compute the amount of any net operating loss carryforwards at year-end. In this case, the net operating loss carryforwards increased by $10 during the year.

Step 3:   Multiply the temporary differences and the net operating loss carryforward by the company's tax rate to compute the deferred tax assets and liabilities. In this case, the tax rate for the year has changed from 35 percent to 36 percent. Therefore, all of the temporary differences and the net operating loss carryforward are multiplied by the new 36 percent rate.

Step 4:   Determine the valuation allowance. In this case, management expects that it is more likely than not that 10 percent of the deferred tax assets relating to the net operating loss carryforward will be realized in the future. Ten percent of the new deferred tax asset of $21 is equal to $2. This means that a valuation allowance for the remaining 90 percent of the deferred tax asset (equal to $21 − $2 = $19) is required.

Step 5:   Determine the net deferred tax asset or liability at year-end.

Step 6:   Compute the change in the net deferred tax asset or liability. This is the deferred income tax expense or benefit.

Step 7:   Add the deferred tax expense to the current tax expense to arrive at the total income tax expense for the year. (If there is a deferred tax benefit it would be subtracted from the current tax expense.)

These steps are all illustrated in the table on the next page.

The following table shows the computation of the income tax expense for 2000 based on the previously stated assumptions:

	TEMPORARY DIFFERENCES AND DEFERRED TAX ASSETS AND LIABILITIES FOR 2000				
Temporary Difference Related to	**Prior Year (taxable) Deductible Temporary Difference**	**Changes for 2000**	**Year 2000 (taxable) Deductible Temporary Difference**	**Tax Rate**	**Deferred Tax (liability) Asset**
Depreciation	(503)	(80)	(583)	36%	(210)
Pensions	(349)	—	(349)	36	(126)
Other	(511)	—	(511)	36	(184)
Deferred tax liabilities					(520)
Benefits and compensation	597	—	597	36	215
Restructuring accruals	89	20	109	36	39
Tax loss carryforwards	49	10	59	36	21
Unearned rent revenue	—	30	30	36	11
Other	143	—	143	36	51
Gross deferred tax assets					337
Valuation allowance					(19)
Net deferred tax assets					318
Net deferred tax liability					(202)
Deferred tax liability from prior year					(187)
Increase in deferred tax liability (this is the deferred tax expense)					15
Current tax expense					280
Total income tax expense					295

Here is the journal entry to record income tax expense:

	Journal Entry to Record Income Tax Expense 2000		
+/−	**Accounts [description of account]**	**Debit**	**Credit**
+	Income Tax Expense [income statement expense account]	295	
+	Deferred Tax Asset [balance sheet asset account]	30	
−	Prepaid Income Tax [balance sheet asset account]		190
+	Accrued Income Taxes [balance sheet liability account]		90
+	Deferred Tax Liability [balance sheet liability account]		43
+	Valuation Allowance [balance contra-asset account]		2

The Prepaid Income Tax account represents the cash that has already been paid to the government in taxes during the year. This asset account is eliminated since the taxes are no longer prepaid but are now treated as income tax expense for the year. The Accrued Income Taxes account reflects the liability of the company to pay the remaining income taxes. This is equal to the current income tax expense of $280 minus the $190 already paid. Deferred tax liabilities increased by $520 − $477 = $43, while gross deferred tax assets increased by $337 − $307 = $30. The $2 credit to Valuation Allowance reflects the increase in this account from $17 to $19.

DISCLOSURE OF TAX INFORMATION

Under U.S. GAAP, firms must disclose the following information related to income tax expense:

1. The current and deferred components of income tax expense.
2. The foreign and domestic components of income tax expense.
3. The foreign and domestic components of pretax income.
4. The amounts and expiration dates of any unused net operating loss or credit carryforwards.
5. The components of deferred tax assets and liabilities.
6. A reconciliation of the company's effective tax rate with the statutory rate.

Items 5 (components of deferred tax assets and liabilities) and 6 (reconciliation of the effective tax rate) are discussed in more detail below.

Components of Deferred Tax Assets and Liabilities

We saw earlier that Campbell Soup's deferred tax liabilities were related to depreciation and pension differences, and its deferred tax assets were related to benefits and compensation and restructuring accruals. Under GAAP, all firms must disclose the major items that make up the temporary differences reflected in the deferred tax assets or liabilities on the balance sheet.

In addition, all deferred tax assets and liabilities must be classified as current and noncurrent. The classification is made based on the classification of the asset or liability to which the deferred tax asset or liability relates. For example, since equipment is a noncurrent asset, the deferred tax liability related to depreciation is a noncurrent liability. In those cases where the deferred tax asset or liability is not related to an actual asset or liability (such as for net operating loss carryforwards) the current/noncurrent classification is made based on when the deferred tax asset or liability is expected to reverse. All current deferred tax assets and liabilities are combined into one net current asset or liability on the balance sheet. Similarly, all noncurrent deferred tax assets and liabilities are combined into one net noncurrent asset or liability on the balance sheet.

To illustrate this disclosure, here is some information from the notes to the financial statements of Hershey Foods Corporation:

The tax effects of the significant temporary differences which comprised the deferred tax assets and liabilities were as follows (in thousands):

	December 31	
	1999	**1998**
Deferred tax assets		
Postretirement benefit obligations	$ 84,305	$ 87,954
Accrued expenses and other reserves	103,232	96,843
Accrued trade promotion reserves	34,708	28,118
Other	23,054	21,530
Total deferred tax assets	245,299	234,445
Deferred tax liabilities		
Depreciation	289,369	308,074
Other	201,672	188,967
Total deferred tax liabilities	491,041	497,041
Net deferred tax liabilities	$245,742	$262,596
Included in		
Current deferred tax assets, net	$ 80,303	$ 58,505
Noncurrent deferred tax liabilities, net	326,045	321,101
Net deferred tax liabilities	$245,742	$262,596

Source: Hershey Foods Corporation Form 10-K.

Notice that Hershey Foods has $245,742 thousand of *net* deferred tax liabilities for 1999, comprised of $245,299 thousand of deferred tax assets and $491,041 thousand of deferred tax liabilities. On the balance sheet of Hershey Foods this net deferred tax liability is reported as a *current* deferred tax asset of $80,303 thousand and a *noncurrent* deferred tax liability of $326,045 thousand.

Reconciliation of the Effective Tax Rate

Firms are also required to provide a reconciliation of their effective tax rate with the statutory tax rate. The effective tax rate is equal to the firm's income tax expense divided by pretax accounting income. The statutory tax rate is the corporate tax rate specified under the income tax law. For U.S. corporations, the statutory tax rate would be the U.S. corporate tax rate, currently 35 percent. Since temporary book-tax differences still result in income tax expense being recorded (as deferred tax expense or benefit), differences between the effective tax rate and the statutory tax rate reflect only permanent book-tax differences.

Here is an example of Campbell Soup's reconciliation of the effective tax rate with the statutory U.S. tax rate:

The following is a reconciliation of effective income tax rates on continuing operations with the U.S. federal statutory income tax rate:

	1999	1998	1997
Federal statutory income tax rate	35.0%	35.0%	35.0%
State income taxes (net of federal tax benefit)	1.9	2.0	2.2
Nondeductible divestiture and restructuring charges	.3	1.8	1.6
Non-U.S. earnings taxed at other than federal statutory rate	(.6)	(.4)	(.7)
Tax loss carryforwards	(.3)	(.8)	(.1)
Other	(2.3)	(1.8)	(2.0)
Effective income tax rate	34.0%	35.8%	36.0%

Source: Campbell Soup Company Form 10-K.

For 1999, Campbell Soup's effective tax rate was 34 percent (equal to tax expense of $373 million divided by pretax income of $1,097 million). The above table provides information as to why this rate is different than the statutory U.S. corporate tax rate of 35 percent. One common reconciling item for most companies is state income taxes (net of federal tax benefit), which is 1.9 percent for Campbell Soup for 1999. This is a common reconciling item because the effective tax rate includes state income taxes, while the statutory U.S. tax rate of 35 percent reflects only the federal income tax. A second common reconciling item for multinational corporations is non-U.S. earnings taxed at other than the U.S. federal statutory rate, which is 0.6 percent for Campbell Soup for 1999. Campbell Soup's effective tax rate includes income taxes paid by the company's foreign subsidiaries in foreign countries, and these countries' income tax rates are not the same as the U.S. rate of 35 percent.[4]

Campbell Soup has three additional reconciling items for 1999. First, nondeductible divestiture and restructuring charges equal to 0.3 percent. This represents the income tax effect of expenses recorded by Campbell Soup that are not deductible under income tax rules. Remember that these expenses represent a permanent book-tax difference, meaning that they will never result in a tax deduction in the future. (If these items represented future tax deductions they would be treated as a temporary book-tax difference and would result in a deferred tax asset and a deferred tax benefit in the current year.)

The second additional reconciling item is tax loss carryforwards of 0.3 percent. To the extent that Campbell Soup was able to reduce its income tax expense through the use of net operating loss carryforwards from other years, its effective tax rate will be less than the statutory rate. Note that these tax loss carryforwards are from other countries (or states), since Campbell Soup did not have a tax loss carryforward for U.S. tax purposes.

The third additional reconciling item is other for 2.3 percent, which represents many small permanent book-tax differences that are individually not considered by Campbell Soup's managers to be material in amount. Obviously, such a large reconciling item with no explanation provides no useful information to users of Campbell Soup's financial statements, since it is not possible to predict whether these items will persist into the future.

---

[4] In cases where the earnings of a foreign subsidiary are expected to be paid as a dividend to the U.S. parent corporation, so that the foreign earnings will become subject to U.S. tax in the future, a deferred tax expense and liability must be recorded. Paying earnings from a foreign subsidiary to a U.S. parent is referred to as *repatriation*.

In some cases, companies will provide a reconciliation of the actual income tax expense *amount,* rather than the effective tax rate, with the tax amount that would result from multiplying pretax accounting income by the statutory tax rate. Reconciliation of the tax amount or the effective tax rate are both acceptable under GAAP. Here is an example of a reconciliation of the tax amount for Intel Corporation:

The provision for taxes reconciles to the amount computed by applying the statutory federal rate of 35% to income before taxes as follows (in millions):

	1999	1998	1997
Computed expected tax	$3,930	$3,198	$3,731
State taxes, net of federal benefits	255	208	249
Foreign income taxed at different rates	(239)	(339)	(111)
Nondeductible acquisition-related costs . . .	274	74	—
Other	(306)	(72)	(155)
Provision for taxes	$3,914	$3,069	$3,714

Source: Intel Corporation Form 10-K.

Disclosure Example

As an example of the income tax disclosure required under GAAP, presented below is the entire income tax note to IBM's financial statements for 2000. This note illustrates all of the disclosures mentioned above in one place.

Notes to Consolidated Financial Statements
O. Taxes
(in millions)

	For the Year Ended December 31		
	2000	1999	1998
Income before income taxes			
U.S. operations	$ 5,871	$ 5,892	$2,960
Non-U.S. operations	5,663	5,865	6,080
	$11,534	$11,757	$9,040
The provision for income taxes by geographic operations is as follows:			
U.S. operations	$ 1,692	$ 2,005	$ 991
Non-U.S. operations	1,749	2,040	1,721
Total provision for income taxes	$ 3,441	$ 4,045	$2,712

The components of the provision for income taxes by taxing jurisdiction are as follows (in millions):

	For the Year Ended December 31		
	2000	**1999**	**1998**
U.S. federal			
Current	$ 613	$1,759	$1,117
Deferred	286	(427)	(475)
	899	1,332	642
U.S. state and local			
Current	192	272	139
Deferred	47	7	(260)
	239	279	(121)
Non-U.S.			
Current	2,607	2,727	2,062
Deferred	(304)	(293)	129
	2,303	2,434	2,191
Total provision for income taxes	3,441	4,045	2,712
Provision for social security, real estate, personal property and other taxes	2,766	2,831	2,859
Total provision for taxes	$6,207	$6,876	$5,571

The effect of tax law changes on deferred tax assets and liabilities did not have a significant effect on the company's effective tax rate.

The significant components of activities that gave rise to deferred tax assets and liabilities that are recorded on the balance sheet were as follows (in millions):

	At December 31	
	2000	**1999**
Deferred Tax Assets		
Employee benefits	$ 3,673	$ 3,737
Alternative minimum tax credits	1,424	1,244
Bad debt, inventory and warranty reserves	953	1,093
Capitalized research and development	848	880
Deferred income	837	870
General business credits	655	605
Infrastructure reduction charges	617	918
Foreign tax loss carryforwards	489	406
Equity alliances	437	377
Depreciation	376	326
State and local tax loss carryforwards	246	227
Intracompany sales and services	149	153
Other	2,809	2,763
Gross deferred tax assets	13,513	13,599
Less: Valuation allowance	572	647
Net deferred tax assets	$12,941	$12,952

	At December 31	
	2000	**1999**
Deferred Tax Liabilities		
Retirement benefits	$3,447	$3,092
Sales-type leases	2,450	2,914
Depreciation	1,179	1,237
Software costs deferred	306	250
Other	1,836	2,058
Gross deferred tax liabilities	$9,218	$9,551

The valuation allowance at December 31, 2000, principally applies to certain state and local, and foreign tax loss carryforwards that, in the opinion of management, are more likely than not to expire before the company can use them.

A reconciliation of the company's effective tax rate to the statutory U.S. federal tax rate is as follows:

	For the Year Ended December 31		
	2000	**1999**	**1998**
Statutory rate	35%	35%	35%
Foreign tax differential	(6)	(2)	(6)
State and local	1	1	1
Valuation allowance related items	(1)	—	(1)
Other	1	—	1
Effective rate	30%	34%	30%

For tax return purposes, the company has available tax credit carryforwards of approximately $2,079 million, of which $1,424 million have an indefinite carryforward period and the remainder begin to expire in 2004. The company also has state and local, and foreign tax loss carryforwards, the tax effect of which is $735 million. Most of these carryforwards are available for more than 5 years or have an indefinite carryforward period.

Undistributed earnings of non-U.S. subsidiaries included in consolidated retained earnings were $15,472 million at December 31, 2000, $14,900 million at December 31, 1999, and $13,165 million at December 31, 1998. These earnings, which reflect full provision for non-U.S. income taxes, are indefinitely reinvested in non-U.S. operations or will be remitted substantially free of additional tax.

Source: IBM Corporation Form 10-K.

INTRAPERIOD TAX ALLOCATION

Recall from Chapter 2 that discontinued operations, extraordinary items, and the cumulative effect of a change in accounting principle are all reported after income tax expense, and that these items are reported net of tax. This is referred to as *intraperiod tax allocation,* since the income tax expense for the year is being allocated among different items on the income statement within the same accounting period.[5] What this means is that the income tax expense on the income statement reflects only the taxes associated with the company's pretax income, and does not reflect taxes associated with discontinued operations, extraordinary items, or the cumulative effect of a change in accounting principle.

It is important to recognize this fact for two reasons. First, when computing a company's tax expense, the tax effect of discontinued operations, extraordinary items, and cumulative effect of a change in accounting principle must be

---

[5] Deferred tax assets and liabilities are sometimes referred to as *interperiod tax allocation.*

subtracted from the other tax expense and allocated to these items separately. Second, the income tax reported on the income statement does not represent the total income tax to the extent the company reports discontinued operations, extraordinary items, or cumulative effect of a change in accounting principle.

ACCOUNTING FOR INCOME TAXES IN OTHER COUNTRIES

Financial reporting standards in most other countries follow some form of the liability method and record deferred tax assets and liabilities. In some countries, such as Germany and Japan, the same accounting rules are followed for both financial reporting purposes and income tax purposes, so that book-tax differences do not arise.

To illustrate accounting for income taxes in other countries, information from the financial statement notes for three non-U.S. companies is presented below. The three companies are Michelin Group (French GAAP), Reed Elsevier (Dutch/ U.K. GAAP), and Nestlé Group (Swiss GAAP).

Here is the note describing the method of accounting for income tax expense for Michelin. Notice that income tax expense includes both due, that is, current, and deferred charges. Deferred taxes are recognized by the liability method (as in the United States) and represent the tax effects of temporary differences and tax loss carryforwards. Finally, the note states that deferred tax assets and liabilities are not discounted.

---

m. Corporate Income Tax

Tax on corporate income includes both due and deferred charges. Deferred taxes are recognized by the liability method on a company-by-company basis with regard to:

Temporary differences between the book value and tax basis of assets and liabilities.

Tax loss carryforwards whose recovery is deemed likely.

Amounts thus determined are not discounted to present-day value.

Source: Michelin Group annual report.

What follows is the detail of Michelin's income tax expense, as well as a reconciliation of the actual tax with the statutory tax, and a summary of deferred tax assets and liabilities. Notice that Michelin does not give a breakdown of the components of deferred tax assets and liabilities but simply lists those attributable to temporary differences, tax credits, and tax loss carryforwards. Also, notice that Michelin discloses unrecognized deferred tax assets. Under U.S. GAAP, these deferred tax assets would have been recorded, but they would have been offset by a valuation allowance.

12. Corporate Income Tax

The breakdown of corporate income tax is as follows:

	At Dec. 31, 2000	At Dec. 31, 1999
Tax due	309,359	275,325
Deferred taxes	−18,912	−61,950
Total	290,447	213,375

The reconciliation between the theoretical tax charge and the book tax charge is as follows:

	Dec. 31, 2000
Theoretical tax on contribution of group entities to consolidated income, calculated in accordance with local tax rates	285,178
Effect of permanent differences	−27,972
Effect of unrecognized deferred tax assets	34,314
Effect of changes on actual local tax rates	7,900
Other effects	−8,973
Tax on corporate income	290,447

	Dec. 31, 2000	Dec. 31, 1999
Total value of unrecognized deferred tax assets:	473,533	517,266

The breakdown of deferred tax assets and liabilities by category is as follows:

	Dec. 31, 2000	Dec. 31, 1999
Deferred tax assets	1,352,494	1,296,940
Deferred tax liabilities	−62,990	−145,669
Net amount	1,289,504	1,151,271
Broken down into		
Temporary differences	966,090	731,006
Tax credits	−21,249	85,110
Tax loss carryforwards	344,663	335,155

Source: Michelin Group annual report.

Reed Elsevier describes its method of accounting for income tax expense in the note on the next page, using the terminology *timing differences* rather than *temporary differences*. (The two terms mean the same thing.) The note also discusses the fact that "No provision is made for tax which would become payable on the distribution of retained profits by foreign subsidiaries, associates or joint ventures, unless there is an intention to distribute such retained earnings giving rise to a charge." This means that the U.K. or Dutch tax rate is not applied to earnings taxed in low-tax-rate foreign countries unless the earnings will later become subject to U.K. or Dutch taxation. This rule is similar to U.S. GAAP.

Consistent with U.K. GAAP, "deferred tax assets are only recognised to the extent that they are considered recoverable in the short term." Under U.S. GAAP, all deferred tax assets would be recognized, with a valuation allowance for those not expected to provide a tax benefit in the future. Finally, the note states that the deferred tax balances are not discounted.

Taxation

Deferred taxation is provided in full for timing differences using the liability method. No provision is made for tax which would become payable on the distribution of retained profits by foreign subsidiaries, associates or joint ventures, unless there is an intention to distribute such retained earnings giving rise to a charge. Deferred tax assets are only recognised to the extent that they are considered recoverable in the short term. Deferred taxation balances are not discounted.

Source: Reed Elsevier annual report.

Here are the details of Reed Elsevier's tax expense, as well as the components of deferred tax assets and liabilities. There is no reconciliation to the statutory tax rate, although the note states "The total tax charge for the year is high as a proportion of profit before tax principally due to non-tax deductible amortisation and the non-recognition of potential deferred tax assets." This provides some information about the differences between the effective tax rate and the statutory tax rate.

8.	Tax on profit on ordinary activities			
	2000 (£m)	1999 (£m)	**2000 (€ m)**	1999 (€ m)
United Kingdom	66	62	**108**	94
The Netherlands	53	50	**87**	76
Rest of world	56	67	**92**	102
Subtotal (including deferred tax of £3m/€ 5m (1999 £16m/€ 24m))	175	179	**287**	272
Share of tax attributable to joint ventures	4	3	**7**	5
Tax on ordinary activities before exceptional items	179	182	**294**	277
Net tax credit on exceptional items	(20)	(15)	**(33)**	(23)
Total	159	167	**261**	254

The total tax charge for the year is high as a proportion of profit before tax principally due to non-tax deductible amortisation and the non-recognition of potential deferred tax assets.

Deferred taxation is analysed as follows:

	2000 (£m)	1999 (£m)	**2000 (€ m)**	1999 (€ m)
Deferred taxation liabilities				
Pension prepayment	37	36	60	58
Revaluation gains	42	33	67	53
	79	69	127	111
Deferred taxation assets				
Excess of amortisation over related tax allowances	(8)	(9)	(13)	(14)
Acquisition related provisions	(34)	(24)	(54)	(39)
	(42)	(33)	(67)	(53)
Total	37	36	60	58

Source: Reed Elsevier annual report.

Nestlé discusses its method of accounting for income tax expense in the note on the next page. As with Michelin and Reed Elsevier, deferred taxes are computed under the liability method. Also, "Deferred tax assets are recognised on all deductible temporary differences provided that it is probable that future taxable income will be available." This is similar to the requirement in the United States for a valuation allowance in cases where it is not more likely than not that the future tax benefit will be realized.

Taxes

This includes current taxes on profit and other taxes such as taxes on capital. Also included are actual or potential withholding taxes on current and expected transfers of income from Group companies and tax adjustments relating to prior years. Deferred taxation is the tax attributable to the temporary differences that appear when taxation authorities recognise and measure assets and liabilities with rules that differ from those of the Consolidated accounts. Deferred taxes are calculated under the liability method at the rates of tax expected to prevail when the temporary differences reverse. Any changes of the tax rates are recognised to the income statement. Deferred tax liabilities are recognised on all taxable temporary differences excluding non deductible goodwill. Deferred tax assets are recognised on all deductible temporary differences provided that it is probable that future taxable income will be available.

Source: Nestlé Group annual report.

Shown below are the details of Nestlé's tax expense, the components of deferred tax expense, and the reconciliation with the statutory tax amount. Notice that only the components of the deferred tax *expense* are given, rather than the components of the deferred tax assets and liabilities. Also, notice that the tax expense includes amounts representing changes in future tax rates.

5.	Taxes (in millions of CHF)		
		2000	**1999**
Components of tax expense			
Current tax		2,395	1,910
Deferred tax		(44)	(64)
Transfers (from)/to unrecognised tax assets		2	79
Changes in deferred tax rates		(13)	10
Prior years tax		18	(36)
Other tax (a)		403	415
		2,761	2,314
Deferred tax by types			
Tangible fixed assets		20	(118)
Goodwill and intangible assets		33	71
Employee benefits liabilities		(68)	(34)
Inventories, receivables, payables and provisions		(148)	(40)
Unused tax losses and tax credits		44	39
Other		75	18
		(44)	(64)
Reconciliation of tax expense			
Tax at the theoretical domestic rates applicable to profits of taxable entities in the countries concerned		2,390	1,889
Tax effect on non-deductible amortisation of goodwill		165	146
Tax effect on non-allowable items		(168)	(125)
Transfers (from)/to unrecognised tax assets		2	79
Difference in tax rates		(49)	(54)
Other tax (a)		421	379
		2,761	2,314

(a) Includes withholding tax levied on transfer of income.

Source: Nestlé Group annual report.

Nestlé provides information about the components of deferred tax assets and liabilities in a separate note to the financial statements, presented below. Normally, for a U.S. company all tax-related information would be presented in a single financial statement note.

21. Deferred taxes (in millions of CHF)	2000	1999
Tax assets by types of temporary differences		
Tangible fixed assets	40	41
Intangible assets	190	230
Employee benefits	957	900
Inventories, receivables, payables and provisions	894	739
Unused tax losses and unused tax credits	71	120
Other	300	394
	2,452	2,424
Tax liabilities by types of temporary differences		
Tangible fixed assets	907	941
Intangible assets	44	52
Employee benefits	105	94
Inventories, receivables, payables and provisions	130	126
Other	247	245
	1,433	1,458
Net assets	1,019	966
Reflected in the balance sheet as follows		
Deferred tax assets	2,569	2,293
Deferred tax liabilities	1,550	1,327
Net assets	1,019	966
Temporary differences for which no deferred tax is recognised		
On investments in affiliated companies (taxable temporary difference)	5,815	4,776
On unused tax losses, tax credits and other items	1,118	820
Unused tax losses expire mainly within 2 to 5 years.		

Source: Nestlé Group annual report.

INCOME TAXES AND THE CASH FLOWS STATEMENT

Income tax expense affects the cash flows statement in several ways. First, deferred income tax expense and deferred income tax benefits are noncash items that affect net income. Therefore, these items must be added back to net income to arrive at cash flows from operating activities. Second, to the extent that the current income tax expense results in an increase or decrease in the liability for income taxes payable, this also represents a noncash item affecting net income that must be added back in arriving at cash flows from operating activities.

Third, income taxes are always classified as an operating activity for purposes of the statement of cash flows, regardless of the classification of the income giving rise to the tax. For example, if a firm sells assets at a gain, the cash proceeds from the sale are classified as cash flows from investing activities. However, the income tax expense associated with the gain is still classified as an operating activity.

Here is a portion of the cash flows statement from Campbell Soup for 1999. Notice that the deferred tax expense of $78 million is added back to net income to arrive at cash flows from operating activities. Also, the $21 million deferred tax benefit in 1998 is subtracted from net income to arrive at cash flows from operating activities. Finally, the adjustment for changes in working capital accounts for other current assets and liabilities for $216 million includes the change in income taxes payable from $163 million at the end of 1998 to $136 million at the end of 1999.

CAMPBELL SOUP COMPANY
Consolidated Statements of Cash Flows
(in millions)

	1999	1998	1997
Cash flows from operating activities			
Net earnings, excluding discontinued operations . . .	$ 724	$ 678	$ 634
Noncash charges to net earnings			
Cumulative effect of accounting change	—	11	—
Restructuring charges	36	262	204
Depreciation and amortization	255	261	283
Deferred taxes	**78**	**(21)**	**(33)**
Other, net	5	53	95
Changes in working capital			
Accounts receivable	108	(159)	(37)
Inventories	(58)	(29)	(48)
Other current assets and liabilities	**(216)**	**(154)**	**(89)**
Net cash provided by operating activities	$ 932	$ 902	$1,009

Source: Campbell Soup Company Form 10-K.

Shown on the next page is a portion of the cash flows statement from IBM Corporation for 1999. In the computation of cash flows from operating activities, IBM subtracts $4,791 million for gain on disposition of fixed and other assets. The gain is subtracted from net income because gains from selling assets are properly classified as investing activities. In the cash flows from investing section, IBM reports proceeds from the disposition of plant, rental machines, and other property of $1,207 million, proceeds from marketable securities and other investments of $2,616 million, and proceeds from sale of the Global Network of $4,880 million. However, notice that the income taxes associated with the gains are not reported as investing activity cash flows. Income taxes are always considered operating activity cash flows.

INTERNATIONAL BUSINESS MACHINES CORPORATION AND SUBSIDIARY COMPANIES Consolidated Statement of Cash Flows (in millions)			
	At December 31		
	1999	**1998**	**1997**
Cash flow from operating activities			
Net income	$ 7,712	$ 6,328	$ 6,093
Adjustments to reconcile net income to cash provided from operating activities:			
Depreciation	6,159	4,475	4,018
Amortization of software	426	517	983
Deferred income taxes	(713)	(606)	358
Gain on disposition of fixed and other assets	(4,791)	(261)	(273)
Other changes that (used) provided cash:			
Receivables	(1,677)	(2,736)	(3,727)
Inventories	301	73	432
Other assets	(130)	219	(378)
Accounts payable	(3)	362	699
Other liabilities	2,827	902	660
Net cash provided from operating activities	$10,111	$ 9,273	$ 8,865
Cash flow from investing activities			
Payments for plant, rental machines and other property	(5,959)	(6,520)	(6,793)
Proceeds from disposition of plant, rental machines and other property	1,207	905	1,130
Investment in software	(464)	(250)	(314)
Purchases of marketable securities and other investments	(3,949)	(4,211)	(1,617)
Proceeds from marketable securities and other investments	2,616	3,945	1,439
Proceeds from sale of the Global Network	4,880	—	—
Net cash used in investing activities	$ (1,669)	$(6,131)	$(6,155)

Source: IBM Corporation Form 10-K.

USING INFORMATION ABOUT INCOME TAXES TO MAKE DECISIONS

Understanding a firm's income tax expense and effective tax rate can help users to forecast a firm's future income tax expense and future net income. Also, by understanding the pattern of changes in a firm's deferred tax assets and liabilities, future cash flows associated with income taxes can be forecast.

A firm's effective tax rate is also an indication of how well managers of a firm are managing the income tax expense. If a firm has an effective tax rate that is higher than those of other firms in the same industry, it may indicate that managers are not actively seeking out opportunities to minimize the firm's income tax expense.

However, a low effective tax rate is not necessarily a signal that one firm is more profitable than another, since a low effective tax rate does not necessarily translate into higher net income. For example, suppose a multinational firm expands operations into a low-tax-rate foreign country, thus reducing the firm's tax expense and effective tax rate. It is possible that the firm will incur substantial nontax costs of doing business in the low-tax-rate country. For example, transportation, communications, and employee training may all be more costly in the low-tax-rate country. In fact, taking all of these nontax costs into consideration, the firm's net income may actually be higher in a high-tax-rate country.

Summary

This chapter presents the GAAP rules for recording income tax expense under the liability method, using deferred tax assets and deferred tax liabilities. Deferred taxes are necessary because financial accounting income and taxable income are rarely the same, and information about the actual income taxes incurred during the year may not be useful to decision makers.

Deferred tax assets and liabilities reflect the tax effects of temporary differences. Temporary differences are differences between the book value of assets and liabilities and the tax basis of the assets and liabilities. Temporary differences also arise from net operating loss carryforwards.

Under the liability method, income tax expense for the year is equal to the current tax expense plus the deferred tax expense or minus the deferred tax benefit. The current tax expense is the taxes actually reflected on the company's income tax returns for the current year. The deferred tax expense is the net increase in deferred tax liabilities or net decrease in deferred tax assets. The deferred tax benefit is the net decrease in deferred tax liabilities or net increase in deferred tax assets.

A valuation allowance is required for deferred tax assets unless, in the opinion of management, it is more likely than not that the future tax benefits represented by the deferred tax assets will actually be realized.

Discussion Questions

1. Explain why taxable income may not be the same as pretax financial accounting income.
2. Give some examples of differences between financial accounting rules and income tax accounting rules.
3. What financial reporting problems arise when taxable income and financial accounting income differ?
4. The financial statement income tax expense might be based on taxable income or financial accounting income. Which measure is more relevant? Which is more reliable?
5. What is meant by the *tax basis* of an asset or liability? Why might the tax basis of an asset or liability differ from its book value?
6. Explain what is meant by a *temporary difference*.
7. Explain the terms *taxable temporary difference* and *deductible temporary difference*. Give examples of each type.
8. How do *deferred tax assets* and *deferred tax liabilities* relate to temporary differences?
9. What tax rate is used in computing deferred tax assets and liabilities?
10. Why aren't deferred tax assets and liabilities discounted?
11. Under GAAP, how is income tax expense computed?
12. Explain what is meant by *current* income tax expense.
13. How are deferred income tax expense and deferred income tax benefit computed?
14. What is a *permanent* difference, and how does it affect the computation of income tax expense?
15. What is a net operating loss? How are net operating losses treated under U.S. tax law?
16. What is the financial accounting treatment for a firm with a net operating loss carryforward?

17. Can a firm with positive net income still have a net operating loss carryforward? Explain.

18. Explain how a valuation allowance is used with respect to the tax benefit for a net operating loss carryforward.

19. What tax-related items must be disclosed in the financial statement notes under GAAP?

20. What is a company's effective tax rate? What is the statutory tax rate?

21. Explain why the effective tax rate may not be equal to the statutory rate.

22. How does deferred income tax expense affect the cash flows statement?

23. Are deferred tax assets and liabilities considered current or noncurrent?

Problems

1. At the end of the year, a corporation has taxable temporary differences of $180,000 and deductible temporary differences of $240,000. The tax rate is 30 percent. Compute the deferred tax asset and deferred tax liability at the end of the year.

2. At the end of the year, a corporation has taxable temporary differences of $265,000 and deductible temporary differences of $380,000. The tax rate is 40 percent. Compute the deferred tax asset and deferred tax liability at the end of the year.

3. At the end of the year, a corporation has taxable temporary differences of $490,000 and deductible temporary differences of $205,000. The tax rate is 50 percent. Compute the deferred tax asset and deferred tax liability at the end of the year.

4. The table below shows the book values and tax bases for assets and liabilities of a corporation as of the end of the current year:

		Book Value	Tax Basis
Equipment	Asset	950,000	870,000
Warranty liability	Liability	180,000	0

a. Identify each book-tax difference as a deductible difference or a taxable difference.

b. Compute the deferred tax asset and deferred tax liability of the corporation using a tax rate of 35 percent.

5. The table below shows the book values and tax bases for assets and liabilities of a corporation as of the end of the current year:

		Book Value	Tax Basis
Buildings	Asset	1,600,000	1,450,000
Unearned revenue	Liability	90,000	0
Restructuring charge	Liability	350,000	0

a. Identify each book-tax difference as a deductible difference or a taxable difference.

b. Compute the deferred tax asset and deferred tax liability of the corporation using a tax rate of 40 percent.

6. The table below shows the book values and tax bases for assets and liabilities of a corporation as of the end of the current year:

		Book Value	Tax Basis
Installment receivable	Asset	230,000	0
Employee benefits	Liability	160,000	0

a. Identify each book-tax difference as a deductible difference or a taxable difference.

b. Compute the deferred tax asset and deferred tax liability of the corporation using a tax rate of 30 percent.

7. A corporation has deferred tax liabilities of $450,000 at the beginning of the year and deferred tax liabilities of $490,000 at the end of the year. What is the amount of the deferred tax expense or deferred tax benefit for the year?

8. A corporation has deferred tax liabilities of $675,000 at the beginning of the year and deferred tax liabilities of $595,000 at the end of the year. What is the amount of the deferred tax expense or deferred tax benefit for the year?

9. A corporation has deferred tax liabilities of $350,000 at the beginning of the year and deferred tax liabilities of $370,000 at the end of the year. What is the amount of the deferred tax expense or deferred tax benefit for the year?

10. A corporation has deferred tax assets of $220,000 at the beginning of the year and deferred tax assets of $265,000 at the end of the year. What is the amount of the deferred tax expense or deferred tax benefit for the year?

11. A corporation has deferred tax assets of $120,000 at the beginning of the year and deferred tax assets of $95,000 at the end of the year. What is the amount of the deferred tax expense or deferred tax benefit for the year?

12. A corporation has deferred tax assets of $760,000 at the beginning of the year and deferred tax assets of $770,000 at the end of the year. What is the amount of the deferred tax expense or deferred tax benefit for the year?

13. The table below shows the balances of deferred tax assets and deferred tax liabilities for a corporation at the beginning and the end of the year.

	Beginning of Year	End of Year
Deferred tax assets	95,000	120,000
Deferred tax liabilities	140,000	180,000

The current income tax expense for the year is $55,000. What is the total income tax expense for the year?

14. The table below shows the balances of deferred tax assets and deferred tax liabilities for a corporation at the beginning and the end of the year.

	Beginning of Year	End of Year
Deferred tax assets	320,000	295,000
Deferred tax liabilities	465,000	405,000

The current income tax expense for the year is $120,000. What is the total income tax expense for the year?

15. The table below shows the balances of deferred tax assets and deferred tax liabilities for a corporation at the beginning and the end of the year.

	Beginning of Year	End of Year
Deferred tax assets	210,000	190,000
Deferred tax liabilities	60,000	90,000

The current income tax expense for the year is $80,000. What is the total income tax expense for the year?

16. The table below shows the balances of deferred tax assets and deferred tax liabilities for a corporation at the beginning and the end of the year.

	Beginning of Year	End of Year
Deferred tax assets	133,000	145,000
Deferred tax liabilities	235,000	218,000

The current income tax expense for the year is $36,000. What is the total income tax expense for the year?

17. The table below shows the balances of deferred tax assets and deferred tax liabilities for a corporation at the beginning and the end of the year.

	Beginning of Year	End of Year
Deferred tax assets	205,000	185,000
Deferred tax liabilities	350,000	380,000

The current income tax expense for the year is $90,000. What is the total income tax expense for the year?

18. The table below shows the balances of deferred tax assets and deferred tax liabilities for a corporation at the beginning and the end of the year.

	Beginning of Year	End of Year
Deferred tax assets	760,000	735,000
Deferred tax liabilities	440,000	405,000

The current income tax expense for the year is $130,000. What is the total income tax expense for the year?

19. The table below shows the taxable and deductible temporary differences and the deferred tax assets and liabilities for a corporation at the beginning of the year:

Balances at Beginning of Year

Temporary Difference Related to	(Taxable) Deductible Temporary Difference	Tax Rate	Deferred Tax (liability) Asset
Depreciation	(385,000)	35%	(134,750)
Pensions	(120,000)	35	(42,000)
Installment receivables	(80,000)	35	(28,000)
Deferred tax liabilities			(204,750)
Restructuring liabilities	100,000	35	35,000
Unearned revenue	90,000	35	31,500
Tax loss carryforwards	50,000	35	17,500
Warranty liabilities	140,000	35	49,000
Gross deferred tax assets			133,000
Valuation allowance			(17,500)
Net deferred tax assets			115,500
Net deferred tax liability			(89,250)

The activity related to the current year is shown in the table below:

Current-Year Activity	
Tax depreciation exceeded book depreciation by	65,000
Balance of prepaid pension asset decreased by	(15,000)
Balance of installment receivables increased by	20,000
Balance of restructuring liability increased by	15,000
Balance of unearned revenue increased by	25,000
Tax loss carryforward increased by	10,000
Balance of warranty liabilities decreased by	(30,000)
Valuation allowance equals 75% of NOL DTA	
Tax rate changes to 34%	
Current tax expense	180,000

Compute the deferred tax asset and liability balances and the total tax expense for the year.

20. The table below shows the taxable and deductible temporary differences and the deferred tax assets and liabilities for a corporation at the beginning of the year:

Balances at Beginning of Year

Temporary Difference Related to	(Taxable) Deductible Temporary Difference	Tax Rate	Deferred Tax (liability) Asset
Depreciation	(480,000)	35%	(168,000)
Pensions	(210,000)	35	(73,500)
Installment receivables	(60,000)	35	(21,000)
Deferred tax liabilities			(262,500)
Restructuring liabilities	120,000	35	42,000
Unearned revenue	40,000	35	14,000
Tax loss carryforwards	—	35	—
Warranty liabilities	80,000	35	28,000
Gross deferred tax assets			84,000
Valuation allowance			—
Net deferred tax assets			84,000
Net deferred tax liability			(178,500)

The activity related to the current year is shown in the table below:

Current-Year Activity	
Book depreciation exceeded tax depreciation by	25,000
Balance of prepaid pension asset increased by	40,000
Balance of installment receivables decreased by	(10,000)
Balance of restructuring liability decreased by	(20,000)
Balance of unearned revenue decreased by	(10,000)
Tax loss carryforward increased by	35,000
Balance of warranty liabilities increased by	15,000
Valuation allowance equals 100% of NOL DTA	
Tax rate changes to 36%	
Current tax expense	260,000

Compute the deferred tax asset and liability balances and the total tax expense for the year.

21. The table on the next page shows the taxable and deductible temporary differences and the deferred tax assets and liabilities for a corporation at the beginning of the year:

Temporary Difference Related to	Balances at Beginning of Year		
	(Taxable) Deductible Temporary Difference	Tax Rate	Deferred Tax (liability) Asset
Depreciation	(240,000)	35%	(84,000)
Pensions	(60,000)	35	(21,000)
Installment receivables	(80,000)	35	(28,000)
Deferred tax liabilities			(133,000)
Restructuring liabilities	140,000	35	49,000
Unearned revenue	60,000	35	21,000
Tax loss carryforwards	30,000	35	10,500
Warranty liabilities	220,000	35	77,000
Gross deferred tax assets			157,500
Valuation allowance			(10,500)
Net deferred tax assets			147,000
Net deferred tax liability			14,000

The activity related to the current year is shown in the table below:

Current-Year Activity	
Tax depreciation exceeded book depreciation by	40,000
Balance of prepaid pension asset increased by	25,000
Balance of installment receivables decreased by	(80,000)
Balance of restructuring liability increased by	35,000
Balance of unearned revenue decreased by	(60,000)
Tax loss carryforward remained unchanged	—
Balance of warranty liabilities increased by	60,000
No valuation allowance required	
Tax rate remains at 35%	
Current tax expense	365,000

Compute the deferred tax asset and liability balances and the total tax expense for the year.

Research Reports

1. In its SEC Form 10-K for 2002, General Electric Company reported earnings before income taxes for 2002 of $18,891 million and a provision for income taxes of $3,758 million (a tax rate of 20 percent). For 2001, the company reported earnings before income taxes of $19,701 million and a provision for income taxes of $5,573 million (a tax rate of 28 percent).

   a. Obtain the financial statements for General Electric Company for 2002.

   b. Explain why General Electric Company reported effective tax rates of 20 percent and 28 percent when the statutory U.S. federal income tax rate is 35 percent.

   c. Explain why General Electric Company's effective tax rate decreased from 28 percent to 20 percent from 2001 to 2002.

2. The March 31, 2003, issue of *Business Week* magazine contains a special report on corporate taxes. Locate this issue and read the article titled "The Corporate Tax Game: How Blue-Chip Companies Are Paying Less and Less of the Nation's Tax Bill."

   a. Explain how corporate tax departments are able to increase the net income of their companies through corporate tax shelters.

   b. Discuss the *quality* of accounting earnings generated through corporate tax shelter activities.

   c. Explain how financial statement users can figure out whether a company is engaging in tax shelter activities.

3. Obtain the financial statements for Amazon.com for 2001.

   a. Why didn't Amazon.com report any income tax expense or income tax benefit on the income statement?

   b. Did Amazon.com have any deferred tax assets and liabilities?

   c. What is the amount of Amazon.com's net operating loss? How did the company report the deferred tax asset associated with the net operating loss.

4. Obtain the financial statements for El Paso Corporation for 2000.

   a. What is the amount of income tax expense that El Paso Corporation reported for 2000?

   b. Of this amount, how much was actually paid to the federal and state governments with respect to 2000 income?

   c. Explain how El Paso Corporation's income tax expense could be so different from the income taxes the corporation actually paid.

   d. Discuss the usefulness of the income tax information reported by El Paso Corporation.

5. Obtain the financial statements for Tootsie Roll Industries Inc. for 2002, 2001, and 2000. Tootsie Roll Industries reported a deferred income tax expense for both 2000 and 2001 (see the income tax note in the notes to the financial statements). However, the company reported a deferred income tax benefit for 2002. Use the information contained in the notes to the financial statements to explain why Tootsie Roll Industries' deferred income tax expense changed to a deferred income tax benefit in 2002.

Rex Rystedt/Timepix/Getty Images

Chapter Learning Objectives

After reading this chapter you should understand

1. The accounting definition of an intangible asset.
2. The five types of identifiable intangible assets.
3. The accounting definition of goodwill.
4. The problems associated with accounting for intangible assets.
5. The difference between purchased and internally developed intangibles.
6. The accounting treatment for purchased identifiable intangible assets.
7. The accounting treatment for purchased goodwill.
8. The accounting treatment for research and development (R&D) expenditures.
9. The accounting treatment for computer software development costs.

Chapter 10

Investments in Intangible Assets

Focus Company: Amazon.com

Introduction

Shown below is the asset section of the balance sheet of Amazon.com, Inc., for 2000 and 1999. Notice that at the end of 1999, Amazon listed goodwill for $535 million and other intangibles for $195 million, a total of $730 million. Yet one year later, these same assets had a book value of $159 million and $96 million, a total of $255 million. The book value of these two groups of assets, both of which represent a category called *intangible assets*, decreased by $475 million (or 65 percent of their book value) in one year.

AMAZON.COM, INC.
Consolidated Balance Sheets
(in thousands, except per share data)

	December 31	
	2000	**1999**
Assets		
Current assets		
Cash and cash equivalents	$ 822,435	$ 133,309
Marketable securities	278,087	572,879
Inventories	174,563	220,646
Prepaid expenses and other current assets	86,044	79,643
Total current assets	1,361,129	1,006,477
Fixed assets, net	366,416	317,613
Goodwill, net	**158,990**	**534,699**
Other intangibles, net	**96,335**	**195,445**
Investments in equity-method investees	52,073	226,727
Other equity investments	40,177	144,735
Other assets	60,049	40,154
Total assets	$2,135,169	$2,465,850

Source: Amazon.com Form 10-K.

What exactly do goodwill and other intangibles represent? And why did their book values decrease so much in 2000? Recall that assets represent expected future benefits to the company. What were the expected future benefits represented by these assets, and why did these expected future benefits go away?

This chapter answers these questions by investigating the GAAP rules related to intangible assets. The chapter begins with a basic discussion of what an intangible asset is and how the unique economics of intangible assets affect their accounting treatment. The GAAP rules relating to intangible assets were substantially changed by the Financial Accounting Standards Board in early 2001, with the new rules becoming effective July 1, 2001. Therefore, the material in this chapter is based on the new rules rather than on the previous rules. However, the examples presented from actual company financial statements reflect the old rules.

THE ECONOMICS OF INTANGIBLE ASSETS

This section discusses the economic factors that tend to cause intangible assets to differ from other types of assets and why these economic factors create difficulties for accountants. The section begins with the question: What exactly is an intangible asset?

Definition of *Intangible Asset*

Although the term *intangible* refers generally to something lacking physical substance, when accountants use the term *intangible asset* they have a more restrictive definition in mind. A useful definition of an intangible asset is: Any asset, whether current or noncurrent, that lacks physical substance, *other than financial instruments*. The term *financial instruments* as it relates to assets means cash, ownership interests in another company (such as shares of stock), and contracts for the future receipt of cash (such as accounts receivable, notes receivable, or debt securities).[1]

Intangible assets for financial accounting purposes generally[2] consist of six types of assets, five of which are called *identifiable intangible assets.* These five identifiable intangible assets are

1. *Marketing-related assets,* such as trademarks, package design, or noncompetition agreements.
2. *Customer-related assets,* such as customer lists, order backlogs, or contractual customer relationships.
3. *Artistic-related assets,* such as copyrights for books, musical works, or motion pictures.
4. *Contract-related assets,* such as licensing agreements, franchise agreements, broadcast rights, or mineral rights.
5. *Technology-based assets,* such as patents, internet domain names, unpatented technology, databases, trade secrets, formulas, processes, or recipes.

These identifiable intangible assets can be further divided into two different categories. The first category is assets that arise from contractual or other legal rights. Examples of these assets are trademarks, noncompetition agreements, contractual customer relationships, copyrights, licensing agreements, franchises, mineral rights, patents, and trade secrets.

The second category is intangible assets that (1) do *not* arise from contractual or other legal rights but that (2) are capable of being separated from the company and sold, transferred, licensed, rented, or exchanged. Examples of this category are customer lists, noncontractual customer relationships, unpatented technology, and databases.

---

[1] The definition of *financial instruments* also includes liabilities for the payment of cash in the future. Financial instruments will be covered in more detail in Chapter 13.

[2] In some cases, companies record deferred charges, such as capitalized start-up costs, capitalized advertising, or bond issue costs, as intangible assets. These types of intangible assets are not discussed in this chapter.

Although there may be other assets that are neither tangible assets nor financial instruments, unless they fall into one of the two categories discussed above—that is, arise from contractual or legal rights, or are capable of being separated—they may not be recorded as identifiable intangible assets; instead, they must be combined as part of an intangible asset called *goodwill* (discussed below). For example, having a highly skilled workforce in place may result in a future economic benefit to a company, but since the benefit does not result from a contractual or legal right, and is not capable of being separated, it would be combined with goodwill.

Another way to categorize intangible assets is to classify them as either being internally developed by the company or purchased from outside of the company. Under GAAP, only intangible assets that are purchased from outside the company are recorded as assets. As a general rule, internally developed intangible assets, including goodwill, are not recorded on the balance sheet.

Goodwill

The sixth type of intangible asset, called *goodwill,* has a very specific definition in financial accounting. Goodwill is the *excess* of (1) the *fair value* of an entire company (as an ongoing business) over (2) the sum of the *market values* of all of the company's identifiable assets (net of liabilities). *Identifiable assets* refers to the sum of tangible assets, financial instruments, and identifiable intangible assets, whether recorded on the balance sheet or not. For example, if the market value of Amazon's common stock was $1,000 million, and the sum of the market values of all of Amazon's identifiable assets (reduced by Amazon's liabilities) was $800 million, Amazon's goodwill would be $200 million. Goodwill will only be recorded on a company's balance sheet if it is acquired as part of the purchase of an entire business. Internally developed goodwill is never recorded on the balance sheet.

The following is a note from Amazon's 1999 financial statements showing the amounts of goodwill recorded on Amazon's balance sheet at the end of 1998 and 1999. During 1999, goodwill increased from $216 million to $748 million, an increase of $532 million for the year.

	December 31	
	1999	**1998**
	(in thousands)	
Goodwill	**$747,720**	**$215,637**
Less accumulated amortization	(213,021)	(41,585)
Goodwill, net	534,699	174,052
Other purchased intangibles	**239,717**	**5,600**
Less accumulated amortization	(44,272)	(1,014)
Other purchased intangibles, net	$195,445	$ 4,586

Source: Amazon.com Form 10-K.

To show where this $532 million increase in goodwill came from, the table on the next page, based on information in the notes to Amazon's 1999 financial statements, lists all of the acquisitions made by Amazon during 1999. The purchase price paid in each acquisition represents the fair value of each of the target companies at the time of the acquisition. The fair values of all of the acquired companies totaled $780 million.

ALLOCATION OF PURCHASE PRICE, AMAZON.COM 1999 ACQUISITIONS		
Target	**Merger Date**	**Purchase Price (in millions)**
Exchange.com	5/14	$ 145
LiveBid	5/14	40
Accept.com	6/9	189
Alexa	6/10	250
Tool Crib, Back to Basics	10/1, 11/8	112
Immaterial acquisitions	Various	44
Total purchase price		$ 780
Allocated to		
Tangible assets and financial instruments		(14)
Identifiable intangible assets		(234)
Residual-allocated to goodwill		$532

Source: Amazon.com annual report.

Amazon acquired $780 million of net assets (that is, assets minus liabilities) during 1999. What sorts of assets were these? Of the total, $14 million represented tangible assets, such as equipment, and financial instruments, such as cash and accounts receivable. Since these assets represent less than 2 percent of the total purchase price, it is obvious that the value of the companies that Amazon was acquiring was represented almost entirely by intangible assets.

Of the $780 million total value, $234 million represented identifiable intangible assets. These are intangible assets other than goodwill. In most cases, these identifiable assets are some type of technology-based assets, such as patents or technological know-how with respect to Internet commerce. These identifiable intangible assets that Amazon acquired in 1999 increased the balance sheet book value of Purchased Intangibles from $6 million at the end of 1998 to $240 million at the end of 1999.

It is now possible to measure the increase in Amazon's goodwill for 1999. The total fair values of all of the acquired companies is $780 million. Subtracting the values of the identifiable assets ($14 million of tangible assets and financial instruments plus $234 million of identifiable intangible assets) equals the amount of goodwill, $532 million.

The following diagrams summarize the relationship between goodwill and other types of assets:

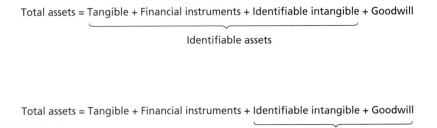

What Distinguishes Intangible Assets?

What is it about intangible assets that causes accountants to treat them differently from other types of assets? Recall that assets represent expected future economic benefits for a company. In the case of intangible assets there tends to be a high degree of uncertainty regarding the future benefits expected to be derived from the assets. This uncertainty has three general causes:

1. The future benefits represented by intangible assets often change dramatically due to competitive conditions. For example, the value of the Nintendo 64 game technology declined when a competitor (Sony) introduced a newer game technology (the PlayStation 2). Often, a company with a large competitive advantage reflected in intangible assets will see that advantage reduced over time by competitors.

2. The future benefits represented by intangible assets may be of use only to the company that owns the asset. For example, Apple Computers made an investment in designing a distinctive shape and appearance for its iMac line of computers. However, it is unlikely that this design would be of value to any other company.

3. It is often extremely difficult to predict the useful life of an intangible asset. For example, consider the copyrights for the Pokémon cartoon character, or the television show *Survivor*. How long will these property rights continue to have value for the owners of the copyrights? An investment in a motion picture may continue to produce revenue for years into the future, or it may be nearly worthless after one week at the box office.

Consider how these factors affecting the value of intangible assets cause problems for accountants. This discussion compares intangible assets with tangible noncurrent assets, such as equipment. Current assets, such as accounts receivable and inventory, are expected to be converted into cash within one year, and so they present fewer problems with respect to future expected benefits.

Assume that Amazon invests $1,000 in new computer equipment. What types of statements can we make about this asset? First, we know that the equipment is worth $1,000, at least at the time that Amazon buys it. We know this because, assuming the purchase was an arm's-length transaction between unrelated parties, $1,000 is the price that other purchasers of similar equipment are willing to pay. Second, we know what future economic benefits Amazon can expect from the equipment. Assume these benefits are faster connection for customers and the ability to service more customers at the same time. Third, based on their experience, the managers of Amazon have some estimate of how long the new equipment will provide a benefit. Assume that Amazon's managers expect the equipment to provide a benefit for three years, after which time it will be obsolete and replaced by newer equipment.

This type of asset presents few problems for accountants. Through the process of depreciation, the cost of the asset is allocated to the future accounting periods in which the asset is expected to provide a benefit, in this example, three years. At the end of that time, the asset will have a book value equal to the expected salvage value, the asset will be sold (or scrapped), and a new asset purchased.

Now compare the above example with a situation in which Amazon invests $1,000 in research to develop a new technology for Internet commerce. At the end of the year, does this $1,000 represent an asset to Amazon?

Clearly, Amazon's managers would not have spent the $1,000 without the expectation of some future benefit. The problem is, unlike the $1,000 spent on equipment, it may not be apparent at year-end whether there is a future benefit from the R&D project. Suppose that the engineers developing the technology are still working on the project at year-end. They may expect to ultimately be successful, but there is some chance that the end result will turn out to be worthless. Also, even if they are ultimately successful, it may not be apparent what the future benefits will be, or how long those future benefits are expected to last. Because of this uncertainty surrounding investments in research and development, accountants are reluctant to record such investments as assets.

ACCOUNTING FOR PURCHASED INTANGIBLE ASSETS

This section discusses financial accounting rules relating to intangible assets purchased from third parties, such as inventors, authors, or other companies. Accounting for intangible assets that a company develops internally is discussed in the next section.

Purchased Intangible Assets

A company may purchase intangible assets in one of two ways. First, the company may purchase individual intangible assets from third parties. For example, a company could purchase a patent for a product from the inventor, a book manuscript from an author, or a noncompetition agreement from a former employee. In these cases, the general rule of recording assets at original cost is followed. The amount paid for the asset is recorded on the balance sheet.

The second way a company may purchase intangible assets is through the acquisition of an entire business.[3] In this case, there is a single purchase price paid for the entire business, and this purchase price must be allocated among all of the purchased assets. Under GAAP, the portion of the purchase price equal to the market value of tangible assets, financial instruments, and identifiable intangible assets is first allocated to those assets in amounts equal to the assets' market values. This allocation of the purchase price then becomes the new balance sheet book value for these assets. The excess of the purchase price over the market values of the identifiable assets is recorded on the balance sheet as the book value of goodwill.[4]

After the initial recording of intangible assets, their cost must be allocated to future accounting periods in some manner. The two methods used, one for identifiable intangible assets and a second for goodwill, are discussed below.

Amortization of Identifiable Intangible Assets

The cost of identifiable intangible assets must be allocated to future accounting periods through a process called *amortization*. Amortization is a process of cost allocation similar to depreciation, except that amortization is usually computed on a straight-line basis. In determining the cost of the intangible asset to amortize, the expected residual or salvage value of the asset at the end of its estimated useful life should be taken into account. For example, if a patent has an original cost of $5,000 and an expected salvage value of $300, only $4,700 of cost should be amortized.

An intangible asset is amortized over its estimated useful life. As with depreciation, this means the expected useful life to the company. Unlike tangible assets, there is no wearing-out that occurs with intangible assets. However, many intangible assets do have legal lives—for example, patents, trademarks, and copyrights all have legal lives. In some cases, such as trademarks, the legal life of an intangible asset may be extended at little cost. For purposes of estimating the useful life of an intangible asset, the legal life should be considered, but the expected useful life of the asset to the company may be different from its legal life.

In some cases, identifiable intangible assets will have an indefinite useful life, which means that the expected useful life extends beyond what the managers of the company can forecast. An intangible asset with an indefinite useful life

---

[3] Accounting for business acquisitions is discussed more fully in Chapter 11.

[4] In rare cases, the total purchase price paid for a business will be *less* than the total of the market values of all of the identifiable assets. (This is sometimes called *negative goodwill* or *badwill*.) In this case, no goodwill is recorded, and the difference between the purchase price and market values is allocated as a pro rata reduction of the book value that would otherwise have been assigned to the identifiable assets.

should not be amortized until such time as the managers of the company determine that the asset's life is finite. Two other things should be noted. First, having an *indefinite* useful life is not the same as having an *infinite* useful life. Second, just because a precise finite life is not known does not mean an asset has an indefinite life.

Just as with other assets, identifiable intangible assets may lose their value and become impaired. An impairment test is necessary any time an event occurs that management believes may have decreased the market value of an asset. The impairment rules were discussed in Chapter 6.

A special impairment test is used in cases of intangible assets with indefinite useful lives, since these assets are not subject to amortization. Assets with indefinite useful lives must be tested for impairment annually, as well as when an impairment event occurs. Also, the impairment test for these assets is based on comparing the asset's *market value* with its book value. (Recall that the normal impairment test compares the sum of an asset's expected future cash flows with its book value.) If the market value is less than the book value, the difference should be recognized as an impairment loss.

Goodwill

For financial accounting purposes, goodwill is recorded as an asset *only* when it is acquired in connection with the purchase of another business. As discussed earlier, the book value of goodwill is equal to the difference between the purchase price of the acquired business and the sum of the market values of the identifiable assets.

Once recorded on the balance sheet, goodwill is *not* amortized. Instead, goodwill is subject to an impairment test. For purposes of the impairment test, goodwill must be allocated to one or more reporting units of the acquiring company. A reporting unit is the lowest level of an entity that (1) is a business and (2) can be distinguished (physically, operationally, and for internal reporting purposes) from the other activities, operations, and assets of the acquiring company. Reporting units are often referred to as *business units*, *operating units*, or *divisions*. The goodwill impairment test is made at the operating unit level.

The Goodwill Impairment Test

The impairment test for goodwill is a two-step process. The first step is to compare the fair value of a reporting unit with the book value of the reporting unit's assets. Fair value of the reporting unit means the amount at which the unit as a whole could be bought or sold in a current transaction between willing parties. Because the reporting unit is an ongoing business, it is unlikely that its fair value will equal the sum of the market values of its individual assets.

If the fair value of the reporting unit is greater than the book value of the unit's assets, there is no impairment and no further steps are necessary. If the fair value is less than the book value, a second step is required to measure the amount of the impairment loss.

The second step in the impairment computation is to compare the implied fair value of the reporting unit's goodwill with the book value of the goodwill. The implied fair value of the goodwill is computed in the same way that goodwill is computed in a business acquisition and is equal to the excess of the fair value of the reporting unit over the sum of the market values of the reporting unit's identifiable assets.

To the extent that the implied fair value of the reporting unit's goodwill is less than the book value of the goodwill, an impairment loss is recorded for the difference, and the book value of the goodwill is reduced. The following numerical example illustrates the impairment test for goodwill. Assume that a reporting unit has the following balance sheet:

REPORTING UNIT BALANCE SHEET		
	Book Value	Market Value
Assets		
Cash	$ 10,000	$ 10,000
Accounts receivable	250,000	250,000
Inventory	320,000	400,000
Equipment (net)	1,450,000	1,600,000
Patent	—	80,000
Goodwill	2,000,000	?
Total assets	4,030,000	
Liabilities		
Accounts payable	170,000	170,000
Notes payable	1,800,000	1,800,000
Total liabilities	1,970,000	
Shareholders' equity		
Common stock	1,000,000	
Retained earnings	1,060,000	
Total shareholders' equity	2,060,000	
Total liabilities and shareholders' equity	$4,030,000	

Assume that the fair value of the reporting unit is $1,900,000. Step one is to compare this amount with the book value of the reporting unit's assets. The book value of the reporting unit's assets is $4,030,000. Subtracting the book value of the liabilities ($1,970,000) results in a book value for net assets of $2,060,000, which is more than the fair value of the reporting unit. This requires the application of the second step in the impairment test.

The next step requires a computation of the implied fair value of the goodwill, which is equal to the excess of the fair value of the reporting unit over the sum of the market values of the reporting unit's identifiable assets. The market value of the identifiable assets, minus the liabilities, is equal to $370,000, so that the implied fair value of goodwill is $1,530,000 as shown in the table below.

IMPLIED FAIR VALUE OF GOODWILL	
Market values of identifiable assets	
Cash	$ 10,000
Accounts receivable	250,000
Inventory	400,000
Equipment (net)	1,600,000
Patent	80,000
Accounts payable	(170,000)
Notes payable	(1,800,000)
	370,000
Fair value of reporting unit	1,900,000
Implied fair value of goodwill	$ 1,530,000

Since the book value of the goodwill ($2,000,000) is greater than the implied fair value of the goodwill ($1,530,000), an impairment loss equal to the difference ($470,000) is required.

Frequency of Impairment Test for Goodwill

An impairment test for goodwill is required at least annually. There is an exception to the annual impairment test requirement if all of the following criteria have been met:

1. The assets and liabilities that comprise the reporting unit have not changed significantly since the previous impairment test.
2. In the previous impairment test, the reporting unit's fair value exceeded the book value of that unit's assets by a substantial amount, making it highly unlikely that a new fair value computation would result in an impairment.
3. Since the previous impairment test, no adverse events have occurred that would indicate a likelihood that the goodwill is impaired.

On the other hand, an impairment test is required more frequently than annually under the following circumstances:

1. An event or circumstance occurs that would more likely than not reduce the fair value of a reporting unit below its book value. Examples are change in the business climate, a legal issue, action by regulators, or loss of key personnel.
2. A more-likely-than-not expectation arises that a reporting unit, or portion of that unit, will be sold or otherwise disposed of.
3. A significant asset group within a reporting unit is tested for an impairment loss under the regular impairment loss rules discussed in Chapter 6.
4. A goodwill impairment loss is recognized by a subsidiary of a reporting unit.

Any time a reporting unit is disposed of, the goodwill allocated to that unit should be included with the book values of the assets being disposed of for purposes of determining the gain or loss on the disposition.

ACCOUNTING FOR INTERNALLY DEVELOPED INTANGIBLE ASSETS

The rules discussed above relate to intangible assets purchased from outside the company. However, just as companies often construct their own tangible assets, companies also develop their own intangible assets. This section discusses the GAAP rules relating to internally developed intangible assets.

The first rule is that goodwill may never be recorded except in connection with the purchase of another business. For example, all of the goodwill recorded on Amazon's balance sheet is related to the acquisition of other businesses by the company. Amazon may also have a substantial amount of goodwill that it has developed internally, through technological innovation, marketing, employee training, and customer service. This internally developed goodwill, although representing a valuable intangible asset of the company, is never recognized.

The second important rule about internally developed intangible assets is that all research and development expenditures are always treated as a period expense under GAAP. This means that the cost of developing patents or other intellectual property is never recorded as an asset on the balance sheet.[5] As a consequence, companies in industries such as pharmaceuticals, computer chips, or biotechnology will have all of their investments in R&D expensed on the income statement each year, and none of the intangible assets developed through these R&D activities will be reflected as assets on the balance sheet.

Sometimes in connection with the purchase of a business, the purchasing company will acquire the target company's research and development projects that are only partially complete. In this case, the company has purchased what is known as *in-process R&D*. In-process R&D is treated as a current period expense by the acquiring company, just as its own R&D would be. However, if the acquired R&D project has been completed by the target company prior to the acquisition, an identifiable intangible asset, rather than in-process R&D, has been acquired and should be recorded as a balance sheet asset.

---

[5] An exception is that legal fees related to obtaining the actual patent for a proven technology, as well as legal fees related to defending the patent from infringement, are capitalized.

Here is some information from the notes to Amazon.com's financial statements relating to the acquisition of in-process R&D.

Approximately $2.8 million of the purchase price of the Accept.com and Alexa transactions attributable to in-process research and development efforts has been expensed because, at the time of acquisition, technological feasibility had not been established and no alternative future uses existed. Purchased in-process research and development was identified and valued by independent valuation through discussions with the acquired companies' management and the analysis of data concerning developmental products, their respective stage of development, the time and resources needed to complete them, their expected income generating ability, target markets and associated risks.

Source: Amazon.com Form 10-K.

The following table shows the allocation of the purchase price of a business to in-process R&D for Yahoo! Inc.

The following table summarizes the acquisitions completed during 2000, 1999 and 1998 that were accounted for under the purchase method of accounting (in millions):

	Purchase Price	In-Process Research and Development	Goodwill and Other Intangibles
2000			
VivaSmart, Inc.	$ 8.9	$ —	$ 7.7
1999			
Log-Me-On.com LLC	9.9	9.8	0.1
Yahoo! Canada	18.0	—	18.0
Innovative Systems Services Group, Inc.	14.1	1.2	12.1
1998			
Viaweb, Inc.	48.6	15.0	24.3
HyperParallel, Inc.	8.1	2.3	5.8

Source: Yahoo! Inc. Form 10-K.

An exception to the rule that R&D expenditures must be treated as a current period expense has to do with costs of developing computer software. Under GAAP, software development costs may be capitalized as soon as the software has reached what is known as *technological feasibility.* This means that the company can demonstrate (for example, through a model) that the software being developed will ultimately be successful.

Capitalized software development costs must be amortized over the estimated useful life of the software. For this purpose, a special amortization method must be used if it results in a greater amortization expense amount than the straight-line method. Under the special method, amortization expense is equal to the book value of the capitalized software multiplied by a ratio. The numerator of the ratio is the amount of revenue generated by the software in the current year. The denominator of the ratio is the total amount of revenue expected to be generated by the software in the current and all future years.

Here is a discussion of Amazon.com's capitalized software costs from the notes to the financial statements:

Technology and content costs are generally expensed as incurred, *except for certain costs relating to the development of internal-use software,* including those relating to operating the Company's Web sites, that are capitalized and depreciated over two years. For the years ended December 31, 2000 and 1999, capitalized costs related to the development of internal-use software, including those relating to operating the Company's Web sites, net of amortization, were $16 million and $8 million, respectively. No such costs were capitalized during 1998. (emphasis added)

Source: Amazon.com Form 10-K.

For another example of capitalized software costs, here is a note from the financial statements of Yahoo! Inc.

Internal Use Software Costs

The Company has capitalized certain internal use software and Web site development costs totaling $3.5 million and $3.2 million during the years ended December 31, 2000 and 1999, respectively. The estimated useful life of costs capitalized is evaluated for each specific project and ranges from one to three years. During the years ended December 31, 2000 and 1999, the amortization of capitalized costs totaled $1.7 million and $0.7 million, respectively.

Source: Yahoo! Inc. Form 10-K.

DISCLOSURE REQUIREMENTS

The new GAAP rules relating to purchased intangibles contain some specific disclosure requirements. The aggregate amount of goodwill should be presented as a separate line item on a company's balance sheet. The aggregate amount of goodwill impairment losses should be presented as a separate line item in the operating section of the income statement, unless it is included as part of discontinued operations. Other intangible assets should be aggregated and presented as a separate line item on the balance sheet, although multiple lines could be used for major classes of intangibles.

For companies with intangible assets subject to amortization, the notes to the financial statements should disclose (1) the total gross book value and accumulated amortization by major class of intangible asset, (2) the total amortization expense for the accounting period, and (3) the aggregate amortization expense for each of the five succeeding annual accounting periods.

For companies with intangible assets that are *not* subject to amortization, the notes to the financial statements should disclose the total book value of each major class of intangible asset.

For companies with recorded goodwill, the notes to the financial statements should disclose the changes in the book value of goodwill during the accounting period. This disclosure should include (1) the aggregate amount of goodwill acquired during the accounting period, (2) the aggregate amount of impairment losses recognized, and (3) the amount of goodwill included in gains or losses on the disposition of a reporting unit.

During an accounting period in which an impairment loss occurs, the following information should be disclosed in the notes to the financial statements: (1) a description of the facts leading to the impairment, (2) the amount of the loss, (3) the method of determining the loss, and (4) whether the loss is based on estimates that have not been finalized at the balance sheet date.

PRIOR GAAP RULES AND TRANSITION PERIOD

The rules presented above are applicable as of July 1, 2001. However, many companies have goodwill and other intangible assets recorded from acquisitions made prior to that date. The prior accounting rules for goodwill and other intangible assets was to amortize them over their estimated useful lives. For this purpose, the estimated useful life of an intangible asset could not exceed 40 years. On the basis of this rule, many companies were amortizing goodwill over a 40-year period.

Once the new accounting rules became effective, several changes resulted in the treatment of existing intangible assets. First, goodwill stopped being amortized and instead became subject to the impairment test discussed previously. Second, intangible assets with indefinite useful lives stopped being amortized. Third, any recorded intangible assets that do not meet the requirements of an identifiable intangible asset discussed above—that is, do *not* arise from contractual or other legal rights and are *not* capable of being separated from the company—must be combined with goodwill.

The major change to existing financial statements will come as a result of the requirement that goodwill no longer be amortized. Companies will see their net income increase, since a major item of expense, that is, goodwill amortization, will be eliminated from the income statement.

Amazon.com's 2000 Intangibles

The beginning of this chapter raised the question of what happened to $475 million of Amazon's intangible assets between 1999 and 2000. Part of the answer is due to amortization. Amortization expense recorded for the year 2000 would reduce the book value of the intangible assets on the balance sheet. In the notes relating to business acquisitions in its 1999 financial statements, Amazon reported that it was amortizing goodwill and other purchased intangibles over three years. The gross book value of goodwill and other intangibles (before accumulated amortization) at the end of 1999 was $987 million. Amortizing this amount over three years would result in an amortization expense, and reduction in book value, of approximately $329 million. Therefore, approximately two-thirds of the $475 million decrease in goodwill and other intangibles in 2000 can be attributed to amortization expense.

The balance of the reduction reflects an impairment loss recorded by Amazon in 2000. Shown below is the income statement of Amazon for 2000. Notice first that the amount for amortization of goodwill and other intangibles is $322 million, indicating that Amazon was amortizing its intangibles over an approximately three-year life. Second, notice the loss of $200 million for impairment-related and other expenses.

AMAZON.COM, INC.
Consolidated Statements of Operations
(in thousands, except per share data)

	Years Ended December 31		
	2000	**1999**	**1998**
Net sales	$ 2,761,983	$1,639,839	$ 609,819
Cost of sales	2,106,206	1,349,194	476,155
Gross profit	655,777	290,645	133,664
Operating expenses:			
Marketing and fulfillment	594,489	413,150	132,654
Technology and content	269,326	159,722	46,424
General and administrative	108,962	70,144	15,618
Stock-based compensation	24,797	30,618	1,889
Amortization of goodwill and other intangibles	**321,772**	**214,694**	**42,599**
Impairment-related and other	**200,311**	**8,072**	**3,535**
Total operating expenses	1,519,657	896,400	242,719
Loss from operations	(863,880)	(605,755)	(109,055)
Interest income	40,821	45,451	14,053
Interest expense	(130,921)	(84,566)	(26,639)
Other income (expense), net	(10,058)	1,671	—
Non-cash gains and losses, net	(142,639)	—	—
Net interest expense and other	(242,797)	(37,444)	(12,586)
Loss before equity in losses of equity-method investees, net	(1,106,677)	(643,199)	(121,641)
Equity in losses of equity-method investees, net	(304,596)	(76,769)	(2,905)
Net loss	$(1,411,273)	$ (719,968)	$(124,546)

Source: Amazon.com Form 10-K.

Shown below is the note from Amazon's 2000 financial statements discussing goodwill and other intangibles. Accumulated amortization of goodwill increased from $213 million to $454 million, indicating amortization expense of $241 million for the year. Accumulated amortization of other intangibles increased from $44 million to $124 million, indicating amortization expense of $80 million. The total amortization expense related to intangibles was therefore $241 million plus $80 million, or a total $321 million, the amount reflected on the income statement shown on the previous page.

Note 5—Goodwill and Other Intangibles

Goodwill and other intangibles were as follows (in thousands):

	December 31	
	2000	**1999**
Goodwill	$ 776,208	$ 747,720
Accumulated amortization	(454,433)	(213,021)
Impairment adjustments	(162,785)	—
Goodwill, net	$ 158,990	$ 534,699
Other intangibles	$ 241,357	$ 239,717
Accumulated amortization	(123,848)	(44,272)
Impairment adjustments	(21,174)	—
Other intangibles, net	$ 96,335	$ 195,445

Source: Amazon.com Form 10-K.

In addition to the amortization expense, the above note also indicates impairment adjustments of $163 million for goodwill and $21 million for other intangibles, a total of $184 million for the year. The following note explains how this impairment loss was arrived at:

During the fourth quarter of 2000, the Company identified indicators of possible impairment of its recorded goodwill and other intangibles. Such indicators included the general slowdown in the retail economy evidenced by general declines in consumer spending, the Company's decline in market capitalization as determined by the quoted market price for its common stock, the pervasive and significant declines in e-commerce valuations in comparison with the market valuations at the time the Company invested in its acquisitions, and changes in the Company's strategic plans for certain of the acquired businesses. Based on the results of its discounted cash flow analyses, the Company identified certain levels of impairment corresponding with the business-unit goodwill and other intangibles initially recorded in connection with the following acquisitions: Alexa, Back to Basics, Tool Crib and Livebid. Accordingly, the Company recorded an impairment loss of $184 million during the fourth quarter of 2000 included in "Impairment-related and other" on the consolidated statements of operations. No impairments were identified in the Company's enterprise-level goodwill and other intangibles, and no impairments of goodwill and other intangibles were recorded in 1999 and 1998.

Source: Amazon.com Form 10-K.

The total reduction in intangible assets for 2000 was therefore $184 million in impairment losses plus $321 million in amortization, for a total of $505 million. Recall that the beginning of the chapter showed that Amazon's goodwill and other intangibles had decreased by $475 million from the previous year. To reconcile that $475 million decrease with the $505 million for amortization and impairment losses, we also have to take into account that the gross amount of goodwill and other intangibles increased by $30 million for the year. The $30 million increase netted against the $505 million decrease results in the net decrease of $475 million for the year.

INTANGIBLE ASSETS AND INCOME TAX EXPENSE

When one publicly traded company acquires another, the transaction is often structured as a tax-free reorganization for income tax purposes. This means that the selling shareholders often receive shares of stock in the acquiring company rather than cash, and they can thus avoid recognizing a gain and paying a tax on the appreciation in value of their shares in the target company.

One consequence of this tax-free treatment is that the acquiring company has the same tax basis in the acquired assets as the target company did. For example, if the target company has a patent with a tax basis of zero and a market value of $10 million, the acquiring company will also have a tax basis of zero in the acquired patent, despite the fact that it paid $10 million worth of stock for it. Since the patent will have a book value on the balance sheet of the acquiring company of $10 million, a taxable temporary difference will arise, since future amortization expense on the income statement will be based on the $10 million book value, while no future tax deductions will be available because the patent has a tax basis of zero.

Because the recording of acquired intangible assets often results in assets with a book value in excess of their tax basis, generating a taxable temporary difference, GAAP rules require the recording of a deferred tax liability equal to the tax effect of the temporary difference. Continuing the above example, with a $10 million book value, a zero tax basis, and a 35 percent tax rate, a deferred tax liability equal to $3.5 million would be required ($10 million taxable temporary difference $\times$ 35% tax rate = $3.5 million).

In future years when the patent is amortized, the book value will gradually decrease, reducing the taxable temporary difference and reducing the deferred tax liability. This reduction in the deferred tax liability will result in a deferred tax benefit, reducing the reported income tax expense. This means that the company's actual future tax payments will be greater than the income tax expense on the income statement, reflecting the fact that the amortization expense does not reduce taxable income.

To illustrate the recording of deferred tax liabilities for acquired intangibles, here is a portion of the income tax note from Intel's financial statements showing the composition of deferred tax assets and liabilities. Notice the deferred tax liability of $214 million in 1999 for acquired intangibles.

(in millions)	1999	1998
Deferred tax assets		
Accrued compensation and benefits	$ 111	$ 117
Accrued advertising	66	62
Deferred income	182	181
Inventory valuation and related reserves	91	106
Interest and taxes	48	52
Other, net	175	100
	673	618
Deferred tax liabilities		
Depreciation	(703)	(911)
Acquired intangibles	**(214)**	—
Unremitted earnings of certain subsidiaries	(172)	(152)
Unrealized gain on investments	(2,041)	(324)
	(3,130)	(1,387)
Net deferred tax (liability)	$(2,457)	$ (769)

Source: Intel Form 10-K.

Permanent Differences

U.S. tax law does not allow a tax deduction for amortization of goodwill acquired prior to 1993. Therefore, any amortization expense related to pre-1993 goodwill taken for financial reporting purposes results in a permanent book-tax difference. Since permanent book-tax differences do not give rise to deferred tax assets or liabilities, the effective tax rate is increased by goodwill amortization. Many public companies, in reconciling their effective tax rates to the statutory tax rate, show a reconciling item for goodwill amortization.

To illustrate this reconciliation, consider the information presented below from the financial statement notes of General Electric Company for 1993. This portion of the note reconciles the effective tax rate, called the *actual tax rate* in the note, with the statutory U.S. federal tax rate. You can see that General Electric's effective tax rate was 1.5 percent greater in 1993 as a result of amortization of goodwill. The increase in the effective tax rate is due to the fact that the amortization expense did not provide General Electric with any tax savings.

Reconciliation of U.S. Federal Statutory Rate to Actual Tax Rate			
	Consolidated		
	1993	**1992**	**1991**
Statutory U.S. federal income tax rate	35.0%	34.0%	34.0%
Increase (reduction) in rate resulting from:			
Inclusion of after-tax earnings of GECS in before-tax earnings of GE	—	—	—
Rate increase—deferred taxes	1.5	—	—
Amortization of goodwill	**1.5**	**1.3**	**1.4**
Tax-exempt income	(2.8)	(2.6)	(2.9)
Foreign Sales Corporation tax benefits	(1.2)	(1.1)	(1.1)
Dividends received not fully taxable	(0.7)	(0.3)	(0.4)
All other—net	(0.6)	0.1	(0.6)
	(2.3)	(2.6)	(3.6)
Actual income tax rate	32.7%	31.4%	30.4%

Source: General Electric Company Form 10-K.

Goodwill related to post-1993 acquisitions may be amortized over 15 years for U.S. tax purposes. This means that post-1993 goodwill will give rise to temporary book-tax differences, and deferred tax assets or liabilities, to the extent the financial statement amortization expense, or impairment expense, differs from the income tax amortization expense.

ACCOUNTING FOR INTANGIBLE ASSETS IN OTHER COUNTRIES

Shown on the next page is a summary of the principal differences between U.K./Dutch GAAP and U.S. GAAP relating to goodwill and intangible assets. This summary comes from the notes to the Form 20-F filed with the U.S. Securities and Exchange Commission by Reed Elsevier. As you can see from the summary, the treatment of goodwill and other intangibles under U.K./Dutch GAAP is similar to that under the old U.S. GAAP, except that the maximum amortization life of 20 years is substantially shorter than the maximum life of 40 years previously allowed under U.S. GAAP.

Summary of the Principal Differences between U.K. and Dutch GAAP and U.S. GAAP

Goodwill and Other Intangible Assets

In the 1998 fiscal year, Reed Elsevier adopted the new UK financial reporting standard FRS 10: Goodwill and Intangible Assets, and changed its accounting policy for goodwill and intangible assets. Under the new policy, goodwill and intangible assets are being amortised through the profit and loss account over their estimated useful lives, up to a maximum of 20 years. In view of this and the consideration given to the determination of appropriate prudent asset lives, the remaining asset lives for U.S. GAAP purposes were reviewed and determined consistently with those adopted for the new U.K. and Dutch GAAP treatment.

This re-evaluation of asset lives under U.S. GAAP, which was effective from 1 January 1998, significantly increased the periodic amortisation charge, as the unamortised value of existing assets, which were previously being amortised over periods up to 40 years, are now amortised over shorter periods.

Source: Reed Elsevier Form 20F.

Shown below is the information contained in the notes to Reed Elsevier's financial statements relating to goodwill and intangible assets. Goodwill is computed in a manner similar to U.S. GAAP, as the excess purchase consideration. According to this note Reed Elsevier's nongoodwill intangible assets consist primarily of publishing rights and titles, databases, exhibition rights, and other intangible assets.

Goodwill and Intangible Assets

On the acquisition of a subsidiary, associate, joint venture or business, the purchase consideration is allocated between the underlying net tangible and intangible assets on a fair value basis, with any excess purchase consideration representing goodwill.

In accordance with FRS10: Goodwill and Intangible Assets, acquired goodwill and intangible assets are capitalised and amortised systematically over their estimated useful lives up to a maximum period of 20 years, subject to impairment review.

Intangible assets comprise publishing rights and titles, databases, exhibition rights and other intangible assets, which are stated at fair value on acquisition and are not subsequently revalued.

	Goodwill ('L'm)	Intangible Assets ('L'm)	Total ('L'm)
Cost			
At 1 January 2000	2,899	3,081	5,980
Acquisitions	680	318	998
Sale of businesses	(42)	(74)	(116)
Exchange translation differences	193	183	376
At 31 December 2000	3,730	3,508	7,238
Accumulated amortisation			
At 1 January 2000	1,197	1,383	2,580
Sale of businesses	(39)	(42)	(81)
Charge for the year	255	210	465
Exchange translation differences	65	82	147
At 31 December 2000	1,478	1,633	3,111
Net book amount			
At 1 January 2000	1,702	1,698	3,400
At 31 December 2000	2,252	1,875	4,127

Source: Reed Elsevier Form 20-F.

To provide further illustrations of accounting for intangible assets in other countries, presented below are portions of the notes to financial statements for Nestlé, Nokia, and Michelin. These notes explain the accounting for intangible assets and research and development. As you can see from these examples, the accounting for goodwill in other countries is generally similar to the old U.S. GAAP rule of capitalization and amortization. The main difference was that most non-U.S. companies were amortizing goodwill over periods of not more than 20 years, while in the United States the amortization period could not exceed 40 years. This capitalization and amortization treatment differs with the new U.S. GAAP rule that requires capitalization and annual testing for impairment.

Intangible Assets

This heading includes separately purchased intangible assets such as software, intellectual property rights and rights to carry on an activity (i.e., exclusive rights to sell products or to perform a supply activity). They are amortised over their useful life, the depreciation being allocated to the relevant headings in the income statement. Internally generated intangibles are recognised only under rare circumstances and provided that a given project and its cost are well identified. They consist mainly of data processing software.

Research and Development

Research and development costs are charged to the income statement in the year in which they are incurred. Development costs related to new products are not capitalised because the availability of future economic benefits is evident only once the products are on the market place.

Source: Nestlé annual report.

Goodwill

Goodwill represents the excess of the purchase cost over the fair value of assets less liabilities of acquired companies. Goodwill is amortized on a straightline basis over its expected useful life. Useful lives vary between two and five years depending upon the nature of the acquisition, unless a longer period not exceeding 20 years can be justified. Expected useful lives are reviewed at each balance sheet date and where these differ significantly from previous estimates, amortization periods are changed accordingly.

Research and Development

Research and development costs are expensed in the financial period during which they are incurred, except for certain development costs which are capitalized when it is probable that a development project will be a success, and certain criteria, including commercial and technological feasibility, have been met. Capitalized development costs are amortized on a systematic basis over their expected useful lives. The amortization period is between 2 and 5 years.

Source: Nokia annual report.

---

a. Goodwill

On first consolidation of an acquisition, goodwill consists of the difference between cost and the fair value of the assets acquired. Goodwill arising on the first consolidation of industrial companies is capitalized and amortized on a straight-line basis over 20 years. In light of annual reassessments of book value, the amortization period may be shortened. Goodwill arising on acquisitions of other companies in the course of the financial year is amortized within that year. Badwill is shown in the balance sheet as a provision and written back as necessary, reflecting changes in the risk associated with the acquired companies.

b. Intangible Fixed Assets

Items shown in the balance sheet under the heading "Intangible Fixed Assets" are mainly the values of computer software, amortized over periods between one and three years, and some items of goodwill, written down in the year of acquisition. Research and development expenses are not included under this heading.

Source: Michelin annual report.

INTANGIBLE ASSETS AND THE CASH FLOWS STATEMENT

Shown below is a portion of Amazon's cash flows statement for 2000. Like depreciation expense, amortization of intangible assets is a noncash expense that must be added back to net income to arrive at cash flows from operating activities. On the statement, $322 million of amortization is added back for 2000.

The impairment loss is also a noncash expense that must be added back to net income to arrive at cash flows from operating activities. For 2000 there is an amount for impairment-related and other for $200 million.

If intangible assets are purchased for cash during the year this would be reflected as a reduction in cash flows from investing activities. However, Amazon's acquisitions of other businesses were mainly done using Amazon's common stock as the consideration rather than cash. Therefore, the acquisition of the goodwill and other intangibles did not necessarily use up Amazon's cash. This is reflected at the bottom of the cash flows statement in the section identified as "supplemental cash flow information." You can see that in 1999, $774 million of assets were acquired using stock, and this did not have a cash flow impact on Amazon.

AMAZON.COM, INC.
Consolidated Statements of Cash Flows
(in thousands)

	Years Ended December 31		
	2000	**1999**	**1998**
Cash and cash equivalents, beginning of period	$ 133,309	$ 71,583	$ 110,119
Operating activities			
Net loss	(1,411,273)	(719,968)	(124,546)
Adjustments to reconcile net loss to net cash provided by (used in) operating activities:			
Depreciation of fixed assets and other amortization	84,460	36,806	9,421
Amortization of deferred stock-based compensation	24,797	30,618	2,386
Equity in losses of equity-method investees, net	304,596	76,769	2,905
Amortization of goodwill and other intangibles	**321,772**	**214,694**	**42,599**
Impairment-related and other	**200,311**	**8,072**	**1,561**
Amortization of previously unearned revenue	(108,211)	(5,837)	—
Loss (gain) on sale of marketable securities, net	(280)	8,688	271
Non-cash investment gains and losses, net	142,639	—	—
Non-cash interest expense and other	24,766	29,171	23,970
Changes in operating assets and liabilities			
Inventories	46,083	(172,069)	(20,513)
Prepaid expenses and other current assets	(8,585)	(54,927)	(16,758)
Accounts payable	22,357	330,166	78,674
Accrued expenses and other current liabilities	93,967	95,839	31,232
Unearned revenue	97,818	6,225	—
Interest payable	34,341	24,878	(167)
Net cash provided by (used in) operating activities	(130,442)	(90,875)	31,035
Supplemental cash flow information:			
Stock issued in connection with business acquisitions	**32,130**	**774,409**	**217,241**

Source: Amazon.com Form 10-K.

USING INFORMATION ABOUT INTANGIBLE ASSETS TO MAKE DECISIONS

Information about intangible assets provided in financial statements prepared under GAAP has been criticized as not being useful for decision making. There are several reasons for this criticism. First, users of financial statements argue that valuable internally developed intangible assets are left off the balance sheet through the expensing of research and development. Second, users argue that intangible assets such as goodwill recorded on balance sheets of U.S. companies do not represent future economic benefits to the company, but are simply the excess purchase price paid in an acquisition years ago. Third, users argue that amortization expense for goodwill distorts current and expected future earnings of U.S. companies, since goodwill amortization is a noncash expense having nothing to do with current operations. Finally, because internally developed intangibles are in most cases excluded from the balance sheet, while externally purchased intangibles are recorded as assets, the balance sheets of similar companies can look much different depending on how the companies acquired their intangible assets.

All of these arguments have to do with the concept of relevance of accounting information. Users are arguing that the information provided under GAAP is not useful in their decisions. However, the GAAP rules for intangibles are primarily based on the concept of reliability. Intangible assets are recorded only when purchased in an arm's-length transaction with an independent party. This assures users that the book values recorded for intangible assets are based on some objective measure of expected future value. The trade-off between relevance and reliability that exists throughout financial reporting is especially troublesome with respect to intangible assets.

The changes being implemented in 2001 are designed to eliminate one of the criticisms of prior accounting: the amortization of goodwill. Under the new rules, goodwill will not be amortized but will remain on the balance sheet until it becomes impaired. This treatment of goodwill is similar to the way land is currently treated. In effect, U.S. standard setters are saying that goodwill does not wear out over time, and therefore any attempt to amortize it only results in an arbitrary expense each year that provides little information to users.

Unbooked Intangibles

Since internally developed intangible assets are not in general recorded under GAAP, this has several implications for users of financial statements. One consequence is that the market value of a company's common stock may greatly exceed the book value of the assets recorded on the company's balance sheet. The ratio of these two numbers, called the *market-to-book ratio*, can be thought of as a measure of how much unrecorded goodwill a company has.

The fact that intangibles are left off the balance sheet also has an impact on measures such as the return on assets or return on equity ratios. If a company develops a valuable drug, for example, and expenses all of the R&D costs in the year they are incurred, the revenues and earnings related to the drug will appear to be very high in relation to the company's recorded assets or equity. For this reason, companies in certain industries, such as pharmaceuticals or computer software, may appear to have unusually high return on asset or return on equity measures.

Summary   This chapter covers the GAAP rules relating to intangible assets. Intangible assets are those assets that lack physical substance, other than financial instruments. Intangible assets are classified broadly into two categories: (1) identifiable intangible assets, consisting of items such as intellectual property or contractual rights, and (2) goodwill. Goodwill represents the purchase price of a business that is in excess of the market values of the identifiable assets of the business.

Under GAAP, intangible assets are generally recorded only when they are purchased from outside parties, such as inventors, or when they are acquired as part of the acquisition of a business. Internally developed intangible assets are usually not recorded, with an exception for certain computer software costs.

The reason for not recording internally developed intangible assets is because there is too much uncertainty about the expected future economic benefits for these assets. Because of this uncertainty, GAAP rules require that all research and development expense be treated as a period expense in the year incurred. Therefore, an investment made in developing new products or technologies is treated as an expense rather than an asset.

Under new accounting rules effective in 2001, goodwill is no longer subject to amortization but is instead subject to a periodic impairment test. Under this test, if goodwill is found to be impaired an impairment loss is recorded in that year. Other intangible assets are amortized over their estimated useful lives, but they are also subject to the general impairment rules.

Discussion Questions

1. Define an intangible asset for accounting purposes.
2. Why isn't accounts receivable an intangible asset?
3. Explain the five types of identifiable intangible assets.
4. Explain how intangible assets can also be classified based on contractual or other legal rights.
5. How is the concept of separability important for defining intangible assets?
6. Explain the accounting treatment for an intangible asset that is (*a*) not represented by a contractual or legal right and (*b*) not separable.
7. Explain what goodwill represents. What types of intangible assets are classified as goodwill?
8. How is goodwill defined for accounting purposes?
9. For purposes of computing goodwill, what assets are considered identifiable assets?
10. What characteristics of intangible assets make accounting for them difficult?
11. What is the difference between a purchased intangible asset and an internally developed intangible asset?
12. Discuss the difference in the accounting treatment (if any) for an intangible asset that is (*a*) acquired as a single asset from the inventor or creator of the asset, or (*b*) acquired as part of the acquisition of all of the assets of an entire business.
13. Explain the accounting treatment for purchased identifiable intangible assets.
14. Explain the accounting treatment for purchased goodwill.
15. Explain how the goodwill impairment test works.
16. Explain how often the goodwill impairment test is required.
17. Explain the accounting treatment for internally developed intangible assets.
18. Explain the accounting treatment for research and development expenditures.
19. What is in-process R&D, and how is it accounted for?
20. Explain the accounting treatment for computer software development costs.
21. Explain the disclosure requirements for purchased intangible assets.
22. Explain how accounting for intangible assets may affect income tax expense.
23. Explain how accounting for intangible assets may affect cash flows.

Problems

1. A company acquires a business for a total purchase price of $950,000. The values of the acquired assets are shown in the table below. The estimated useful life of the identifiable intangible assets is 8 years.

Tangible assets	290,000
Financial instruments	120,000
Identifiable intangibles	360,000

a. What amount will the company record for goodwill?

b. What is the amortization expense each year associated with intangible assets?

2. A company acquires a business for a total purchase price of $2,350,000. The values of the acquired assets are shown in the table below. The estimated useful life of the identifiable intangible assets is 12 years.

Tangible assets	1,600,000
Financial instruments	320,000
Identifiable intangibles	280,000

a. What amount will the company record for goodwill?

b. What is the amortization expense each year associated with intangible assets?

3. A company acquires a business for a total purchase price of $5,840,000. The values of the acquired assets are shown in the table below. The estimated useful life of the identifiable intangible assets is 15 years.

Tangible assets	4,200,000
Financial instruments	850,000
Identifiable intangibles	315,000

a. What amount will the company record for goodwill?

b. What is the amortization expense each year associated with intangible assets?

4. A corporation has a reporting unit with goodwill recorded as an asset. Apply the impairment test for goodwill based on the values in the table below.

Fair value of reporting unit	8,600,000
Book value of assets of reporting unit	9,300,000
Implied fair value of reporting unit's goodwill	120,000
Book value of goodwill	160,000

5. A corporation has a reporting unit with goodwill recorded as an asset. Apply the impairment test for goodwill based on the values in the table below.

Fair value of reporting unit	3,400,000
Book value of assets of reporting unit	3,800,000
Implied fair value of reporting unit's goodwill	215,000
Book value of goodwill	235,000

6. A corporation has a reporting unit with goodwill recorded as an asset. Apply the impairment test for goodwill based on the values in the table below.

Fair value of reporting unit	6,200,000
Book value of assets of reporting unit	5,800,000
Implied fair value of reporting unit's goodwill	140,000
Book value of goodwill	150,000

Research Reports

1. Using library research, answer the following questions:

a. What is the difference between a patent, a trademark, and a copyright?

b. What are the legal lives of patents, trademarks, and copyrights?

c. Is it possible for the owners of patents, trademarks, and copyrights to have these legal lives extended?

d. Explain the costs and benefits to society of (*i*) allowing the owners of patents, trademarks, and copyrights to have a period of exclusive benefit, and (*ii*) allowing that period to expire after a finite number of years.

e. Explain how the legal life of a patent, trademark, or copyright affects the financial accounting treatment.

2. Before a pharmaceutical company can begin selling a new drug, it must first obtain government approval by conducting clinical trials.

a. Locate a news article about a pharmaceutical company that announces either (*i*) failure of a new drug in a clinical trial, or (*ii*) failure to obtain governmental approval for a new drug.

b. How did the company's stock price respond to the news article? Look at the stock price change over the three-day period beginning the day prior to the news article appearing in the press. Compare the company's stock price movement over this three-day period with the movement of a stock market index such as the S&P 500. What can you conclude about the impact of the news on the value of the company?

c. Obtain the financial statements of the company for the year containing the news article. How much did the company spend on research and development for the year?

d. Discuss the costs and benefits of the GAAP treatment of R&D expenditures in the context of the spending on the new drug in the news article.

e. Think up your own alternative method of accounting for R&D expenditures. Compare the costs and benefits of your alternative method in the context of the spending on the new drug in the news article.

3. Obtain the Form 10-K for AOL Time Warner for 2002.

a. What categories of intangible assets does AOL Time Warner list on its balance sheet?

b. What is the amount of amortization related to intangible assets during 2002?

c. Are there any impairment losses related to intangibles for 2002? If so, how much?

d. Explain how the amortization and impairment losses affected AOL Time Warner's cash flows from operations for 2002.

e. Using information in the notes to the financial statements, identify the business segments that experienced goodwill impairment losses and the amount of each segment's loss.

f. Using information in the notes to the financial statements, identify the major types of intangible assets that AOL Time Warner has recorded.

g. Using information in the notes to the financial statements, explain how the cumulative effect of accounting change relates to intangible assets.

4. Locate the website of the Financial Accounting Standards Board (www. fasb.org) which contains information about the board's Project Updates (www.fasb.org/project). Find the explanation of the project on "Disclosures about Intangible Assets" (www.fasb.org/project/intangibles.shtml).

a. In your own words, summarize the purpose of this project.

b. Explain what decisions the board has made at this time with respect to this project.

c. What is the current status of the project?

d. Explain the costs and benefits associated with this project.

5. Locate one or more articles in the financial press that discuss the use of the measure called EBITDA by security analysts.

   a. Explain what is meant by EBITDA.

   b. Explain how EBITDA differs from net income.

   c. Explain how EBITDA differs from cash flows from operating activities.

   d. How is EBITDA related to the accounting rules for intangible assets?

   e. For what industries do you think managers would prefer that investors use EBITDA rather than net income as a measure of firm performance? Explain why. Also, explain how financial reporting rules impact your answer.

   f. What does the use of measures like EBITDA suggest about the usefulness of net income as a measure of firm performance?

   g. What are some criticisms of the use of EBITDA?

   h. Discuss the costs and benefits of EBITDA relative to net income.

© David Samuel Robbins/CORBIS

Chapter Learning Objectives

After reading this chapter you should understand

1. Reasons for one corporation to invest in the stock of another corporation.
2. Why accounting for intercompany investments is based on the amount of influence one company has over another company.
3. The five accounting methods available for intercompany investments.
4. How and when to apply the two versions of the fair value method of accounting.
5. How and when to apply the cost method of accounting.
6. How and when to apply the equity method of accounting.
7. How and when to apply the consolidation method of accounting.
8. How different accounting methods affect the balance sheet and income statement.
9. The accounting methods available for investments in debt securities.

Chapter 11

Investments in Other Companies

Focus Company: The Coca-Cola Company

Introduction

Presented below is part of the balance sheet of The Coca-Cola Company for 2000. Under the heading Investments and Other Assets, Coke lists three types of investments: equity method investments, cost method investments, and marketable securities. Consider one of the equity method investments listed on the balance sheet: Coca-Cola Enterprises, Inc.

Coca-Cola Enterprises, the world's largest bottler of soft drinks, is a publicly traded (NYSE) U.S. corporation with 40 percent of its common stock owned by Coke. The book value of this investment on the balance sheet of Coke was $707 million at the end of 2000. What exactly does the $707 million book value represent?

THE COCA-COLA COMPANY AND SUBSIDIARIES
Consolidated Balance Sheets
(in millions, except share data)

	December 31	
	2000	1999
Investments and Other Assets		
Equity method investments		
Coca-Cola Enterprises Inc.	**707**	**728**
Coca-Cola Amatil Limited	617	1,133
Coca-Cola HBC S.A.	758	788
Other, principally bottling companies . . .	3,164	3,793
Cost method investments, principally bottling companies	519	350
Marketable securities and other assets	2,364	2,124
	8,129	8,916

Source: The Coca-Cola Company Form 10-K.

Consistent with the focus of GAAP on original cost, you might expect that the $707 million represents the original cost of Coke's investment in Coca-Cola Enterprises. Original cost is a very reliable measure of the investment. However, in this case the $707 million does *not* represent the original cost of the investment.

Another alternative, consistent with the usefulness of market value information for decision making, is that the $707 million represents the market value of Coke's investment in Coca-Cola Enterprises. Market value information is extremely relevant to users of financial accounting information. However, in this case the market value of Coke's investment was $3,200 million at the end of 2000. Therefore, the balance sheet book value does *not* represent the market value of the investment.

If the book value of the investment is neither the original cost nor the market value, perhaps looking at the decrease in book value from $728 million at the end of 1999 to $707 million at the end of 2000 can provide some information about the valuation method. Coke did not sell any of its investment during the year, and there were no impairment losses recorded. During 2000, Coke-Cola Enterprises reported net income of $236 million and paid dividends of $70 million. Why then did the book value of the investment decrease?

This chapter explores GAAP rules dealing with one company's investment in the common stock of another company. The chapter shows that there are in fact *five* different ways of accounting for such an equity investment; further, one of those five methods, called the *equity method*, provides the answer to the question of what the $707 million represents and why the book value decreased during 2000. Before covering the details of the different accounting methods, the chapter first discusses reasons one company might invest in the stock of another company.

REASONS FOR EQUITY INVESTMENTS

There are several reasons why a large publicly traded corporation might choose to invest in the common stock, or some other type of ownership interest, of another company. Some of these reasons are discussed below.[1]

1. *Short-term investments.* The simplest reason for investing in the stock of another company is to earn an investment return through the receipt of dividends or appreciation in the value of the stock. Public companies often find they need to accumulate cash for anticipated business needs, and managers will invest this cash to earn the highest expected return for a given amount of risk. At the end of 2000, Coke had $215 million worth of equity securities held as short-term investments. These are included under the heading Marketable Securities on the balance sheet shown above. Often, short-term equity investments consist of preferred stock rather than common stock, since the return on preferred stock is more predictable than the return on common stock.[2]

2. *Corporate control.* One corporation may buy stock in another corporation to achieve some degree of control over the investee.[3] For example, it is extremely important for Coke to have some control over the quality of the bottlers that actually sell its soft drinks to the public. By owning a portion of the voting common stock of Coca-Cola Enterprises and other bottlers, Coke is able to influence the managers of the bottling companies. In some cases, an investor will acquire more than 50 percent of the voting common stock of an investee, thus allowing the investor to have a majority vote on the investee's board of directors.[4] For example, Coke provided the following information in its 2000 annual report: "In October 2000, the Company purchased a 58 percent interest in Paresa, a bottler located in Paraguay. In December 2000, the Company made a tender offer for the remaining 42 percent of the shares in Paresa. In January 2001, we completed the tender offer. We currently own approximately 95 percent of Paresa."

[1] The GAAP rules deal with investments by one company in a *security* of another company. This chapter will focus almost exclusively on investments in a particular type of security: common stock. Investments in debt securities are discussed later in the chapter.

[2] U.S. tax rules allow corporations a deduction for dividends received from other U.S. corporations, effectively reducing the tax rate on dividend income. This makes preferred stock an attractive short-term investment for corporate taxpayers.

[3] The company making the equity investment, that is, buying stock, is referred to as the *investor;* the company whose stock is being acquired is referred to as the *investee.*

[4] For U.S. income tax purposes, a parent company must own 80 percent or more of the voting stock of a subsidiary corporation to include that subsidiary in the parent's consolidated federal income tax return. This provides a tax-motivated reason to own more than 50 percent of the investee's stock.

3. *Joint ventures.* Sometimes two or more companies will combine their activities to form a type of partnership called a *joint venture,* with each partner having an ownership interest in the venture. For example, Coke reported the following information in its 2000 annual report: "During 2000, the Company entered into a joint venture in China with China National Oils and Foodstuffs Imports/Exports Corporation (COFCO), completion of which is subject to satisfaction of certain conditions. COFCO is contributing to the joint venture its minority equity interests in 11 Chinese bottlers. Our Company is contributing its equity interests in two Chinese bottlers plus cash in exchange for a 35 percent equity interest in the venture."

4. *Strategic alliances.* Two companies may agree to work together without any sort of investment by one company in the other. This is known as a *strategic alliance.* For example, Caterpillar announced its strategic alliance with Daimler-Chrysler as follows: "In the fourth quarter of 2000, we announced an agreement to create a global alliance with the commercial vehicle division of DaimlerChrysler to develop, manufacture, market and distribute medium-duty engines and fuel systems for sale to third-party customers and for captive use. The alliance will create a medium-duty engine joint venture, a fuel systems joint venture, research and engineering cooperation, and combined purchasing volume focused on procurement synergies. The alliance is expected to be finalized during the second quarter of 2001." Notice that this strategic alliance involves research and engineering cooperation and combined purchasing volume as well as the formation of two joint ventures.

5. *Foreign subsidiaries.* When a company expands into other countries, it is often more efficient to purchase an existing foreign corporation than to start new operations from scratch. For example, Coke expanded into Paraguay through the purchase of Paresa, as discussed above. In another example, Nokia announced its expansion into Brazil in the following note in its annual report: "In October, Nokia increased its ownership of the Brazilian handset manufacturing joint venture NG Industrial (NGI) from 51 percent to 100 percent by acquiring all the shares of NGI held by Gradiente Telecom S.A. for US$415 million. Obtaining full ownership of NGI was an important step for Nokia to increase its presence in Brazil."

CORPORATE INFLUENCE AND ACCOUNTING FOR EQUITY INVESTMENTS

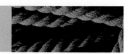

Under GAAP, the way to account for an equity investment is determined by the amount of *influence* that the investor has over the investee. Influence is exercised over a corporation through the ability to elect members of the board of directors of the investee. Therefore, GAAP rules use the percentage of voting stock owned as the measure of influence exerted by the investor over the investee.[5] Under GAAP, there are three levels of influence recognized, and each level has a different financial accounting treatment:

1. *No influence or control (less than 20 percent).* This category is applied to investments representing less than 20 percent of the voting stock of the investee. The accounting methods available for this category of investment are the fair value method (two different versions) and the cost method (in certain circumstances). These methods are discussed below.

---

[5] There are other ways for one corporation to influence another corporation besides investing in voting stock. For example, major customers may influence the actions of corporations from which they purchase products.

2. *Significant influence but not control (20–50 percent).* This category is applied to investments representing between 20 and 50 percent of the voting stock of the investee. Ownership of 20 percent or more is considered enough to give the investor some influence over the operations of the investee, but owning less than 51 percent does not give the investor control of the investee. The accounting method available for this category of investment is the equity method, discussed below. Recall that Coke owned 40 percent of the stock of Coca-Cola Enterprises and used the equity method to account for that investment. Coke had significant influence over Coca-Cola Enterprises but could not elect a majority of the board of directors.

3. *Control of investee (more than 50 percent).* This category is applied to investments representing more than 50 percent of the voting stock of the investee. Ownership of more than 50 percent of the voting stock allows the investor to elect a majority of the board of directors of the investee, thus giving the investor the ability to control the operations of the investee. The accounting method available for this category of investment is the consolidation method, discussed below.

The following table summarizes these rules:[6]

Percentage of Investee Voting Stock Owned	Accounting Methods Available
1. Less than 20%	Fair value method (or cost method)
2. Between 20 and 50%	Equity method
3. More than 50%	Consolidation method

FAIR VALUE METHOD: NO INFLUENCE OR CONTROL

The fair value method of accounting for equity securities is used for securities that have readily determinable fair values. The fair value of an equity security is considered to be readily determinable if the security is traded on a U.S. or foreign security exchange, or on the national over-the-counter market. Under the fair value method an equity security must be classified as one of two types: trading securities and available-for-sale securities. Each of these classifications is discussed below.

1. *Trading securities.* Trading securities are defined as securities that are bought and held principally for the purpose of selling them in the near term and are therefore held for only a short period of time. Trading securities are actively and frequently bought and sold with the objective of profiting from short-term price changes.

2. *Available-for-sale securities.* Available-for-sale securities are all equity securities that have a readily determinable fair value and are *not* classified as trading securities.

Under the fair value method, both trading securities and available-for-sale securities are initially recorded at their original cost. On each subsequent balance sheet date, the book values of the securities are adjusted to equal their fair values at year-end.[7] Increases in fair values are recorded as unrealized gains, while decreases are recorded as unrealized losses.

---

[6] These represent the general rules under GAAP. There may be unusual situations in which an investor owns less than 20 percent of an investee's voting stock but still has significant influence. Similarly, there may be situations in which an investor owns 20 percent or more of an investee's voting stock but does not have significant influence.

[7] This method is sometimes referred to as the *mark-to-market method.*

The accounting method difference between trading securities and available-for-sale securities relates to how the unrealized gains and losses are recorded. For trading securities, any unrealized gains and losses are recorded on the income statement as part of net income. For available-for-sale securities, any unrealized gains and losses are recorded as part of other comprehensive income in the shareholders' equity section of the balance sheet. The following table summarizes this rule:

Type of Securities	Where Unrealized Gains and Losses Are Recorded
1. Trading securities	Included in net income on income statement
2. Available-for-sale securities	Included in other comprehensive income as part of shareholders' equity on the balance sheet

It is easier to understand this accounting method if you have an understanding of what accounting standard setters were trying to accomplish in selecting the method and what obstacles they were facing. First, standard setters recognized that market value information about investments in equity securities was much more relevant to decision making than original cost information. Also, for securities that are publicly traded, market values are reliable since they are published each trading day in the financial press (such as *The Wall Street Journal*). Therefore, there seemed to be no reason *not* to use fair value accounting for these assets.

The problem with fair value accounting is this: Managers of public companies do not want their companies' net income being affected by changes in the market values of equity investments. For example, assume a manager of a public company has done an extremely good job of managing the company during the year, so that the company's net income has increased over the previous year. Now consider what would happen if stock market prices suddenly decrease at year-end, so that the fair values of the company's marketable securities decrease from the previous year, requiring the recording of an unrealized loss. If this unrealized loss reduces net income, it may (in the mind of the manager) conceal the great job the manager has done running the company. Managers want net income to reflect their efforts as much as possible; they do not want net income changing every time the stock market goes up or down. This posed a problem for standard setters. How could they find an accounting method that provided relevant and reliable market value information while at the same time avoiding the perceived problem associated with reflecting unrealized gains and losses in net income?

The compromise solution arrived at was to record all securities at fair value on the balance sheet, but to remove unrealized gains and losses associated with available-for-sale securities from the computation of net income. Although net income is not affected, Other Comprehensive Income, a shareholders' equity account, is affected, so that users of financial statements can still incorporate this information into their decisions.

Example: Available-for-Sale Securities

Here is a comprehensive example applying fair value accounting to available-for-sale securities. Assume that Coke buys marketable equity securities when it has excess cash to invest and sells the securities when a cash need arises. Since Coke intends to hold these securities for an indefinite period of time, management has classified them as available-for-sale securities rather than trading securities. The table below gives actual stock prices for several public companies from June 1998 through December 2000. These prices are used in the example that follows.

Company	Symbol	Closing Stock Prices (adjusted for splits)					
		6/30/98	12/31/98	6/30/99	12/31/99	6/30/00	12/31/00
Amazon.com	AMZN			62.56	76.13		
Boeing	BA	43.37	31.75	42.96	40.71	41.37	65.63
Campbell Soup	CPB	49.01	51.13	43.53			
Chevron	CHV					82.31	83.23
Goodyear	GT			53.61	25.93	18.94	22.44

Source: Yahoo! Finance.

Assume that on June 30, 1998, Coke bought 100 shares of Boeing for $43.37 per share and 100 shares of Campbell Soup for $49.01 per share. Here are the journal entries to record the purchase of the shares.

Journal Entry to Record Purchase of Boeing Stock			
+/−	Accounts [description of account]	Debit	Credit
+	Marketable Securities [balance sheet asset account]	4,337	
−	Cash [balance sheet asset account]		4,337

Journal Entry to Record Purchase of Campbell Soup Stock			
+/−	Accounts [description of account]	Debit	Credit
+	Marketable Securities [balance sheet asset account]	4,901	
−	Cash [balance sheet asset account]		4,901

At December 31, 1998 (the balance sheet date) the prices on the New York Stock Exchange for shares of Boeing and Campbell Soup were $31.75 and $51.13, respectively. This means that the fair value of the Boeing shares decreased since the shares were purchased (from $43.37 to $31.75), while the fair value of the Campbell Soup shares increased (from $49.01 to $51.13) over that same time period. There was an unrealized loss on the Boeing shares and an unrealized gain on the Campbell Soup shares at year-end.

Since these unrealized gains and losses related to available-for-sale securities, they were *not* included in net income but instead treated as part of Other Comprehensive Income, a shareholders' equity account. Shown on the next page are the entries to record the unrealized gains and losses. A contra-asset account called Unrealized Losses and an asset account called Unrealized Gains are used to keep track of the unrealized gains and losses on the balance sheet. The Marketable Securities account continues to reflect the original cost of the securities. Combining the accounts for Unrealized Gains and Unrealized Losses with the Marketable Securities account has the effect of restating the book value of marketable securities from original cost to fair value at year-end.

Recording securities at fair value rather than original cost will cause the book values of marketable securities to differ from the tax bases of the securities, creating a temporary book-tax difference requiring a Deferred Tax Asset (for unrealized losses) or a Deferred Tax Liability (for unrealized gains). In this example, assume Coke's tax rate was 35 percent.

Journal Entry to Record Unrealized Loss on Boeing Stock

+/−	Accounts [description of account]	Debit	Credit
−	Other Comprehensive Income [balance sheet shareholders' equity account]	1,162	
+	Unrealized Losses [balance sheet contra-asset account]		1,162
+	Deferred Tax Asset [balance sheet asset account]	407	
+	Other Comprehensive Income [balance sheet shareholders' equity account]		407

Journal Entry to Record Unrealized Gain on Campbell Soup Stock

+/−	Accounts [description of account]	Debit	Credit
+	Unrealized Gains [balance sheet asset account]	212	
+	Other Comprehensive Income [balance sheet shareholders' equity account]		212
−	Other Comprehensive Income [balance sheet shareholders' equity account]	74	
+	Deferred Tax Liability [balance sheet liability account]		74

The transactions and adjustments from the example up to this point are summarized in the table below.

EXAMPLE OF PURCHASES OF AVAILABLE-FOR-SALE SECURITIES

Date	Action	100 Shares BA	100 Shares CPB
6/30/98	Purchase—original cost	$ 4,337	$4,901
12/31/98	Unrealized gain or (loss)	(1,162)	212
12/31/98	Fair value at year-end	$ 3,175	$5,113

At the end of 1998, the balance sheet book value of these two investments is equal to their original cost ($4,337 + $4,901) reduced by the contra-asset account balance for Unrealized Losses ($1,162) and increased by the asset account balance for Unrealized Gains ($212) for a total book value of $8,288. This is the same book value that would result from multiplying the year-end stock price times the number of shares ($31.75 × 100 + $51.13 × 100 = $8,288).

Continuing with the example, assume that on June 30, 1999, Coke sold the 100 shares of Campbell Soup for $43.53 per share and purchased 100 shares of Amazon.com for $62.56 per share and 100 shares of Goodyear for $53.61 per share. Here are the journal entries to record the purchases of stock.

Journal Entry to Record Purchase of Amazon.com Stock

+/−	Accounts [description of account]	Debit	Credit
+	Marketable Securities [balance sheet asset account]	6,256	
−	Cash [balance sheet asset account]		6,256

Journal Entry to Record Purchase of Goodyear Stock

+/−	Accounts [description of account]	Debit	Credit
+	Marketable Securities [balance sheet asset account]	5,361	
−	Cash [balance sheet asset account]		5,361

The entry to record the sale of the Campbell Soup shares is more complex. The discussion up until this point has been about *unrealized* gains and losses. However, upon the actual sale of an investment any gains and losses from prior periods become *realized* gains and losses and must be reflected in net income. For available-for-sale securities, the realized gains or losses are the difference between the selling price of the security and its *original cost*.[8] Campbell Soup's original cost was $49.01 per share and the selling price was $43.53 per share, resulting in a realized loss of $5.48 per share, or $548 for the 100 shares owned by Coke. This realized loss is reflected in Coke's net income in the year the stock is sold.

Since prior-year *unrealized* gains and losses on these shares were already reflected in Other Comprehensive Income, and since the *realized* gain or loss was recorded as part of net income, in effect the same increase or decrease in stock price was recorded twice. To avoid this double counting, any unrealized gains or losses that have been recorded in prior years must be reversed from Other Comprehensive Income in the year the stock is sold. Also, since the stock has been sold, the Deferred Tax Liability is no longer necessary. Here is the journal entry to record the sale of the Campbell Soup shares:

	Journal Entry to Record Realized Loss on Sale of Campbell Soup Stock		
+/−	**Accounts [description of account]**	**Debit**	**Credit**
+	Cash [balance sheet asset account]	4,353	
+	Loss on Sale [income statement loss account]	548	
−	Other Comprehensive Income [balance sheet shareholders' equity account]	138	
−	Deferred Tax Liability [balance sheet liability account]	74	
−	Unrealized Gains [balance sheet asset account]		212
−	Marketable Securities [balance sheet asset account]		4,901

Continuing the example, assume that on December 31, 1999, Coke sold the 100 shares of Amazon.com for $76.13 per share. The difference between the selling price and the original cost is a realized gain ($76.13 − $62.56 = $13.57 per share, or $1,357 for all 100 shares). Since the stock was purchased on June 30, 1999, no unrealized gains or losses have been recorded with respect to this stock. The entry to record the sale is therefore,

	Journal Entry to Record Realized Gain on Sale of Amazon.com Stock		
+/−	**Accounts [description of account]**	**Debit**	**Credit**
+	Cash [balance sheet asset account]	7,613	
+	Gain on Sale [income statement gain account]		1,357
−	Marketable Securities [balance sheet asset account]		6,256

On December 31, 1999, Coke still had investments in Boeing and Goodyear. These investments had to be restated to fair value at the balance sheet date. The market price of the Boeing shares was $40.71 per share and the market price of the Goodyear shares was $25.93 per share. This means that the Boeing investment experienced an unrealized gain, since the market price increased from $31.75 at December 31, 1998, to $40.71 at December 31, 1999. The Goodyear investment experienced an unrealized loss, since the market price decreased from $53.61 (the original cost) to $25.93. Here is the activity in the marketable securities account through December 31, 1999:

---

[8] There is a different rule for trading securities, discussed below.

EXAMPLE OF PURCHASES AND SALES OF AVAILABLE-FOR-SALE SECURITIES

Date	Action	100 Shares BA	100 Shares CPB	100 Shares AMZN	100 Shares GT
6/30/98	Purchase—original cost	$ 4,337	$ 4,901		
12/31/98	Unrealized gain or (loss)	(1,162)	212		
12/31/98	Fair value at year-end	3,175	5,113		
6/30/99	Purchase—original cost			$ 6,256	$ 5,361
6/30/99	Sold (book value)		(5,113)		
12/31/99	Sold (book value)			(6,256)	
12/31/99	Unrealized gain or (loss)	896			(2,768)
12/31/99	Fair value at year-end	$ 4,071	—	—	$ 2,593

Here are the journal entries to record the unrealized gains and losses, assuming a 35 percent tax rate:

	Journal Entry to Record Unrealized Gain on Boeing Stock		
+/−	**Accounts [description of account]**	**Debit**	**Credit**
+	Unrealized Gains [balance sheet asset account]	896	
+	Other Comprehensive Income [balance sheet shareholders' equity account]		896
−	Other Comprehensive Income [balance sheet shareholders' equity account]	314	
+	Deferred Tax Liability [balance sheet liability account]		314

	Journal Entry to Record Unrealized Loss on Goodyear Stock		
+/−	**Accounts [description of account]**	**Debit**	**Credit**
−	Other Comprehensive Income [balance sheet shareholders' equity account]	2,768	
+	Unrealized Losses [balance sheet contra-asset account]		2,768
+	Deferred Tax Asset [balance sheet asset account]	969	
+	Other Comprehensive Income [balance sheet shareholders' equity account]		969

To complete the example, assume that on June 30, 2000, Coke purchased 100 shares of Chevron stock for $82.31 per share. Here is the entry to record the purchase:

	Journal Entry to Record Purchase of Chevron Stock		
+/−	**Accounts [description of account]**	**Debit**	**Credit**
+	Marketable Securities [balance sheet asset account]	8,231	
−	Cash [balance sheet asset account]		8,231

The market prices of Coke's investments at December 31, 2000, were as follows: Boeing $65.63 per share, Chevron $83.23 per share, and Goodyear $22.44 per share. This means that both the Boeing and Chevron investments experienced unrealized gains, while the Goodyear investment experienced an unrealized loss. The following table reflects the activity in the marketable securities account for the entire example:

EXAMPLE OF PURCHASES AND SALES OF AVAILABLE-FOR-SALE SECURITIES

Date	Action	100 Shares BA	100 Shares CPB	100 Shares AMZN	100 Shares GT	100 Shares CHV
6/30/98	Purchase—original cost	$ 4,337	$ 4,901			
12/31/98	Unrealized gain or (loss)	(1,162)	212			
12/31/98	Fair value at year-end	3,175	5,113			
6/30/99	Purchase—original cost			$ 6,256	$ 5,361	
6/30/99	Sold (book value)		(5,113)			
12/31/99	Sold (book value)			(6,256)		
12/31/99	Unrealized gain or (loss)	896			(2,768)	
12/31/99	Fair value at year-end	4,071	—	—	2,593	
6/30/00	Purchase—original cost					$8,231
12/31/00	Unrealized gain or (loss)	2,492			(349)	92
12/31/00	Fair value at year-end	$ 6,563	—	—	$ 2,244	$8,323

Here are the journal entries to record the unrealized gains and losses at December 31, 2000:

Journal Entry to Record Unrealized Gain on Boeing Stock

+/−	Accounts [description of account]	Debit	Credit
+	Unrealized Gains [balance sheet asset account]	2,492	
+	Other Comprehensive Income [balance sheet shareholders' equity account]		2,492
−	Other Comprehensive Income [balance sheet shareholders' equity account]	872	
+	Deferred Tax Liability [balance sheet liability account]		872

Journal Entry to Record Unrealized Gain on Chevron Stock

+/−	Accounts [description of account]	Debit	Credit
+	Unrealized Gains [balance sheet asset account]	92	
+	Other Comprehensive Income [balance sheet shareholders' equity account]		92
−	Other Comprehensive Income [balance sheet shareholders' equity account]	32	
+	Deferred Tax Liability [balance sheet liability account]		32

Journal Entry to Record Unrealized Loss on Goodyear Stock

+/−	Accounts [description of account]	Debit	Credit
−	Other Comprehensive Income [balance sheet shareholders' equity account]	349	
+	Unrealized Losses [balance sheet contra-asset account]		349
+	Deferred Tax Asset [balance sheet asset account]	122	
+	Other Comprehensive Income [balance sheet shareholders' equity account]		122

Example: Trading Securities

Assume that all of the facts in the above example are the same except that Coke invested in the shares with the intention to profit from short-term price increases, and that the management of Coke therefore classified the securities as trading securities. There are two differences in the accounting treatment between available-for-sale securities (illustrated above) and trading securities. First, *unrealized* gains and losses for trading securities are recorded on the income statement as part of net income rather than as part of Other Comprehensive Income. Second, *realized* gains and losses on sales of trading securities are computed as the difference between the selling price and the book value of the security at the time of sale. This means that the realized loss on the sale of the Campbell Soup shares on June 30, 1999, would be the $43.53 selling price less the $51.13 book value as of December 31, 1998, resulting in a realized loss of $7.60 per share, or $760 for the 100 shares. This can be compared with the realized loss of $548 recorded above under the assumption the Campbell Soup shares were available-for-sale securities.

Dividends

Dividends received from investments accounted for under the fair value method are recorded as investment income on the income statement. For example, if Chevron paid a dividend of $0.15 per share in December 2000, Coke would make the following entry to record the receipt of the dividend:

+/−	Journal Entry to Record Dividend from Chevron		
	Accounts [description of account]	**Debit**	**Credit**
+	Cash [balance sheet asset account]	15	
+	Dividend Income [income statement revenue account]		15

Transfers between Accounts

Managers may change their intentions with respect to investments in equity securities. For example, a security may be purchased as a trading security but may later be reclassified as an available-for-sale security. Similarly, securities initially recorded as available-for-sale securities may later be reclassified as trading securities.

Since unrealized gains and losses are reflected in net income for trading securities but in Other Comprehensive Income for available-for-sale securities, it could be a problem if managers were able to affect reported net income simply by changing the classification of a security. For example, if a trading security had decreased in value during the year, reclassifying it as an available-for-sale security could cause the unrealized loss to be reflected in Other Comprehensive Income rather than net income. Similarly, transferring a security that had increased in value from available-for-sale securities to trading securities could cause the unrealized gain to be reflected in net income rather than Other Comprehensive Income.

To avoid these potential problems, accounting standard setters adopted the following rule. When securities are transferred between accounts, the fair value of the transferred security at the date of transfer becomes the security's new book value and is treated as the security's original cost for all subsequent computations.

If the transfer is from trading securities to available-for-sale securities, the difference between the security's book value and the fair value at the date of the transfer is treated as a realized gain or loss. This means that transferring a security whose price has declined does not avoid recognizing the unrealized loss in net income.

If the transfer is from available-for-sale securities to trading securities, any prior unrealized gains or losses previously recorded as part of Other Comprehensive Income must be reversed, and any unrealized gain or loss existing at the date of transfer is treated as a realized gain or loss.

Here is an example. Assume that the 100 shares of Goodyear in the previous example were transferred from available-for-sale securities to trading securities on December 31, 2000. Here are the accounting entries required:

	Journal Entry to Record Reclassification of Goodyear		
+/−	**Accounts [description of account]**	**Debit**	**Credit**
+	Marketable Securities [balance sheet asset account]	2,244	
+	Loss on Transfer [income statement loss account]	3,117	
−	Marketable Securities [balance sheet asset account]		5,361
−	Unrealized Losses [balance sheet contra-asset account]	3,117	
−	Deferred Tax Asset [balance sheet asset account]		1,091
+	Other Comprehensive Income [balance sheet shareholders' equity account]		2,026

Coke's Marketable Securities

The following note to Coke's 2000 financial statements gives information about investments in both equity and debt securities, referred to as *held-to-maturity securities* (discussed later in the chapter). Notice that all of Coke's equity investments were available-for-sale securities—Coke had no trading securities.

Certain Debt and Marketable Equity Securities

Investments in debt and marketable equity securities, other than investments accounted for by the equity method, are categorized as either trading, available-for-sale or held-to-maturity. On December 31, 2000 and 1999, we had no trading securities. Securities categorized as available-for-sale are stated at fair value, with unrealized gains and losses, net of deferred income taxes, reported as a component of accumulated other comprehensive income. Debt securities categorized as held-to-maturity are stated at amortized cost.

On December 31, 2000 and 1999, available-for-sale and held-to-maturity securities consisted of the following (in millions):

	Cost	Gross Unrealized Gains	Gross Unrealized Losses	Estimated Fair Value
2000				
Available-for-sale securities				
Equity securities	$248	$57	$(90)	$215
Collateralized mortgage obligations . . .	25	—	(2)	23
Other debt securities	15	—	—	15
	$288	$57	$(92)	$253
Held-to-maturity securities				
Bank and corporate debt	$1,115	$—	$—	$1,115
	$1,115	$—	$—	$1,115

Source: The Coca-Cola Company Form 10-K.

At December 31, 2000, Coke had investments in available-for-sale equity securities that had an original cost of $248 million. These securities had a total of $57 million in unrealized gains and $90 million in unrealized losses. The fair value of these securities was $215 million at year-end. The difference between the original cost and the fair value of the securities ($248 million − $215 million = $33 million unrealized loss) has been reflected in Coke's other comprehensive income, part of shareholders' equity, after being reduced by a deferred tax asset.

In its 2000 statement of shareholders' equity, Coke reported under the heading Comprehensive Income a $60 million loss for net change in unrealized gain on securities. The table below shows how this $60 million unrealized loss was computed. At December 31, 1999, Coke's available-for-sale securities had net unrealized gains of $55 million. By December 31, 2000, this unrealized net gain had become an unrealized net loss of $35 million, which means Coke's available-for-sale securities decreased in value by $90 million during the year. This $90 million unrealized loss was offset by a $30 million Deferred Tax Asset,[9] leaving a net loss of $60 million as part of other comprehensive income.

COKE'S OTHER COMPREHENSIVE INCOME FOR 2000		
	2000	**1999**
Unrealized gains	$57	$ 69
Unrealized losses	(92)	(14)
Net gain (loss)	(35)	55
Change 99–00	(90)	
Deferred tax asset	30	
Net of tax loss	$(60)	

Cost Method: No Influence or Control

In some cases, there are no market prices available for equity securities. Thus, the fair value method cannot be applied, and the cost method is used instead. Under the cost method, equity securities are recorded at their original cost. No unrealized gains or losses are recorded. When the security is sold, a realized gain or loss is recorded for the difference between the selling price and the original cost of the security.

EQUITY METHOD: INFLUENCE BUT NOT CONTROL

At the beginning of the chapter it was noted that Coke accounts for its investment in Coca-Cola Enterprises using the equity method. The equity method is used in cases where the investor owns between 20 and 50 percent of the investee. Owning 20 percent or more of the voting stock allows the investor to exercise significant influence over the investee; but since the investor cannot elect a majority of the investee's board of directors, the investor does not control the investee.

To understand the reasoning behind the equity method, recall that under the fair value method investment revenue was recognized when the investee paid a dividend. This system works well when the investor cannot influence the investee, since the payment of dividends is completely at the discretion of the investee's board of directors. However, in cases where the investor can exercise significant influence over the investee, measuring investment income based on dividend payments may not be useful.

---

[9] More correctly, there was a combination of a reduction of a prior-year Deferred Tax Liability and an increase in a current-year Deferred Tax Asset that totaled $30 million.

For example, consider a case in which the investee had a net loss during the year. If the investor can use its influence over the investee to cause the investee to pay a dividend, the investor would report investment income even though the investee was losing money. Similarly, an investee may be extremely profitable and the investor may prefer that the investee retain all of its earnings to reinvest in the business. In this situation, no investment income would be recognized even though the investee was making money. The fact that dividends might be paid by investees with losses while profitable investees might not pay dividends makes dividends a poor measure of an investment's economic performance.

Under the equity method, an investment is initially recorded at original cost. In each subsequent year, the investor recognizes as income the investor's proportionate share of the investee's accounting net income. The balance sheet investment account is increased by the amount of investment income recognized. For example, if Coke owns 40 percent of the stock of Coca-Cola Enterprises, and Coca-Cola Enterprises has net income of $234 million for a year, Coke would report income from equity investments of 40% × $234 million = $94 million for the same year. Here is the journal entry to record this hypothetical equity income:

	Journal Entry to Record Equity Income		
+/−	Accounts [description of account]	Debit	Credit
+	Investment in Coca-Cola Enterprises [balance sheet asset account]	94	
+	Equity Income [income statement revenue account]		94

Similarly, if the investee reports a net loss for the year, the investor recognizes an investment loss equal to the investor's proportionate share of the loss. In this case, the Investment account is decreased by the investment loss. For example, if Coca-Cola Enterprises has a net loss of $90 million for a year, Coke would report a loss from equity investments of 40% × $90 million = $36 million for the same year. Here is the journal entry to record this hypothetical equity loss:

	Journal Entry to Record Equity Loss		
+/−	Accounts [description of account]	Debit	Credit
+	Equity Loss [income statement loss account]	36	
−	Investment in Coca-Cola Enterprises [balance sheet asset account] ...		36

Here is Coke's equity method income and loss reported on the income statements for 2000, 1999, and 1998. Coke reported equity losses for 2000 and 1999 and equity income for 1998.

THE COCA-COLA COMPANY AND SUBSIDIARIES			
Consolidated Statements Of Income			
(in millions, except per share data)			
	Year Ended December 31		
	2000	**1999**	**1998**
Equity income (loss)	(289)	(184)	32

Source: The Coca-Cola Company Form 10-K.

Receipt of Dividends

Under the equity method, any time the investee pays a dividend the investor's investment account is *decreased* by the amount of the dividend. Under this view, a payment of cash simply reduces one balance sheet asset (the Investment account) and increases another balance sheet asset (Cash). No revenue is recognized for the payment of the dividend. Under the equity method, income from an investment is recognized only for the investor's proportionate share of the investee's net income.

For example, assume Coca-Cola Enterprises paid a $28 million cash dividend to Coke during the year. Here is the entry to record the dividend:

	Journal Entry to Record Dividend under Equity Method		
+/−	Accounts [description of account]	Debit	Credit
+	Cash [balance sheet asset account]	28	
−	Investment in Coca-Cola Enterprises [balance sheet asset account] . . .		28

Difference between Investor Cost and Investee Book Value

Applying the equity method to real companies is more complicated than is apparent from the above examples. When the price per share paid by the investor for the stock of the investee differs from the book value per share of the investee (as it almost always will), additional accounting entries are necessary. Continue with Coke's investment in Coca-Cola Enterprises as an example.

The net book value of common shareholders' equity of Coca-Cola Enterprises at December 31, 2000, was $2,790 million. If Coke purchased 40 percent of the stock of Coca-Cola Enterprises on December 31, 2000, the purchased stock would represent net assets with a *book value* of $1,116 million (that is, 40% × $2,790 = $1,116). However, the *market value* of 40 percent of Coca-Cola Enterprises' stock at December 31, 2000, was $3,177 million. The difference between the cost of the stock to Coke ($3,177 million) and the book value of 40 percent of the underlying assets on the balance sheet of Coca-Cola Enterprises ($1,116 million) represents assets not recorded on the balance sheet of Coca-Cola Enterprises but reflected in the market value of the stock. For example, goodwill or other types of intangible assets might not be recorded. In addition, there may be assets that are recorded on the balance sheet of Coca-Cola Enterprises but with a book value that is less than their current market value. The following table illustrates these relationships:

BOOK VALUE AND MARKET VALUE OF COCA-COLA ENTERPRISES (IN MILLIONS}		
	100%	40%
Book value of Coca-Cola Enterprise's assets at 12/31/00	$ 22,162	$ 8,865
Book value of Coca-Cola Enterprise's liabilities* at 12/31/00	(19,372)	(7,749)
Net book value of Coca-Cola Enterprises at 12/31/00	2,790	1,116
Market value of Coca-Cola Enterprises at 12/31/00	7,943	3,177
Excess of market value over book value	$ 5,153	$ 2,061

*Includes preferred stock of 44.

Continuing this example, the investment is recorded under the equity method at the price Coke paid for the stock ($3,177 million). However, the 40 percent share of Coca-Cola Enterprises' net income that Coke recognizes for the year reflects only the book value of Coca-Cola Enterprises' assets. For example, depreciation expense for Coca-Cola Enterprises is based on the book value of depreciable assets, even though the market value of the assets (reflected in the price Coke paid for the stock) may be higher. Also, amortization of goodwill and other intangibles is based only on those intangible assets actually recorded on the balance sheet, even though the price Coke paid for the stock reflects all intangible assets, both recorded and unrecorded, at their market values.

Assume that $310 million of the $2,061 million excess purchase price represented depreciable equipment and $2,861 million represented goodwill. Since the excess purchase price does not result in an increase in the tax basis of these assets, there is also an unrecorded deferred income tax liability equal to ($310 million + $2,861 million) $\times$ 35% = $1,110 million (see the table below).

COCA-COLA ENTERPRISES
Assets, Liabilities, and Preferred Stock at December 31, 2000
(in millions)

	Book Value 100%	Market Value 100%	Excess	Coke's 40% Investment Share		
				Book Value 40%	Market Value 40%	Excess
Assets						
Cash and cash investments, at cost	$ 294	$ 294	—	$ 117	$ 117	—
Trade accounts receivable	1,297	1,297	—	519	519	—
Amounts receivable from The Coca-Cola Company	47	47	—	19	19	—
Finished goods inventory	408	408	—	163	163	—
Raw materials and supplies inventory	194	194	—	78	78	—
Current deferred income tax assets	116	116	—	46	46	—
Prepaid expenses and other current assets	275	275	—	110	110	—
Land	364	364	—	146	146	—
Buildings and improvements	1,470	1,470	—	588	588	—
Machinery and equipment	7,704	8,479	$ 775	3,082	3,392	$ 310
Less allowances for depreciation	(4,059)	(4,059)	—	(1,624)	(1,624)	—
Construction in progress	304	304	—	122	122	—
Franchises and other noncurrent assets	13,748	20,901	7,153	5,499	8,360	2,861
Total assets	$22,162	$30,090	$7,928	$8,865	$12,036	$3,171
Liabilities and preferred stock						
Accounts payable and accrued expenses	$ 2,321	$ 2,321	—	$ 928	$ 928	—
Current portion of long-term debt	773	773	—	309	309	—
Long-Term Debt, Less Current Maturities	10,348	10,348	—	4,139	4,139	—
Retirement and Insurance Programs and Other	1,112	1,112	—	445	445	—
Long-Term Deferred Income Tax Liabilities	4,774	7,549	$2,775	1,910	3,020	$1,110
Preferred stock	44	44	—	18	18	—
Total liabilities and preferred stock	$19,372	$22,147	$2,775	$7,749	$ 8,859	$1,110
Common shareholders' equity	$ 2,790	$ 7,943	$5,153	$1,116	$ 3,177	$2,061

Assume the depreciable equipment has an estimated useful life of five years, while the goodwill (under the GAAP rules existing prior to July 2001) would be amortized over a period of 40 years. The additional depreciation would be $62 million per year, and the additional goodwill amortization would be $72 million per year. Assuming a 35 percent tax rate, the after-tax effect of this additional depreciation and amortization would be $134 million $\times$ (1 − 0.35) = $87 million of additional (after-tax) expense. Coca-Cola Enterprises would have recognized this expense as part of net income *if the book value of its assets equaled the price paid by Coke for its stock.*

To account for this difference, the investor must adjust its share of the investee's net income by any additional depreciation or amortization expense that would result from the excess of the purchase price of the stock over the book value of the underlying assets. This additional depreciation and amortization (net of income tax expense) has the effect of reducing the equity income (or increasing the equity loss) on the income statement of the investor as well as reducing the investor's balance sheet investment account.

We are now in a position to answer the question posed at the beginning of the chapter regarding the accounting method used to record Coke's investment in Coca-Cola Enterprises. Here is an analysis of the actual investment account of Coke in Coca-Cola Enterprises for 2000.

ANALYSIS OF COKE'S INVESTMENT ACCOUNT IN COCA-COLA ENTERPRISES FOR 2000	
Beginning book value, January 1, 2000	$728
Increase: 40% of net income of Coca-Cola Enterprises	94
Decrease: 40% of dividends paid by Coca-Cola Enterprises	(28)
Decrease: Additional depreciation and amortization	(87)
Ending book value, December 31, 2000	$707

The investment account was increased by Coke's 40 percent share of Coca-Cola Enterprises' net income for the year and decreased by the dividends paid by Coca-Cola Enterprises to Coke. In addition, the account was reduced to reflect additional amortization or depreciation based on the excess of Coke's purchase price for the stock over Coca-Cola Enterprises' book value in the underlying assets.

CONSOLIDATION METHOD: CONTROL OF INVESTEE

Once the investor owns in excess of 50 percent of the voting stock of the investee, the investor has control of the investee through the ability to elect a majority of the members of the board of directors. Because of this control, GAAP rules require any investee that is more than 50 percent owned to be consolidated with the investor.

Consolidation means that all of the assets and liabilities of the investee are added to the assets and liabilities of the investor in preparing the consolidated balance sheet. Also, the revenues and expenses of the investee are added to the revenues and expenses of the investor in preparing the consolidated income statement.

To illustrate the consolidation method, we briefly leave The Coca-Cola Company and turn to Caterpillar Inc. as an example. Presented on the next page is a portion of the income statement from the annual report of Caterpillar for 1998. The left-hand column gives the *consolidated* revenues and expenses that the company is required to report under GAAP. However, Caterpillar's management felt that consolidating, that is, adding together, the operating results of the machinery and engine operations with the financial products operations might not be useful to investors. Therefore, Caterpillar also provided separate revenue and expense information for both the machinery and engine operations (column 3) and the financial products operations (column 4). This provides a nice example of how consolidated financial statements are prepared. For purposes of illustrating the consolidation method, assume that machinery and engines is a single corporation (the investor) and that financial products is a single 100 percent owned subsidiary (the investee).

CATERPILLAR INC.
Consolidated Results of Operations
Year Ended December 31, 1998
(in millions)

		Supplemental Consolidating Data		
	Consolidated	**Eliminations**	**Machinery and Engines**	**Financial Products**
Sales and revenues				
Sales of Machinery and Engines	$19,972	—	$19,972	—
Revenues of Financial Products	1,005	$(112)	—	$1,117
Total sales and revenues	20,977	(112)	19,972	1,117
Operating costs				
Cost of goods sold	15,031	—	15,031	—
Selling, general, and administrative expenses	2,561	(26)	2,210	377
Research and development expenses	643	—	643	—
Interest expense of Financial Products	489	(12)	—	501
Total operating costs	18,724	(38)	17,884	878
Operating profit	2,253	(74)	2,088	239
Interest expense excluding Financial Products	264	—	264	—
Other income (expense)	185	74	46	65
Consolidated profit before taxes	2,174	—	1,870	304
Provision for income taxes	665	—	554	111
Profit of consolidated companies	1,509	—	1,316	193
Equity in profit of unconsolidated affiliated companies	4	—	4	—
Equity in profit of Financial Products' subsidiaries	—	(193)	193	—
Profit	$1,513	$(193)	$1,513	$193

Notice that the two right-hand columns are *not* simply added together to arrive at the consolidated column. There is an additional column for eliminations. This eliminations column for the income statement serves two purposes. First, any revenues and expenses resulting from transactions between the Machinery and Engines operations and the Financial Products operations must be eliminated from the consolidated income statement. In other words, Caterpillar cannot generate revenues by selling from one part of its business to another. In the above income statement, $112 million of the financial products revenue was derived from the machinery and engines operation and is therefore eliminated in consolidation.[10]

The second type of income statement elimination is to avoid counting the same income twice. Notice that the Machinery and Engines column reports $193 million of income from equity in profit of Financial Products' subsidiaries. This is because on the *separate* financial statements of the Machinery and Engines operations, the investment in the Financial Products operations would be reported using the equity method. This is not allowed under GAAP for the company's external financial statements, since consolidated financial statements are required for more than 50 percent owned subsidiaries; nevertheless, the investor will always account for its investment in the investee using the equity method *on the separate accounting records of the investor.*[11]

[10] These same adjustments to eliminate intercompany profits are also necessary under the equity method. However, we ignored them in the Coke example presented earlier to avoid adding additional complexity to the example.

[11] Another way to think about this issue is that consolidation is something that is only done at the time financial statements are issued to the public. On the separate internal accounting records of the investor, all investments of more than 20 percent ownership are accounted for using the equity method.

Since the $193 million net income of the Financial Products operations is also included in the $1,513 million net income of the Machinery and Engines operations, it is eliminated in consolidation to avoid double counting. Notice that the net income of the investor ($1,513 million) is exactly the same as the net income on the consolidated income statement. This is an important feature of the equity method. Under the equity method, net income is exactly the same as under the consolidation method. The only difference is that the consolidation method reports the revenues and expenses of the investee as separate income statement items, while the equity method reports the revenues and expenses combined as part of income from equity investments.

Notice the consolidated balance sheet of Caterpillar shown on page 348. Just as with the income statement, the assets and liabilities of the investor and investee are not simply added together; elimination entries are also necessary. Balance sheet eliminations remove the effects of intercompany transactions from the consolidated assets and liabilities. For example, an account receivable from the investee on the investor's balance sheet will also be reflected as an account payable on the balance sheet of the investee. Similarly, any profits that one company makes from selling inventory to the other company must be removed from the inventory book value when consolidating.

A second type of balance sheet elimination is to avoid double counting the investment account in the investee. Notice that there is an asset on the separate balance sheet of the investor for $1,269 for investments in Financial Products' subsidiaries. This is exactly the same amount as the net book value of the total stockholders' equity on the balance sheet of the investee. Since the assets and liabilities represented by this net book value will be included in the individual assets and liabilities on the consolidated balance sheet, the amount is eliminated from both the investment account of the investor and the stockholders' equity account of the investee.

Notice another feature of the consolidation method: The stockholders' equity account balance of $5,131 million on the balance sheet of the investor is exactly the same as the stockholders' equity balance on the consolidated balance sheet. Just as the consolidation method does not change reported net income, it also does not change reported stockholders' equity. Only the balances of individual asset and liability accounts are changed. The book value of the investor's stockholders' equity is unaffected regardless of whether the consolidation method or the equity method are used.[12]

Less than 100 Percent Ownership

If the investor owns more than 50 percent of the stock of the investee but less than 100 percent, the investee is still consolidated with the investor. All of the investee's assets and liabilities (adjusted for intercompany eliminations) are added to those of the investor, even though the investor does not own 100 percent. This is done on the theory that, although the investor does not own these assets and liabilities, the investor does control them by virtue of ownership of more than 50 percent of the voting stock of the investee.

Since the investor is not entitled to 100 percent of the revenues and expenses of the investee, a separate line item called *minority interest* is subtracted prior to the computation of net income on the consolidated income statement. This minority interest income statement amount represents the share of the investee's net income that does not belong to the investor. Similarly, a balance sheet minority interest line is necessary as part of shareholders' equity to represent the portion of the investee's shareholders' equity that is not owned by the investor.

---

[12] Because the equity and consolidation methods result in the same reported net income and shareholders' equity, the equity method is sometimes referred to as a *one-line consolidation*.

CATERPILLAR INC.
Financial Position at December 31, 1998
(in millions)

	Consolidated	Supplemental Consolidating Data		
		Eliminations	Machinery and Engines	Financial Products
Assets				
Current assets				
Cash and short-term investments	$ 360	—	$ 303	$ 57
Receivables—trade and other	3,660	$ (819)	2,604	1,875
Receivables—finance	3,516	—	—	3,516
Deferred income taxes and prepaid expenses	1,081	(18)	1,081	18
Inventories	2,842	—	2,842	—
Total current assets	11,459	(837)	6,830	5,466
Property, plant, and equipment—net	4,866	—	4,125	741
Long-term receivables—trade and other	85	—	85	—
Long-term receivables—finance	5,058	—	—	5,058
Investments in unconsolidated affiliated companies	773	—	773	—
Investments in Financial Products' subsidiaries	—	(1,269)	1,269	—
Deferred income taxes	955	(33)	980	8
Intangible assets	1,241	—	1,241	—
Other assets	691	—	316	375
Total assets	$25,128	$(2,139)	$15,619	$11,648
Liabilities				
Current liabilities				
Short-term borrowings	$ 809	—	$ 49	$ 760
Accounts payable and accrued expenses	3,558	(693)	3,440	811
Accrued wages, salaries, and employee benefits	1,217	—	1,208	9
Dividends payable	107	—	107	—
Deferred and current income taxes payable	15	—	(19)	34
Deferred liability	—	(143)	—	143
Long-term debt due within one year	2,239	—	60	2,179
Total current liabilities	7,945	(836)	4,845	3,936
Long-term debt due after one year	9,404	—	2,993	6,411
Liability for postemployment benefits	2,590	—	2,590	—
Deferred income taxes and other liabilities	58	(34)	60	32
Total liabilities	19,997	(870)	10,488	10,379
Stockholders' equity				
Common stock of $1.00 par value	1,063	(683)	1,063	683
Profit employed in the business	6,123	(615)	6,123	615
Accumulated other comprehensive income	1	29	1	(29)
Treasury stock at cost	(2,056)	—	(2,056)	—
Total stockholders' equity	5,131	(1,269)	5,131	1,269
Total liabilities and stockholders' equity	$25,128	$(2,139)	$15,619	$11,648

ACCOUNTING FOR INVESTMENTS IN DEBT SECURITIES

Although this chapter deals with investments in equity securities, the fair value accounting method discussed earlier also applies to investments in debt securities, such as corporate or government bonds. However, for debt securities there is an alternative accounting method available for what are called *held-to-maturity securities.*

Held-to-maturity securities are debt securities that the investor intends to hold until the debt securities mature. This means that the investor will receive the principal on the debt security at maturity rather than selling the security prior to maturity. Because there is no intention of selling the security, restating the book value of these securities to market value each year would (in the opinion of accounting standard setters) not provide useful information to users of financial statements.

For example, assume that Coke invests in a government bond that matures in five years and is purchased to yield 8 percent. Coke initially records the investment in the bond at original cost. Assume further that Coke intends to hold the bond for the next five years and to receive the principal from the bond at the maturity date. If market interest rates increase later in the year, the market value of the bond will decrease, meaning if Coke tried to sell the bond it would realize a loss on the sale. However, since Coke does not intend to sell the bond, but intends to hold it to maturity, this unrealized loss will never be realized.

The GAAP accounting treatment for held-to-maturity securities is to record them at amortized cost, which means original cost increased each year by any discount amortization or decreased each year by any premium amortization. Amortized cost is the same accounting method (applied to an asset) as that used for accounting for bonds payable discussed in Chapter 5. Debt securities not classified as held-to-maturity must be classified as either trading securities or available-for-sale securities, and their book value must be restated to market value at the end of each year. At December 31, 2000, Coke had held-to-maturity securities on its balance sheet with a book value of $1,115 million, consisting of bank and corporate debt.

INTERCOMPANY INVESTMENTS AND INCOME TAX EXPENSE

There are several ways in which accounting for equity investments affect a company's income tax expense. First, for marketable securities reported under the fair value method, the unrealized gains and losses from restating book values to market value at the end of each year result in temporary differences that require deferred income tax assets or liabilities. However, since the unrealized gains and losses for available-for-sale securities are reflected in Other Comprehensive Income, a shareholders' equity account, rather than on the income statement, changes in deferred tax assets and liabilities associated with available-for-sale securities do not affect reported income tax expense.

Second, under the equity method differences between the purchase price paid for the investee's stock and the investor's share of the investee's underlying assets and liabilities will also result in temporary differences that require deferred income tax assets and liabilities. Third, under the equity method the investor reports as income its share of the investee's *net* income, which is after the investee's income tax expense amount. However, on the income statement of the investor this equity income is included as part of pretax income. This can sometimes distort the relationship between pretax income and income tax expense, since in effect the investor's share of the investee's income tax expense is used to reduce pretax income rather than increasing the investor's income tax expense.

To illustrate these tax effects, a portion of the income tax note from Coke's financial statements is presented below.

A reconciliation of the statutory U.S. federal rate and effective rates is as follows:

	Year Ended December 31		
	2000	**1999**	**1998**
Statutory U.S. federal rate	35.0%	35.0%	35.0%
State income taxes—net of federal benefit	.8	1.0	1.0
Earnings in jurisdictions taxed at rates different from the statutory U.S. federal rate	(4.0)	(6.0)	(4.3)
Equity income or loss (1)	**2.9**	**1.6**	—
Other operating charges (2)	1.9	5.3	—
Other—net	(.6)	(.6)	.3
	36.0%	36.3%	32.0%

(1) Includes charges by equity investees. See Note 15.

The tax effects of temporary differences and carryforwards that give rise to deferred tax assets and liabilities consist of the following (in millions):

	December 31	
	2000	**1999**
Deferred tax assets		
Benefit plans	$ 261	$ 311
Liabilities and reserves	456	169
Net operating loss carryforwards	375	196
Other operating charges	321	254
Other	126	272
Gross deferred tax assets	1,539	1,202
Valuation allowance	(641)	(443)
Total deferred tax assets	$ 898	$ 759
Deferred tax liabilities		
Property, plant and equipment	$ 425	$ 320
Equity investments	**228**	**397**
Intangible assets	224	197
Other	129	99
Total deferred tax liabilities	$1,006	$1,013
Net deferred tax asset (liability) (1)	$ (108)	$ (254)

(1) Deferred tax assets of $250 million and $244 million have been included in the consolidated balance sheet caption "Marketable securities and other assets" at December 31, 2000 and 1999, respectively.

Source: The Coca-Cola Company Form 10-K.

Dividend income received by one U.S. corporation from another U.S. corporation is subject to a dividend-received deduction that reduces the tax rate on dividends below the statutory U.S. tax rate. Also, to the extent that the consolidated financial statements contain earnings of foreign (that is, non-U.S.) subsidiaries, the consolidated effective tax rate will reflect foreign tax rates, which may differ substantially from the U.S. rate.

ACCOUNTING FOR INTERCOMPANY INVESTMENTS IN OTHER COUNTRIES

There are several differences between the U.S. GAAP rules discussed above and the financial reporting rules used in other countries. First, in some countries the lower of cost or market rule, rather than the fair value rule, is applied to investments in marketable securities. For example, here are some descriptions of accounting methods from non-U.S. corporations:

Michelin

Stockholdings and Other Investments

Non-consolidated shareholders' and other investments are recorded at the lower of cost and net realizable value.

Source: Michelin annual report.

Nestlé

Marketable securities, which are held to maturity, are valued at the lower of cost or market value, while those held for trading purposes are carried at market value. Any resulting gains or losses are recognised in the income statement.

Source: Nestlé annual report.

Reed Elsevier

Investments

Fixed asset and short term investments are stated at the lower of cost and estimated net realisable value.

Source: Reed Elsevier Form 20-F.

The equity method is also used in other countries. Here is some information from the notes to the financial statements of Reed Elsevier providing information about its equity investments in joint ventures. Notice that the book value is increased by the investor's share of the profits of the investee and decreased by dividends received from the investee as well as amortization of goodwill and other intangibles.

Associates and Joint Ventures

Investments which are held for the long term and where the Combined Businesses exercise significant influence or joint control with other parties represent interests in associates or joint ventures and are accounted for under the equity and gross equity methods respectively.

13. Fixed Asset Investments

(in pound millions)	Investments in Joint Ventures	Other Investments	Total
At January 1, 1999	75	12	87
Share of attributable profit	4	—	4
Amortisation of goodwill and intangible assets	(4)	—	(4)
Dividends received from joint ventures	(4)	—	(4)
Additions	19	22	41
Disposals	—	(4)	(4)
Exchange translation differences	(1)	0	(1)
At December 31, 1999	89	30	119

The principal joint ventures at December 31, 1999 are Giuffre (a 40% shareholding in an Italian legal publisher) and REZsolutions, Inc. (a 67% shareholding in a hotel reservations and marketing business which is in the process of being sold).

The cost and net book amount of goodwill and intangible assets in joint ventures were (pound) 74 million and (pound) 49 million respectively (1998 (pound) 58 million and (pound) 36 million).

Source: Reed Elsevier Form 20-F.

The consolidation method is also used in other countries. Below are portions of the income statement and balance sheet of Reed Elsevier showing the minority interest amount for less than 100 percent owned investees:

REED ELSEVIER
Combined Profit and Loss Accounts
(in pound millions)

	Year Ended December 31		
	1997	**1998**	**1999**
Profit on ordinary activities before taxation	86	1,044	105
Tax on profit on ordinary activities	(99)	(271)	(167)
(Loss)/profit on ordinary activities after taxation	(13)	773	(62)
Minority interests and preference dividends	(1)	(1)	(1)
(Loss)/profit attributable to parent companies' shareholders	(14)	772	(63)

Combined Balance Sheets

	At December 31	
	1998	**1999**
Total assets less current liabilities	2,969	2,596
Creditors: amounts falling due after more than one year	(797)	(620)
Provisions for liabilities and charges	(36)	(113)
Minority interests	(6)	(8)
Net assets	2,130	1,855

Source: Reed Elsevier Form 20-F.

INTERCOMPANY INVESTMENTS AND THE CASH FLOWS STATEMENT

Unrealized gains and losses from marketable securities have no cash flow consequences. Realized gains and losses are eliminated from net income in arriving at cash flows from operating activities since they are not considered to be operating activities. The cash received from sales of marketable securities is reflected on the cash flows statement under cash flows from investing activities.

Income or loss reported under the equity method has no cash flow consequences and must therefore be eliminated when net income is reconciled with cash flows from operating activities. Also, dividends received from investees accounted for under the equity method must be added to net income to arrive at cash flows from operating activities.

There are no unusual cash flow effects associated with the consolidation method other than the requirement to prepare a consolidated statement of cash flows. All of the cash flow effects of accounting for equity investments are shown on the next page in the operating and investing sections of Coke's cash flows statement:

THE COCA-COLA COMPANY AND SUBSIDIARIES
Consolidated Statements of Cash Flows
(in millions)

	Year Ended December 31		
	2000	1999	1998
Operating Activities			
Net income	$ 2,177	$ 2,431	$ 3,533
Depreciation and amortization	773	792	645
Deferred income taxes	3	97	(38)
Equity income or loss, net of dividends	**380**	**292**	**31**
Foreign currency adjustments	196	(41)	21
Gains on issuances of stock by equity investees	**—**	**—**	**(27)**
Gains on sales of assets, including bottling interests	**(127)**	**(49)**	**(306)**
Other operating charges	916	799	73
Other items	119	119	51
Net change in operating assets and liabilities	(852)	(557)	(550)
Net cash provided by operating activities	$ 3,585	$ 3,883	$ 3,433
Investing Activities			
Acquisitions and investments, principally trademarks and bottling companies	**(397)**	**(1,876)**	**(1,428)**
Purchases of investments and other assets	**(508)**	**(518)**	**(610)**
Proceeds from disposals of investments and other assets	**290**	**176**	**1,036**
Purchases of property, plant and equipment	(733)	(1,069)	(863)
Proceeds from disposals of property, plant and equipment	45	45	54
Other investing activities	138	(179)	(350)
Net cash used in investing activities	$(1,165)	$(3,421)	$(2,161)

Source: The Coca-Cola Company Form 10-K.

USING INFORMATION ABOUT INTERCOMPANY INVESTMENTS TO MAKE DECISIONS

The use of the fair value method to value marketable securities provides useful balance sheet information about the values of investment assets at year-end. The fact that unrealized gains and losses are reported in shareholders' equity as part of other comprehensive income means that the income statement impact of changes in the values of marketable securities is not readily apparent. Information providing the details of other comprehensive income allows the user to adjust reported net income to take these unrealized gains and losses into account.

It is not clear how useful the information provided by the equity method is for users of financial statements. Clearly, such information is more useful than simply reporting dividends as investment income. However, for equity method investees whose stock is publicly traded, using the market value rather than the equity method book value may provide more useful information. For example, users of Coke's financial statements may find it more useful to know that the market value of Coke's investment in Coca-Coca Enterprises is $3,177 million rather than that the book value of the investment is $707 million.

However, one problem with applying market value in this case is the fact that Coke is such an important shareholder in Coca-Coca Enterprises that it is unlikely a buyer would be willing to pay the market price ($3,177 million) for Coke's 40 percent interest in Coca-Cola Enterprises.

With respect to the consolidation method there are three issues to consider. First, at what level of stock ownership does control occur? In other words, just because Coke only owns 40 percent of Coca-Cola Enterprises, is it meaningful to say that Coke does not control the investee? There may be other indicators of control, such as the extent of business relationships, that are more important than the percentage of stock owned. For example, in the early 1980s Apple Computer was forced to give up the look and feel of its Macintosh operating system to Microsoft, and this system was ultimately incorporated into the Windows operating system. Although Microsoft did not control Apple under the accounting definition of more than 50 percent ownership of voting stock, it was so vital to Apple that Microsoft continue to produce its Word and Excel applications in a Macintosh version that Apple found it very difficult to say no to Microsoft's demands.

A second issue about the consolidation method relates to 100 percent consolidation and the use of minority interest. For example, if an investor owns 75 percent of the stock of an investee, under GAAP 100 percent of the investee's revenues, expenses, assets, and liabilities are reported by the investor, with adjustments for minority interests. An alternative consolidation method, called *proportionate consolidation*, would only include 75 percent (in this example) of the investee's revenues, expenses, assets, and liabilities in the consolidated financial statements, and no minority interests would be reported. Proportionate consolidation is not allowed under GAAP.

A third issue about the consolidation method relates to which investees ought to be combined in a consolidated financial statement. Under GAAP, all investees that are more than 50 percent owned must be consolidated. However, for some companies with diverse lines of business many people feel that consolidation distorts the financial statement income rather than making it more useful. For example, Caterpillar's managers believe that it is more useful for investors to see separately the results for the Machinery and Engines operations and the Financial Products operations. Similar examples would be consolidating an insurance company (Allstate) with a department store (Sears), or consolidating a financial services company (General Electric Credit Corporation) with a manufacturer of washing machines (General Electric). For this reason, many companies provide supplemental information in their financial statements or notes to allow users to unconsolidate the consolidated financial statement to some extent. This issue is particularly troublesome for manufacturers that also have finance subsidiaries to finance purchases of their products, such as General Motors and GMAC.

Summary

This chapter covers GAAP rules relating to investments by one company in the stock of another company. There are five different methods that might be applied to these investments: two versions of the fair value method, the cost method, the equity method, and the consolidation method.

The fair value method is applied to investments that represent less than 20 percent of the voting stock of the investee. Under this method, securities that have a readily determinable market value are recorded at their market value at year-end. The treatment of unrealized gains and losses from this restatement depends on the classification of the securities. Securities classified as trading securities have unrealized gains and losses reported as part of net income. Securities classified as available-for-sale securities have unrealized gains and losses reported in shareholders' equity as a component of other comprehensive income. Securities with no readily determinable market value are reported under the cost method. Dividends received are reported as investment income.

The equity method applies to investments representing between 20 and 50 percent of the voting stock of the investee. Under this method, the book value of the investment is originally recorded at cost and is increased by the investor's share of the investee's accounting net income (or decreased by the investor's share of the investee's accounting loss) for the year. The investee's accounting net income or loss must be adjusted for additional depreciation or amortization in cases where the purchase price for the shares did not equal the book value of the underlying assets and liabilities of the investor at the time the investment was made. Under the equity method, dividends received are treated as a reduction in the book value of the investment.

The consolidation method applies in cases where the investor owns more than 50 percent of the voting stock of the investee. Under this method, the investee's revenues, expenses, assets, and liabilities are combined with those of the investor in a single consolidated set of financial statements. Appropriate eliminations must be made to avoid double counting items included in both the investor's and investee's financial statements, as well as to eliminate any intercompany profits, assets, or liabilities resulting from transactions between the investor and the investee.

Discussion Questions

1. Discuss some reasons for one corporation to invest in the stock of another corporation.
2. Explain why the amount of influence that one company has over another company should affect the accounting treatment.
3. Why doesn't the concept of *influence* occur in accounting for other types of assets or liabilities?
4. Explain the accounting method that applies for each of the following levels of influence: (*a*) less than 20 percent ownership, (*b*) between 20 and 50 percent ownership, and (*c*) more than 50 percent ownership.
5. Explain the accounting rules under the fair value method.
6. Explain the difference between trading securities and available-for-sale securities.
7. Explain the income statement and balance sheet differences under the fair value method for trading securities compared with available-for-sale securities.
8. Why is fair value used to record securities but not other types of assets?
9. Explain why unrealized gains and losses for available-for-sale securities are not reflected in net income. Include the concepts of relevance and reliability in your explanation.
10. When available-for-sale securities or trading securities are sold, how is the gain or loss computed? How is the gain or loss reported in the financial statements?
11. Explain how the receipt of a dividend is reported for trading securities or available-for-sale securities.
12. Explain the accounting treatment of securities that are transferred between the trading securities and available-for-sale securities accounts.
13. What is the cost method of accounting for securities, and when is it applicable?
14. When is the equity method of accounting used?
15. Explain the basic accounting rules under the equity method.
16. Is the equity method more relevant or reliable than the fair value method? If yes, explain why. If not, why is it used?
17. Explain how the receipt of a dividend is treated under the equity method.
18. Explain the accounting treatment under the equity method when the investor's cost of the securities differs from the investee's book value.
19. When is the consolidation method of accounting used?

20. Is the consolidation method more relevant or reliable than the fair value method? If yes, explain why. If not, why is it used?

21. Is the consolidation method more relevant or reliable than the equity method? If yes, explain why. If not, why is it used?

22. Will the net income of the investor differ between the consolidation method and the equity method? If not, why not? If yes, explain how.

23. Will the net assets of the investor differ between the consolidation method and the equity method? If not, why not? If yes, explain how.

24. Explain why the investor will always account for its greater than 50 percent investment in the investee using the equity method in the investor's separate books. Explain how the consolidation method gets reflected in the financial statements.

25. Explain how intercompany eliminations affect consolidated financial statements.

26. What is a minority interest, and how is it accounted for?

27. Explain the accounting rules for investments in debt securities.

28. How does the fair value method affect the investor's income tax expense?

29. How does the equity method affect the investor's income tax expense?

30. How does the fair value method affect the cash flows statement?

31. How does the equity method affect the cash flows statement?

Problems

1. An investor corporation purchases 100 shares of the common stock of a public company at a price of $35 per share. The investment represents less than 20 percent of the shares of the investee. At year-end the stock is worth $40 per share. The investor has a 35 percent tax rate.
   a. Give the journal entry to record the purchase of the stock.
   b. Give the journal entry required at year-end assuming the shares are classified as trading securities.
   c. Give the journal entry required at year-end assuming the shares are classified as available-for-sale securities.

2. An investor corporation purchases 200 shares of the common stock of a public company at a price of $20 per share. The investment represents less than 20 percent of the shares of the investee. At year-end the stock is worth $30 per share. The investor has a 35 percent tax rate.
   a. Give the journal entry to record the purchase of the stock.
   b. Give the journal entry required at year-end assuming the shares are classified as trading securities.
   c. Give the journal entry required at year-end assuming the shares are classified as available-for-sale securities.

3. An investor corporation purchases 300 shares of the common stock of a public company at a price of $80 per share. The investment represents less than 20 percent of the shares of the investee. At year-end the stock is worth $88 per share. The investor has a 35 percent tax rate.
   a. Give the journal entry to record the purchase of the stock.
   b. Give the journal entry required at year-end assuming the shares are classified as trading securities.
   c. Give the journal entry required at year-end assuming the shares are classified as available-for-sale securities.

4. An investor corporation purchases 400 shares of the common stock of a public company at a price of $30 per share. The investment represents less than 20 percent of the shares of the investee. At year-end the stock is worth $25 per share. The investor has a 35 percent tax rate.

a. Give the journal entry to record the purchase of the stock.

b. Give the journal entry required at year-end assuming the shares are classified as trading securities.

c. Give the journal entry required at year-end assuming the shares are classified as available-for-sale securities.

5. An investor corporation purchases 500 shares of the common stock of a public company at a price of $45 per share. The investment represents less than 20 percent of the shares of the investee. At year-end the stock is worth $20 per share. The investor has a 35 percent tax rate.

a. Give the journal entry to record the purchase of the stock.

b. Give the journal entry required at year-end assuming the shares are classified as trading securities.

c. Give the journal entry required at year-end assuming the shares are classified as available-for-sale securities.

6. An investor corporation purchases 600 shares of the common stock of a public company at a price of $60 per share. The investment represents less than 20 percent of the shares of the investee. At year-end the stock is worth $44 per share. The investor has a 35 percent tax rate.

a. Give the journal entry to record the purchase of the stock.

b. Give the journal entry required at year-end assuming the shares are classified as trading securities.

c. Give the journal entry required at year-end assuming the shares are classified as available-for-sale securities.

7. Assume the same facts as given in problem 1. In the subsequent year, all of the stock is sold for $45 per share.

a. Give the journal entry to record the sale of the stock assuming the shares are classified as trading securities.

b. Give the journal entry to record the sale of the stock assuming the shares are classified as available-for-sale securities.

8. Assume the same facts as given in problem 2. In the subsequent year, all of the stock is sold for $25 per share.

a. Give the journal entry to record the sale of the stock assuming the shares are classified as trading securities.

b. Give the journal entry to record the sale of the stock assuming the shares are classified as available-for-sale securities.

9. Assume the same facts as given in problem 3. In the subsequent year, all of the stock is sold for $90 per share.

a. Give the journal entry to record the sale of the stock assuming the shares are classified as trading securities.

b. Give the journal entry to record the sale of the stock assuming the shares are classified as available-for-sale securities.

10. Assume the same facts as given in problem 4. In the subsequent year, all of the stock is sold for $28 per share.

a. Give the journal entry to record the sale of the stock assuming the shares are classified as trading securities.

b. Give the journal entry to record the sale of the stock assuming the shares are classified as available-for-sale securities.

11. Assume the same facts as given in problem 5. In the subsequent year, all of the stock is sold for $15 per share.

a. Give the journal entry to record the sale of the stock assuming the shares are classified as trading securities.

b. Give the journal entry to record the sale of the stock assuming the shares are classified as available-for-sale securities.

12. Assume the same facts as given in problem 6. In the subsequent year, all of the stock is sold for $40 per share.

a. Give the journal entry to record the sale of the stock assuming the shares are classified as trading securities.

b. Give the journal entry to record the sale of the stock assuming the shares are classified as available-for-sale securities.

13. The following table shows prices per share for three publicly traded securities (AAA Company, BBB Company, and CCC Company) at various dates:

	June 30 2001	Dec. 31 2001	June 30 2002	Dec. 31 2002	June 30 2003	Dec. 31 2003
AAA Company	20	23	27	31	28	25
BBB Company	45	40	38	33	36	39
CCC Company	70	75	74	73	72	71

A corporation had the following purchase and sale transactions in these securities:

June 30, 2001	Purchase 100 shares AAA
Dec. 31, 2001	Purchase 80 shares BBB
	Purchase 60 shares CCC
June 30, 2002	Sell 100 shares AAA
June 30, 2003	Sell 60 shares CCC

a. Compute the realized and unrealized gains and losses for 2001, 2002, and 2003 using the fair value method, assuming the securities are trading securities.

b. Compute the realized and unrealized gains and losses for 2001, 2002, and 2003 using the fair value method, assuming the securities are available-for-sale securities.

14. The following table shows prices per share for four publicly traded securities (DDD Company, EEE Company, FFF Company, and GGG Company) at various dates:

	June 30 2001	Dec. 31 2001	June 30 2002	Dec. 31 2002	June 30 2003	Dec. 31 2003
DDD Company	30	33	37	40	36	32
EEE Company	15	12	10	11	18	20
FFF Company	55	60	65	70	75	80
GGG Company	90	85	80	75	70	65

A corporation had the following purchase and sale transactions in these securities:

June 30, 2001	Purchase 200 shares DDD
	Purchase 300 shares EEE
	Purchase 400 shares FFF
June 30, 2002	Sell 300 shares EEE
	Purchase 100 shares GGG
June 30, 2003	Sell 200 shares DDD

a. Compute the realized and unrealized gains and losses for 2001, 2002, and 2003 using the fair value method, assuming the securities are trading securities.

b. Compute the realized and unrealized gains and losses for 2001, 2002, and 2003 using the fair value method, assuming the securities are available-for-sale securities.

15. The following table shows prices per share for 5 publicly traded securities (HHH Company, JJJ Company, KKK Company, LLL Company, and MMM Company) at various dates:

	June 30 2001	Dec. 31 2001	June 30 2002	Dec. 31 2002	June 30 2003	Dec. 31 2003
HHH Company	33	37	41	44	46	52
JJJ Company	66	62	59	56	52	48
KKK Company	77	87	90	85	80	88
LLL Company	23	26	25	24	27	28
MMM Company	76	60	80	85	70	60

A corporation had the following purchase and sale transactions in these securities:

June 30, 2001	Purchase 300 shares HHH
	Purchase 200 shares JJJ
Dec. 31, 2001	Purchase 100 shares KKK
	Purchase 400 shares LLL
Dec. 31, 2002	Sell 200 shares JJJ
	Sell 100 shares KKK
	Purchase 500 shares MMM

a. Compute the realized and unrealized gains and losses for 2001, 2002, and 2003 using the fair value method, assuming the securities are trading securities.

b. Compute the realized and unrealized gains and losses for 2001, 2002, and 2003 using the fair value method, assuming the securities are available-for-sale securities.

16. At the beginning of 2001, Investor Corporation purchased 30 percent of the stock of Investee Corporation for $3,000,000. At the time of the purchase, the book value of Investee Corporation was $10,000,000. The following table shows the net income of and dividends paid by Investee Corporation for 2001, 2002, and 2003.

	Net Income (loss)	Dividends
2001	80,000	10,000
2002	(30,000)	12,000
2003	65,000	14,000

a. What is the amount of income or loss that Investor Corporation will report under the equity method for 2001, 2002, and 2003?

b. What is the book value of the investment asset account on the books of Investor Corporation at the end of 2001, 2002, and 2003?

17. At the beginning of 2001, Investor Corporation purchased 40 percent of the stock of Investee Corporation for $16,000,000. At the time of the purchase, the book value of Investee Corporation was $40,000,000. The following table shows the net income of and dividends paid by Investee Corporation for 2001, 2002, and 2003.

	Net Income (loss)	Dividends
2001	140,000	30,000
2002	240,000	30,000
2003	(90,000)	40,000

a. What is the amount of income or loss that Investor Corporation will report under the equity method for 2001, 2002, and 2003?

b. What is the book value of the investment asset account on the books of Investor Corporation at the end of 2001, 2002, and 2003?

18. At the beginning of 2001, Investor Corporation purchased 25 percent of the stock of Investee Corporation for $6,250,000. At the time of the purchase, the book value of Investee Corporation was $25,000,000. The following table shows the net income of and dividends paid by Investee Corporation for 2001, 2002, and 2003.

	Net Income (loss)	Dividends
2001	(80,000)	45,000
2002	(70,000)	45,000
2003	110,000	45,000

a. What is the amount of income or loss that Investor Corporation will report under the equity method for 2001, 2002, and 2003?

b. What is the book value of the investment asset account on the books of Investor Corporation at the end of 2001, 2002, and 2003?

19. Assume the same facts as given in problem 16 except that at the time of the purchase the book value of Investee Corporation was $9,000,000 (rather than $10,000,000). Assume that any additional purchase price was attributable to depreciable assets with a useful life of 12 years and no salvage value. Assume a 35 percent tax rate.

a. What is the amount of income or loss that Investor Corporation will report under the equity method for 2001, 2002, and 2003?

b. What is the book value of the investment asset account on the books of Investor Corporation at the end of 2001, 2002, and 2003?

20. Assume the same facts as given in problem 17 except that at the time of the purchase the book value of Investee Corporation was $38,000,000 (rather than $40,000,000). Assume that any additional purchase price was attributable to depreciable assets with a useful life of 15 years and no salvage value. Assume a 35 percent tax rate.

a. What is the amount of income or loss that Investor Corporation will report under the equity method for 2001, 2002, and 2003?

b. What is the book value of the investment asset account on the books of Investor Corporation at the end of 2001, 2002, and 2003?

21. Assume the same facts as given in problem 18 except that at the time of the purchase the book value of Investee Corporation was $23,000,000 (rather than $25,000,000). Assume that any additional purchase price was attributable to depreciable assets with a useful life of 20 years and no salvage value. Assume a 35 percent tax rate.

a. What is the amount of income or loss that Investor Corporation will report under the equity method for 2001, 2002, and 2003?

b. What is the book value of the investment asset account on the books of Investor Corporation at the end of 2001, 2002, and 2003?

22. Shown below are the separate financial statements of Investor Corporation and its 100 percent owned subsidiary Investee Corporation. Use this information to prepare the consolidated financial statements for Investor Corporation and Subsidiary. There are no elimination entries.

Balance Sheet	Investor Corporation	Investee Corporation
Cash	$ 200,000	$ 100,000
Accounts receivable	340,000	120,000
Inventories	290,000	200,000
Property and equipment (net)	1,350,000	850,000
Investment in subsidiary	400,000	—
Total assets	$2,580,000	$1,270,000
Accounts payable	$280,000	$180,000
Debt	1,350,000	690,000
Total liabilities	1,630,000	870,000
Common stock	600,000	180,000
Retained earnings	350,000	220,000
Total shareholders' equity	950,000	400,000
Total liabilities and shareholders' equity	$2,580,000	$1,270,000

Income Statement		
Sales	$1,000,000	$ 800,000
Cost of goods sold	(490,000)	(650,000)
Selling and administrative expense	(445,000)	(96,154)
Income from equity investments	35,000	—
Income before income taxes	100,000	53,846
Income tax expense	(35,000)	(18,846)
Net income	$ 65,000	$ 35,000

23. Shown below are the separate financial statements of Investor Corporation and its 100 percent owned subsidiary Investee Corporation. Use this information to prepare the consolidated financial statements for Investor Corporation and Subsidiary. There are no elimination entries.

Balance Sheet	Investor Corporation	Investee Corporation
Cash	$ 300,000	$ 80,000
Accounts receivable	210,000	140,000
Inventories	250,000	190,000
Property and equipment (net)	1,600,000	900,000
Investment	500,000	—
Total assets	$2,860,000	$1,310,000
Accounts payable	$ 300,000	$ 165,000
Debt	1,210,000	645,000
Total liabilities	1,510,000	810,000
Common stock	500,000	200,000
Retained earnings	850,000	300,000
Total shareholders' equity	1,350,000	500,000
Total liabilities and shareholders' equity	$2,860,000	$1,310,000

Income Statement		
Sales	$1,300,000	$ 950,000
Cost of goods sold	(490,000)	(700,000)
Selling and administrative expense	(445,000)	(280,000)
Income from equity investments	(19,500)	—
Income before income taxes	345,500	(30,000)
Income tax expense	(120,925)	10,500
Net income	$ 224,575	$ (19,500)

24. Shown below are the separate financial statements of Investor Corporation and its 100 percent owned subsidiary Investee Corporation. Use this information to prepare the consolidated financial statements for Investor Corporation and Subsidiary. There are no elimination entries.

Balance Sheet	Investor Corporation	Investee Corporation
Cash	$ 800,000	$ 50,000
Accounts receivable	950,000	60,000
Inventories	780,000	70,000
Property and equipment (net)	4,500,000	500,000
Investment	300,000	—
Total assets	$7,330,000	$ 680,000
Accounts payable	$ 650,000	$ 40,000
Debt	1,480,000	340,000
Total liabilities	2,130,000	380,000
Common stock	900,000	200,000
Retained earnings	4,300,000	100,000
Total shareholders' equity	5,200,000	300,000
Total liabilities and shareholders' equity	$7,330,000	$ 680,000

Income Statement		
Sales	$4,000,000	$ 700,000
Cost of goods sold	(3,600,000)	(450,000)
Selling and administrative expense	(500,000)	(150,000)
Income from equity investments	65,000	—
Income before income taxes	(35,000)	100,000
Income tax expense	12,250	(35,000)
Net income	$ (22,750)	$ 65,000

Research Reports

1. Obtain the Form 10-K for General Electric for 2002, and locate the financial statements. In the following notes to its financial statements, General Electric explains how its financial statements are presented:

Financial data and related measurements are presented in the following categories:

- **GE** This represents the adding together of all affiliates other than General Electric Capital Services, Inc. (GECS), whose operations are presented on a one-line basis.
- **GECS** This affiliate owns all of the common stock of General Electric Capital Corporation (GE Capital) and GE Global Insurance Holding Corporation (GE Global Insurance Holding), the parent of Employers Reinsurance Corporation. GE Capital, GE Global Insurance Holding and their respective affiliates are consolidated in the GECS columns and constitute its business.
- **CONSOLIDATED** This represents the adding together of GE and GECS.

The effects of transactions among related companies within and between each of the above-mentioned groups are eliminated. Transactions between GE and GECS are immaterial and consist primarily of GECS services for material procurement and trade payables and receivables management, aircraft engines and medical equipment manufactured by GE that are leased to others, buildings and equipment leased by GE from GECS, and GE investments of cash in GECS commercial paper.

Assume that the financial statements for GE represent the separate financial statements of the parent corporation, while the financial statements for GECS represent the financial statements of a 100 percent owned subsidiary corporation. Assume there are no elimination entries required.

a. Use a computer spreadsheet to show how the separate balance sheets of GE and GECS can be combined to result in a consolidated balance sheet.

b. Use a computer spreadsheet to show how the separate income statements of GE and GECS can be combined to result in a consolidated income statement.

2. Obtain the financial statements for Microsoft Corporation for the year ended June 30, 2002. Microsoft's income statement reports the following (in millions):

	Year Ended June 30		
	2000	2001	2002
Losses on equity investees and other	(57)	(159)	(92)
Investment income/(loss)	3,326	(36)	(305)

Microsoft's stockholders' equity statement reports the following (in millions):

	Year Ended June 30		
	2000	2001	2002
Other comprehensive income:			
Net unrealized investment gains/(losses)	(283)	(1,460)	5

a. Use the information contained in the notes to Microsoft's financial statements to explain what is represented by the above numbers.

b. Use the information contained in the notes to Microsoft's financial statements to prepare a schedule showing the detail of realized and unrealized gains and losses for 2002.

3. Obtain the financial statements of Waxman Industries, Inc., for the year ended June 30, 2000. Waxman is a supplier of specialty plumbing, hardware, and other products to the repair and remodeling market in the United States. In the notes to its financial statements, Waxman made the following statement:

The accompanying consolidated financial statements include the accounts of Waxman Industries, Inc. ("Waxman Industries") and its wholly-owned subsidiaries (collectively, the "Company"). As of June 30, 2000, the Company owned 44.2% of the common stock of Barnett Inc. ("Barnett Common Stock"), a direct marketer and distributor of plumbing, electrical and hardware products, and accounts for Barnett Inc. ("Barnett") under the equity method of accounting.

Obtain the financial statements of Barnett Inc. for the year ended June 30, 2000.

a. Verify that Waxman has reported its share of Barnett's net income correctly under GAAP. If the reported amount does not appear to be correct, suggest some possible reasons for the difference.

b. Verify that Waxman's investment account reflects the correct balance at year-end. If the balance does not appear to be correct, suggest some possible reasons for the difference.

c. Comment on the relevance and reliability of the equity method. In Waxman's case, does the use of the equity method provide users with useful information?

    d. Look at the financial statements of Waxman for the years ended June 30, 2001 and 2002. Is there any information in these financial statements that would change your answer in (*c*) above?

4. Obtain the financial statements of Crown Resources Corporation for 2000. In the notes to its financial statements, Crown Resources made the following statement:

Crown Resources Corporation (the "Company" or "Crown") engages principally in the acquisition, exploration and development of mineral properties, which presently exist in the western United States and Mexico. Prior to October 18, 2000 Crown held properties in Peru through Solitario Resources Corporation ("Solitario"), which is currently a 41.3%-owned unconsolidated subsidiary.

On October 18, 2000,("the Effective Date") Solitario, completed a Plan of Arrangement ("the Plan") with Altoro Gold Corp. of Vancouver, Canada ("Altoro"), whereby Altoro became a wholly-owned subsidiary of Solitario. In connection with the Plan, Solitario issued 6,228,894 shares to Altoro shareholders and option holders. Solitario also reserved 825,241 Solitario shares for issuance upon the exercise of 825,241 warrants issued in exchange for Altoro warrants. On October 24, 2000, Solitario issued 261,232 shares upon the exercise of the above warrants and 286,231 the warrants expired unexercised. After the issuance of the shares in connection with the Arrangement and exercise of the warrants discussed above, Solitario has 23,344,647 shares outstanding of which Crown owns 9,633,585 shares. Primarily as a result of the issuance of Solitario shares in connection with the Plan, Crown's ownership percentage in Solitario was reduced from 57.2% to 41.3% at December 31, 2000.

Basis of Presentation

Accordingly, Crown has accounted for its investment in Solitario under the equity method since the Effective Date. Solitario's income, expense and minority interest are included in the Consolidated Statement of Operations of Crown through the Effective Date. Crown's interest in the net assets of Solitario are shown the Consolidated Balance Sheet as of December 31, 2000 as equity in unconsolidated subsidiary. Crown's share of Solitario's net loss from the Effective Date through December 31, 2000 is shown as equity in loss of unconsolidated subsidiary in the Consolidated Statement of Operations.

---

    a. In your own words, explain why the above transaction is consistent with GAAP reporting for investments in subsidiaries.

    b. Explain how Crown's income statement and balance sheet would be different if its investment in Solitario had not decreased below 50 percent during the year.

    c. Discuss the costs and benefits of using a different accounting method for a 57.2 percent ownership interest relative to a 41.3 percent ownership interest.

5. Locate the financial statements for Merrill Lynch & Co., Inc., for the year ended December 27, 2002. Use the financial statements and notes to answer the following questions:

    a. What is the fair value of Merrill Lynch's available-for-sale securities and trading securities at the end of 2002?

    b. What is the total amount of *unrealized* gains and losses from available-for-sale securities recognized for 2002?

    c. What is the total amount of *realized* gains and losses from available-for-sale securities recognized for 2002?

    d. What is the total amount of *unrealized* gains and losses from trading securities that was included in net income for 2002?

    e. Comment on the relevance and reliability of Merrill Lynch's reporting of investment information.

Getty Images

Chapter Learning Objectives

After reading this chapter you should understand

1. The economics of leasing.
2. The difference between a capital lease and an operating lease.
3. The four lease capitalization criteria applicable to lessees.
4. The two additional lease capitalization criteria applicable to lessors.
5. The accounting treatment of capital leases for lessees.
6. The difference between a sales type lease and a direct financing lease.
7. The accounting treatment of capital leases for lessors.
8. How residual value of the leased asset affects accounting treatment.
9. The accounting treatment for operating leases.

Chapter 12

Investments in Leased Assets

Focus Company: UAL Corporation

Introduction

Shown below is a portion of the 1999 consolidated balance sheet of UAL Corporation (the parent of United Airlines) disclosing operating property and equipment with a net book value of $14,865 million. Notice that $2,377 million (or 16 percent) of this total is represented by something called *capital leases*.

UAL CORPORATION AND SUBSIDIARY COMPANIES
Statements of Consolidated Financial Position
(in millions)

	December 31	
	1999	**1998**
Assets		
Operating property and equipment		
Owned		
Flight equipment	$13,518	$12,006
Advances on flight equipment	809	985
Other property and equipment	3,368	3,134
	17,695	16,125
Less—Accumulated depreciation and amortization	5,207	5,174
	12,488	10,951
Capital leases		
Flight equipment	2,929	2,605
Other property and equipment	93	97
	3,022	2,702
Less—Accumulated amortization	645	599
	2,377	**2,103**
	$14,865	$13,054

Source: UAL Corporation Form 10-K.

On the liability side of UAL's balance sheet (shown on the next page), the company reported $2,337 million of long-term obligations under capital leases at the end of 1999, an amount that is nearly equal to the total long-term debt of $2,650 million. From this example you can see that capital leases have a major impact on balance sheet assets and liabilities of UAL, and in fact leases play an important role in the financial statements of most large public corporations. As shown later in the chapter, accounting for capital leases also affects reported revenues and expenses on the income statement.

UAL CORPORATION AND SUBSIDIARY COMPANIES Statements of Consolidated Financial Position (in millions)		
	December 31	
	1999	1998
Liabilities and Stockholders' Equity		
Long-term debt	$2,650	$2,858
Long-term obligations under capital leases ...	**$2,337**	**$2,113**

Source: UAL Corporation Form 10-K.

This chapter investigates the accounting issues that arise when companies use leased assets in their business. It analyzes leasing from the standpoint of both the legal owner of the leased assets (the lessor) and the user of the leased assets (the lessee) and shows how GAAP rules separate leases into two basic types: capital leases and operating leases. The chapter begins with a brief discussion of the economics of leasing.

THE ECONOMICS OF LEASING

In a typical leasing transaction, one corporation (the lessor) owns an asset that is used by another corporation (the lessee) in exchange for a payment from the lessee to the lessor. Although the payment can take many forms, assume for now that the lease payment is made periodically (that is, once a month or once a year), that the payment is the same amount each period, and that the payment is made at the *beginning* of each period.[1] Recall from Chapter 5 that a series of equal payments made at equal time intervals constitutes an annuity. Later in the chapter we will take advantage of the fact that lease payments are annuities to compute the present value of a lease.

The Lessee

Consider the economics of leasing from the lessee's standpoint. Assume that United needs a new 777 aircraft. One alternative is to purchase the aircraft from Boeing. There are three alternative ways to purchase the aircraft. First, United could simply pay Boeing cash equal to the purchase price of the aircraft. Second, United could purchase the aircraft and give Boeing a note payable for the purchase price. In this way, United could make payments to Boeing over some time period. However, in addition to the purchase price United would also incur interest expense on the outstanding note balance. Third, United could borrow the money to purchase the aircraft from a third party, for example, GE Capital. GE Capital would pay Boeing the purchase price of the aircraft, and United would make payments to GE Capital, including interest, over some time period.

Notice that the second and third methods of purchasing the aircraft are similar. In both cases, United gets the use of the aircraft in exchange for making periodic payments, including interest, to a lender—either Boeing (the manufacturer of the aircraft) or GE Capital. In both of these cases, although United would be the legal owner of the aircraft, the corporation providing financing (that is, Boeing or GE Capital) would have a security interest in the aircraft.

Compare this with a situation in which United leases an aircraft. There are two different forms that the lease could take. First, United could lease the aircraft di-

---

[1] For example, when you rent an apartment you usually pay rent each month on the first day of the month. Contrast this with a loan payment (on an auto loan, for example) where the payment is usually due at the end of each month.

rectly from Boeing, with Boeing keeping ownership of the aircraft and United using it in exchange for making periodic lease payments to Boeing. Second, a third party such as GE Capital could purchase the aircraft from Boeing and then lease it to United. In this situation, GE Capital would be the owner of the aircraft while United would use it in exchange for lease payments. Although these payments would not be designated as principal or interest payments, the lease payments would include an amount to compensate GE Capital for the use of its money over the lease term.

Notice that economically the lease situations are quite similar to the last two purchase situations. In each case, United gets the use of an aircraft in exchange for making periodic payments that include an interest factor—either explicitly in the form of interest on a loan, or implicitly as part of a lease payment. There are certain legal differences relating to the ownership interests in the aircraft. In the case of a purchase, United would be the legal owner, while either Boeing or GE Capital would have a security interest in the aircraft. In the case of a lease, the lessor (Boeing or GE Capital) would be the legal owner of the aircraft while United would simply have a right to use it for the term of the lease. (This right is an example of an intangible asset).

One important difference between the purchase and lease examples discussed above is what happens to the aircraft at the end of the lease. If United purchases the aircraft, it acquires what are sometimes referred to as the *burdens* and *benefits* (or risks and rewards) of ownership. If the value of a used 777 aircraft goes up over time, United will benefit from the increase in value. Similarly, if the value of the aircraft goes down more than was expected, United will suffer the loss in value.[2] In the lease situation, it is the lessor who has the burdens and benefits of ownership, since at the end of the lease United returns the aircraft to the lessor and has no further ownership interest.

There are ways to make the lease even more similar to the purchase by transferring the burdens and benefits of ownership to the lessee. One way is through a *bargain purchase option,* which works like this: Suppose United leases the aircraft from Boeing or GE Capital for 20 years, and at the end of the 20-year lease term United has the option to purchase the aircraft for five dollars. Since even a 20-year-old aircraft will obviously be worth more than five dollars, United is certain to exercise its option and purchase the aircraft at the end of the 20-year lease term. Therefore, if the value of the aircraft increases or decreases unexpectedly, United will suffer the decrease or gain the increase in value.

Another way to transfer the burden of ownership to the lessee is through a *guaranteed residual value provision* in the lease. For example, assume that United leases the 777 from GE Capital for 20 years, and that at the start of the lease term GE Capital estimates that in 20 years a 20-year-old 777 aircraft will be worth $8 million. This $8 million is called the *residual value.* Under the lease terms, United might be required to guarantee that the residual value of the aircraft at the end of the lease will be at least $8 million. This means that if the aircraft is worth less than $8 million, United will have to pay GE Capital the difference between $8 million and the actual value of the aircraft. A guaranteed residual value provision in a lease transfers the burden of ownership, but not the benefit, to the lessee.

Tax Issues

If United purchases a new aircraft and finances the purchase with debt, it will make periodic payments of interest and principal to either the manufacturer or the lender. If United leases a new aircraft, it will make periodic lease payments to the lessor. It may be that the lease payments are the same amount as

---

[2] Another burden of ownership is risk of loss from the destruction of the aircraft. However, in both the purchase and lease situations, United is likely to cover this risk through some form of insurance.

the combined principal and interest payments on the loan. However, the *tax treatment* of the two transactions is quite different, and this difference in tax treatment is a major reason that companies lease assets rather than purchase them.

Assume first that United borrows money to purchase an aircraft. For tax purposes, the aircraft will generate tax deductions for (1) interest payments on the loan and (2) depreciation expense computed under tax depreciation rules. During the early years of the loan, the interest portion of the loan payment will be large, since the outstanding principal balance will be high. Also, accelerated tax depreciation will be high during the early years of the asset's life, since the tax depreciation system uses the double declining balance method with no salvage value. This means that the total tax benefits available to United (interest expense plus depreciation expense) will be quite large in the early years of the aircraft's life and will become smaller over time as both interest expense and depreciation decrease.

Contrast this tax treatment of an asset purchase with the tax treatment of lease payments. If United leases a new aircraft, the lease payments result in tax deductions. However, since each lease payment is the same amount, the tax benefits will be spread evenly over the life of the aircraft. What this means is that, because the tax benefits of ownership are concentrated in the early years of an asset's life, the present value of the tax benefits available to an owner are greater than the present value of tax benefits available to a lessee, even though the total tax benefits over the entire life of the asset may be the same.

You might think that this tax result would mean that corporations would always choose to purchase assets rather than lease them. However, corporations sometimes find that they cannot use all of the tax benefits available to the purchaser of a new asset. This usually occurs when the corporation has experienced tax losses. For a corporation with tax losses, any additional tax deductions have a low value, since they do not result in an immediate reduction in income taxes but must be carried forward and used to offset future taxable income when, and if, the corporation becomes profitable again. Leasing provides a way for a corporation in this situation to transfer the tax benefits to another corporation that has a high tax rate and is therefore able to utilize the tax deductions associated with ownership of the asset.

For example, assume that GE Capital has high taxable income and is paying taxes at a rate of 35 percent, while UAL has tax losses and is not currently paying any taxes. If United purchases a new aircraft, all of the tax benefits associated with the interest and depreciation will not provide an immediate benefit, since they will only increase United's tax loss carryforward. However, if GE Capital purchases the aircraft and leases it to United, GE Capital (as the owner of the aircraft) receives an immediate 35 percent tax benefit for all of the tax deductions associated with ownership. United can negotiate a lower lease payment from GE Capital because GE Capital is receiving the tax benefits that would have been wasted on United. Leasing thus provides a means for low-tax-rate corporations to transfer tax benefits to high-tax-rate corporations in exchange for lower lease payments. Taxes thus provide a strong economic incentive for many corporations to engage in lease transactions.

The Lessor

Now consider the economics of leasing from the standpoint of the lessor, focusing on two different situations. In the first situation, the lessor is the manufacturer of the leased asset. In the second, the lessor is a third-party financial institution.

Manufacturer Lessor

Assume that Boeing leases a new 777 aircraft to United for 20 years. At this point, it might be helpful to put some numbers in the lease example. Assume that the purchase price for a new 777 aircraft is $30 million and that Boeing estimates that a used 777 aircraft will be worthless in 20 years.[3] Finally, assume the cost of manufacturing a 777 aircraft is $20 million.

If Boeing simply sells the aircraft to United for cash, here is the entry that Boeing would use to record the transaction:

	Journal Entry to Record Sales Revenue (in millions)		
+/−	**Accounts [description of account]**	**Debit**	**Credit**
+	Cash [balance sheet asset account]	30	
+	Cost of Goods Sold [income statement expense account]	20	
+	Sales Revenue [income statement revenue account]		30
−	Inventory [balance sheet asset account]		20

A second possibility is for Boeing to sell the aircraft to United and to take back a note receivable for the purchase price. United would then make payments on the note, including interest, to Boeing until the note is paid off. Here is the journal entry to record the sale under this example:

	Journal Entry to Record Sales Revenue (in millions)		
+/−	**Accounts [description of account]**	**Debit**	**Credit**
+	Notes Receivable [balance sheet asset account]	30	
+	Cost of Goods Sold [income statement expense account]	20	
+	Sales Revenue [income statement revenue account]		30
−	Inventory [balance sheet asset account]		20

For Boeing to agree to lease the aircraft to United, Boeing would have to be in the same economic position after the lease as it would be after a sale. How can the company achieve this? One possibility might be to charge United 20 annual lease payments with each payment equal to $30,000,000/20 = $1,500,000. However, from Chapter 5 it is clear that, because of the time value of money, 20 payments of $1,500,000 each over a 20-year period do not have the same present value as $30,000,000 cash received in the current year.

What is it that makes the note receivable worth $30 million while 20 payments of $1.5 million each are not? The answer is that the note receivable will also require the payment of interest to compensate Boeing for the fact that it will receive the sales price over 20 years. Charging interest on the note causes the *present value* of the note payments to equal $30 million. For the lease to be economically equivalent to a sale then, the *present value* of the lease payments must also equal $30 million.

Suppose that United agrees to pay Boeing 20 annual lease payments equal to $2,829,228.02 each, with the first payment due at the beginning of the lease. The following table shows the present value of this series of 20 payments, assuming an interest rate of 8 percent.

---

[3] Obviously, this is not realistic assumption, and it is made here for simplicity only. Later, the assumption will be relaxed, and the value of the aircraft at the end of the lease will be allowed to differ from zero.

EXAMPLE OF AIRCRAFT LEASE PAYMENTS

Years in Future	Amount of Payment	8% Present Value Factor	Present Value
0	$ 2,829,228.02	1.00	$ 2,829,228.02
1	2,829,228.02	0.93	2,619,655.58
2	2,829,228.02	0.86	2,425,607.02
3	2,829,228.02	0.79	2,245,932.42
4	2,829,228.02	0.74	2,079,567.06
5	2,829,228.02	0.68	1,925,525.05
6	2,829,228.02	0.63	1,782,893.57
7	2,829,228.02	0.58	1,650,827.38
8	2,829,228.02	0.54	1,528,543.87
9	2,829,228.02	0.50	1,415,318.40
10	2,829,228.02	0.46	1,310,480.00
11	2,829,228.02	0.43	1,213,407.40
12	2,829,228.02	0.40	1,123,525.37
13	2,829,228.02	0.37	1,040,301.27
14	2,829,228.02	0.34	963,241.92
15	2,829,228.02	0.32	891,890.67
16	2,829,228.02	0.29	825,824.69
17	2,829,228.02	0.27	764,652.49
18	2,829,228.02	0.25	708,011.57
19	2,829,228.02	0.23	655,566.26
Total	$56,584,560.46		$30,000,000.00

As the table shows, the total of these 20 lease payments is $56 million, but their present value (using an 8 percent interest rate) is only $30 million, the value of the aircraft. Therefore, if Boeing leases the aircraft to United under these terms, Boeing is in the same position economically as if it had sold the aircraft to United and taken back a note receivable with an 8 percent interest rate.

Recall that the series of lease payments illustrated above constitutes an annuity. We can take advantage of this fact to make it easier to compute the present value, since there is a formula (from Chapter 5) for the present value of an annuity. The formula is

$$\text{Present value of ordinary annuity} = \text{Amount of one payment} \times \left[\frac{1 - \frac{1}{(1 + i)^n}}{i} \right]$$

However, an ordinary annuity is one for which the payments occur at the *end* of each period. In the case of a lease, the payments occur at the *beginning* of each period. An annuity with payments at the beginning of the period is called an *annuity due*. Here is the formula for the present value of an annuity due:

$$\text{Present value of annuity due} = \text{Amount of one payment} \times \left\{ 1 + \left[\frac{1 - \frac{1}{(1 + i)^{n - 1}}}{i} \right] \right\}$$

Substituting $i = 8\%$ and $n = 20$ into the above formula, the value of the term in brackets (called the *present value factor*) is equal to 10.6035992. Multiplying 10.6035992 × $2,829,228.02 = $30 million.

This formula can be used to compute the amount of a lease payment for a lease of a given term provided the value of the asset being leased (the present value of the lease payments) and the interest rate are known. Divide the present value of the lease payments by the present value factor to arrive at the amount of each lease payment. In fact, that is how the figure of $2,829,228.02 was computed for the lease in the example. The present value of the lease payments was $30 million, and the present value factor was 10.6035992. The lease payment is computed as $30 million/10.6035992 = $2,829,228.02.

Finance Company Lessor

Suppose a finance company such as GE Capital made a $30 million loan to United to allow United to purchase a new aircraft. If the term of the loan was for 20 years and the interest rate on the loan was 8 percent, United would make payments to GE Capital of $3,055,566.26 per year. Here is the amortization schedule for the loan in this example:

		EXAMPLE OF LOAN AMORTIZATION		
Years in Future	Amount of Payment	Interest at 8%	Reduction in Principal	Principal Balance
				$30,000,000.00
1	$ 3,055,566.26	$ 2,400,000.00	$ 655,566.26	29,344,433.74
2	3,055,566.26	2,347,554.70	708,011.57	28,636,422.17
3	3,055,566.26	2,290,913.77	764,652.49	27,871,769.68
4	3,055,566.26	2,229,741.57	825,824.69	27,045,944.99
5	3,055,566.26	2,163,675.60	891,890.67	26,154,054.32
6	3,055,566.26	2,092,324.35	963,241.92	25,190,812.40
7	3,055,566.26	2,015,264.99	1,040,301.27	24,150,511.13
8	3,055,566.26	1,932,040.89	1,123,525.37	23,026,985.76
9	3,055,566.26	1,842,158.86	1,213,407.40	21,813,578.35
10	3,055,566.26	1,745,086.27	1,310,480.00	20,503,098.36
11	3,055,566.26	1,640,247.87	1,415,318.40	19,087,779.96
12	3,055,566.26	1,527,022.40	1,528,543.87	17,559,236.09
13	3,055,566.26	1,404,738.89	1,650,827.38	15,908,408.71
14	3,055,566.26	1,272,672.70	1,782,893.57	14,125,515.15
15	3,055,566.26	1,130,041.21	1,925,525.05	12,199,990.09
16	3,055,566.26	975,999.21	2,079,567.06	10,120,423.04
17	3,055,566.26	809,633.84	2,245,932.42	7,874,490.62
18	3,055,566.26	629,959.25	2,425,607.02	5,448,883.60
19	3,055,566.26	435,910.69	2,619,655.58	2,829,228.02
20	3,055,566.26	226,338.24	2,829,228.02	0.00
Total	$61,111,325.29	$31,111,325.29	$30,000,000.00	

As an alternative, GE Capital could purchase the aircraft from Boeing for $30 million and then lease it to United for 20 years. As shown earlier, the lease payments would be $2,829,228.02. At first glance it may appear that the value of the lease to GE Capital is different from the value of the loan (since the loan payments are $3,055,566.26) and that the higher payments might cause GE Capital to favor the loan over the lease. However, this difference in payments is due entirely to the fact that the lease payments are made at the *beginning* of each year, whereas the loan payments are made at the *end* of each year. In effect, the lease is fully paid off after only 19 years, whereas the loan is only paid off after 20 years. Since GE Capital is loaning money for a longer period of time with the loan, it should receive higher payments. To see that the difference is due to the timing of the payments, here is the same $30 million loan amortization schedule computed on the assumption that the payments are made at the beginning, rather than at the end, of each year. Since the first payment is due at the start of the loan, there is no interest expense associated with the first payment.

EXAMPLE OF LOAN AMORTIZATION				
Years in Future	Amount of Payment	Interest at 8%	Reduction in Principal	Principal Balance
				$30,000,000.00
0	$ 2,829,228.02	$ 0.00	$ 2,829,228.02	27,170,771.98
1	2,829,228.02	2,173,661.76	655,566.26	26,515,205.71
2	2,829,228.02	2,121,216.46	708,011.57	25,807,194.15
3	2,829,228.02	2,064,575.53	764,652.49	25,042,541.66
4	2,829,228.02	2,003,403.33	825,824.69	24,216,716.96
5	2,829,228.02	1,937,337.36	891,890.67	23,324,826.30
6	2,829,228.02	1,865,986.10	963,241.92	22,361,584.38
7	2,829,228.02	1,788,926.75	1,040,301.27	21,321,283.11
8	2,829,228.02	1,705,702.65	1,123,525.37	20,197,757.73
9	2,829,228.02	1,615,820.62	1,213,407.40	18,984,350.33
10	2,829,228.02	1,518,748.03	1,310,480.00	17,673,870.33
11	2,829,228.02	1,413,909.63	1,415,318.40	16,258,551.94
12	2,829,228.02	1,300,684.15	1,528,543.87	14,730,008.07
13	2,829,228.02	1,178,400.65	1,650,827.38	13,079,180.69
14	2,829,228.02	1,046,334.46	1,782,893.57	11,296,287.12
15	2,829,228.02	903,702.97	1,925,525.05	9,370,762.07
16	2,829,228.02	749,660.97	2,079,567.06	7,291,195.01
17	2,829,228.02	583,295.60	2,245,932.42	5,045,262.59
18	2,829,228.02	403,621.01	2,425,607.02	2,619,655.58
19	2,829,228.02	209,572.45	2,619,655.58	0.00
Total	$56,584,560.46	$26,584,560.46	$30,000,000.00	

CLASSIFYING LEASES UNDER GAAP

Under GAAP, all leases must be classified as either (1) an operating lease or (2) a capital lease. A series of rules determines when a lease is considered to be a capital lease. All leases that are not capital leases are operating leases.

The Accounting Problem with Leases

Before discussing the accounting rules for leases, it is important to understand the purpose of the rules. The discussion above showed that there may be very little difference economically between purchasing an asset (and financing the purchase with debt) and leasing the same asset. This is especially true if most of the burdens and benefits of ownership are transferred to the lessee. If these two types of transactions are economically so similar, a problem arises if the accounting treatment is different depending on the legal form of the transaction (a lease or a purchase).

The problem has to do with recording a liability for future lease payments. Consider United's balance sheet if United borrows $30 million to purchase a new aircraft. In addition to recording the asset, United also records a $30 million liability on the balance sheet. However, liabilities for future lease payments would generally not be recorded on the balance sheet, since a lease is considered to be a mutually unexecuted contract.

For example, assume that United signs a contract for $1,000 to have one of its aircraft repainted in the following year. Even though United is obligated to pay the $1,000, it has this obligation only after the other party to the transaction (in this example, a painting company) has completed its part of the contract. Until the aircraft is painted, United has no obligation to pay the painting company. Therefore, the contract is mutually unexecuted (that is, neither party has performed their portion of the contract) and no liability is recorded under GAAP.

Now apply this same reasoning to a lease. Assume that United enters into an agreement to lease a fuel truck next year for $1,000. Even though United is obligated to pay the $1,000, it has this obligation only after it has started using the truck. Until it starts using the truck, United has no obligation to pay the truck leasing company. Therefore, the lease contract is mutually unexecuted and no liability is recorded under GAAP.

The lease of the aircraft for 20 years would be treated the same way. United has contracted to use an aircraft each year for 20 years in exchange for 20 annual lease payments. Each year that United uses the aircraft it is obligated to make another lease payment. However, the remaining future lease payments represent mutually unexecuted contracts and would not be recorded as liabilities.

This is the reason for an accounting difference between borrowing money to purchase an asset and leasing that same asset. Since borrowing money gives rise to a liability under GAAP, but entering into a lease contract does not, a different balance sheet treatment could result for what is economically a very similar transaction.

To prevent this result, accounting standard setters developed the concept of a *capital lease*. If a lease is considered a capital lease, *it is accounted for as though the lessee had taken out a loan and purchased the asset*. This means that the lessee must record a balance sheet liability for future lease payments. Also, the lessee records the leased asset as a balance sheet asset (part of property and equipment) and depreciation expense is recorded on the lessee's income statement. In this situation, accounting rules ignore the legal form of the transaction and account for it based on its economic substance.

Rules for Determining Capital Lease—Lessee

There are four tests to determine if a lease is a capital lease for a lessee. If any one of the four tests is met, the lease is a capital lease and must be accounted for by the lessee as a purchase. The tests are designed to identify those situations in which the economic substance of a lease is essentially that the lessee has purchased the asset. These tests only apply to leases that are noncancelable; a lease that can be canceled at any time will always be an operating lease. Here are the four tests and the rationale behind each:

1. *There is a transfer of ownership of the asset from the lessor to the lessee.* Since a transfer of ownership means the lessee also receives the burdens and benefits of ownership, the lease is essentially equivalent to a purchase of the asset. The transfer of ownership will usually occur at the end of the lease.

2. *The lease contains a bargain purchase option.* A bargain purchase option means that the lessee has the right to purchase the leased asset for a price that is substantially less than the asset's expected market value at the time the option is exercisable. Since the option gives the lessee the right to purchase an asset for less than its expected market value, it is reasonable to assume that the lessee will exercise the option and become the owner of the property at some time during the lease.

3. *The lease period is 75 percent or more of the asset's estimated useful life.* For example, if the estimated useful life of a new 777 aircraft is 20 years, a lease for 15 years or more (that is, 75% × 20 = 15) will constitute a capital lease. This rule takes the view that the use of an asset for substantially all of its useful life is essentially the same as purchasing the asset. For purposes of determining the lease period, any bargain renewal options must be included.

4. *The present value of the minimum lease payments required under the lease is 90 percent or more of the asset's fair market value.* For example, if the fair market value of a new 777 aircraft is $30 million, a lease where the present value of the minimum lease payments is $27 million or more (that is, 90% × 30 = 27) will constitute a capital lease. This rule takes the view that the payment of

substantially the entire fair market value of an asset is essentially the same as purchasing the asset.

For purposes of this test, the minimum lease payments include: (1) all payments required under the lease, (2) any bargain purchase payment, and (3) any guarantee of the asset's residual value. Minimum lease payments do not include payments made by the lessee to maintain the property, such as repairs or insurance. In making the present value computation, the lessee's incremental borrowing rate is used. The incremental borrowing rate is the interest rate that the lessee would have incurred in borrowing the money to purchase the asset, assuming loan terms similar to the lease terms. There is one exception to this rule. If the implicit interest rate used by the lessor in the lease can be determined, and if this rate is *less than* the lessee's incremental borrowing rate, the implicit interest rate must be used for the present value computation. The implicit interest rate is the interest rate that causes the present value of the minimum lease payments, plus any expected residual value that is not guaranteed, to equal the fair market value of the asset at the start of the lease.

Rules for Determining Capital Lease—Lessor

To determine if a lease is a capital lease or an operating lease for purposes of recording it on the financial statements of the lessor, the four tests discussed above are also used. However, for classifying leases for lessors there are two additional tests that must be applied. To be treated as a capital lease by the lessor, the lease must meet one of the four tests discussed above and must also meet *both* of the additional tests discussed below.

The reason for a stricter test for lessors is that the potential problem of unrecorded lease liabilities does not arise for lessors. Instead, a capital lease would be treated as a note receivable on the balance sheet of the lessor, and, as will be shown below, the lessor may also recognize sales revenue and gross profit when a capital lease is recorded. Therefore, accounting standard setters wanted to make certain that the lease payments would likely be collected by the lessor before allowing capital lease treatment. Because there are two additional tests for the lessor, it is possible that some leases will be classified as capital leases for the lessee and operating leases for the lessor.

Here are the two additional tests for capital lease treatment for a lessor. Both of these tests must be met, in addition to one of the four tests discussed earlier, for the lease to be classified as a capital lease:

1. *Collectibility of the lease payments is reasonably certain.* This test is similar to the test for revenue recognition. Since a lease receivable will be recorded and revenue recognized, collectibility of the lease payments must be likely.
2. *There are no material uncertainties relating to future costs required to be incurred by the lessor.* Since revenue will be recognized by the lessor under the lease, it is important that all of the lessor's costs under the lease be estimated with reasonable certainty.

Any lease that fails to satisfy both of these tests will be classified as an operating lease by the lessor.

ACCOUNTING BY LESSEES

This section explains in more detail the accounting treatment of leases by lessees, beginning with the treatment of operating leases.

Operating Leases

An *operating lease* is any lease that does not meet one of the four tests for determining a capital lease. The accounting treatment for operating leases is to treat the lease as a mutually unexecuted contract. Therefore, no liability is recorded for any future lease payments, and no asset is recorded for the use of the leased asset.

Under an operating lease, the lessee records rent expense as the asset is used. For example, if United leases a new aircraft for $2,829,228.02 per year and the lease is considered an operating lease, United will record the lease payment with the following entry:

Journal Entry to Record Rent Payment for Operating Lease			
+/−	Accounts [description of account]	Debit	Credit
+	Prepaid Rent [balance sheet asset account]	2,829,228	
−	Cash [balance sheet asset account]		2,829,228

As the leased asset is used, United will record rent expense of $2,829,228.02 each year using the following entry:

Journal Entry to Record Rent Expense for Operating Lease			
+/−	Accounts [description of account]	Debit	Credit
+	Rent Expense [income statement expense account]	2,829,228	
−	Prepaid Rent [balance sheet asset account]		2,829,228

Capital Leases

If a lease meets one of the four tests to be classified as a capital lease the lessee must account for the lease as though the asset was purchased by the lessee. Both a balance sheet asset and a balance sheet liability are recorded at an amount equal to *the present value of the minimum lease payments.*

Consider the example shown earlier where United leased a new aircraft for 20 years at an annual payment of $2,829,228.02. The implicit interest rate in this lease was 8 percent, and the present value of the lease payments was $30 million. Here is how United would initially record this lease:

Journal Entry to Record Capital Lease (in millions)			
+/−	Accounts [description of account]	Debit	Credit
+	Flight Equipment [balance sheet asset account]	30	
+	Long-Term Obligations under Capital Leases [balance sheet liability account]		30

United is required to make the first lease payment at the beginning of the first year of the lease. Here is the entry to record the first lease payment:

Journal Entry to Record First Lease Payment			
+/−	Accounts [description of account]	Debit	Credit
−	Long-Term Obligations under Capital Leases [balance sheet liability account]	2,829,228	
−	Cash [balance sheet asset account]		2,829,228

At this point, the balance of the liability is equal to the original balance of $30,000,000 minus the first payment of $2,829,228.02 for a balance of $27,170,771.98. Since under the accounting method for capital leases United is treated as having incurred this liability, interest expense must also be recorded. The interest rate used is the same rate that was used to determine the present value of the future minimum lease payments (8 percent in this example) and interest is computed under the effective interest rate method discussed in Chapter 5. Under this method, the interest expense for the year is equal to the interest rate multiplied by the book value of the liability at the beginning of the year.

In this example, interest expense for the first year of the lease would be computed as $8\% \times \$27,170,771.98 = \$2,173,661.76$. Here is the entry to record the interest expense for the first year of the lease. The entry would be made at the end of the first year of the lease term.

Journal Entry to Record Interest Expense on Capital Lease			
+/−	Accounts [description of account]	Debit	Credit
+	Interest Expense [income statement expense account]	2,173,662	
+	Long-Term Obligations under Capital Leases [balance sheet liability account]		2,173,662

At the beginning of the second year of the lease term, United would make a second lease payment. Here is the entry to record the second lease payment:

Journal Entry to Record Second Lease Payment			
+/−	Accounts [description of account]	Debit	Credit
−	Long-Term Obligations under Capital Leases [balance sheet liability account]	2,829,228	
−	Cash [balance sheet asset account]		2,829,228

After recording this entry, the balance of the lease liability is $27,170,771.98 (the balance at the beginning of the previous year) + $2,173,661.76 (the interest expense for the previous year) − $2,829,228.02 (the payment for the second year) = $26,515,205.71. Each year interest expense and lease payments would be recorded in the same manner. The schedule on page 379 shows the amortization of the lease liability over the 20-year period of the lease.

In using a lease amortization table such as this it is important to keep in mind that financial statement interest expense is recognized in an accounting period based on the accrual method, not in the accounting period when the cash payment is made. This means that the interest expense of $2,173,661.76 associated with the second lease payment (made at the beginning of year 2 of the lease term) is properly recorded as interest expense for the first year of the lease.

Depreciation

Since the lease is being accounted for as if United purchased the aircraft, depreciation expense must be recorded. A question arises as to what is the useful life of a leased asset. Since United will return the aircraft to the lessor at the end of the lease, the general rule is to depreciate the leased asset over the lease term.[4] In this

---

[4] Exceptions would be in cases where title passes to the lessee at the end of the lease, or where the lease contains a bargain purchase option. In these cases, it is assumed that the lessee will continue to use the asset past the end of the lease term, so that depreciation is based on the useful life of the asset.

EXAMPLE OF LEASE LIABILITY AMORTIZATION

Years in Future	Amount of Lease Payment	Interest at 8%	Reduction in Liability	Liability Balance
				$30,000,000.00
0	$ 2,829,228.02	$ 0.00	$ 2,829,228.02	27,170,771.98
1	2,829,228.02	2,173,661.76	655,566.26	26,515,205.71
2	2,829,228.02	2,121,216.46	708,011.57	25,807,194.15
3	2,829,228.02	2,064,575.53	764,652.49	25,042,541.66
4	2,829,228.02	2,003,403.33	825,824.69	24,216,716.96
5	2,829,228.02	1,937,337.36	891,890.67	23,324,826.30
6	2,829,228.02	1,865,986.10	963,241.92	22,361,584.38
7	2,829,228.02	1,788,926.75	1,040,301.27	21,321,283.11
8	2,829,228.02	1,705,702.65	1,123,525.37	20,197,757.73
9	2,829,228.02	1,615,820.62	1,213,407.40	18,984,350.33
10	2,829,228.02	1,518,748.03	1,310,480.00	17,673,870.33
11	2,829,228.02	1,413,909.63	1,415,318.40	16,258,551.94
12	2,829,228.02	1,300,684.15	1,528,543.87	14,730,008.07
13	2,829,228.02	1,178,400.65	1,650,827.38	13,079,180.69
14	2,829,228.02	1,046,334.46	1,782,893.57	11,296,287.12
15	2,829,228.02	903,702.97	1,925,525.05	9,370,762.07
16	2,829,228.02	749,660.97	2,079,567.06	7,291,195.01
17	2,829,228.02	583,295.60	2,245,932.42	5,045,262.59
18	2,829,228.02	403,621.01	2,425,607.02	2,619,655.58
19	2,829,228.02	209,572.45	2,619,655.58	0.00
Total	$56,584,560.46	$26,584,560.46	$30,000,000.00	

example, the lease term is 20 years, so depreciation expense is $30 million divided by 20 years, or $1.5 million per year (assuming United uses straight-line depreciation). However, since the right to use leased assets is technically an intangible asset, some companies use the term *amortization* rather than *depreciation* when allocating the cost of assets held under capital leases to future accounting periods. Notice that United's balance sheet, shown at the beginning of the chapter, uses the heading "accumulated amortization" with respect to assets under capital leases.

Here is the entry United would make to record depreciation of the leased aircraft:

Journal Entry to Record Depreciation on Leased Asset (in millions)

+/−	Accounts [description of account]	Debit	Credit
+	Amortization Expense [income statement expense account]	1.5	
+	Accumulated Amortization—Flight Equipment [balance sheet contra-asset account]		1.5

Comparison with Operating Lease

Comparing the capital lease accounting treatment with that for an operating lease, the most noticeable difference has to do with the balance sheet—capital lease accounting records the leased asset and the lease liability, whereas operating lease accounting does not. However, there is also an income statement difference. Notice that the total expense United recorded for an operating lease was the lease payment in the amount of $2,829,228.02. However, under capital lease accounting United recorded interest expense in the first year of $2,173,661.76 plus depreciation expense of $1,500,000 for a total first-year expense associated with the lease of $3,673,661.76. Here is a schedule comparing the total expense under both methods over the whole 20-year lease term. Notice that the total expense at the end of 20 years is exactly the same under both methods. The difference is that the operating lease method reports a constant rent expense amount over the term of the lease, whereas the capital lease method reports more expense in the early years of the lease term and less expense in the later years.[5]

COMPARISON OF EXPENSE—OPERATING VERSUS CAPITAL LEASE

Year of Lease	Operating Lease Rent Expense	Capital Lease		
		Interest Expense	Depreciation Expense	Total Expense
1	$ 2,829,228.02	$ 2,173,661.76	$ 1,500,000.00	$ 3,673,661.76
2	2,829,228.02	2,121,216.46	1,500,000.00	3,621,216.46
3	2,829,228.02	2,064,575.53	1,500,000.00	3,564,575.53
4	2,829,228.02	2,003,403.33	1,500,000.00	3,503,403.33
5	2,829,228.02	1,937,337.36	1,500,000.00	3,437,337.36
6	2,829,228.02	1,865,986.10	1,500,000.00	3,365,986.10
7	2,829,228.02	1,788,926.75	1,500,000.00	3,288,926.75
8	2,829,228.02	1,705,702.65	1,500,000.00	3,205,702.65
9	2,829,228.02	1,615,820.62	1,500,000.00	3,115,820.62
10	2,829,228.02	1,518,748.03	1,500,000.00	3,018,748.03
11	2,829,228.02	1,413,909.63	1,500,000.00	2,913,909.63
12	2,829,228.02	1,300,684.15	1,500,000.00	2,800,684.15
13	2,829,228.02	1,178,400.65	1,500,000.00	2,678,400.65
14	2,829,228.02	1,046,334.46	1,500,000.00	2,546,334.46
15	2,829,228.02	903,702.97	1,500,000.00	2,403,702.97
16	2,829,228.02	749,660.97	1,500,000.00	2,249,660.97
17	2,829,228.02	583,295.60	1,500,000.00	2,083,295.60
18	2,829,228.02	403,621.01	1,500,000.00	1,903,621.01
19	2,829,228.02	209,572.45	1,500,000.00	1,709,572.45
20	2,829,228.02	—	1,500,000.00	1,500,000.00
Total	$56,584,560.46	$26,584,560.46	$30,000,000.00	$56,584,560.46

ACCOUNTING BY LESSORS

This section explains in more detail the accounting treatment of leases by lessors, beginning with the treatment of operating leases.

Operating Leases

Under an operating lease, the lessor records rent income as the asset is used. For example, if Boeing leases a new aircraft to United for $2,829,228.02 per year and the lease is considered an operating lease, Boeing will record the receipt of the lease payment with the following entry:

Journal Entry to Record Receipt of Rent Payment for Operating Lease			
+/−	Accounts [description of account]	Debit	Credit
+	Cash [balance sheet asset account]	2,829,228	
+	Unearned Rent [balance sheet liability account]		2,829,228

[5] The difference for income tax purposes between the two methods would be even greater since accelerated MACRS tax depreciation (rather than straight-line) would result in more tax depreciation expense in the early years of the lease.

As the leased asset is used, Boeing will record rent income of $2,829,228.02 each year using the following entry:

+/−	Journal Entry to Record Rent Revenue for Operating Lease		
	Accounts [description of account]	Debit	Credit
−	Unearned Rent [balance sheet liability account]	2,829,228	
+	Rent Revenue [income statement revenue account]		2,829,228

In addition, since the lessor is the owner of the leased asset, it must record depreciation each year on the leased asset.

Capital Leases

The accounting rules for lessors distinguish between two types of capital leases: sales-type leases and direct-financing leases. The difference between the two has to do with whether the lessor earns a profit because the value of the leased asset is greater than the lessor's cost of the asset. If the value of the asset is greater than the lessor's cost, the lease is a sales-type lease. Otherwise the lease is a direct-financing lease.

In an earlier example it was assumed that Boeing sold a new aircraft to United and took back a $30 million note receivable. It was also assumed that the cost of the aircraft to Boeing was $20 million. Here is the journal entry used to illustrate the sale. Notice that Boeing records a gross profit on this transaction of $10 million, equal to the $30 million selling price less the $20 million cost of goods sold. In addition to this profit, Boeing will also recognize interest revenue as the note is collected.

+/−	Journal Entry to Record Sales Revenue (in millions)		
	Accounts [description of account]	Debit	Credit
+	Notes Receivable [balance sheet asset account]	30	
+	Cost of Goods Sold [income statement expense account]	20	
+	Sales Revenue [income statement revenue account]		30
−	Inventory [balance sheet asset account]		20

If instead of selling the aircraft Boeing leases it to United under a capital lease, the transaction would be treated as a sale by Boeing for financial accounting purposes. Boeing would therefore recognize the same $10 million of gross profit on the transfer of the aircraft as it would if the aircraft was actually sold. Therefore, this lease is a sales-type lease for Boeing. Usually, sales-type leases arise when manufacturers or dealers lease products to customers as a way of financing a purchase of an item from inventory.

Contrast this with a situation in which GE Capital purchases a new aircraft from Boeing for $30 million and immediately leases it to United. In this case, GE Capital has no profit from the transfer of the aircraft because the value of the aircraft is equal to GE Capital's cost. The only profit GE Capital receives from this lease is the interest element related to the lease receivable, just as it would if it had loaned the $30 million to United. Therefore, this lease is a direct-financing lease for GE Capital. Usually, direct-financing leases arise when banks or other financial institutions acquire an asset that is then leased to a lessee.

The lessor in a capital lease will record a lease receivable, just as the lessee recorded a lease liability. The lease receivable is equal to (1) the total of the minimum lease payments due under the lease and (2) the expected residual value of the property at the end of the lease. (The lease examples to this point have assumed a zero residual value.) In the example used above (leasing an aircraft to United for 20 years at an annual lease payment of $2,829,228.02), the gross lease receivable would be equal to 20 × $2,829,228.02 = $56,584,560.40.

Although this lease receivable represents the future lease payments that the lessor will receive, a portion of these future payments represents future interest income to the lessor, and this interest has not been earned at the beginning of the lease. Therefore, the portion of the lease receivable representing unearned interest revenue must also be recorded. The unearned interest revenue is the difference between (1) the gross lease receivable and (2) the fair market value of the leased asset. In the United aircraft lease example, this is equal to the difference between $56,584,560.40 and $30,000,000.00, or $26,584,560.40. The net lease receivable is the difference between the gross lease receivable and the unearned interest.

The entry to record the lease depends on whether it is a sales-type lease or a direct-financing lease. Since the direct-financing lease is easier, it is presented first. Assume that GE Capital purchases a new aircraft from Boeing for $30 million and leases it to United for 20 years at an annual lease payment of $2,829,228.02. (Continue the assumption that the residual value of the aircraft at the end of the lease will be zero.)

Here is the entry that GE Capital makes to record the lease:

	Journal Entry to Record Direct-Financing Lease		
+/−	Accounts [description of account]	Debit	Credit
+	Gross Lease Receivable [balance sheet asset account]	56,584,560	
−	Property and Equipment [balance sheet asset account]		30,000,000
+	Unearned Interest [balance sheet contra-asset account]		26,584,560

At the beginning of the lease, GE Capital receives the first lease payment. Here is the journal entry to record the payment:

	Journal Entry to Record First Lease Payment		
+/−	Accounts [description of account]	Debit	Credit
+	Cash [balance sheet asset account]	2,829,228	
−	Gross Lease Receivable [balance sheet asset account]		2,829,228

At the end of the first year, GE Capital has earned one year's worth of interest revenue on the lease receivable. The amount of interest revenue is determined using the effective interest rate method. The interest rate used to value the lease was 8 percent. The balance of the lease receivable at the beginning of the year was the initial balance $56,584,560.46 minus the unearned interest revenue of $26,584,560.46 and minus the first lease payment of $2,829,228.02 for a net balance of $27,170,771.98. The interest revenue for the first year is therefore 8% × $27,170,771.98 = $2,173,661.76. (Note that this is the same amount of interest expense recognized by United as the lessee in the first year of the lease.)

	Journal Entry to Record Interest Revenue from Capital Lease		
+/−	Accounts [description of account]	Debit	Credit
−	Unearned Interest [balance sheet contra-asset account]	2,173,662	
+	Interest Revenue [income statement revenue account]		2,173,662

Here is the entry to record the receipt of the second lease payment by GE Capital:

	Journal Entry to Record Second Lease Payment		
+/−	Accounts [description of account]	Debit	Credit
+	Cash [balance sheet asset account]	2,829,228	
−	Gross Lease Receivable [balance sheet asset account]		2,829,228

Similar entries are made each year to record the receipt of the lease payments and to record interest revenue and reduce the balance in the lease receivable and the unearned interest accounts.

To illustrate accounting for a sales-type lease, assume the same lease was entered into between Boeing (the manufacturer of the leased aircraft) and United. Here is the entry to record the lease on the accounting records of Boeing:

	Journal Entry to Record Sales-Type Lease		
+/−	Accounts [description of account]	Debit	Credit
+	Gross Lease Receivable [balance sheet asset account]	56,584,560	
+	Cost of Goods Sold [income statement expense account]	20,000,000	
+	Sales Revenue [income statement revenue account]		30,000,000
+	Unearned Interest [balance sheet contra-asset account]		26,584,560
−	Inventory [balance sheet asset account]		20,000,000

The rest of the entries would be the same as the direct-financing lease already illustrated.

RESIDUAL VALUE

Up to this point, it has been assumed that the residual value of the leased asset is zero. Residual value is the amount that the lessor expects the leased asset to be worth at the end of the lease. For lease accounting purposes, there are two types of residual value: guaranteed residual value and unguaranteed residual value. *Guaranteed residual value* is the amount that the lessee (or a third party) agrees the asset will be worth at the end of the lease. If the asset is worth less than this amount, the lessee (or a third party) must pay the lessor the difference between the guaranteed residual value and the actual value of the asset at the end of the lease. The *unguaranteed residual value* is the total residual value less any guaranteed residual value. Any guaranteed residual is included in the minimum lease payments for purposes of recording the lease liability of the lessee. The gross lease receivable recorded by the lessor includes the minimum lease payments as well as any unguaranteed residual value.

In accounting for a sales-type lease, the sales price recorded by the lessor is equal to the present value of the minimum lease payments. This means that the sales price *does not* include any unguaranteed residual value. The reason for this rule is that the unguaranteed residual value is an estimate by management of the future value of an asset, and as such is not a reliable measure for recording sales revenue. However, the cost of goods sold is *reduced* by the present value of the unguaranteed residual value. Reducing the cost of goods sold has the same effect on net income as increasing sales revenue. Therefore, although the unguaranteed residual value does not increase sales revenue, it does increase gross profit and net income.

For example, assume that Boeing leases a new 777 aircraft to United for 20 years, but that Boeing estimates the used aircraft will be worth $5,000,000 at the end of 20 years. This $5,000,000 is the residual value of the asset. If United (or a third party) does not guarantee that the aircraft will be worth $5,000,000 in 20 years, the residual is unguaranteed and is therefore not included as part of the minimum lease payments. However, the unguaranteed residual value is included as part of the gross lease receivable.

The $5,000,000 residual value of the aircraft is included by Boeing in the gross lease receivable. Therefore, the gross lease receivable is equal to $56,584,560.46 + $5,000,000 = $61,584,560.46. The unearned interest revenue is the difference between the gross lease receivable and the fair market value of the leased asset. In this example, the fair market value of the leased asset is no longer $30,000,000, because, in addition to the lease payments, Boeing also expects to receive the $5,000,000 residual value at the end of the lease. Therefore, the fair market value of the asset is $30,000,000 plus the present value of the $5,000,000 at the end of 20 years.

The present value of $1 at the end of 20 years is $1/(1.08)^{20} = 0.214548207$, so the present value of $5,000,000 is $1,072,741.04. This means that the market value of the leased asset is $31,072,741.04. The unearned interest revenue is therefore $61,584,560.46 − $31,072,741.04 = $30,511,819.42. Notice that this interest revenue that Boeing will recognize over the term of the lease is different from the amount of interest expense that United will recognize over the term of the lease. This occurs in the case of an unguaranteed residual value in a sales-type lease. In effect, Boeing is earning interest on the $5,000,000 residual value over the 20-year term of the lease.

Here is the lease amortization table for the lease in this example:

EXAMPLE OF LEASE LIABILITY AMORTIZATION: $5 MILLION RESIDUAL				
Years in Future	Amount of Payment	Interest at 8%	Reduction in Liability	Liability Balance
				$31,072,741.04
0	$ 2,829,228.02	$ 0.00	$ 2,829,228.02	28,243,513.01
1	2,829,228.02	2,259,481.04	569,746.98	27,673,766.03
2	2,829,228.02	2,213,901.28	615,326.74	27,058,439.29
3	2,829,228.02	2,164,675.14	664,552.88	26,393,886.41
4	2,829,228.02	2,111,510.91	717,717.11	25,676,169.30
5	2,829,228.02	2,054,093.54	775,134.48	24,901,034.82
6	2,829,228.02	1,992,082.79	837,145.24	24,063,889.59
7	2,829,228.02	1,925,111.17	904,116.86	23,159,772.73
8	2,829,228.02	1,852,781.82	976,446.20	22,183,326.53
9	2,829,228.02	1,774,666.12	1,054,561.90	21,128,764.63
10	2,829,228.02	1,690,301.17	1,138,926.85	19,989,837.77
11	2,829,228.02	1,599,187.02	1,230,041.00	18,759,796.77
12	2,829,228.02	1,500,783.74	1,328,444.28	17,431,352.49
13	2,829,228.02	1,394,508.20	1,434,719.82	15,996,632.67
14	2,829,228.02	1,279,730.61	1,549,497.41	14,447,135.26
15	2,829,228.02	1,155,770.82	1,673,457.20	12,773,678.06
16	2,829,228.02	1,021,894.24	1,807,333.78	10,966,344.28
17	2,829,228.02	877,307.54	1,951,920.48	9,014,423.80
18	2,829,228.02	721,153.90	2,108,074.12	6,906,349.68
19	2,829,228.02	552,507.97	2,276,720.05	4,629,629.63
20	5,000,000.00	370,370.37	4,629,629.63	0.00
Total	$61,584,560.46	$30,511,819.42	$31,072,741.04	

Here is the journal entry that Boeing would make to record this lease. Remember, under GAAP the sales price cannot be increased for the unguaranteed residual value. Instead, the cost of goods sold is reduced by the present value of the unguaranteed residual value. This makes the cost of goods sold equal to

$20,000,000 - $1,072,741.04 = $18,927,258.96. Therefore, the gross profit on the sale is $30,000,000 - $18,927,258.96 = $11,072,741.04. (Note that this is the same gross profit that would result if the unguaranteed residual value was included in the sales price, but the cost of goods sold remained at $20,000,000.)

+/−	Journal Entry to Record Sales-Type Lease with Unguaranteed Residual		
	Accounts [description of account]	Debit	Credit
+	Gross Lease Receivable [balance sheet asset account]	61,584,560	
+	Cost of Goods Sold [income statement expense account]	18,927,259	
+	Sales Revenue [income statement revenue account]		30,000,000
+	Unearned Interest [balance sheet contra-asset account]		30,511,819
−	Inventory [balance sheet asset account]		20,000,000

SALE-LEASEBACK

In this chapter you have seen that a corporation can acquire the use of an asset by either purchase or lease. It is also possible for the corporation to change from one form to the other while continuing to use the asset. For example, a corporation that is leasing an asset might decide to stop leasing and purchase the asset instead. Similarly, a corporation that owns an asset might decide to sell the asset and instead lease a similar asset. Owning an asset financed by debt, or leasing an asset, are different ways of financing the asset's use.

When the legal owner of an asset sells the asset and then leases the same asset back from the purchaser, this is known as a *sale-leaseback*. For example, a corporation that owns the office building that houses the corporation's headquarters might sell the building and then lease the same building back from the purchaser. There are several reasons for a corporation to engage in a sale-leaseback. First, it is a way for the corporation to obtain immediate cash from the sale, as an alternative to borrowing. Second, the corporation might decide that it wants to transfer the burdens and benefits of ownership to a lessor that might be better able to manage them. Third, as was discussed earlier, the tax benefits of owning and leasing are quite different, and a corporation that owns an asset might find that the tax benefits would be worth more if they could be sold to a lessor.

The financial accounting issue related to sale-leasebacks has to do with the recognition of gain or loss on the sale. To the extent the sales price of the asset is higher or lower than the net book value, a gain or loss will result. For example, assume United owns an office building with a net book value of $5,000,000 and a market value of $8,000,000. Selling the building for $8,000,000 and leasing it back results in a gain of $3,000,000. Should United be allowed to increase its earnings by this gain?

The answer is no. Accounting standard setters were concerned that sale-leaseback transactions are a change in legal form but not in economic substance. In the example above, United continues to use the same asset after the sale as it used before the sale. And although United might have $8,000,000 of cash from the sale, it has also entered into a lease obligating it to make future lease payments with a present value $8,000,000. The transaction is essentially the same as if United had borrowed $8,000,000 through a mortgage on the building.

Under GAAP, any gain on a sale-leaseback is deferred and recognized in future years over the term of the lease. If the lease is a capital lease, the deferred gain will result in less depreciation expense as the capitalized asset is depreciated. If the lease is an operating lease, the deferred gain will reduce rent expense in future years. Following the conservatism principle, any loss on a sale-leaseback is recognized in the year of the sale.

DISCLOSURE REQUIREMENTS

Under GAAP, there are requirements to disclose information about leases and leased assets in the financial statements of both lessees and lessors. In most cases, these disclosures are made in the notes to the financial statements. A general description of the company's leasing arrangements is required for both capital and operating leases. Examples of items that should be disclosed are the details of any contingent rental agreements, the details of any subleases, and the existence and terms of any purchase options.

For operating leases, the future minimum rental payments required on all noncancelable leases must be disclosed. These future amounts must be disclosed in the aggregate and also by year for the five years subsequent to the balance sheet date. In addition, lessors must disclose the cost, book value, and accumulated depreciation of leased property.

For capital leases, the future minimum lease payments must be disclosed, in aggregate and also by year for the five years subsequent to the balance sheet date. Lessees must disclose the cost, book value, and accumulated depreciation of assets recorded under capital leases. Lessors must disclose the amount of unguaranteed residual values that are expected from capital leases, as well as the amount of unearned revenue related to the lease receivable.

Here is an example of the lessee's lease disclosure in the notes to the financial statements of UAL:

---

10. Lease Obligations

The Company leases aircraft, airport passenger terminal space, aircraft hangars and related maintenance facilities, cargo terminals, other airport facilities, real estate, office and computer equipment and vehicles.

Future minimum lease payments as of December 31, 1999, under capital leases (substantially all of which are for aircraft) and operating leases having initial or remaining noncancelable lease terms of more than one year are as follows (in millions):

	Operating Leases		Capital Leases
	Aircraft	**Nonaircraft**	**Leases**
Payable during			
2000	$ 912	$ 458	$ 350
2001	884	442	445
2002	871	401	385
2003	912	389	286
2004	946	376	296
After 2004	9,874	5,628	1,906
Total minimum lease payments	$14,399	$7,694	3,668
Imputed interest (at rates of 5.3% to 12.2%)			(1,141)
Present value of minimum lease payments			2,527
Current portion			(190)
Long-term obligations under capital leases			$ 2,337

As of December 31, 1999, United leased 317 aircraft, 76 of which were under capital leases. These leases have terms of 10 to 26 years, and expiration dates range from 2000 through 2020.

In connection with the financing of certain aircraft accounted for as capital leases, United had on deposit at December 31, 1999 an aggregate 39 billion yen ($379 million), 326 million German marks ($167 million), 64 million French francs ($10 million), 27 million Euro ($27 million) and $11 million in certain banks and had pledged an irrevocable security interest in such deposits to certain of the aircraft lessors. These deposits will be used to pay off an equivalent amount of recorded capital lease obligations.

Amounts charged to rent expense, net of minor amounts of sublease rentals, were $1.412 billion in 1999, $1.385 billion in 1998 and $1.416 billion in 1997. Included in 1999 rental expense was $11 million in contingent rentals, resulting from changes in interest rates for operating leases under which the rent payments are based on variable interest rates.

Source: UAL Corporation Form 10-K.

As an example of disclosure by a lessor, here is the lease information from the financial statement notes of International Shipholding Corporation:

Note G—Leases

In 1998, the Company entered into a direct-financing lease of a foreign flag PCTC expiring in 2018. In 1999, the Company entered into another direct-financing lease of a foreign flag PCTC expiring in 2019. The schedule of future minimum rentals to be received under these two direct-financing leases in effect at December 31, 2000, is as follows (all amounts in thousands):

	Receivables under Financing Leases
Year ended December 31	
2001	$ 17,192
2002	17,192
2003	17,142
2004	16,593
2005	16,548
Thereafter	195,496
Total minimum lease payments receivable	280,163
Estimated residual values of leased properties	4,103
Less unearned income	(172,539)
Total net investment in direct financing leases	111,727
Current portion	(3,621)
Long-term net investment in direct-financing leases at December 31, 2000	$108,106

Source: International Shipholding Corporation Form 10-K.

ACCOUNTING FOR LEASES IN OTHER COUNTRIES

Most other countries have leasing rules that are similar to those in the United States. As an example of lease accounting in another country, shown below is some information from the financial statements of KLM, a large Dutch airline with worldwide operations.

Like other airlines, KLM leases aircraft to use in their business. Shown below are the financial statement disclosures relating to the accounting methods used for aircraft. As you can see, the category "aircraft" also includes aircraft held under financial lease agreements, which would be similar to a capital lease under U.S. accounting rules. The note says these aircraft are carried at cost which, for a leased aircraft, is the net present value, discounted at the contract interest rate.

Aircraft are carried at cost (including purchase expenses, such as financing expenses up to the date the aircraft is taken into service) less depreciation or value in use if structurally lower. Aircraft held under financial lease agreements are also included under this heading following the same valuation policy.

Financial lease obligations are initially stated at net present value, discounted at the contracted interest rate. Loans to finance companies in this respect are set off against lease obligations, provided offsetting of receivables and debts is legally permitted or agreed upon.

Source: KLM annual report.

The following note shows KLM's tangible fixed assets, which under U.S. terminology would be referred to as property and equipment. Notice that aircraft under financial lease arrangements are not shown separately in this schedule, but the book value of these aircraft is disclosed at the bottom of the table.

2. Tangible Fixed Assets (continued)

	Aircraft, Spare Engines, and Spare Parts	Buildings and Land	Inventories, Machines, and Installations	Vehicles and Other Tangible Fixed Assets	Total
Purchase value as of March 31, 2000	6,597	788	615	136	8,136
Accumulated depreciation and diminution in value through 1999/2000	2,499	341	388	78	3,306
Book value as of March 31, 2000	4,098	447	227	58	4,830
Changes in book value					
Additions	720	18	70	23	831
Disposals	(121)	(3)	(8)	(4)	(136)
Depreciation and diminution in value	(330)	(28)	(59)	(12)	(429)
Exchange rate differences	42	1	—	—	43
Changes in the group of consolidated holdings	—	(55)	(20)	(8)	(83)
Other	(13)	—	(4)	(1)	(18)
Total changes	298	(67)	(21)	(2)	208
Purchase value as of March 31, 2001	7,032	738	623	126	8,519
Accumulated depreciation and diminution in value through 2000/2001	2,636	358	417	70	3,481
Book value as of March 31, 2001	4,396	380	206	56	5,038

This overview includes aircraft for which financial lease agreements have been concluded. Their book value amounts to EUR 2,850 million (last year EUR 2,765 million).

Source: KLM annual report.

The next note details KLM's long-term debt. Notice that a substantial portion of its long-term debt consists of financial lease commitments. These are the same as lease liabilities recorded for capital leases under U.S. GAAP.

8. Long-Term Debt

	March 31, 2001	March 31, 2000
Perpetual debt		
Subordinated perpetual loans	560	916
Other long-term debt		
Debenture loans	92	96
Bank loans	57	73
Financial lease commitments	2,977	2,460
Other loans	293	302
	3,419	2,931
of which maturing in 2001/2002 and 2000/2001, respectively	293	135
	3,126	2,796
	3,686	3,712

Source: KLM annual report.

The final note is information that KLM provided about the difference between its financial statements prepared under Dutch GAAP and the information that would be required under U.S. GAAP. There were no differences in net income between U.S. and Dutch GAAP having to do with lease accounting, which is an indication that the net income effect of lease accounting is similar under both types of GAAP. However, Dutch GAAP requires fewer disclosures about leases than U.S GAAP. To reconcile the two types of GAAP, KLM provided additional lease disclosure in the note on the next page. (The term *SFAS* stands for statement of financial accounting standards. SFAS 13 and SFAS 125 deal with lease accounting.)

The following are additional disclosures to comply with generally accepted accounting principles in the United States of America:

Accounting for Leases (SFAS 13 / SFAS 125)

As per March 31, 2001 and 2000 the Company had financial lease commitments for EUR 3,635 million and EUR 2,947 million, respectively. Financial lease commitments are stated at net present value.

The redemption of financial leases for each of the following fiscal years are (in millions):

2001	419
2002	152
2003	263
2004	140
2005	421
2006 and later	2,240

As of March 31, 2001 and 2000 the book value of assets (aircraft) for which financial lease commitments have been concluded amounted to EUR 2,850 million and EUR 2,765 million, respectively.

The majority of the Company's financial lease commitments had fixed interest rates which ranged from 4.5% to 11.4%. Variable rate commitments averaged, after taking interest rate contracts into account, 5.0% for fiscal 2001. The overall average interest percentage on financial lease commitments was 5.1%.

Source: KLM annual report.

LEASES AND THE CASH FLOWS STATEMENT

There are few cash flow effects of operating leases since cash flows for lease payments generally occur in the same period as the rental revenue or expense is recorded. To the extent there is an increase in prepaid rent or rent receivable, cash flows from operating activities will differ from net income. For lessors under operating leases, the depreciation on the leased assets will be a noncash expense that will reconcile net income to cash flows from operating activities. Also, to the extent that leased assets are acquired or sold by the lessor, cash flows from investing activities will be affected.

With respect to capital leases, the depreciation (or amortization) expense that the lessee records is a noncash expense that will reconcile net income with cash flows from operating activities. However, since assets under capital leases are (by definition) not acquired for cash there will not be an impact on cash flows from investing activities. Instead, cash flows from financing activities will be reduced by the principal payments made on the lease liability. Here is the cash flows from financing activities section of the cash flows statement for UAL showing the reduction in cash flows for the principal payments on the lease liability. In addition, UAL is required to make deposits with the lessor, and these are also shown as reductions in cash flows from financing activities.

Cash flows from financing activities			
Reacquisition of preferred stock	—	(3)	—
Repurchase of common stock	(261)	(459)	(250)
Proceeds from issuance of long-term debt	286	928	597
Repayment of long-term debt	(513)	(271)	(301)
Principal payments under capital leases	**(248)**	**(322)**	**(147)**
Purchase of equipment certificates under Company operating leases	(47)	(693)	—
Increase (decrease) in short-term borrowings	(123)	184	—
Aircraft lease deposits	**(20)**	**(154)**	**(112)**
Cash dividends	(10)	(10)	(10)
Other, net	59	19	23
	(877)	(781)	(200)

Source: UAL Form 10-K.

With respect to a lessor, cash flows from investing activities will be decreased by investments in direct financing leases and increased by principal payments received on lease receivables.

LEASES AND INCOME TAX EXPENSE

Provided leases are treated in the same manner for both tax and financial reporting, there are few book-tax differences related to leasing. For example, a lease that is an operating lease for tax purposes will generally recognize rental expense or rental revenue in the same period as the financial statements. An exception is rental revenue received in advance, which is included in taxable income when received but is treated as unearned revenue (a liability) on the financial statements.

Similarly, a capital lease for tax purposes will be treated in much the same manner as a capital lease for financial reporting purposes. The major book-tax difference related to capital leases is the use of tax depreciation rather than financial statement depreciation. Also, leased assets acquired in a business acquisition may have a tax basis that differs from their book value and so require the recording of a deferred tax asset or liability at the time of the acquisition.

Major book-tax differences can arise, however, in cases where leases are classified differently for book and tax purposes. For example, leases may be operating leases on the financial statements but capital leases for tax purposes, or vice versa. This can occur because the tax rules for classifying leases are similar to but not exactly the same as the financial accounting rules. This results in, or allows, leases that meet one set of rules but not the other. In many cases, this is done deliberately to achieve the tax benefits of asset ownership that come with a capital lease (accelerated depreciation and interest deductions) while avoiding recording a balance sheet lease liability. Leases that are capital leases for tax purposes but operating leases for financial reporting purposes are sometimes called *synthetic leases*.

USING INFORMATION ABOUT LEASES TO MAKE DECISIONS

There are two main areas in which information about leases is useful in making decisions. First, information about leases makes it easier to determine the income statement and cash flows effects of leased assets. This aids in forecasting earnings and cash flows for a single company and also makes it easier to compare companies with similar operations but different ways of financing asset acquisitions (purchases, capital leases, or operating leases).

Using information about the future minimum lease payments under operating leases allows the user to estimate the present value of the future minimum lease payments. An estimate of the depreciation and interest expense that would result if the leases were treated as capital leases can then be made.

The second way lease information is useful is in determining the amount of liabilities a company has for purposes of risk analysis. For example, a company with a substantial amount of noncancelable operating leases with large future minimum lease payments due under the leases may in fact have just as large a liability as another company that has financed its operations using conventional debt, but the operating leases will not appear on the balance sheet of the lessee. Therefore, in analyzing leverage and making other decisions based on the amount of liabilities a company has, information about future minimum lease payments may be used to increase the reported balance sheet liabilities.

Summary

This chapter covers GAAP rules for recording leases. All leases are classified as either operating leases or capital leases. Operating leases result in rental expense for lessees and rental revenue for lessors.

A capital lease is economically similar to a purchase of the leased asset using debt. Under capital lease accounting, the leased asset is recorded as an asset on the balance sheet of the lessee at an amount equal to the present value of the future lease payments. A lease liability in the same amount is also recorded. The lessee records depreciation expense on the leased asset and interest expense on the lease liability.

From the lessor's standpoint, a capital lease is either a sales-type lease or a direct-financing lease. A sales-type lease is treated as if the lessor had sold the leased asset to the lessee and taken back a note receivable for the total of the future lease payments. The lessor recognizes gross profit on the difference between the fair market value of the leased asset and its cost to the lessor. In addition, the lessor recognizes interest revenue over the term of the lease.

The lessor in a direct-financing lease is treated as a lender, recording a lease receivable equal to the future lease payments due under the lease. The lessor recognizes interest revenue over the term of the lease.

Most other countries have GAAP rules requiring capital lease treatment for leases that are essentially purchases of assets. However, the disclosures required under U.S. GAAP are usually more extensive than those in other countries.

Lease information can be used to estimate lease liabilities, depreciation, and interest expense for lessees reporting operating leases. Also, the present value of future required lease payments can be added to measures of balance sheet leverage for purposes of risk analysis.

Discussion Questions

1. Explain the four lease capitalization criteria applicable to lessees.
2. For each of the four lease capitalization criteria, explain why accounting standard setters think that meeting the criteria should result in capitalization.
3. Why don't we simply capitalize all leases? Explain the costs and benefits of such a policy.
4. Why do we capitalize any leases? Explain the costs and benefits of capitalization.
5. Explain the two additional lease capitalization criteria applicable to lessors.
6. For each of the two additional lease capitalization criteria applicable to lessors, explain why accounting standard setters think that failing to meet the criteria should prevent capitalization.
7. Explain what accounts are affected if a lease is capitalized. Answer separately for the lessee and the lessor.
8. Applying GAAP lease capitalization criteria can sometimes result in inconsistent treatment between lessors and lessees. For example, a lease might be capitalized on the lessee's books but not be capitalized on the lessor's books. Do you think this is a problem? Why or why not?
9. Explain why future lease payments required under an operating lease are not considered an accounting liability. Do you agree with this treatment? Why or why not?

Problems

1. A lease requires annual payments at the beginning of each year for 10 years. The interest rate used in the lease is 8 percent, and the value of the asset being leased (equal to the present value of the lease payments) is $90,000. Compute the amount of the lease payment.

2. A lease requires annual payments at the beginning of each year for eight years. The interest rate used in the lease is 12 percent, and the value of the asset being leased (equal to the present value of the lease payments) is $75,000. Compute the amount of the lease payment.

3. A lease requires annual payments at the beginning of each year for 15 years. The interest rate used in the lease is 11 percent, and the value of the asset being leased (equal to the present value of the lease payments) is $120,000. Compute the amount of the lease payment.

4. A lease requires annual payments at the beginning of each year for nine years. The interest rate used in the lease is 7 percent, and the amount of each lease payment is $9,323.94. Compute the present value of the lease payments.

5. A lease requires annual payments at the beginning of each year for 12 years. The interest rate used in the lease is 9 percent, and the amount of each lease payment is $10,249.59. Compute the present value of the lease payments.

6. A lease requires annual payments at the beginning of each year for 14 years. The interest rate used in the lease is 8.5 percent, and the amount of each lease payment is $12,656.84. Compute the present value of the lease payments.

7. A lease requires annual payments at the beginning of each year for six years. The value of the asset being leased (equal to the present value of the lease payments) is $95,000, and the amount of each lease payment is $20,130.28. Compute the interest rate used in the lease.

8. A lease requires annual payments at the beginning of each year for seven years. The value of the asset being leased (equal to the present value of the lease payments) is $75,000, and the amount of each lease payment is $12,015.12. Compute the interest rate used in the lease.

9. A lease requires annual payments at the beginning of each year for 13 years. The value of the asset being leased (equal to the present value of the lease payments) is $150,000, and the amount of each lease payment is $16,377.82. Compute the interest rate used in the lease.

10. Using a computer spreadsheet, prepare an amortization schedule for the lease described in problem 1 above.

11. Using a computer spreadsheet, prepare an amortization schedule for the lease described in problem 2 above.

12. Using a computer spreadsheet, prepare an amortization schedule for the lease described in problem 3 above.

13. Using the lease described in problem 4 above, show the journal entries necessary to record the lease on the books of the lessee for the first two years of the lease. Assume that the lessee uses straight-line depreciation and that the asset will be worthless at the end of the lease. Show the entries assuming that the lease is (a) a capital lease and (b) an operating lease. (Remember to record interest expense using the accrual method.)

14. Using the lease described in problem 5 above, show the journal entries necessary to record the lease on the books of the lessee for the first two years of the lease. Assume that the lessee uses straight-line depreciation and that the asset will be worthless at the end of the lease. Show the entries assuming that the lease is (a) a capital lease and (b) an operating lease. (Remember to record interest expense using the accrual method.)

15. Using the lease described in problem 6 above, show the journal entries necessary to record the lease on the books of the lessee for the first two years of the lease. Assume that the lessee uses straight-line depreciation and that the asset will be worthless at the end of the lease. Show the entries assuming that the lease is (a) a capital lease and (b) an operating lease. (Remember to record interest expense using the accrual method.)

16. Using the lease described in problem 7 above, show the journal entries necessary to record the lease on the books of the lessor for the first two years of the lease. Assume that the lessor produced the asset at a cost equal to 50 percent of the asset's value. Further assume that the lessor uses straight line depreciation and that the asset will be worthless at the end of the lease. Show the entries assuming that the lease is (a) a capital lease and (b) an operating lease. (Remember to record interest income using the accrual method.)

17. Using the lease described in problem 8 above, show the journal entries necessary to record the lease on the books of the lessor for the first two years of the lease. Assume that the lessor produced the asset at a cost equal to 50 percent of the asset's value. Further assume that the lessor uses straight line depreciation and that the asset will be worthless at the end of the lease. Show the entries assuming that the lease is (a) a capital lease and (b) an operating lease. (Remember to record interest income using the accrual method.)

18. Using the lease described in problem 9 above, show the journal entries necessary to record the lease on the books of the lessor for the first two years of the lease. Assume that the lessor produced the asset at a cost equal to 50 percent of the asset's value. Further assume that the lessor uses straight line depreciation and that the asset will be worthless at the end of the lease. Show the entries assuming that the lease is (a) a capital lease and (b) an operating lease. (Remember to record interest income using the accrual method.)

19. Using a computer spreadsheet, complete the following steps:

   a. Compute the total expense for a lessee (interest plus depreciation) each year associated with the lease described in problem 1, assuming the lease is a capital lease. (Assume straight-line depreciation over the term of the lease with no salvage value. Also, remember to record interest expense using the accrual method.)

   b. Assume that the lessee has a 35 percent corporate income tax rate. Compute the tax savings each year due to the expense from step a.

   c. Compute the present value of the annual tax savings from step b. (Use the same interest rate as that used in the lease.)

   d. Repeat steps a through c assuming the lease is an operating lease.

   e. If a manager's goal was to minimize tax payments, which type of lease would be preferred?

20. Using a computer spreadsheet, complete the following steps:

   a. Compute the total expense for a lessee (interest plus depreciation) each year associated with the lease described in problem 3, assuming the lease is a capital lease. (Assume straight-line depreciation over the term of the lease with no salvage value. Also, remember to record interest expense using the accrual method.)

   b. Assume that the managers of the lessee receive a bonus each year equal to 10 percent of the lessee's pretax income. Compute the reduction in the managers' bonus each year due to the expense from step a.

   c. Compute the present value of the annual bonus reductions from step b. (Use the same interest rate as that used in the lease.)

   d. Repeat steps a through c assuming the lease is an operating lease.

   e. If a manager's goal was to maximize manager bonuses, which type of lease would be preferred?

21. Assume a corporation with $100,000 of cash flows from operating activities each year is considering entering into the lease described in problem 2 (as a lessee).

a. Compute the corporation's cash flows from operating activities each year assuming that it enters into the lease and the lease is a capital lease. (Assume no change in income tax expense.)

b. Compute the corporation's cash flows from operating activities each year assuming that it enters into the lease and the lease is an operating lease. (Assume no change in income tax expense.)

c. If the cash flows numbers in a and b are different, explain why. In other words, how can different accounting methods result in differences in cash flows?

Research Reports

1. Using the SEC's EDGAR database, obtain the financial statements for a corporation that discloses future lease obligations (as a lessee) under operating leases in the financial statement notes. Choose a company that reports future lease obligations that extend more than five years into the future.

   a. Compute the ratio of total liabilities to total shareholders' equity for the most recent year.

   b. Compute an average interest rate for the corporation. This can be computed by dividing the total interest expense for the year by the average balance of interest-bearing debt on the balance sheet. (Interest-bearing debt would exclude such liabilities as accounts payable and deferred income taxes.)

   c. Estimate how long the obligation for future operating lease payments will last beyond year 5. To do this, divide the future lease payments due beyond year 5 by the future lease payments due in year 5. For example, if the company reports future lease payments due in year 5 equal to 10 million, and future lease payments due beyond year 5 equal to 32 million, the lease payments would be expected to continue for 3.2 years beyond year 5 (that is, 32/10 = 3.2).

   d. Use the information about future lease payments from the financial statement notes and from step c to compute the present value of the future lease payments under operating leases. Assume that all lease payments are made on the first day of the year. Use the average interest rate from step b in the computation.

   e. Adjust the balance sheet of the company by adding the present value of operating lease payments as an additional liability and also as an additional asset.

   f. Recompute the ratio of total liabilities to total shareholders' equity.

   g. Explain why the ratio changed. Discuss how this change might affect managers' preferences for capital leases relative to operating leases.

2. Locate articles in the financial press that deal with the leasing industry. From these articles identify the types of assets that are most likely to be leased. Also, identify the types of assets that are least likely to be leased. What are the major differences, if any, between these two groups of assets? Have the assets represented by these two groups changed over time? Comment on any trends that you identify in the leasing industry.

3. Using library research, explain what is meant by the term *synthetic lease*. How are synthetic leases used, and why are they popular? Explain the criticism of synthetic leases and some of the steps that have been proposed to limit their use. Evaluate these criticisms and the costs and benefits associated with their proposed restrictions. In your judgment, should synthetic leases be allowed?

4. Obtain a copy of *Statement of Financial Accounting Standards No. 13 Accounting for Leases*. Locate Appendix B "Basis for Conclusions," which contains a section titled "Criteria for Classification." In paragraphs 72 through 90, the

Financial Accounting Standards Board discusses many of the criteria for lease capitalization that were initially considered.

a. List each of the criteria that the board considered.

b. For each of the criteria, discuss the board's decision with respect to that particular item. Did the board finally adopt the item as one of the criteria for classification of a lease? If so, why? If not, why not?

5. In a direct-financing lease, the lessor buys an asset and leases it to a lessee. In these types of leases, the lessor will usually borrow the money that is used to purchase the leased asset.

a. Locate articles in the financial press that discuss ways that lessors use to finance the purchase of the leased assets. Explain the different financing options that are available.

b. Are there ways of financing leased assets that are different from other types of borrowing? If so, what are the unique characteristics of leased assets that lead to this type of financing?

6. Corporations often engage in a transaction called a *sale-leaseback*.

a. Explain how a sale-leaseback transaction works from the standpoint of the company making the sale.

b. Find an example in the financial press of a sale-leaseback. Explain the reasons for the transaction. Also, explain the accounting treatment that was used in this transaction.

c. What alternative transaction might a company use if it wanted to avoid a sale-leaseback? Would the accounting treatment for this alternative transaction differ from that used in the transaction in part b?

Sabina Dowell

Chapter Learning Objectives

After reading this chapter you should understand

1. The nature of a financial instrument.
2. The preferred accounting method for financial instruments.
3. The nature of a derivative.
4. The three characteristics for derivative classification in financial statements.
5. The nature of a hedge.
6. The financial reporting rules for derivatives *not* classified as hedges.
7. The three types of hedges recognized for financial reporting purposes.
8. The accounting treatment for fair value hedges.
9. The accounting treatment for cash flow hedges.

Chapter 13

Financial Instruments and Derivative Securities

Focus Company: The Procter & Gamble Company

Introduction

On April 12, 1994, Procter & Gamble (P & G), a large multinational manufacturer of consumer products, surprised investors with the following press release:

> The Procter & Gamble Company announced today that its third quarter earnings will be reduced by $102 million after tax due to a one-time charge to close-out two interest rate swap contracts. These transactions were negatively affected by the recent dramatic increase in interest rates.

Procter & Gamble's net income for that same quarter was $482 million, which means that the two interest rate swaps cost P&G an amount equal to 21 percent of quarterly net income. The management of P&G explained this loss in the same press release as follows:

> Procter & Gamble, like many large corporations, has successfully used interest rate swaps to manage exposure to interest and exchange rates, and reduce the cost of borrowing. Unlike the other swaps the company has historically used, it turned out that the two leveraged swaps in question were based on highly complex formulas that multiplied the effect of interest rate increases. These types of transactions are inconsistent with the company's policy.
>
> Derivatives like these are dangerous and we were badly burned. We won't let this happen again . . . . We have thoroughly reviewed the company's remaining swap contracts with an outside financial advisor. Based on this review, we are certain the remaining portfolio is consistent with the company's policy.

Interest rate swaps are examples of financial contracts known collectively as *derivatives*. The reason the $102 million loss came as a surprise was that, under the financial accounting rules in existence in 1994, the swaps did not appear on the financial statements of P&G. Therefore, it was difficult for users of P&G's financial statements to understand the potential loss that the company faced by investing in the swaps. In fact, according to the press release, it is not clear whether P&G's managers understood, or were even aware of, the potential loss that the swaps represented.

The problem of accounting for swaps and other derivatives led U.S. standard setters in 1998 to issue Statement of Financial Accounting Standards No. 133, "Accounting for Derivative Instruments and Hedging Activities." In this statement, the standard setters laid out a comprehensive, and quite complex, set of rules for accounting for derivative securities.

This chapter begins with an explanation of what a derivative financial instrument is and how and why derivatives are used. Since the concept of a hedge is important in accounting for derivatives, hedging is also discussed. Finally, the accounting rules for derivative financial instruments are outlined, with examples provided. Important questions related to derivative accounting are (1) Do derivatives constitute assets and liabilities? and (2) What is the most relevant valuation measure for a derivative?

FINANCIAL INSTRUMENTS

Since derivatives are a special type of financial instrument, it is useful to understand the general accounting rules applicable to financial instruments before proceeding to the more detailed rules applicable to derivatives. Financial instruments were introduced in Chapter 10 in connection with the discussion of intangible assets. Recall that financial instruments consist of either financial assets or financial liabilities. Financial assets are cash; ownership interests in another company, such as shares of stock; and contracts for the future receipt of cash, such as accounts receivable, notes receivable, and other types of debt securities. Financial liabilities are contracts for the future payment of cash, such as accounts payable, notes payable, bonds payable, and other types of debt securities.

The position of U.S. accounting standard setters is that fair value is the most relevant valuation method in accounting for financial instruments. Despite this preference for fair value as a valuation method, GAAP rules apply a combination of different valuation methods to financial instruments. The table that follows shows some common types of financial instruments and the valuation methods required under GAAP.

Type of Financial Instrument	GAAP Valuation Method
Cash	Fair value
Accounts receivable	Amount expected to be collected after recording an allowance for uncollectible accounts; since receivables are expected to be collected relatively quickly, this approximates fair value
Notes receivable	Original cost adjusted for amortization of discount or premium
Marketable equity securities	Fair value if available-for-sale or trading securities; equity method for investments representing more than 20 percent of the investee
Marketable debt securities	Fair value if available-for-sale or trading securities; amortized cost if held-to-maturity securities
Accounts payable	Expected payment amount; since payables are expected to be paid relatively quickly, this approximates fair value
Notes or bonds payable	Original amount borrowed adjusted for amortization of discount or premium

As you can see from this analysis, there are some types of financial instruments that are *not* valued at fair value under GAAP. For example, the fair value of a bond payable will not equal its book value if either market interest rates or the riskiness of the bond have changed since the bond was issued.

If GAAP rules require valuation methods that differ from fair value, even though fair value is the most relevant (or useful) valuation measure for financial instruments, users of financial statements are not being provided with the most relevant information for decision making. This failure to provide relevant information could be justified if the relevant information is not considered reliable. However, financial instruments represent contracts to receive cash or pay cash in the future. Therefore, the fair value of most financial instruments can be estimated by a present value computation.[1] Also, for companies with publicly traded bonds, the fair value of bonds payable is easily determined by reference to market prices.

Because fair value information is more relevant for decision making, and because estimating the fair value of financial instruments is considered reliable (because financial instruments represent future cash flows, making present value computations possible), GAAP rules require companies to *disclose*[2] in their

---

[1] More complex financial instruments require mathematical formulas to approximate their value. The Black-Scholes option pricing formula is an example.

[2] To *disclose* an item means to put the information in the notes to the financial statements. Putting the information in the financial statements themselves is referred to as *recording* or *recognizing*.

financial statements the fair value of all financial instruments. Here is the fair value disclosure of Procter & Gamble in the notes to its 2001 annual report. In this note, P&G refers to *risk management instruments,* which is another term for derivatives.

Fair Values of Financial Instruments

Fair values of cash equivalents, short and long-term investments and short-term debt approximate cost. The estimated fair values of other financial instruments, including debt, equity and risk management instruments, have been determined using available market information and valuation methodologies, primarily discounted cash flow analysis. These estimates require considerable judgment in interpreting market data, and changes in assumptions or estimation methods may significantly affect the fair value estimates.

The fair value of the long-term debt was $10,164 and $9,024 at June 30, 2001 and 2000, respectively.

Source: The Procter & Gamble Company annual report.

To provide a more comprehensive illustration of a company with an extensive disclosure of fair values of financial instruments, portions of the notes from General Electric's 2000 financial statements are presented below. The first item presented is a discussion by General Electric of how it computes fair values for financial instruments that are not, in general, publicly traded. As you can see from this note, estimating fair values is sometimes a complicated process despite the fact that present value techniques can be applied.

---

30. Additional Information about Financial Instruments

This note contains estimated fair values of certain financial instruments to which GE and GECS are parties. Apart from certain borrowings by GE and GECS and certain marketable securities, relatively few of these instruments are actively traded. Thus, fair values must often be determined by using one or more models that indicate value based on estimates of quantifiable characteristics as of a particular date. Because this undertaking is, by its nature, difficult and highly judgmental, for a limited number of instruments, alternative valuation techniques may have produced disclosed values different from those that could have been realized at December 31, 2000 or 1999. Assets and liabilities that, as a matter of accounting policy, are reflected in the accompanying financial statements at fair value are not included in the following disclosures; such items include cash and equivalents, investment securities and separate accounts.

A description of how values are estimated follows.

Borrowings. Based on quoted market prices or market comparables. Fair values of interest rate and currency swaps on borrowings are based on quoted market prices and include the effects of counterparty creditworthiness.

Time Sales and Loans. Based on quoted market prices, recent transactions and/or discounted future cash flows, using rates at which similar loans would have been made to similar borrowers.

Investment Contract Benefits. Based on expected future cash flows, discounted at currently offered discount rates for immediate annuity contracts or cash surrender values for single premium deferred annuities.

Financial Guarantees and Credit Life. Based on future cash flows, considering expected renewal premiums, claims, refunds and servicing costs, discounted at a market rate.

All Other Instruments. Based on comparable transactions, market comparables, discounted future cash flows, quoted market prices, and/or estimates of the cost to terminate or otherwise settle obligations to counterparties.

Source: General Electric Form 10-K.

The second example from General Electric's financial statement notes is a table that summarizes the fair values of all of the company's different financial instruments. In the following table, the term *carrying amount* refers to the balance sheet book value of the asset or liability. Notice that GE provides two measures of estimated fair value: a high measure and a low measure. In most cases, these two numbers are either the same or quite close in amount. The term *notional amount* in the table applies only to derivatives and will be explained in the discussion of derivatives that follows.

Financial Instruments
December 31, 2000 (in millions)

		Assets (Liabilities)		
		Carrying	Estimated Fair Value	
	Notional Amount	Amount (net)	High	Low
GE				
Investment related				
Investments and notes receivable	$ (a)	$ 2,012	$ 2,060	$ 2,026
Cancelable interest rate swap	1,046	6 4 4		
Borrowings and related instruments				
Borrowings (b) (c)	(a)	(1,781)	(1,781)	(1,781)
Interest rate swaps	786	—	(38)	(38)
Currency swaps	172	—	(4)	(4)
Recourse obligations for receivables sold . .	589	(42)	(42)	(42)
Financial guarantees	2,345	—	—	—
Other firm commitments				
Forwards and options	6,961	37	30	30
Financing commitments	1,492	—	—	—
GECS				
Assets				
Time sales and loans	(a)	92,912	93,539	92,360
Integrated swaps	22,911	(44)	(771)	(771)
Purchased options	9,832	105	164	164
Mortgage-related positions				
Mortgages acquired for resale	(a)	1,267	1,250	1,245
Options, including "floors"	21,984	202	208	208
Interest rate swaps and futures	2,798	29	38	38
Other financial instruments	(a)	10,940	11,130	11,102
Liabilities				
Borrowings and related instruments				
Borrowings (b) (c)	(a)	(205,371)	(207,670)	(207,670)
Interest rate swaps	52,681	—	(208)	(208)
Currency swaps	24,314	—	(957)	(957)
Currency forwards	27,902	—	381	381
Investment contract benefits	(a)	(27,575)	(26,144)	(26,144)
Insurance—financial guarantees				
and credit life	239,940	(2,759)	(2,797)	(2,910)
Credit and liquidity support—				
securitizations	37,667	(630)	(630)	(630)
Performance guarantees (d)	7,895	—	—	—
Other financial instruments	2,982	(1,184)	(1,114)	(1,114)
Other firm commitments				
Currency forwards	1,585	8	47	47
Currency swaps	647	292	275	275
Ordinary course of business				
lending commitments	9,450	—	—	—
Unused revolving credit lines				
Commercial	11,278	—	—	—
Consumer—principally credit cards . . .	188,421	—	—	—

a. Not applicable.
b. Includes effects of interest rate and currency swaps, which also are listed separately.
c. See note 19.
d. Includes letters of credit.

Source: General Electric Form 10-K.

DERIVATIVES

Derivatives are complex financial contracts whose value depends on (or is *derived* from—hence the name derivative) *changes* in the value of something called an *underlying*.[3] The underlying can be just about anything. For example, you could enter into a contract with someone that required you to pay the other party (called the *counterparty*) $1 for every degree that the average daily temperature in New York in the month of July exceeded 90 degrees. The underlying in this example is the average daily temperature in New York.[4]

A more realistic example, and one familiar to most students, is an option to purchase stock. Suppose you hold an option to purchase 100 shares of Procter & Gamble common stock. Assume that the exercise price of the option is equal to the current market price of the stock ($40 per share) and the option expires in 30 days.

The option is an example of a derivative. The underlying is the price of a share of Procter & Gamble common stock. If the price of the stock increases above the $40 exercise price, the contract increases in value. The value of the contract is based on the value of 100 shares of stock. In derivative terminology, the 100 shares is called the *notional amount*, the amount that is used to compute the value of the derivative. If the P&G stock price increases to $48 per share, the value of the option is equal to the change in the value of the underlying ($48 − $40 = $8) times the notional amount (100), or $800.

Statement 133 gives examples of common types of underlyings: interest rates, security prices, commodity prices, foreign exchange rates, and indexes of prices or rates. According to the Statement, an underlying may be a price or rate of an asset or liability but is not the asset or liability itself. The Statement also defines a notional amount as a number of currency units, shares, bushels, pounds, or other units. In some contracts, the notional amount is called the *face amount.*

Here are some examples of different types of derivatives, their underlyings, and their notional amounts:

Type of Contract	Underlying	Notional Amount
Option to buy stock	Price of stock	Number of shares of stock
Commodity futures contract	Price of a commodity	Quantity of the commodity
Interest rate swap	Interest rate	Principal amount of debt
Currency swap	Currency exchange rate	Amount of currency

How Derivatives Are Used

Since derivatives only derive their value from future *changes* in the value of the underlying, they initially have no value or a relatively small value. For this reason, the general GAAP accounting rules, based on original cost, failed to record derivatives as assets or liabilities.

You might wonder why anyone would ever enter into a derivative contract if they have no value. The reason is that derivatives allow firms to reduce the impact of future price changes. Here is how it works.

Assume you have a firm that uses copper as a raw material in manufacturing and that the price of copper is currently $1 per pound. One risk you face is the risk that the price of copper will increase in the future. You could reduce this risk by entering into a contract with someone who agrees to sell you copper in the

---

[3] The term *underlying* may seem strange at first. In English, *underlying* is usually used as an adjective. However, in connection with derivatives it is used as a noun.

[4] While this example may seem silly, Statement 133 specifically discusses contracts where the underlying on which the settlement of the contract is based is a climatic or geological variable.

future for $1 per pound. Why would someone agree to such a contract? The reason is that someone who owns a copper mine also faces a risk related to the future price of copper—the risk that the price will decrease. Therefore, the copper mine owner wants to find someone willing to enter into a contract to buy copper in the future for $1 per pound. You each enter into contracts (you to buy copper, the mine owner to sell copper) based on a future price of $1 per pound. The contracts make both you and the mine owner better off because you have both removed the risk of changes in the future price of copper.

Notice that neither of you is trying to profit from the future price movements of copper. If the price of copper drops in the future, you are better off because you can now get your raw materials cheaper. However, your gain from the decrease in the price of copper is offset by the loss you face on the copper futures contract—you have to buy copper for $1 per pound when the current market price is less. Similarly, if the price of copper increases, the mine owner has gained since his inventory is worth more, but this gain is offset by the loss the mine owner faces on the copper futures contract—the mine owner has to sell copper for $1 per pound when the current market price is higher. Entering into these contracts protects each of you from the effects of future price changes, both good and bad. Removing the risks of future price changes in this manner is called *hedging*, and the contracts are referred to as *hedges*.

Not all derivatives represent hedges. Someone might invest in a contract to buy copper for $1 per pound because he believes that the price of copper will increase in the future. If the investor is right, the value of the contract will increase, because the investor could buy copper for the contract price of $1 per pound and sell it at the higher current market price. However, if the price of copper decreases, there will be a loss on the contract. People who invest in derivative securities with the intention of profiting from future price changes of the underlying are referred to as *speculators*.

Definition of a Derivative

For purposes of Statement 133, a derivative is defined as a financial instrument or other contract with *all three* of the following characteristics:

1. It has one or more underlyings and one or more notional amounts.
2. It requires no initial net investment (or a relatively small initial net investment).
3. It requires or permits net settlement (or a settlement similar to a net settlement).

The first two requirements—that the contract have underlyings and notional amounts, and that there be no initial net investment—have already been discussed. The third requirement for a financial instrument to be treated as a derivative is that there must be the possibility of net settlement.

A financial instrument is considered to have the possibility of net settlement if it has *one* of the following three features:

1. Neither party is required to actually deliver an asset represented by the underlying to the other party.
2. One of the parties is required to deliver an asset represented by the underlying, but there exists a market mechanism that facilitates net settlement. For example, the manufacturer who entered into a contract to buy copper for $1 per pound could utilize the market for copper futures to later enter into a contract to sell copper for $1 per pound. The two contracts to buy and sell the same amount of copper at the same price would offset one another, and in effect cancel out. The manufacturer would not actually have to buy copper from anyone or sell copper to anyone.
3. One of the parties is required to deliver an asset represented by the underlying, but that asset is readily convertible into cash.

ACCOUNTING FOR DERIVATIVES

Under GAAP, all derivatives must be valued at fair value and recorded as assets or liabilities on the balance sheet. Except for derivatives designated as hedges (discussed below), the gains and losses associated with changes in the fair value of derivatives must be reported as part of net income each year. Under these rules, investors are provided with information about the values of derivatives and the gains and losses arising from changes in those values.

Hedge Accounting

As noted above, gains and losses associated with changes in the value of hedges are subject to special accounting rules. A hedge is a derivative whose value moves in the opposite direction from the item being hedged. In the example of the copper mine owner, the contract to sell copper in the future for $1 would increase in value if the price of copper declined, and it would decrease in value if the price of copper increased. In this way, any gain or loss from the copper futures contract would offset the change in the value of the mine owner's copper inventory.

Under Statement 133, there are three types of hedges that are recognized for financial reporting purposes. These are (1) a fair value hedge, (2) a cash flow hedge, and (3) a foreign currency hedge. If a hedge is designated by the company as one of these types of hedges, it is subject to special hedge accounting rules.

Fair Value Hedges

A fair value hedge is a hedge that has been designated by the company to protect against changes in the fair value of a specified asset or liability. For example, a cereal manufacturer with a large inventory of corn may want to hedge against the possibility of future changes in the fair value of its corn inventory due to changes in the market price of corn. Similarly, a company with bonds payable may wish to hedge against the possibility of future changes in the value of the bonds due to changes in market interest rates.[5]

Under GAAP, any gain or loss from the change in value of a fair value hedge is included in net income. However, any change in the value of the hedged asset or liability is also included in net income, in effect offsetting the gain or loss on the hedge. In the corn inventory example, if the price of corn increased, the value of the hedge instrument (a futures contract to sell corn at a specified price) will decrease. Both the loss from the decrease in the value of the hedge and the gain from the increase in the value of the inventory will be included in net income in the same year.

Notice that this accounting rule requires the hedged asset or liability to be recorded at fair value on the balance sheet. Normally, increasing the book value of inventory to reflect price changes, or changing the book value of bonds payable to reflect changes in market interest rates, is not allowed under GAAP. However, the standard accounting rules are overridden by this special hedge accounting rule in Statement 133.

Cash Flow Hedges

A cash flow hedge is a hedge that has been designated by the company to protect against the risk of future changes in expected cash flows. The future cash flows being hedged may be related to an existing asset or liability, or they may relate to a forecasted future transaction. For example, an airline may expect to purchase large quantities of aviation fuel over the next year and wants to hedge against

---

[5] Even though the accounting *book value* of a bond payable does not change due to a change in market interest rates, the *economic value* of the liability will change, and hence the market value of the company will change as well.

increases in the price. It could do so through a cash flow hedge by entering into a futures contract for the future purchase of aviation fuel at a fixed price.

Under GAAP, all gains and losses from changes in the value of cash flow hedges are recorded in the other comprehensive income section of shareholders' equity, a balance sheet account. These gains and losses are deferred until the accounting period in which the cash flows being hedged are reported. In that accounting period, the deferred gains and losses from the hedge are reversed out of other comprehensive income and reported as part of net income. In this way, the gains and losses from the hedge are matched against the decreases and increases in cash flows that were being hedged.

Using the airline example, assume that the price of aviation fuel increased during the year, so that the value of the hedge increased (that is, the owner of the contract could buy aviation fuel at the contract price and sell it at the higher market price). At year-end, the hedge is recorded at fair value and a gain is reported in Other Comprehensive Income. The next year the airline buys aviation fuel at the high market price and records this as an expense on the income statement. Under GAAP, the prior-year gain on the hedge contract is reversed out of Other Comprehensive Income and is recorded as part of net income, offsetting the higher fuel expense.

Foreign Currency Hedges

Foreign currency hedges are hedges designated by the company to protect against the risk of future changes in foreign currency exchange rates. Since the financial accounting rules related to foreign currency are typically covered in an advanced accounting course, the details of reporting foreign currency hedges are not discussed in this textbook.

Distinguishing between Types of Hedges

How can you distinguish between a fair value hedge and a cash flow hedge? The difference depends on the purpose for which the hedge was entered into, and this purpose must be documented by management when the hedge is established. It is possible that the same type of asset or liability could be subject to both kinds of hedges. For example, a bond payable with a fixed interest rate could be subject to a fair value hedge to protect against an increase in the value of the liability if interest rates decrease. A bond payable with a variable interest rate could be subject to a cash flow hedge to protect against an increase in future interest payments if interest rates increase. In both cases the hedge relates to an existing liability, but in one case the hedge protects against a change in value, and in the other it protects against future cash flow changes.

It is also possible for the same derivative to provide a fair value hedge in one situation and a cash flow hedge in another situation. For example, a firm holding an inventory of corn that wants to hedge against a possible decrease in the value of the inventory could acquire a futures contract to sell corn at a fixed price in the future. If the price of corn decreases, the value of the derivative will increase and offset the decrease in the value of the inventory. If the same firm planned on selling the inventory in the future and wanted to hedge against a decrease in the expected future selling price, the same type of futures contract could also be used for a cash flow hedge. The purpose of the hedge, documented at the time the hedge was entered into, will determine the proper accounting treatment.

Highly Effective Hedges

Only hedges that are expected to be *highly effective* qualify for the special hedge accounting rules. A highly effective hedge is one for which the change in value of the derivative is expected to offset the change in value of the underlying asset or liability being hedged. Statement 133 gives the following example of a hedge that is *not* highly effective. A company with natural gas stored in west Texas enters into a hedge by selling a futures contract for the sale of natural gas. The price of the natural gas specified in the futures contract is based on delivery at a terminal in Louisiana. Since the price of natural gas in Louisiana may not be the same as the price of natural gas in west Texas, the contract is *not* highly effective in hedging future price changes for the company's natural gas inventory.

Gains and losses from changes in the fair value of derivatives that are not highly effective do not qualify for hedge accounting treatment, and they must be recognized in income currently. If a derivative is highly effective, but is not perfectly effective, the ineffective portion will be recognized in income currently.

Disclosure of Information about Derivatives

Statement 133 has specific disclosure requirements for derivatives. Companies with derivatives must disclose the gains and losses associated with the derivatives. In addition, if the company holds derivatives that qualify for special hedge accounting treatment, it must disclose its objectives for holding or issuing the derivatives, the context needed to understand those objectives, and the strategies for achieving those objectives.

EXAMPLES

This section presents two examples of accounting for hedges, both of which come from Statement 133. The first example is a fair value hedge of fixed-rate interest-bearing debt using an interest rate swap. The second example is a cash flow hedge of a forecasted sale of wheat. Finally, an example from the actual financial statements of Procter & Gamble is shown.

Fair Value Hedge Example

Assume that on July 1, 2001, a company issues a $1,000,000 face amount three-year note payable with a fixed interest rate of 8 percent payable semiannually. The semiannual interest payments under the note (using a 4 percent semiannual rate) are $40,000. All of the principal is payable at the end of the three-year note term.

Managers are concerned about possible changes in interest rates over the three-year term of the note and the effect these changes will have on the fair value of the note. If interest rates should decrease, the company would find itself paying the higher fixed rate for the full three years and would suffer an economic loss since the fair value of the note payable would increase.

To hedge against this risk of a change in the value of the note payable, the company enters into what is called an *interest rate swap*.[6] An interest rate swap is a contract under which Company A pays a fixed interest rate to Company B, while Company B pays a variable interest rate to Company A. The interest rates are based on a specified notional (or face) amount of debt. The swap is a derivative with the underlying being the interest rate.

Since the example company is already paying a fixed interest rate on its debt and wants to hedge against changes in future interest rates, it will want to enter into what is called a *receive-fixed, pay-variable swap*. Under this type of a swap, the company will receive a fixed interest rate equal to the rate on the note payable and will pay a variable interest rate.[7] Using the swap will thus convert what was a fixed interest rate into a variable interest rate.

---

[6] The simple interest rate swap in this example is not the same as the leveraged swap that led to the loss of $102 million suffered by Procter & Gamble in 1994.

[7] You may wonder who the other party to the swap contract would be. Anyone with a variable-rate liability who wanted to eliminate the risk of having to pay larger interest payments if interest rates increased would want a swap that was a receive-variable, pay-fixed swap.

Assume that on July 1, 2001, the company enters into a receive-fixed, pay-variable swap with a notional amount of $1,000,000 and interest computed semi-annually. The fixed rate in the swap is an 8 percent annual rate, while the variable rate is the LIBOR rate (the London Interbank Offer Rate, an interest rate often used in swaps). Assume that the LIBOR rate on July 1, 2001, is also 8 percent. The swap has a three-year term to correspond with the term of the note payable. Thus, the swap is considered by managers to be highly effective in hedging the risk of changes in the value of the note payable.

Here is how the swap hedges the fair value of the note payable. If interest rates decrease in the future, the company will continue to receive the 8 percent fixed rate under the swap (offsetting the 8 percent fixed rate on the note payable). The company will pay the lower variable rate under the swap. The value of the note payable will increase, but the value of the swap (an asset) will also increase by the same amount. Therefore, there will be no change in the value of the company's net assets.

Similarly, if interest rates increase in the future, the company will continue to receive the 8 percent fixed rate but will now have to pay a higher variable rate. The value of the note payable will decrease, reducing the value of liabilities, but this decrease in the value of the note payable is exactly offset by a decrease in the value of the swap.

The following table summarizes the impact of interest rate changes on both the value of the liability and the value of the swap.

Future Change in Interest Rates	Effect on Value of Note Payable	Effect on Value of Swap
Increase	Decrease	Decrease
Decrease	Increase	Increase

Here is the journal entry to record the note payable. Since the swap has no value initially, there is no accounting entry to record the swap at the time it is entered into.

	Journal Entry to Record Note Payable		
+/−	**Accounts [description of account]**	**Debit**	**Credit**
+	Cash [balance sheet asset account]	1,000,000	
+	Note Payable [balance sheet liability account]		1,000,000

At the end of the first semiannual period, the company makes an interest payment equal to $40,000. Here is the entry to record the payment:

	Journal Entry to Record Interest Payment on Note Payable		
+/−	**Accounts [description of account]**	**Debit**	**Credit**
+	Interest Expense [income statement expense account]	40,000	
−	Cash [balance sheet asset account]		40,000

Assume that the LIBOR interest rate has increased from 8 percent to 9 percent over the six-month period. This means that the company will receive a fixed rate on the swap equal to $40,000 and will pay a variable rate on the swap equal to $45,000. However, since swaps are contracts that allow net settlement, the two parties to the contract do not actually make these payments. Rather, the party that owes the larger amount makes a payment of the net difference to the other party. This means that the example company will make a payment on the swap equal to $45,000 − $40,000 = $5,000. This has the effect of increasing the interest rate on the note from the 8 percent fixed rate to a 9 percent rate, at least for this semiannual period. Here is the entry to record the payment on the swap:

	Journal Entry to Record Net Payment on Swap		
+/−	Accounts [description of account]	Debit	Credit
+	Interest Expense [income statement expense account]	5,000	
−	Cash [balance sheet asset account]		5,000

On the company's December 31, 2001, financial statements, the swap has to be recorded as an asset or liability at its fair value. Since the variable rate that the company has to pay on the swap is more than the fixed rate received, the swap represents a liability. What is the value of the swap liability? As the following table shows, the present value of the remaining swap payments (discounted at a 4.5 percent semiannual interest rate) is $21,949.88.

	VALUE OF SWAP 4.50%		
	Swap Payment	Present Value Factor	Present Value
7/1/2002	$5,000	0.9569	$ 4,784.69
12/31/2002	5,000	0.9157	4,578.65
7/1/2003	5,000	0.8763	4,381.48
12/31/2003	5,000	0.8386	4,192.81
7/1/2004	5,000	0.8025	4,012.26
Value of swap			$21,949.88

Under Statement 133, the company must record this swap as a liability at fair value. The change in the value of the swap is a loss that is included in net income. Here is the journal entry to record the change in the value of the swap.

	Journal Entry to Record Change in Value of Swap		
+/−	Accounts [description of account]	Debit	Credit
+	Loss on Hedging [income statement expense account]	21,950	
+	Swap Contract [balance sheet liability account]		21,950

However, the increase in the value of the swap liability is offset by a decrease in the value of the note payable. Since the hedge is highly effective, the decrease in the value of the note payable is exactly equal to the increase in the value of the swap liability. The table on page 408 demonstrates this.

Although changes in the value of notes payable are not recognized under GAAP, the special hedge accounting rules under Statement 133 provide an exception to the general rule. The change in the value of the note payable and the unrealized gain are recognized in the financial statements and offset the loss from the hedging transaction. The entry to record the change in the note payable value is shown on page 408.

VALUE OF NOTE			
		4.50%	
	Note Payment	**Present Value Factor**	**Present Value**
7/1/2002	$ 40,000	0.9569	$ 38,277.51
12/31/2002	40,000	0.9157	36,629.20
7/1/2003	40,000	0.8763	35,051.86
12/31/2003	40,000	0.8386	33,542.45
7/1/2004	1,040,000	0.8025	834,549.09
Value of Note			978,050.12
Original Note Value			1,000,000.00
Change in Note Value . . .			$ (21,949.88)

Journal Entry to Record Change in Value of Note Payable			
+/−	**Accounts [description of account]**	**Debit**	**Credit**
−	Note Payable [balance sheet liability account]	21,950	
+	Gain on Hedging [income statement gain account]		21,950

Since the gain from the note exactly equals the loss from the swap, there is no income statement net impact under the hedge accounting rules. Similarly, the decrease in the note payable is offset by the increase in the swap liability, leaving the balance sheet unchanged.

This example made sure that the hedge was highly effective. To the extent that the value of the swap was not the same as the change in the value of the note payable, the difference in values would represent hedge ineffectiveness. Any hedge ineffectiveness will affect the current period's net income, since the gains and losses will no longer exactly offset.

One final point: In this example, management wanted to hedge against changes in the value of the note payable. Consider an alternative transaction in which management issued a note payable with a variable interest rate. In that case, management might want to hedge against changes in future cash flows due to interest rate changes. An interest rate swap that was a receive-variable, pay-fixed swap could be used for this purpose. This type of hedge would represent a cash flow hedge rather than a fair value hedge. Accounting for a cash flow hedge is illustrated next.

Cash Flow Hedge Example

This second example illustrates the rules for reporting a cash flow hedge. Assume that on July 1, 2001, a company owns 1,000,000 bushels of wheat that it expects to sell in March 2002 for $6 per bushel. The company's managers would like to hedge against a change in the price of wheat so they can remove the risk that future cash flows will be different from the $6,000,000 expected amount.

On July 1, 2001, the company enters into a contract to sell 1,000,000 bushels of wheat in March 2002 for a price of $6 per bushel. This contract is a derivative, the underlying is the price of a bushel of wheat, and the notional amount is 1,000,000 bushels. The company's managers designate this as a cash flow hedge. Since the contract calls for a sale of the same grade and type of wheat owned by the company, and for delivery at the company's normal place of delivery, the derivative is expected to be highly effective in hedging the cash flow risks associated with the future sale of wheat.

Assume that there is no value to the contract on July 1, 2001, so that there is no accounting entry to record. Assume further that on December 31, 2001, the price of wheat has decreased to $5.50 per bushel. This means that the value of the derivative has increased by $0.50 per bushel, or $500,000 for 1,000,000 bushels. Under Statement 133, the company is required to include the derivative as an asset on its balance sheet at December 31, 2001, and to value this asset at fair value, $500,000 in this example. Here is the entry to record the change in the value of the hedge. The $500,000 gain is recorded as part of other comprehensive income (OCI).

	Journal Entry to Record Change in Value of Wheat Hedge		
+/−	**Accounts [description of account]**	**Debit**	**Credit**
+	Hedge Contract [balance sheet asset account]	500,000	
+	Gain on Hedging-OCI [balance sheet shareholders' equity account] . .		500,000

By recording the income effect of the hedge in other comprehensive income, net income is not affected. On March 1 the price of wheat is still $5.50 per bushel, and the company sells its 1,000,000 bushels and closes out the derivative. At this time, the prior gain from the hedge contract is removed from other comprehensive income and reported as part of net income, offsetting the reduction in cash flows due to the decline in the price of the wheat. Here are the entries to record the sale of the wheat and the closing out of the derivative:

	Journal Entry to Record Sale of Wheat		
+/−	**Accounts [description of account]**	**Debit**	**Credit**
+	Cash [balance sheet asset account]	5,500,000	
+	Sales Revenue [income statement revenue account]		5,500,000

	Journal Entry to Record Change in Value of Wheat Hedge		
+/−	**Accounts [description of account]**	**Debit**	**Credit**
+	Cash [balance sheet asset account]	500,000	
−	Gain on Hedging-OCI [balance sheet shareholders' equity account]	500,000	
−	Hedge Contract [balance sheet asset account]		500,000
+	Gain on Hedging [income statement gain account]		500,000

Notice that the total of the $5,500,000 cash from selling the wheat plus the $500,000 of cash from closing out the derivative equals the $6,000,000 cash flow that the company expected to receive for selling the wheat. Thus, the hedge has been effective in removing the risk of changes in cash flows.

Actual Procter & Gamble Example

Shown on page 410 is a portion of the note from Procter & Gamble's financial statements explaining its accounting for derivatives. You can see that P&G has adopted Statement 133, and that it has both cash flow hedges and fair value hedges. Also, you can see that it uses interest rate swaps to hedge against changes in interest rates. All of its hedges are 100 percent effective.

Note 6 Risk Management Activities

Effective July 1, 2000, the Company adopted SFAS No. 133, "Accounting for Derivative Instruments and Hedging Activities," as amended, which requires that all derivative instruments be reported on the balance sheet at fair value and establishes criteria for designation and effectiveness of hedging relationships. The cumulative effect of adopting SFAS No. 133 as of July 1, 2000, was not material.

The Company is exposed to market risks, such as changes in interest rates, currency exchange rates and commodity pricing. To manage the volatility relating to these exposures, the Company nets the exposures on a consolidated basis to take advantage of natural offsets. For the residual portion, the Company enters into various derivative transactions pursuant to the Company's policies in areas such as counterparty exposure and hedging practices. Designation is performed on a specific exposure basis to support hedge accounting. The changes in fair value of these hedging instruments are offset in part or in whole by corresponding changes in the fair value or cash flows of the underlying exposures being hedged. The Company does not hold or issue derivative financial instruments for trading purposes.

Interest Rate Hedging The Company's policy is to manage interest cost using a mix of fixed-and variable-rate debt. To manage this mix in a cost efficient manner, the Company enters into interest rate swaps in which the Company agrees to exchange, at specified intervals, the difference between fixed and variable interest amounts calculated by reference to an agreed-upon notional principal amount.

At June 30, 2001, the Company had swaps with a fair value of $125 designated as fair value hedges of underlying fixed-rate debt obligations and recorded as long-term assets. The mark-to-market values of both the fair value hedging instruments and the underlying debt obligations are recorded as equal and offsetting gains and losses in the interest expense component of the income statement. All existing fair value hedges are 100% effective. As a result, there is no impact to earnings due to hedge ineffectiveness.

Source: Procter & Gamble Form 10-K.

Here is a portion of the statement of shareholders' equity showing P&G's other comprehensive income for the year ended June 30, 2001. Notice that one of the components is net investment hedges. These represent foreign currency hedges that have not yet been recognized as part of net income.

THE PROCTER & GAMBLE COMPANY AND SUBSIDIARIES
Consolidated Statements of Shareholders' Equity
(dollars in millions/shares in thousands)

	Accumulated Other Comprehensive Income
Balance June 30, 2000	$(1,842)
Other comprehensive income	
Financial statement translation	(715)
Net investment hedges, net of $276 tax	460
Other, net of tax	(23)
Balance June 30, 2001	$(2,120)

Source: Procter & Gamble Form 10-K.

Finally, here is an example of P&G's cash flow hedging activities with respect to commodity prices.

Commodity Price Management

Raw materials used by the Company are subject to price volatility caused by weather, supply conditions, political and economic variables and other unpredictable factors. To manage the volatility related to anticipated inventory purchases, the Company uses futures and options with maturities generally less than one year and swap contracts with maturities up to five years. These market instruments are designated as cash flow hedges. The mark-to-market gain or loss on qualifying hedges is included in other comprehensive income to the extent effective, and reclassified into cost of products sold in the period during which the hedged transaction affects earnings. Qualifying cash flow hedges currently deferred in OCI are not material. These amounts will be reclassified into earnings as the underlying transactions are recognized. The mark-to-market gains or losses on non-qualifying, excluded and ineffective portions of hedges are recognized in cost of products sold immediately. No cash flow hedges were discontinued during the year ended June 30, 2001. Commodity hedging activity is not material to the Company's financial statements.

Source: Procter & Gamble Form 10-K.

FINANCIAL INSTRUMENTS AND THE CASH FLOWS STATEMENT

Statement 133 does not have a major impact on the cash flows statement. Since derivatives are required to be accounted for at fair value, with changes in value accounted for on the income statement, net income may reflect unrealized gains and losses from derivatives that have not been realized in the form of cash. This will require an adjustment on the cash flows statement to reconcile net income with cash flows from operating activities.

However, recall that to the extent that derivatives are designated as hedges, and the hedges are highly effective, gains and losses from the hedges will offset losses and gains on the hedged assets and liabilities, so that there will be no effect on net income. The cash flows realized from closing out derivative contracts will also be reflected on the cash flows statement.

ACCOUNTING FOR FINANCIAL INSTRUMENTS IN OTHER COUNTRIES

Accounting for derivatives in other countries is varied and in general is not as comprehensive as the accounting rules contained in Statement 133. However, the general approach is usually some sort of offsetting of gains and losses and deferral of net losses until contracts have been completed.

For an example of French accounting for risks, here is a note from the annual report of the Michelin Group.

i. Financial Instruments

Foreign exchange risks

Group policy is to hedge foreign exchange exposure. Accordingly, various market instruments are used, mainly exchange rate forward contracts or options.

In general, foreign currency receivables and payables are of a similar term and nature, giving rise to an offset. Only the net exposure is hedged and contracts are accounted for on completion of the transactions concerned.

The resulting gains and losses, realized or unrealized, together with the costs of hedging are recorded in the income statement.

Investments by holding companies in foreign affiliates are financed in the currency of the holding companies' accounts.

Interest rate risks

Interest rate exposure for periods of less than one year is managed locally. The maximum amount to be financed at fixed rate for more than one year is set for each foreign currency.

Group policy concerning interest rate exposure is coordinated and controlled centrally.

Source: Michelin Group annual report.

The following note from the KLM Royal Dutch Airlines' financial statement explains that KLM will be adopting Standard 133 even though this standard is not required under Dutch GAAP.

New U.S. Accounting Standards (not yet applied)

In June 1998, the Financial Accounting Standards Board issued Financial Accounting Standards (SFAS) No. 133 "Accounting for Derivative Instruments and Hedging Activities". SFAS No. 133 standardizes the accounting for derivative instruments, including certain derivative instruments embedded in other contracts and for hedging activities. Under the standard, entities are required to carry all derivative instruments in the statement of financial position at fair value.

As of April 1, 2001, KLM will account for derivatives in accordance with SFAS 133 of the Financial Accounting Standards Board. In view of international developments in accounting for derivatives, KLM believes it should apply these accounting and reporting requirements for its derivative financial instruments in the Netherlands. The effect of this change on KLM's results and equity will be limited.

Source: KLM Form 20-F.

The following note from KLM's financial statements provides the fair value disclosure information for financial instruments that is required under U.S. GAAP.

---

27. Differences between Netherlands GAAP and U.S. GAAP

Disclosure on the fair value of financial instruments (SFAS 107)

Fair value is defined as the amount at which a financial instrument could be exchanged in a current transaction between willing parties, other than in a forced sale or liquidation, and is best evidenced by a quoted market price, if one exists. Fair value estimates are made at a specific point in time, based on relevant market information and information about the financial instruments.

Although management uses its best judgment in estimating the fair value of these financial instruments, there are inherent weaknesses in any estimation technique. Therefore the estimates presented are not necessarily indicative of the amounts that the Company could realise in a current market exchange or the value that ultimately will be realised by the Company upon maturity or disposition.

The following table summarises the carrying amounts and estimated fair values of the Group's financial instruments:

| | March 31, 2001 | | March 31, 2000 | |
Assets	Carrying Amount	Estimated Fair Value	Carrying Amount	Estimated Fair Value
Financial fixed assets				
Receivables from holdings	101	101	39	39
Other financial fixed assets	454	489	583	641
Marketable securities	6	6	63	63
Cash	839	839	667	667
Liabilities (excluding leases)				
Perpetual debt	560	447	916	1,106
Financial lease commitments (see note 8)				
Other long-term debt	442	453	471	500
Maturing within one year	(152)	(152)	(28)	(28)
Current liabilities (excluding leases)	1,949	1,949	2,136	2,136

Source: KLM Form 20-F.

FINANCIAL INSTRUMENTS AND INCOME TAX EXPENSE

To the extent that the unrealized gains and losses from fair value adjustments related to derivatives are included in financial statement income (either net income or other comprehensive income) but are not reflected in taxable income, a temporary book-tax difference will arise, requiring the recording of either a deferred tax asset or a deferred tax liability. Unrealized gains and losses that are reflected in other comprehensive income should be recorded net of a deferred tax expense or deferred tax benefit.

USING INFORMATION ABOUT FINANCIAL INSTRUMENTS TO MAKE DECISIONS

The information that a company is required to disclose relating to how it manages exposure to future risks provides a great deal of information for users of the company's financial statements. For example, the fact that Procter & Gamble's management has to discuss the company's exposure to the risk of changes in commodity prices may provide users with information that might not have been available in the past. Also, by requiring derivatives to be recorded at fair value, with unrealized gains and losses reflected in net income (or other comprehensive income), and by reporting the ineffective portion of hedges as part of net income, users are able to evaluate how effective management has been in hedging these risks.

Summary

This chapter examines the complex new financial reporting rules for derivative financial instruments. Under these rules, derivatives are recorded as assets and liabilities on the balance sheet at their fair values, and changes in these values are reported as part of net income. Special hedge accounting rules apply to qualifying fair value hedges, cash flow hedges, and foreign currency hedges.

For fair value hedges, gains and losses on changes in the values of the hedges are offset against losses and gains on changes in the values of the hedged assets and liabilities, so only the ineffective portion of the hedge is reflected in net income. For cash flow hedges, gains and losses from changes in the values of the hedges are included in other comprehensive income, a shareholders' equity balance sheet account. These gains and losses are reversed and taken into net income in the year the cash flows that are being hedged are realized.

Discussion Questions

1. Explain what is meant by a financial instrument.
2. In general, what valuation method do U.S. accounting standard setters prefer for valuing financial instruments? Are all financial instruments valued using this method? If not, why not?
3. What are some of the difficulties associated with determining fair values of financial instruments? How do these difficulties affect the relevance and reliability of the fair value disclosures in financial statements.
4. Explain what derivatives are. In your explanation, include a discussion of the following terms: *counterparty, underlying,* and *notional amount.*
5. What causes a derivative to increase or decrease in value?
6. What is a hedge? How are hedges used by businesses to reduce risks? Explain how derivatives are used in hedges.
7. Do all derivatives represent hedges? If yes, what is the difference between a derivative and a hedge? If no, explain why derivatives may not represent hedges.
8. What are the three characteristics for derivative classification under GAAP?
9. Explain what is meant by the term *net settlement.*
10. Explain the financial reporting rules for derivatives that are *not* classified as hedges. What are the balance sheet and income statement consequences of this treatment?

11. Explain the three types of hedges recognized for financial reporting purposes.

12. Classification as a particular type of hedge depends on the managers' intentions as to what is being hedged: asset (or liability) values or future cash flows. Explain.

13. Explain the accounting rules for fair value hedges.

14. Explain the accounting rules for cash flow hedges.

15. What are the balance sheet and income statement consequences of a hedge being classified as a fair value hedge rather than a cash flow hedge?

16. Explain the concept of a *highly effective* hedge.

17. What happens if a hedge is not highly effective?

18. What happens if a hedge is highly effective but not perfectly effective?

19. Explain how a commodity futures contract works. How could it be used in a fair value hedge? How could it be used in a cash flow hedge?

20. Explain how an interest rate swap works. How could it be used in a fair value hedge? How could it be used in a cash flow hedge?

21. Explain how an option to buy or sell shares of stock is a derivative.

22. Explain how the hedge accounting rules affect the cash flows statement.

23. Explain how the hedge accounting rules affect the computation of income tax expense.

Problems

1. A corporation sold $1,000,000 principal amount of 10-year bonds on January 1, 2001. The bonds have a coupon rate of 8 percent and pay interest semiannually on June 30 and December 31. The market interest rate when the bonds were issued was 8 percent. On December 31, 2002, market interest rates have changed to 6 percent.

   a. What is the book value of the bonds on December 31, 2002?

   b. What is the fair value of the bonds on December 31, 2002?

2. A corporation sold $1,000,000 principal amount of 10-year bonds on January 1, 2001. The bonds have a coupon rate of 8 percent and pay interest semiannually on June 30 and December 31. The market interest rate when the bonds were issued was 10 percent. On December 31, 2002, market interest rates have changed to 12 percent.

   a. What is the book value of the bonds on December 31, 2002?

   b. What is the fair value of the bonds on December 31, 2002?

3. A corporation sold $1,000,000 principal amount of 10-year bonds on January 1, 2001. The bonds have a coupon rate of 8 percent and pay interest semiannually on June 30 and December 31. The market interest rate when the bonds were issued was 7 percent. On December 31, 2002, market interest rates have changed to 5 percent.

   a. What is the book value of the bonds on December 31, 2002?

   b. What is the fair value of the bonds on December 31, 2002?

4. A corporation sold $1,000,000 principal amount of five-year bonds on July 1, 2001. The bonds have a coupon rate of 10 percent and pay interest semiannually on December 31 and June 30. The market interest rate when the bonds were issued was 10 percent. Managers of the company are concerned about possible changes in interest rates over the term of the bond and the effect these changes will have on the fair value of the bond.

   To hedge against this risk of a change in the value of the bond, the company enters into a receive-fixed, pay-variable swap on July 1, 2001, with a notional amount of $1,000,000 and interest computed semi-annually. The fixed rate in the swap is an 10 percent annual rate, while the variable rate is the LIBOR rate. The LIBOR rate on July 1, 2001, is 10 percent. The swap has a five-year term to correspond with the term of the bonds. The swap is considered by the company's managers to be highly effective in hedging the risk of changes in the value of the bonds.

On December 31, 2001, the LIBOR rate has increased to 12 percent.

a. Compute the fair value of the swap at December 31, 2001.

b. Compute the fair value of the bonds at December 31, 2001.

c. Show the journal entries required at December 31, 2001, under the GAAP rules for hedge accounting.

5. Assume the same facts as given in problem 4 except that on December 31, 2001, the LIBOR rate has decreased to 8 percent.

a. Compute the fair value of the swap at December 31, 2001.

b. Compute the fair value of the bonds at December 31, 2001.

c. Show the journal entries required at December 31, 2001, under the GAAP rules for hedge accounting.

6. Assume the same facts as given in problem 4 except that on December 31, 2001, the LIBOR rate has decreased to 7.5 percent.

a. Compute the fair value of the swap at December 31, 2001.

b. Compute the fair value of the bonds at December 31, 2001.

c. Show the journal entries required at December 31, 2001, under the GAAP rules for hedge accounting.

7. On July 1, 2001, a company owns 100,000 barrels of oil that it expects to sell in February 2002 for $25 per barrel. The company's managers would like to hedge against a change in the price of oil so they can remove the risk that future cash flows will be different from the $2,500,000 expected amount. On July 1, 2001, the company enters into a contract to sell 100,000 barrels of oil in February 2002 for a price of $25 per barrel. The company's managers designate this as a cash flow hedge, and it is expected to be highly effective.

a. Assume that on December 31, 2001, the price of oil has decreased to $23 per barrel. Show the journal entry required at December 31, 2001, under the GAAP rules for hedge accounting.

b. Assume that the oil is sold in February 2002 for $23 per barrel. Show the journal entries required to record the sale of the oil and the closing out of the hedge in February 2002.

8. Assume the same facts as given in problem 7 except that on December 31, 2001, the price of oil has increased to $28 per barrel.

a. Show the journal entry required at December 31, 2001, under the GAAP rules for hedge accounting.

b. Assume that the oil is sold in February 2002 for $28 per barrel. Show the journal entries required to record the sale of the oil and the closing out of the hedge in February 2002.

9. Assume the same facts as given in problem 7 except that on December 31, 2001, the price of oil has increased to $30 per barrel.

a. Show the journal entry required at December 31, 2001, under the GAAP rules for hedge accounting.

b. Assume that the oil is sold in February 2002 for $30 per barrel. Show the journal entries required to record the sale of the oil and the closing out of the hedge in February 2002.

Research Reports

1. Obtain the most recent financial statements of a public company that uses hedges.

   a. Explain the types of risks the company faces.

   b. Explain the types of hedges used.

   c. Explain how the hedge accounting rules have affected the company's financial statements.

   d. Comment on how useful the risk-related disclosures in the notes to the financial statements are. Consider usefulness from the standpoint of an investor trying to value the company's common stock.

   e. Are there risks that the company cannot hedge?

2. Find an article in the financial press that discusses derivatives and their use by public companies. (Do *not* use an article that discusses derivatives as investments for individual investors.)

   a. Why does the article say derivatives are used?

   b. What are the risks of using derivatives?

   c. Based on your knowledge of the financial accounting rules for derivatives, do you think the derivative disclosures required under GAAP are adequate?

   d. After reading the article, develop an alternative way of accounting for derivatives. Discuss the costs and benefits of your new accounting method and compare them with the costs and benefits of the current GAAP rules.

3. Obtain the financial statements of El Paso Corporation for 2000. The cash flows statement contains the following item for 2000: "Change in price risk management activities, net (1,787)." This means that changes in the price of something called *risk management activities* resulted in a decrease in cash flows from operating activities of $1,787 million that was not reflected in net income.

   a. Using information in the financial statements and notes, as well as any additional information you can obtain, explain what caused the decrease in cash flows.

   b. Comment on how useful the accounting information was with respect to this item. Was there any way that investors or other users of El Paso's financial statements could have anticipated this decrease in cash flows based on the information provided?

   c. Explain why this large decrease in cash flows was not reflected in net income.

4. Obtain the financial statements of General Mills, Inc., for the year ended May 26, 2002.

   a. General Mills reports unrealized losses on hedge derivatives. Explain what this represents and why it is recorded as part of other comprehensive income.

   b. Using the information contained in the notes to the financial statements, explain the types of hedging activities that General Mills engages in.

   c. For each type of hedging activity described in *b* above, explain the financial accounting rules that apply.

   d. Explain how the new FASB rules relating to accounting for derivatives affected General Mills' financial statements for the year.

AP Photo/Fabian Bimmer

Chapter Learning Objectives

After reading this chapter you should understand

1. How a defined benefit pension plan works.
2. How the liability for future pension benefits (the PBO) is computed.
3. What items make up a company's net pension cost or pension income.
4. How pension plan investment earnings affect the income statement and balance sheet.
5. What is meant by overfunded or underfunded pension plans.
6. The minimum pension liability.
7. The pension disclosures required by GAAP.
8. The accounting rules for defined contribution pension plans.
9. The accounting rules for other postemployment benefits.

Chapter 14

Pension and Other Postemployment Benefits

Focus Company: International Business Machines Corporation

Introduction

On September 20, 1999, *The Wall Street Journal* published the following in an article concerning IBM's attempt to change the type of pension plan offered to employees:

> On Friday, International Business Machines Corp. gave in to the protests of middle-aged employees and significantly revised its plan to switch to cash-balance pensions, a controversial new type of pension system . . . even when a company has a huge pension surplus, and thus doesn't need to contribute to the pension plan at all, it can benefit by converting to a cash-balance plan. That is because companies can take a credit on their income statements when pension income exceeds current liabilities. Cutting benefit obligations through conversion to a cash-balance plan reduces liabilities, fattens the surplus and thus can boost the earnings still more.

As you can see from the article, even though changing plan types would not affect IBM's cash contributions to the pension plan, the change would cause IBM's reported earnings to increase. To see why this is the case, it is necessary to understand both how pension plans work and how they are accounted for under GAAP.

Accounting for pension plans is one of the most complex areas in financial reporting, even though pension plans themselves are relatively simple to understand. The complexity comes from the fact that standard setters have tried to minimize the impact of pension plan accounting on (1) the volatility of reported earnings of the employer and (2) reported balance sheet assets and liabilities of the employer. Under GAAP, the pension information recorded in the financial statements does not always reflect the underlying economic activity of the pension plan. As a consequence, GAAP rules require extensive pension-related disclosures in the notes to the financial statements as a way of providing financial statement users with additional pension information.

This chapter first describes how a pension plan operates and what constitutes pension-related cash flows, assets, and liabilities. Next, the GAAP rules related to pension plans are explained, showing how these underlying cash flows, assets, and liabilities are reflected in the financial statements of the employer. Finally, financial reporting rules applicable to other types of benefits provided to retired employees, called *other postemployment benefits,* are discussed.

HOW PENSION PLANS WORK

In any corporate pension plan, the employer promises to make payments to the employee when the employee retires.[1] The plan is a legal contract between the employer and the employee and therefore creates a liability on the part of the

---

[1] Pension plans also typically contain provisions for payments to employees (or their beneficiaries) upon the disability or death of the employee.

employer for future pension payments. Accrual accounting views the future pension payment as an expense associated with the accounting period during which the employee worked to earn the pension, rather than as an expense of the period in which the pension is actually paid to the employee. Since the pension represents cash payments to be made in the future, present value concepts are applied in determining the pension expense and the pension liability. The two main financial reporting issues with respect to pension plans are (1) how and when to record the liability for future pension benefits and (2) how to measure the pension expense for the year.

Pension plans can be classified into two general types—called *defined contribution plans* and *defined benefit plans*—and the computation of the liability for expected future pension payments differs depending on which type of plan the employer uses. The sections below discuss the accounting rules for defined benefit plans. The accounting rules for defined contribution plans are discussed later in the chapter.

Under a defined benefit plan, the employer contracts to pay each employee a certain dollar amount upon retirement, usually determined under a formula that takes into account the number of years the employee has worked for the employer and the employee's compensation level. The plan is called a *defined benefit plan* because the benefit amount, that is, the retirement payment, is defined by the plan contract. For example, a plan could contain an annual pension benefit determined as follows:

> Multiply the employee's average annual compensation for the five-year period prior to retirement by a percentage equal to two percentage points for each year that the employee has worked for the employer.

Assume a new employee works for this employer for one year (2001) and that the average of the employee's annual compensation for the five years prior to retirement is expected to be $80,000. Assume that the employee is expected to work 10 years before retiring, with retirement occurring at the end of 2010.

Under the above formula, when the employee retires she would be entitled to a pension each year equal to 20 percent (2% × 10 years) of average annual compensation ($80,000), or $16,000. However, not all of the $16,000 pension is due to the work the employee performed during 2001. The $16,000 amount is based on the assumption that the employee works for 10 years and under accrual accounting is considered to be earned over that 10-year period. The portion of the pension payment applicable to 2001 is equal to 2% × $80,000, or $1,600.

Since the employer will pay this pension payment each year, beginning with the year the employee retires and ending with the employee's death, the actual amount of future pension payments will depend on how long the retired employee lives after retirement. Assume that the employee is expected to live for 12 years after retirement, with the first payment in 2011 and the last payment in 2022. Under this assumption, the total retirement payments over the employee's lifetime that are attributed to work performed in 2001 are 12 × $1,600, or $19,200.

Since the $19,200 will be paid over a period of 12 years, beginning in 2011, the present value of the expected pension payments at the date of retirement will be less than $19,200. At the date of retirement (the end of 2010), the pension represents an annuity of 12 equal payments. The present value of an annuity of $1,600 for 12 periods (assuming a 10 percent discount rate) is $10,902. This is the present value of the expected pension payments at the time of retirement (end of 2010) that relate to work performed in 2001.

At the end of 2001, when the employer wants to record the pension liability and expense, the employee has already worked one of her expected ten years, so the expected retirement date is nine years in the future. This means that the present value of the expected future pension payments *as of the end of 2001* will be less than the present value at the time of retirement (end of 2010). The present value of a payment of $10,902 made nine years in the future (assuming a 10 percent discount rate) is only $4,623.

These computations are illustrated in the following table:

End of Year		Annual Pension Payment*	Years in Future from 2010	10% Present Value Factor	Present Value
	PRESENT VALUE OF FUTURE PENSION PAYMENTS				
2022	Pension payment	$1,600	12	0.3186	$ 510
2021	Pension payment	1,600	11	0.3505	561
2020	Pension payment	1,600	10	0.3855	617
2019	Pension payment	1,600	9	0.4241	679
2018	Pension payment	1,600	8	0.4665	746
2017	Pension payment	1,600	7	0.5132	821
2016	Pension payment	1,600	6	0.5645	903
2015	Pension payment	1,600	5	0.6209	993
2014	Pension payment	1,600	4	0.6830	1,093
2013	Pension payment	1,600	3	0.7513	1,202
2012	Pension payment	1,600	2	0.8264	1,322
2011	Pension payment	1,600	1	0.9091	1,455
2010	Present value of future pension payments				$10,902
	Present value factor nine years in future (10%)				× 0.4241
2001					$ 4,623

*2% × $80,000 = $1,600.

Based on this example, the pension expense for 2001 would be $4,623, and the employer would have a liability at the end of 2001 for future pension payments with a present value of $4,623. Under GAAP, this liability is called the *projected benefit obligation* (PBO). The PBO is the present value of the pension benefits that the employees have earned and that the employer expects to pay in future years.

One of the problems in computing the PBO is that the employer does not know until an employee actually retires either (1) how long the employee will work before retiring or (2) what the employee's average compensation for the years prior to retirement will be. In addition, the employer does not know how long the employee will live after retirement. Therefore, employers must hire professional consultants, called *actuaries,* to compute the PBO.

The actuaries estimate the future pension payments on the basis of a set of assumptions about how long an average employee will work, what her average compensation will be, and how long she will live after retirement. These assumptions are based on statistical estimation techniques, and, although the assumptions will result in over- or underestimations of PBOs for individual employees, the assumptions will result in an estimate of the *total* PBO that is highly accurate.

Since the PBO is a present value, it is sensitive to changes in the discount rate used in the computation. If the discount rate used in the example above changed from 10 percent to 8 percent, the value of the PBO increases to $6,032. Therefore, assumptions by managers about the discount rate used in the present value computation can have a large impact on the amount of the PBO.

Shown on page 422 is some information about the discount rate used by IBM for its U.S. plans. As you can see, the discount rate has changed from 6.5 percent in 1998 to 7.75 percent in 1999 to 7.25 percent in 2000.

Weighted-Average Actuarial Assumptions, U.S. Plans			
	As of December 31		
	2000	**1999**	**1998**
Discount rate	7.25%	7.75%	6.5%
Expected return on plan assets	10.0	9.5	9.5
Rate of compensation increase	6.0	6.0	5.0

Source: IBM Corporation Form 10-K.

Most pension plans contain a provision that requires the employee to work for the employer for a certain minimum number of years before the employee is entitled to receive a pension. This minimum period of employment necessary to receive pension benefits is referred to as the *vesting period,* and an employee who has worked the required number of years is said to be *vested.* Employees who stop working for the employer before they are vested will forfeit any pension benefits they may have earned.

Pension Trusts

Companies rarely make pension payments directly to their retired employees. Instead, they establish what is called a *pension trust,* a separate legal entity under the direction of a trustee or group of trustees.[2] The trust works in the following way. The employer makes periodic cash payments to the trust during the periods when employees are working and earning future pension benefits. These cash payments from the employer to the pension trust are referred to as *funding the trust.* The trustee of the trust invests the cash in a portfolio of investments such as stocks, bonds, and treasury bills. Over time, the cash contributions from the employer, together with the earnings from the trust investments, build up assets within the trust. As employees retire, these trust assets are then used to make pension payments to the retired employees.

The tables below lay out the pension-related cash flows and assets and liabilities associated with the employer and the pension trust.

PENSION-RELATED CASH FLOWS	
Employer	**Pension Trust**
Decreased by cash payments to pension trust	Increased by cash payments from employer
	Decreased by investments made
	Increased by earnings from investments and sales of investments
	Decreased by pension payments to retired employees

PENSION-RELATED ASSETS AND LIABILITIES	
Employer	**Pension Trust**
Assets	
Cash contributed to pension trust in excess of pension expense (a prepaid expense)	Cash received from employer plus investment assets
Liabilities	
Pension expense in excess of cash contributed to pension trust (an accrued expense)	Obligation to make future pension payments to retired employees (PBO)

[2] Both the U.S. Department of Labor and Internal Revenue Service have strict rules that employers must follow in the establishment and operation of pension trusts, as well as requirements for the amount of cash that employers must contribute to the trust each period. These rules are designed to ensure that employees actually receive the promised pension payments in the event the employer becomes bankrupt or otherwise insolvent.

ACCOUNTING FOR PENSION COSTS

The basic accounting entries to record the pension expense, called *net pension cost* under GAAP, are shown below. In each case, a net pension cost is recorded as an expense, and cash is decreased for the amount contributed to the trust for the year. In both examples, the net pension cost for the year is assumed to be $4,623. The first entry illustrates a situation in which the cash contributed to the pension trust (assumed to be $3,000) is less than the net pension cost, resulting in a liability called *unfunded accrued pension cost*. The second entry illustrates a situation in which the cash contributed to the pension trust (assumed to be $5,000) is more than the net pension cost, resulting in an asset called *prepaid pension cost*.[3]

	Journal Entry to Record Pension Cost		
+/−	**Accounts [description of account]**	**Debit**	**Credit**
+	Net Pension Cost [income statement expense account]	4,623	
−	Cash [balance sheet asset account]		3,000
+	Unfunded Accrued Pension Cost [balance sheet liability account] . .		1,623

	Journal Entry to Record Pension Cost		
+/−	**Accounts [description of account]**	**Debit**	**Credit**
+	Net Pension Cost [income statement expense account]	4,623	
+	Prepaid Pension Cost [balance sheet asset account]	377	
−	Cash [balance sheet asset account]		5,000

GAAP rules view the pension trust as an entity separate and distinct from the employer and treat the assets and liabilities of the pension trust as being separate from the assets and liabilities of the employer. For example, in the first entry above, the pension trust would have assets of $3,000 and liabilities of $4,623, while the employer would report only the net unfunded accrued pension cost of $1,623. In the second entry, the pension trust would have assets of $5,000 and liabilities of $4,623, while the employer would report only the net prepaid pension cost of $377.

Shown on page 424 is financial statement information about some of IBM's balance sheet accounts. As you can see, IBM had a balance in prepaid pension assets equal to $6,806 million at December 31, 2000. This represents (with some accounting modifications discussed below) the excess of the IBM pension trust's investment assets over the trust's PBO.

To further illustrate how the accounting entries made on the financial statements of the employer relate to the assets and liabilities of the pension trust, a pension worksheet will be used. The pension worksheet has two parts. The columns on the left side keep track of items that are recorded on the financial statements of the employer, either as part of the net pension cost for the year or as a cash payment during the year. The left side also keeps track of the balance of the employer's prepaid pension cost or unfunded accrued pension cost. The change to this asset or liability each year is equal to the difference between the net pension cost for the year and the cash contribution made to the plan.

---

[3] The cash contributed to the plan is rarely equal to the net pension cost. Cash contribution amounts are often based on tax considerations, since the employer gets a tax deduction for the contribution. The net pension cost is determined under GAAP.

Investments and Sundry Assets (in millions)		
	At December 31	
	2000	**1999**
Deferred taxes	$ 2,968	$ 2,654
Prepaid pension assets	**6,806**	**5,636**
Alliance investments		
Equity method	629	595
Other	909	1,439
Goodwill (less accumulated amortization)	848	1,045
Marketable securities—noncurrent	171	113
Software	782	663
Other assets	1,334	1,527
Total	$14,447	$13,672

Source: IBM Corporation Form 10-K.

The right side of the pension worksheet keeps track of the assets and liabilities of the pension trust. The liability represents the PBO. The assets represent cash and investments of the trust. Here is a pension worksheet reflecting the first journal entry shown above:

PENSION WORKSHEET					
	Employer Accounting Records			**Additional Information**	
	Net Pension Cost	**Cash**	**Prepaid Pension Cost (unfunded accrued pension cost)**	**PBO (plan liability)**	**Plan Assets**
Beginning balance			0	0	0
Pension cost	4,623			(4,623)	
Cash contribution		(3,000)			3,000
	4,623	(3,000)	(1,623)		
Ending balance			(1,623)	(4,623)	3,000

Service Cost and Interest Cost

Although the rules discussed above are relatively straightforward, the actual computation of the prepaid pension cost or unfunded accrued pension cost on the employer's balance sheet is much more complicated. First, as mentioned earlier, the accounting rules for measuring balance sheet pension assets or liabilities are designed to minimize the volatility of earnings that might result from recording assets or liabilities at their market values. Second, the computation of the PBO is complicated. This section discusses in more detail how net pension cost and PBO are computed by focusing on two components: service cost and interest cost.

Service Cost

The $4,623 amount computed in the above example is called the *service cost* for the year. The service cost, one of the components of both net pension cost and the PBO, is the increase in the present value of expected future pension benefits earned by working for the company for an additional year. Since the example is the first year of employment, the entire amount of the present value of expected future pension benefits is the service cost.

The same example can be used to compute the service cost for the second year (2002). By working another year the employee earns an additional pension payment equal to 2% × $80,000, or $1,600. This is the same amount as the first year, since the estimate of the average annual compensation is still expected to be $80,000. Assuming that the employee is still expected to live for 12 years after retiring, the total of retirement payments over the employee's lifetime is 12 × $1,600, or $19,200, the same the first year, and the present value of this amount at the time of retirement (end of 2010) is still $10,902.

One change that must be taken into account in computing the service cost for the second year is the fact that the employee is one year closer to retiring. Therefore, the present value of the $10,902 future amount will be computed assuming retirement eight years in the future, rather than the nine years used in the first computation. The present value of a payment of $10,902 made eight years in the future (assuming a 10 percent discount rate) is $5,086. This is the service cost for the second year (2002).

Interest Cost

Since the PBO is a present value, the passage of time causes the present value to increase. This increase due to the passage of time is called the *interest cost*. Consider the $4,623 PBO from the example at the end of 2001. Even if it is assumed that the employee will not earn any additional pension benefits after that date, the present value of expected future pension benefits would increase each year as the time to retirement came closer. At the end of 2002, the $4,623 PBO would increase by the 10 percent discount rate, or by $462 (10% × $4,623). The interest cost increases both the net pension cost and the PBO.

The combined effect of the service cost of $5,086 and the interest cost of $462 is a total of $5,548 for 2002. Since this amount will increase both the net pension cost and the PBO, another way to demonstrate this effect is to compute the PBO at the end of 2002. At the end of 2002, the employee will have earned a future pension payment equal to 4 percent of average compensation (2% × 2), or $3,200 (4% × $80,000), payable for 12 years. The present value of this annuity is $21,804 as of the date of retirement (end of 2010). The retirement date is eight years in the future. The present value of a payment of $21,804 made eight years in the future is $10,172. The table below illustrates these computations:

PRESENT VALUE OF FUTURE PENSION PAYMENTS (2ND YEAR)

End of Year		Annual Pension Payment*	Years in Future from 2010	10% Present Value Factor	Present Value
2022	Pension payment	$3,200	12	0.3186	$ 1,020
2021	Pension payment	3,200	11	0.3505	1,122
2020	Pension payment	3,200	10	0.3855	1,234
2019	Pension payment	3,200	9	0.4241	1,357
2018	Pension payment	3,200	8	0.4665	1,493
2017	Pension payment	3,200	7	0.5132	1,642
2016	Pension payment	3,200	6	0.5645	1,806
2015	Pension payment	3,200	5	0.6209	1,987
2014	Pension payment	3,200	4	0.6830	2,186
2013	Pension payment	3,200	3	0.7513	2,404
2012	Pension payment	3,200	2	0.8264	2,645
2011	Pension payment	3,200	1	0.9091	2,909
2010	Present value of future pension payments				$21,804
	Present value factor eight years in future (10%)			×	0.4665
2002					$10,172

*4% × $80,000 = $3,200.

The change in the PBO from 2001 to 2002 is $10,172 − $4,623 = $5,549. This change is composed of the service cost of $5,086 and the interest cost of $462 (plus a $1 rounding difference). The effect of the service cost and the interest cost for 2002 are illustrated on the pension worksheet below.

| | **PENSION WORKSHEET** | | | **Additional Information** | |
| | **Employer Accounting Records** | | | | |
	Net Pension Cost	Cash	Prepaid Pension Cost (unfunded accrued pension cost)	PBO (plan liability)	Plan Assets
Beginning balance, 2001 . . .			(1,623)	(4,623)	3,000
Service cost	5,086			(5,086)	
Interest cost	462			(462)	
	5,548		(5,548)		
Ending balance, 2002			(7,171)	(10,171)	3,000

Plan Assets

The focus so far has been on the liability side of the pension trust, the PBO. However, the employer makes cash contributions to the plan at regular intervals, and the cash is used to make investments that (1) provide liquid assets to allow the plan to pay future pensions and (2) generate a return on the investment that can be used to pay future pensions. This section focuses on accounting for the plan assets.

As the worksheet below illustrates, cash contributions from the employer increase plan assets, while payments made to retired employees decrease plan assets. Neither employer cash contributions nor payments of pension benefits affects net pension cost. Continuing with the numbers from the previous examples, assume the employer contributes an additional $3,000 to the plan in 2002, and the plan pays benefits of $2,000. The cash contribution reduces the employer's cash and increases the plan assets, while the payment of benefits decreases both the plan assets and the PBO.

| | **PENSION WORKSHEET** | | | **Additional Information** | |
| | **Employer Accounting Records** | | | | |
	Net Pension Cost	Cash	Prepaid Pension Cost (unfunded accrued pension cost)	PBO (plan liability)	Plan Assets
Beginning balance, 2001 . . .			(1,623)	(4,623)	3,000
Service cost	5,086			(5,086)	
Interest cost	462			(462)	
Cash contribution		(3,000)			3,000
Payment of benefits				2,000	(2,000)
	5,548	(3,000)	(2,548)		
Ending balance, 2002			(4,171)	(8,171)	4,000

The treatment of investment gains and losses is more complex. The plan assets are accounted for by the plan at fair value, taking into account both realized and unrealized gains and losses. Plan assets are increased by investment gains and decreased by investment losses during the year. However, under GAAP the net pension cost is reduced by the *expected* investment gains for the year, based on the assumptions used by the plan actuaries. The difference between the actual gain or loss realized by the plan for the year and the expected gain used in the actuarial computations is an unrecognized (or deferred) gain or loss. For example, if the actuaries expected plan assets to generate a return of 8 percent for the year, but the actual return on plan assets turns out to be 11 percent, net pension cost for the year would be reduced by the 8 percent expected return, while the difference of 3 percent would be treated as a deferred gain.

To see why this rule was adopted, consider the example of IBM for 2000. The fair value of IBM's U.S. plan assets at the beginning of 2000 was $45,584 million. IBM's actuaries expected these assets to generate investment returns in 2000 equal to $3,902 million, and this amount reduced IBM's net pension cost for the year. However, IBM's actual return on plan assets for 2000 was only $1,395 million. If IBM computed its net pension cost based on the actual returns, these actual returns would fluctuate as interest rates or stock prices increased and decreased in the economy, events that IBM's managers have little control over. Therefore, to minimize the impact of fluctuations in actual returns, GAAP rules call for the computation of net pension costs on the basis of the *expected* rate of return.

What happens if (as was the case for IBM in 2000) the actual rate of return is more or less than the expected rate of return? In that case, the difference is deferred until a future accounting period. In some years, the actual rate of return will exceed the expected rate of return; in other years, the reverse will be true. Thus, the balance of cumulative net deferred gains (or deferred losses) will fluctuate each year.

GAAP requires only amortization of the net deferred gain or loss if the deferred gain or loss becomes very large. This approach, known as the *corridor method* of amortization, requires amortization of the balance of net deferred gains or losses if the balance exceeds 10 percent of the fair value of pension assets or pension liabilities, whichever is larger. The amortization period is the average remaining service period of active employees expected to receive benefits under the plan.

For example, the balance of IBM's deferred gains at the end of 1999 was $7,003 million. This exceeded 10 percent of the fair value of plan assets (10 percent of $45,584 million = $4,558 million). Therefore, IBM would have been required to amortize a portion of the deferred gains for 1999 over the average remaining service period of active employees. The balance of deferred gains for 2000 is only $2,768 million, less than 10 percent of the fair value of plan assets, so no amortization is required.

To illustrate how actual and expected gains and losses affect the worksheet, assume the example company's expected return was 11 percent, and it experienced a gain of $600 for 2002. The plan assets at the beginning of the year were $3,000, so an expected return of 11 percent would be a gain of $330. This expected gain reduces the net pension cost for the year. The actual gain of $600 increases the plan assets for the year. The difference of $270 is a deferred gain. The pension worksheet on page 428 incorporates these effects. Also shown on page 428 is the journal entry to record net pension cost for 2002.

Other Items

To reduce the volatility of the net pension cost, GAAP rules allow firms to spread the effect of certain pension-related items over a number of accounting periods rather than recognizing them all in one year. These items are (1) prior service cost, (2) transition liabilities, and (3) deferred gains and losses. Amortization of deferred gains and losses has already been discussed. Prior service cost represents the portion of the pension liability that relates to years worked by employees prior to the time the pension plan was adopted, but for which they are owed a pension benefit. This amount is amortized over the expected service lives of the

PENSION WORKSHEET

	Employer Accounting Records			Additional Information		
	Net Pension Cost	Cash	Prepaid Pension Cost (unfunded accrued pension cost)	PBO (plan liability)	Plan Assets	Deferred (Gains)/ Losses
Beginning balance, 2001..			(1,623)	(4,623)	3,000	
Service cost	5,086			(5,086)		
Interest cost	462			(462)		
Cash contribution		(3,000)			3,000	
Payment of benefits				2,000	(2,000)	
Investment gains	(330)				600	(270)
	5,218	(3,000)	(2,218)			
Ending balance, 2002 . . .			(3,841)	(8,171)	4,600	(270)

	Journal Entry to Record Net Pension Cost		
+/−	Accounts [description of account]	Debit	Credit
+	Net Pension Cost [income statement expense account]	5,218	
−	Cash [balance sheet asset account]		3,000
+	Unfunded Accrued Pension Cost [balance sheet liability account] . .		2,218

employees. Transitional liabilities are the pension liabilities that arose when the company first adopted the current GAAP rules for accounting for pension plans.

Summary

The following tables summarize the items that increase and decrease net pension cost, plan assets, and the PBO.

COMPONENTS OF NET PENSION COST

Increases
  Service cost
  Interest cost
  Amortization of deferred losses
  Amortization of prior service cost
  Amortization of transition liability
Decreases
  Expected return on plan assets
  Amortization of deferred gains
  Amortization of transition asset

ITEMS CAUSING INCREASES AND DECREASES IN PLAN ASSETS AND PBO

	Plan Assets	PBO
Increases	Cash received from employer	Service cost
	Actual gains	Interest cost
Decreases	Payment of pension benefits	Payment of pension benefits
	Actual losses	

IBM'S PENSION ACCOUNTING

This section illustrates financial reporting for pension plans by examining IBM's U.S. pension plans for 2000.

Projected Benefit Obligation

IBM's PBO, called the *benefit obligation* in the table below, was $34,434 million for U.S. plans at the beginning of 2000. During 2000, the PBO increased by the service cost of $563 million and the interest cost of $2,553 million and decreased by payments of benefits of $2,421 million. In addition to these increases and decreases, there were several other changes in the PBO for 2000. First, there were net acquisitions/divestitures arising from transactions made by IBM to acquire new businesses or dispose of existing businesses. For example, if IBM acquires a new subsidiary, the pension liability is increased by the present value of the future pension benefits payable to the newly acquired employees.

Another item causing a change in IBM's pension liability is amendments. Changes in the provisions of the plan contract could result in an increase or decrease in the amount of future pension benefits payable. Finally, there are actuarial losses and gains. These represent changes in the expected future pension payment amounts due to changes made by the actuaries in their assumptions, or amortization of deferred gains and losses.

Here is the information from the notes to IBM's financial statements detailing the changes in the PBO for 2000 and 1999 for the company's U.S. pension plans.

The changes in the benefit obligations of the U.S. defined benefit plans for 2000 and 1999 were as follows (in millions):

	U.S. Plan	
	2000	**1999**
Change in benefit obligation		
Benefit obligation at beginning of year	$34,434	$36,561
Service cost	563	566
Interest cost	2,553	2,404
Acquisitions/divestitures, net	36	68
Amendments	645	75
Actuarial losses/(gains)	1,729	(2,766)
Benefits paid from trust	(2,421)	(2,474)
Benefit obligation at end of year	$37,539	$34,434

Source: IBM Corporation Form 10-K.

Plan Assets

The table on page 430 shows the changes in the plan assets of IBM's U.S. pension plans for 2000 and 1999. The fair value of plan assets at the beginning of 2000 was $45,584 million. The actual return on plan assets of $1,395 million is the sum of the investment income (interest and dividends) as well as gains and losses. Acquisitions and divestitures represents the pension plan assets of acquired companies. The plan assets are reduced by benefits paid from trust in the amount of $2,421, the same amount as the reduction in the PBO shown above. There is no increase for cash payments from IBM to the trust because the company did not make a cash contribution to the trust during 2000 or 1999.

The changes in plan assets of the U.S. defined benefit plans for 2000 and 1999 were as follows (in millions):

	U.S. Plan	
	2000	**1999**
Change in plan assets		
Fair value of plan assets at beginning of year . . .	$45,584	$41,593
Actual return on plan assets	1,395	6,397
Acquisitions/divestitures, net	36	68
Benefits paid from trust	(2,421)	(2,474)
Fair value of plan assets at end of year	$44,594	$45,584

Source: IBM Corporation Form 10-K.

Net Pension Cost

The following table shows the computation of IBM's net pension cost for the prior three years. The service cost of $563 million and the interest cost of $2,553 million are the same as the increase in the PBO shown earlier. The net pension cost is reduced by the expected return on plan assets of $3,902 million. Notice that this amount is different from the actual return of $1,395 shown above. Since IBM's expected return on plan assets (a reduction in pension expense) is larger than the service cost and the interest cost, the company reports pension *income* rather than pension cost. The amount of pension income is also affected by amortization of the transition asset and amortization of prior service cost. The net pension income for 2000 is $896 million.

(Income) / Cost of Pension Plans (in millions)			
	U.S. Plan		
	2000	**1999**	**1998**
Service cost	$ 563	$ 566	$ 532
Interest cost	2,553	2,404	2,261
Expected return on plan assets	(3,902)	(3,463)	(3,123)
Amortization of transition assets	(141)	(140)	(140)
Amortization of prior service cost	31	(21)	16
Recognized actuarial losses	—	16	—
Net periodic pension (income) — U.S. plan . . .	$ (896)	$ (638)	$ (454)

Source: IBM Corporation Form 10-K.

As a clear example of the smoothing effect of GAAP pension accounting, notice that had IBM used the actual return on plan assets of $1,395 million rather than the expected return of $3,902 million, the company would have reported a net pension *cost* rather than pension income. Also, notice that, as pointed out in the introduction to this chapter, IBM's reported net income is increased through the recording of pension income.

Recording Pension Expense or Income

Here is the entry that IBM would make to record its net pension income for the year:

	Journal Entry to Record Pension Income (in millions)		
+/−	**Accounts [description of account]**	**Debit**	**Credit**
+	Prepaid Pension Cost [balance sheet asset account]	896	
+	Pension Income [income statement revenue account]		896

Pension Worksheet for IBM

The following worksheet records all of the pension activity for IBM's U.S. pension plans for 2000. The entries to the worksheet reflect the items that have been discussed above and are taken from the notes to IBM's financial statements. There is no reduction in cash for 2000 because IBM did not make a cash contribution to the plan for the year. IBM's pension income of $896 million and prepaid pension cost of $4,680 million are shown at the bottom of the left side of the worksheet. The right side of the worksheet shows the trust assets of $44,594 million and PBO of $37,539 million, as well as the unrecognized gains and losses, unrecognized prior service cost, and unrecognized transition asset.

WORKSHEET ANALYSIS OF IBM'S PENSION ACCOUNTING FOR 2000 (in millions)							
	Employer Accounting Records			**Additional Accounting Information**				
	Net Pension Cost/ (Income)	**Cash**	**Prepaid Pension Cost (unfunded accrued pension cost)**	**PBO (plan liability)**	**Plan Assets**	**Unrecognized (Gain)/ Loss**	**Unrecognized Prior Service Cost**	**Unrecognized Net Transition Asset**
Balances, 12/31/99			3,784	(34,434)	45,584	(7,003)	269	(632)
Service cost	563			(563)				
Interest cost	2,553			(2,553)				
Return on plan assets	(3,902)				1,395	2,507		
Benefits paid				2,421	(2,421)			
Amortization of prior service cost	31						(31)	
Amortization of transition assets	(141)							141
Acquisitions/divestures				(36)	36			
Amendments				(645)			645	
Actuarial losses				(1,729)		1,729		
	(896)		896					
Balances, 12/31/00			4,680	(37,539)	44,594	(2,767)	883	(491)

FUNDING STATUS AND MINIMUM LIABILITY

Funding Status of the Plan

To the extent a plan's assets exceed the PBO, the plan is said to be *overfunded*. To the extent the PBO exceeds a plan's assets, the plan is said to be *underfunded*. You can see from the information discussed above that at the end of 2000 the value of IBM's U.S. plan assets was $44,594 million, while the corresponding PBO was $37,539 million, meaning the company's U.S. plans were overfunded. This overfunded status is the reason that IBM did not make a cash contribution to the plan for 2000—the value of plan assets was more than enough to pay the expected future pension liability.[4]

---

[4] One reason plans are overfunded is tax incentives. Firms with excess cash can make contributions to their pension trust and receive a tax deduction. In effect, these firms are prepaying future pension expenses and receiving a current tax benefit. A return on plan assets that is higher than expected can also lead to overfunding.

Although the $7,055 million difference between the $44,594 million fair value of plan assets and the $37,539 million pension liability reflects the overfunded status of the plan, this amount is *not* the amount reflected on IBM's balance sheet as a prepaid pension cost. IBM's actual prepaid pension cost on its balance sheet for 2000 is $4,679 million, as shown in the following table:

Fair value of plan assets in excess of benefit obligation ...	$ 7,055	$11,150
Unrecognized net actuarial gains	(2,768)	(7,003)
Unrecognized prior service costs	883	269
Unrecognized net transition asset	(491)	(632)
Net prepaid pension asset recognized in the Consolidated Statement of Financial Position	$ 4,679	$ 3,784

Source: IBM Corporation Form 10-K.

The reason the actual asset recorded on IBM's balance sheet differs from the overfunded amount is because of the unusual accounting treatment mentioned earlier to try and smooth out the impact of changes in plan assets and liabilities. As the above table shows, there are three items that reconcile IBM's overfunded amount of $7,055 million with the actual prepaid pension cost recorded on the balance sheet of $4,679 million: (1) unrecognized net actuarial gains, (2) unrecognized prior service costs, and (3) unrecognized net transition asset.

Unrecognized net actuarial gains is the cumulative difference between the expected gains (used in the actuarial plan computations) and the actual gains and losses realized by the plan. Prior service cost represents the portion of the pension liability that relates to years worked by employees prior to the time the pension plan was adopted, but for which they are owed a pension benefit. Transitional assets are the pension assets that arose when the company first adopted the current GAAP rules for accounting for pension plans.

Minimum Pension Liability

Since future pension benefits payable are based on the employees' salaries at the time of retirement, rather than their current salaries, the actuaries must estimate how future salaries will grow and consider these future salary increases in their computation of expected future pension payments. If future salaries remained the same as current salaries, the present value of the pension liability would be smaller. This smaller measure of the pension liability, computed without taking into account expected future salary increases, is known as the *accumulated benefit obligation* (ABO). Although the ABO is used for certain computations (discussed below), the number used to provide information about the present value of the expected pension liability is the PBO.

Standard setters were concerned that the deferral of losses or prior service costs could result in a recorded pension liability on the employer's balance sheet that was misleading to users of financial statements. They therefore included a requirement for a minimum pension liability. If the actual net pension liability recorded on the employer's balance sheet is less than the minimum liability, the recorded liability must be increased to the amount of the minimum liability.[5] IBM recorded an additional $90 million liability in 2000 in connection with the minimum liability for non-U.S. plans.

The minimum pension liability is the excess of the accumulated benefit obligation over the fair value of plan assets. Recall that the ABO is the liability of the pension trust to pay future benefits, but computed *without* taking into account

[5] This computation is made after the normal net pension cost or income is recorded for the year.

future salary increases. For example, assume that after recording net pension cost for the year, the accrued pension cost on the balance sheet of the employer is $10,000. Assume further that the ABO is $180,000 and the fair value of plan assets is $165,000. This excess of $15,000 is the minimum liability. Since this exceeds the actual liability of $10,000, an additional $5,000 liability must be recorded on the balance sheet of the employer. The debit part of the accounting entry is to an intangible pension asset (another balance sheet account). This entry is as follows:

	Journal Entry to Record Minimum Pension Liability		
+/−	**Accounts [description of account]**	**Debit**	**Credit**
+	Intangible Pension Asset [balance sheet asset account]	5,000	
+	Additional Pension Liability [balance sheet liability account]		5,000

Under GAAP, the intangible pension asset cannot be larger than the balance of unrecognized prior service cost for the plan. If the intangible pension asset would exceed the balance of unrecognized prior service cost, any additional minimum pension liability is recorded as a reduction in other comprehensive income, a shareholders' equity account.

PENSION DISCLOSURES

Under GAAP, firms are required to disclose the following information with respect to pension plans:

- A reconciliation showing the changes in the PBO during the accounting period.
- A reconciliation showing the changes in plan assets during the accounting period.
- A comparison of the PBO with the plan assets so that the funded status of the plan can be determined.
- A reconciliation of the overfunded or underfunded amount with the accrued pension cost or prepaid pension cost recorded on the balance sheet of the employer.
- The actuarial assumptions on which the PBO is based. These include the interest rate used in the present value computation, the expected return on plan assets, and the expected rate of increase in employee compensation.
- The major components of net pension cost or net pension income.

Although many of the parts of IBM's pension disclosure have been shown earlier in the chapter, the tables on pages 434–435 present the entire pension disclosure for IBM.

(Income) / Cost of Pension Plans (in millions)	U.S. Plan			Non-U.S. Plans		
	2000	**1999**	**1998**	**2000**	**1999**	**1998**
Service cost	$ 563	$ 566	$ 532	$ 445	$ 475	$ 399
Interest cost	2,553	2,404	2,261	1,234	1,282	1,213
Expected return on plan assets	(3,902)	(3,463)	(3,123)	(2,042)	(1,937)	(1,739)
Amortization of transition assets	(141)	(140)	(140)	(10)	(11)	(10)
Amortization of prior service cost	31	(21)	16	24	25	26
Recognized actuarial losses	—	16	—	4	28	5
Settlement (gains)/losses	—	—	—	(25)	(23)	10
Net periodic pension (income)/cost— U.S. plan and material non-U.S. plans	$ (896)	$ (638)	$ (454)	$ (370)	$ (161)	$ (96)
Cost of other defined benefit plans	72	68	59	23	37	54
Total net periodic pension (income)/cost for all defined benefit plans	$ (824)	$ (570)	$ (395)	$ (347)	$ (124)	$ (42)
Cost of defined contribution plans	$ 294	$ 275	$ 258	$ 149	$ 131	$ 90
Total retirement plan (income)/cost recognized in the Consolidated Statement of Earnings	$ (530)	$ (295)	$ (137)	$ (198)	$ 7	$ 48

Source: IBM Corporation Form 10-K.

The changes in the benefit obligations and plan assets of the U.S. and material non-U.S. defined benefit plans for 2000 and 1999 were as follows (in millions):

	U.S. Plan		Non-U.S. Plans	
	2000	**1999**	**2000**	**1999**
Change in benefit obligation				
Benefit obligation at beginning of year	$34,434	$36,561	$21,770	$22,048
Service cost	563	566	445	475
Interest cost	2,553	2,404	1,234	1,282
Plan participants' contributions	—	—	28	29
Acquisitions/divestitures, net	36	68	(65)	(47)
Amendments	645	75	63	—
Actuarial losses/(gains)	1,729	(2,766)	243	522
Benefits paid from trust	(2,421)	(2,474)	(728)	(737)
Direct benefit payments	—	—	(218)	(257)
Foreign exchange impact	—	—	(1,626)	(1,552)
Plan curtailments/settlements/termination benefits	—	—	4	7
Benefit obligation at end of year	$37,539	$34,434	$21,150	$21,770
Change in plan assets				
Fair value of plan assets at beginning of year	$45,584	$41,593	$27,843	$25,294
Actual return on plan assets	1,395	6,397	(196)	5,184
Employer contribution	—	—	66	143
Acquisitions/divestitures, net	36	68	(50)	(36)
Plan participants' contributions	—	—	28	29
Benefits paid from trust	(2,421)	(2,474)	(728)	(737)
Foreign exchange impact	—	—	(2,015)	(1,995)
Settlements	—	—	(115)	(39)
Fair value of plan assets at end of year	$44,594	$45,584	$24,833	$27,843
Fair value of plan assets in excess of benefit obligation	7,055	11,150	3,683	6,073
Unrecognized net actuarial gains	(2,768)	(7,003)	(1,860)	(4,597)
Unrecognized prior service costs	883	269	168	140
Unrecognized net transition asset	(491)	(632)	(56)	(72)
Adjustment to recognize minimum liability	—	—	(90)	(84)
Net prepaid pension asset recognized in the Consolidated Statement of Financial Position	$ 4,679	$ 3,784	$ 1,845	$ 1,460

Source: IBM Corporation Form 10-K.

Actuarial assumptions used to determine costs and benefit obligations for principal pension plans follow:
Weighted-Average Actuarial Assumptions (as of December 31)

	U.S. Plan			Non-U.S. Plans		
	2000	**1999**	**1998**	**2000**	**1999**	**1998**
Discount rate	7.25%	7.75%	6.5%	4.5– 7.1%	4.5– 7.3%	4.5– 7.5%
Expected return on plan assets	10.0	9.5	9.5	5.0–11.0	6.0–10.5	6.5–10.0
Rate of compensation increase	6.0	6.0	5.0	2.6– 6.1	2.6– 6.1	2.7– 6.1

The company evaluates its actuarial assumptions on an annual basis and considers changes in these long-term factors based upon market conditions and the requirements of SFAS No. 87, "Employers' Accounting for Pensions."

The change in expected return on plan assets and the discount rate for the 2000 U.S. plan year had an effect of an additional $(195) million and $(26) million of net retirement plan (income)/cost, respectively, for the year ended December 31, 2000. This compares with an additional $46 million and $65 million of net retirement plan (income)/cost for the year ended December 31, 1999, as a result of plan year 1999 changes in the rate of compensation increase and the discount rate, respectively.

Net periodic pension cost is determined using the Projected Unit Credit actuarial method.

Funding Policy

It is the company's practice to fund amounts for pensions sufficient to meet the minimum requirements set forth in applicable employee benefits laws and local tax laws. From time to time, the company contributes additional amounts as it deems appropriate. Liabilities for amounts in excess of these funding levels are accrued and reported in the company's Consolidated Statement of Financial Position. The assets of the various plans include corporate equities, government securities, corporate debt securities and real estate.

Other

At December 31, 2000, the material non-U.S. defined benefit plans in which the fair value of plan assets exceeded the benefit obligation had obligations of $16,941 million and assets of $20,915 million. The material non-U.S. defined benefit plans in which the benefit obligation exceeded the fair value of plan assets had obligations of $4,209 million and assets of $3,919 million.

At December 31, 1999, the material non-U.S. defined benefit plans in which the fair value of plan assets exceeded the benefit obligation had obligations of $21,168 million and assets of $27,400 million. The material non-U.S. defined benefit plans in which the benefit obligation exceeded the fair value of plan assets had obligations of $602 million and assets of $443 million.

The change from 1999 to 2000 was the result of the company's pension plan in Japan. In 1999, the Japan pension plan assets exceeded its benefit obligation by approximately 15 percent. In 2000, the benefit obligation exceeded assets by approximately 3 percent. Total assets of this plan at December 31, 2000 exceeded $3,500 million.

Source: IBM Corporation Form 10-K.

DEFINED CONTRIBUTION PLANS

Under a defined contribution plan, the amount payable to an employee at retirement is not fixed by the plan. Rather, an account (similar to a savings account at a bank) is established for each employee, and the employer makes contributions to this account each year. Often, the amount of the contribution is based on the employee's compensation for the year. For example, the plan may require the employer to contribute an amount equal to 5 percent of each employee's compensation for the year. Alternatively, the contribution may be based on a percentage of the earnings of the employer, making the retirement plan a profit sharing plan.

In a defined contribution plan, the plan contract will contain rules that determine how much the employer must contribute to the plan each year and how this contribution is to be allocated to the accounts of the individual employees. The plan is called a *defined contribution plan* because the contribution amount is defined by the plan contract.

From an accounting standpoint, the key feature of a defined contribution plan is that the employer has not promised to pay a specific amount at the time the employee retires. The amount available to pay to each retired employee is the amount in each employee's pension account under the plan. Those employees who have large account balances will receive large pension payments. This means that the amount of the employer's liability for future pension payments to a retired employee is exactly equal to the amount of assets in that employee's account. Therefore, with a defined contribution plan there is no prepaid pension cost or unfunded accrued pension cost.

Here is an example from the notes to IBM's financial statements of how the company's new cash balance plan works.

Effective July 1, 1999, the company amended the IBM Retirement Plan to establish the IBM Personal Pension Plan (the U.S. Plan). The new plan establishes a new formula for determining pension benefits for many of its employees. Under the amended U.S. Plan, a new formula was created whereby retirement benefits are credited to each employee's cash balance account monthly based on a percentage of the employee's pensionable compensation.

Source: IBM Corporation Form 10-K.

ACCOUNTING FOR OTHER POSTEMPLOYMENT BENEFITS

In addition to providing pensions to retired employees, firms often provide other types of benefits to their retired workers, such as medical insurance. These nonpension retirement benefits are known as *other postemployment benefits* or *nonpension postretirement benefits*. IBM describes its plans as follows: "The company has a defined benefit postretirement plan that provides medical, dental and life insurance for U.S. retirees and eligible dependents." This section discusses the financial reporting rules relating to these benefits.

The principal difference between pension benefits and nonpension benefits is that firms do not usually fund their nonpension benefits by contributing cash to a pension trust. Instead, firms usually make payments directly to insurance companies that provide the benefits. Therefore, firms generally have a cash outflow each year equal to the cost of the benefits for employees that have already retired.

For financial reporting purposes, the main issue relating to nonpension benefits is the accrual of future costs relating to employees who have not yet retired. Under accrual accounting, these future costs should be matched against revenues generated during the accounting periods in which the employees provided services to the firm.

Just as with pension liabilities, actuaries estimate the expected future payments that the firm will make with respect to their current employees, and the present value of these expected future payments is recorded as a liability on the employer's balance sheet. Shown in the following table are the changes in IBM's liability for other postemployment benefits. There are two important things to notice about this information. First, the types of changes in the benefit obligation (that is, the liability for future payments) are the same as those for the pension liability discussed earlier: service cost, interest cost, and actuarial gains and losses. Second, although IBM estimated the liability for future benefits to be $6,443 million at the end of 2000, it had plan assets of only $4 million. The liability recorded on the balance sheet of IBM for future benefits is $6,254 million. As with pension benefits, this number does not reflect deferred actuarial losses or prior service costs.

The changes in the benefit obligation and plan assets of the U.S. plan for 2000 and 1999 are as follows (in millions):

	2000	1999
Change in benefit obligation		
Benefit obligation at beginning of year	$ 6,178	$ 6,457
Service cost	50	48
Interest cost	449	424
Amendments	—	(127)
Actuarial gains	(69)	(445)
Actuarial losses	432	371
Benefits paid from trust	(87)	(325)
Direct benefit payments	(510)	(225)
Benefit obligation at end of year	6,443	6,178
Change in plan assets		
Fair value of plan assets at beginning of year	$ 105	$ 123
Actual loss on plan assets	(14)	(18)
Employer contributions	—	325
Benefits paid, net of employee contributions	(87)	(325)
Fair value of plan assets at end of year	4	105
Benefit obligation in excess of plan assets	(6,439)	(6,073)
Unrecognized net actuarial losses	986	631
Unrecognized prior service costs	(801)	(948)
Accrued postretirement benefit liability recognized in the Consolidated Statement of Financial Position	$(6,254)	$(6,390)

Source: IBM Corporation Form 10-K.

Shown in the following table is the expense recorded by IBM for other postemployment benefits. Notice that the components of the expense—service cost, interest cost, and so forth—are the same as the components of the pension expense. The main difference between this expense and the pension expense is the expected return on plan assets is so low because there are almost no assets in the plan.

The net periodic postretirement benefit cost for the U.S. plan for the years ended December 31 include the following components (in millions):

	2000	1999	1998
Service cost	$ 50	$ 48	$ 42
Interest cost	449	424	427
Expected return on plan assets	(2)	(6)	(5)
Amortization of prior service cost	(147)	(143)	(133)
Recognized actuarial losses	24	19	—
Net periodic postretirement benefit cost	$ 374	$ 342	$ 331

Source: IBM Corporation Form 10-K.

One difference in the disclosure requirements between pensions and other postemployment benefits is the following. Under GAAP, firms must disclose how their expense and liability for other postemployment benefits would change if there was a one-percentage-point change in their estimate of the rate of increase in health care costs. Since the principal component of other postemployment benefits is the cost of health insurance, and since future health insurance costs will reflect future increases in health care costs, the computation of the expense and liability are usually quite sensitive to this assumption. Here is the disclosure for IBM:

A one-percentage-point change in the assumed health care cost trend rate would have the following effects as of December 31, 2000 (in millions):

	One-Percentage-Point Increase	One-Percentage-Point Decrease
Effect on total service and interest cost	$ 8	$(10)
Effect on postretirement benefit obligation	52	(65)

Source: IBM Corporation Form 10-K.

PENSIONS AND THE CASH FLOWS STATEMENT

If the cash a firm contributes to a pension trust is not equal to the amount of pension expense reported on the income statement, an adjustment is necessary to reconcile net income with cash flows from operating activities on the statement of cash flows. For example, in 2000 IBM did not contribute any cash to its pension trust. However, as shown earlier, IBM recorded pension income of $896 million. Therefore, an adjustment is necessary to reconcile IBM's net income with IBM's cash flows. Since IBM reports a prepaid pension cost, this adjustment is reflected in the changes to other assets on IBM's cash flows statement.

For another example of the cash flow effects of postretirement benefits, the cash flows statement of The Boeing Company shows an adjustment for the change in accrued retiree health care. To the extent the company accrues a liability for future retiree health care expenses without making a cash payment, an adjustment on the cash flows statement is necessary.

THE BOEING COMPANY AND SUBSIDIARIES
Consolidated Statements of Cash Flows
(in millions)

	Year Ended December 31		
	1999	1998	1997
Cash flows—operating activities			
Net earnings (loss)	$2,309	$1,120	$ (178)
Adjustments to reconcile net earnings (loss)			
to net cash provided by operating activities			
Share-based plans	209	153	(99)
Depreciation	1,538	1,517	1,354
Amortization of goodwill and intangibles	107	105	104
Customer and commercial financing valuation provision	72	61	64
Gain on dispositions, net	(87)	(13)	
Changes in assets and liabilities—			
Short-term investments	179	450	154
Accounts receivable	(225)	(167)	(240)
Inventories, net of advances and progress billings	2,030	652	(96)
Accounts payable and other liabilities	217	(840)	1,908
Advances in excess of related costs	(36)	(324)	(139)
Income taxes payable and deferred	462	145	(451)
Other	(597)	(479)	(272)
Accrued retiree health care	**46**	**35**	**(4)**
Net cash provided by operating activities	$6,224	$2,415	$2,105

Source: The Boeing Company Form 10-K.

PENSION ACCOUNTING IN OTHER COUNTRIES

Pension accounting in other countries is similar to that in the United States in that a liability for future pension payments is recorded. However, many of the details of how this liability is determined differ in other countries. Shown below is the pension note from the financial statements of Reed Elsevier explaining the main differences between U.S. pension accounting (following the requirements of SFAS 87) and U.K. accounting (following the requirements of SSAP24).

Pensions

The combined businesses account for pension costs under the rules set out in SSAP24. Its objectives and principles are broadly in line with SFAS 87, Employers' Accounting for Pensions. However, SSAP24 is less prescriptive in the application of the actuarial methods and assumptions to be applied in the calculation of pension costs.

Under U.S. GAAP, plan assets are valued by reference to market-related values at the date of the financial statements. Liabilities are assessed using the rate of return obtainable on fixed or inflation-linked bonds. Under U.K. GAAP, pension plan assets and liabilities are based on the results of the latest actuarial valuation. Pension assets are valued at the discounted present value determined by expected future income. Liabilities are assessed using the expected rate of return on plan assets.

Source: Reed Elsevier Form 20-F.

In the following financial statement note, Reed Elsevier explains the many actuarial assumptions on which its pension expense and pension liability is based. Under U.K. terminology, pension plans are referred to as *schemes*.

---

6. Pension Schemes

A number of pension schemes are operated around the world. The major schemes are of the defined benefit type with assets held in separate trustee administered funds. The two largest schemes, which cover the majority of employees, are in the U.K. and U.S. The main U.K. scheme was subject to a valuation by Watson Wyatt Partners as at 5 April 2000. The main U.S. scheme was subject to a valuation by Towers Perrin as at 1 January 2000.

The principal valuation assumptions for the main UK scheme were:

Actuarial method	Projected unit method
Annual rate of return on investments	6.60%
Annual increase in total pensionable remuneration	5.00%
Annual increase in present and future pensions in payment	3.00%

The principal valuation assumptions used for the U.S. scheme were a rate of return on investments of 8%, increase in pensionable remuneration of 4.5%, and increase in present and future pensions in payment of 2%.

The actuarial values placed on scheme assets were sufficient to cover 121% and 117% of the benefits that had accrued to members of the main U.K. and U.S. schemes, respectively. Actuarial surpluses are spread as a level amount over the average remaining service lives of current employees. The market values of the schemes' assets at the valuation dates, excluding assets held in respect of members' additional voluntary contributions, were 'L'1,723m and 'L'158m in respect of the U.K. and U.S. schemes, respectively.

Assessments for accounting purposes in respect of other schemes, including the Netherlands scheme, have been carried out by external qualified actuaries using prospective benefit methods with the objective that current and future charges remain a stable percentage of pensionable payroll. The principal actuarial assumptions adopted in the assessments of the major schemes are that, over the long term, investment returns will marginally exceed the annual increase in pensionable remuneration and in present and future pensions. The actuarial value of assets of the schemes approximated to the aggregate benefits that had accrued to members, after allowing for expected future increases in pensionable remuneration and pensions in course of payment.

The net pension charge was 'L'35m (1999 'L'28m; 1998 'L'22m), including a net 'L'1m (1999 'L'3m; 1998 'L'4m) SSAP24 credit related to the main U.K. scheme. The net SSAP24 credit on the main U.K. scheme comprises a regular cost of 'L'23m (1999 'L'16m; 1998 'L'15m), offset by amortisation of the net actuarial surplus of 'L'24m (1999 'L'19m; 1998 'L'19m). Pension contributions made in the year amounted to 'L'36m (1999 'L'31m; 1998 'L'26m). A prepayment of 'L'128m (1999 'L'127m; 1998 'L'124m) is included in debtors falling due after more than one year, representing the excess of the pension credit to the profit and loss account since 1988 over the amounts funded to the main U.K. scheme.

Source: Reed Elsevier Form 20-F.

Although this accounting is similar to U.S. accounting, there are some significant differences. The following shows the reconciliation of Reed Elsevier's net income and shareholders' equity with U.S. GAAP. Notice that one of the adjustments is a difference in net income and shareholders' equity due to pension accounting differences. The effect of pension accounting is to increase U.S. GAAP net income and shareholders' equity over that of U.K. and Dutch GAAP.

Effects on net income of material differences between U.K. and Dutch GAAP and U.S. GAAP (in 'L'm):

	2000	1999	1998
Net income/(loss) under U.K. and Dutch GAAP	33	(63)	772
U.S. GAAP adjustments			
Amortisation of goodwill and other intangible assets	(78)	(83)	(477)
Deferred taxation	85	67	77
Pensions	**22**	**6**	**30**
Other items	(2)	—	(4)
Net income/(loss) under U.S. GAAP	60	(73)	398

Effects on combined shareholders' funds of material differences between U.K. and Dutch GAAP and U.S. GAAP (in 'L'm):

	2000	1999
GAAP adjustments		
Goodwill and other intangible assets	604	553
Deferred taxation	(203)	(180)
Pensions	**86**	**63**
Other items	2	5
Ordinary dividends not declared in the period	177	127
Combined shareholders' funds under U.S. GAAP	3,707	2,423

Source: Reed Elsevier Form 20-F.

PENSIONS AND INCOME TAX EXPENSE

In general, U.S. tax law allows firms a tax deduction for the amount of cash contributed to a pension trust. However, as shown in this chapter, the firm's pension expense will likely differ from the amount of cash contributed. Therefore, a deferred tax asset or deferred tax liability will arise with respect to pension expense, since a firm's tax deduction for pension expense will seldom be the same as the firm's pension expense for financial reporting purposes.

IBM has overfunded its pension plan, so that no current cash contributions to the plan are necessary. This means that the pension expense on IBM's income tax returns in past years has exceeded the pension expense that the firm has recorded under GAAP, resulting in a deferred tax liability for the tax effect of the difference. The financial statement note on page 441 indicates that IBM had a deferred tax liability related to retirement benefits of $3,447 million at the end of 2000.

Unlike they do for pension benefits, firms seldom overfund other postretirement benefits. In most cases, firms record a liability under GAAP for future benefits but do not actually pay these benefits until the employees retire. U.S. tax law allows a tax deduction for these benefits only when they are paid. Therefore, other postretirement benefits usually result in a deferred tax asset on the balance sheet. Shown on page 441 is IBM's deferred tax asset related to employee benefits in the amount of $3,673 million at the end of 2000:

Deferred Tax Liabilities (in millions)		
	(At December 31)	
	2000	**1999**
Retirement benefits	**$3,447**	**$3,092**
Sales-type leases	2,450	2,914
Depreciation	1,179	1,237
Software costs deferred	306	250
Other	1,836	2,058
Gross deferred tax liabilities	$9,218	$9,551

Source: IBM Corporation Form 10-K.

Deferred Tax Assets (in millions)		
	(At December 31)	
	2000	**1999**
Employee benefits	**$ 3,673**	**$ 3,737**
Alternative minimum tax credits	1,424	1,244
Bad debt, inventory and warranty reserves	953	1,093
Capitalized research and development	848	880
Deferred income	837	870
General business credits	655	605
Infrastructure reduction charges	617	918
Foreign tax loss carryforwards	489	406
Equity alliances	437	377
Depreciation	376	326
State and local tax loss carryforwards	246	227
Intracompany sales and services	149	153
Other	2,809	2,763
Gross deferred tax assets	$13,513	$13,599

Source: IBM Corporation Form 10-K.

USING INFORMATION ABOUT PENSIONS TO MAKE DECISIONS

Using pension information to make decisions about the firm is particularly difficult. As shown above, GAAP rules attempt to smooth out the volatility of reported pension expense. One way this is accomplished is through the deferral of actual gains and losses to the extent they exceed the expected return on plan assets. Another way is through the amortization of prior service costs. Therefore, the pension cost reported by the firm in any particular year can be thought of as a long-run average pension cost rather than the pension expense related to that particular year.

Another problem with using reported pension cost for decision making is that the information is sensitive to changes in management's actuarial assumptions. For example, changes in the expected return on plan assets, the expected rate of increase in compensation, and the discount rate used for present value computations will all have an impact on the reported pension cost. Users of financial statement information must determine whether management's assumptions are reasonable. For example, IBM used an expected return on plan assets of 10 percent for 2000 while Reed Elsevier used 8 percent.

Probably the most important item of information about pensions is the amount of cash required by firms to fund their pension liability in future years. Unfortunately, GAAP rules do not require firms to report this information. However, the firms do have to disclose the funding status of the plan, and for any plan that is underfunded (that is, plan assets are less than the PBO), it is likely that cash contributions to the plan in the future will have to be increased at some time.

Although pension accounting is complex and confusing, many firms are moving away from defined benefit plans to defined contribution plans, as IBM did with its cash balance plan. Therefore, in the future the way pension plans are accounted for may become less important.

Summary

This chapter shows how firms with defined benefit pension plans incur a liability for the present value of future pension benefits owed to their employees and the way firms satisfy this liability through the use of a pension trust. Firms make periodic cash contributions to the pension trust, and the trustees of the trust invest this cash and use it in the future, together with the earnings from the investments, to pay pension benefits to the firms' retired employees.

Under GAAP, the liability for future pension benefits is offset against the fair value of assets in the pension trust, and only the net liability is reflected on the balance sheet of the employer. In cases where the fair value of plan assets exceeds the pension liability, the excess is a prepaid pension asset that is recorded on the balance sheet of the employer.

GAAP rules are designed to smooth out the volatility in pension expense by computing pension expense using the expected return on plan assets, rather than the actual return, and by deferring and amortizing prior service costs. To the extent that the pension liability (without regard to expected future increases in employee compensation) exceeds the fair value of plan assets, a minimum pension liability must be recorded.

The pension expense recorded under GAAP consists of the service cost for the year and the interest cost related to the prior year's pension liability, reduced by the expected return on plan assets. To the extent that there are deferred gains and losses from prior years, or unrecognized prior service costs, the amortization of these items may also affect reported pension expense.

If an employer provides nonpension postretirement benefits to employees, the present value of the expected future payments for these other postemployment benefits must be recorded as a liability by the employer.

Discussion Questions

1. Explain the accounting issues associated with pension plans.
2. What is a defined benefit pension plan? What features of the plan are important for accounting purposes?
3. What is the projected benefit obligation (PBO) and how is it computed?
4. What is the role of an actuary in the computation of the PBO?
5. Explain how changes in interest rate assumptions can affect the PBO.
6. What is a pension trust and how is it used? How are the cash flows, assets, and liabilities of the pension trust related to those of the employer?
7. Explain the terms *net pension cost, unfunded accrued pension cost,* and *prepaid pension cost.*
8. What does a balance in unfunded accrued pension cost represent?
9. What does a balance in prepaid pension cost represent?
10. Explain what a pension worksheet is and what the various columns of the worksheet represent. Why is the worksheet useful?

11. Explain what is meant by *service cost* in connection with pension accounting.
12. Explain what is meant by *interest cost* in connection with pension accounting.
13. Explain what causes the balance in plan assets to increase or decrease.
14. Explain what factors cause the PBO to increase or decrease.
15. How do gains and losses from investing pension assets affect (a) the net pension cost and (b) the balance of plan assets?
16. Explain the difference between expected gains and losses and actual gains and losses. Explain how deferred gains and losses are accounted for.
17. Explain the term *prior service cost* and its effect on pension accounting.
18. Explain the term *transition liability* and its effect on pension accounting.
19. What are the components of net pension cost?
20. Explain how a company can record pension income rather than pension cost.
21. Explain the terms *overfunded* and *underfunded* as they relate to pension plans.
22. Explain the differences between a plan's overfunded or underfunded status and the employer's unfunded accrued pension cost or prepaid pension cost.
23. What is a minimum pension liability?
24. What is the accounting treatment to record a minimum pension liability?
25. Explain the pension disclosures required by GAAP.
26. What is a defined contribution pension plan?
27. Explain the accounting rules for defined contribution pension plans.
28. Explain the accounting rules for other postemployment benefits.
29. What differences (if any) are there between accounting for pension plans and accounting for other postemployment benefits?
30. Explain how pension accounting rules affect the cash flows statement.
31. Explain how pension accounting rules affect income tax expense.

Problems

1. A corporation's defined benefit pension plan pays benefits based on the following formula: Multiply the employee's average annual compensation for the five-year period prior to retirement by a percentage equal to three percentage points for each year that the employee has worked for the employer.

   Assume a new employee works for the employer for one year (2001) and that the average of the employee's annual compensation for the five years prior to retirement is expected to be $65,000. The employee is expected to work 15 years before retiring, with retirement occurring at the end of 2015. The employee is expected to live for 12 years after retirement, with the first payment in 2016 and the last payment in 2027. The discount rate is 7 percent.

   a. What is the PBO for this employee at the end of 2001?

   b. What is the service cost for this employee for 2001?

2. A corporation's defined benefit pension plan pays benefits based on the following formula: Multiply the employee's average annual compensation for the five-year period prior to retirement by a percentage equal to one and one-half (1.5) percentage points for each year that the employee has worked for the employer.

   Assume a new employee works for the employer for one year (2001) and that the average of the employee's annual compensation for the five years prior to retirement is expected to be $70,000. The employee is expected to work 12 years before retiring, with retirement occurring at the end of 2012. The employee is expected to live for eight years after retirement, with the first payment in 2013 and the last payment in 2020. The discount rate is 8 percent.

   a. What is the PBO for this employee at the end of 2001?

   b. What is the service cost for this employee for 2001?

3. A corporation's defined benefit pension plan pays benefits based on the following formula: Multiply the employee's average annual compensation for the five-year period prior to retirement by a percentage equal to two and one-half (2.5) percentage points for each year that the employee has worked for the employer.

   Assume a new employee works for the employer for one year (2001) and that the average of the employee's annual compensation for the five years prior to retirement is expected to be $90,000. The employee is expected to work eight years before retiring, with retirement occurring at the end of 2008. The employee is expected to live for 11 years after retirement, with the first payment in 2009 and the last payment in 2019. The discount rate is 5 percent.

   a. What is the PBO for this employee at the end of 2001?

   b. What is the service cost for this employee for 2001?

4. A corporation's net pension cost is $150,000 for the year, and it contributes $120,000 in cash to its pension trust. Give the journal entry to record the pension cost for the year.

5. A corporation's net pension cost is $1,600,000 for the year, and it contributes $2,000,000 in cash to its pension trust. Give the journal entry to record the pension cost for the year.

6. A corporation's net pension cost is $8,400,000 for the year, and it contributes $7,000,000 in cash to its pension trust. Give the journal entry to record the pension cost for the year.

7. Assume the same facts as given in problem 1, except that the employee works for a second year (2002). All other assumptions remain the same.

   a. Compute the service cost for 2002.

   b. Compute the interest cost for 2002.

   c. Use a pension worksheet to record the pension activity for this employee for 2001 and 2002.

8. Assume the same facts as given in problem 2, except that the employee works for a second year (2002). All other assumptions remain the same.

   a. Compute the service cost for 2002.

   b. Compute the interest cost for 2002.

   c. Use a pension worksheet to record the pension activity for this employee for 2001 and 2002.

9. Assume the same facts as given in problem 3, except that the employee works for a second year (2002). All other assumptions remain the same.

   a. Compute the service cost for 2002.

   b. Compute the interest cost for 2002.

   c. Use a pension worksheet to record the pension activity for this employee for 2001 and 2002.

10. A corporation has a defined benefit pension plan. For 2001, the service cost was $8,000, the interest cost was $480, and the corporation funded the plan for $9,000. During 2001, the plan paid benefits of $2,500.

    a. Complete the pension worksheet below to show the ending balances for 2001.

	Employer Accounting Records			Additional Information
	Net Pension Cost	Cash	Prepaid Pension Cost (unfunded accrued pension cost)	PBO (plan liability)	Plan Assets
Beginning balance, 2001			(4,000)	(6,000)	2,000

b. Give the journal entry to record net pension cost for 2001.

11. A corporation has a defined benefit pension plan. For 2001, the service cost was $25,000, the interest cost was $5,950, and the corporation funded the plan for $20,000. During 2001, the plan paid benefits of $4,500.

a. Complete the pension worksheet below to show the ending balances for 2001.

	Employer Accounting Records			Additional Information	
	Net Pension Cost	Cash	Prepaid Pension Cost (unfunded accrued pension cost)	PBO (plan liability)	Plan Assets
Beginning balance, 2001			12,000	(85,000)	97,000

b. Give the journal entry to record net pension cost for 2001.

12. A corporation has a defined benefit pension plan. For 2001, the service cost was $15,000, the interest cost was $5,400, and the corporation funded the plan for $25,000. During 2001, the plan paid benefits of $3,000.

a. Complete the pension worksheet below to show the ending balances for 2001.

	Employer Accounting Records			Additional Information	
	Net Pension Cost	Cash	Prepaid Pension Cost (unfunded accrued pension cost)	PBO (plan liability)	Plan Assets
Beginning balance, 2001			(1,000)	(60,000)	59,000

b. Give the journal entry to record net pension cost for 2001.

13. A corporation has a defined benefit pension plan. For 2001, the service cost was $32,000, the interest cost was $15,300, and the corporation funded the plan for $30,000. During 2001, the plan paid benefits of $8,500. Expected gains on plan assets were $13,940, while actual gains were $9,000. During 2001, $400 of the prior service cost was amortized.

a. Complete the pension worksheet below to show the ending balances for 2001.

	Employer Accounting Records			Additional Information		
	Net Pension Cost	Cash	Prepaid Pension Cost (unfunded accrued pension cost)	PBO (plan liability)	Plan Assets	Deferred (Gains)/ Losses	Unrecognized Prior Service Cost
Beginning balance, 2001			(12,000)	(180,000)	164,000	1,600	2,400

b. Give the journal entry to record net pension cost for 2001.

14. A corporation has a defined benefit pension plan. For 2001, the service cost was $40,000, the interest cost was $26,000, and the corporation funded the plan for $55,000. During 2001, the plan paid benefits of $16,000. Expected gains on plan assets were $27,780, while actual gains were $35,000. During 2001, $240 of the prior service cost was amortized.

a. Complete the pension worksheet below to show the ending balances for 2001.

	Employer Accounting Records			Additional Information		
	Net Pension Cost	Cash	Prepaid Pension Cost (unfunded accrued pension cost)	PBO (plan liability)	Plan Assets	Deferred (Gains)/ Losses	Unrecognized Prior Service Cost
Beginning balance, 2001			15,000	(260,000)	277,800	(4,600)	1,800

b. Give the journal entry to record net pension cost for 2001.

15. A corporation has a defined benefit pension plan. For 2001, the service cost was $80,000, the interest cost was $45,750, and the corporation funded the plan for $90,000. During 2001, the plan paid benefits of $8,500. Expected gains on plan assets were $43,485, while actual gains were $41,000. During 2001, $700 of the prior service cost was amortized.

a. Complete the pension worksheet below to show the ending balances for 2001.

	Employer Accounting Records			Additional Information		
	Net Pension Cost	Cash	Prepaid Pension Cost (unfunded accrued pension cost)	PBO (plan liability)	Plan Assets	Deferred (Gains)/ Losses	Unrecognized Prior Service Cost
Beginning balance, 2001			(30,000)	(610,000)	579,800	(3,800)	4,000

b. Give the journal entry to record net pension cost for 2001.

Research Reports

1. Obtain the latest financial statements for a public company with one or more defined benefit pension plans. (Do not use IBM.)

   a. What is the funding status of the plan? Is it over- or underfunded and by how much?

   b. What is reflected on the balance sheet of the employer? Is there an unfunded accrued pension cost, or a prepaid pension cost, and how much?

   c. What is the net pension cost (or pension income) for the year?

   d. Using the information available in the notes to the financial statement, complete a pension worksheet for the plan for the most recent year.

2. Locate an article in the financial press that discusses a public company changing the terms of its pension plan.

   a. Explain the reason for the change in the plan.

   b. Explain any financial accounting consequences of the plan change.

   c. Explain any cash flow consequences of the plan change.

   d. Obtain the financial statements for the company in the article. Is the information in the financial statements consistent with the information in the article?

3. Locate an article in the financial press that discusses the other post employment benefits of a public company.

   a. Explain the types of postemployment benefits offered.

   b. Discuss the accounting issues that relate to these benefits.

   c. Obtain the financial statements for the company in the article. Is the information in the financial statements consistent with the information in the article?

4. Obtain recent financial statements for three public companies with defined benefit pension plans.

a. What interest rates are used in the actuarial assumptions in the plans? Do all three companies use the same rates for the same years? If not, can you explain the difference?

b. What is the assumed rate of return on plan assets in the plans? Do all three companies use the same rates for the same years? If not, can you explain the difference?

c. How do the assumed rates of return on plan assets compare with the actual rates of return on plan assets?

d. How have the interest rates and assumed rates of return changed over the prior three-year period?

e. Assume all of the corporations had to use the same interest rate and assumed rate of return on plan assets. Prepare a schedule estimating what the effect of this would be on each company's projected benefit obligation and net pension cost.

5. Develop your own alternative set of financial accounting rules for pensions.

a. Explain how your accounting rules would address the following questions: (i) What is the liability for future pension benefits? and (ii) What is the pension expense for the year?

b. Explain the major effects on the financial statements of the employer if companies adopted your accounting rules.

c. Discuss the costs and benefits of your proposed accounting rules. Compare these costs and benefits with those of the current GAAP pension accounting rules.

d. Discuss how pension accounting rules are affected by managers' incentives.

Chapter Learning Objectives

After reading this chapter you should understand

1. The major components of shareholders' equity.
2. What *other comprehensive income* represents.
3. The accounting treatment for cash dividends.
4. The accounting treatment for stock dividends and stock splits.
5. The accounting treatment for stock repurchases (treasury stock).
6. The fair value method of accounting for employee stock options.
7. The intrinsic value method of accounting for employee stock options.
8. How basic earnings per share is computed.
9. How diluted earnings per share is computed.

Chapter 15

Shareholders' Equity

Focus Company: Intel Corporation

Introduction

During 1999, the shareholders' equity[1] section (part of the balance sheet) of Intel Corporation increased from $23,377 million to $32,535 million, an increase of $9,158 million. However, as shown in the table below, this increase consisted of a combination of increases and decreases in nine different items, separated into three distinct components: common stock and capital in excess of par value, retained earnings, and accumulated other comprehensive income.

Consolidated Statements of Stockholders' Equity
(in millions)

	Common Stock and Capital in Excess of Par Value	Retained Earnings	Accumulated Other Comprehensive Income	Total
Balance at December 26, 1998	$4,822	$17,952	$ 603	$23,377
Components of comprehensive income				
Net income	—	7,314	—	7,314
Change in unrealized gain on available-for-sale investments, net of tax	—	—	3,188	3,188
Proceeds from sales of shares through employee stock plans, tax benefit of $506 and other	1,049	—	—	1,049
Proceeds from sales of put warrants	20	—	—	20
Reclassification of put warrant obligation, net	7	64	—	71
Repurchase and retirement of common stock	(1,076)	(3,536)	—	(4,612)
Issuance of common stock in connection with Level One Communications acquisition	1,963	—	—	1,963
Stock options assumed in connection with acquisitions	531	—	—	531
Cash dividends declared ($0.110 per share)	—	(366)	—	(366)
Balance at December 25, 1999	$7,316	$21,428	$3,791	$32,535

Source: Intel Corporation Form 10-K.

This chapter explains GAAP rules relating to shareholders' equity accounts. To aid in the analysis, the chapter is divided into four parts, each dealing with a major shareholders' equity accounting issue. The four parts are (1) the nature of shareholders' equity, (2) distributions of cash or stock, (3) employee stock options, and (4) earnings per share.

[1] The terms *shareholders' equity* and *stockholders' equity* are used interchangeably.

THE NATURE OF SHAREHOLDERS' EQUITY

The shareholders of a corporation are sometimes referred to as the *residual claimants*. This means that the shareholders have the legal right to the assets of the firm that remain (or are left over) after all of the firm's creditors are paid off. This residual claim on the corporation's assets is represented by the shareholders' equity section of the balance sheet and generally consists of three components: (1) common stock and capital in excess of par value,[2] (2) retained earnings, and (3) accumulated other comprehensive income. Each of these components is discussed below.

Common Stock and Capital in Excess of Par Value

Each shareholder's ownership interest in the corporation is evidenced by a number of shares of stock, and the total of all of the shares owned by all of the shareholders is the number of shares issued and outstanding. For example, at the end of 1999 Intel Corporation had 3,334 million shares of common stock issued and outstanding.

The number of shares issued and outstanding is an arbitrary number with no important economic significance. For example, if Firm A has twice as many shares of stock issued and outstanding as Firm B, it does *not* mean that Firm A is worth more or is larger than Firm B. The more shares a firm has issued and outstanding, the less each share will be worth. Also, a firm can change the number of shares issued and outstanding by means of a stock split, where each old share of stock is replaced by a different number of new shares. For example, a firm can double the number of shares outstanding by means of a 2-for-1 stock split. Each old share of stock is exchanged for two new shares of stock. Since there are twice as many shares outstanding, each new share is only worth half as much as each old share.

Shares of stock sometimes have a par value associated with them. Like the number of shares outstanding, the par value of a share has no economic significance. Stock may also be issued without a par value, known as *no-par value stock*. Both par value and no-par value shares are common for U.S. public corporations.

Preferred Stock

Sometimes, firms have more than one class or type of stock. All firms have what is known as *common stock*, but firms can have different classes of common, such as class A common and class B common. The different classes often have different voting rights or different priority in liquidation.

Stock that has preferences in dividends payments or liquidation proceeds is usually called *preferred stock*. Preferred stock is often nonvoting and usually has a stated dividend per share that the firm intends to pay to the preferred shareholders, expressed either as a dollar amount or as a percentage of the stock's face amount or par value.[3]

If a firm pays dividends, preferred stockholders must receive a dividend before the common shareholders do, and any preferred dividends not paid from prior years, *called dividends in arrears*, must usually be made up before dividends may be paid to common shareholders. Preferred shareholders also have a right to receive assets in liquidation before the common shareholders. Preferred stock

---

[2] The total of common stock and capital in excess of par value is sometimes referred to as *contributed capital*.

[3] One reason firms are thought to issue preferred stock is because of a demand for dividend income, rather than interest income, by investors that are corporations. Dividend income received by corporations is taxed at a very low rate. Because of this low tax rate, the dividend yield on preferred stock can be lower than the interest rate on debt. For firms with tax loss carryforwards that do not receive an immediate tax benefit for interest payments on debt, the cost of dividends on preferred stock may be less than the after-tax cost of interest on debt.

may be convertible into common stock, may be callable by the firm, or may be redeemable at a certain time in the future, making it quite similar to debt.

As an example of the different features that preferred stock can have, here is a description of preferred stock issued by Wells Fargo:

Adjustable-Rate Cumulative Preferred Stock, Series B

These shares are redeemable at the option of the Company at $50 per share plus accrued and unpaid dividends. Dividends are cumulative and payable quarterly on the 15th of February, May, August and November. For each quarterly period, the dividend rate is 76% of the highest of the three-month Treasury bill discount rate, 10-year constant maturity Treasury security yield or 20-year constant maturity Treasury bond yield, but limited to a minimum of 5.5% and a maximum of 10.5% per year. The average dividend rate was 5.6% during 2001 and 2000 and 5.5% in 1999.

Source: Wells Fargo Form 10-K.

This stock has several features that make it different from common stock. First, the stock is redeemable for $50 plus accrued and unpaid dividends. Second, dividends are cumulative, meaning that any dividends that are missed must be made up in the future. Third, the dividend rate is adjustable and is based on the yields of U.S. Treasury bills and bonds.

Here is a portion of the shareholders' equity section of Intel's balance sheet showing the company's preferred and common stock:

	1999	1998
Stockholders' equity		
Preferred stock, $0.001 par value, 50 shares authorized; none issued	—	—
Common stock, $0.001 par value, 4,500 shares authorized; 3,334 issued and outstanding (3,315 in 1998) and capital in excess of par value	7,316	4,822

Source: Intel Corporation Form 10-K.

The first thing to notice is that Intel is legally authorized to issue 50 million shares of preferred stock with a par value of $0.001 per share. However, no preferred shares have been issued. Firms usually have more shares of stock authorized than issued. Having unissued shares already authorized makes it easy for the firm to issue additional shares in the future as the need arises.

Intel has 4,500 million shares of common stock authorized, and 3,334 million of these shares are issued and outstanding. The common stock has a par value of $0.001 per share.

Issuing Stock

When common stock is issued, the accounting entry is to increase cash for the proceeds, increase the Common Stock account for an amount equal to the par value per share times the number of shares issued, and increase Capital in Excess of Par Value for the amount of the proceeds in excess of the par value of the shares issued.[4] For example, if Intel issues 1,000 shares of common stock at a price of $30 per share, the total proceeds of $30,000 will be accounted for as follows:

---

[4] This account is often referred to as Additional Paid-In Capital or simply Paid-In Capital.

Journal Entry to Record Issue of Common Stock			
+/−	Accounts [description of account]	Debit	Credit
+	Cash [balance sheet asset account]	30,000	
+	Common Stock [balance sheet shareholders' equity account]		1
+	Capital in Excess of Par Value [balance sheet shareholders' equity account]		29,999

The $1 increase in the Common Stock account represents the $0.001 par value per share multiplied by the 1,000 shares issued. The balance of the $30 per share is recorded in the Capital in Excess of Par Value account.[5]

Subscribed Stock

A firm may agree to sell shares of stock where cash is not received immediately. Instead, the investors agree to purchase the stock, and the stock is not issued until the purchase price is received. When an agreement is entered into to sell stock in this way, the stock is called *subscribed stock,* and the firm records a receivable for the subscription price. This receivable is not considered to be an asset but rather is recorded as a contra-shareholders' equity account on the balance sheet.

Stock Issued for Property or Services

Firms do not always issue stock for cash. Stock can be issued for services, or it can be used to purchase assets. For example, Intel's common stock and capital in excess of par value accounts increased by $1,963 million in connection with the Level One Communications acquisition. When stock is issued for other than cash, the transaction is recorded at the market value of the stock issued.[6] For example, if Intel issued 1,000 shares of common stock in exchange for a new piece of equipment, and on the date of the acquisition Intel's stock was trading at $30 per share, the transaction would be recorded as follows:

Journal Entry to Record Issue of Common Stock for Equipment			
+/−	Accounts [description of account]	Debit	Credit
+	Equipment [balance sheet asset account]	30,000	
+	Common Stock [balance sheet shareholders' equity account]		1
+	Capital in Excess of Par Value [balance sheet shareholders' equity account]		29,999

Retained Earnings

Retained earnings represents accumulated net income from prior years that has not been distributed to shareholders. Retained earnings is increased by net income and is reduced by dividends. Retained earnings may also be reduced by other shareholders' equity transactions, such as the repurchase and retirement of stock, as explained later in the chapter. Under state corporation laws, a corporation often cannot pay a dividend in excess of the firm's retained earnings. If a firm has a loss (that is, negative net income), retained earnings is reduced. Firms with losses may have negative retained earnings. For example, Amazon.com had negative retained earnings, called *accumulated deficit,* of $2,293 million at the end of 2000.

---

[5] For firms that issue no-par value stock, all of the proceeds would be recorded in the Common Stock account.

[6] In some cases, it may be easier to value the property or services received than to value the stock issued. In that case, the transaction is recorded at the value of the property or services received.

It is important to keep in mind that, although retained earnings represents the portion of shareholders' equity available to pay dividends, it does *not* represent cash. The retained earnings have been reinvested in productive assets like equipment and inventory. A firm with retained earnings is *legally* allowed to pay dividends, but the payment of dividends depends on the availability of cash.

Accumulated Other Comprehensive Income

Other comprehensive income represents changes in balance sheet asset and liability accounts that, for various reasons, U.S. accounting standard setters have decided to segregate from net income. Usually this is done to minimize the impact of the balance sheet changes on the volatility of net income. For example, the unrealized gains and losses from available-for-sale marketable securities are recorded as part of other comprehensive income rather than part of net income. Contrast this treatment with unrealized gains and losses from trading securities, which are included as part of net income.

Items that affect other comprehensive income are (1) unrealized gains and losses from available-for-sale marketable securities, (2) foreign currency translation gains and losses,[7] (3) gains and losses from derivatives qualifying as cash flow hedges, and (4) adjustments to a firm's minimum pension liability.[8] Items are recorded as other comprehensive income on a net-of-tax basis—that is, reduced by the applicable income tax effect. Here is how Intel explained the components of other comprehensive income for 1999 in the notes to its financial statements:

The components of other comprehensive income and related tax effects were as follows (in millions):	**1999**
Gains on investments during the year, net of tax of $(2,026)	$3,762
Less: adjustment for gains realized and included in net income, net of tax of $309	(574)
Other comprehensive income	$3,188

Accumulated other comprehensive income presented in the accompanying consolidated balance sheets consists of the accumulated net unrealized gain on available-for-sale investments

Source: Intel Corporation Form 10-K.

Under the view adopted by U.S. standard setters, a firm's total earnings is represented by what is called *comprehensive income*. Comprehensive income consists of two parts: (1) net income and (2) changes in other comprehensive income. For example, in its statement of shareholders' equity shown earlier, Intel reported two components of comprehensive income: net income of $7,314 million and change in unrealized gain on available for sale investments, net of tax of $3,188 million.

DISTRIBUTIONS OF CASH OR STOCK

There are two ways for corporations to distribute cash to their shareholders: cash dividends and stock repurchases. The accounting rules related to these two types of cash distributions are outlined below. Firms may also distribute additional shares of stock as a dividend as an alternative to distributing cash. The accounting rules relating to stock dividends are also discussed below, together with the

---

[7] Accounting for foreign currency translation is usually covered in an advanced accounting course.

[8] Recall that when a minimum pension liability is recorded, the debit is made to an intangible pension asset to the extent of unrecognized prior service costs. To the extent the minimum liability entry exceeds this amount, the debit is made to shareholders' equity as part of other comprehensive income.

rules applicable to stock splits, since stock dividends and stock splits are similar transactions that differ only in form.

Cash Dividends

Unlike interest payments on debt, a corporation is under no legal obligation to pay dividends to its shareholders. Dividends are paid at the discretion of the board of directors and only after the board has authorized the dividend at a formal meeting. Therefore, unlike interest expense, which is accrued as an expense with the passage of time, a dividend is recorded only upon its authorization by the board of directors.

Another difference between a dividend and interest is that a dividend is not considered an expense in arriving at net income, whereas interest is. A dividend is a distribution of the profits of the firm rather than an expense used to measure those profits. This treatment is consistent with the view that shareholders are the residual claimants of the firm. Net income is a measure of what is left over after payment of all of the firm's expenses, including interest expense paid to lenders. Thus, the distribution of this net income to the shareholders does not result in an expense.

A dividend is recorded when it is declared by the board of directors, although it is not paid until a later date. Therefore, recording a dividend involves a Dividends Payable account. Here is an example of recording Intel's 1999 dividend of $0.11 per share:

+/−	Journal Entry to Record Declaration of Dividend (in millions)		
	Accounts [description of account]	**Debit**	**Credit**
−	Retained Earnings [balance sheet shareholders' equity account]	366	
+	Dividend Payable [balance sheet liability account]		366

The dividend reduces retained earnings.[9] When the dividend is paid in cash, the following entry is made:

+/−	Journal Entry to Record Payment of Dividend (in millions)		
	Accounts [description of account]	**Debit**	**Credit**
−	Dividend Payable [balance sheet liability account]	366	
−	Cash [balance sheet asset account]		366

Stock Repurchases

Public companies in the United States may repurchase their stock for several different reasons: (1) they may need shares of stock to issue to employees who are exercising employee stock options; (2) managers may feel that the company's stock price is too low; (3) managers may be attempting to reduce the number of shares outstanding; or (4) managers may be trying to distribute cash to shareholders in a way that minimizes the taxes the shareholders have to pay on the transaction.[10]

---

[9] In practice, firms often record the dividend in a separate shareholders' equity account called Dividends Declared or simply Dividends. This account is closed out to retained earnings at the end of the accounting period.

[10] While dividends are taxed to individual shareholders at the ordinary income tax rate, stock repurchases usually qualify for lower tax rates as long-term capital gains.

Here is some information from Intel's financial statement notes discussing the company's stock repurchase program:

Stock repurchase program

The company has an ongoing authorization, as amended, from the Board of Directors to repurchase up to 760 million shares of Intel's common stock in open market or negotiated transactions. During 1999, the company repurchased 71.3 million shares of common stock at a cost of $4.6 billion. As of December 25, 1999, the company had repurchased and retired approximately 659.9 million shares at a cost of $18.2 billion since the program began in 1990. As of December 25, 1999, after allowing for 2 million shares to cover outstanding put warrants, 98.1 million shares remained available under the repurchase authorization.

Source: Intel Corporation Form 10-K.

Whatever the reason for the repurchase, the accounting treatment is the same. The repurchased stock is called *treasury stock*. Treasury stock is still considered to be issued but is no longer outstanding. The firm may keep the treasury stock to reissue in the future, or it may cancel the treasury stock, a process known as *retirement*.

Even though treasury stock is something that the firm purchases, it is *not* treated as an asset nor as an expense. Treasury stock represents a reduction in shareholders' equity. The fact that the firm can resell the treasury stock in the future is not considered to be an economic benefit; it is simply another potential form of financing, similar to unissued shares of stock or an unused line of credit. Also, a firm cannot realize a gain (or loss) from selling treasury stock. For example, if Intel repurchases its own stock at $40 per share and later resells the same stock at $45 per share, the $5 increase in price is *not* a gain but is treated as in-crease in paid in capital.

Cost Method

There are two methods under GAAP for recording a treasury stock purchase: the cost method and the par value method. The cost method is the most commonly used method and is illustrated first. Assume that Intel originally sold 10,000 shares of stock for $20 per share. Here is the entry for the original sale:

	Journal Entry to Record Issue of Common Stock		
+/−	**Accounts [description of account]**	**Debit**	**Credit**
+	Cash [balance sheet asset account]	200,000	
+	Common Stock [balance sheet shareholders' equity account]		10
+	Capital in Excess of Par Value [balance sheet shareholders' equity account]		199,990

Assume further that Intel repurchases 5,000 shares of stock for $60 per share. Here is the entry to record the purchase:

	Journal Entry to Record Purchase of Treasury Stock—Cost Method		
+/−	**Accounts [description of account]**	**Debit**	**Credit**
+	Treasury Stock [balance sheet contra-shareholders' equity account] . .	300,000	
−	Cash [balance sheet asset account]		300,000

Intel could either keep the treasury stock for reissuance at a later date or retire the shares. Assume that 1,000 of the shares are reissued for $65 per share. The

Treasury Stock account is credited for the $60 cost of the shares ($60 × 1,000 = $60,000). The balance of the credit is to the Paid-In Capital Treasury Stock account. Here is the entry to record the transaction:

+/−	Journal Entry to Record Reissue of Common Stock—Cost Method		
	Accounts [description of account]	Debit	Credit
+	Cash [balance sheet asset account]	65,000	
−	Treasury Stock [balance sheet contra-shareholders' equity account]		60,000
+	Paid-In Capital Treasury Stock [balance sheet shareholders' equity account]		5,000

Assume that another 1,000 of the shares are reissued for $45 per share. The Treasury Stock account is credited for the $60 cost of the shares ($60 × 1,000 = $60,000). The difference between the $45 issue price and the $60 purchase price is debited to Paid-In Capital Treasury Stock to the extent that account has a credit balance. Otherwise, the debit is to the Retained Earnings account. Here is the entry to record the transaction:

+/−	Journal Entry to Record Reissue of Common Stock—Cost Method		
	Accounts [description of account]	Debit	Credit
+	Cash [balance sheet asset account]	45,000	
−	Paid-In Capital Treasury Stock [balance sheet shareholders' equity account]	5,000	
−	Retained Earnings [balance sheet shareholders' equity account]	10,000	
−	Treasury Stock [balance sheet contra-shareholders' equity account]		60,000

Assume that the remaining 3,000 shares of treasury stock are retired. The journal entry to record the retirement of the 3,000 shares is as follows:

+/−	Journal Entry to Record Retirement of Treasury Stock—Cost Method		
	Accounts [description of account]	Debit	Credit
−	Common Stock [balance sheet shareholders' equity account]	3	
−	Capital in Excess of Par Value [balance sheet shareholders' equity account]	59,997	
−	Retained Earnings [balance sheet shareholders' equity account]	120,000	
−	Treasury Stock [balance sheet contra-shareholders' equity account]		180,000

Notice that the retirement has no impact on the book value of shareholders' equity. It simply reclassifies the Treasury Stock account balance to other shareholders' equity accounts. Also, notice that the repurchase and retirement of the treasury stock reduces retained earnings in a way that is similar to the treatment of a dividend. If the stock had originally been repurchased at a price that was less than the $20 original issue price, the above transaction would have a credit to the Paid-In Capital Treasury Stock account rather than a debit to Retained Earnings.

Par Value Method

The second method allowed under GAAP for recording treasury stock is the par value method. These examples will use the same facts as the examples used to illustrate the cost method. Assume that Intel originally sold 10,000 shares of stock for $20 per share. Here is the entry for the original sale:

Journal Entry to Record Issue of Common Stock			
+/−	Accounts [description of account]	Debit	Credit
+	Cash [balance sheet asset account]	200,000	
+	Common Stock [balance sheet shareholders' equity account]		10
+	Capital in Excess of Par Value [balance sheet shareholders' equity account]		199,990

Assume further that Intel repurchases 5,000 shares of stock for $60 per share. The Treasury Stock account is debited for the par value of the repurchased stock ($0.001 \times 5,000 = \$5$). The Capital in Excess of Par Value account is debited for the amount of capital in excess of par value per share that was originally recorded when the stock was issued ($20 − \$0.001 = \$19.999$). Further, $5,000 \times \$19.999 = \$99,995$. The difference between the $60 repurchase price and the $20 issue price ($40) is a debit to retained earnings ($5,000 \times \$40 = \$200,000$). Here is the entry to record the purchase:

Journal Entry to Record Purchase of Treasury Stock—Par Value Method			
+/−	Accounts [description of account]	Debit	Credit
+	Treasury Stock [balance sheet contra-shareholders' equity account] ..	5	
−	Capital in Excess of Par Value [balance sheet shareholders' equity account]	99,995	
−	Retained Earnings [balance sheet shareholders' equity account]	200,000	
−	Cash [balance sheet asset account]		300,000

If the repurchase price was less than the $20 issue price, the difference would be credited to the Paid-In Capital Treasury Stock account.

Assume that 1,000 of the shares are reissued for $65 per share. The Treasury Stock account is credited for the $0.001 par value of the shares ($0.001 \times 1,000 = \$1$). The balance of the credit is to the Capital in Excess of Par Value account, just as with the original issuance of stock. Here is the entry to record the transaction:

Journal Entry to Record Reissue of Common Stock—Par Value Method			
+/−	Accounts [description of account]	Debit	Credit
+	Cash [balance sheet asset account]	65,000	
−	Treasury Stock [balance sheet contra-shareholders' equity account]		1
+	Capital in Excess of Par Value [balance sheet shareholders' equity account]		64,999

Assume that another 1,000 of the shares are reissued for $45 per share. The Treasury Stock account is credited for the $0.001 par value of the shares ($0.001 \times 1,000 = \$1$). The balance of the credit is to the Capital in Excess of Par Value account, just as with the original issuance of stock. Here is the entry to record the transaction:

+/−	Journal Entry to Record Reissue of Common Stock—Par Value Method		
	Accounts [description of account]	**Debit**	**Credit**
+	Cash [balance sheet asset account]	45,000	
−	Treasury Stock [balance sheet contra-shareholders' equity account]		1
+	Capital in Excess of Par Value [balance sheet shareholders' equity account]		44,999

Assume that the remaining 3,000 shares of treasury stock are retired. The journal entry to record the retirement of the 3,000 shares is as follows:

+/−	Journal Entry to Record Retirement of Treasury Stock—Par Value Method		
	Accounts [description of account]	**Debit**	**Credit**
−	Common Stock [balance sheet shareholders' equity account]	3	
−	Treasury Stock [balance sheet contra-shareholders' equity account]		3

Notice that the retirement has no impact on the book value of shareholders' equity. It simply reclassifies the Treasury Stock account balance to the Common Stock Account.

Stock Dividends and Stock Splits

In some cases, the board of directors of a corporation wants to declare a dividend even though the corporation doesn't have the cash available to pay one. In this case, the board might declare what is known as a *stock dividend*. A stock dividend results in a distribution of additional shares of stock to the existing shareholders. For example, a firm might declare a dividend of one new share for every 10 shares of stock owned (a 10 percent stock dividend). A shareholder owning 500 shares of stock would receive 50 additional shares.

The important thing to recognize about a stock dividend is that, although there are more shares of stock outstanding, each shareholder's percentage ownership in the firm remains unchanged. Also, the total value of the firm is unchanged. Therefore, a stock dividend has no economic significance. Accordingly, the accounting treatment is to simply reclassify a portion of retained earnings to common stock and capital in excess of par value.

Assume that Intel declares and pays a stock dividend of one new share for each 50 existing shares owned (a 2 percent stock dividend). That means that for the 3,334 million shares outstanding Intel would issue an additional 66.68 million shares. Assume further that the market value of Intel's stock at the time the dividend is declared is $30 per share. The accounting treatment under GAAP is to reclassify the market value of the newly issued shares from Retained Earnings to the Common Stock and Paid-In Capital accounts.

In this example, the value of the stock issued is 66.68 million × $30 = $2,000,400,000. The par value of the shares issued is $0.001 × 66.68 million = $66,680. Here is the entry to record the transaction:

	Journal Entry to Record Stock Dividend (in thousands)		
+/−	Accounts [description of account]	Debit	Credit
−	Retained Earnings [balance sheet shareholders' equity account] ...	2,000,400	
+	Common Stock [balance sheet shareholders' equity account] ...		67
+	Capital in Excess of Par Value [balance sheet shareholders' equity account]		2,000,333

This type of accounting treatment is only applied to what are known as *small stock dividends,* which means stock dividends of less than 25 percent. Stock dividends of greater than 25 percent are treated as stock splits, under rules discussed below.

Stock Splits

In a stock split, the corporation recalls its old shares and reissues a larger number of new shares. For example, in a 2-for-1 stock split each old share of stock is replaced by two new shares of stock. Since the total value of the firm is unchanged and there are twice as many shares outstanding, each new share should be worth one-half as much as each old share.[11] Also, the par value of the new shares would be only one-half as much as the par value of the old shares. For example, if Intel had a 2-for-1 stock split the par value of its stock would decrease from $0.001 per share to $0.0005 per share. Since the number of shares outstanding would be doubled, the total balance of the Common Stock account would remain unchanged. Because a stock split has no effect on the balances of the Shareholders' Equity accounts, no accounting entries are necessary to record a stock split.

As an alternative to a 2-for-1 split a firm could have a 100 percent stock dividend, with each shareholder receiving one additional share for each share already owned. Because large stock dividends are essentially the same as stock splits, the accounting treatment for large stock dividends and stock splits is similar. Under GAAP, a *large stock dividend* is considered to be one greater than 25 percent.

The one difference between a stock split and a stock dividend is that the par value per share does not change with a stock dividend. Therefore, with a 100 percent stock dividend the Common Stock account (reflecting the par value of the outstanding shares) would double. Since the Common Stock account balance changes, an accounting entry is necessary to transfer an amount equal to the par value of the new shares from Retained Earnings to the Common Stock account. No adjustment is made to the Paid-In Capital account.

The following financial statement note reflects Intel's stock splits during 1999 and 1997.

Stock distribution

On April 11, 1999, the company effected a two-for-one stock split in the form of a special stock distribution to stockholders of record as of March 23, 1999. On July 13, 1997, the company effected a two-for-one stock split in the form of a special stock distribution to stockholders of record as of June 10, 1997. All share, per share, common stock, stock option and warrant amounts herein have been restated to reflect the effects of these splits.

Source: Intel Corporation Form 10-K.

---

[11] This decrease in the per-share price of the stock is thought to be one of the main reasons that firms split their stock. Absent stock splits, as the firm grows the price per share would continue to increase. An extremely high price per share is thought to discourage many investors from purchasing the stock.

EMPLOYEE STOCK OPTIONS

Accounting for employee stock options is one of the most controversial issues in accounting standard setting in the United States. Under GAAP, managers may choose one of two different accounting methods. The accounting method preferred by standard setters is not generally chosen by managers of public companies; the vast majority of managers choose the alternative method. The major difference between the two methods is whether the value of stock options granted to employees should be included as compensation expense in the computation of net income. Under the alternative method, firms are able to give away millions of dollars worth of stock options to employees without any impact on reported net income.

The section below first explains the nature of employee stock options. Next, the accounting rules favored by U.S. standard setters are presented, based on Statement of Financial Accounting Standards (SFAS) No. 123 (called the *fair value method*). Finally, the alternative accounting treatment is presented, based on Accounting Principles Board (APB) Opinion No. 25 (called the *intrinsic value method*). Firms may choose to use either method in the computation of net income, although the vast majority of firms use the intrinsic value method. Firms that use the intrinsic value method must disclose in the notes to the financial statements what their net income would have been had the fair value method been used. The net income computed under the fair value method is referred to as *pro forma income*.

The intense debate over the method of accounting for employee stock options is a good example of why people think that financial accounting has real economic effects. Since the method of accounting for options has no effect on the cash flows, including income taxes, of a firm, and since the effect of the fair value method must be disclosed in the notes to financial statements, the value of a firm should be unchanged regardless of which accounting method is used. Nevertheless, managers of public companies have threatened to eliminate employee stock options if forced to adopt the fair value method, and members of Congress have threatened to intervene in the standard-setting process. Apparently, accounting methods affect the behavior of managers and other financial statement users in ways that are not fully understood.

The Nature of Employee Stock Options

A stock option is a contractual right to purchase a specified number of shares of a company's stock for a specified price for a specified time period. For example, an option might allow the holder to purchase 100 shares of common stock at a price of $20 per share for the next two years. If the market price of the company's stock increases above $20 per share in the next two years, the holder of the option can buy the stock for $20 and sell it for the higher current market price, thus making a profit on the transaction. The purchase of stock by the holder of an option is referred to as the *exercise* of the option. The price that the holder must pay to receive the stock is called the *exercise price* or the *strike price*.

Public corporations in the United States frequently grant stock options to their employees as a type of compensation. Options help align the incentives of employees with the incentives of the shareholders, since both groups will profit if the company's stock price increases. However, options have less risk for the employee than ownership of the company's stock, since an employee cannot lose money from owning a stock option. If the stock price decreases below the exercise price, the employee will not exercise the option. Therefore, options are a way for employees to profit when the stock price increases, but they protect the employees from losses should the stock price decrease.

Employees who are granted options must usually wait some period of time after the grant before they may exercise their options. This waiting time is referred to as a *vesting period,* and employees who have the right to exercise their options are referred to as being *vested.* The vesting period is a way to ensure that the employees remain with the company, since if they leave they forfeit their rights to their options. Employee stock options are not publicly traded and may usually not be transferred to anyone other than the employee who was granted the option. Therefore, stock options with a long vesting period are an effective way to keep valuable employees from leaving the company. Employees who leave the company have their options canceled.

Here is some information about Intel's employee stock options for 1999:

Stock option plans

Intel has a stock option plan under which officers, key employees and non-employee directors may be granted options to purchase shares of the company's authorized but unissued common stock. The company also has a stock option plan under which stock options may be granted to employees other than officers and directors. Under all of the plans, the option exercise price is equal to the fair market value of Intel common stock at the date of grant.

Options granted by Intel currently expire no later than 10 years from the grant date and generally vest within 5 years. Proceeds received by the company from exercises are credited to common stock and capital in excess of par value. Additional information with respect to stock option plan activity was as follows:

		Outstanding Options	
	Shares Available for Options (in millions)	Number of Shares (in millions)	Weighted Average Exercise Price
December 26, 1998	267.2	312.5	$18.13
Grants	(40.6)	40.6	63.91
Options assumed in acquisitions	—	12.8	25.74
Exercises	—	(48.0)	6.64
Cancellations	12.3	(12.3)	32.85
December 25, 1999	238.9	305.6	25.73

The range of option exercise prices for options outstanding at December 25, 1999, was $0.15 to $84.97. The following tables summarize information about options outstanding at December 25, 1999:

	Outstanding Options		
Range of Exercise Prices	Number of Shares (in millions)	Weighted Average Contractual Life (in years)	Weighted Average Exercise Price
$0.15–$7.58	59.6	2.4	$ 4.28
$8.66–$15.09	62.9	4.8	10.46
$15.12–$37.45	91.4	6.7	25.61
$37.47–$84.97	91.7	8.6	50.28
Total	305.6	6.0	25.73

These options will expire if not exercised at specific dates through December 2009.

Source: Intel Corporation Form 10-K.

Employee stock options have some important income tax features that should be understood. For tax purposes, there are two types of employee stock options: (1) *incentive stock options* (ISOs) and (2) *nonqualified options.* When an employee exercises nonqualified options, the *employer* is allowed an income tax deduction for the difference between the exercise price paid by the employee and the market price of the shares issued by the company. For example, if an employee exercises a nonqualified option to purchase 100 shares at an exercise price of $20 per share when the stock is currently selling for $30 per share, the employee will pay the company 100 × $20 = $2,000 and receive stock worth 100 × $30 = $3,000. The employer corporation is allowed an income tax deduction for the excess of the $3,000 market value of the stock over the $2,000 exercise price paid by the employee. No tax deduction is allowed if the options exercised are incentive stock options.[12]

As an alternative to using stock options to compensate employees, some firms use what are called *stock appreciation rights* (SARs). Stock appreciation rights are contracts that promise to make a future payment to the employee in an amount equal to the increase in value of a share of the company's stock over some specified price. In effect, SARs provide the same economic benefit to the employee as stock options, since the employee receives the increase in the stock price but does not suffer a loss from a decrease in stock price. However, SARs do not result in the issuance of additional shares of stock, as is required with stock options. For financial reporting purposes, SARs are treated as compensation expense and are not subject to the stock option reporting rules discussed below.

Accounting for Employee Stock Options: Fair Value Method

U.S. accounting standard setters have recognized that employee stock options have value even in cases in which the exercise price is greater than or equal to the market price, and therefore this value should be recognized as a compensation expense by the employer. Modern finance theory has developed models to estimate the value of stock options, the most common being the Black-Scholes model.[13] By applying these models to the employee stock options granted, firms can estimate the value of the options they are giving to their employees when the options are granted. This is the basic idea underlying the fair value method (SFAS No. 123).

Under the fair value method, firms record compensation expense equal to the fair value of the options granted to employees, where the fair value is determined under an option pricing model such as Black-Scholes. The compensation expense amount is allocated to the accounting periods over which the options vest. In Intel's case, this vesting period is five years.

Assume that 10,000 options with a fair value of $15 each are granted to employees and that the options vest over five years. The total compensation expense associated with the options is 10,000 × $15 = $150,000. The company would record $150,000/5 = $30,000 of compensation expense each year for five years as follows:

+/−	**Journal Entry to Record Stock Option Compensation Expense**		
	Accounts [description of account]	**Debit**	**Credit**
+	Compensation Expense [income statement expense account]	30,000	
+	Paid-In Capital Stock Options [balance sheet shareholders' equity account]		30,000

[12] Incentive stock options have tax benefits for the employee. Stock options must meet certain requirements specified in the tax law to be treated as ISOs. In general, the tax laws make nonqualified options more attractive to the employer and ISOs more attractive to the employee.

[13] Students not familiar with the Black-Scholes option pricing model should consult a basic textbook in finance.

At the end of the five-year vesting period, the balance in the Paid-In Capital Stock Options account would be $150,000. If the options expire unexercised, the balance in Paid-In Capital Stock Options would be transferred to the Capital in Excess of Par Value account.

If the options are nonqualified, a deferred tax asset would also be recorded. Assuming a 35 percent tax rate, the deferred tax asset is equal to $35\% \times \$30,000 = \$10,500$ each year. Here is the entry that would be made each year for five years:

	Journal Entry to Record Stock Option Deferred Tax Asset		
+/−	Accounts [description of account]	Debit	Credit
+	Deferred Tax Asset [balance sheet asset account]	10,500	
−	Income Tax Expense [income statement expense account]		10,500

In the event the options expire unexercised, the above entry would be reversed.

No expense is recognized when the options are exercised. The cash received by the company for the exercise price is recorded as an increase in the Capital in Excess of Par Value account. Assume that during the year employees exercised 1,000 of the nonqualified options with an exercise price of $20 per share when the stock is worth $45 per share. This means that the employer will receive cash of $20 \times 1,000 = \$20,000$ and (using Intel's par value of $0.001 per share) issue shares with a par value of $0.001 \times 1,000 = \$1$. Recall that $15 per share has already been recorded as compensation in the Paid-In Capital Stock Options account. Here is the entry that would be made to record the exercise of the options:

	Journal Entry to Record Stock Option Exercise		
+/−	Accounts [description of account]	Debit	Credit
+	Cash [balance sheet asset account]	20,000	
−	Paid-In Capital Stock Options [balance sheet shareholders' equity account]	15,000	
+	Common Stock [balance sheet shareholders' equity account]		1
+	Capital in Excess of Par Value [balance sheet shareholders' equity account]		34,999

The employer will also receive a tax deduction of $25 per share ($45 − $20), and the tax savings from this deduction is $35\% \times \$25 = \$8.75$ per share. Recall that a deferred tax asset of $35\% \times \$15 = \$5.25$ per share has already been recorded. Here is the entry to record the tax effects of the stock option exercise:

	Journal Entry to Record Tax Benefit of Stock Option Exercise		
+/−	Accounts [description of account]	Debit	Credit
−	Income Taxes Payable [balance sheet liability account]	8,750	
+	Paid-In Capital Stock Options [balance sheet shareholders' equity account]		3,500
−	Deferred Tax Asset [balance sheet asset account]		5,250

Notice that the additional income tax benefit does not reduce income tax expense. If the tax benefit from the exercise was less than the deferred tax asset, the difference would be debited to the Income Tax Expense account.

Accounting for Employee Stock Options: Intrinsic Value Method

Under the intrinsic value method (APB Opinion No. 25), the accounting method used by almost all public U.S. corporations,[14] no compensation expense is recognized on the granting of an option provided the exercise price is *greater than or equal to* the stock's market price when the option is granted. For example, a note in Intel's financial statement reports that "under all of the plans, the option exercise price is equal to the fair market value of Intel common stock at the date of grant." Therefore, under the intrinsic value method Intel does not recognize any compensation expense on the granting of the options. Also, no income is recognized when the options are exercised. Cash is debited and Common Stock and Capital in Excess of Par Value are credited. Any income tax benefit from the exercise is credited to Paid-In Capital Stock Options.

To the extent options are granted with an exercise price in excess of the current market price, the intrinsic value method does recognize compensation expense. For example, if 10,000 options were granted with an exercise price of $25 when the current market price was $20, compensation expense of $5 per share would be recognized over the time period that the options vested. The journal entries in this situation are similar to those presented for the fair value method.

Intel's Stock Options

Intel uses the intrinsic value method to record stock options. Here is the information from the company's statement of shareholders' equity showing the impact of stock options on shareholders' equity:

Consolidated Statements of Stockholders' Equity (in millions)				
	Common Stock and Capital in Excess of Par Value	Retained Earnings	Accumulated Other Comprehensive Income	Total
Proceeds from sales of shares through employee stock plans, tax benefit of $506 and other	1,049	—	—	1,049

Source: Intel Corporation Form 10-K.

Notice that Intel received a tax savings of $506 million from the tax deduction associated with the exercise of nonqualified options and that this tax benefit is added to capital in excess of par value. It does not reduce the company's income tax expense.

Under GAAP, firms that use the intrinsic value method to determine their compensation expense must also disclose in their financial statement notes what their net income would have been if the fair value method had been used. This revised net income amount is referred to as *pro forma net income.* Intel's disclosure of its fair value method pro forma net income is shown on page 465.

The net income for 1999 would have been $6,860 under the fair value method. Comparing this with the reported 1999 net income of $7,314 shows that the value of employee stock option compensation related to 1999 was $454 million. The $454 is an after-tax number, meaning the actual pretax cost to Intel (assuming a 35 percent tax rate) was $698 million. Under the intrinsic value method, this $698 value of options given to employees is never recorded as an expense.

---

[14] Beginning in 2002, some public companies announced that they were switching from the intrinsic value method to the fair value method in response to the accounting scandals that had reduced investor confidence in reported earnings. The Coca-Cola Company was the first major corporation to make the switch.

For purposes of pro forma disclosures, the estimated fair value of the options is amortized to expense over the options' vesting periods. The company's pro forma information follows (in millions, except per share amounts):

	1999	1998	1997
Pro forma net income	$6,860	$5,755	$6,735
Pro forma basic earnings per share	2.06	1.73	2.06
Pro forma diluted earnings per share	1.98	1.66	1.88

Source: Intel Corporation Form 10-K.

EARNINGS PER SHARE

Under GAAP, firms are required to report net income on a per share basis on the income statement.[15] This per share net income is referred to as *earnings per share* (EPS). From an information standpoint, it is not clear why per share income is a useful number, since firms may change their reported earnings per share by simply utilizing a stock split or stock dividend. Also, one firm may report higher earnings per share than another firm simply because it has fewer shares of stock outstanding. Finally, users of financial statements can compute their own measure of EPS by dividing net income by the number of shares outstanding.

One reason why a per share net income number may be useful is because stock prices are also reported on a per share basis. Reporting earnings per share allows users of the firm's financial statements an easy way of comparing the firm's per share net income with the firm's per share stock price, usually in the form of a price–earnings (PE) or earnings-price (EP) ratio. For example, as shown in the following table, Intel's EPS for 2000 was $2.20 per share. Intel's stock price at the end of 1999 was $82 per share, resulting in a price–earnings ratio of 82/2.20 = 37 and an earnings–price ratio of 2.20/82 = 0.027. These ratios can be compared with those of other corporations in Intel's industry as one measure of the relative market value of Intel's accounting earnings.

Three years ended December 25, 1999 (in millions, except per share amounts):

	1999	1998	1997
Net income	$7,314	$6,068	$6,945
Basic earnings per common share	$ 2.20	$ 1.82	$ 2.12
Diluted earnings per common share	$ 2.11	$ 1.73	$ 1.93
Weighted average common shares outstanding	3,324	3,336	3,271
Weighted average common shares outstanding, assuming dilution	3,470	3,517	3,590

Source: Intel Corporation Form 10-K.

As you can see from the above table, firms must report two different measures of earnings per share: basic EPS and diluted EPS. For Intel for 1999, basic EPS

---

[15] GAAP rules also require firms to report the following on a per share basis: (1) earnings before extraordinary items, (2) discontinued operations, (3) extraordinary items, and (4) the cumulative effect of a change in accounting method.

was $2.20 while diluted EPS was $2.11. The discussion below explains the rules for computing each of these measures.

Basic Earnings per Share

In the basic EPS computation, the numerator is the net income available for common shareholders, and the denominator is the weighted average number of shares outstanding during the year. Net income available for common shareholders is equal to net income less any dividends declared on preferred stock. Since Intel has no preferred stock outstanding, net income available for common shareholders is the same as net income and is equal to $7,314 million.

The weighted average number of shares outstanding takes into account increases or decreases in the number of shares outstanding during the year. For example, if new shares are issued or existing shares are repurchased, the number of outstanding shares will change. The weighted average computation takes into account these changes.

Here is how to compute weighted average shares outstanding:

1. Start with the number of shares outstanding at the beginning of the year.
2. For any increases or decreases in shares, multiply the increase or decrease by the length of time remaining to the end of the year, expressed as a percentage of a year.
3. Add the increase to (or subtract the decrease from) the number of shares at the beginning of the year.

For example, assume Intel begins the year with 3,315 million shares outstanding. Assume that Intel issues 1,000 million new shares on February 1, 301 million new shares on June 1, and 500 million new shares on October 1. Assume further that Intel repurchases 800 million shares on March 1 and 1,300 million shares on August 1. Here is the computation of the weighted average number of shares outstanding for the year:

CALCULATION OF WEIGHTED AVERAGE SHARES OUTSTANDING

Date	Transaction	Increase (Decrease) in Number of Shares	Months to Year End	Fraction of Year	Weighted Average Shares
Beginning		3,315	12	100.00%	3,315
Feb. 1	Issue new shares	1,000	11	91.67	917
Mar. 1	Repurchase shares	(800)	10	83.33	(667)
June 1	Issue new shares	301	7	58.33	176
Aug. 1	Repurchase shares	(1,300)	5	41.67	(542)
Oct. 1	Issue new shares	500	3	25.00	125
Weighted average shares					3,324

Using this number for the weighted average shares outstanding during 1999, along with the net income from 1999, Intel's 1999 basic EPS is $7,314/3,324 = $2.20.[16]

If a company has stock splits or stock dividends during the year, the number of shares outstanding is restated as of the beginning of the year to reflect the new number of shares from the first day of the year. Assume that on April 1 Intel issued a 25 percent stock dividend. This means that the beginning number of shares used in the computation above would have to be increased to 1.25 × 3,315 = 4,144. Similarly, the February 1 issue of new shares and the March 1

---

[16] Since both the numerator and denominator are expressed in millions, no adjustment is necessary.

repurchase would also have to be adjusted. Here is how the weighted average shares computation would look with the 25 percent stock dividend on April 1:

	WEIGHTED AVERAGE SHARES OUTSTANDING-AFTER STOCK DIVIDEND					
Date	Increase (Decrease) in Number of Shares	25% Stock Dividend Factor*	Adjusted for Stock Dividend	Months to Year End	Fraction of Year	Weighted Average Shares
Beginning	3,315	1.25	4,144	12	100.00%	4,144
Feb. 1	1,000	1.25	1,250	11	91.67	1,146
Mar. 1	(800)	1.25	(1,000)	10	83.33	(833)
June 1	376	**	376	7	58.33	219
Aug. 1	(1,625)	**	(1,625)	5	41.67	(677)
Oct. 1	625	**	625	3	25.00	156
weighted average shares						4,155

*25% stock dividend on April 1.
**After dividend, no adjustment necessary.

Diluted Earnings per Share

To understand the accounting rule for diluted EPS it is first necessary to understand the concept of dilution as it relates to shareholders of a corporation. The concept of dilution can best be explained using a numerical example. Assume that you own 200 shares of the stock of a corporation with 2,000 shares outstanding (that is, you own 10 percent of the stock) and that the whole corporation is worth $100,000. Your stock is therefore worth 10% × $100,000 = $10,000, or $50 per share.

Now assume that the corporation issues 100 shares to an employee as compensation, and that the employee pays nothing for the shares. The corporation is still worth $100,000, but now there are 2,100 shares outstanding. Your 200 shares now represents 200/2,100 = 9.524% of the total stock and is therefore worth 9.524% × $100,000 = $9,524, or $47.62 per share. Your stock is suddenly worth less because there are more shares outstanding and you did not receive a proportionate part of those new shares. This decrease in the value of your stock when more shares are issued is called *dilution*.

Dilution does not always occur when new shares are issued—only when they are issued for less than their market value. In the above example, assume that the employee who received the 100 shares had to pay the market value of $50 for the shares. This means that the corporation would receive $50 × 100 = $5,000 in cash. The value of the corporation would therefore increase from $100,000 to $105,000. Your 9.524 percent of this value would equal $10,000, or $50 per share. When the shares are issued for their market value, there is no dilution.

Consider what happens when employees exercise stock options. In the above example, assume the employee had an option to acquire the 100 shares for $15 per share rather than their market value of $50. The corporation receives a total of $1,500 in cash from the employee for the shares, making the value of the corporation $101,500. Your 9.524 percent of this value is $9,667, or $48.33 per share. Thus, the fact that employees exercise stock options reduces, or dilutes, the value of the shares of the existing shareholders. This dilution is a cost to the existing shareholders that is not reported in the financial statements.

Accounting standard setters in the United States were worried about the effect that dilution has on earnings per share. To the extent that options are exercised, for example, the number of shares outstanding goes up, which has the effect of reducing EPS. Therefore, under GAAP firms must report an amount called *diluted EPS*. Diluted EPS reflects the potential impact that dilution could have on the reported basic EPS amount.

Dilutive Securities in General

A corporation's diluted EPS will differ from its basic EPS to the extent that the firm has what are called *dilutive securities* in its capital structure. Dilutive securities are basically any securities that (1) can be converted into shares of common stock and (2) whose conversion would result in a decrease in basic EPS.[17] This section presents the accounting treatment for two types of dilutive securities: employee stock options and convertible bonds.

Employee stock options have already been discussed earlier in the chapter. Convertible bonds are debt instruments that may, at the option of the debtholder, be converted into a specified number of shares of common stock. Since the computations for diluted EPS are different for both stock options and convertible bonds, each of these computations is discussed separately below.

Dilutive Stock Options

Employee stock options are dilutive and therefore have to be included in the diluted EPS computation if the exercise price is less than the market price during the year.[18] Dilutive options are assumed to have been exercised at the beginning of the accounting period. The proceeds that would result from the exercise are assumed to be used to purchase treasury stock at the market price. Although the assumed exercise of the options increases shares outstanding, the assumed purchase of treasury stock decreases shares outstanding. Therefore, the closer the market price is to the exercise price, the smaller the net increase in outstanding shares and the lower the dilution effect will be.

Here is an example. The following table shows that at the end of 1999 Intel had outstanding employee stock options for 305.6 million shares outstanding with a weighted average exercise price of $25.73. If all of these options had been exercised at the beginning of 1999, Intel would have received proceeds of 305.6 million × $25.73 = $7,863 million. Assume that at the beginning of 1999 Intel's common stock price was $49 per share. This means with these proceeds the firm could have repurchased 160.4 million shares (7,863/49 = 160.4). The dilutive effect of the stock options is therefore 305.6 million − 160.4 million = 145 million additional shares.

	Outstanding Options	
	Number of Shares (in millions)	Weighted Average Exercise Price
December 25, 1999	305.6	$25.73

Source: Intel Corporation Form 10-K.

Intel's EPS can be recomputed after taking into account the dilutive effect of the stock options. The numerator of the EPS computation remains at $7,314. The denominator becomes 3,324 + 145 = 3,469. The EPS would be $7,314/3,469 = $2.11. The dilutive effect of the stock options has decreased the earnings per share by $0.09.

---

[17] Not all convertible securities result in dilution. Securities that would result in an *increase* in EPS if converted into common stock are referred to as antidilutive securities and are not taken into account for the diluted EPS computation.

[18] For this purpose, the average market price during the year is used.

Dilutive Convertible Bonds

From the above computation it is apparent that the computations related to dilutive stock options affect the denominator of the EPS computation but not the numerator. The computations required for convertible bonds affect both the numerator (that is, net income available for common shareholders) as well as the denominator (weighted average shares outstanding).

The denominator effect is the number of additional shares that would be issued if the convertible bonds were converted into shares of common stock. The numerator effect is to add back the net-of-tax interest expense associated with the converted bonds. For example, if the interest expense associated with convertible bonds was $1,000,000 for the year, and the company's tax rate was 35 percent, the after-tax interest would be $1,000,000 \times (1 - 35\%) = \$650,000$.

Since the effects of convertible bonds increase both the numerator and the denominator of the EPS computation, some convertible bonds may not be dilutive. It is possible to tell if a convertible bond is dilutive by computing the ratio of the numerator effect and the denominator effect. If the ratio is less than the basic EPS, the bonds are dilutive. If the ratio is greater than the basic EPS, the bonds are antidilutive and should not be included in the diluted EPS computation.

Here is an example. Intel's basic EPS is $2.20 per share. Assume that a convertible bond had a numerator effect of $200,000 (that is, the after-tax interest from the bonds) and a denominator effect of 300,000 shares. The ratio of these two is $200,000/300,000 = 0.67$. Since this is less than 2.20, the bonds are dilutive. If the denominator effect was 50,000 shares, the ratio would be $200,000/50,000 = 4$, which is greater than 2.20, making the bonds antidilutive.

Sometimes companies have more than one convertible bond, and each one might appear to be dilutive when compared with the basic EPS number. However, when they are all included in the computation, some of the bonds may actually be antidilutive. For this reason, convertible bonds should be ranked by how dilutive they are (based on the ratio of the numerator effect and the denominator effect) and should be added to the diluted EPS computation one at a time, starting with the most dilutive, to check for dilution effects.

In the case of Intel's convertible notes, a note to the company's financial statements indicates that conversion would increase outstanding shares by 1 million. Here is what the financial statements say about this convertible debt:

During 1999, the company assumed 4% convertible subordinated notes with a principal amount of $115 million as a result of the Level One Communications, Inc. acquisition (see "Acquisitions"). The value assigned to the notes was approximately $212 million, based upon the assumed conversion price at the date of acquisition. Amortization of the premium substantially offsets the interest expense on the notes. The notes are convertible into common stock of the company at a conversion price of $31.01 per share. After September 2000, the notes are redeemable at the option of the company.

Source: Intel Corporation Form 10-K.

Here is how Intel would compute the additional shares due on conversion of the notes. Each note is convertible into common stock of the company at a conversion price of $31.01. The total face amount of the notes is $115,000,000. This means that on conversion the note holders could receive $115,000,000/31.01 = 3.7$ million shares of Intel common stock. However, the assumption of the notes from Level One Communications occurred in August 1999, and we have to weight the additional shares by the length of time until the end of the year. Therefore, the convertible notes were only outstanding for 4/12 of the year, and $4/12 \times 3.7$ million = 1.2 million shares, which Intel has rounded to 1 million in its computation.

Since Intel recorded these notes at a premium, the amortization of the premium reduces the interest expense recorded for the note coupon payments. Thus, the interest expense recorded on the notes is so small that Intel states "the add-back of the after-tax interest expense related to these convertible notes would not have a material impact on net income."

As an example of how the dilution computation should be made for convertible bonds, assume that Intel did not record the convertible notes at a premium. The coupon rate on the notes was 4 percent, meaning Intel pays coupon interest payments of $0.04 \times \$115$ million $= \$4.6$ million each year, or $\$1.5$ million for 4/12 of the year. The $\$1.5$ million has to be adjusted for Intel's tax rate of 35 percent. Under these assumptions, Intel would add $\$1.5$ million $\times (1 - 0.35) = \$1$ million back to net income. The ratio of the numerator effect and the denominator effect in this case is $1/1 = 1$, which is less than the 2.11 EPS computed after the dilution effect of the stock options. Therefore, the notes are dilutive. Increasing net income by $\$1$ million and increasing shares outstanding by 1 million would result in an EPS of

$$\frac{\$7,314 + 1}{3,324 + 1} = \$2.20$$

Because the dilution adjustment for the convertible notes in this example is so small, rounding to the nearest $0.01 results in no change to Intel's basic EPS.

Firms sometimes issue convertible preferred stock, which can also be dilutive. Convertible preferred stock is treated in the same way as convertible bonds. The numerator effect for convertible preferred stock is the amount of preferred dividends that were declared for the year. The denominator effect is the number of common shares that would result from the conversion.

Intel Example

The dilution effects of both the stock options and the convertible bonds can be combined to arrive at Intel's diluted EPS. The computation would look like this:

$$\frac{\$7,314 + 1}{3,324 + 145 + 1} = \$2.11$$

Here is the information from Intel's financial statement notes showing the computation of its weighted average shares used in the diluted EPS computation:

Earnings per share

The shares used in the computation of the company's basic and diluted earnings per common share are reconciled as follows (in millions):

	1999
Weighted average common shares outstanding	3,324
Dilutive effect of Employee stock options	145
Convertible notes	1
Weighted average common shares outstanding, assuming dilution	3,470

Weighted average common shares outstanding, assuming dilution, includes the incremental shares that would be issued upon the assumed exercise of stock options, as well as the assumed conversion of the convertible notes. For the three year period ended December 25, 1999, certain of the company's stock options were excluded from the calculation of diluted earnings per share because they were antidilutive, but these options could be dilutive in the future. Net income for the purpose of computing diluted earnings per common share is not materially affected by the assumed conversion of the convertible notes.

Source: Intel Corporation Form 10-K.

SHAREHOLDERS' EQUITY AND THE CASH FLOWS STATEMENT

Increases in shareholders' equity for new stock issued and decreases for dividends and stock repurchases are reflected in the cash flows from financing activities section of the cash flows statement. Here are Intel's cash flows related to shareholders' equity for 1999:

Cash flows provided by (used for)	
financing activities	
Proceeds from sales of shares through employee stock plans and other	543
Proceeds from sales of put warrants	20
Repurchase and retirement of common stock	(4,612)
Payment of dividends to stockholders	(366)

Source: Intel Corporation Form 10-K.

One exception to this rule is the cash flow effects associated with the tax deduction the company receives when its employees exercise nonqualified stock options. This tax benefit is shown in the cash flows from operating activities section, as follows:

Adjustments to reconcile net income to net cash provided by (used for) operating activities	
Depreciation	3,186
Amortization of goodwill and other acquisition-related intangibles	411
Purchased in-process research and development	392
Gains on sales of marketable strategic equity securities	(883)
Net loss on retirements of property, plant and equipment	193
Deferred taxes	(219)
Changes in assets and liabilities	
Accounts receivable	153
Inventories	169
Accounts payable	79
Accrued compensation and benefits	127
Income taxes payable	726
Tax benefit from employee stock plans	**506**
Other assets and liabilities	(819)
Total adjustments	4,021

Source: Intel Corporation Form 10-K.

ACCOUNTING FOR SHAREHOLDERS' EQUITY IN OTHER COUNTRIES

The balance sheet shareholders' equity accounts often look much different under GAAP in other countries. For example, here is the shareholders' equity section of the Reed Elsevier balance sheet for 2000:

	Note	2000 ('L'm)	1999 ('L'm)
Capital and reserves			
Combined share capitals		185	168
Combined share premium accounts . . .		1,621	341
Combined reserves		1,235	1,346
Combined shareholders' funds	28	3,041	1,855

Source: Reed Elsevier Form 20-F.

To explain the changes in combined shareholders' funds, Reed Elsevier presents the following reconciliation:

**Combined Shareholders' Funds Reconciliation
For the Year Ended 31 December 2000**

	2000 ('L'm)	1999 ('L'm)	1998 ('L'm)
Profit/(loss) attributable to parent companies' shareholders	33	(63)	772
Ordinary dividends paid and proposed	(245)	(234)	(349)
Issue of ordinary shares, net of expenses and less capital redemptions . . .	1,285	5	18
Exchange translation differences	113	17	(3)
Net increase/(decrease) in combined shareholders' funds	1,186	(275)	438
Combined shareholders' funds at 1 January	1,855	2,130	1,692
Combined shareholders' funds at 31 December	3,041	1,855	2,130

Source: Reed Elsevier Form 20-F.

As you can see from this reconciliation, shareholders' funds increased by the £33 million of profit, the £1,285 million for new shares issued, and the £113 million for foreign currency translation adjustments, and shareholders' funds decreased by £245 million dividends. All of these items would also affect shareholders' equity under U.S. GAAP.

As with U.S. firms, Reed Elsevier does not report compensation expense for employee stock options. As the following note explains, the company has adopted the Statement 123 disclosure of pro forma income:

Stock Based Compensation

SFAS 123: Accounting for Stock Based Compensation, establishes a fair value based method of computing compensation cost. It encourages the application of this method in the profit and loss account instead of intrinsic value based methods. Where fair value based methods are not applied in the profit and loss account, the proforma effect on net income is disclosed.

The disclosure only provisions of SFAS 123 have been adopted. If compensation costs based on fair value at the grant date had been recognised in the profit and loss account, net income under U.S. GAAP would have been reduced by 'L'23m in 2000 (1999 'L'5m; 1998 'L'2m).

Source: Reed Elsevier Form 20-F.

One difference between U.S. and U.K. GAAP is the timing for recording dividends. The following financial statement note explains this difference:

Ordinary Dividends

Under U.K. and Dutch GAAP, dividends are provided for in the year in respect of which they are proposed by the directors. Under U.S. GAAP, such dividends would not be provided for until they are formally declared by the directors.

Source: Reed Elsevier Form 20-F.

Finally, under U.K. and Dutch accounting standards firms do not report other comprehensive income. However, to comply with U.S. GAAP Reed Elsevier provide the following additional information in its financial statement notes:

Comprehensive Income Information

SFAS 130: Reporting Comprehensive Income, requires that all items that are required to be recognised as components of comprehensive income under U.S. accounting standards are reported in a separate financial statement. Under U.S. GAAP, the comprehensive gain for the year ended 31 December 2000 would be 'L'182m (1999 'L' (46)m; 1998 'L'389m). Comprehensive income under U.S. GAAP comprises net income for the financial year, adjustments to the fair value of marketable securities and exchange translation differences.

Under U.S. GAAP, the following amounts would be reported:

	2000 ('L'm)	1999 ('L'm)	1998 ('L'm)
Net income/(loss) under U.S. GAAP	60	(73)	398
Unrealised gains on marketable securities			
Arising in the year	—	1	11
Recognised in net income/(loss)	—	(3)	(7)
Exchange translation differences	122	29	(13)
Comprehensive income/(loss) under U.S. GAAP	182	(46)	389

Source: Reed Elsevier Form 20-F.

SHAREHOLDERS' EQUITY AND INCOME TAX EXPENSE

The main income tax effect of shareholders' equity comes from the tax deduction that employers receive when employees exercise nonqualified stock options. As shown above, Intel's cash flows from operating activities were increased by $506 million in 1999 due to this tax benefit.

However, despite the large tax savings Intel received, there was no impact on the company's reported income tax expense. Looking at Intel's income tax note for 1999 you would find that there is no evidence from either the company's effective tax rate or its deferred tax assets and liabilities that its taxes were reduced by $506 million.

USING SHAREHOLDERS' EQUITY INFORMATION TO MAKE DECISIONS

The shareholders' equity balance sheet amount is useful primarily as a component of financial statement ratios. For example, the return on equity (ROE) is equal to net income divided by shareholders' equity, and the debt to equity ratio is equal to total debt divided by shareholders' equity. Investors want to know how much the firm is earning given the amount of capital the shareholders have contributed, either directly (as common stock and capital in excess of par value) or through retained earnings. Similarly, those who want some measure of the riskiness of the firm will compare the relative amounts of capital provided by lenders with capital provided by shareholders.

One important use of shareholders' equity information is the Other Comprehensive Income account. Users of the company's financial statements can look here for items affecting the value of assets or liabilities that are not included in net income. For example, an unrealized loss in the company's available-for-sale marketable securities portfolio would be reflected as a decrease in other comprehensive income.

Users of financial statements should also be cautious about how to treat the tax savings associated with employees' exercise of nonqualified stock options, which is an increase in shareholders' equity rather than a reduction in income tax expense. Because this tax savings is likely to occur only in periods when the company's stock price is high, users must decide whether or not to remove this item from forecasts of future cash flows from operating activities.

One common use that is made of the book value of shareholders' equity is to compare it with the market value of the company's stock in the form of a market/book ratio (or price/book ratio). The market/book ratio is often used as a way of separating companies into what are called *growth stocks* and *value stocks*. Firms with high market/book ratios are those with a share price greater than the book value of equity, and the high share price for these firms is due to investors' expectations of future growth in earnings. Firms with low market/book ratios have a share price that is low compared with the book value of equity, and these companies are seen as being relatively low priced.

Summary

This chapter explores the rules relating to accounting for the various shareholders' equity accounts: common stock, capital in excess of par value, retained earning, and other comprehensive income.

Common stock and capital in excess of par value are increased by new shares issued and are decreased by share repurchases and retirements. Retained earnings is increased by net income and decreased by dividends and share repurchases and retirements. Other comprehensive income is affected by unrealized gains and losses from available-for-sale marketable securities, gains and losses from cash flow hedges, and the minimum pension liability.

The chapter also investigates the accounting rules for employee stock options, both the intrinsic value method of APB 25 and the fair value method of Statement 123. Although U.S. public firms can choose either method, almost all use the intrinsic value method, which usually does not result in recording compensation expense. However, the effects of the fair value method on net income must be disclosed in the notes to the financial statements. A major item associated with nonqualified stock options is the tax savings the employer receives when employees exercise the options. This tax savings does not affect the firm's income tax expense but does affect shareholder's equity and cash flows from operating activities.

The requirement to disclose earnings per share, both basic and diluted, is covered. The chapter also explains the computation of weighted average shares outstanding, the method used to identify dilutive securities, and the method used to adjust shares outstanding in the computation of diluted earnings per share.

Discussion Questions

1. Explain why shareholders are considered residual claimants of the firm.
2. What are the major components of the shareholders' equity section of the balance sheet?
3. Does the number of shares of stock a firm has outstanding have any economic significance?
4. Explain what preferred stock is. How does it differ from common stock?

5. Explain the accounting treatment when a firm issues common stock for cash.

6. Explain the accounting treatment when a firm issues common stock for property or services.

7. What does retained earnings represent?

8. Is it possible for retained earnings to be negative? If no, why not? If yes, what does negative retained earnings represent?

9. What is the relationship between retained earnings and the payment of dividends?

10. Explain what other comprehensive income represents.

11. What are the items that affect the balance of other comprehensive income under GAAP?

12. Explain how dividends are different from interest from the standpoint of the paying corporation.

13. Explain the accounting treatment when a firm declares and pays a cash dividend.

14. What are some possible reasons for a corporation to purchase its own stock?

15. Explain why treasury stock is not an asset of the firm.

16. What are the two GAAP accounting methods available to account for treasury stock?

17. Explain the accounting treatment to record the repurchase of common stock under (a) the cost method and (b) the par value method.

18. Explain the accounting treatment to record the reissuance of common stock under (a) the cost method and (b) the par value method.

19. Treasury stock may be reissued at a price that is greater than or less than the price at which the firm reacquired the stock. Explain whether there are differences in the accounting treatment for these two situations.

20. Explain the difference (if any) between a stock dividend and a stock split.

21. Why do firms utilize stock dividends and stock splits?

22. What are the economic consequences of stock dividends and stock splits.

23. What is the accounting treatment of small stock dividends?

24. What is the accounting treatment of large stock dividends and stock splits?

25. Explain how an employee stock option works.

26. Explain why employee stock options are used.

27. Explain the following terms as they relate to employee stock options: *grant date, exercise date, exercise price, vesting, incentive stock option,* and *nonqualified stock option.*

28. Explain the employer's income tax treatment with respect to stock options.

29. Explain the fair value method of accounting for employee stock options.

30. Explain the intrinsic value method of accounting for employee stock options.

31. Explain what is meant by the term *earnings per share.*

32. How is the weighted average number of shares outstanding computed?

33. How is basic earnings per share computed?

34. Explain what dilution is as it relates to earnings per share.

35. Explain how stock options affect the diluted earnings per share computation.

36. Explain how convertible bonds affect the diluted earnings per share computation.

37. Securities may sometimes be antidilutive. Explain what this means. Explain how antidilutive securities affect the diluted earnings per share computation.

38. Explain how shareholders' equity transactions affect the cash flows statement.

Problems

1. A corporation issued 10,000 shares of common stock with a par value of $0.01 per share. The stock was sold for $25 per share. Give the journal entry to record the sale of the stock.

2. A corporation issued 2,000 shares of common stock with a par value of $1.00 per share. The stock was sold for $80 per share. Give the journal entry to record the sale of the stock.

3. A corporation issued 5,000 shares of common stock with a par value of $0.50 per share. The stock was sold for $60 per share. Give the journal entry to record the sale of the stock.

4. Assume the corporation in problem 1 repurchased 2,000 of the shares for $30 per share.
   a. Give the journal entry to record the repurchase using the cost method.
   b. Give the journal entry to record the repurchase using the par value method.
   c. Assume that 1,000 of the repurchased shares were later resold for $35 per share. Give the journal entry to record the resale of the shares using (i) the cost method and (ii) the par value method.
   d. Assume that the remaining repurchased shares were retired by the corporation. Give the journal entry to record the retirement of the shares using (i) the cost method and (ii) the par value method.

5. Assume the corporation in problem 1 repurchased 1,200 of the shares for $90 per share.
   a. Give the journal entry to record the repurchase using the cost method.
   b. Give the journal entry to record the repurchase using the par value method.
   c. Assume that 400 of the repurchased shares were later resold for $100 per share. Give the journal entry to record the resale of the shares using (i) the cost method and (ii) the par value method.
   d. Assume that the remaining repurchased shares were retired by the corporation. Give the journal entry to record the retirement of the shares using (i) the cost method and (ii) the par value method.

6. Assume the corporation in problem 1 repurchased 3,000 of the shares for $70 per share.
   a. Give the journal entry to record the repurchase using the cost method.
   b. Give the journal entry to record the repurchase using the par value method.
   c. Assume that 2,000 of the repurchased shares were later resold for $75 per share. Give the journal entry to record the resale of the shares using (i) the cost method and (ii) the par value method.
   d. Assume that the remaining repurchased shares were retired by the corporation. Give the journal entry to record the retirement of the shares using (i) the cost method and (ii) the par value method.

7. A corporation grants 25,000 nonqualified stock options to employees. The options have an exercise price of $25 and a fair value of $20; they vest over an eight-year period. The corporation's tax rate is 35 percent. The corporation's stock has a market value of $25 per share and a par value of $1 per share.
   a. Give the journal entry that would be made each year to record compensation expense under the fair value method.
   b. Give the journal entry that would be made each year to record the tax effect of the option compensation under the fair value method.

c. Assume that 800 of the options are exercised at a time when the market value of the stock is $60 per share. Give the journal entry to record the exercise. (Include the income tax effect of the exercise.)

8. A corporation grants 100,000 nonqualified stock options to employees. The options have an exercise price of $12 and a fair value of $10; they vest over a four-year period. The corporation's tax rate is 35 percent. The corporation's stock has a market value of $12 per share and a par value of $0.01 per share.

   a. Give the journal entry that would be made each year to record compensation expense under the fair value method.

   b. Give the journal entry that would be made each year to record the tax effect of the option compensation under the fair value method.

   c. Assume that 3,000 of the options are exercised at a time when the market value of the stock is $80 per share. Give the journal entry to record the exercise. (Include the income tax effect of the exercise.)

9. A corporation grants 50,000 nonqualified stock options to employees. The options have an exercise price of $30 and a fair value of $20; they vest over a five-year period. The corporation's tax rate is 35 percent. The corporation's stock has a market value of $30 per share and a par value of $1 per share.

   a. Give the journal entry that would be made each year to record compensation expense under the fair value method.

   b. Give the journal entry that would be made each year to record the tax effect of the option compensation under the fair value method.

   c. Assume that 2,000 of the options are exercised at a time when the market value of the stock is $75 per share. Give the journal entry to record the exercise. (Include the income tax effect of the exercise.)

10. A corporation has changes in the number of shares outstanding during the year as shown in the table below. Compute the weighted average number of shares outstanding during the year for purposes of computing earnings per share.

Date	Transaction	Increase (Decrease) in Number of Shares
Beginning		35,000
Apr. 1	Issue new shares	3,000
May 1	Issue new shares	2,000
Aug. 1	Repurchase shares	(4,000)
Oct. 1	Repurchase shares	(500)
Nov. 1	Issue new shares	5,000

11. A corporation has changes in the number of shares outstanding during the year as shown in the table below. Compute the weighted average number of shares outstanding during the year for purposes of computing earnings per share.

Date	Transaction	Increase (Decrease) in Number of Shares
Beginning		80,000
Jan. 31	Repurchase shares	(6,000)
Apr. 30	Repurchase shares	(3,000)
Sep. 30	Issue new shares	12,000
Oct. 31	Repurchase shares	(2,000)
Nov. 30	Repurchase shares	(1,000)

12. A corporation has changes in the number of shares outstanding during the year as shown in the table below. Compute the weighted average number of shares outstanding during the year for purposes of computing earnings per share.

Date	Transaction	Increase (Decrease) in Number of Shares
Beginning		100,000
Mar. 1	Issue new shares	10,000
May 1	Repurchase shares	(10,000)
Jul. 1	Issue new shares	5,000
Sep. 1	Repurchase shares	(5,000)
Nov. 1	Issue new shares	3,000

13. A corporation has net income of $28,000,000 for the year and weighted average common shares outstanding of 11,300,000. There are no preferred dividends. The corporation also has outstanding 1,500,000 employee stock options with a weighted average exercise price of $36. The company's common stock price is $62. Compute the basic and diluted earnings per share.

14. A corporation has net income of $46,000,000 for the year and weighted average common shares outstanding of 15,000,000. There are no preferred dividends. The corporation also has outstanding 4,000,000 employee stock options with a weighted average exercise price of $26. The company's common stock price is $48. Compute the basic and diluted earnings per share.

15. A corporation has net income of $28,000,000 for the year and weighted average common shares outstanding of 11,300,000. There are no preferred dividends. The corporation also has outstanding 1,500,000 employee stock options with a weighted average exercise price of $36. The company's common stock price is $62. Compute the basic and diluted earnings per share.

16. A corporation has net income of $55,000,000 for the year and weighted average common shares outstanding of 16,000,000. There are no preferred dividends. The corporation also has outstanding (since the beginning of the year) convertible bonds with a conversion rate of $28 and a face amount of $4,600,000.

    a. Compute the basic earnings per share.

    b. Compute the ratio of the numerator effect and denominator effect of dilution, and determine if the convertible bonds are dilutive.

    c. Compute the diluted earnings per share.

17. A corporation has net income of $76,000,000 for the year and weighted average common shares outstanding of 37,000,000. There are no preferred dividends. The corporation also has outstanding (since the beginning of the year) convertible bonds with a conversion rate of $16 and a face amount of $12,000,000.

    a. Compute the basic earnings per share.

    b. Compute the ratio of the numerator effect and denominator effect of dilution, and determine if the convertible bonds are dilutive.

    c. Compute the diluted earnings per share.

18. A corporation has net income of $23,000,000 for the year and weighted average common shares outstanding of 19,000,000. There are no preferred dividends. The corporation also has outstanding (since the beginning of the year) convertible bonds with a conversion rate of $12 and a face amount of $10,000,000.

    a. Compute the basic earnings per share.

b. Compute the ratio of the numerator effect and denominator effect of dilution, and determine if the convertible bonds are dilutive.

c. Compute the diluted earnings per share.

Research Reports

1. Obtain the financial statements for Tootsie Roll Industries, Inc., for 2002.
   a. Tootsie Roll has two classes of stock. Explain the difference between the two.
   b. Explain why Tootsie Roll has two classes of stock.
   c. Prepare a schedule showing the changes to Tootsie Roll's other comprehensive income for 2000, 2001, and 2002.
   d. How does Tootsie Roll account for treasury stock?
   e. Tootsie Roll has an unusual policy with respect to stock dividends. Explain the policy. What are the economic consequences of the policy? Why do you think Tootsie Roll has this policy?

2. Locate one or more articles in the financial press that discuss the accounting treatment for employee stock options in the United States.
   a. Outline the arguments both for and against treating the value of stock options issued as an expense.
   b. Discuss the costs and benefits of treating the value of stock options issued as an expense.
   c. Discuss some alternative ways that stock options might be accounted for.
   d. Do you think the recent accounting scandals among public companies have affected people's views as to whether stock options should be expensed? Explain.
   e. Give your opinion as to what is the most useful (from the perspective of financial statement users) method of accounting for stock options.

3. Obtain the financial statements of Intel Corporation for 2002.
   a. What were Intel's basic earnings per share for 2002, 2001, and 2000?
   b. What would Intel's basic earnings per share have been if Intel had accounted for employee stock options using the fair value method?
   c. Compute the percentage difference in Intel's basic earnings per share under the two different accounting methods.
   d. Where in the financial statements did you locate the information about Intel's earnings per share under the fair value method? (Be specific.)
   e. Where in the financial statements is the information about Intel's employee stock option plan, such as numbers of options granted and outstanding and average exercise prices of options? (Be specific.)
   f. Comment on why you think the information in d above is in a different place than the information in e above?

4. Obtain the financial statements of The Coca-Cola Company for 2002.
   a. What method does Coca-Cola use to account for employee stock options?
   b. Why do you think Coca Cola changed its method of accounting for employee stock options?
   c. Locate one or more articles in the financial press that discusses Coca-Cola's change in accounting method for employee stock options. What reasons do the articles give for the change?
   d. Comment on whether you think other companies will change their accounting methods for employee stock options? Explain why or why not.

5. Obtain the financial statements for Microsoft Corporation for the year ended June 30, 2002.

   a. What were Microsoft's basic and diluted earnings per share for the year ended June 30, 2002.

   b. Using information from the notes to the financial statements (and any other information you need, such as stock prices), prepare a schedule that shows how Microsoft's basic and diluted earnings per share were computed. State any assumptions that you use in your schedule.

   c. Were any of Microsoft's stock options antidilutive? If yes, explain why. If no, explain why not. As part of your answer, explain what *antidilutive* means.

Chapter Learning Objectives

After reading this chapter you should understand

1. What is meant by the term *earnings management.*
2. How earnings management is related to incentives of managers.
3. Ways that managers use to manage earnings.
4. How earnings management differs from accounting fraud.
5. Why earnings management may undermine investor confidence in reported earnings.
6. Why allowing managers flexibility in accounting choices may be useful.

Chapter 16

Earnings Management

Focus Company: General Electric Company

Introduction

The following chart shows the earnings per share from continuing operations for General Electric Company[1] from 1990 through 2000, adjusted for stock splits. What is remarkable about this information is that over this 11-year period, GE's earnings per share increased every year.

General Electric EPS

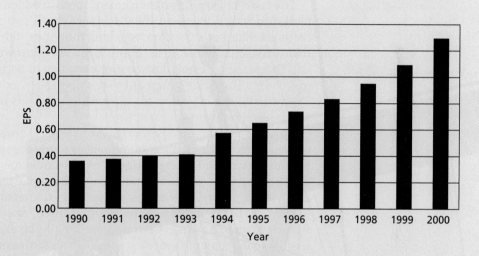

GE's earnings per share over this time period exhibit a trait known as *smoothness,* meaning the earnings do not fluctuate up and down from year to year but follow a consistent pattern. In contrast to GE's accounting earnings, the chart on the next page shows GE's cash flows from operating activities from 1991 through 2000. Notice that GE's cash flows do not exhibit the same smoothness that earnings per share do. Changes in cash flows appear more random—higher in some years and lower in others.

The fact that the pattern of GE's earnings is smoother than the pattern of its cash flows should not be surprising, since one of the purposes of accrual accounting is to smooth out the lumpiness in cash flows. Therefore, we might expect the pattern of a company's cash flows to exhibit more randomness, or volatility, than the pattern of accrual accounting earnings.

However, sometimes managers of public companies make accounting method choices and accounting estimates with the express purpose of *making* their earnings look smoother than they would otherwise be, or to achieve an earnings per share number that meets or exceeds the earnings expected by security analysts. This activity by managers—taking specific actions to achieve desired income statement financial reporting results—is referred to as *earnings management.*

---

[1] Nothing in this chapter is intended as a criticism of General Electric Company or its accounting policies. GE is widely admired for the quality of its financial statement disclosure.

GE Cash Flow from Operating Activities

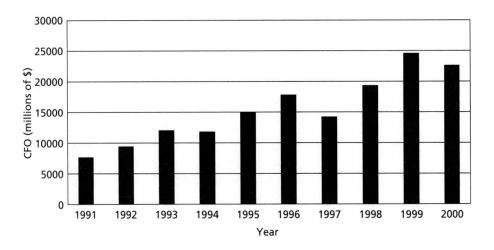

The issue of earnings management took on added importance in 2001 with the bankruptcy of Enron and the disclosure that Enron had been using accounting methods that made the company look more profitable, and less highly leveraged, than was actually the case. Many large, well-known companies, such as Xerox and Qwest, have restated prior-year earnings to correct what are perceived to be misleading financial statements. In some cases, companies such as WorldCom appear to have used incorrect accounting methods in a way that misled investors and other financial statement users.

This chapter focuses on the issue of earnings management from several viewpoints. First, the incentives of managers to manage financial statement earnings are addressed, and the techniques used to manage earnings are explained. Understanding why and how managers manage earnings helps students to better understand the arguments against earnings management. Second, the arguments against earnings management are presented, specifically those raised by the Securities and Exchange Commission. Finally, an argument suggesting that some level of management flexibility with respect to financial reporting is beneficial to the workings of capital markets is presented. Understanding the arguments surrounding the practice of earnings management helps students make better ethical decisions.

WHY MANAGE EARNINGS?

This section briefly outlines five reasons that have been suggested to explain earnings management. These suggested reasons are (1) bonus plans, (2) debt contracts, (3) income smoothing, (4) a pattern of earnings growth, and (5) meeting analysts' forecasts. Each of these reasons are discussed below.

Bonus Plans

As was pointed out in Chapter 1, managers' compensation is often tied to accounting earnings through bonus plans. For example, here is some information about the compensation of Michael Eisner, CEO of The Walt Disney Company, for 1999 through 2001:

Executive Compensation Summary Table			
Name and Principal Position	**Fiscal Year**	**Salary**	**Bonus**
Michael D. Eisner,	2001	$1,000,000	$ 0
Chief executive officer	2000	813,462	8,500,000
and chairman of the board	1999	750,000	0

Source: The Walt Disney Company proxy statement.

As you can see, Eisner received a bonus of $8,500,000 in 2000 but no bonus in 2001. In the company's proxy statement, the compensation subcommittee of Disney's board of directors explained the reason for not paying Eisner a bonus as follows:

For fiscal 2001, the Subcommittee established an overall performance target based upon the achievement of a specified level of net income and an additional financial target based upon adjusted net income. After the end of the fiscal year, the Subcommittee determined that the 2001 targets had not been achieved, primarily due to non-cash charges associated with the discontinuation of go.com and certain one-time charges relating to reduction of the Company's workforce. Consequently, no annual bonuses were paid under the plan.

Source: The Walt Disney Company proxy statement.

According to the proxy statement, the bonus was based on achievement of a specified level of net income and adjusted net income. Since Disney did not achieve these net income levels, Eisner did not receive a bonus.

At first glance, it may appear that any managers compensated under a bonus plan based on accounting earnings have an incentive to increase reported net income. More net income usually means a larger bonus. However, that is not always the case. Consider a manager who is compensated under the following bonus arrangement:

Employer's Reported Net Income	**Bonus Amount**
Less than $1,000,000	Zero
More than $1,000,000 but less than $2,000,000	10% of excess of net income over $1,000,000
More than $2,000,000	$100,000

Under this plan, if the employer reports net income of $1,300,000, the manager receives a bonus equal to $(1,300,000 - 1,000,000 = 300,000) \times 10\% = \$30,000$. Suppose that the manager is unsure whether the allowance for doubtful accounts at the end of the year should be decreased by $10,000. Decreasing the allowance for doubtful accounts will have the effect of increasing net income (ignoring income tax expense) by $10,000, which will result in an additional bonus of $10,000 \times 10\% = \$1,000$ for the manager. Therefore, the bonus plan provides the manager with an incentive to increase reported accounting net income.

However, suppose that the employer's net income in the example is only $800,000, rather than $1,300,000, and that the manager will not receive a bonus, since net income is less than $1,000,000. In that case, an increase in net income from $800,000 to $810,000 will still result in a bonus of zero for the manager. Therefore, in this situation the bonus plan provides no incentive for the manager to reduce the allowance for doubtful accounts. This is an important point, since the mere fact that the manager's bonus is based on accounting earnings will not necessarily result in an incentive for the manager to increase reported earnings. The incentive effect of the bonus depends on the terms of the bonus plan and how close the employer's actual earnings are to the targets in the bonus plan.[2]

Debt Contracts

Many lenders require borrowers to enter into debt contracts, also called *debt covenants*, that specify financial statement target amounts or ratios that the borrower must maintain. Violation of the terms of the debt contract can result in costly renegotiation of the debt, with a possible increase in the interest rate or an acceleration of payment terms. Therefore, the presence of accounting-based debt contracts provides an incentive for managers to manage earnings to avoid violation of the terms of the contract.

Here is an example of a debt contract entered into by Lucent Technologies Inc. with respect to a borrowing referred to as Credit Facilities:

> The Credit Facilities contain affirmative and negative covenants, including financial covenants requiring the maintenance of specified consolidated minimum net worth and minimum earnings before interest, taxes, depreciation and amortization (EBITDA).
>
> Source: Lucent Technologies Form 10-Q.

In this example, the covenant is based on both net worth, that is, shareholders' equity, and earnings. If Lucent's earnings or net worth are too low, the covenant will be violated and Lucent will either have to repay the debt or renegotiate the terms of the debt with the lender. Both of these alternatives would be costly for Lucent. If Lucent's financial statement earnings or net worth are close to those specified in the covenant, the managers of Lucent have an incentive to use accounting methods that increase earnings or net worth as a way of avoiding the costly violation.

Income Smoothing

Another reason for earnings management is to minimize the volatility, or variability, of earnings changes. The idea behind income smoothing is that investors want to be able to predict future earnings. If the earnings change from period to period is relatively constant, it makes it much easier for investors to predict future earnings. Under this view, investors are willing to pay more for shares of stock in a company with smooth earnings.

If managers want smooth earnings, there is an incentive to decrease reported earnings in periods when earnings are unexpectedly high. Similarly, there is an incentive to increase reported earnings in periods when earnings are unexpectedly low. This pattern of earnings management, where earnings are reduced in unusually high years and increased in unusually low years, may result in no change in the total amount of net income reported over some time period. However, even though the total amount of net income is the same, the pattern of the net income from year to year will look much different to investors.

Pattern of Earnings Growth

This argument is related to the income smoothing argument discussed above. The idea is that investors are willing to pay more for shares of stock in a company that exhibits a pattern of earnings growth. There is some evidence that when firms break a pattern of earnings growth—by reporting a decrease in earnings for one year—their stock price drops by a large amount.

---

[2] In the example bonus plan, the maximum bonus that the manager can receive is $100,000 when reported earnings are $2,000,000. Therefore, this bonus plan provides no incentive to increase reported earnings above $2,000,000.

For managers of firms with a pattern of earnings growth over several years there is an incentive to continue to report increasing earnings each year. One way to accomplish this is to manage earnings down in years with earnings increases, and to manage earnings up in years with earnings decreases.

The following chart illustrates the difference between smoothing earnings and a pattern of earnings growth. Each of the three lines represents a hypothetical pattern of earnings over a 10-year period, and the total earnings over the time period are the same for each pattern. The solid line illustrates unmanaged earnings. The dashed line represents these same earnings after they have been smoothed. The dotted line represents the same earnings after they have been managed to reflect a pattern of earnings growth. Since the total earnings for each firm are exactly the same, any difference in the stock prices of these three hypothetical firms at the end of the period would be due to the differences in the earnings pattern over time.

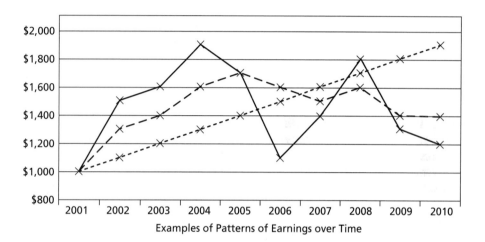

Examples of Patterns of Earnings over Time

Meeting Analysts' Forecasts

Security analysts often forecast what they expect the earnings of public companies to be for the next quarter or year. These forecasts are made available to the public and are aggregated into what is known as a *consensus forecast*, which is just the average of all of the forecasts of the different analysts. Since this consensus forecast is public information, managers know what earnings analysts are expecting the company to report before the company actually reports its earnings.

In the news article shown below, American Express reported fourth quarter earnings of 22 cents per share. According to the article, this earnings number was a penny below the consensus analyst forecast, meaning that analysts expected the company to report 23 cents per share. As the article explains, the stock price of American Express fell by 70 cents a share, which represented nearly 2 percent of the shares' value. If managers believe that the company's share price will drop significantly if reported earnings are less than analysts' forecasted earnings, this provides an incentive to manage earnings to always meet or exceed analysts' forecasts.

American Express 4Q Earnings Down
NEW YORK (AP)—American Express said Monday that its earnings for the fourth quarter and the year were down significantly because of the drop in travel after the Sept. 11 terrorist attacks.

The giant financial services company said its net profits totaled $297 million, or 22 cents a share, in the fourth quarter, a 56 percent drop from a year earlier. The results were a penny a share below the estimate from analysts surveyed by Thomson Financial/First Call.

In the year-earlier period, earnings were $677 million, or 50 cents a share.

American Express stock fell 70 cents, or nearly 2 percent, to $36.29 at the close of regular trading on the New York Stock Exchange.

The majority of earnings announcements are at amounts that equal or exceed the consensus forecast. This implies one of two things: Either (1) analysts are consistently underestimating companies earnings,[3] or (2) managers are managing earnings to meet or exceed analysts' forecasts. It is likely that both of these things are going on simultaneously.

HOW DO MANAGERS MANAGE EARNINGS?

After understanding the incentives that managers have to manage earnings, it is important to understand exactly how earnings management is accomplished. By understanding how managers can manage reported earnings, you will be better able to (1) detect earnings management when it exists (that is, you will know where to look for it) and (2) make adjustments to reported financial statement numbers to adjust for the impact of earnings management.

There are four main ways to manage a company's reported earnings: (1) valuation allowance accounts, (2) accounting method choices, (3) accounting estimates, and (4) real economic decisions. Each of these categories is discussed in more detail below.

Valuation Allowances

Valuation allowances are balance sheet accounts with credit balances that either reduce the amount of reported assets (that is, contra-asset accounts) or increase reported liabilities. Since the account has a credit balance, the entry to establish (or increase) the account also involves a debit that increases an income statement expense account. Valuation allowances are sometimes referred to as *reserves* by the financial press, although most accountants feel the term *reserve* is somewhat misleading and try to avoid its use.

The following are examples of valuation allowances that have been discussed in previous chapters:

Valuation Allowance	Associated Expense
Allowance for doubtful accounts	Bad debt expense
Liability for future warranty payments	Warranty expense
Liability for restructuring	Severance payment expense
Deferred tax asset valuation allowance	Deferred income tax expense
Allowance for inventory write-downs	Cost of goods sold

The reason valuation allowances are often used for managing earnings is that (1) they are based almost solely on management estimates and (2) their balances increase and decrease from year to year. Increases in the balances result in the recording of additional expenses in the current year, while decreases in the balances may result in the recording of a smaller expense in the current year. For example, if the allowance for doubtful accounts is increased in 2001, bad debt expense is recorded in 2001. If it is later determined in 2002 that the balance in the allowance for doubtful accounts is too high, a smaller bad debt expense, or perhaps no bad debt expense, will be recorded in 2002.

Accounting Method Choice

Another way managers can manage reported accounting earnings is through their selection of accounting methods. For example, the choice of the LIFO

---

[3] You might wonder why analysts would consistently underestimate earnings. The reason is they may have incentives to either (1) make managers look good (by allowing managers to always meet the forecast) or (2) make their clients who purchased the company's shares happy (since a company that always meets or exceeds earnings forecasts is likely to experience stock price increases).

inventory cost flow assumption will result in lower earnings when costs are increasing compared with the FIFO cost flow assumption. Similarly, the choice of an accelerated depreciation method will result in lower earnings in the early years of an asset's life compared with the straight-line method.

Unlike valuation allowances, the effects of accounting method choices cannot be easily reversed in future years. Firms cannot arbitrarily change accounting methods from year to year. Also, the income statement impact of a change in accounting method must be disclosed in the financial statements (as the cumulative effect of a change in accounting principle), and this highlights the impact of the change for financial statement users.

Accounting Estimates

Changes in accounting estimates are another way that managers can affect reported accounting earnings. For example, managers must estimate the useful lives and salvage values of all depreciable assets, and changes in these estimates will affect depreciation expense. Similarly, managers must make estimates for the expected return on pension plan assets, and changes in these expected returns will affect pension plan expense.

Unlike changes in accounting methods, changes in estimates do not require special treatment in the financial statements—that is, there is no cumulative effect of a change in estimate in the same way there is for a change of accounting method. However, if the effect of the change in estimate is material, it should be disclosed in the notes to the financial statements.

Real Economic Decisions

All of the methods for managing earnings discussed above affect only the financial statement numbers—they have no impact on the company's underlying cash flows.[4] However, there are things that managers can do to affect accounting earnings that also affect the firm's cash flows. Because the firm's cash flows are affected, these decisions are said to have real economic effects.

For example, a manager who wants to increase her firm's reported earnings could reduce the firm's spending on research and development. Since R&D spending is treated as an expense in the period incurred, a reduction in R&D spending will reduce R&D expense, which will increase reported earnings. Notice, however, that this decision has affected the firm's cash flows, since less is being spent on R&D. Although the firm reports higher earnings and cash flows, the reduction in R&D spending may actually be a bad thing for the firm, putting it behind its competitors in technological innovation and ultimately reducing expected future cash flows from new products. Thus, a decision that may be harmful to the firm in the long run (reducing R&D spending) will make the firm look more profitable in the short run by reducing recorded R&D expense.

Another example of a decision that has both accounting consequences and real economic effects is the decision to sell some of the firm's assets. Suppose the firm has a profitable asset that is worth more than the asset's book value. By selling the asset, the firm will realize a gain, which increases net income.[5] Therefore, the firm will look more profitable. However, if the asset was one that was important to the firm's future success, this may be a bad decision with respect to long-run profitability.

---

[4] The statement that earnings management has no effect on cash flows ignores the effects of accounting methods on tax payments. For example, adopting the LIFO inventory cost flow assumption in a period of rising costs can reduce the firm's cash payments for taxes.

[5] A similar result occurs when a firm retires debt at a gain.

Management Decisions and Accounting Earnings: An Example

To provide an example of how decisions by a company's managers can affect reported accounting earnings, look again at the pattern of General Electric's earnings per share and cash flows. As was pointed out earlier, the earnings per share numbers exhibit a constantly increasing pattern, whereas the cash flows are more variable—higher in some years and lower in others.

Notice that GE's cash flows decreased in 1997, but accounting earnings continued the trend of increases. This may be the result of normal accounting accruals smoothing out the lumpiness of cash flows; or it may reflect management actions that resulted in an increase in reported accounting earnings. Look more closely at GE's income statement and see if you notice anything unusual about the year 1997.

GENERAL ELECTRIC COMPANY
Statement of Earnings
For the Years Ended December 31
(in millions; per share amounts in dollars)

	General Electric Company and Consolidated Affiliates		
	1998	1997	1996
Revenues			
Sales of goods	$43,749	$40,675	$36,106
Sales of services	14,938	12,729	11,791
Other income (note 2)	649	2,300	638
Earnings of GECS	—	—	—
GECS revenues from services (note 3)	41,133	35,136	30,644
Total revenues	100,469	90,840	79,179
Costs and expenses (note 4)			
Cost of goods sold	31,772	30,889	26,298
Cost of services sold	10,508	9,199	8,293
Interest and other financial charges	9,753	8,384	7,904
Insurance losses and policyholder and annuity benefits	9,608	8,278	6,678
Provision for losses on financing receivables (note 7)	1,609	1,421	1,033
Other costs and expenses	23,477	21,250	17,898
Minority interest in net earnings of consolidated affiliates	265	240	269
Total costs and expenses	86,992	79,661	68,373
Earnings before income taxes	13,477	11,179	10,806
Provision for income taxes (note 8)	(4,181)	(2,976)	(3,526)
Net earnings	$ 9,296	$ 8,203	$ 7,280

Source: General Electric Form 10-K.

You can see that GE's total revenues and net earnings have increased each year from 1996 to 1998. However, notice the item labeled "other income" under the revenues category. This amount increased from $638 million in 1996 to $2,300 million in 1997 and then dropped back down to $649 million in 1998. The 1997 amount for other income is approximately $1,600 million *greater* than the amounts for the other two years. The source of this additional income is discussed in note 2 of GE's financial statements:

2. GE Other Income (in millions)

	1998	1997	1996
Residual licensing and royalty income			
RCA licensing	$250	$ 287	$265
Other	51	54	60
Associated companies	(9)	50	50
Marketable securities and bank deposits	114	78	72
Customer financing	19	26	29
Other investments			
Dividends	8	62	79
Interest	8	1	18
Other items	243	1,749	56
	$684	$2,307	$629

Source: General Electric Form 10-K.

You can see that the increase in other income for 1997 is due to something labeled "other items" in the above table. Note 2 explains this item as follows:

> Included in the "Other items" caption for 1997 is a gain of $1,538 million related to a tax-free exchange between GE and Lockheed Martin Corporation (Lockheed Martin). In exchange for its investment in Lockheed Martin Series A preferred stock, GE acquired a Lockheed Martin subsidiary containing two businesses, an equity interest and cash to the extent necessary to equalize the value of the exchange, a portion of which was subsequently loaned to Lockheed Martin.

Source: General Electric Form 10-K.

Nearly 100 percent of the increase in other income for 1997 relates to a gain from an exchange between GE and Lockheed Martin Corporation. This exchange transaction was announced by GE in a press release on November 3, 1997. As part of the transaction, GE received approximately $1,600 million of cash from Lockheed Martin, most of which was immediately loaned back to Lockheed Martin.

Since this gain was structured as a tax-free exchange, the pretax gain of $1,538 million is also the amount by which net income increased for the year—that is, there is no income tax expense associated with the gain; it represents a permanent book-tax difference. Subtracting the $1,538 million gain from GE's reported 1997 earnings of $8,203 million results in an amount of $6,665 million, which is *less than* the 1996 net income of $7,280.

What does this example show about the relationship between management decisions and reported earnings? GE had a record of annual earnings increases that would not have continued in 1997 if the company had not entered into the Lockheed Martin exchange transaction by the end of 1997. Although the transaction did have cash flow consequences to GE (since it received $1,600 million in cash from Lockheed Martin), GE immediately loaned the cash back to Lockheed Martin. Since the transaction was tax free, GE did not incur an additional tax expense due to the gain. Therefore, because of this transaction GE's reported earnings for 1997 increased by $1,538 million without any significant cash flow implications for the company.

How did GE explain this transaction to investors? GE's then-chairman John F. Welch is quoted in the company's November 3, 1997, press release as saying "the gain from this transaction will give us the opportunity to restructure our industrial businesses to position them for the global competition in the next decade." GE's management is saying that the gain resulted from a strategic business decision. There is no suggestion that the gain was realized based on the financial accounting impact. However, had the transaction taken place two months later, in January 1998, the pattern of GE's earnings would have been dramatically different, with a decrease in earnings in 1997 and an increase in 1998. In fact, GE's earnings would have followed a pattern similar to the pattern of cash flows presented earlier. The following chart shows GE's (1) cash flows from operating activities, (2) actual earnings, and (3) what these earnings would have been had the exchange transaction taken place in January 1998 rather than November 1997 (called *adjusted earnings*).

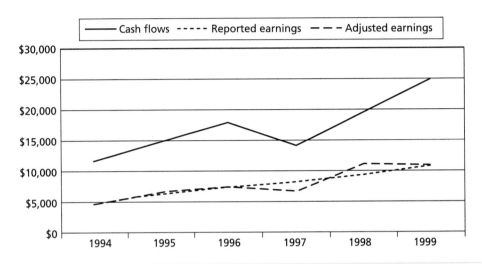

EARNINGS MANAGEMENT AND ACCOUNTING FRAUD

For all of the earnings management techniques discussed above, it is assumed that a company's audit firm is fully aware of the decisions made by management and that these decisions do not result in financial statements that are materially misleading. Unfortunately, in some cases managers may go beyond these earnings management techniques and simply record earnings that do not exist. There have been cases in which managers have recorded sales revenue and accounts receivables for sales that were never made.

Any time managers knowingly present financial accounting reports that are intended to mislead users, it constitutes accounting fraud. Managers found guilty of accounting fraud face large fines or prison terms, or both. Knowing the difference between an optimistic estimate of the allowance for doubtful accounts and a fraudulent attempt by management to misstate earnings is not easy. This is one reason why financial statements of public companies are required to be audited by independent accounting experts. Theoretically, the independent audit firm can make an unbiased judgment as to whether the financial statements fairly present the results of operations of the company.[6]

The SEC has attempted to deal with accounting fraud by clarifying exactly when firms should recognize revenue in a variety of circumstances. Recall from Chapter 2 that the SEC issued Staff Accounting Bulletin (SAB) No. 101, in December 1999 based on the results of a March 1999 study of accounting fraud. The study found that over half of the cases of financial reporting fraud involved overstating revenue. The provisions of SAB 101 generally have the effect of delaying the time of revenue recognition until later accounting periods. Recently, Congress has attempted to address the issue of accounting fraud by enacting legislation requiring managers of public companies to sign a statement certifying the accuracy of their companies' financial statements.

---

[6] This assumes that the audit firm knows about all of the company's transactions. In many cases of accounting fraud, the audit firm is misled by the client and has no knowledge of the fraudulent transactions.

ARGUMENTS AGAINST EARNINGS MANAGEMENT

Earnings management may be harmful to the workings of U.S. capital markets. Recent accounting-related stories in the financial press have shaken investor confidence in the reliability of reported earnings of public firms. In recent years, a strong opponent of earnings management has been the Securities and Exchange Commission. This section presents an outline of the SEC's opposition to earnings management, as reflected in speeches given by Arthur Levitt, the former chairman of the SEC. Levitt refers to earnings management as a "numbers game"; others often call earnings management "cooking the books."

The "Numbers Game"

Here is an example of Levitt's concerns about earnings management:[7]

> Increasingly, I have become concerned that the motivation to meet Wall Street earnings expectations may be overriding common sense business practices. Too many corporate managers, auditors, and analysts are participants in a game of nods and winks. In the zeal to satisfy consensus earnings estimates and project a smooth earnings path, wishful thinking may be winning the day over faithful representation.

Levitt fears that (1) "we are witnessing an erosion in the quality of earnings, and therefore, the quality of financial reporting," (2) "managing may be giving way to manipulation," and (3) "integrity may be losing out to illusion." He talks about a "gray area between legitimacy and outright fraud . . . where the accounting is being perverted; where managers are cutting corners; and, where earnings reports reflect the desires of management rather than the underlying financial performance of the company."

All of the above comments indicate the seriousness with which the SEC views the trend in earnings management in U.S. public companies in recent years. Here is Levitt's explanation for why earnings management is such a potentially serious problem:

> If a company fails to provide meaningful disclosure to investors about where it has been, where it is and where it is going, a damaging pattern ensues. The bond between shareholders and the company is shaken; investors grow anxious; prices fluctuate for no discernible reasons; and the trust that is the bedrock of our capital markets is severely tested.

Levitt points out five of the most abusive types of earnings management: (1) "big bath" restructuring charges, (2) creative acquisition accounting, (3) "cookie jar" reserves, (4) "immaterial" misapplications of accounting principles, and (5) the premature recognition of revenue. Each of these earnings management issues is discussed in detail below.

Big Bath Restructuring Charges

Levitt explains the problem with restructuring charges as follows:

> Companies remain competitive by regularly assessing the efficiency and profitability of their operations. Problems arise, however, when we see large charges associated with companies restructuring. These charges help companies "clean up" their balance sheet—giving them a so-called "big bath." Why are companies tempted to overstate these charges? When earnings take a major hit, the theory goes Wall Street will look beyond a one-time loss and focus only on future earnings. And if these charges are conservatively estimated with a little extra cushioning, that so-called conservative estimate is miraculously reborn as income when estimates change or future earnings fall short.

---

[7] All of the quotes in this section are from a speech given by Arthur Levitt on September 28, 1998, at the NYU Center for Law and Business.

As an example of restructuring charges, the following financial statement note shows the restructuring charges taken by IBM Corporation in 1992 and 1993:

J. Restructuring actions

In 1993 and 1992, the company recorded restructuring charges of $8.9 billion before taxes ($8.0 billion after taxes or $14.02 per common share) and $11.6 billion before taxes ($8.3 billion after taxes or $14.51 per common share), respectively, as part of restructuring programs to streamline and reduce resources utilized in the business. These charges and their subsequent utilization are summarized in the following table (in billions):

	Amounts Charged in 1993 and 1992	Amounts Utilized at Year-End 1994	Amounts to Be Utilized in 1995
Workforce related	$11.5	$10.5	$1.0
Manufacturing capacity	4.9	4.0	.9
Excess space	3.4	3.0	.4
Other	.7	.7	—
Total restructuring charges	$20.5	$18.2	$2.3

Source: IBM Corporation Form 10-K.

IBM recorded a total of $20.5 billion of expenses in 1992 and 1993 related to the company's restructuring activities. As of the end of 1994, the company had actually incurred $18.2 billion of costs related to the restructuring. Therefore, the remaining $2.3 billion was expected to be utilized in 1995. However, to the extent that management overestimated the restructuring expenses in 1992 and 1993, the company's earnings in 1995 and future years would be greater by the amount of the excess.

Creative Acquisition Accounting

The SEC's concern about acquisition accounting is explained by Levitt as follows:

> Some acquirers . . . engage in another form of "creative" accounting. I call it "merger magic." . . . So what do they do? They classify an ever-growing portion of the acquisition price as "in-process" Research and Development, so—you guessed it—the amount can be written off in a "one-time" charge—removing any future earnings drag [that is, future amortization].

To illustrate the expensing of purchased in-process R&D, a portion of Intel Corporation's income statement for 1997–1999 is shown on page 495. Notice that Intel recorded an expense for purchased in-process research and development of $392 million in 1999 and $165 million in 1998. If this amount were not expensed as R&D in the year of the acquisition, U.S. accounting principles would require it to be capitalized as goodwill and (under accounting standards in effect prior to 2001) to be amortized over future accounting period.

Cookie Jar Reserves

Levitt explains the problem of cookie jar reserves as follows:

> A third illusion played by some companies is using unrealistic assumptions to estimate liabilities for such items as sales returns, loan losses or warranty costs. In doing so, they stash accruals in cookie jars during the good times and reach into them when needed in the bad times. I'm reminded of one U.S. company who took a large one-time loss to earnings to reimburse franchisees for equipment. That equipment, however, which included literally the kitchen sink, had yet to be bought. And, at the same time, they announced that future earnings would grow an impressive 15 percent per year.

INTEL CORPORATION
Consolidated Statements of Income
Three Years Ended December 25, 1999
(in millions—except per share amounts)

	1999	1998	1997
Net revenues	$29,389	$26,273	$25,070
Cost of sales	11,836	12,088	9,945
Research and development	3,111	2,509	2,347
Marketing, general and administrative	3,872	3,076	2,891
Amortization of goodwill and other acquisition-related intangibles	411	56	—
Purchased in-process research and development	392	165	—
Operating costs and expenses	19,622	17,894	15,183
Operating income	$ 9,767	$ 8,379	$ 9,887

Source: Intel Corporation Form 10-K.

The idea here is that by setting up reserves, usually accrued liabilities, on the balance sheet, management can increase future reported earnings by debiting future expenses to the liability account rather than to an expense account.

As an example of an inappropriate use of reserves to manage earnings, the following is an explanation of the restatement of earnings by National Steel Corporation in connection with its use of reserves:

The report found certain misapplications of generally accepted accounting principles and accounting errors, including excess reserves, which have been corrected by the restatements as discussed below. The report found that the accretion of excess reserves to income during the first, second and third quarters of 1997 as described in the amended Forms 10-Q for those quarters may have had the effect of management of earnings as the result of errors in judgment and misapplications of generally accepted accounting principles. However, these errors do not appear to have involved the intentional misstatement of the Company's accounts.

Source: National Steel Corporation Form 10-K/A.

Immaterial Misapplications of Accounting Principles
Levitt explains how the abuse of the concept of materiality can cause problems with earnings management:

Let me turn now to the fourth gimmick—the abuse of materiality—a word that captures the attention of both attorneys and accountants. Materiality is another way we build flexibility into financial reporting. Using the logic of diminishing returns, some items may be so insignificant that they are not worth measuring and reporting with exact precision. But some companies misuse the concept of materiality. They intentionally record errors within a defined percentage ceiling. They then try to excuse that fib by arguing that the effect on the bottom line is too small to matter. If that's the case, why do they work so hard to create these errors? Maybe because the effect can matter, especially if it picks up that last penny of the consensus [analysts' earnings] estimate. When either management or the outside auditors are questioned about these clear violations of GAAP, they answer sheepishly, "It doesn't matter. It's immaterial."

As an example of the use of materiality in financial statements, the following is the financial statement note reconciling General Motors' income tax expense with the statutory rate amount for the years 1996–1998. Notice that for the year

1997 GM shows a reconciling item called "other adjustments" equal to $226 million. Since this item represents more than 20 percent of the actual income tax expense, it is not clear why GM did not disclose the nature of this other adjustment. Presumably management felt the items making up this category were not material.

Note 6. Income Taxes

A reconciliation of the provision for income taxes compared with the amounts at the U.S. federal statutory rate was as follows (in millions):

	Years Ended December 31		
	1998	**1997**	**1996**
Tax at U.S. federal statutory income tax rate	$ 1,614	$ 2,727	$ 2,272
Hughes Defense spin-off	—	(1,494)	—
Foreign rates other than 35%	60	(123)	(285)
Taxes on unremitted earnings of subsidiaries	98	44	49
Tax effect of the 1995 contribution of Class E common stock to the U.S. hourly pension plan	—	—	(245)
Research and experimentation credits	(237)	(311)	(165)
Subsidiary settlement of affirmation claim with IRS	(92)	—	—
Other adjustments	20	226	97
Total income tax	$ 1,463	$ 1,069	$ 1,723

Source: General Motors Form 10-K.

Premature Recognition of Revenue

The last problem area discussed by Levitt is explained as follows:

> Lastly, companies try to boost earnings by manipulating the recognition of revenue. Think about a bottle of fine wine. You wouldn't pop the cork on that bottle before it was ready. But some companies are doing this with their revenue—recognizing it before a sale is complete, before the product is delivered to a customer, or at a time when the customer still has options to terminate, void or delay the sale.

The following is an example of a company changing its revenue recognition accounting to be consistent with the SEC's Staff Accounting Bulletin No. 101. The example is from the notes to the financial statements of Lucent Technologies.

---

5. Accounting changes

Staff Accounting Bulletin 101, "Revenue Recognition in Financial Statements" (SAB 101)

In December 1999, the Securities and Exchange Commission issued SAB 101, which provides guidance on the recognition, presentation and disclosure of revenues in financial statements. During the fourth quarter of fiscal year 2001, Lucent implemented SAB 101 retroactively to the beginning of fiscal year 2001, resulting in a cumulative effect of a change in accounting principle of a $68 loss (net of a tax benefit of $45), or $0.02 loss per basic and diluted share, and a reduction in the 2001 loss from continuing operations of $11, or $0.00 per basic and diluted share. For the fiscal year ended September 30, 2001, Lucent recognized $116 in revenue that is included in the cumulative effect adjustment as of October 1, 2000. The cumulative effect adjustment results primarily from the change in revenue recognized on intellectual property license agreements that included settlements for which there was no objective evidence of the fair value of the settlement. Under SAB 101, in the absence of objective evidence of fair value of the settlement, revenue is recognized prospectively over the remaining term of the intellectual property license agreement. In addition, revenue recognition was deferred for certain products for multiple element agreements where certain services, primarily installation and integration, were deemed to be essential to the functionality of delivered elements.

Source: Lucent Technologies Form 10-K.

BENEFITS OF FLEXIBILITY IN FINANCIAL REPORTING

The arguments by Levitt presented in the previous section make the case that earnings management is something that should be eliminated from U.S. financial reporting. Certainly, the earnings restatements by large public companies that have appeared so frequently in the financial press, and the damage done to investor confidence by these restatements, underscore the seriousness of the earnings management problem. However, there is also another side to the earnings management debate. This section presents an argument in favor of allowing managers some flexibility in financial reporting decisions.

Ask yourself this question: If earnings management is bad, why don't investors punish managers who engage in earnings management? In other words, why aren't stock prices *lower* for companies that report a smooth pattern of increasing earnings year after year? Why does the stock market reward companies that report smooth earnings with higher stock prices?

Perhaps the best way to think about earnings management is to return to an idea that was presented in Chapter 1—that a primary objective of financial reporting is to solve the problem of information asymmetry. Recall that information asymmetry refers to the fact that managers have access to more information about the actual performance of a company than do people outside the company. Financial reporting provides a means for managers to convey their private information to users of financial statements.

If financial reporting does not allow managers some degree of flexibility, it is harder for managers to convey their information about company performance to users of financial statements. Because the same accounting procedure may not provide the most useful information in all circumstances, GAAP rules allow managers to apply their judgment in a variety of financial reporting situations. By allowing managers some flexibility with respect to financial reporting—such as estimating useful lives and salvage values for depreciation purposes, establishing the correct ending balance in the allowance for doubtful accounts, or choosing LIFO rather than FIFO as an inventory cost flow assumption—users of financial statements may actually get a better idea of how the company is performing.

Also, arguments against earnings management do not consider that in many cases investors are provided with enough information to understand exactly what financial reporting actions managers have taken. For example, consider the case of General Electric's 1997 earnings. Since users of GE's financial statements knew about the Lockheed Martin gain and the effect it had on GE's reported earnings, they could easily have recomputed GE's earnings without the gain had they wanted to do so. Similarly, firms disclose the estimated useful lives used for depreciation purposes, the balances in their allowance for doubtful accounts and other valuation accounts, and the methods of accounting used in the financial statements. Therefore, it is not clear why investors should be "fooled" by the effect that these types of accounting choices have on reported earnings.

There are large differences in the types of earnings management in which companies engage. WorldCom misclassified expenses as capital improvements, which is clearly not in accordance with GAAP. Compare this with Qwest's recording of revenue related to swaps of fiber-optic cable capacity, an accounting treatment that Qwest argued was consistent with GAAP. Even though these are very different types of earnings management, both resulted in restatements of earnings. At the other extreme, a company could sell an asset at the end of a year in which its reported earnings would otherwise have declined and clearly disclose the sale in the financial statements. As a future user of financial accounting information, you should understand the differences between these types of earnings management and what the implications are for the reliability of the companies' financial statement information.

EARNINGS MANAGEMENT AND CASH FLOWS

In most cases, earnings management does not affect a company's cash flows. Therefore, to the extent users of financial statements make decisions based on cash flows from operations, earnings management should not affect their decisions. An exception to this is the case in which earnings management is accomplished by the sale of assets. In this case, cash flows from investing activities should increase in an amount equal to the sales proceeds from the assets disposed of. In the case of early retirement of debt at a gain, cash flows from financing activities should decrease by the amount paid for to retire the debt.

Even if total cash flows are not affected by earnings management, cash flows from operating activities can be affected in some cases. For example, if a company enters into capital leases rather than operating leases, cash flows from operations are not reduced by the portion of the lease payment that is considered to be a repayment of loan principal. Also, to the extent repair items are capitalized rather than expensed, cash flows from operating activities are increased.

EARNINGS MANAGEMENT IN OTHER COUNTRIES

Some studies of earnings management suggest that it is more prevalent in countries other than the United States. For example, Germany, France, and Japan are often cited as countries in which earnings management, particularly, the smoothing of income, is widely practiced. However, there is some evidence that this practice is decreasing as capital markets in different countries become more integrated.

EARNINGS MANAGEMENT AND INCOME TAX EXPENSE

Many of the earnings management techniques discussed in this chapter do not affect the company's taxable income and, therefore, the current income tax expense. However, accounting accruals to manage earnings may result in deferred tax assets or liabilities, which affect the deferred income tax expense. Therefore, one measure of earnings management is the ratio of current income tax expense to total income tax expense.

The following chart shows this ratio for General Electric. Notice that this ratio varies from year to year, unlike GE's earnings pattern.

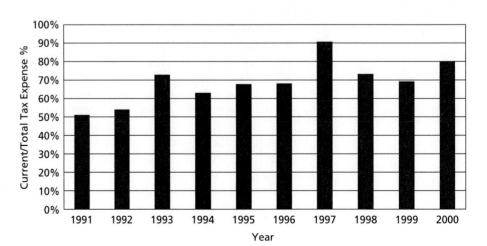

GE Current/Total Tax Expense

EARNINGS MANAGEMENT AND THE USEFULNESS OF ACCOUNTING INFORMATION

Obviously, the effect of earnings management on the usefulness of accounting information depends on the extent to which managers engage in earnings management to provide more useful information rather than to mislead users of the company's financial statements. If earnings management is undertaken to provide a more accurate picture of the company's performance, accounting information may actually be more useful than unmanaged earnings numbers. However, to the extent that managers attempt to mislead users as to the company's actual performance, earnings management decreases the usefulness of accounting information, and, as Arthur Levitt warned, could seriously impair U.S. capital markets.

Summary

This chapter explores the complex topic of earnings management. Incentives for earnings management include: (1) bonus plans, (2) debt contracts, (3) income smoothing, (4) a pattern of earnings growth, and (5) meeting analysts' forecasts. Techniques used by managers to manage earnings include: (1) valuation allowance accounts, (2) accounting methods, (3) accounting estimates, and (4) economic decisions. The SEC argues that earnings management will erode the quality of reported earnings and reduce investor confidence in capital markets. Major earnings management problems identified by the SEC include: (1) excessive restructuring charges, (2) acquisition accounting for in-process R&D, (3) use of reserves, (4) immaterial misapplications of accounting principles, and (5) premature recognition of revenue. Finally, the chapter makes an argument that some degree of manager flexibility with respect to financial reporting may actually improve the usefulness of accounting information.

Discussion Questions

1. Explain what is meant by the term *earnings management*.
2. Explain how earnings management is related to incentives of managers.
3. What are some of the incentives that managers may have to manage earnings?
4. Explain how bonus plans affect managers' incentives to manage earnings.
5. Explain what is meant by smoothing of earnings.
6. Explain how earnings forecasts by security analysts affect manager incentives to manage earnings.
7. What are some of the ways that managers could use to manage earnings?
8. Explain how changes in valuation allowances affect reported earnings.
9. Explain how choices of accounting methods can affect reported earnings.
10. Explain how the use of estimates can affect reported earnings.
11. Explain how managers' real economic decisions can affect reported earnings.
12. How is earnings management different from accounting fraud?
13. Explain why earnings management may undermine investors' confidence in reported earnings.
14. Explain how earnings management may reduce the efficiency of capital markets.
15. Explain how a "big bath" restructuring charge may result in earnings management.
16. Explain how expensing in-process R&D may result in earnings management.
17. Explain what is meant by a "cookie jar" reserve and how this may result in earnings management.
18. Explain how the recording of immaterial items may result in earnings management.

19. Explain why allowing managers some degree of flexibility in making accounting estimates and choosing accounting methods might be useful. Consider relevance and reliability.

Problems

For problems 1–6, assume a corporation pays managers a bonus according to the terms in the following table:

Employer's Reported Net Income	Bonus Amount
Less than $1,000,000	Zero
More than $1,000,000 but less than $2,000,000	10% of excess of net income over $1,000,000
More than $2,000,000	$100,000

1. Assume that managers expect earnings in the current year to be $1,500,000 and earnings next year to be $1,600,000. Explain what incentives there are, if any, for managers to
   a. Increase reported earnings in the current year and decrease reported earnings next year.
   b. Decrease reported earnings in the current year and increase reported earnings next year.

2. Assume that managers expect earnings in the current year to be $700,000 and earnings next year to be $1,200,000. Explain what incentives there are, if any, for managers to
   a. Increase reported earnings in the current year and decrease reported earnings next year.
   b. Decrease reported earnings in the current year and increase reported earnings next year.

3. Assume that managers expect earnings in the current year to be $2,600,000 and earnings next year to be $1,300,000. Explain what incentives there are, if any, for managers to
   a. Increase reported earnings in the current year and decrease reported earnings next year.
   b. Decrease reported earnings in the current year and increase reported earnings next year.

4. Assume that managers expect earnings in the current year to be $2,200,000 and earnings next year to be $3,000,000. Explain what incentives there are, if any, for managers to
   a. Increase reported earnings in the current year and decrease reported earnings next year.
   b. Decrease reported earnings in the current year and increase reported earnings next year.

5. Assume that managers expect earnings in the current year to be $600,000 and earnings next year to be $700,000. Explain what incentives there are, if any, for managers to
   a. Increase reported earnings in the current year and decrease reported earnings next year.
   b. Decrease reported earnings in the current year and increase reported earnings next year.

6. Assume that managers expect earnings in the current year to be $1,990,000 and earnings next year to be $1,500,000. Explain what incentives there are, if any, for managers to
   a. Increase reported earnings in the current year and decrease reported earnings next year.
   b. Decrease reported earnings in the current year and increase reported earnings next year.

Research Reports

1. Give your own opinion as to the answers to the following questions:
   a. Can an action be unethical without being illegal?
   b. When making accounting decisions, do managers have a responsibility to consider the social consequences of their decisions?
   c. Do you think it is possible for managers to make accounting estimates and choose accounting methods without taking into consideration the effects their choices will have on the firm's financial statements?

2. Locate an article or articles in the financial press that discusses a restatement of earnings by a public company.
   a. Explain what caused the earnings restatement. Be specific with respect to the accounting method that was affected.
   b. Explain the dollar amounts and years involved in the restatements.
   c. Obtain the financial statements from the year that is being restated. Is there any information in the financial statement that would have alerted users of the financial statements that the accounting methods used might later be questioned?
   d. In your opinion, why did the managers of the company decide to use the accounting method that was later questioned?
   e. Discuss any consequences of the restatement for the company's managers. For example, were criminal charges filed? Were managers fired or forced to resign?

3. Obtain a recent proxy statement for a public company. (Proxy statements are found on the SEC's EDGAR database. They are referred to as "DEF 14A.") The proxy statement will contain a discussion of manager compensation.
   a. Explain how the managers of the company are compensated.
   b. Explain the amounts and types of compensation received by the company's top managers.
   c. Discuss how the manager compensation arrangement may result in incentives to manage earnings.

4. Locate an article or articles in the financial press discussing recent federal legislation to regulate financial reporting. (This is sometimes known as Sarbanes-Oxley legislation.)
   a. Explain the main provisions of the legislation.
   b. Explain why the legislation was thought necessary.
   c. What effect do you think this legislation will have on earnings management activities?

5. Design your own set of accounting rules that would completely eliminate any opportunity for earnings management.
   a. Compare your accounting rules with GAAP in terms of relevance and reliability of accounting information.
   b. Comment on whether your system is detailed enough to deal with the following items:
      i. Determining the amount of a restructuring charge for a year.
      ii. Determining the correct discount rate to use in computing a company's projected benefit obligation (PBO) for a defined benefit pension plan.
      iii. Determining the expected volatility of the company's common stock price for purposes of applying the Black-Scholes option pricing model to determine compensation expense under the fair value method of reporting employee stock options.

Appendix A

Who Makes Accounting Standards and Why Do They Do It?

INTRODUCTION

Throughout this book, accounting standards called generally accepted accounting principles (GAAP) have been discussed. Although the Financial Accounting Standards Board has been mentioned in connection with some of the standards, the fundamental questions of (1) Who makes accounting standards? and (2) Why do they do it? have not been addressed.

This appendix briefly discusses standard setting in the United States, and also contrasts the U.S. standard-setting process with those used in other countries. In addition to describing who makes the standards and the process they go through to arrive at them, the appendix also discusses why standard setting is necessary.

WHAT MAKES UP GAAP?

In the United States, generally accepted accounting principles come from two sources. First, some accounting principles are based on prior accounting practices that have been consistently followed by accountants over a long period of time. For example, businesses have been recording depreciation as an expense since at least the early 1900s. Recording an expense for depreciation would therefore be considered a generally accepted accounting principle even without any explicit standard from the Financial Accounting Standards Board. Since most professional accountants would agree with the principle of recording depreciation expense, it is considered to be "generally accepted" by the accounting community.

The second source of GAAP is a set of standards issued by a standard-setting body. In the United States, the major standard-setting bodies are the Securities and Exchange Commission (SEC), the Financial Accounting Standards Board (FASB), and the American Institute of Certified Public Accountants (AICPA).[1] The SEC is an agency of the federal government and is therefore in the public sector. The FASB and AICPA are *not* governmental agencies and are therefore in the private sector. Each of these organizations are discussed in more detail below.

The SEC

The Securities and Exchange Commission was established under the Securities Exchange Act of 1934. This act empowers the SEC with broad authority over all aspects of the securities industry, including the power to register, regulate, and

---

[1]Other organizations may also set accounting standards. For example, stock exchanges may have accounting requirements for companies listing their shares on the exchange.

oversee brokerage firms, transfer agents, and clearing agencies as well as the nation's various stock exchanges.[2]

The act also empowers the SEC to require periodic reporting of information by companies with publicly traded securities, which includes the authority to establish accounting and reporting standards. However, throughout its history the SEC's policy has been to rely on the private sector for this function.

The SEC deals with accounting standards chiefly through the Office of the Chief Accountant, the principal adviser to the Commission on accounting and auditing matters. The Office of the Chief Accountant also works closely with domestic and international private sector accounting and auditing standard-setting bodies—such as the Financial Accounting Standards Board, the International Accounting Standards Board, and the American Institute of Certified Public Accountants.

The SEC periodically issues accounting-related rules and interpretations, which are designed to supplement, rather than replace, standards issued by the private sector. These rules and interpretations are also used to implement disclosure requirements that the SEC considers necessary to carry out its mission. These accounting requirements are contained in a document called Regulation S-X, which governs the form and content of financial statements filed with the SEC.

Another task of the SEC is to oversee the private sector accounting standard-setting process, which in the United States is carried out by the FASB. The SEC oversees the FASB's activities to determine whether the process that the FASB is following is operating in an open, fair, and impartial manner. The SEC also ensures that each standard is within an acceptable range of alternatives that serves the public interest and protects investors. For example, the SEC staff recently oversaw the FASB's adoption of a new standard dealing with accounting for goodwill and other intangibles acquired in business combinations.

The FASB

The Financial Accounting Standards Board was established in 1973 as an independent private sector body whose mission is to issue financial accounting standards in the United States.[3] Both the SEC and the AICPA have officially recognized standards issued by the FASB as being authoritative, meaning these standards must be followed by companies that are registered with the SEC or that are audited by accountants who are members of the AICPA.[4]

The FASB has seven full-time members who are appointed for five-year terms by the Financial Accounting Foundation (FAF). The FAF is a an independent, not-for-profit organization that, in addition to appointing the members of the FASB, is responsible for funding the FASB's activities and for generally overseeing the operations of the FASB. In addition to overseeing the FASB, the FAF also oversees the operation of a second standard-setting organization, the Governmental Accounting Standards Board (GASB).

The process that the FASB follows to arrive at a standard is a long and complicated one, as outlined below:

1. The board receives recommendations and comments from various constituencies as to what accounting issues it should consider. These constituencies include the general public, the investment community, public companies, the accounting profession, and the SEC.

2. The board makes a decision to add an item to its agenda. In making this decision, the board considers such things as the pervasiveness of the issue,

---

[2]Much of the material in this section is taken from publicly available documents from the SEC.

[3]Prior to 1973, financial accounting standards in the United States were issued by the Committee on Accounting Procedures of the AICPA (1936–59) and the Accounting Principles Board of the AICPA (1959–73).

[4]Much of the material in this section is taken from publicly available documents from the FASB.

alternative solutions available, technical feasibility, practical consequences, convergence possibilities, cooperative opportunities, and resources.

3. The board discusses the item at one or more meetings. These meetings are open to the public. The staff of the FASB provides written analyses of the issue being discussed at the meeting. The board may ask questions of staff members about the issue.

4. When the board has reached a conclusion about a standard, through a vote of the board members, the staff prepares an Exposure Draft for public comment. The Exposure Draft sets out the proposed standard as well as background information and an explanation of the basis of the board's conclusions. The public is invited to provide written comments on the Exposure Draft.

5. After the exposure period has ended, usually 60 days, the board considers all of the comments that have been received on the Exposure Draft. This is again done through meetings that are open to the public. The board will then decide to either revise the Exposure Draft and reissue it, or to adopt the standard in either its original or modified form. A vote of four (out of seven) board members is required to adopt a standard.

6. Once the standard is adopted, it is issued to the public in the form of a Statement of Financial Accounting Standards (SFAS). More than 100 of these Standards have been issued by the FASB since 1973.

The AICPA

The American Institute of Certified Public Accountants is a professional organization of certified public accountants (CPAs) in the United States. Certified public accountants are people who have met certain educational requirements as well as having passed an examination to be licensed by a state to practice public accounting. CPAs are the only people who can conduct audits of public companies in accordance with SEC rules. Therefore, the members of the AICPA have a strong interest in accounting standards. The AICPA is involved in selecting some of the trustees that serve on the Financial Accounting Foundation. The AICPA also issues standards, called *generally accepted auditing standards* (GAAS), that must be followed in conducting financial statement audits.

Prior to the formation of the FASB, the AICPA was the organization responsible for issuing financial accounting standards in the United States. However, it was thought that under that system the accounting profession exercised too much control over what standards were adopted. Under the current system, the FASB is primarily responsible for U.S. accounting standards. However, the AICPA still issues guidelines about financial accounting matters, and these pronouncements of the AICPA are considered to be part of GAAP.

ASSESSING COSTS AND BENEFITS OF NEW STANDARDS

In any standard-setting process, it is important to ensure that the benefits that will be realized from the new standard are greater than the costs that will be incurred to implement the standard. However, it is not clear how benefits and costs of new accounting standards can be measured or compared. In some cases, the benefits of a new standard may be realized by one group (for example, potential shareholders) while the costs of implementing the standard may be imposed on a different group (for example, current shareholders). To the extent a standard results in information that makes capital markets operate more efficiently, society as a whole may benefit.

Accounting information, like other types of information, suffers from what is known in economics as the *free-rider* problem. This means that there is no way to effectively charge the people who benefit from the information for the cost of providing the information. Once a firm's financial statements are made public, the information they contain is freely available to anyone who wants to use it. Therefore, there is a tendency for users of financial statements to demand as much information as possible, since they do not pay for the information. This makes it very difficult to compare costs and benefits of information.

The costs of new accounting standards go beyond simply the additional book-keeping or recordkeeping costs involved in gathering and summarizing the information required by the standard. Information required by a new accounting standard may be used by a company's competitors as well as by investors. Providing some types of information may harm the competitiveness of the company, making the shareholders worse off. Similarly, information about the impact of employee stock options on net income may impose costs on the company's managers to the extent the information causes the board of directors to grant fewer options.

STANDARD SETTING AS A POLITICAL PROCESS

Accounting standards are set in the United States through a political process. This means that various interested parties have the opportunity to lobby the FASB to adopt standards that they favor and to vote against standards to which they are opposed. These interested parties all have different levels of ability to influence the decisions made by individual members of the FASB. Those parties that are more influential will be more likely to have standards adopted that favor their interests, and they will be more likely to defeat efforts to adopt standards to which they are opposed.

One consequence of standard setting being a political process is that we do not always end up with the "best" standards as determined by some objective criteria. We simply end up with the standards that a majority of the members of the FASB are persuaded to vote for. Because of the political nature of the standard-setting process, the FASB goes to great lengths to ensure that all interested parties have a chance to make their views on a particular standard known to the board.

WHY IS STANDARD SETTING NECESSARY?

Providing financial accounting information is a regulated industry. In recent years, there has been a movement by governments to deregulate many other regulated industries, such as airlines, long-distance telephone service, or natural gas production. This leads to the question of why regulation of accounting standards is necessary.

Why doesn't the market for accounting information work in such a way that each public company would have incentives to provide exactly the right amount of information without regulation? Firms that failed to provide the information that investors demanded would find that no one would invest in their shares. These firms would have to either provide the information demanded or lose their ability to raise additional capital.

Unfortunately, markets do not always work to produce the optimal amount of goods and services, and this may be true of the market for accounting information. When this happens it is referred to as a *market failure*. One cause of market failure is the free-rider problem, which has already been discussed. In an efficiently functioning market, accounting information would continue to be produced until the point where the marginal benefit of more information was exactly equal to the marginal cost of the information. In a situation where the users of the information do not pay the cost, this may not occur.

Another problem with the market for accounting information is that the private value of the information may differ from the value of the information to society. If society as a whole benefits from more information, in the form of more efficient capital markets, but the cost of the information is borne by individual firms, the optimal amount of information (from society's standpoint) might not be produced.

Accountants continue to debate the question of whether the market for accounting information suffers from market failure. However, to the extent that market failure is present, regulation may be necessary to force companies to produce more or better information than they would in the absence of such regulation.

STANDARD SETTING IN OTHER COUNTRIES

The standard-setting model used in the United States is to allow the private sector (the FASB) to set accounting standards, subject to oversight by the public sector (the SEC). Private sector standard setting is also used in other countries, such as the U.K., where the Accounting Standards Board (ASB) sets financial accounting standards. Also, the International Accounting Standards Board (IASB) is a private sector organization.

However, in some countries accounting standard-setting is done directly by the government, or it is done through governmental agencies. This is the case in Germany and Japan. In cases where accounting standards are set by the public sector, financial accounting rules tend to be the same as income tax accounting rules, and the interest of the government is to make sure firms do not underreport their taxable income. Requiring the same accounting standards for both financial reporting and income tax reporting may result in accounting standards that are less useful for decision making. In terms of relevance and reliability, accounting standards designed to ensure the collection of income taxes by the government may be reliable but may not be relevant.

Appendix B

Recording Accounting Transactions

INTRODUCTION

This appendix briefly outlines how accounting transactions are recorded. If you have previously taken a course in financial accounting, the material in this appendix will serve to refresh your memory. If this is your first accounting course, this material will provide you with a basic understanding of how accountants record business transactions.

Keep in mind that not everything that happens to a business is recorded in the financial statements. There are many important events that affect the value of a public corporation that are not considered transactions for financial accounting purposes. Some examples are the signing a new contract, the death of a key officer, or the introduction of a new product. While this type of information is important for anyone interested in valuing a public company, the information will not be reflected in the company's financial statements.

THE ACCOUNTING EQUATION

Accountants represent the financial position of a firm by using the following equation (also called the *balance sheet equation*):

$$\text{Assets} = \text{Liabilities} + \text{Owners' Equity}$$

Assets represent the financial resources of a corporation, while Liabilities and Owners' Equity represent the claims against those financial resources. The terms in this equation can be abbreviated as A = L + OE.

A key factor to keep in mind when recording accounting transactions is that the accounting equation must always be kept in balance, which means that the total of the items on the left side of the equation (Assets) must always equal the total of the items on the right side of the equations (the sum of Liabilities and Owners' Equity). The process of recording accounting transactions is designed to keep the equation in balance, through a mechanism called *double-entry book-keeping*. Using double-entry bookkeeping, every time a transaction is recorded in one part of the accounting equation, one or more additional entries must be made to keep the equation in balance.

For example, if a company issues common stock (a type of Owners' Equity) for cash, both the Assets part of the equation and the Owners' Equity part of the equation will increase by the same amount, keeping the equation in balance. Similarly, if a company uses cash to purchase equipment, the Assets part of the equation will both increase (for the equipment) and decrease (for the cash) by the same amount, keeping the equation in balance.

It is useful to expand the accounting equation still further to incorporate the concept of Revenues, Expenses, and Dividends. Since Owners' Equity consists of two components, Contributed Capital (CC) and Retained Earnings (RE), the accounting equation can be expanded as follows:

$$A = L + CC + RE$$

Retained Earnings can be expanded still further. A company's retained earnings is increased by Net Income (NI) for a year and decreased by Dividends (D) for the year. Therefore, the Retained Earnings at any time consists of the Beginning Retained Earnings (BRE) as of the end of the prior accounting period, plus Net Income, less Dividends. This results in

$$A = L + CC + BRE + NI - D$$

Finally, Net Income consists of Revenues (R) minus Expenses (E). Incorporating these terms into the equation results in

$$A = L + CC + BRE + R - E - D$$

RECORDING TRANSACTIONS

The expanded equation can now be used to record some simple transactions to show how the equation is kept in balance through the use of double entries. Here is the first transaction:

a. Issue 1,000 shares of common stock for $50,000 cash.

In this transaction, an Asset (cash) increases by $50,000 and Contributed Capital (common stock) also increases by $50,000. Here is how the transaction would be recorded using the accounting equation:

	A	=	L	+ CC	+ BRE	+ R	− E	− D
a.	50,000	=		50,000				

The second transaction is

b. Borrow $40,000 cash from the bank.

In this transaction, an Asset (cash) increases by $40,000 and a Liability (bank loan) also increases by $40,000. Here is how the transaction would be recorded using the accounting equation:

	A	=	L	+ CC	+ BRE	+ R	− E	− D
b.	40,000	=	40,000					

The third transaction is

c. Purchase $20,000 of equipment for cash.

In this transaction, an Asset (equipment) increases by $20,000 and an Asset (cash) decreases by $20,000. Here is how the transaction would be recorded using the accounting equation:

	A	=	L	+ CC	+ BRE	+ R	− E	− D
	20,000							
c.	(20,000)							

The remaining transactions, shown below, are all recorded in the same way:

d. Purchase $15,000 worth of inventory using an account payable.

e. Sell inventory costing $10,000 for accounts receivable of $18,000.

f. Pay $15,000 of cash to pay off accounts payable.

g. Collect $17,500 of accounts receivable in cash.

h. Write off $500 of accounts receivable as a bad debt expense.

i. Record $2,000 of depreciation expense on equipment.

j. Pay wages of $1,500 in cash.

k. **Pay $2,100 of interest expense in cash.**

l. **Pay $400 dividend in cash.**

The table below shows all of the accounting transactions recorded using the accounting equation. As you can see from the table, the total of the transactions recorded on the left side of the equation ($91,500) equals the total of the transactions recorded on the right side of the equation ($91,500). (Remember that Expenses and Dividends are *subtracted* from the right side of the equation.)

	A	=	L	+ CC	+ BRE	+ R	− E	− D
a.	50,000	=		50,000				
b.	40,000	=	40,000					
c.	20,000							
	(20,000)							
d.	15,000	=	15,000					
e.	18,000	=				18,000		
	(10,000)	=					10,000	
f.	(15,000)	=	(15,000)					
g.	17,500							
	(17,500)							
h.	(500)	=					500	
i.	(2,000)	=					2,000	
j.	(1,500)	=					1,500	
k.	(2,100)	=					2,100	
l.	(400)	=						400
	$91,500	=	$40,000	$50,000	—	$18,000	$16,100	$400
	$91,500	=	$91,500					

One problem with using the accounting equation method to record transactions for actual companies is that there is no way to tell what the balance is in a single account, such as cash or interest expense. One solution is to have a separate column for each asset, liability, expense, and so forth. However, this would result in an enormous number of columns for a large public company.

THE GENERAL LEDGER

To achieve the same result, but without all of the columns, accountants put each column on a separate page in a book; each column (page) is called an *account,* and the book called a *general ledger.* Each account keeps track of increases on one side of the page and decreases on the other side. The following is an example of the cash account used to record the example transactions shown above. Increases in cash are recorded on the left side of the page, and decreases are recorded on the right side.[1]

Cash	
50,000	20,000
40,000	15,000
17,500	1,500
	2,100
	400
107,500	39,000
68,500	

[1]Because the lines on the page are in the shape of the letter T, the account is sometimes referred to as a *T-account.*

Using this system, the balance in cash is found on the Cash account page. This is the page in the ledger on which all the increases and decreases in cash are recorded.

One problem with this method is that it loses track of all of the various parts of the transaction. Only the increases and decreases in cash are shown, but not what caused those increases or decreases or what other accounts are affected. The solution to this problem is to record the entire transaction in one place and then transfer the various parts of the transaction to the individual accounts in the general ledger. The place where the transactions are recorded is called a *journal*, and transferring the parts of the transactions to the individual accounts in the general ledger is called *posting*.

DEBITS AND CREDITS

To record transactions in the journal and transfer the parts of the transaction to the individual general ledger accounts requires a rule that shows whether the transaction is increasing or decreasing a particular account. The rule is as follows: Increases in asset and expense accounts are recorded on the left side of the account, while increases in liability, owners' equity, and revenue accounts are recorded on the right side of the account. Conversely, decreases in asset and expense accounts are recorded on the right side of the account, while decreases in liability, owners' equity, and revenue accounts are recorded on the left side. The following table summarizes these rules:

	Left Side (debit)	Right Side (credit)
Increase	Assets Expenses	Liabilities Equity Revenue
Decrease	Liabilities Equity Revenue	Assets Expense

Accountants use the term *debit* to refer to an entry on the left side of an account and *credit* to refer to an entry on the right side of an account. These terms have no other meaning. When crediting your account to increase it and debiting your account to decrease it, a bank is following the rules from the above table— your account is a liability on the bank's financial statements.

The next page shows how the above transactions would be recorded using journal entries:

Accounts	Debit	Credit
Cash	50,000	
Common Stock		50,000
Cash	40,000	
Bank Loan		40,000
Equipment	20,000	
Cash		20,000
Inventory	15,000	
Accounts Payable		15,000
Accounts Receivable	18,000	
Cost of Goods Sold	10,000	
Sales Revenue		18,000
Inventory		10,000
Accounts Payable	15,000	
Cash		15,000
Cash	17,500	
Accounts Receivable		17,500
Bad Debt Expense	500	
Allowance for Doubtful Accounts		500
Depreciation Expense	2,000	
Accumulated Depreciation		2,000
Wages Expense	1,500	
Cash		1,500
Interest Expense	2,100	
Cash		2,100
Dividends	400	
Cash		400

Index